THE

SCIENCE

OF

PSYCHOLOGY

THE

SCIENCE

OF

PSYCHOLOGY

AN INTRODUCTION

by William S. Ray

Professor of Psychology
The University of North Carolina at Greensboro

THE MACMILLAN COMPANY, NEW YORK
COLLIER-MACMILLAN LIMITED, LONDON

First Printing

DESIGNED BY MARY A. BROWN

Library of Congress catalog card number: 64-14962

THE MACMILLAN COMPANY, NEW YORK
COLLIER-MACMILLAN CANADA, LTD., TORONTO, ONTARIO

Printed in the United States of America

Preface

Homo sapiens as infant, child, student, parent, trainee, salesman, or other individual is the subject under study in this introduction to scientific psychology. As primate, mammal, vertebrate, and animal, he is assumed to have his proper place in comparative psychology—a field of knowledge about relationships among the different kinds of animals. Consequently, psychological theory and fact concerning chimpanzees, dogs, cats, rats, pigeons, snakes, salmon, cockroaches, and other infrahuman animals has not been included here.

The behavior of man has been given the central position. Consciousness has been given a lesser position as one source of psychological concepts and theory. Although theory and fact pertaining to behavior form the major content, methods of investigation are discussed extensively.

The over-all plan of the book is a progression from simpler to more complex topics. After establishing that the discussion is to be centered on behavior, the topics, in order, are observation, measurement, prediction in nonexperimental research, and prediction and control in experimental research. The purpose is twofold: first, to confront the student with the major forms of psychological knowledge; second, to emphasize the distinctiveness of experimental knowledge as it has to do with the control of behavior.

Certain of the student's difficulties in studying psychology are treated as problems in language. This results in considerable discussion of definitions, ambiguities, and levels of abstraction. Where issues have not yet been clearly resolved in current practice, the existing situation is described and, in some cases, solutions are suggested.

The formation of psychological concepts is one important goal of an introductory course. It is accomplished, in some instances, by means of definitions and simple logic; in others, by means of examples and abstraction from them. Especially in the formation of empirical concepts about behavior are examples valuable. Consequently, accounts of specific events and procedures have been employed liberally.

The function concept is developed in simple terms to insure the student's understanding of it before its use in prediction is described. It is a concept of great importance, not only in modern psychology but in many other fields of study and many areas of life. Some students are, of course, prepared to interpret functions without special discussion. Many are not so prepared. It is hoped that all will benefit by the systematic, though elementary, treatment of the topic.

The original materials out of which the text was constructed were developed in connection with the teaching of two different introductory courses at the University of North Carolina at Greensboro. One was a two-semester course with laboratory; the other, a one-semester course without laboratory. Students in both courses were exposed to the ideas and provided many valuable reactions.

The author wishes to acknowledge his indebtedness to others in bringing this book to completion:

The University's Council on Research provided material assistance in the production of the manuscript.

The staff of the University's excellent library made the task of surveying literature much easier than was anticipated.

Professor Kendon Smith of the University's Department of Psychology provided many valuable suggestions and criticisms.

Miss June Rubin, formerly an art-education major at the University, gave extensive assistance in the preliminary selection and preparation of illustrations.

Betty M. Ray, wife of the author, shared a large part of every phase of the arduous task. Without this assistance, the project could not have been brought to completion until far into the future.

Finally, the author wishes to acknowledge the benefit he derived from writing the book. The first-hand examination of hundreds of research reports and the required concentration on the task of defining and describing scientific psychology for college students constituted a whole education in themselves.

WILLIAM S. RAY

Greensboro, N. C.

Contents

THE

SCIENCE

OF

PSYCHOLOGY

PART 1

PRELIMINARY
DEFINITIONS

1

Psychological
Knowledge

PSYCHOLOGY IS ONE OF THE FIELDS OF KNOWLEDGE IN WHICH THE objects of investigation are living animal organisms. Because there already exists a substantial body of evidence concerning relations between certain psychological characteristics of these organisms and their physicochemical characteristics and because there may be new additions to this body of evidence in the future, psychology has a connection with biology and must take account of developments in its various fields, including anatomy, biochemistry, genetics, neurology, and physiology. Because of this connection and their interest in it, some psychologists classify psychology as a biological science. Other psychologists are especially interested in the interactions of animal organisms. These psychologists, many of whom concentrate their efforts on the investigation of human person-to-person and person-to-group relations, prefer to classify psychology as a social science.

The history of psychology, which constitutes an important part of the history of scientific thought, has been written at length and in detail by Boring[1,2]. The historical origins of many topics in modern psychology can be traced to other fields of knowledge. Psychology had beginnings in physiology's studies of the functions of sense organs, nerves, and brains, in astronomy's studies of errors of observation, and in physics' studies of light

3

and sound. Its principal antecedents, however, were in philosophy, especially that branch in which the theory of the association of ideas developed. In the early part of the nineteenth century there were not yet any psychologists, only physiologists investigating the body and philosophers discussing the mind. In 1879, at the University of Leipzig, Germany, Wilhelm Wundt established the first psychological laboratory. Wundt, a former physiologist, was the first to call himself a psychologist. In 1890 there occurred an important event in the early development of psychology in America: the publication of a very successful and widely read textbook, *Principles of Psychology,* by William James, the Harvard philosopher and psychologist.

In the last years of the nineteenth century the connections between philosophy and psychology were still strong, but in the early years of the twentieth century the two disciplines began to go their separate ways, developing different topics and attacking different problems. Today they have a new relationship. Psychology, as well as other fields of science, has become dependent on philosophy in two matters. Psychologists, along with all other scientists, make extensive use of the principles of formal logic and look to philosophers for leadership in the formulation of a philosophy of science. All the sciences are indebted to philosophy for the development of subjects such as the nature of knowledge, methods of acquiring knowledge, and the role of language in this endeavor.

From its beginning, psychology has had its quantitative developments, and these have continued to expand and multiply in recent years. The principal quantitative areas are measurement of psychological characteristics and evaluation of research data. Since psychology offers many opportunities for applications of mathematics, training in mathematics is considered an important part of a research psychologist's background.

That modern psychology, to a considerable degree, is quantitative deserves emphasis. In everyday life, it is a common practice to describe people or animals in terms of qualities or kinds. Although psychologists do make some use of qualitative descriptions, in much of their research they try to assess the quantity or degree of a given psychological characteristic or circumstance; that is, they try to give expression to their knowledge in terms of numbers. Qualitative description appears to be easier than quantitative description. One learns early to put people in categories. This classifying is usually quite crude. One may think in terms of the good and the bad, the right and the wrong, the honest and the dishonest, the loyal and the disloyal, the bright and the dull, the friendly and the unfriendly, the bold and the shy, the brave and the cowardly, the successful and the unsuccessful, and so on. Thus in everyday life the possibility that psychological characteristics may vary in degree is often overlooked, and use is seldom made of quantitative description.

In addition to being the subject of teaching and research, activities which are carried on in nearly all colleges and universities, psychology is a field of many practical applications. Psychologists work in business, industry, government, the military services, and psychiatric agencies and institutions of varied kinds. Furthermore, psychology is a basic subject in the training of professional personnel in education, physical education, home economics, industrial engineering, and the health sciences, including medicine and psychiatry as well as the related fields of nursing and social work.

Psychology is a large and complex field. Its subject matter has been fractionated into many parts, thus reflecting the specialized interests of its members. Despite the high degree of specialization among psychologists, there is much agreement among them as to the general character of psychology. This agreement is manifest in the wide acceptance of a standard for the continuing development of psychology.

A Standard for Psychology

It is important to distinguish between two kinds of knowledge: empirical and rational. Empirical knowledge is the agreement in reports of repeated observations made by two or more persons. Rational knowledge is the agreement in results of problem solving by two or more persons. The fundamental procedure in the obtaining of empirical knowledge is observation. The fundamental procedure in the obtaining of rational knowledge is logical thinking or deduction. Psychology is an empirical field of knowledge. It follows that psychological knowledge derives from observation. Chemistry is also an empirical field. An example of an empirical fact from chemistry is the repeated observation that water boils at a temperature of 100 degrees centigrade at sea level. Mathematics is an example of a rational field of knowledge. An example of a rational fact from arithmetic is the result obtained by adding a set of numbers. The fact that two plus three plus four equals nine is established by a process of logical thinking. Both kinds of knowledge are subject to error. Error in empirical knowledge is associated with the occasions on which observations are obtained. One part of this error can be attributed to the observer and his instruments; another part can be attributed to extraneous influences operating at the time of observation. The error in rational knowledge is attributed to the drawing of illogical conclusions.

Although psychology is basically an empirical field of knowledge, it does have something to do with rational knowledge. In the planning of research and the extensive use of computation and other quantitative methods in the evaluation of research data, strong demands are made on the reasoning powers of psychologists. It is not only usage in research, however, which accounts for psychology's concern with rational knowledge. Theory is important to psychology, and logical thinking or deduction is important in theorizing. Indeed, the value of a theory is determined, in part, by the nature of the deductions obtained from that theory. The value of a theory may be questioned if it does not yield rigorously deduced hypotheses which can be tested in research. If a theorizer does not deduce his hypotheses correctly, then his theorizing is a wasted effort.

The quest of the psychologist for new empirical knowledge is marked by a desire for accuracy. Although knowledge is never perfect and the psychologist's propositions setting forth his knowledge always contain error (sometimes little and sometimes much), those propositions which are highly inaccurate and are demonstrated to be contrary to the evidence are denied a place in psychology. Furthermore, the psychologist's quest for knowledge is, in large part, a continuing effort to reduce the amount of error in his propositions.

The psychologist's goal is a body of fact. Psychology is to be realistic. Sophistry is not to be permitted: psychology will not be based upon argument which is plausible but fallacious; it will be based upon observation guided by logic.

Psychology is to be objective in that its propositions are to be impersonal and unprejudiced, thereby encouraging intellectual acceptance and agreement. It is not to be subjective, for if its propositions were to contain personal beliefs such as moral judgments of good and bad, personal attitudes of approval and disapproval, or expressions of liking and disliking, they would surely be the subject of opposition and controversy. Objective data provide one common basis for agreement among men. Subjective data are usually a source of disagreement. Agreement arising out of objectivity is considered a desirable end.

The quest for new empirical knowledge is marked by a desire for order. To this end the propositions of psychology are to be systematically organized. It is not sufficient to collect facts, no matter how accurate they may be. The achievement of knowledge in its highest form requires that the facts be organized and integrated. Systematic organization implies the achievement of generalizations consistent with the facts.

The standard for psychology extends to its use of rational methods. Psychologists are constantly alert to detect logical fallacies in the planning and evaluation of research. In theorizing, hypotheses and conclusions found to be illogical are quickly rejected.

All of this amounts to saying that, to the extent that it is possible, psychology is to be scientific. This is the standard against which psychologists' efforts to build a field of knowledge are to be evaluated. It is a standard established and supported by a majority of men and women with advanced training in the field.

The agreement among psychologists extends to what psychology is not. Psychology is not phrenology, the old study of the conformation of the skull to learn about the faculties of the mind. It is not astrology, the pseudoscience of the influences of the stars on human affairs. It is not palmistry, the practice of telling fortunes and judging human traits by studying the palm of the hand. It is not magic, the production of effects by either legerdemain or the mastery of secret forces in nature. It is not parapsychology, the study of the perception of objects and events by some mysterious sense not as yet identified with any organ of the body as, for example, sight is identified with the eyes.

Psychology has nothing to do with mental telepathy, the affecting of one mind by the thoughts or feelings of another outside the ordinary channels of communication; with mind reading, the art of perceiving another's thought without communication in the normal manner; with spiritualism, a belief that the spirits of the dead communicate with the living through physical phenomena, trances, or mediums; or with so-called psychical research, the investigation of phenomena on the hypothesis that there is mental activity quite apart from the body.

Psychology is not religion; it is not meant to be a substitute for religion; it is neither ally nor adversary of religion. Psychology has nothing to say concerning the validity of religious doctrines and beliefs unless they are inconsistent with established facts. Psychology is a field of empirical knowledge whereas religion, of course, has much to do with matters of faith. The characteristics of people revealed by their participation in religious activities may be investigated, however, and the results may constitute important and valuable knowledge.

Acting in a manner consistent with the standard that psychology is a scientific field of knowledge, the great majority of psychologists endeavor to do research and teaching free of subjectivity, superstition, dogmatism, provincialism, chauvinism, ethnocentrism, and undisciplined speculation.

There is abundant popular literature in which psychology is given a treatment that renders it temporarily intriguing and exciting. It may be portrayed as dealing primarily with bizarre, morbid, mysterious, or taboo topics. It may be given a superficial appearance of intellectual respectability through emphasis on theories so abstruse as to be of questionable value. Unfortunately, it may take on the appearance of an esoteric body of knowledge quite attractive to the novice. Unfortunately, too, the impression may be conveyed to scientists in other fields that psychology is a cult devoted to ideas which, in the end, constitute no more than a series of intellectual fads. Developed along these lines, its entertainment value is considerable, but its benefits are not those of a well-grounded and well-balanced field of knowledge. These mildly sensationalistic treatments are avoided in the main stream of modern psychological writing. In general the journals and textbooks which serve the profession of psychology reveal a commitment to serious and responsible scholarship in the pursuit of knowledge. Psychology is given a straightforward and representative treatment, which ultimately many people find to be interesting, satisfying, practical, and profitable.

The object of study in psychology is a living (human or infrahuman) animal organism. When it is being investigated, the organism is referred to as a *subject*. Man has been the central subject of the psychologist's investigations but chimpanzees, monkeys, dogs, cats, rats, cockroaches, ants, paramecia, and other lower animals have also received considerable study. This text deals only with human organisms. Unless explicit reference is made to lower animals, the student can assume that the discussion refers to humans.

Fundamental Terms

Before a definition of psychology can be presented in an understandable form, it is necessary to introduce and distinguish between two fundamental terms: consciousness and behavior.

Consciousness means *the awareness of events within one's self. Experience* is employed widely as an equivalent term. On certain occasions requiring an adjective, *experiential* is valuable. When one wishes to refer to a person who advocates the study of consciousness or emphasizes its importance, *phenomenologist* is useful. *Consciousness, experience, experiential,* and *phenomenologist* are the terms which will be regularly employed in the discussion to follow.

One may report the events of consciousness as they occur. As he does so, it is said that he is *introspecting* or *using the method of introspection.* For example, during a brief period, as I sit at my desk, it is possible for me to report what I see, hear, smell, and otherwise sense, what I feel, and what I think. What I see includes a table, a radio, a window, trees, houses, birds, and a cat. What I hear are voices in the distance, the noise of a typewriter, a passing automobile, the closing of a door, and a motor starting. What I smell are cooking odors from the house next door. As for what I feel, I have, at the moment, no intense feelings, but only a pleasant sense of well-being and friendly disposition toward my surroundings and the people in them. What I think includes an idea about the international situation, the prospects of a good breeze for sailing later in the day, and the order of topics for an outline I must construct. This introspective report is brief, informal, and sketchy. Only prominent events are noted. An introspective report can be much more systematic and complete. It can be limited to only one kind of event, or it can be expanded to cover a wide variety of events. An introspective report could, of course, be quite detailed. For example, I could try to analyze my visual experience into lights, shadows, dots, lines, contours, colors, patterns, textures, and spatial arrangements.

If one takes the point of view that psychology is to be developed as a science, then an important feature of experience is that it is private. The experiencer is the sole witness to these inner events: the one having the experience is the only knower. Other people cannot share the experience itself; they can only witness a report of it. The report, of course, may or may not correspond to the experience. How completely and accurately an individual reports on any occasion is a matter of conjecture, for the fidelity of the experiencer's report of inner events cannot be checked. Occasionally, one encounters a person who seriously believes that psychiatrists, psychoanalysts, and psychologists know powerful methods for what may be crudely described as reading a person's mind, and who believes that it is possible to force another individual into revealing what he is really experiencing. This is a mistaken notion. There are no such methods. Consciousness is private.

Although consciousness is private, man can at least report to other men concerning it. The lower animals, of course, cannot report to human observers concerning their experiences. Consequently, the nature of consciousness among the lower animals, and even its existence, can be debated. No good purpose would be served by trying to settle these issues here. When consciousness is discussed in this text, it is the consciousness of humans, not that of the lower animals.

Earlier an extended statement was made of a standard for psychology. In brief, it was that psychology is to be scientific. Stating that experience is private implies that it cannot be investigated scientifically. Consequently, experience is not an object of study in a scientific psychology. One cannot be accurate about the experience of others. Factual knowledge about the experience of others is impossible to attain.

Early in the history of psychology strenuous attempts were made to investigate experience scientifically. These attempts did not succeed and gave no promise of success. Indeed, the conclusion of some psychologists was that there was no possibility of success. A reaction followed.

John Watson was the first of many psychologists who decided that experience should be eliminated from psychology. In the years between 1913 and 1919 he took the position that the existence of consciousness was an assumption which could not be proved. Others were not so extreme. They agreed that psychology should be scientific and that experience posed a serious problem, but they were unwilling to say that experience was irrelevant to psychology. The whole matter has been controversial for half a century.

Although experience cannot be investigated scientifically, it has remained on the psychological scene. What is the explanation of this apparent inconsistency? If experience can be investigated, then psychologists should get on with the job. If it cannot be investigated, should they not eliminate it? The seemingly contradictory facts are that the scientific investigation of experience is impossible and that the language of experience continues as a substantial part of the language of most psychologists. In fact, many who agree that the scientific study of experience is impossible continue to use experiential terms. Actually the facts are not contradictory. Experience is relevant to psychology, but not as an object of study. Its relevance lies in its being immediately a source of language and ultimately a source of theory. The position taken here is that experience has an important place in psychology as one source of abstract concepts and, consequently, identifies a major division of psychological theory.

The statement that experience cannot be investigated scientifically does not imply that an individual cannot have personal knowledge of his own experience. Awareness is a kind of knowledge or might be so considered. It is not what is meant, however, by scientific knowledge. Some psychologists prefer to limit the word *knowledge* to its scientific use. They would say that one knows only what one can publicly demonstrate or verify. The issue is one of definition. One way of resolving the issue is to distinguish between personal knowledge and scientific knowledge.

Although this personal knowledge is private and must remain so, individuals persist in trying to share it. How successful the attempts at communication and accumulation are cannot be determined. In judging the degree of this success, one may be misled by the agreement in reports of experience. For example, ten men asked by an examiner to name the color of a card may all say, "Red." Two statements may now be made about the situation. The first is that all ten men saw red. The second is that all ten men said they saw red. Which is the better statement of what was observed by the examiner? The second, of course. It is uncontroversial. One may view this distinction as trivial, but in another situation where the same men are asked to sort cards of various colors into separate piles, one or more of the men may be observed to fail in separating red cards from green ones. His failure is easily described in terms of what he did but not of what he saw. Furthermore, the statement of what he said in the first situation does not contradict a statement about his failure in the second situation. A statement about what he actually saw in both situations would be very difficult to formulate. The validity of personal knowledge will always be debatable because there are no standards for its acquisition. If the criterion of scientific knowledge is applied, of course, personal knowledge is discredited. The attempted pooling of personal knowledge may account for a substantial part of the body of ideas and beliefs shared by the members of a society.

The Language of Experience

Although experience is private, everyday discourse exhibits considerable agreement among people regarding certain of its prominent features. In fact, a substantial vocabulary has developed for conversing about experience. This vocabulary is used freely but tentatively. In listening to someone give an introspective report, people often assume that the reporter is being reasonably accurate. Sometimes, however, in special circumstances the listeners are highly skeptical regarding the accuracy of the report. There is, as has already been said, no absolute criterion for accuracy.

Many of the words employed in everyday life for conversing about experience have been adopted in psychology but, in the process, have undergone a special kind of redefinition. This statement does not imply that the words have been deprived of their original everyday meaning. The statement does imply that the original meaning is not adequate for the psychologist's special purposes in developing a science of psychology. Additional meaning, necessary for those purposes, is provided by the redefinition. The words retain their original experiential referents as hypothesized referents. Their definitions are sophisticated, however, to provide them with public referents, thereby making them acceptable in scientific psychology. The nature of this special kind of redefinition of experiential terms will be described in Chapter 4.

In Chapter 2, an account will be given of the categories of experience as these are distinguished and labeled by psychologists. This account will also include a brief description of the salient properties of experience within each category and their physical and physiological correlates. The account is intended as a starting point for the transition from use of the terms in ordinary discourse about experience to their technical use in psychology after redefinition.

Behavior

Behavior has two definitions. The everyday meaning is deportment, the way in which one complies with the conventions of social living. If an adolescent obeys his parents, displays good manners, respects the property and rights of others, and abides by the regulations of his school, he is considered to exhibit proper behavior. Improper behavior is misbehavior. In psychology, however, the technical meaning of behavior involves no notion of conventions or standards. It has no connotation of propriety.

In psychology behavior refers to any overt action on the part of an animal organism. The action may be simple or complex. At one extreme, it may be blinking an eye, flexing a finger, tilting the head, swallowing some water, taking a step, uttering a sound, or putting a mark on an answer sheet. At the other extreme, it may be singing a song on a television show, attempting a ten-foot putt on the eighteenth hole in a golf tournament, bargaining for an automobile on a used car lot, taking a final examination in a freshman history course, painting a still life in an attic studio, or piloting an ocean liner from New York to Liverpool. From this point on, the word behavior will be used with the psychological meaning of overt action.

To observe is to see, hear, or otherwise perceive an object or event which is external to oneself. Although an object or event can be observed by only one person, it must be public in the sense that it could be perceived by others if they were present. An object or event which can be perceived by man is said to be observable. It follows that behavior is observable.

The psychologist, in his research, observes behavior. Although it is possible for him to observe his own behavior, the standard practice is for the investigator to observe the behavior of an organism distinguishable from himself. Very infrequently does he observe his own behavior to obtain data; self-observation is not, therefore, an important source of facts in psychology. Observation of the behavior of another person encounters less criticism than does self-observation. When he observes himself, there is the risk that the investigator, knowing the purposes and circumstances of the research, will be suspected of behaving to produce the desired results, and there is the additional risk that he will be charged with subjectivity more often than when he observes others. Finally, observation of a number of subjects provides a more adequate base for generalization than self-observation does.

Observation and behavior are the foundations of a public psychological knowledge of others. Observing behavior is what people can do together, in an attempt to acquire psychological knowledge, with confidence in the outcome of their endeavor. The individual can think about himself and observe himself in self-study; but he cannot fully share his self-study with anyone else, and he cannot fully share any other person's self-study. He *can* join on equal terms with other individuals in the study of the behavior of still other organisms. This public endeavor with all investigators on an equal footing accounts for most of modern psychological research. Thus the field of psychology is essentially the domain of public knowledge concerning the actions of animals—human and infrahuman.

Basing psychological knowledge on the observation of behavior does not achieve certainty for that knowledge. The observing of behavior, even under the best conditions, is subject to error. The psychologist's only recourse is replication, the repetition of research by himself and others. Psychological knowledge becomes more and more dependable as the research on which it is based is repeated and the results are confirmed by other investigators.

Earlier, in the discussion of consciousness, or experience, the label *phenomenologist* was applied to the psychologist who emphasizes the importance of experience in psychology. The label *behaviorist* is applied to the psychologist who emphasizes behavior and rejects experience. This use of labels does not imply that it is possible to classify psychologists as either phenomenologists or behaviorists. Psychologists vary in their support of these two extreme positions. The differentiation of these positions does imply that psychologists are not in complete agreement on the definition of psychology.

No matter how one defines psychology, if he engages in any active study of people or the lower animals, he observes behavior. His language may suggest otherwise, but to the extent that it does, it will be erroneous and misrepresentative of the situation. He may think about people or the lower animals without reference to their behavior. He may expound and argue theoretically about experience at great length, but when he moves to gather information, what he does is observe and what he observes is behavior.

A psychological investigation, if it is not just idle speculation, always involves concrete apparatus and particular situations, definite operations or procedures, and specific actions on the part of the organisms investigated. The psychologist cannot ignore the apparatus, the operations, and the actions. He must give an account of them in his report of his findings, no matter what the terms of his theory are or how general his interpretation is. The significance of his results is determined in large part by the realities of his research.

One way of viewing the continuing debate between the phenomenologist and the behaviorist is in terms of their use of language. The behaviorist has insisted on setting forth in clear and unmistakable terms the realities of the research, as well as giving close attention to the significance imparted by these features. In this respect, the behaviorist's position is unassailable because the research cannot take place without apparatus, operations, and actions. Research cannot occur without the observing of behavior. The behaviorist has also insisted on minimizing or even eliminating experiential language. In addition, he has explored the possibilities of, and shown a preference for, theory expressed without use of experiential language. In actual practice, however, psychologists rarely, if ever, succeed in being pure behaviorists. In their writing and teaching, they do not avoid completely and absolutely the use of experiential terms. The behaviorist actually has great difficulty in describing many complex forms of behavior without employing the language of experience.

On the other side of the debate, the phenomenologist has insisted on the potential value of experiential language. He cannot validly argue that a psychologist must use concepts associated with experience as the behaviorist can argue with respect to operational and behavioral terms. Although it has not been done, it is conceivable that a behavioristic psychology could be written without a single experiential word in it. An experiential psychology could not be written without an account of the observation of behavior. If it were written, it would not be based on research. The phenomenologist can argue, however, that the concepts associated with experience are valuable, especially in formulating theory. In short, the behaviorist can say that one must use operational and behavioral terms; the phenomenologist can say that one may find value in experiential terms for theoretical purposes.

There is the possibility that an individual may acquire knowledge based on his own observations of the behavior of others under circumstances in which he is the only observer and in which research cannot be done. These circumstances obtain wherever custom has established areas of strict privacy and confidence in relations among people. This knowledge may be communicated widely in a society. It may become a part of the working knowledge of counselors of all types, including priests, rabbis, pastors, lawyers, social workers, psychiatrists, psychoanalysts, and clinical psychologists. As long as areas of life are closed to research, however, this knowledge will be suspect and it will not be accorded the status of scientific knowledge. These statements are not meant to imply that research cannot be done in clinical and counseling situations; it can be and is being done. When it is, the results may add to scientific psychological knowledge. When research is not possible, however, the unsupported observations of one clinician or counselor are subject to serious question.

The Definition of Psychology

It is now possible to present a definition of psychology based on all the considerations of the preceding discussion regarding a standard for psychology, the nature of experience, the nature of behavior, and the nature of scientific knowledge about animals.

Psychology is the science of the behavior of living animals. Behavior, not consciousness, is the activity investigated. Both behavior and consciousness have important places, however, in psychological theory. Some psychologists prefer behavioral theory; some prefer experiential theory.

Relativism in Psychology

All sciences are relativistic in the sense that every fact obtains only under some specified set of conditions. These conditions, which are called parameters, are sometimes quite numerous. Under different conditions, a different fact obtains. A fact having no parameters would have great generality. A fact having a thousand parameters would have great specificity. A fact having a few parameters is not necessarily more important in any respect than one having many, but generality is valued more highly than specificity. Here is an example from chemistry. Water boils at 100 degrees centigrade. Is this statement acceptable? If it were, the implication would be that there are no parameters and that this fact has very great generality. The statement is not acceptable, however, for it is important to indicate the condition of atmospheric pressure under which the fact obtains, as in this corrected statement: Water boils at 100 degrees centigrade at sea level or when the atmospheric pressure is 1034 grams per square centimeter. At lower pressures, like those encountered high on a mountain, the boiling point is lower. Although other parameters might be specified, statements of boiling points of water with the parameter of atmospheric pressure given have very great generality.

In a physical science like chemistry, parameters have to do with materials and circumstances. In the laboratory these can often be rigorously controlled. When they are specified and standardized, a fact can often be demonstrated to hold true in laboratories all over the world. In chemical engineering, strict control of a few parameters may make possible the practical application of chemical knowledge in a wide variety of everyday circumstances.

In a field such as psychology, the situation is quite different. The materials are people or lower animals. The circumstances are those of the situation in which they live. Especially with people, the parameters may be quite numerous. People cannot be purified or homogenized as chemicals can be. Their life circumstances cannot be manipulated even in the psychological laboratory as can conditions in the chemistry laboratory. Consequently, many of the facts of psychology are specific, and psychology gives the impression of being far more relativistic than chemistry.

Psychologists value generality and work constantly toward the achievement of higher levels. Because their field is highly relativistic, however, psychologists often emphasize method instead of facts. It becomes important to know and to teach, not a fact specific to one situation, but a method which could be applied in a variety of situations to obtain the facts appropriate to those situations. For example, it may be much more valuable to teach, not the degree of demonstrated reliability of a certain psychological test on a particular occasion, but the method by means of which the degree of reliability of a test can be determined for any situation. Psychology's relativism shifts a great deal of attention from fact to method. In practical situations in education, business, industry, and government, the psychologist may value methods by means of which he can obtain facts for those situations more than he values facts obtained at other times and places for people and circumstances which may be quite different from those with which he is concerned. These comments are not meant to imply that there are no psychological facts having generality. They do imply that there are two ways in which generality may be obtained: one involves facts; the other, methods.

Three Kinds of Discourse

It is useful to distinguish between three kinds of discourse on psychological matters: the common lore, technical material, and introductory exposition.

The common lore is a hodgepodge of ideas about people, including some facts, much misinformation, many misconceptions, and a variety of beliefs and values. The lore varies from person to person, but people in groups such as families, communities, and nations have much in common. The ideas cover many areas of life: if you spare the rod, you spoil the child; Negroes are inferior to whites; Southerners are hospitable; the American soldier is the best in the world; democratic procedures for making decisions are better than authoritarian procedures; politicians are dishonest; for every woman there is the right man; labor acts only in self-interest; management acts only in self-interest; Democrats are spendthrifts; New Englanders are thrifty; children should respect their parents; children should be required to earn their allowances; a mother's love cannot be equaled; woman's place is in the home.

Most people, if not all, participate in the exchange and propagation of the lore. Most people think they understand it and think they know something in understanding it. What they actually know, if it were sorted out by any reasonable standard, would constitute only a very small part of the whole. Most people accept the lore somewhat uncritically as a general practice. Some are skeptical of it and quick to admit being so. Some are committed to it and react defensively if it is questioned.

Psychology is not a study of the lore and does not undertake to confirm or contradict it in whole or by parts. One could know a great deal of psychology and have little to say about the lore or any part of it. Practical applications of psychology do not necessarily pertain to it and are not necessarily anticipated by it.

As one studies psychology, it is not difficult to see the possibility of a connection between certain facts and some idea in the lore. If one accepts this tenuous connection somewhat uncritically, the facts may appear to justify or condemn the idea. There is nothing inherently wrong with this kind of interpretation except that it is farfetched. Furthermore, a reasonably intelligent person needs no special help in making the connection, since it is so easily made.

Scientific psychology has not developed subservient to the lore. It has developed as men have found ways of obtaining knowledge in an atmosphere of freedom to seek that knowledge wherever it is to be found. There are tremendous gaps between knowledge and the lore. It is suggested that the student do some conjecturing about the possibilities of connections, without committing himself to an uncritical acceptance of them.

Technical material in psychology can be divided into three parts: the methods, results, and conclusions of research; theories, or references to them, and statements of hypotheses tested in research; and generalizations and principles. This technical material is psychology.

Introductory exposition is discourse intended to facilitate the student's transition from involvement with the common lore to an understanding and appreciation of the technical material which is psychology. Much introductory exposition must necessarily be below the level of technical discourse. As one might anticipate, the presentation of scientific psychology in the chapters which follow combines introductory exposition and technical material. The former is the means; the latter, the end.

Chapter Summary

Psychology is a science in the making. Observation is its fundamental procedure. Since consciousness is private and not observable, it cannot be the subject of investigation in a scientific psychology. Behavior, which is public and observable, is the subject of investigation and is also the base for a large part of psychological theory. Consciousness does, however, have a place of importance in psychology. Experiential terms are employed in many concepts for which behavioral terms are either clumsy or inadequate. These experiential terms have undergone redefinition, a process which will be discussed at length in Chapter 4. Experiential language is also the base for another large part of psychological theory. Scientific psychology has no necessary connection with the common lore.

References

1. Boring, E. G. *Sensation and Perception in the History of Experimental Psychology.* New York: Appleton-Century-Crofts, Inc., 1942.
2. ———. *A History of Experimental Psychology,* 2nd ed. New York: Appleton-Century-Crofts, Inc., 1950.

Consciousness

ALTHOUGH MANY EXPERIENTIAL TERMS IN EVERYDAY LANGUAGE are also used in psychology, their technical meanings are different from their common meanings. The differences come about in the process of redefinition, which will be described in Chapter 4. As preparation for that redefinition, there will be undertaken next the establishment of a basic vocabulary of experiential words. Common meanings will be reviewed and clarified, and some new words will be introduced. The purpose of this discussion is to provide a starting point for the transition from everyday language to the technical language. Discussing consciousness in this way is not psychology, strictly speaking, but it is valuable preparation for psychology. The transition only begins here; it does not end until redefinition has been presented.

Establishing a vocabulary of experiential terms is the main purpose of this chapter, but it is not the only purpose. There are two others: the recognition of biological correlates of properties of experience; and the specification of physical correlates of those properties.

Categories and Properties of Experience

Since experience is immaterial and complex, it is difficult to analyze and classify. Many attempts at analysis and classification by psychologists in the past have produced different schemes to take account of the varieties of experience as well as the characteristics of the situation in which the experience occurs. No one of these schemes can be said to be correct in an absolute sense. A large part of everyday language provides a highly detailed classification of experience, but one cannot be confident that the exact shades of meaning intended by many of these terms can actually be respected or fulfilled.

The schemes which have been devised by psychologists in the past have varied somewhat with respect to the number of categories and their names, but the schemes have had much in common. Three categories which appear frequently in these schemes will be employed here. The names of the three categories are perception, feeling, and thought. Other terms have been used by other writers. Sensation has been linked with perception to constitute one category. Emotion and motivation have been linked with feeling or used in place of it as a major heading. Thought has sometimes referred principally to reasoning, but it is used here in a broader sense to cover a number of conscious activities. Some writers prefer terms such as perceiving, feeling, and thinking in the form of present participles because they may convey the idea of a continuing process or activity better than terms such as perception, emotion, and thought, which may incorrectly suggest static entities. Whatever the specific form, these words are intended to refer to continuing inner events and not to entities in any other sense.

PERCEPTION

Perception is the category of the familiar senses of seeing, hearing, smelling, tasting, and touching. Two unfamiliar senses are also included in the category: the sense of position or movement of the limbs and other parts of the body; and the sense of body rotation and head tilt. Psychologists have special terms for these senses as indicated by the following equivalents: seeing, vision; hearing, audition; smelling, olfaction; tasting, gustation; touching, cutaneous sensitivity; the sense of position and movement, kinesthesis; the sense of body rotation and head tilt, static sensitivity.

The various experiences of each sense have properties which can be identified and distinguished. These properties can be classified as either *qualities* or *quantities*. A qualitative property is one that varies in kind; a quantitative property is one that varies in degree. A quantitative property is also known as a *dimension*.

Biological Correlates

In addition to being differentiated in experience, the senses are differentiated in terms of their association with parts and processes of the body. It is this association to which we refer in speaking of the biological correlates of experience. Biological correlates fall into three groups: anatomical, physiological, and biochemical. It is a commonplace that man sees with his eyes, hears with his ears, tastes with his tongue, smells with his nose, and has a variety of experiences through the surface of his body. These are, of course, only gross descriptions of the organs involved in the several perceptions. Much research has been directed toward establishing in detail the anatomical, physiological, and biochemical correlates of experience. The specific details of organic structure and function relating to sensory experience constitute a major topic of study in the specialized area of physiological psychology as well as in physiology itself. Much of the investigation of sensory physiology is microscopic in level since it deals with cells, the structural and functional units of a living organism.

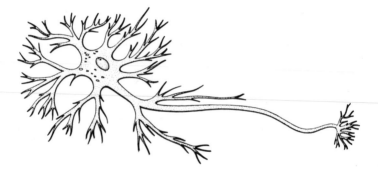

Figure 2-1. A schematic drawing of a neuron. The numerous small branches at the left are dendrites, the receivers of impulses. The large branch extending to the right is the axon, the transmitter of impulses to other neurons.

There is extensive knowledge concerning three classes of cells which figure prominently in the functioning of the body during sensory experiences: *one,* receptors, the anatomical points of origin of experience in the body; *two,* sensory neurons, the transmitters of electrochemical impulses from the receptors to the brain directly, or indirectly by way of the spinal cord; and *three,* neurons which make up the masses of tissue called the brain and the spinal cord. Figure 2-1 is a schematic drawing of a neuron. There is, of course, great variation in the shape and size of neurons. Each neuron has two parts: a cell body and fibers. There are two types of fibers: dendrites, the receivers of stimulation; and axons, the deliverers of stimulation. A neuron conducts its electrochemical impulse at a fairly high speed. When the neuron discharges—that is, when an impulse starts to travel in it—it cannot immediately discharge again, but it soon recovers its capability. The tiny gap between one neuron and the next in a transmission

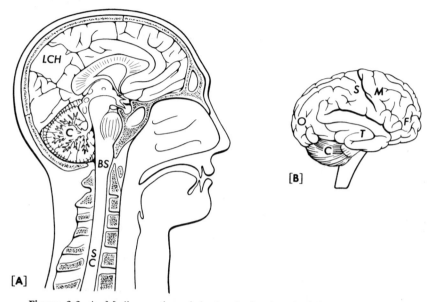

Figure 2-2. A: Median section of the head, showing the left cerebral hemisphere (*LCH*), the cerebellum (*C*), the brain stem (*BS*), and the spinal cord (*SC*). [Adapted from a drawing by Denoyer-Geppert Company, Chicago.] **B:** The right cerebral cortex, showing the occipital lobe (*O*), the cerebellum (*C*), the temporal lobe (*T*), the somesthetic area (*S*), the motor area (*M*), and the frontal lobe (*F*).

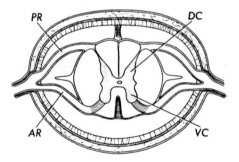

Figure 2-3. Cross section of the spinal cord showing a nerve's posterior root (*PR*) which contains sensory neurons, a nerve's anterior root (*AR*) which contains motor neurons, the dorsal column (*DC*) of the cord, and the ventral column (*VC*) of the cord. [Adapted from a drawing by Denoyer-Geppert Company, Chicago.]

series is called a synapse. The impulse does not cross the synapse but the adjacent neuron may be discharged by it. A bundle of neurons is called a nerve.

Impulses from visual, auditory, olfactory, gustatory, and static receptors travel by way of the various cranial nerves directly to the brain. Impulses from the cutaneous receptors of the face also travel directly to

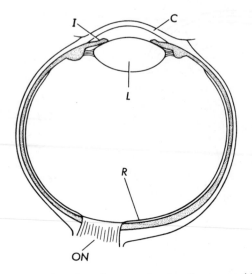

Figure 2-4. Horizontal section of an eye showing the cornea (*C*), the iris (*I*), the lens (*L*), the retina (*R*), and the optic nerve (*ON*). [From E. Gardner, *Fundamentals of Neurology*. Philadelphia: W. B. Saunders Company, 1947.]

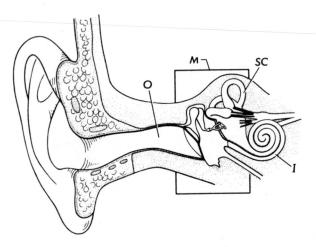

Figure 2-5. Schematic representation of the ear showing the canal of the outer ear (*O*), the region of the middle ear (*M*), the cochlea of the inner ear (*I*), and the semi-circular canals (*SC*). [Adapted from H. Davis, and S. R. Silverman, *Hearing and Deafness*. New York: Holt, Rinehart & Winston, Inc., 1960.]

the brain, but those from the cutaneous receptors of the body, excluding the face, and those from the kinesthetic receptors travel by way of the spinal cord to the brain. Various crudely defined areas of the cortex or outer layer of the brain are known to be associated with the various senses.

The parietal lobe contains areas involved in the cutaneous sense and kinesthesis; the occipital lobe, those involved in vision; and the temporal lobe,
those involved in audition. Figure 2-2A is a median section of the head
showing the position of the brain and spinal cord, and 2-2B is a drawing
of the cortex showing its sensory areas. Figure 2-3 is a cross section of
the spinal cord. Sensory neurons in the thirty-one pairs of spinal nerves
distributed along the spinal cord at regular intervals enter the spinal cord
from the rear or dorsal side of the spine and go to their locations in the
brain. (Sensory neurons are also called afferent neurons.)

The correlate of vision is action on the part of the receptor cells in
the retina of the eye, nerve fibers in the occipital lobes of the brain, and
nerve fibers connecting the retina and the brain. Figure 2-4 is a horizontal

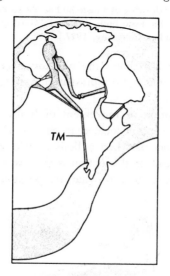

Figure 2-6. Schematic drawing of the region of the middle ear showing the tympanic
membrane or eardrum (*TM*). The three ossicles can be seen above the eardrum. [Adapted
from A. Keith, in T. Wrightson, *An Enquiry into the Analytical Mechanism of the Internal
Ear.* New York: The Macmillan Company, 1918.]

section of the eye. Receptors are distributed over the area called the
retina.

The correlate of audition is action on the part of receptor cells in the
inner ear, nerve fibers in the temporal lobes of the brain, and nerve fibers
connecting the inner ear and the brain. Figure 2-5 shows the relative positions of the outer, middle, and inner ears. An enlarged cross section of the
middle ear is presented in Figure 2-6.

In a similar fashion, neural paths function for gustation, olfaction, and
cutaneous sensitivity. Figure 2-7 is a schematic representation of the receptor cells and supporting cells which constitute a taste bud on the surface

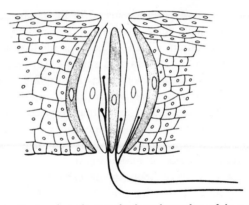

Figure 2-7. Schematic drawing of a taste bud on the surface of the tongue. Receptors for taste are contained in the taste buds. [From E. Gardner, *Fundamentals of Neurology.* Philadelphia: W. B. Saunders Company, 1947.]

of the tongue. Figure 2-8 shows the olfactory receptor cells of the nasal cavity. Figure 2-9 is a schematic representation of receptor cells for cutaneous sensitivity.

The sense of position or movement of limbs and other parts of the body has its special receptors located in the muscles, tendons, and joints. Action in these cells occurs when a limb is held in a certain position or is moved. A concomitant of this action is that as a person moves his arm, he is aware of where it is and what its position is after he stops the

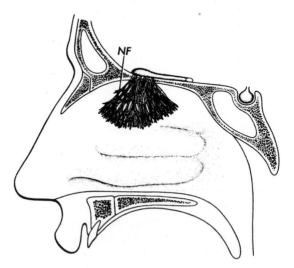

Figure 2-8. Olfactory structures in the nasal cavity showing the olfactory nerve filaments (*NF*). [From E. Gardner, *Fundamentals of Neurology.* Philadelphia: W. B. Saunders Company, 1947.]

movement. His awareness is associated with the sensitivity of receptor cells in the muscles, tendons, and joints.

The static sense has its receptor cells located in the head, in certain cavities of the innermost section of the ear. These cavities include three semicircular canals and two small chambers, all filled with a liquid (see Figure 2-5). Rotation of the head in any direction is accompanied by changes in the liquid of one or more of the canals and by movement of the end hairs of receptor cells located there. The tilt of the head at any moment is reflected in the two small chambers by the position of end hairs weighted with tiny particles of calcium and is accompanied by the action

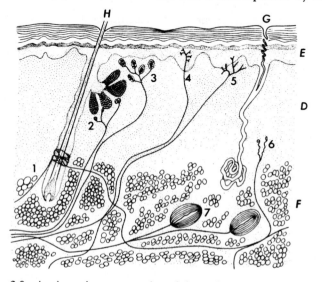

Figure 2-9. A schematic representation of the various receptors ·and nerves of the skin, showing epidermis (*E*), dermis (*D*), subcutaneous fat (*F*), duct of a sweat gland (*G*), hair (*H*), nerve ending around hair (*1*), end bulbs of Krause (*2*), Meissner's corpuscle (*3*), tactile discs (*4*), free nerve endings (*5*), Ruffini ending (*6*), and Pacinian corpuscle (*7*). [Adapted from E. Gardner, *Fundamentals of Neurology.* Philadelphia: W. B. Saunders Company, 1947; modified from original by Woolard, et al., *Journal of Anatomy,* **74**, 1940.]

of certain receptors. The corresponding features of experience are that one is aware of rotation and the tilt of his head at any given moment.

Theorizing about the detailed biological correlates of experience has produced many hypotheses. That every variation in experience may correspond to some variation in the structure or function of cells, the connections between cells, and the patterns of interaction among cells has been taken into account in much of the theorizing. Many important research findings have been reported but, of course, much remains to be discovered. Detailed consideration of this theory and evidence is ordinarily undertaken in physiological psychology.

Physical Correlates

The senses are also differentiated in terms of the circumstances, external to the organism, in which receptors act and experiences occur. It is known that various physical and chemical conditions are involved. The radiant energy which we commonly call light is known to be transmitted by the cornea, lens, and fluid of the eyeball, all of which constitute a kind of optical system, and is projected by this system as a pattern on the retina of the eye where light-sensitive cells, the receptors, are located. It is known that a vibrating object may produce rapid alternating increases and decreases in the pressure of the air and that the occurrence of these pressure changes near the ear is accompanied by movements of the eardrum or tympanic membrane. These movements are transmitted mechanically by a system of three tiny connected bones in the middle section of the ear and by the liquid of the spiral bony structure called the cochlea, in the innermost section of the ear, to the end hairs of the receptor cells which serve as points of origin for the experience of hearing. When certain substances in solution are introduced into the mouth and onto the surface of the tongue, chemically sensitive receptor cells act, and the experience of tasting occurs. When certain mixtures of air and gas are breathed into the nasal passages or are injected there by laboratory methods, cells high in the nasal passages connecting the nostrils and the throat act, and the action is accompanied by the experience of smelling. When the skin of the body is deformed by a hard object, certain cells act, and the experience is that of pressure on the body. When an object such as a metal rod is heated and applied to the skin, other cells act, and there occurs the feeling of warmth. When a cube of ice is applied to the skin, still other cells act, and there occurs the experience of cold. When a pin prick is administered to certain cells, pain occurs. Much research has been done on the effects of external physical and chemical conditions on the various sense organs and receptor cells. Widespread agreement has developed concerning the experiential correlates of variations in these conditions.

The external object (or event) whose presence (or occurrence) is the occasion for action of sensory receptors is called a *stimulus*. The plural form is *stimuli*. The concomitant action of a receptor cell is called a response to the stimulus. The action of a neuron connected with a receptor cell is considered to be a response to the stimulus provided by the action of that receptor. Similarly, the action of a neuron may be a response to the stimulation provided by another neuron.

Vision

Visual perception is the first of seven senses to be considered in the preliminary study of consciousness represented by this chapter. As already stated, the purpose of the preliminary study is to establish a vocabulary of experiential terms defined in nontechnical language. Although a number of properties of visual experience will be identified and described here, the actual psychology of vision will be presented in later chapters.

Some properties of visual experience—such as hue, brightness, size, distance, and distinctness—vary with remarkable regularity as changes occur in certain simple physical correlates. One might say that seeing is, in these respects, quite consistent with physical events. Sometimes, however, things are not seen as they are. An interrupted light is seen as continuous. Stationary lights give the appearance of movement. Lines of the same length appear to be different. These experiences, being inconsistent with physical stimulation, are called illusions. There are other properties —such as pattern, movement, and object quality—which have very complex physical correlates. In other words, for these experiences it is very difficult or even impossible to say exactly what the physical stimulation is. There are also occasions on which no change in visual perception occurs, although a change in stimulation actually does occur; that is, some aspect of experience remains constant when physical stimulation does not. For example, as one walks about a room, stimulation from furniture and other objects changes, but their shapes are seen as remaining the same. Finally, a change in visual experience may occur with no change in stimulation. The same things may be seen differently, as when a person shifts his attention from one feature of an object to another. These various kinds of visual experience are described in the sections which follow.

HUE. The radiant energy known as light is a stimulus to which receptor cells in the retina of the eye respond during the experience of seeing. The experience of seeing light has two properties with simple physical correlates which can be readily manipulated. One property, that of hue, is qualitative. Light, either emitted or reflected, may be seen as having one of the qualities: violet, blue, green, yellow, orange, red, or some intermediate hue.

In the psychological laboratory, light of a specified hue is often produced by passing white light through an appropriate filter. The light can then be viewed either directly or after reflection off a white screen. In manufacturing the filters, dyes are mixed in gelatin, which is then made into a film. The film may be cemented between pieces of glass for ease in handling and projecting.

Light of a specified hue can also be produced by reflecting white light off special paper. The paper is fixed to a metal disk which rotates at high speed and yields a reflecting surface which appears to be homogeneous. The disk, its motor, and its mount constitute a device commonly called a color wheel. A typical color wheel is shown in Figure 2-10.

The propagation of light of a specified hue from its source to the eye

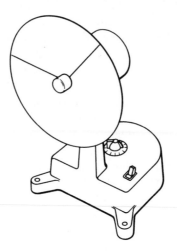

Figure 2-10. A color wheel. [Adapted from C. H. Stoelting Company.]

can be represented abstractly and graphically by a sine curve, a periodic curve consisting of a regular succession of waves. One complete cycle of a sine curve is shown in Figure 2-11. Related to variation in hue is a physical property of the radiation: its wave length, which corresponds to the horizontal distance covered by one cycle of the sine curve. Wave length is expressed in units called millimicrons, which are millionths of a millimeter. Light with a wave length of 430 millimicrons is perceived as violet in hue; that with a wave length of 477 millimicrons is blue; that of 515 millimicrons is green; that of 582 millimicrons is yellow; and that of 660 millimicrons is red. The figures associated with the various hues should be interpreted as locating bands through which there is a gradual transition from one

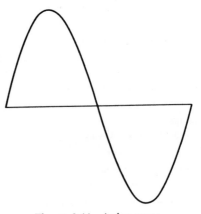

Figure 2-11. A sine curve.

hue to another through intermediate hues. The physical scale of wave length and the corresponding hues characteristic of visual experience are shown in Figure 2-12.

In laboratory work it may be important to know the characteristics of filters in terms of the wave lengths transmitted. The transmission characteristics of the widely used Wratten filters have been determined. For example, a red filter transmits from 590 millimicrons into the infrared with concentration around 617; a deep yellow filter transmits from 510 millimicrons into the infrared with concentration around 585; a green filter transmits from 480 to 620 millimicrons with concentration around 530; a blue filter transmits from 370 to 510 millimicrons with concentration around 440.

The scale of wave length of radiant energy extends in both directions far beyond the scale of that shown in Figure 2-12. The entire range is called the spectrum of electromagnetic radiation. The portion from 400 to 700 millimicrons, approximately, is called the visible spectrum. Immediately below the visible spectrum is ultraviolet radiation; immediately above is infrared.

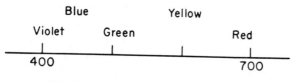

WAVE LENGTH IN MILLIMICRONS

Figure 2-12. The scale of wave length for the visible portion of the electromagnetic spectrum.

BRIGHTNESS. The other property of light with a simple physical correlate is brightness. Since it varies in degree, it is quantitative and is considered a dimension. In the laboratory, the brightness of emitted light may be varied by interposing neutral filters between the source and the eye of the viewer or by changing the voltage of the source of electric power. If the light is reflected from a color wheel, its brightness can be varied by changing the illumination of the wheel. The surface of the disk on a color wheel can also be varied from white through gray to black by combining white and black papers to give sectors of various sizes.

The physical property of the radiation related to variation in brightness is the amplitude of its waves. In Figure 2-11, amplitude is the height or depth to which the curve rises or descends, measured vertically from the horizontal line. For a given wave length, radiation waves of greater amplitude are seen as brighter than those of lesser amplitude. Related to amplitude is the physical measure: the energy level or intensity of the radiation.

Light of any wave length from the visible spectrum is without hue when it is presented to the viewer at a very low but visible intensity in a darkened room. If a uniform low intensity is employed for all wave lengths, the extremes of the spectrum will be dimmer than the middle portion. If this intensity is decreased, the middle portion of the spectrum remains visible longer than the extremes.

MIXTURES OF LIGHT. White light can be produced by mixing or combining lights of different wave lengths. When two lights in combination produce white, they are said to be complementary. Examples of complementary combinations are red and bluish green, yellow and blue, and orange and greenish blue. Mixtures of three or more hues will also yield white. For example, white light can be obtained by mixing red, blue, and green, in the proper intensities. Many other combinations give the same effect.

Not all combinations of two lights are complementary. Many combinations yield intermediate hues. Red and yellow yield an intermediate hue, orange; red and green yield yellow.

The mixing of lights of different hues can be done with either filters or colored papers. If two lights are mixed by means of filters, one filter is placed in front of each source and the transmitted radiation of both is projected on the same area of a white screen. An arrangement of projectors and screen employed in a student laboratory to demonstrate the mixing of light is shown in Figure 2-13. The mixture of light is reflected from the screen to the viewer's eyes. If the mixing is done with colored papers, a color wheel is employed. Two colored papers of different hues are fixed to the disk with each paper exposed on a sector of the disk. The wheel is rotated under white-light illumination, and the rapid alternation of the two kinds of reflected light accomplishes the mixing.

Although the color wheel is widely used in student laboratories, the best work is done with filters. Even so, filters themselves vary in efficiency. Among the most efficient are the Wratten filters. An example of a complementary pair is the combination yellow and blue. The yellow one transmits from 500 millimicrons into the infrared; the blue one, from 370 to 510. The overlap is very small. If they are projected on the same area of a white screen, with an appropriate adjustment of intensity, the projection area appears white. If one filter is placed over the other and the combination is held so that the sun is viewed through it, very little light is transmitted. However, if two *inefficient* filters, one predominantly yellow and the other predominantly blue, are placed in front of a source of white light, the transmitted light may be green. The predominantly yellow filter alone may transmit small amounts of green and orange in addition to yellow. The predominantly blue filter alone may transmit small amounts of violet and green in addition to blue. Together they eliminate all but green. This phenomenon of inefficient yellow and blue filters is the same one produced by the mixing of yellow and blue pigments to obtain green paint.

Combining lights of various hues may be considered to be a kind of synthesis. Thus white light can be said to be synthesized from two or more hues. Corresponding to this synthesis is a kind of analysis. White light passed through a prism and viewed directly or projected on a white screen will be separated into an array of lights of the hues violet, blue, green, yellow, orange, and red. Consequently it is said that white light can be analyzed into its component hues.

Another property of the experience of mixtures of wave lengths is saturation. A color of low saturation is pale or pastel and is said to be

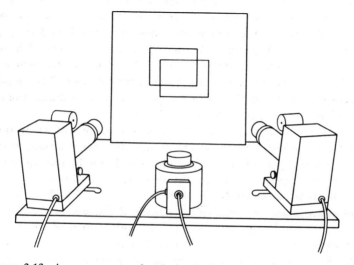

Figure 2-13. An arrangement of projectors and screen for mixing colors in a student laboratory. The area of overlap in the rectangles reflects the mixed light. The rheostat in the center controls the intensity of one of the projectors.

unsaturated. A color of high saturation is rich or vivid and is said simply to be saturated. In the laboratory the saturation of a red light can be reduced by mixing white light with it. The saturation of a red disk on a color wheel can be reduced by dividing the surface of the wheel into white and red sectors or into black and red sectors. In general, saturation is greatest in the middle range of brightness and least at the two extremes.

ANATOMICAL CORRELATES OF COLOR VISION. There has been much theorizing about the nature of the visual receptors with respect to their color sensitivity. One theory is that there are two kinds of receptor cells in the retina of the eye. The one kind of receptor, called a cone, mediates color. The other, called a rod, does not. The theory is widely accepted, but experts caution that rods and cones are not easily distinguished and that while some rods may not mediate any hues, some may mediate certain ones; and while some cones may mediate all hues, some may mediate only certain ones. Other theories have been concerned with the number of different kinds of color receptors. The well-established principles of color mixing have been employed in support of a theory that there are three kinds: red, blue, and green. There is some physiological evidence that supports a number as low as two or as high as four. The situation is further complicated by the fact that much of the physiological evidence has been obtained from the eyes of lower animals.

SIZE. If a large object and a small object are placed at equal distances from the viewer, the large object has the larger image: it occupies a larger part of the viewer's field of vision than does the small and may be seen as larger. This experience of size is related to the reflection of light rays from an object, their transmission into the eyeball, and their projection on the retina. The larger the object, the larger the retinal image and the greater the perceived size of the object. The size of the retinal image is usually expressed in terms of the visual or retinal angle. The visual angle is, approximately, the angle formed by two straight lines drawn from points on the object to the lens of the viewer's eye.

DISTANCE. If two objects identical in size are placed at unequal distances from a viewer, the near object has the larger image; that is, it occupies a larger part of the field of vision and may be seen as nearer. As is true of the experience of size, the experience of distance is related to the visual angle subtended by an object. The nearer the object, the larger the visual angle and the smaller the perceived distance of the object.

Since perceived size and distance are both related to the size of the retinal angle, the conclusion is justified that erroneous perceptions of size and distance may occur; that is, a near small object could be seen as larger than a large far object. That such errors do not occur frequently in ordinary perception indicates that perceived size and distance are related to other conditions in addition to the size of the retinal angle.

DISTINCTNESS. The distinctness of vision varies widely. In one book, the print seems distinct and is quite easy to read; in another, it seems indistinct and is very difficult to read. What are the physical correlates of the experience of legibility and illegibility of print? There are many. Legibility may be related to characteristics of the illumination, the paper, the ink, and the type. One very important factor is the size of the marks made by the type and the separations between those marks, or the sizes of the visual angles subtended by the marks and separations. Many combinations of mark and separation sizes are possible. If the width of marks and the width of separations are equal, then distinctness increases as both widths increase. Distinctness also increases as the printing is moved, relative to the viewer, from a distant point to a near point. These principles have been employed in the construction of devices commonly used in tests of visual acuity. The eye-chart test requires the subject to read lines of letters which vary in size. A device employed in a visual-acuity test, which requires the subject to state the position of a checkerboard in each one of a number of figures of different sizes, is shown in Figure 2-14.

DARK ADAPTATION. When one goes from a brightly lighted room to a dimly lighted room, objects in the latter may be quite indistinct. Within a few seconds, however, objects begin to become more distinct, and within a few minutes one's vision in the dimly lighted room may be relatively good. This change in distinctness after the sudden change from bright to dim illumination is called dark adaptation. In the dimly lighted room, objects

Figure 2-14. A subject being tested for visual acuity by means of an Ortho-Rater. The subject has to correctly identify the position of a checkerboard in a larger figure.

are not seen in their original vivid colors; they are seen very much in terms of grays. This feature of experience is associated primarily with the action of rods, not cones.

FUSION. If a source emits light periodically at a slow rate with a short on-phase and a long off-phase, then the light will be seen as flashing. As the rate of emission increases, the rate of occurrence of flashes will also increase, up to a point. At and beyond some point, the light will be seen as continuous, not flashing. The rate at which the transition occurs is called the critical flicker frequency or *CFF*. The rate at which fusion first occurs depends on many factors, including the brightness of the light, the general illumination, and the ratio of light and dark phases. In the

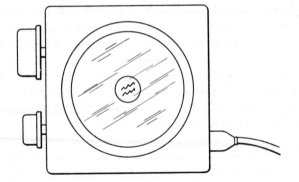

Figure 2-15. A stroboscope. The rate of flashing of the center light can be set by adjustment of one of the knobs on the left.

laboratory, a device called a stroboscope is sometimes used to produce a flashing light. One kind is shown in Figure 2-15. The rate of flashing can be controlled by the simple adjustment of a knob and can be read from a dial. Another laboratory device is the episcotister. It consists of a disk with cutout sectors. The disk is rotated in front of a light source and interrupts that light source. The rate of flashing of the light through the cutout sectors can be controlled by adjusting the speed of rotation. The relation between the on-phase and the off-phase is determined by the relative size of the cutout sector.

APPARENT MOVEMENT. The illusion of apparent movement should be

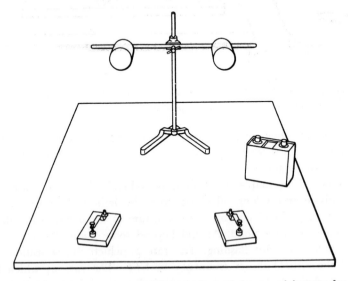

Figure 2-16. An arrangement of lights, telegraph keys, and battery for demonstrating apparent movement in a student laboratory.

familiar to all students because it is involved in moving pictures and the moving objects of many signs employed for advertising purposes. The illusion of movement can be created, when there actually is no movement, by flashing in succession two identical lights located in front of a viewer and some distance apart. An arrangement employed in a student laboratory to demonstrate apparent movement is shown in Figure 2-16. The interval between the flashing of the first light and the flashing of the second light can be adjusted so that the viewer will experience the movement of one light from one location to the other. With longer intervals between flashes, the viewer will experience two lights flashing in succession. With very short intervals, he will experience both lights flashing simultaneously. The magnitude of the interval yielding the illusion of movement depends upon the intensity of the lights, their distance apart, the particular viewer, and other conditions. The phenomenon has received considerable attention from psychologists since the investigations reported in 1912 by Max Wert-

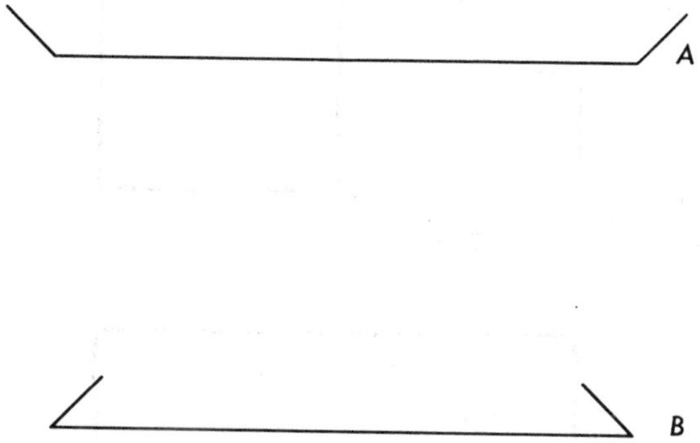

Figure 2-17. Equal horizontal lines which appear unequal.

heimer, who named it the *phi phenomenon*. The illusion of moving pictures is achieved by projecting in succession still pictures in which the position of the figures vary. Conditions are so selected that a very realistic appearance of continuous movement results. Advertising displays create the illusion of moving objects and figures by illuminating different parts of the display in rapid succession.

AN ILLUSION OF A DIFFERENCE IN LENGTH. Examine the drawing of Figure 2-17. The two horizontal and parallel lines are actually equal in length. The line labeled A, however, is commonly viewed as longer than the one labeled B. There is an illusion of a difference in length. If B were gradually increased in length, it would eventually appear equal to A; that is, the illusion can be overcome by increasing the length of the apparently shorter line. Thus the extent of the illusion can be expressed in terms of the increase required to overcome it. The illusion also depends

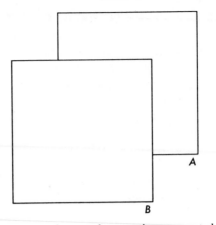

Figure 2-18. Interposition, a feature of perspective represented in two dimensions.

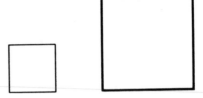

Figure 2-19. Images of different sizes, a feature of perspective represented in two dimensions.

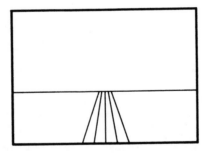

Figure 2-20. Converging lines, a feature of perspective represented in two dimensions.

on the length and angle of the lines attached to the horizontal. Several theories have been formulated regarding the illusion. The drawing in Figure 2-17 is a modification of the famous Müller-Lyer illusion.

PERSPECTIVE.   The appearance of objects with respect to their form in three dimensions and their relative positions in three-dimensional space has several features which correspond to specific characteristics of the situation in which the viewing is done. These characteristics can be implied by certain representations in two-dimensional drawings or pictures.

1. *Interposition*. In three-dimensional space, a near object may partially block the view of a far object. Examine Figure 2-18, which is a drawing in two-dimensional space. If one interprets the drawing as representing two complete squares, then one overlaps the other and is viewed as nearer. In other words, *B*, if it is seen as interposed between *A* and the viewer, appears to be nearer than *A*.

2. *Size*. In three-dimensional space, the nearer of two objects of the same actual size has a larger visual image and may be seen as nearer.

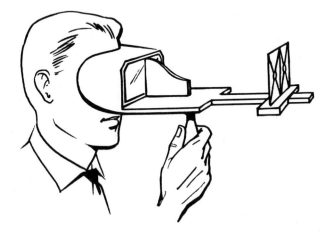

Figure 2-21. A subject viewing a card in a stereoscope. [Adapted from H. E. Garrett, *General Psychology*. New York: American Book Company, 1955.]

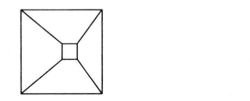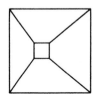

Figure 2-22. Drawings from a stereoscopic card. When the images fuse, the viewer sees the outline of a three-dimensional rectangular pyramid, as seen from above. [Adapted from C. H. Stoelting Company.]

Examine Figure 2-19, a drawing in two-dimensional space. If one interprets the drawing as representing two squares of equal size, then the larger of the two is seen as nearer. Can you destroy the perspective in your view of them? Does the thickness of the lines have anything to do with the perspective? In Figure 2-20 there is a set of converging lines. The separations of the lines in the lower part of the drawing are larger than those in the upper part. Can you see the lines as receding in the distance? Can you destroy the perspective in your view of them?

3. *Binocular disparity.* Normally, the individual's view of his surroundings with both eyes is unified and gives no indication that it is actually based on views which differ from one eye to the other. It is easy to demonstrate for oneself this disparity in the two views. First, cover the left eye and take note of the view obtained, with particular attention to the edges and sides of near objects. Second, cover the right eye and note again the edges and sides. With the left eye covered, one sees more of the right edges and sides than with the right one covered. With the right eye covered, one sees more of the left edges and sides than with the left one covered. With both eyes uncovered, however, one experiences a unified view. Disparate pictures of an object can be obtained by photographing it from two slightly different angles. If both photographs are viewed simultaneously, each photograph being exposed to only one of the viewer's eyes, a unified view with an impressive quality of depth results. This principle has been applied in the design of the stereoscope (see Figure 2-21). Simple line drawings with appropriate disparities can be employed in the same way. Figure 2-22 shows two drawings from a stereoscopic card.

PATTERN AND MOVEMENT. Variations in hue and brightness have simple physical correlates and are not difficult to describe verbally. In many situations variations in perceived size and distance correspond to variations in actual size and distance and are not difficult to describe. Variations in certain other properties, however, may have quite complex physical correlates and may be quite difficult to describe. Consider the patterns of light reflected from two different surfaces. A piece of red cloth and a piece of red paper may be much alike in hue and brightness but markedly different in terms of texture. Although the two materials may be distinguished easily, the surface of each may reflect light in a pattern which is so complex as to defy description. The movement of light is another of these complex properties. Variations in the direction and rate of movement of light in the field of vision can be as complicated as the patterning of surface textures. The multicolored lights of a ferris wheel in motion are not likely to be confused with a multicolored display of fireworks, yet the differences may be very difficult to specify in terms of physical correlates and may be very difficult to describe verbally.

OBJECTS. The seeing of objects, a major feature of visual experience, is commonly taken for granted. Objects are seen as whole and separate entities. Thus wholeness and separateness are qualities which belong to objects. Objects are also seen as having dimensions, colors, boundaries, surfaces, and shapes. Varying the physical correlate of a specific dimension such as perceived length may be easy, whereas varying the physical correlate of a general quality like wholeness presents a very difficult problem. In fact, even identifying or expressing the correlates of wholeness is very difficult.

CONSTANCY. Given some amount of white-light illumination, a white object reflects more light to the eye than does a gray object. Imagine that the level of illumination for both objects is increased until the gray object reflects more light than the white object did formerly. It is not true that the gray object is now seen as white. The gray object is still seen as gray and the white object is still seen as white. The amount of light reflected by the white object has, of course, also increased. Although changes in illumination result in changes of amount of light being reflected to the eye, relations among objects are perceived as unchanged. This phenomenon is an example of brightness constancy. It is consistent with the fact that relative amounts of light reflected by objects under the same illumination remain constant with changes in illumination.

As a balloon is inflated in one's presence, the visual angle it subtends becomes larger and it may be seen as becoming larger. The inference that an increase in the size of the angle is always accompanied by the perception of an increase in size is erroneous. As an automobile approaches, the visual angle becomes larger but the automobile is usually seen as coming nearer, not as growing in size. This phenomenon is an example of size constancy.

A flexible circular hoop can be deformed so that its shape is seen as changed from a circle to an ellipse. When the circle changes to an ellipse, the pattern of stimulation on the retina undergoes a corresponding change. The inference that a change in the projection from a circle to an ellipse will always be perceived as a change in shape is erroneous. A rigid circular hoop can be tilted so that its representation in the field of vision becomes an ellipse but its position, not its shape, is seen as changed. The pattern of light projected on the retina changes from a circle to an ellipse, but the viewer's perception of the hoop's shape remains unchanged. This phenomenon is an example of shape constancy.

The constancy phenomena are evidence that the extent of the relation between certain visual experiences and certain specified changes in physical stimuli varies. The extent of the relation is related to other variables such as unspecified changes in the physical stimuli or interpretations the viewer has learned to make. Thus it is possible that thought or at least learning to respond to a complex set of stimuli, as well as perception, is involved in the constancy phenomena.

ATTENTION. Two prominent and common features of visual experience are the focusing of attention on some detail of the environment and the shifting of attention from one detail to another. As I sit at my desk I see before me a radio. Across the front of the radio is printed the word transistor. I look at the *n,* and while I do so, the other letters seem not as prominent. I now look at the *a* and, as I do so, the *a* is prominent and the *n* seems less prominent than it was before. Notice that the experiences of focusing and shifting attention do not depend on changes in the letters or in their illumination. Actually no changes occurred in the physical stimulus provided by light reflected from the front of the radio. The experiences appear to depend solely on my actions or on processes within my body.

Figure 2-23. Objects for introspecting about focusing and shifting attention (see text).

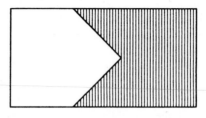

Figure 2-24. A partially shaded rectangle for introspecting about figure and ground (see text).

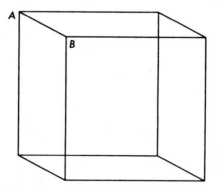

Figure 2-25. Necker's cube, a two-dimensional drawing which may give the illusion of three dimensions in either of two ways (see text).

Figure 2-23 contains a circle and a square. Look at the circle. While you look at it, are you also aware of the square? Is the square as prominent as the circle? Now look at the square. Is it more prominent now than it was before? Is the circle less prominent as you focus on the square?

Focusing attention on one detail out of many and shifting attention from one to another are experiences so familiar they are usually taken for granted. What actually happens when visual attention is shifted? The drawings do not change. It has been found that eye movements are correlates of shifts of visual attention.

FIGURE AND GROUND. The drawing in Figure 2-24 is a rectangle divided into two areas, one shaded and the other unshaded. It can be seen in either of two ways. One can see a pointed white object on a shaded background or a dented shaded object on a white background. What is seen as an object is called a figure, and what is seen as the background is called a ground. Ordinarily, a viewer can shift from one perception to the other at will. Note that the change of experience of figure and ground is

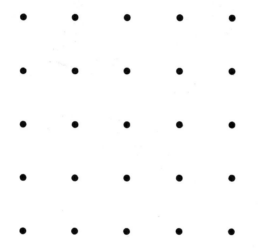

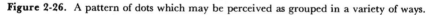

Figure 2-26. A pattern of dots which may be perceived as grouped in a variety of ways.

not related to any change in the drawing itself. The change must be in the viewer.

A REVERSIBLE FIGURE. Figure 2-25 is a drawing containing twelve straight lines on a two-dimensional surface. There are three sets of parallel lines and the four lines within each set are equal in length. The drawing can be seen, however, as a three-dimensional figure: a cube. In fact, it can be seen as a cube in either of two ways. It can be seen as a cube with corner *A* closer to the viewer than *B*, or with corner *B* closer than *A*. Note that the reversing is accomplished with no change in the drawing itself. The reversal must therefore involve some change in the viewer.

ORGANIZATION. The viewer of a relatively homogeneous pattern of objects can vary his perception with respect to the grouping of the objects. In Figure 2-26 is a pattern of similar dots which are subject to several kinds of visual grouping. They may be grouped by fours, rows, and columns, and possibly in other ways. Grouping is a familiar experience in the counting of a collection of objects. One may visually group the objects in pairs and count by twos, or group into threes and count by threes, and so on. Note that change from one kind of grouping to another does

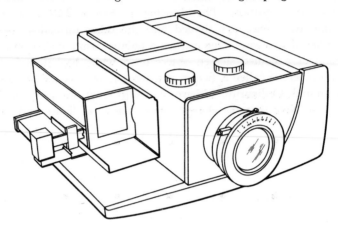

Figure 2-27. A slide-projecting tachistoscope permitting the control of exposure time and focus. (Intensity could be controlled by adding a rheostat.)

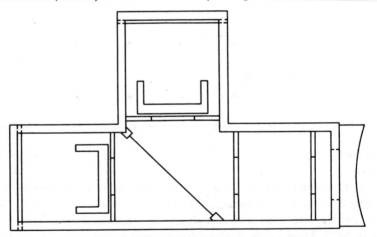

Figure 2-28. Schematic top view of a mirror tachistoscope. The subject views from a position next to the curve at the left. The object to be viewed is placed in the chamber at the bottom. The diagonal line represents the sheet of glass. [Adapted from Karlin.[5]]

not involve changes of any kind in the physical stimuli. There must be organismic correlates in the viewer.

THE PRESENTATION OF MATERIALS FOR VIEWING. The tachistoscope is a device often used by psychologists for exposing materials to be viewed by subjects. The device permits very strict control of the duration of exposure, the time between exposures, and the brightness of the viewing field. A modern slide-projecting tachistoscope is shown in Figure 2-27. It can be used for projecting colors, drawings, symbols, words, pictures, and other kinds of material on a screen for viewing by a single subject or a group.

A different type is the mirror tachistoscope which exposes material to the direct view of a single subject. Psychologists sometimes build their own equipment to meet their special needs. A plan for a mirror tachistoscope described by Karlin[5] and used at New York University is presented in Figure 2-28. The drawing is a view from above with the top removed.

A mirror tachistoscope is based on the principle that a sheet of glass placed at an angle to one's line of vision is transparent if lighted from the rear, but it acts as a mirror if lighted from the front. In Figure 2-28 the diagonal line in the center is the sheet of glass. The subject viewed from a position on the left. Two compartments, one at the right and one at the bottom of the drawing, could be lighted one at a time, but not simultaneously. Material to be viewed was placed at the end of the right compartment. An object which the viewer was asked to fixate before each exposure was placed at the end of the compartment at the bottom. When the light in the bottom compartment was on, the subject could see only the fixation object reflected from the sheet of glass. When the light in the right compartment was on, he could see only the material the psychologist wished to present.

SUMMARY OF VISUAL PERCEPTION. Certain properties of visual experience, such as hue, brightness, and size, have relatively simple physical correlates. Others, such as perspective, have relatively complex connections with the physical characteristics of what is viewed. The constancy phenomena superficially appear to be experiences which contradict one's expectations based on characteristics of the stimuli. It may be, however, that they actually have physical correlates more complex than those ordinarily specified when expectations are contradicted. It is also possible that perception is not the only kind of experience involved in constancy. Finally, certain experiences, such as the reversing of figure and ground, occur clearly without changes in stimuli. These experiences are known or assumed to be related to changes in the organism.

Audition

As already noted, the main purpose of this chapter is to establish a vocabulary of experiential terms defined in everyday language. Perception, the category of the senses, has been introduced. Vision, one of the seven senses, has been described. Auditory perception is the second sense to be considered. The properties of auditory experience include pitch, loudness, combinations of tones, noise, masking, distance, direction, rhythm, melody, and attention. In the several sections which follow, these properties will be defined. (The psychology of audition will be presented in later chapters.)

PITCH. Rapid pressure changes in the air, occurring in the vicinity of the eardrum, are accompanied by the experience of hearing. The experience has two properties with simple specific physical correlates which can be readily manipulated. Both properties are quantitative; that is, they vary in degree. Both can therefore be called dimensions. The first of these dimensions to be discussed is pitch.

Pitch is the property of sounds which is said to vary from low to high. The conspicuous difference between a bass voice and a soprano voice is the difference in pitch. The bass voice has a relatively low pitch; the soprano voice has a relatively high pitch. Alto and tenor voices are intermediate in pitch with, of course, the tenor lower than the alto. The flute and the piccolo differ in pitch with the flute generally lower than the piccolo. The trumpet, trombone, and tuba vary in pitch from high to low in the order given, as do the violin, viola, cello, and contrabass. Of course, there is some overlap in the ranges of the various voices and instruments. The notes of the piano and the organ vary from low to high going from left to right on their keyboards.

Pressure changes which are the stimulus for hearing may be produced by the regular and sustained vibration of an object. As an object vibrates, the air near it is alternately compressed and expanded. This action radiates from the vibrating object in all directions through the air unless it is blocked in some way. The alternate compressing and expanding of the air constitute changes in pressure. These changes are called condensations and rarefactions.

The movement of pressure changes in the air produced by an object vibrating at a constant rate can be represented abstractly as having the wave form of a simple periodic curve called a sine function (see Figure 2-11). The sound produced is called a pure tone. The physical correlate of the pitch of a pure tone is the relative frequency of occurrence of complete cycles of pressure change expressed as cycles per second. Referred to a sine curve, relative frequency is the number of waves advancing per second. Relative frequency corresponds to the vibration rate of the sound's source.

A tone of thirty cycles per second is very low; a tone of 15,000 cycles per second is fairly high. The upper and lower limits of audible tones vary from person to person. It is unusual for someone to hear tones of frequencies less than twenty cycles per second or greater than 20,000 cycles per second.

A familiar quality of auditory experience is tonality, the striking similarity of tones quite different in frequency. Tones which differ in that the frequency of one is an integral multiple of the other are heard as being very much alike, even though one is higher than the other. For example, a tone of 880 cycles per second is heard as being very much like a tone of 440 or 220. In music, the 880 tone is said to be one octave higher than the 440 one; and 440 is one octave higher than 220.

LOUDNESS. A second dimension of auditory experience is loudness. A tone may vary in loudness from being faint, soft, or subdued, to being blatant, piercing, or resounding. The physical correlate of loudness is the change in air pressure expressed in units of force per square unit of surface. This physical measure is usually referred to as the intensity of the stimulus. Referred to a sine curve, intensity is related to the amplitude of

Figure 2-29. A student adjusts the frequency of an audio-oscillator. An identical oscillator is on the right. The device in the center provides a visual display of frequency. Speakers or earphones, not shown in the drawing, deliver the sound stimulation to a subject.

the curve. Referred to the sound's source, intensity is related to the extent of the movement of the vibrating object. The unit of force commonly used is the dyne, which is approximately equal to one-thousandth of a gram. The unit of area is the square centimeter. A 1000-cycle-per-second tone is just audible for many people at an intensity of .001 dynes per square centimeter. The intensity becomes unbearable at 1000 dynes per square centimeter. The intensity scale is not usually expressed as pressure in absolute terms. A relative measure, the ratio of the given pressure to a standard of .002 dynes per square centimeter, is often employed. Furthermore, conventional practice is to transform the ratio of the two pressures to a logarithm and then multiply it by twenty. This new intensity scale has units called decibels.

Tones are produced by many kinds of vibrating objects. The vocal cords of a singer, the lips of the trumpeter, the strings of the violin, the air column of the flute, and the reed of the clarinet are some of the vibrating objects which produce musical tones. In the psychological laboratory, traditional methods of producing a tone have included striking a tuning fork and blowing a whistle. At the present time, an electronic device known as an audio-oscillator is employed. It can be readily adjusted to produce a tone of specified frequency and intensity (see Figure 2-29).

BIOLOGICAL CORRELATES OF PITCH AND LOUDNESS. There are two kinds of theory about pitch and its representation in the inner ear, the auditory nerve, and the brain. One kind of theory holds that the frequency of the stimulus is represented by the frequency of impulses in the nerve fibers. The other kind of theory holds that different frequencies stimulate different places in the cochlea of the inner ear, the division of the ear shaped like the coil of a snail shell (see Figure 2-5). The basilar membrane which extends from the base to the apex of the cochlea has been considered as one possibility for the organ on which these places are differentiated. The physiological evidence regarding the frequency of impulses in the fibers of the auditory nerve does not support a frequency theory for the perception of pitch at high frequencies, although the theory may apply at low frequencies. The evidence of differential stimulation of the cochlea and differential localization in the brain does support a place theory.

There is more agreement on theory about loudness and its biological correlates. The physiological evidence is that an increase in the intensity of the auditory stimulus is accompanied by an increase in the number of fibers stimulated and the frequency of impulses in the fibers.

COMBINATIONS OF TONES. Two vibrating objects can propagate pressure changes in the air at the same time. The two combine and yield a variety of auditory experiences.

If the two vibrating objects have the same frequency and their condensations and rarefactions correspond exactly, the experience of the listener will be that of a tone much louder than that produced by either object alone. The effect can be represented by the combining of two sine curves. At each point the amplitude of one adds to the corresponding amplitude of the other. The waves are then said to be "in phase." If they have the same frequency and the condensations produced by one correspond exactly to the rarefactions of the other, they will cancel one another and no tone will be audible. The canceling can be thought of as the combining of the positive amplitude of one wave with the negative amplitude of the other. The waves are then said to be "out of phase." The location of the listener with reference to the two sources is a critical factor in the way the two tones combine, for the phase relation varies with that location.

If the two vibrating objects have slightly different vibration rates, then condensations may occur together at one instance but become progressively separated with time. In the succession of waves, one amplitude augments the other by decreasing amounts until it begins to cancel the other. The waves may be in phase at one moment, producing for the hearer a louder tone than either would be separately, and out of phase a moment later, producing an inaudible or barely audible tone. Thus two vibrating objects of slightly different frequencies may produce a pulsating tone, varying considerably in loudness. The pulses or waxing-and-waning units can be counted and occur with a frequency per second equal to the difference in vibration rate of the two objects. These audible pulses are called beats. Two tones of 440 and 441 cycles per second, respectively, produce one waxing-and-waning unit per second.

If two or more vibrating objects have substantially different vibration rates, a corresponding number of tones is heard simultaneously. An example is a musical chord produced by a pianist, a string quartet, a vocal chorus, or an orchestra.

In a combination of several different frequencies, where the higher ones are integral multiples of the lowest and are also of lesser intensity than the lowest, the combination may be heard as a single tone of pitch corresponding to the lowest frequency but of a quality different from that of a pure tone. The lowest frequency of the combination is called the fundamental; the higher frequencies are called partials, overtones, or harmonics. The higher frequencies are not usually distinguished by the hearer, but they impart a distinctive quality to the sound. This quality is called timbre.

Musical instruments usually produce combinations of frequencies, not pure tones. Timbre is the quality which, in large part, distinguishes the clarinet, the flute, the trumpet, the violin, and other instruments. Instruments are also distinguished by their differences in resonance. One instrument may amplify partial frequencies different from those amplified by another instrument.

NOISE. Noise is the sound of irregular or aperiodic pressure changes. It can be obtained by combining many different frequencies which augment and diminish one another with no discernible pattern. Because white light is composed of radiant energy of varied wave lengths from the range of the visible spectrum, noise synthesized of many different frequencies throughout the audible range is often called white noise.

MASKING. The loudness of a tone depends on the presence or absence of other auditory stimulation. A single tone unaccompanied by any other stimulation may be audible at a very low intensity. If another tone, a combination of tones, or noise is introduced, the original tone may become much reduced in loudness or actually inaudible. This phenomenon is called masking. The extent to which a tone is masked can be measured by determining the increase in intensity necessary for the masked tone to become audible.

DISTANCE. A source of loud sounds is often interpreted as near the hearer; a source of faint sounds, as distant from him. It is, of course, a matter of common experience that an approaching sound source increases in loudness and a receding sound source decreases. In other words, loudness is at times related to the distance of a sound source from the hearer.

DIRECTION. Auditory experience also includes the localization of sound sources with respect to their directions from the hearer. A source may, of course, be located to his right or left, above or below him, or in front or back of him at various angles. A person with normal hearing can demonstrate fairly good accuracy in determining the direction of the source if it is, to some degree, to the right or left of him, not directly above or below him and directly in front or in back of him. These facts are consistent with the idea that the experience of right or left direction is related to the differential stimulation of the hearer's two ears, and with the demonstration that certain kinds of differential stimulation contrived in the laboratory are accompanied by the experience of direction without any actual location for the sound. If two clicks are produced in rapid succession, the first in a listener's left earphone and the second in his right earphone, he experiences one click localized to his left. If a tone is produced with one intensity in a listener's left earphone and with a lesser intensity in his right earphone, he experiences the tone localized to his left. Thus experience of direction is related to time and intensity differences in the stimulation of the listener's two ears. In everyday situations both kinds of differences depend on the distances of the two ears from the source.

RHYTHM AND MELODY. Tones of the same frequency and intensity, occurring in sequence, may define for the hearer a rhythm, a recurring temporal pattern of sounds; tones of varied frequency occurring in a temporal pattern may define a melody. It is an interesting constancy phenomenon that the perception of a melody depends on the relations among the frequencies of the musical notes and not on their absolute frequencies. Thus the same melody can be transposed up or down the musical scale to suit the convenience of singers and musicians without affecting one's perception of it.

AUDITORY ATTENTION. Auditory experience at any moment may consist of a wide variety of sounds. Even so, the listener can often focus his attention on one aspect of the experience to the partial exclusion of other aspects, and he can shift his attention from one aspect to another. A musically sophisticated member of the audience at a symphony concert can, with some ease and as a matter of choice, single out and focus attention on one instrument or section of instruments while to a considerable extent holding others in the background. At other times that person may choose to shift his attention to another instrument, to another section, or to the whole orchestra.

SUMMARY OF AUDITORY PERCEPTION. Terms commonly employed to denote properties of auditory experience have been introduced. They include pitch, loudness, beats, chords, timbre, noise, masking, distance, melody, and attention. Thus far, the preliminary study of consciousness has covered visual and auditory perception. It continues with the five remaining senses: gustation, olfaction, cutaneous sensitivity, kinesthesis, and static sensitivity. The description of perception, one of three major categories of consciousness, will be terminated with a consideration of the experience of control.

Gustation

There is general agreement that there are four qualitatively different and prominent taste experiences: salt, sweet, sour, and bitter. When a solution of any one of a number of chemical substances is applied to the surface of the tongue, receptor cells located there are stimulated, and a particular taste quality is experienced. A solution of sodium chloride tastes salty; a solution of sucrose (cane sugar) tastes sweet; a solution of quinine tastes bitter; a solution of hydrochloric acid tastes sour. Although these substances are commonly used in laboratory demonstrations and investigations, many other substances can also evoke these experiences or combinations of them. Acids, which in solution yield hydrogen ions, evoke the experience of sour. No unique physical or chemical property has been connected with salt, sweet, or bitter. It has been established that receptor cells for each taste quality are distributed nonuniformly over the surface of the tongue. Receptors for salt are at the front of the tongue; those for bitter at the back. Receptors for sweet are concentrated on the tip of the tongue; those for sour on the sides.

Each of the four taste qualities may vary in intensity. For example, the saltiness of a solution varies with the concentration of salt—that is, the amount of salt relative to the amount of water in the solution tasted.

In the laboratory, solutions are presented for tasting by a variety of methods. A small brush is one simple device which may be employed to deposit the liquid on the tongue. A dropper may also be used. To achieve greater control fairly complicated devices have been constructed which administer a known amount of a solution to a specified area of the tongue. Much use has been made, however, of the method of having subjects sip from small containers. Usually in extensive testing, the liquid is expectorated after a brief period and not swallowed. Sometimes subjects are required to rinse their mouths with water between tastings to insure maintenance of a normal degree of sensitivity.

Taste experiences are characterized by adaptation, blending, and contrast. Adaptation is the diminishing of the strength of a taste quality, with repeated stimulation. The extent to which adaptation occurs varies from substance to substance. The blending of qualities commonly occurs in connection with the seasoning of foods. Sometimes the taster can successfully identify the separate qualities. When, as often happens, there is a blend of taste qualities associated with odors, it may be very difficult to analyze the blend into its components. Contrast is the enhancing of one taste by a

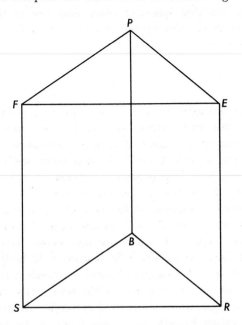

Figure 2-30. Henning's odor prism showing the hypothesized relations among the qualities: fragrant (*F*), ethereal (*E*), spicy (*S*), resinous (*R*), putrid (*P*), and burned (*B*).

prior taste. A bitter substance is more bitter following the tasting of a sweet substance than it is following a neutral substance. Sour is more sour following sweet than it is following a neutral substance. There are other possibilities as everyday experience reveals. The enjoyment of food is sometimes increased by the deliberate choice of combinations or sequences providing such contrasts.

Olfaction

The qualities of olfactory experience are not so well-defined as are those of taste. A system proposed in 1915 by Hans Henning had six qualities: fragrant, ethereal, resinous, spicy, putrid, and burned. These six words were not intended to designate separate categories. According to Henning, a given odor could be described by relating it to some combination of the labels. The six labels were conceptualized as being located at the corners of a triangular prism, and odorous substances were placed on the faces at appropriate points (see Figure 2-30). Cinnamon is spicy; orange oil is ethereal; thyme is between spicy and fragrant but closer to fragrant; acetone is between ethereal and resinous on another edge. A system proposed in 1927 by E. C. Crocker and L. F. Henderson had four qualities: fragrant, acid, burnt, and caprylic. These four qualities were said to be represented by musk, vinegar, roast coffee, and sweat. No classification system of olfactory qualities has proved to be completely satisfactory.

The physical stimulus for olfactory experience is some property of a mixture of air and an odorous substance in gaseous form. The strength of an odor varies with the concentration of the substance in air. Since the qualities of olfactory experience are not clearly defined, it is impossible to determine specific physical and chemical correlates. Furthermore, no general physical or chemical property of olfactory stimuli has yet been isolated.

Odors are subject to adaptation, masking, and blending. Adaptation to some olfactory stimuli is quite rapid and extensive. This diminishing of the strength of an odor with repeated or continued stimulation has its advantages when one encounters substances with obnoxious odors. It has its disadvantages, too, when one wishes to have a pleasant odor endure. One odor may mask another. In the presence of one olfactory stimulus, a person may not smell another stimulus also present. Odors blend. Until the fundamental qualities of odors are established, however, the nature of blending cannot be determined.

In the laboratory, an odorant may be presented to the subject by a variety of methods. Some complicated apparatus has been devised to mix a gas with air under controlled temperature and to inject a specific amount of the mixture with a standard pressure into the nasal cavities. In many class demonstrations and in much research, however, the subject simply sniffs at a bottle or a container of some sort.

An odorless and odor-proof room, equipped for the controlled presentation of olfactory stimuli, was constructed in the psychological laboratory at Cornell University. It was called an olfactorium and has been described by Foster, Scofield, and Dallenbach[3]. Figure 2-31 shows a subject in the olfactorium.

The olfactorium was divided into two parts: the glass chambers and the air-treatment unit. The two glass chambers were constructed of tempered plate glass and polished steel. A door entered the smaller antechamber and another opened into the larger main chamber. Great effort was made to eliminate the presence of contaminating or unintended odors. Joints between metal and metal and between glass and metal were sealed with a special paste. Felt gaskets were placed on the doors. An air-conditioning system provided air from outdoors or indoors. The building containing the olfactorium was located on a hill in an area relatively free of soot and other ground contaminants.

The incoming air passed through a mechanical filter for removal of gross impurities—a spray of water, a drier, a heater, and a series of canisters of activated carbon intended to remove any remaining odors. Steam was employed for deodorizing the apparatus after use.

Odorants were introduced through small openings in the sides and ceilings of the larger chamber. The air, which was circulated by a fan in

Figure 2-31. The Cornell olfactorium showing a subject clothed in a special suit and an investigator placing an odorant in one of the ducts. [Adapted from Foster, Scofield, and Dallenbach. [3]]

the main chamber, could be sampled for chemical analysis through a hole connecting the two chambers. Odorants could also be introduced into the incoming stream of air by means of an atomizing unit in the air duct leading to the larger chamber. Each subject took a shower and put on an envelope made of an odorless plastic before he entered the olfactorium. The envelope, which resembled an Eskimo's parka, covered all parts of the subject's body and head except his face.

Cutaneous Sensitivity

Speaking of a sense of touch does not do justice to the category of experiences associated with the stimulation of the skin. Actually, there have been distinguished four qualitatively different and prominent experiences: warmth, cold, pain, and pressure. Receptor cells corresponding to the four qualities are distributed nonuniformly on or near the surface of the skin. It was once thought that punctuate or discrete areas of sensitivity could be identified, but it is now thought that sensitivity varies in degree over the body surface.

Adaptation is a familiar feature of the cutaneous experiences. Taking a hot or cold shower usually involves a considerable change in sensitivity. Clothing produces light pressure on many parts of the wearer's body, but the awareness of pressure soon diminishes or disappears. Adaptation to mild pain, such as that produced by an antiseptic applied to a wound, is also possible.

In the student laboratory a temperature cylinder, a small brass rod which tapers to a blunt point at one end, is often employed for thermal stimulation. It may be heated or cooled in a water bath. (Figure 2-32 shows a temperature cylinder being applied to the surface of a subject's

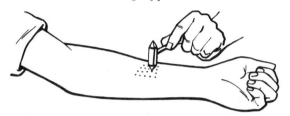

Figure 2-32. Stimulating a subject's arm with a temperature cylinder in a student laboratory. The grid is stamped on the arm to permit identification of spots stimulated.

forearm.) Pain may be produced by the prick of a sharp needle. Light pressure may be produced by applying a stiff hair or some other pointed object to the skin so that the skin is deformed or dented. A special device called an aesthesiometer is employed to produce light pressure at two points simultaneously. When two near points on the skin are stimulated simultaneously by an aesthesiometer, the experience may be that of two points, or it may be only one point. This phenomenon indicates the existence of a property of experience which could be called tactual distinctness.

Special apparatus for the presentation of thermal stimuli, developed and described by Burton, Hall, and Dallenbach[1,4], is shown in Figure 2-33A. It was cooled by water which flowed from the regular main into a small open reservoir through a valve, by means of which the rate of flow could be varied by small amounts. The reservoir was attached to a vertical rod by means of a clamp so that it could be raised or lowered. Water which cooled the applicator flowed through the apparatus, while excess water entered an overflow pipe which projected from the bottom of the reservoir. By adjusting the height of the reservoir, the investigators could control the rate and pressure of the flow of water and the temperature of the applicator. Greater height gave lower temperatures. The temperature of the water was taken just before it entered the applicator and again as it left. Since the two thermometers were equidistant from the applicator point, the two readings were averaged to obtain an estimate of the temperature of the point. Warm water could also be introduced into the system.

The applicator was brought into contact with the subject's skin by means of an adjustable stand, shown in Figure 2-33B. Constancy of pres-

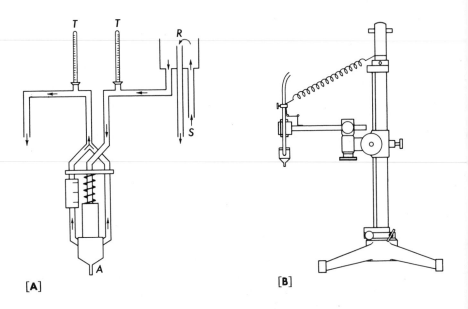

[A]   **[B]**

Figure 2-33. Diagrams showing apparatus for controlling stimulus temperature. **A:** Schematic drawing of the applicator showing the thermometers (T), the water reservoir (R), the water supply (S), and the applicator point (A). **B:** The adjustable stand and applicator. [Adapted from Burton, Hall, and Dallenbach. [1,4]]

sure of the point against the skin was obtained by lowering the applicator until the spring which carried the weight of the instrument was compressed to a given point on an adjacent scale.

The blindfolded subject sat at a table with his left hand and forearm in a plaster cast made especially for him. In one series of investigations, the skin area selected for stimulation was located on the dorsal surface of the forearm. The area was shaved and a small grid with cross-section lines was stamped upon it. The investigator could then follow a systematic plan for stimulating spots in the squares of the grid.

Kinesthesis

The experiences of position and movement are not characterized by salient qualities and are not associated with external physical stimuli as are vision, hearing, gustation, olfaction, and cutaneous sensitivity. Since the receptor cells are located in the muscles, tendons, and joints, those cells are stimulated as some position is maintained or some movement of a part of the body occurs. While no physical stimulus can be changed to produce a kinesthetic experience, it is possible to institute and control, by instruction or actual manipulation, the position and movement of parts of the body of a cooperative subject.

Static Sensitivity

The experience associated with body rotation does not possess distinctive qualities, except for the experience of dizziness which may sometimes occur. One simply knows whether or not he is being rotated, and, if he is, the direction and relative speed of rotation. The experiences of head tilt, also, do not vary qualitatively. One simply knows the direction and degree of tilt of his head. With neither experience is there an external stimulus as in vision, hearing, gustation, olfaction, and cutaneous sensitivity. The experience of rotation is related to the change in speed of the actual rotation. The experience of head tilt varies with the direction and degree of actual head tilt.

The Experience of Control in Perception

Under ordinary circumstances, a person can control his perceptual experiences in many ways and is aware that he can do so. He can institute, change, and terminate perceptual experiences by his own actions, which may include manipulation of his environment. He can turn a light on or off; he can change stations on his radio or television set; he can go to a movie and, if he doesn't like what he sees and hears, he can leave before the show is over; he can provide music for himself by playing an instrument, going to a concert, or putting a record on a phonograph; he can view paintings, watch a sunset, and gaze at the stars; he can choose food and drink, as well as the seasonings for them, to suit his taste; he can exercise a preference regarding the scent of his soap and other toilet articles. He can avoid intense stimulation by a variety of simple measures: When light is too bright, he can close his eyes, turn his head, put on dark glasses, adjust the visor on his car, go indoors, or pull the window shades. When noises are too loud, he can cover his ears, insert plugs in his ears, move away from the sound source, go indoors, or close the windows. He can often avoid contact with objects which are too cold, hot, rough, or sharp for his comfort. He can put on clothing, seek shelter, and turn on the heat to control the cold of winter; he can take off clothing, seek shade, and turn on air conditioning to control the heat of summer. He can don gloves, shoes, a mask, or a helmet for special protection of the surface of his body from pricking, burning, freezing, or abrasion. He can hold his nose or leave the site of an obnoxious odor. He can spit out an unpleasant tasting substance and rinse his mouth with water.

The awareness of control may involve an awareness of purpose and effort. The viewer may try to see. The listener may try to hear. A man may make a special effort to smell smoke if he suspects the presence of fire in his house. A housewife may make a special effort in tasting milk if she suspects that it has started to sour.

The awareness of control and effort may lead to awareness of limits on that control. One becomes aware that he cannot always avoid or terminate perceptual experiences and that he cannot always achieve the kind or degree of perception he may desire. No matter how hard he tries, he may not be able to distinguish a very small separation between marks on a paper, see a very dim light, hear a very faint sound, hear a very slight difference in the frequency of two tones, or detect a small difference in temperature.

In certain situations of everyday life, the perceiver's control of his experience leaves much to be desired. The student who wishes to study may not be able to shut out the music from his roommate's radio. The business man who wishes to sleep may not be able to shut out noise from a party next door. The driver of a car who must be alert for traffic control signs on a highway cannot avoid seeing billboards. The traveler who must listen for train announcements in a railroad station cannot avoid hearing advertising on the public address system.

There are extraordinary circumstances, under which the control of perception by the experiencer is severely limited. In illnesses, accidents, battles, explosions, fires, floods, and storms, the efforts of a victim to control his perception may be futile. He may be forced to endure intense, unpleasant, painful, and even harmful stimulation.

Under ordinary circumstances, an individual permits external agents or agencies to manipulate his perceptual experience for a large part of the time and in many different ways. For example, a student may cooperate with a psychologist and allow his experience to be determined in some specific way. The psychologist may display a colored paper, present a tone of a certain frequency and intensity, or apply a temperature cylinder to a spot on the subject's arm. The psychologist, given the cooperation of his subject, can manipulate the physical correlates of a number of perceptual experiences and the subject's experiences will vary concomitantly. In everyday life, of course, there are many situations in which people willingly allow their perceptual experience to be manipulated.

Summary

A description of three major categories of experience has been undertaken. An account of one of the three, perception, has been completed. The salient properties of seven senses have been presented. Two major categories, feeling and thought, remain to be described.

The main purpose of the account of perception was to establish a vocabulary of terms. Emphasis was given, however, to the physical correlates of perception: the characteristics of physical stimuli or other external conditions to which variations in perceptual experience are related. In addition, brief mention was made of certain biological correlates of perception: the anatomical and physiological characteristics to which variations in perceptual experience are related.

FEELING

Feeling designates a category of experiences which are familiar and distinctive but difficult to define and differentiate verbally. Perception is to a large extent a category of experiences of outer objects or events, whereas feeling, as defined here, is exclusively a category of experiences of inner activities. As experienced, these inner activities are attributed largely to the organs of the chest, the organs of the abdomen, and the genital organs, and only slightly to the head, neck, and limbs. The experiencer perceives objects and events external to himself but feels activity within himself. The objects and events he perceives may affect or involve him, but the activity he *feels* is his own.

The experiences of feeling are difficult to classify. Efforts to give expression to them are represented by hundreds of words in everyday language. Many attempts have been made at classification, but none of the resulting schemes is perfect and many appear to be equally satisfactory. The category does have one general property which is widely agreed upon: the dimension of hedonic tone or pleasantness-unpleasantness. One usually experiences a feeling as being to some degree pleasant or unpleasant.

A list of words employed in everyday life to designate feelings would include hunger, thirst, suffocation, and the like; the urge to eliminate, the sexual urge, fatigue, drowsiness, monotony, and the like; fear, anger, anxiety, joy, love, and the like. The grouping evident in the preceding sentence suggests one way of classifying feelings. The experiences of hunger, thirst, and suffocation are associated with material requirements of an organism for food, water, and air. The urge to eliminate, the sexual urge, fatigue, drowsiness, and monotony are associated with requirements of instituting, changing, or terminating actions such as urination, copulation, rest, sleep, exercise, and so on. Other feelings, such as satisfaction, relief, and alertness, are associated with the supply of these needed materials or actions.

The experiences associated with material and action requirements will be called need states. Fear, anger, anxiety, joy, love, and others make up a group which will be called the emotions. Emotions are not closely associated with either material requirements or action requirements, as are the need states. For example, fear does not indicate to the experiencer a material need, as hunger indicates the need for food; anger does not indicate a need for beginning, changing, or ceasing action, as fatigue indicates the need for rest.

The biological correlates of specific feelings can be identified only to a limited extent. Hunger is associated with stomach contractions and low blood sugar. Thirst is associated with dryness of the mouth and general dehydration of the body. Fatigue is associated with increases in the amount of oxygen required to do a given amount of work and the quantity of certain wastes produced by the body. Although these correlates are specific and differentiable, the correlates of some feelings are complex, diffuse, and overlapping. Fear and anger are associated with pulse rate, blood pressure, muscle tension, dryness of the mouth, amount of perspiration, the electrical activity of the brain, frequency of urination, extent of dilation of the pupil of the eye, respiration rate, and the amount of adrenalin discharged into the blood; but the patterns are not fixed, distinct, and mutually exclusive.

As already noted, stomach contractions are a correlate of hunger. That they are a correlate was demonstrated in a classic investigation reported in 1912 by Cannon and Washburn[2]. Washburn was himself the subject in their investigation.

Every day for several weeks, Washburn introduced into his stomach a soft rubber balloon attached to a small tube. On each occasion the tube and ballon were kept in position for two or three hours. After this preliminary period, he reported that the introduction and presence of the tube were not disturbing to him.

When the action of his stomach was to be recorded, the balloon was moderately inflated with air and connected with a pressure gauge, which registered contractions of the stomach. A pneumograph, a device usually placed around the chest to record respiratory movements, was fastened below the subject's ribs to record movements of his abdomen. On the days of observation, he ate little or no breakfast, and no lunch. Observation began at two o'clock in the afternoon. The subject sat with one hand at a key. When he experienced a hunger pang he pressed the key. Figure 2-34 shows the subject and the arrangement of apparatus.

Four records were made on a kymograph, an instrument which registers movement graphically. One record showed the occurrence of stomach contractions; another, movements of the abdomen. The two remaining records were of time signals and the subject's pressing of a key. All recording arrangements were out of the subject's sight. The results showed that when the subject indicated he was hungry, contractions of the stomach were invariably registered. Increases in pressure on the balloon in his stomach occurred with a frequency of 11 to 13 in twenty minutes. Typically, the contraction nearly reached its maximum pressure before the subject pressed the key.

The Control of Feelings

It was pointed out earlier that in ordinary circumstances perceptions are experienced under the partial but effective control of the experiencer.

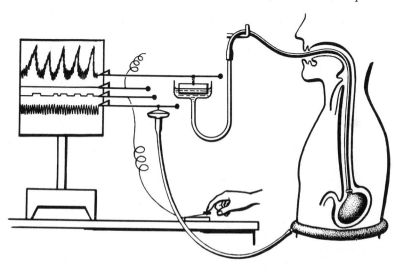

Figure 2-34. Schematic drawing of subject and apparatus in recording stomach contractions. The kymograph record on the left shows changes in the volume of the balloon in the subject's stomach, a time line, the reports of hunger pangs given by the subject's pressing of the key, and movements of the abdominal wall as detected by the pneumograph. [Adapted from W. B. Cannon in C. Murchison, *A Handbook of General Experimental Psychology.* Worcester, Mass.: Clark University Press, 1934.]

Feelings, however, in ordinary circumstances, are experienced under less certain and less effective control. The need states can be controlled, but not always immediately upon their occurrence and very frequently only after an unpleasant delay. The experience of hunger includes an awareness of what should be done about it; that is, the hungry person knows that food will satisfy his need. Food, however, may or may not be available. If it is not, he must delay eating and endure the hunger. He may be able to carry on other activities but he cannot terminate the hunger. As time passes, the intensity of the experience of hunger may grow until all activity is devoted to the seeking of food. The tired person is usually aware that he can satisfy his need by resting. He may or may not have the immediate opportunity to do so. Conditions over which he has no control may prevent him from resting. If so, he may continue to function in many ways, but he must endure the fatigue; he cannot terminate it. As time passes, the intensity of the experience of fatigue may grow until the individual seeks rest regardless of his situation.

Control of the emotions is even more precarious than control of the need states. The person who is afraid of some situation and wishes to avoid it is often unable to do so. He may simply have to endure the fear, not once but many times. He may continue to function in that situation but may not be able to eliminate the fear. If the fear becomes unbearable, he may resort to flight, even though the practical consequences are disastrous. Another person, who is afraid all of the time regardless of the situation, may have no idea what he can do to obtain relief and may be subject to chronic suffering. An angry person often does not know what to do about his anger. He may restrain its overt expression so as to minimize the undesirable consequences, but if the anger becomes very intense, he may act in a way which creates many additional serious problems for himself.

Furthermore, there may be no one who can tell the fearful or angry person what to do. Someone may say, in effect, "Don't be afraid," or "Don't be angry," but that is not like saying, "Go to the bathroom" when a child has the urge to urinate, or "Eat some candy" when a companion becomes hungry on a long trip. If one does not wish to see and hear a television program, he can often shut off the set or leave the room. If one becomes too sleepy to continue a card game, he can usually leave the game and go to bed. If one becomes afraid or angry, there is often no escape from the unpleasantness. Even if one cannot escape the television program or the card game, enduring the sight and sound or the drowsiness is not usually as unpleasant as fear or anger.

Lack of control is not characteristic of the unpleasant emotions only. Joy and love are not subject to very satisfactory control. It is true that the pleasant emotions are not usually thought of as feelings one would like to terminate, but lack of control of them is sometimes a problem. Either emotion may come and go with what often appears to be little or no control on the part of the experiencer. He may seem to himself to be only a witness.

It was with good reason that the philosopher Benedict De Spinoza, writing an essay on the strength of the emotions, chose the title *Of Human Bondage*. Lack of control of the emotions is more of a problem than is the limit on perceptual control or the interference with control of the need states. It is natural that the emotions should be of intense interest to the student and the layman. The emotions are viewed by many people as focal points of serious and aggravating personal problems. It is understandable that the emotions and the problems which accompany them are seen as important matters for psychological investigation. It is also understandable that perception, with its fewer and less unpleasant problems of control, may be seen by many people as a less important matter for investigation. Although most psychologists would agree with this ordering in terms of importance, if uncertainty of control and unpleasantness of experience are considered, there are other reasons for the amount of attention given to various topics by psychologists. One reason is the availability of physical correlates or external conditions which can be manipulated in research; another is the degree of freedom allowed by society in research on humans.

In the discussion of perception, numerous connections were indicated between variations in experience and variations in either physical stimuli or external circumstances. A psychologist may develop considerable interest in the many possibilities for systematic and gradual manipulation of these physical correlates and their effects on the behavior of his subjects. Some feelings do, of course, have connections with external and manageable conditions. Hunger is related to the length of time a person is deprived of food. Thirst is related to the length of time a person is deprived of water. The urge to urinate is related to the time elapsed since the last act. Fatigue is related to the amount of work done, as measured in physical terms. Monotony is related to the time spent at a simple, repetitious task. There are well-established connections between some other feelings and external conditions. These conditions can be instituted in laboratory and field research, and their effects on behavior can be observed. Not all feelings, however, have such connections. The emotions do not have simple universal connections with conditions like those between hunger and food deprivation, thirst and water deprivation, and fatigue and work. Although, in the normal course of living, situations accompanied by emotional experiences occur continually, it is not easy to institute conditions which will be accompanied by those experiences.

Although conditions known to be connected with certain feelings can be imposed on his subjects by a psychologist, his interest in investigating those conditions may be tempered considerably by the restrictions he must observe. He must be careful in imposing a condition such as food deprivation or work. The condition must not be hazardous, seriously frustrating, offensive, or unpleasant to an extreme degree. The psychologist depends on the cooperation of his subjects; he must avoid public censure; and he must live with his own conscience.

Many conditions permissible in the laboratory may seem trivial compared to life conditions. For example, a mild electric shock administered in a laboratory hardly compares with participation in a war-time bombing mission over enemy country, with respect to the intensity of the accompanying anxiety. A few brief communications given in an approving tone of voice by a psychologist hardly compare with years of approval in word and deed by parents or friends, with respect to the feelings experienced by an adolescent.

There are many possibilities for systematic variation of the correlates of perception, accompanied or followed by observation of behavior. Most of the variations are realistic and practical in the sense that they are identical with or quite similar to those which occur in everyday life. There are not as many possibilities for variation of circumstances associated with feelings. Some of the possibilities are restricted or forbidden. Many of those permitted are of questionable significance. A few are realistic and practical.

THOUGHT

Perception and feeling, two of the three major categories of experience, have now been described. The third category is thought. It includes remembering, recognizing, abstracting, reasoning, reflecting, associating, imagining, dreaming, and the like. There is no one scheme for classifying these experiences. If one employs only a few categories, many kinds of thinking appear to be neglected; if one employs many categories, they overlap and merge.

Thought does not have physical correlates as perception does, or material and action requirements as the need states do. On many occasions thinking occurs with no apparent connections to external events. On other occasions, however, it occurs with obvious connections to materials such as prose, poetry, names, dates, words, pictures, and signs, and to communications such as questions, instructions, messages, and problems.

Relatively little is known about the specific biological correlates of the different kinds of thought. From animal studies, it is known that certain kinds of problem solving are affected adversely by lesions of the cortex of the brain, and that performance in certain tests of remembering, called delayed-reaction tests, is affected adversely by lesions of the prefrontal lobes of the brain. In studies of humans, it has been found that the electroencephalogram, a graphic record of the electrical rhythm picked up by electrodes placed on the skull or cortex, shows changes from sleep to waking and during mental problem solving. In other studies of humans, action potentials in muscles, a kind of electrical activity which can be picked up by electrodes placed on the skin of the tongue and lips, show concomitance with certain occasions of thinking.

A prominent feature of some thought processes—one not nearly as prominent in perception and feeling—is that they change with repetition or continuation of the processes. For example, remembering improves with repeated exposure to materials and with repeated attempts to remember them. By contrast, visual acuity does not improve appreciably with repeated viewing, and hunger does not change in intensity with recurrent periods of food deprivation. Another feature of remembering is that changes may occur with the passage of time. Success in remembering may decline over a period of hours, days, or weeks after the initial exposure to materials and after success in remembering them.

The Control of Thought

Control is a prominent aspect of the experience of thinking, but it is control within limits of which the experiencer may be aware. A student of history may or may not remember an important date. He may experience the intent to remember it and an effort to do so. If he does not succeed, he experiences a limit. He may, of course, think he has remembered correctly, but he may actually not have. A person may experience choosing to think about his work, changing to his social life, and changing again to his hobby. This experience of control extends to the relinquishing of it. One may daydream; that is, he may let his mind wander over many topics. He may follow instructions to think about one matter or another. Sometimes control seems impossible to achieve and the individual continues to think about a matter when he would like to stop.

Although a person may fail or err in remembering, recognizing, reasoning, or abstracting and may thereby incur some unpleasant consequences, he does not usually experience the kind of unpleasantness that is associated with the need states and certain emotions. Thus the thought processes do not constitute an area of serious personal troubles as do the emotions. Earlier it was pointed out that perceptual experiences are not as troubling as emotions. It is not surprising that the psychological interests of many students and laymen focus on emotion and not on perception or thought. Many psychologists, however, are interested in the numerous possibilities for devising materials and observing the actual behavioral demonstrations of subjects' success in remembering, recognizing, reasoning, and abstracting upon presentation of those materials. Furthermore, since these materials have many identifiable counterparts in everyday life, these investigations may possess a high degree of realism and practicality.

Thought is not subject to external control as perception is. A person may see the light from a sign without thinking about its content or hear the sound of a radio announcer without thinking about his message. Thought does not seem to be determined by external events in any immediate, direct, or invariant way. Normally, the experiencer continues to claim adopting his own ideas and reaching his own conclusions regardless of the events surrounding him.

Chapter Summary

A preliminary description of consciousness or experience has been completed. The main purpose was the establishing of a vocabulary of experiential terms. In Chapter 3, a preliminary description of behavior will be given. In Chapter 4, there will be a return to experiential terms in connection with an explanation of their redefinition. Experiential terms are employed in psychology, but always with implicit, if not explicit, behavioral referents.

Experience has been divided into three categories: perception, feeling, and thought. Perception is the category of the experiences of vision, audition, gustation, olfaction, cutaneous sensitivity, kinesthesis, and static sensitivity. Numerous properties of perceptual experience are related to characteristics of physical stimuli and external conditions. Feeling is the category of need states such as hunger, thirst, fatigue, drowsiness, and monotony, and of emotions such as anger, anxiety, fear, joy, and love. As far as the experience is concerned, the need states are clearly related to circumstances involving deprivation and action; the emotions are not. A prominent characteristic of feeling is the degree of pleasantness or unpleasantness experienced. Thought is the category of experiences such as remembering, recognizing, abstracting, reasoning, associating, imagining, and dreaming. Thought does not have stimulus correlates as does perception, or material and action requirements as do the need states. Thought is, however, often associated with materials and communications external to the thinker.

The kind and degree of control by the experiencer are important features of all three categories of experience. In perception and thought, control is positive but limited. In feeling, control is precarious and severely limited. Obstacles may prevent the satisfying of need states. Control of the emotions is, in general, much more difficult than control of perception and thought, and it often seems impossible.

The statements about the exercising and relinquishing of control in perception and thought are intended to characterize salient features of those experiences. They are not intended as contradictions of deterministic views about life processes. Whether one accepts a deterministic view of these processes or not, controlling one's perceptions and thoughts is still an aspect of his experience.

The Awareness of Control of Behavior

A feature of experience which has not yet been described is the awareness of the control of action. One may be conscious of intent, purpose, design, and effort associated with his behavior. Recognition of this feature of experience has nothing to do with the philosophical question of whether or not a person actually does control his actions and is not inconsistent with a deterministic position.

References

1. Burton, N. G., and K. M. Dallenbach. "The Duration of the After-Sensations of Warmth Aroused by Punctiform Stimulation." *The American Journal of Psychology,* 66 (1953), 386-396.

2. Cannon, W. B., and A. L. Washburn. "An Explanation of Hunger." *The American Journal of Physiology,* 29, (1912), 441-454.
3. Foster, D., E. H. Scofield, and K. M. Dallenbach. "An Olfactorium." *The American Journal of Psychology,* 63 (1950), 431-440.
4. Hall, N. B., Jr., and K. M. Dallenbach. "Minor Studies from the Psychological Laboratory of Cornell University, 94." *The American Journal of Psychology,* 60 (1947), 260-271.
5. Karlin, L. "The New York University Tachistoscope." *The American Journal of Psychology,* 68 (1955), 462-466.

3

Behavior

THE STUDY OF PSYCHOLOGY PROPER BEGINS HERE WITH A CONSIDER-
ation of behavior and observation. *Behavior* refers to any overt action on
the part of an animal. *To observe* is to perceive some object or event
external to oneself. Behavior is, therefore, observable. Psychology is an
empirical field of knowledge based on agreements in the reports of numerous investigators who have observed behavior.

To observe behavior is to perceive an action. It is to see a child climbing a tree, hear a violinist playing a concerto, be aware of the pressure of
a man's grip in shaking hands, and sense the body pressures produced by
the starting, accelerating, turning, slowing, and stopping of a car as it is
driven by another person.

Perceiving an intimate concomitant or an immediate effect of some
action is considered equivalent to observing behavior. Watching the movement of an indicator on a device which measures strength of handgrip is
observing behavior; so is watching the path of a signal on a radar screen
as a plane is tracked on its approach for a landing, the maneuvers of a sailboat as it is handled by its captain and crew in a race, and the movement
of the hand on a pressure gauge as a child writes a sentence on a pressure-sensitive surface.

Perceiving the product of an action is also considered to be equivalent
to observing behavior. Tasting a cake baked by a participant in a contest,
inspecting a drawing by a cartoonist, reading a poem written by a college

66

student, listening to the musical composition of a conservatory student as it is played by an orchestra, and inspecting the cloth produced by a weaver are behavioral observations. In these examples, the behaviors observed are baking a cake, drawing a cartoon, writing a poem, composing music, and weaving cloth. The products—the cake, the drawing, the poem, the composition, and the cloth—are, in a sense, records of the behaviors.

It should be evident from the examples given that everyday language is rich with terms which can be employed in psychology to give an account of behavior. Many of these terms can be used with their common definitions. A few must be redefined to have somewhat more precise meanings than they commonly have. Since some redefinition is necessary, the student should be alert for its occurrence, but he can take considerable satisfaction from the fact that his vocabulary already includes many perfectly respectable psychological terms.

Units of Behavior

The behavior of an organism can be thought of as continuous and unified, but any attempt to study it results in focusing on its parts. What are they? Are there natural units into which it can be subdivided? The questions do not have simple answers and have provoked much discussion in the past. There does seem to be some agreement that the division into parts or units depends to a considerable extent on the purposes of the psychologist and the kind of knowledge he seeks. If he wishes to study the behavior of an architect in designing a building, the units will be large and chosen to be closely related to the designing. If he wishes to study the behavior of a child in drawing a line, the units will be smaller. What is the smallest unit? One cannot say, absolutely, but the action of a muscle and the secreting of a gland are certainly far down the scale. Below these units, body activities are usually not thought of as behavior in a psychological sense but as physicochemical processes of primary interest to neurologists and physiologists.

Biological Correlates of Behavior

The obvious correlate of behavior, thought of as continuous and unified, is the biological functioning of the whole organism, but along with the study of behavior in its parts or units, there goes the study of the specific functioning of particular organs and particular parts of the nervous system. While any specific behavioral action is occurring, there is, of course, extensive concomitant physiological and neurological activity, but the interest of psychologists, and especially physiological psychologists, is centered on those processes which might ultimately be important in the prediction and control of specific behavior.

Some of the more important features of the nervous system as it enters into motor activity, the activity of muscles and glands, will be mentioned briefly. It is known that the frontal lobes of the brain contain centers for controlling movements; the cerebellum is a center for motor coordination and maintenance of posture and balance; motor or efferent neurons, which leave the spinal cord on its ventral side or front, carry stimulation to the muscles involved in body and limb movements such as walking, bending, stooping, and grasping. (See Figures 2-2 and 2-3, Chapter 2.)

The autonomic nervous system, a motor system outside the central nervous system, carries stimulation to the blood vessels, heart, glands, and other internal organs. The autonomic system has two parts: the sympathetic and parasympathetic. Action of the sympathetic system, which occurs especially during emotion, increases heart rate and blood pressure, and distributes blood to exterior muscles. Other related changes include interruptions in breathing, enlargement of the pupil of the eye, drying of the mouth, cessation of contractions of the stomach and intestines, discharge of the hormone adrenalin—a stimulant and energizer—by the adrenal glands, and secreting of the sweat glands. Action of the parasympathetic system, especially in periods of calm and relaxation, decreases heart rate and blood pressure, and distributes blood to the interior of the body, including the stomach and intestines.

Categories of Behavior

The actions of people can be classified in many ways. By way of introducing the problem of classification, a few widely used and fundamental schemes will be described briefly in this chapter. Since the classification of behavior provides much of the substance of later chapters, the discussion now undertaken continues throughout a large part of the remainder of the book.

Vocal behavior is distinguished from motor behavior. Vocal behavior includes talking, screaming, mumbling, groaning, singing, shouting, and whispering. Motor behavior includes blinking, grasping, stooping, walking, jumping, shrugging, frowning, smiling, lip biting, and head scratching. There are many other behaviors in each of the two categories. Use of this division does not imply that vocal behavior occurs without muscular movement. Vocal behavior does obviously involve the action of jaws, lips, tongue, throat, and lungs.

Some actions which are clearly not vocal are not adequately characterized by designation simply as motor behavior. A boy may idly throw stones into the air. A baseball pitcher may throw the ball across the inside corner of home plate on signal from the catcher. Both actions involve throwing, but the function of the eyes is quite different in the two cases. The function of the eyes in the boy's throwing is quite possibly insignificant. In fact, the boy may close his eyes on some throws. The function of the eyes in the pitcher's throwing, however, is highly important. It is not likely that he would close his eyes in attempting a throw to a batter in a game. Here is another comparison. A man turns a crank to lower the window of

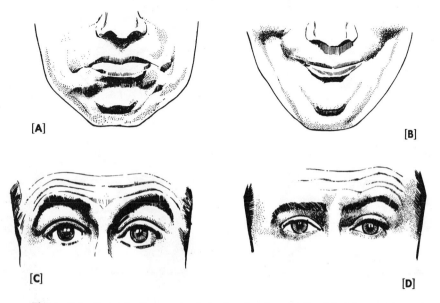

[A]

[B]

[C]

[D]

Figure 3-1. Records of expressive behavior showing details of facial expressions. **A:** depression of the corners of the mouth. **B:** elevation of the corners of the mouth. **C:** elevation of both eyebrows. **D:** elevation of one eyebrow. (What experience do you associate with each?) [Adapted with permission from S. R. Peck, *Atlas of Human Anatomy for the Artist.* New York: Oxford University Press, 1951.]

an automobile; another man turns a crank to adjust the position of a cutting tool on a metal lathe. Both actions, as examples of motor behavior, are quite similar. The man in the automobile, however, does not need his eyes to accomplish the lowering of the window quite satisfactorily. The man at the lathe must use his eyes to effect the very accurate adjustment which may be required by his work. There are many other actions which obviously depend on the eyes, ears, or other sensory organs for their coordination. Of course, motor activity always involves kinesthetic sensitivity in the control and organization of movements themselves. Actions whose coordination requires one or more of the senses in addition to kinesthesis

[A]

[B]

[C]

[D]

Figure 3-2. Records of expressive behavior showing facial expressions. **A:** a smile. **B:** fatigue. **C:** the reaction to a bitter pill. **D:** a response in a religious meeting.

are commonly designated as sensorimotor behavior. Handwriting is another example. Driving a car through heavy city traffic is still another. If a sense is especially important in the performance of a task, then the behavior may be described as sensorimotor.

Logically, one would expect to find employed a category called sensorivocal. Reading aloud from a printed page, singing from the score of an opera, calling balls and strikes in a baseball game, and calling out soundings from a depth finder in a ship are examples of behavior which could be included in this category. Actually the term sensorivocal is seldom, if ever, employed. Common practices in categorizing are not always logically systematic and complete.

Behavior can be classified according to the function it serves. Some possibilities are avoidance, destruction, escape, food-seeking, mating, attention-getting, protection, recreation, selling, locomotion, teaching, and

[A]   [B]

Figure 3-3. Records of expressive behavior. **A:** a broad gesture to emphasize a point about the surrounding country. **B:** the familiar disclaiming gesture involving both hands, palms up, accompanied by raised eyebrows.

communication. Specific teaching behaviors include lecturing, showing slides, writing on the blackboard, and answering questions. Communication has an interesting subcategory: expressive behavior (see Figures 3-1 to 3-6). A person may communicate to others through facial expressions, gestures, and postures.

Behavior can be classified according to the status or role of the persons involved: infant, child, adolescent, adult, parent, athlete, student, criminal, juvenile delinquent, and so on. Records illustrating infant behavior are contained in Figures 3-7 to 3-9; familiar athletic behavior, in Figure 3-10; and student behavior in the psychology laboratory, in Figures 3-11 and 3-12.

Behavior can be classified to represent social institutions: marital, political, legal, religious, military, and economic. Military behavior in-

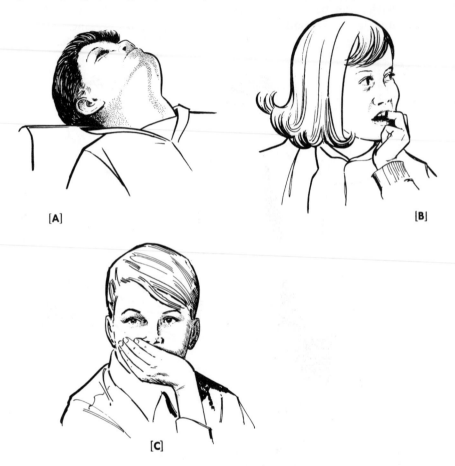

[A]   [B]

[C]

Figure 3-4. Records of expressive behavior in the classroom. Note the position of the head in **A**; the position of the fingers in relation to the mouth in **B**; and the position of the hand, as well as the expression around the eyes, in **C**. (What feeling or thought do you associate with each?)

cludes saluting, standing at attention, drilling, giving commands, parading, firing a rifle, bombing, driving a tank, and parachuting. Economic behavior includes buying, selling, trading, borrowing, advertising, manufacturing, and bookkeeping.

When a considerable amount of research has been done using a particular procedure or special apparatus, the behavior under investigation is sometimes categorized in terms of the procedure or apparatus. For example, one finds in psychological literature references to bar-pressing behavior, maze-running behavior, questionnaire behavior, interview behavior, pursuit-rotor behavior, test-taking behavior, and discrimination behavior.

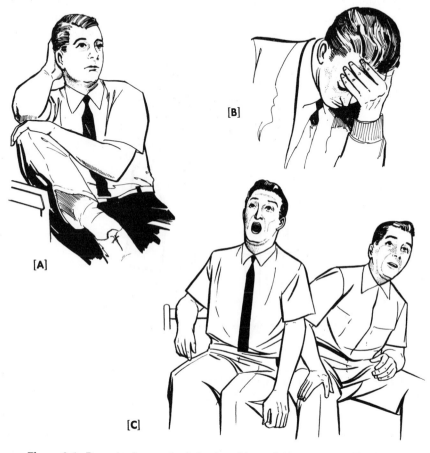

Figure 3-5. Records of expressive behavior with emphasis on posture. The casual pose of the spectator in **A** should be contrasted with the poses of the two spectators in **C**. The reaction of a man under arrest in a police station is shown in **B**.

Reflexive and Operant Behavior

In the description of perception, *stimulus* was defined as an object or event whose presence or occurrence was the occasion of action by sensory receptors. The term has another important usage. An external event which is followed invariably, or nearly so, by the action of a subject without prior instruction or training is also called a stimulus. This kind of stimulus event is specifiable in physical terms. It may be chemical, mechanical, thermal, electrical, or radiant.

The action which follows presentation of a stimulus is called a reflex, a respondent, or a response. *Reflex,* which has a physiological origin, is not used in psychology as much now as formerly. The simplest complete neural system for a reflexive action has three parts: a sensory neuron, an association neuron, and a motor neuron. The three neurons connect sensory stimulation with muscular or glandular action, the whole series of

Figure 3-6. Records of expressive behavior (postures, gestures, and facial expressions) on the part of two women saying farewell to a member of their family going off to war.

events constituting what has been called a reflex arc. It was once thought of as the fundamental unit of behavior. It is now known to be neither typical nor common; most sensorimotor behavior is much more complex. *Respondent* is a broader term than reflex. As it is employed in some theoretical discourse in psychology, it includes reflexes, the internal actions of glands and other organs, and so-called consummatory actions such as eating and copulating. *Response* is in very general use. It has the disadvantage of ambiguity in that it is sometimes equivalent to action or behavior, sometimes equivalent to reflex, and, as in everyday discourse, sometimes equivalent to answer.

Figure 3-7. Records of infant behavior. **A:** orientation of head and eyes in relation to a dangling hoop. **B:** handling of a cube. [Adapted from A. Gesell, *Infant Development*. New York: Harper & Row, 1952.]

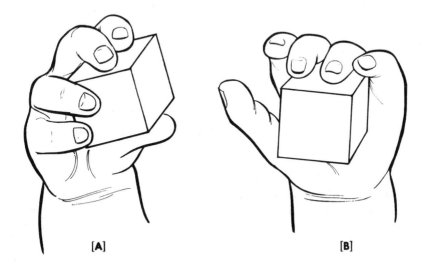

Figure 3-8. Records of infant prehension. **A:** a complete grasp of a cube. **B:** the partial grasp of a cube. [Adapted from A. Gesell, *Infant Development*. New York: Harper & Row, 1952.]

Following are some common stimulus-reflex combinations: light and contraction of the pupil of the eye; a loud noise and a body startle; a blow on the knee and a leg jerk; food in the windpipe and coughing; liquid in the throat and swallowing; dust injected in the nasal passages and sneezing; an air puff applied to the cornea of an eye and an eye blink; a hot metal rod applied to the hand and quick hand withdrawal.

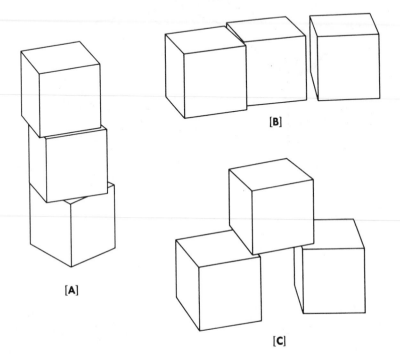

Figure 3-9. Records of infant behavior involving construction with three wooden cubes. **A:** a tower. **B:** a wall. **C:** a bridge. [Adapted from A. Gesell, *Infant Development.* New York: Harper & Row, 1952.]

Action for which a prior stimulus event cannot be identified is called operant behavior. The term is the behaviorist's substitute for *spontaneous,* which is considered by many to be a vague experiential word with philosophical connotations of voluntariness and free will. *Operant* is employed primarily, in company with *respondent,* in the context of a certain kind of psychological theory. Although stimuli cannot be identified for much of behavior, they are assumed by some psychologists to be present. It is also assumed that stimuli will eventually be identified for all actions.

NORMAL AND ABNORMAL BEHAVIOR

Behavior can be classified as normal or abnormal, but the issues which arise in attempting to justify the process are many and complex. Other terms which themselves require clarification must inevitably be considered. All of these terms have been controversial at one time or another. *Crazy* and *mad* are not used by psychologists because of their derogatory conno-

Figure 3-10. Records of athletic behavior. **A:** the discus throw. **B:** the straddle style of running high jump. **C:** the sprint crawl stroke. **D:** the running broad jump, knee tuck style. [**A, B,** and **D** after G. T. Bresnahan, W. W. Tuttle, and F. X. Cretzmeyer, *Track and Field Athletics*, 6th ed., 1964; **C** after D. A. Armbruster, R. H. Allen and, B. Harlan, *Swimming and Diving*, 1958; by permission of the authors and The C. V. Mosby Company, publishers.]

tations. *Sane* and *insane* are seldom used because the terms have been associated with legal procedure in the determination of responsibility and, subsequently, guilt or innocence in criminal trials. In many societies the determination of responsibility and blame before the law is considered to be an important and necessary function. Granting that it is important does not imply that the concepts are relevant to the development of the field of

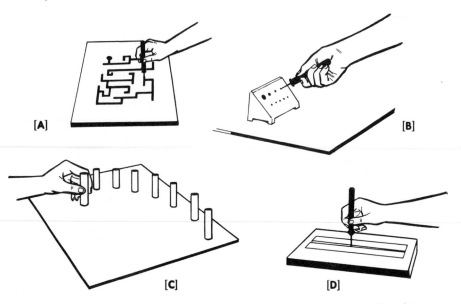

Figure 3-11. Behavior in a student laboratory. **A:** tracing a maze. **B:** holding a stylus steady in the center of a hole. **C:** lifting small weights in the process of making judgments about them. **D:** tracing a narrow converging path in a steadiness test.

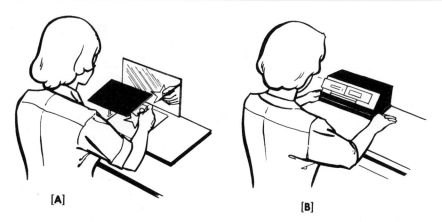

Figure 3-12. Subject and apparatus arrangements for familiar tasks in the student laboratory. **A:** a subject traces a star pattern while viewing its reflection in the mirror. **B:** A subject views nonsense syllables or words as they are exposed in the apertures of a memory drum.

psychological knowledge. Responsibility and blame are not knowledge and are irrelevant to its acquisition. Similarly, evil and sin, which are accorded importance in the religious life of many people, are irrelevant to psychological knowledge, and the terms are not employed in psychology.

Widely accepted by psychologists but still subject to controversy are terms like mental health and mental illness. The latter is thought by some to be more humane than other terms in that it carries no stigma. In saying someone is mentally ill, there is at least the advantage that one avoids the connotations of crazy, mad, guilty, and evil, which could play no useful role in establishing scientific facts. It is possible, of course, that the stigma was eliminated when the term mental illness was first adopted but that the stigma will return gradually as the new term becomes associated with the old behavior.

The trouble with the term mental illness lies in the assumptions one makes in using it and the conclusions one draws from them. There is, as a starting point for the discussion, the whole living organism, a biological unit. One may identify various states and behaviors of the organism, some of which are classed as organic illness and some, as mental illness. It is obvious that all behaviors are associated with a living organism and that any one of them has numerous biological correlates, although its psychological characteristics can be described without reference to those correlates. The issues come into focus when the question is asked how behavior in general and abnormal behavior or mental illness in particular can be influenced in some desired respect.

There is no denying the possibility that some manipulation or treatment of these biological correlates would change behavior in some desired direction. Although little is actually known at present about such treatments, the possibility cannot be denied that more will be discovered in the future. This kind of thinking forms the basis for concluding that mental illness is organic illness and that eventually there will be medical treatments for it. It would, however, be illogical to conclude that no other kind of treatment can be effective, that any other kind of effective treatment should be given only by medical specialists, that medical treatments for all behavioral disorders will necessarily be available by any given date, or that medical treatments, when available, would necessarily be better, in all respects, than any other kind of treatment.

The treatment of organic illness is, by common agreement in the United States, the province of the medical profession. Its methods of treatment are primarily chemical, surgical, and dietary. If every kind of mental illness turns out to be an organic condition which can be treated effectively only by these methods, then it will be reasonable to make it strictly the province of the medical profession. The fact is that little is known at the present time about the successful treatment of mental illness by chemical, surgical, and dietary means. It is true that sedatives and tranquilizers are valuable in the care and comfort of the mentally ill but, with respect to their effects, they are not in a class with the traditional medical treatments for organic illness. It is also true that the mentally ill often require custodial care, one feature of which should certainly be adequate medical care.

There is a possible fallacy in the argument that mental illness requires medical treatment. It is the assumption that there are specific identifiable organic conditions corresponding to characteristics of the behavior of the mentally ill. Mental illness is at present a broad concept embracing many more narrow concepts about behavior. Concepts are ways of thinking and there is no guarantee in nature that these ways of thinking about behavioral disorders will correspond to organic conditions which can be treated. It could be that the concepts of mental illness have their useful treatment correlates, not in the body, but in the ordinary circumstances of life, especially the training of children and the interactions between people. It could be that the useful treatments will turn out to be forms of training such as practice, instruction, education, occupation, and recreation, or forms of interaction such as persuasion, encouragement, discipline, and participation in a confidential relationship with a counselor. Although physicians may use or prescribe these activities, they are not the exclusive province of the medical profession. Although psychologists may engage in them, they are not the exclusive province of the profession of psychology. Parents, teachers, friends, coaches, religious counselors, social workers, lawyers, and many others are involved in these interactions and cannot be excluded. If it does turn out, as many now believe, that training and interpersonal interaction can provide effective treatments for mental illness, it is reasonable, of course, to expect that only persons with the proper training would be allowed to offer their services professionally to the public. Under what circumstances of supervision and control, if any, they should be permitted to practice in our society will not be decided here. There are complicated legal and professional problems which must be solved before decisions can be made on this matter. If forms of training and interpersonal interaction are found to be effective in changing the behavior under consideration, then it would be well to drop the term mental illness with its connotation of organic illness and medical treatment.

Proper use of the words normal and abnormal in psychology entails no connotation of good and bad, praise and blame, or guilt and innocence. One cannot deny, however, the suggestion of standards, the achievement of which is considered highly desirable. *Normality* and *abnormality* refer to variations in behavior of several different kinds:

1. Behavior is normal if it is concordant with the satisfactory biological functioning of the organism. Behavior is abnormal if it accompanies or results in the deterioration, destruction, or death of the organism. For example, excessive drinking of alcoholic beverages may be abnormal, as may excessive eating of rich foods, or excessive work. Taking poison, cutting one's wrists with a razor, or hanging oneself also are abnormal by this standard.

2. Normal behavior is rational in the sense that it accompanies or follows logically sound conclusions. Abnormal behavior is irrational in the sense that it is associated with illogical conclusions. Normal rational behavior is indicated by the statement, "The loss comes as a great disappointment to me but there is no point in bemoaning it. I shall just try harder next time and do my best." Abnormal irrational behavior is indicated by the statement, "I made a fool of myself yesterday and that means the end of everything. I'm going out and get myself good and drunk."

3. Normal behavior is realistic in that it is consistent with known facts. Abnormal behavior is unrealistic in that it is inconsistent with known facts. The realistic statement, "The policeman looked in my direction but, as far as I could tell, gave no sign of objecting to my sitting on the park grass," is normal. The unrealistic statement, "The President of the United States is trying to control my thoughts and is using radio waves to make voices say that I was guilty of incest with my mother," is abnormal.

4. Behavior is normal if it is concordant with the conventions and standards of a rational and realistic community to which the individual belongs. It is abnormal if it deviates widely from the typical and, at the same time, places the individual in such conflict with his group that he is rejected or punished by rational, dispassionate, and impersonal action of the group. Normal behavior involves a degree of accommodation to others, not incessant and irreconcilable conflict with them, and a degree of contact and participation with other people, not extreme withdrawal. In our society, the wearing of clothing in public is normal behavior, whereas going nude is abnormal.

This definition does not imply that every deviation from conventional practice is abnormal, for many deviations are allowed and even ignored. The pattern of allowed and forbidden behaviors may, of course, be quite inconsistent or arbitrary. Since this way of defining abnormal behavior implies a relative, not an absolute, standard, it is highly controversial. It is quite possible that some specific behavior could be typical at one time and place and deviant at another. It does not follow that any behavior which is rejected or punished is to be considered abnormal. A group of people may react irrationally, emotionally, and personally to punish someone for deviant action. In this situation the behavior of the group would be considered abnormal.

5. When behavior exhibits a serious impairment of function with respect to competence, where the impairment is disproportional to physical damage or debility, the behavior is considered abnormal. Thus the formerly successful lawyer who now emits only unintelligible vocalizations but reveals no organic disorder exhibits abnormal behavior.

6. The normal person is, within broad limits, calm, confident, energetic, organized, and productive. The person who is, in the extreme, excited or depressed, insecure or overconfident, apathetic or frantically

active, disorganized or overorganized is abnormal. It is, of course, entirely a matter of the combination of characteristics and the degree of each. Thus classification can in some instances be highly controversial.

The difficulty with classifying behavior as normal or abnormal should now be apparent. There is no single characteristic of behavior on which normality or abnormality can be based. Any one of a number of characteristics and many different combinations of them could be appropriately employed. Furthermore, each of these characteristics can be thought of as varying in degree, a circumstance which insures that there will be many borderline cases.

Summary

Behavior can be classified in many ways. The purpose in listing some of the common schemes has been to confront the student immediately with the fact that there are numerous possibilities, that, while some of them are useful and valuable, they are not absolutes, and that there is nothing difficult to understand about their origin. Whenever there is agreement in labeling a number of different actions according to a common characteristic, a category comes into being. Sometimes there will be several coordinate categories which seem to include much if not all behavior. Usually, however, close examination of the system will reveal inadequacies: some behaviors can be placed in two or more categories; some will not fit at all. The point is that these classifications are man-made schemes intended to provide ways of comprehending the complexity of human behavior. Consequently the psychologist may choose among the presently available schemes to suit his purposes, although he expects new schemes to be invented in the future.

Methods of Observing

Knowledge is based on observation, but it is planned, not casual, observation. The simplest arrangement for observing makes use of a natural setting in which behavior occurs undisturbed in any way by the procedures of the psychologist. He establishes himself at some vantage point to observe the behavior of his subjects: children playing in a park; a crew of men building a house; students taking an examination; a group of women playing bridge; or a crowd of shoppers in a department store. Although there is no contriving by the psychologist to define or limit the behavior which takes place, he must be prepared with a system for observing and recording the aspects of the behavior which are of interest to him. There are other arrangements in which the behavior is defined or limited by the observer's procedures: presenting the subject with a specific task; structuring a situation in which the subject must perform; conducting an interview with the subject; or having the subject complete a questionnaire.

A psychological task is an action required of a person by a psychologist who wishes to observe some aspect of the person's behavior. Typical tasks are solving a problem, tracking a target, memorizing a list of words, telling a story, and judging the size of an object. The subject's behavior may be recorded by the psychologist, by special apparatus, or by the subject himself.

As noted previously, tasks are devised by psychologists to reveal characteristics of behavior which they are interested in studying. How simple tasks can be devised to reveal characteristics such as aggression, avoidance of a threatening situation, self display, and control of another person was demonstrated by Santostefano[6]. He had his subjects, 150 male students selected randomly from the junior and senior classes of two Pennsylvania high schools, choose between ways of actually manipulating or avoiding objects presented to them.

The material for the tasks was presented on the top of a desk. Any one of them could be completed by a single action executed within a few seconds. They were combined into pairs, and a subject was required to choose and perform one task in every pair. Each subject was observed individually. He was urged to make his choices quickly and encouraged to give expression to the feelings he experienced before making his choice.

Aggression was considered to be indicated by the subject's choice of driving a spike in a plank instead of pulling it out; tearing a sheet of paper instead of repairing a torn one; striking a sheet of glass with a mallet instead of refusing to do so; and scattering sawdust over the desk top instead of sweeping it up.

Avoidance was indicated by playing an easy unknown game instead of a difficult one; examining an unfamiliar object instead of breaking a balloon; and looking at a concealed picture instead of exploring with his hand the interior of a box.

Self-display was revealed in the choice of reciting a speech instead of copying one, and reading to the examiner instead of listening to the examiner read.

Control of another person was revealed by a choice of shocking the examiner instead of being shocked by him, and handcuffing the examiner rather than being handcuffed by him.

Situations of many kinds have been contrived by psychologists to make it possible to observe some aspect of behavior of interest to them. In 1939, Maudry and Nekula[2] described a technique for observing the social behavior of children during the first two years of life. Subjects were children at a social agency in Vienna. Each one of twenty-four children called *chief subjects* was observed in play situations with other children called *partners*. There were chief subjects and partners in each of four different age groups from six months to twenty-five months.

Two children were placed in a playpen in the middle of the nursery. The playpen had three rows of movable beads on one side of it. Five observation periods of four minutes each were held. During the first period, no play material was present. At the beginning of the second period, three cubes were distributed: one was offered to each child; the third was placed on the floor between them. At the end of the second period, the cubes were taken away and a bell was given to one of the children. At the end of the third period, the bell was taken away, a drum was placed between the children, and a drumstick was offered to each one. At the end of the fourth period, drum and sticks were removed, and a ball was given to one child after both had been shown how to roll it from one to the other. At the end of the fifth period, the children were taken back to their cribs.

After the investigator placed the children in the playpen and presented the play materials, she left the room and took her position behind an observation screen outside the glass walls of the nursery. She reentered the room when it was time to remove and present the play material, when the children's fighting became so intense that they were in danger, when one fell or cried for some time, or when they definitely turned away from each other. While the investigator organized and supervised the situation, an observer took a detailed record of the behavior of both children. Emphasis was put on observing social behavior.

One record, for a situation in which a bell was given to the partner, revealed the following events: The investigator gave a bell to Erwin. Roland, sitting near the rail and playing with the beads, turned, looked at Erwin, and grasped for the bell. Erwin hid the bell immediately behind his back. Roland turned away, moved toward the bar, and moved the beads back and forth. Erwin examined the bell, watching Roland at the same time; then he rang the bell. Roland turned around to Erwin, and babbled at him. Erwin, deeply engaged in examining the bell, paid no attention to Roland. Roland turned back to the bar and moved the beads back and forth.

An inventory of behavior, consisting of a number of items describing a child's actions in the presence of another child, was devised. The three main categories were disregard of interference, negative social behavior, and positive social behavior. A specific item under disregard of interference was "turning away"; under negative behavior, "biting partner"; and under positive behavior, "smiling at partner."

Situation tests were employed extensively by the assessment staff[4] of the Office of Strategic Services in the selection of personnel during the Second World War. These tests provided opportunity for the observation of behavior judged to be relevant to the success of men who would be operating as agents behind enemy lines. A "construction test," intended to reveal leadership qualities and social relations, required the candidate to direct two uncooperative assistants, who were actually stooges, in helping him erect a wooden structure in a limited period of time. The helpers raised so many questions and provided so many hindrances that no candidate ever succeeded in completing the structure.

Taken from a protocol, which is an original record of what happened in a given testing situation, is the following typical conversation involving Slim, the candidate, and Buster and Kippy, the stooges. The candidate's part of the conversation was an important part of his performance in the situation.

Staff Member (calling toward the barn): Can you come out here and help this man for a few minutes?
Buster and Kippy: Sure, we'll be right out.
Staff Member: O.K., Slim, these are your men. They will be your helpers. You have ten minutes.
Slim: Do you men know anything about building this thing?
Buster: Well, I dunno, I've seen people working here. What is it you want done?
Slim: Well, we have got to build a cube like this and we only have a short time in which to do it, so I'll ask you men to pay attention to what I have to say. I'll tell you what to do and you will do it. O.K.?
Buster: Sure, sure, anything you say, Boss.
Slim: Fine. Now we are going to build a cube like this with five-foot poles for the uprights and seven-foot poles for the diagonals, and use the blocks for the corners. So first we must build the corners by putting a half block and a whole block together like this and cinching them with a peg. Do you see how it is done?
Buster: Sure, sure.
Slim: Well, let's get going.
Buster: Well, what is it you want done, exactly? What do I do first?
Slim: Well, first put some corners together—let's see, we need four on the bottom and four topside—yes, we need eight corners. You make eight of these corners and be sure that you pin them like this one.
Buster: You mean we both make eight corners or just one of us?
Slim: You each make four of them.
Buster: Well, if we do that, we will have more than eight because you already have one made there. Do you want eight altogether or nine altogether?
Slim: Well, it doesn't matter. You each make four of these, and hurry.
Buster: O.K., O.K.
Kippy: What cha in, the Navy? You look like one of them curly-headed Navy boys all the girls are after. What cha in, the Navy?
Slim: Er—no. I am not in the Navy. I'm not in anything.
Kippy: Well, you were just talking about "topside" so I thought maybe you were in the Navy. What's the matter with you—you look healthy enough. Are you a draft dodger? (pp. 105-106)

An interview is a conversation for purposes of obtaining information or providing counseling. It may be conducted with an individual or a group. Most personal interviewing is done face-to-face, but it is possible to do it by telephone. If interviewing is to be successful in providing the observations desired, the interviewer must be properly trained.

In obtaining information, as in employee selection or surveys of public opinion, an interview is usually structured; that is, the interviewer has a predetermined set of questions to be presented in a predetermined order. He may also have a number of rules to follow in recording answers and in dealing with unusual responses.

Interviewing can also be employed to good advantage with children, as demonstrated in 1933 by Jersild, Markey, and Jersild[1]. They studied children's desires, fears, and fancies. In a private interview, each child was asked to give specific details concerning his fears, dreams, daydreams, likes, and dislikes; to describe the unhappiest and the happiest events he had experienced; and to tell about his ambitions for the future, his wishes, and his preferences. Subjects were 400 children, equal numbers of boys and girls at each age from five to twelve, in two schools, one public and one private, in New York City.

A child was interviewed in a private room while school was in session. After his name, age and grade were obtained, the investigator said, "I am going to ask you a few questions and I should like you to answer each one as well as you can. This is not like a school test because you won't be marked or get a grade on it. I just want to ask a few questions and I am going to write down some of the things you say, but no one else is going to know what you say."

The investigator asked the child to elaborate on answers which he gave, with indications of special interest on his part. If a child did not understand a question, it was repeated or rephrased, but no suggestion of a possible answer was given. The investigator recorded answers as well as supplementary questions and prompts. Answers were recorded verbatim when it was possible, but only main points were recorded when a child responded rapidly and at length.

A large part of the interview was made up of questions about dreams. The questions, given here without the pauses required for answers, were: "Tell me what you dream about when you sleep. What else, what other dreams do you have? Tell me about other dreams you have had. Now tell me what good dreams you have had, dreams you liked. What are some of the bad dreams, dreams you don't like? Do you have any dream that comes again and again? Tell me about any dream that comes back one night and then another, so that you have it several times. What do you have most, dreams you like or dreams you don't like, good dreams or bad ones? Do you wish you would never dream?"

The results consisted primarily of the classification of reports according to their content. Dreams, which are the only content considered here, were classified in twenty-nine major categories. The three categories having the largest percentages of the total number of dreams reported were entertainment; everyday matters; and unpleasant events, including accidents, injuries, punishment, and fighting. Entertainment was divided into travel, amusements, adventure, and mischief. Travel included reports of going places on a train, being in Cleveland, going to Africa, and taking a boat to Europe with the family. Among the amusements reported were playing hide and seek, playing house, riding on a horse, being out in the country, having a lot of fun, going fishing and hunting, having a part in the kitchen, and going to the circus. Reports of adventure included the following: I went with my father in a submarine; I was in the woods shooting a lot of lions; I was on a boat pulling the rope and singing sea chanties; I was walking through a jungle in Africa; I am in the West shooting Indians; and I was in a war. Under mischief were the statements: I opened a window instead of doing what mother said; I sneaked out of the front door and rode off in somebody's car; I threw all the food and dishes on the floor and ran to the woods where my mother and father won't find me.

In counseling, interviews vary according to the views or theories of the clinician. Interviews in which the client is given much freedom in choosing the topics and encouraged to do most of the talking are called nondirective, whereas those in which the clinician plays a considerable role in questioning and interpreting are called directive. A part of a protocol from a counseling interview by Carl R. Rogers[5] illustrates the classic nondirective approach, in which he played a foremost pioneering role. The excerpt opens with the subject speaking of the fact that his college work is going more badly than it was earlier.

S: I haven't written to my parents about this at all. In the past they haven't been of any help to me in this respect, and if I can keep it away from them as much as possible, I'll do so. But there's a slight matter of grades to explain, and they're not good, and I don't know how I'm going to explain without telling them about this. [Meaning his upset emotional condition which, he has said, accounts for his problems.] Would you advise me to tell them about it?
C: Suppose you tell me a little more what you had thought about it.
S: Well I think I'm compelled to, because——
C: It's a situation you've really got to face.
S: Yes, there's no use getting around it, even if they can't take it the way they should, because I've already flunked my gym course. I just haven't come. I've just been negligent about it. Now, they'll know that you can't flunk in gym without being negligent about it. They'll ask why.
C: It will be fairly hard for you to tell them.
S: Yes. Oh, I don't know if they're going to sort of condemn me. I think so, be-

cause that's what they've done in the past. They've said, "It's your fault. You don't have enough will power, you're not interested." That's the experience I've had in the past. I've been sort of telling them that I improved in this respect. I was—I was all right the first quarter. Well, I wasn't entirely all right, but I just got worse. (*Pause*)

C: You feel that they'll be unsympathetic and they'll condemn you for your failures.

S: Well, my—I'm pretty sure my father will. My mother might not. He hasn't been—he doesn't experience these things; he just doesn't know what it's like. "Lack of ambition" is what he'd say. (*Pause*)

C: You feel that he could never understand you?

S: No, I don't think he is—is capable of that, because I don't get along with him, don't at all! [pp. 135-136]

A questionnaire is a set of questions designed to obtain opinions or information from an individual. The questions are often concerned with the individual himself, but they may have to do with other matters. A questionnaire may be administered to an individual or a group, and is sometimes distributed by mail. Instructions usually indicate whether or not the form is to be signed by the respondent. Anonymity is considered desirable if the issues covered are sensitive or if there is no need to identify the respondent. Questionnaires are widely used in public opinion surveys and research on consumer preferences.

Aids in Observing

The observation of behavior may be facilitated by special apparatus. Some apparatus produces a permanent record of the behavior. A sound recorder can preserve the vocalizations of a subject for repeated and intensive examination long after the original action takes place. Still photographs can record the successive positions taken by a moving subject. Moving pictures can reproduce the movements of a subject with great fidelity and detail. Still photographs and movie film can be projected in a manner permitting detailed study not possible with the original actions themselves. Mechanical devices can convert movements of parts of the body into movements of a pen on paper. Electronic devices can convert vocal sounds into a pattern of lights and shadows of film. Some apparatus which has been of value in observing and recording behavior is shown in Figures 3-13 to 3-15.

The behavior of an audience has been studied by Meier[3], who designed a compact piece of apparatus for recording the audience's responses to a movie, a stage play, a radio or television program, a concert, or a speech. The unit was contained in a box which could easily be held on a subject's lap and operated in the dark. One unit was required for each subject. Figure 3-16 shows the recorder. It produced a continuous record of a subject's responses on wax-impregnated tape, with time marked by perforations at intervals of one minute. The tape moved at a constant speed and issued from a slot on the side of the recorder. When a subject's task was completed, the tape could be released, drawn clear, and torn off.

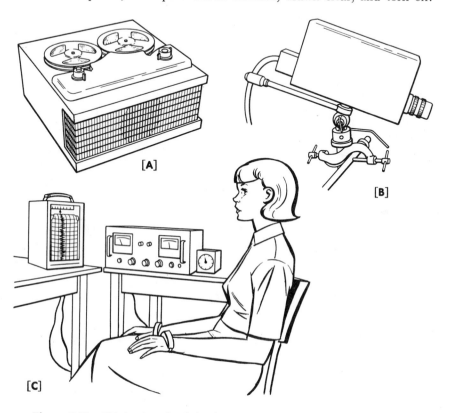

Figure 3-13. Aids in observing behavior. **A:** a tape sound recorder widely used for recording vocalizations. **B:** a television camera, frequently employed in a student laboratory to observe children being tested or for close-ups of facial expressions, manipulatory movements, and other details of behavior. **C:** apparatus for detecting and recording continuously the level of skin resistance. (At left, an Esterline-Angus graphic recorder; in the center, a Fels Dermohmmeter.)

On top of the box was a sliding plate to which a brass stylus was attached. The stylus rested on the tape. On the sliding plate was a knob which the subject held between his index finger and thumb. Attached to the knob was a pointer which could be moved along a scale covered with plexiglass. The scale, which was constructed to suit the purposes of a particular study, displayed a graded set of values. These values were memorized by a subject if the recorder was to be used in the dark. The movement of the stylus was at right angles to the movement of the tape. Figure 3-16 also shows a typical record.

In investigations in which subjects responded to dramatic productions, a research assistant using a stop watch marked the script at intervals so that corresponding points could be located on each subject's record. Records of a number of subjects were combined by superimposing and tracing.

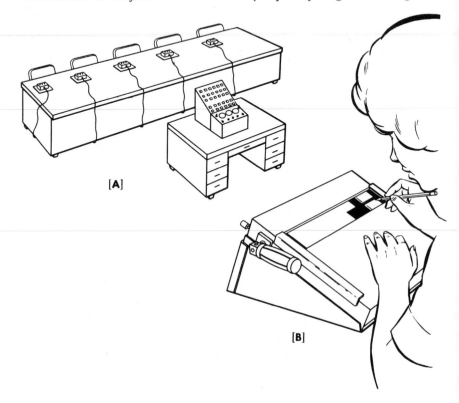

Figure 3-14. Aids in observing behavior in instructional situations. **A:** A device for monitoring student responses in the classroom, developed by Aircraft Armaments, Inc. During a lecture, the teacher asks a question having three alternative answers and the student chooses his answer by depressing one of three buttons on his box. When all students have responded, the teacher can operate a switch which signals on each student box whether or not that student is correct. **B:** The Foringer Teaching Machine employs a program on a continuous web of paper. The student has to make written responses to many small-step items in a prescribed order. [Adapted from AID, 1, 1961, Institute of International Research and Development, Inc. (INRAD), Lubbock, Texas.]

Another valuable class of aids to observation consists of special materials to which a subject responds as the psychologist presents them. Preliminary instructions are, of course, usually necessary. In addition to a variety of printed booklets containing questions or problems of many dif-

Figure 3-15. The Gesell observatory. The examiner and the child can be seen by the outsiders and photographed by the cameraman at the left but cannot see the observers.

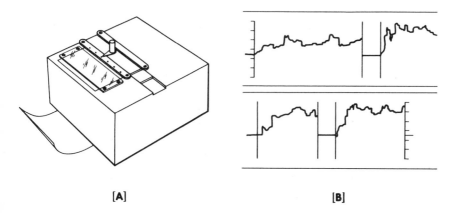

[A]   **[B]**

Figure 3-16. An aid to observing and recording the behavior of members of an audience. **A:** The recorder is operated by a subject's manipulating the pointer. **B:** The subject's choice of answers is recorded on a tape. [Adapted from Meier.[3]]

ferent kinds, with which many college students have already had frequent encounters, there are special pictures, cartoons, puzzles, mazes, blocks, and an assortment of gadgets of various kinds requiring manipulation by the subject. A sampling of these materials is shown in Figures 3-17 and 3-18.

Figure 3-17. Materials to which a subject may respond, thereby providing behavior which can be observed. **A:** The subject is instructed to use his imagination in completing the drawing on the left and writing a title for it. An example of a completed drawing is shown at the right. [Adapted from Horn Art Aptitude Inventory, C. H. Stoelting Company.] **B:** A child is told to look at the picture and find out which of three statements is true. In this example, the true statement is: "The boy broke the window." [Adapted from Davis-Eells Games, *Elementary Test* (1952), Harcourt, Brace and World, Inc., New York.] **C:** A child is told to write in the empty space what he thinks the boy would answer. [Adapted from the Rosenzweig Picture-Frustration Study, Children's Form, copyright 1948 by Saul Rosenzweig. Reproduced by permission.] **D:** As part of playing a game, a child is asked to tell a story about what is going on in the picture. [Adapted from The Children's Apperception Test by Leopold Bellak, M.D.]

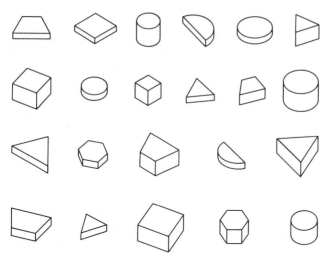

Figure 3-18. Blocks of the Hanfmann-Kasanin Concept Formation Test. A subject is asked to sort the blocks into categories. The level of abstraction he achieves is noted by the psychologist. (The varied colors of the blocks are not revealed in the drawing.) [Adapted from C. H. Stoelting Co.]

Chapter Summary

Behavior, the overt action of a human or infrahuman subject, is observable. To perceive a concomitant or the product of an action is equivalent to observing behavior. Among the smallest units of behavior are the action of a muscle and the secreting of a gland. The biological correlate of behavior is physicochemical activity of the whole organism. Human behavior is classified as vocal and motor; as sensorivocal and sensorimotor; according to its functions; according to the status or role of the person; by social institution; as reflexive and operant; and as normal and abnormal. Observation may take place in a natural setting, without any definition of or limitation on the behavior, but more often the psychologist presents a task to the subject, structures a situation around him, conducts an interview with him, or requests him to complete a questionnaire. The result is always a record of observations of behavior, upon which psychological knowledge is ultimately based.

References

1. Jersild, A. T., F. V. Markey, and C. L. Jersild. "Children's Fears, Dreams, Wishes, Daydreams, Likes, Dislikes, Pleasant and Unpleasant Memories." *Child Development Monographs,* No. 12 (1933).
2. Maudry, M., and M. Nekula. "Social Relations Between Children of the Same Age During the First Two Years of Life." *The Journal of Genetic Psychology,* 54 (1939), 193-215.
3. Meier, N. C. "The Meier Audience-Response Recorder." *The American Journal of Psychology,* 63 (1950), 87-90.

4. The OSS Assessment Staff. *Assessment of Men.* New York: Rinehart and Company, Inc., 1948.
5. Rogers, C. R. *Counseling and Psychotherapy.* Boston: Houghton Mifflin Co., 1942.
6. Santostefano, S. "An Exploration of Performance Measures of Personality." *The Journal of Clinical Psychology,* 16 (1960), 373-377.

4

Psychological
Language

New knowledge of any kind is not obtained easily. The quest for new psychological knowledge, represented by the many research activities of a substantial proportion of psychologists, has had its share of difficulties. Many of these difficulties are easily understood if they are treated as problems of language. This approach involves two assumptions. First, success in obtaining new psychological knowledge depends very much on the psychologist's choice of words, his definition of those words, and the principles he follows in formulating propositions out of the words. Second, formulating certain issues as language problems objicifies the discussion and makes those issues more clearly identifiable and distinguishable.

Reporting Observation

It is possible to observe without reporting what is observed, but the acquisition and systematization of knowledge require that what is observed be made a matter of permanent record so that data may be accumulated, analyzed, and evaluated. Psychological data typically display many irregularities and are therefore often difficult to interpret. The regularities in data, their salient features, are seldom obvious upon inspection. When the amount of data is small, the irregularities may obscure the regularities; when the amount is large, regularities may appear. Extensive accumulation, standard analysis, and strict evaluation of data are usually required for a satisfactory interpretation of research results.

An observation is recorded by expressing it in written language involving words, numbers, or other symbols. In this process the observer's perception of an external object or event is transformed into symbols which can be recorded. The transition from perception to recorded symbols may not appear difficult when it is examined only casually, but it is actually a giant step in the acquisition of knowledge.

One could hardly expect that accurate reporting or recording would follow as an automatic consequence of observing. That it does not is clearly indicated by the amount of disagreement which often appears in reports of the same event by different observers. It is true that inadequate observing could account for the disagreement, but inadequate expression cannot be ruled out and could be the major failure. In everyday life, of course, one's choice of language to represent his observations of people seldom receives the attention that it quite naturally demands of the psychologist in his attempt to represent with accuracy the behavior of his subjects and to communicate his findings to the scientific community.

Although the study of language is itself difficult, certain characteristics of accurate and effective language usage can be made explicit. The characteristics of most importance to students of introductory psychology have to do with semantical as distinguished from syntactical issues. Syntactical issues are concerned with spelling, punctuation, and sentence structure. Semantical issues are concerned with meanings of words and sentences. It will be assumed that students are sufficiently familiar with the syntactical conventions of English as a consequence of their general educational background. Emphasis here will be given to the semantical issues of the technical language of psychology.

Denotation and Connotation

The meaning of a word is given by indicating the word's referent—that is, by stating what the word designates or represents. In this connection, a distinction is made between denotation and connotation. The formally recognized meaning of a word is called its denotation; its additional meaning is called its connotation. Denotation is explicit meaning; connotation is suggested meaning. The denotation of a word may be stable while its connotation fluctuates from one period, group, or region to another.

The denotative meanings of words as used by psychologists are of critical importance to their work. Therefore, an attempt will be made to make explicit the nature of the referents of several different kinds of psychological terms. In addition, the referents of many specific terms will be identified and distinguished.

The connotation of a word may be expressed partially if a lengthy definition is given, but there is no guarantee that it can be expressed completely. The incomplete specification of connotation, however, is not a serious problem. The presence of subjective connotation *is* a problem. Subjective connotation is the suggestion of a positive or negative attitude on the part of the user. A positive attitude is one of approval, liking, deference, or esteem; a negative attitude is one of contempt, disapproval, disliking, or superiority.

In choosing a word to represent behavior, psychologists must take account of its connotation as well as its denotation. On some occasions subjective connotation may influence an audience subtly and improperly in the direction desired by the speaker or writer, but on other occasions it may succeed only in antagonizing the audience. Nothing of value is added to the quest for knowledge by subjective connotation, and since its user may be charged with biased reporting, psychologists carefully avoid it.

Many words with subjective connotation are commonly used to describe behavior. Among those which have had varied connotations, depending upon the time, place, and circumstances of their use, are the words capitalist, communist, socialist, integrationist, segregationist, reactionary, conservative, liberal, radical, isolationist, chauvinist, and pacifist.

It is possible to identify words which have similar denotation but different connotation. Listed below are ten pairs of synonyms selected from Roget's *Thesaurus*[6] and *Webster's Collegiate Dictionary*[7]. The members of each pair vary with respect to the desirableness of their connotations. The pairs are listed with words having neutral connotation in the left column and unfavorable connotation in the right column.

Neutral	*Unfavorable*
absurd	foolish
criticism	censure
deception	deceit
dispute	squabble
plausible	specious
slender	skinny
strange	queer
to admit	to confess
to conciliate	to appease
to leave	to desert

In Chapter 3 in the section on normal and abnormal behavior, some terms were mentioned as having conspicuous subjective connotation: mentally ill, insane, mad, and crazy. *Mentally ill* has, at present, favorable connotation; the others have unfavorable connotation.

Literal and Figurative Language

Verbal expressions can be distinguished as literal and figurative. Literal language involves words employed strictly for their denotative meaning; figurative language involves words which compare the thing being described to something else. There are many situations in which direct expression seems difficult and in which indirect expression appears to be the only recourse. In these circumstances figurative language is tempting, but it is risky when the user is concerned about accuracy. He may have in mind what he means exactly by a given figure of speech but, even if he does, he cannot limit his audience to the particular interpretation which he intends. Furthermore, several interpretations of a figure of speech may be equally valid, but only one may fulfill the intention of the user. It follows that psychological language should be literal: it should express as clearly and directly as possible exactly what its user intends to communicate. Perfection in this respect, of course, can seldom be achieved.

The more commonly encountered forms of figurative language are analogy, simile, and metaphor. An analogy is an extended comparison. It is based on the assumption that two matters, both alike in certain known respects, are alike in other respects known for only one of the two. A simile is a comparison explicitly stated and preceded by *as* or *like*. A metaphor is an implicit comparison very succinctly expressed without *as* or *like*. A simile can often be compressed into a metaphor, and a metaphor can often be expanded into a simile.

Examples of analogy and simile encountered in the psychoanalytic writings of Sigmund Freud, Jolan Jacobi, Carl Jung, and Karl Menninger follow. Psychoanalytic literature contains much figurative language, but choice of that literature as a source of examples does not imply that it is entirely figurative; nor does it imply that psychological literature is completely devoid of figurative language.

The examples of figurative language usage by Sigmund Freud are taken from his book, *A General Introduction to Psychoanalysis*[3]. In his third lecture, which deals with the psychology of errors, he characterizes the conditions under which slips of the tongue occur (p. 42). The analogy begins at the asterisk.

. . . The influence of such physiological predispositions as arise in slight illness, circulatory disturbances and conditions of fatigue, upon the occurrence of slips of the tongue is to be admitted without more ado; everyday personal experience may convince you of it. But how little is explained by this admission! Above all, these are not necessary conditions of errors. Slips of the tongue may just as well occur in perfect health and normal conditions. These bodily factors, therefore, are merely contributory; they only favour and facilitate the peculiar mental mechanism which produces slips of the tongue. I once used an illustration for this state of things which I will repeat here, as I know of no better. *Just suppose that on some dark night I am walking in a lonely neighborhood and am assaulted by a rogue who seizes my watch and money, whereupon, since I could not see the robber's face clearly, I make my complaint at the police-station in these words: "Loneliness and darkness have just robbed me of my valuables." The police officer might reply to me: "You seem to carry your support of the extreme mechanistic point of view too far for the facts. Suppose we put the case thus: Under cover of darkness and encouraged by the loneliness of the spot, some unknown thief has made away with your valuables. It appears to me that the essential thing to be done is to look about for the thief. Perhaps we shall then be able to take the plunder from him again."

In Freud's eleventh lecture, which concerns dreams, there is a simile comparing the form of a dream to the face of a building (p. 161). He states: ". . . that the appearance of a dream can have as little organic connection with the inner content of the dream as exists between the façade of an Italian church and its general structure and ground-plan. . . ."

In the same lecture he objects to attempts to explain one part of a dream by reference to another part as if the dream were a coherent whole. He says, "It is in most cases comparable rather to a piece of Breccia stone, composed of fragments of different kinds of stone cemented together in such a way that the markings upon it are not those of the original pieces contained in it."

In his fourteenth lecture, which deals with wish-fulfillment, Freud characterizes a dream by a brief analogy (p. 194): ". . . . We have compared the dream with a night-watchman, a guardian of sleep, whose purpose it is to protect sleep from interruption. Now night-watchmen also, just like dreams, have to rouse sleepers when they are not strong enough to ward off the cause of disturbance or danger alone. . . ."

In *The Psychology of Jung* by Jolan Jacobi[4], the author discusses the nature and structure of the psyche and, in that connection, describes Jung's concept of the persona as important in the individual's adaptation to the world. The following quotation contains a simile comparing a healthy persona to a healthy skin (p. 20).

. . . A well-fitting and functioning persona, so to speak, is an essential condition for psychic health and is of the greatest importance if the demands of the environment are to be met successfully. As a healthy skin naturally allows the underlying tissues to transpire through its pores and, when it turns into a hardened, dead epidermis, cuts off the life of the inner layers, so a properly "vascularized" persona acts as protector and regulator in the exchange between the inner and outer worlds, but comes to be, if it loses its elasticity and permeability, a troublesome impediment and even a fatal barrier. . . .

In the following quotation from Jacobi, archetypes, which according to Jung are representations of certain instinctive responses, are described in the figurative language of Jung himself (p. 43):

"The form of these archetypes," says Jung, "is perhaps comparable to the axial system of a crystal, which predetermines as it were the crystalline formation in the saturated solution, without itself possessing a material existence. This existence first manifests itself in the way the ions and then the molecules arrange themselves . . . The axial system determines, accordingly, merely the stereometric structure, not, however, the concrete form of the individual crystal, . . . and just so the archetype possesses . . . an invariable core of meaning that determines its manner of appearing always only in principle, never concretely."

In presenting Jung's laws of the psychic processes, Jacobi employs a simile involving physical processes (p. 49): "The structure of the psyche is accordingly for Jung not statically but dynamically constituted. As the building up and tearing down of cells keeps the physical organism in equilibrium, so—as a rough comparison—the distribution of psychic energy determines the relations between the various psychic data, and all disturbances therein lead to pathological phenomena. . ."

In *The Human Mind*, Karl Menninger[5] employs an extended analogy to convey his ideas about the structure and function of the unconscious (p. 279):

Think of the mind as a theatre. Let the field of consciousness be represented by the stage. On it, from time to time, there come and go certain actors (ideas and desires), directed from the wings by a stage-manager (the censor or ego ideal), who has derived his standards and experiences from training and example and precept and pictured ideal—from the lives and mouths of parents, teachers, early friends, and other early influences.

All of the actors—and we infer that there are very many of them—want to act. They will get on to the stage, if possible. The stage-manager holds some of them off stage merely until the proper time for their appearance. They are suppressed *pro tem.,* and they come or go as called. Others never get on the stage at all. They are poor actors, or unclothed and motley, or belong in another show, and so have no business clamouring for admission here. Most of them are not even in the wings (the *fore-conscious*), but are outside the theatre, thrown out, perhaps in the course of previous rehearsals and performances. They noisily demand to be let in, hoping to get on to the stage, but the confusion they create is not heard on the stage or in the audience. These actors, locked outside, are repressed ideas and desires.

These, the repressed, and even the suppressed, actors may trick the stage-manager by disguising themselves in various costumes and masquerading as proper actors in the show. They are never wholly proper, and the keen eye may detect their real identity and trace their origin. But the average playgoer (the ordinary person) will think only that the play is here and there a bit shabby or clumsy or strange.

In the examples from psychoanalytic literature, the figures of speech are prominent and the comparisons are explicit. In psychological usage, although literalness is the goal, figurative meaning may be present and may be very difficult to detect. One can never be certain that he has succeeded in completely avoiding or eliminating it. Consider the term motive. It has been defined, in part, as an internal condition which initiates and controls behavior. *Initiates* and *controls* are the words which are suspect with regard to figurative meaning. Is there, in these two words, the suggestion that the internal condition is an agent or a doer? Is the motive a mover? Expressed crudely, is there the suggestion of a little man inside the organism, pushing buttons and pulling levers? A careful examination of the word and its usage reveals that, in its definition, reference should be made to three components: the behavior of a subject; the related internal biological condition; and the related external circumstance. If the motive is hunger, then the behavior could be a verbal report, the subject's statement that he is hungry; the physiological condition could be his low level of blood sugar; and the circumstance could be a prior period of twenty-four hours of food deprivation. It might be demonstrated that the occurrence of the verbal report is related to the level of blood sugar and the condition of deprivation. If so, an explicit statement could be made of those relations. There is no need to speak of initiation and control, and it is possible that nothing is gained by doing so.

Drive, sometimes used as a synonym for *motive,* poses the same problem. It has been defined as an impetus to behavior, a condition which impels, or a condition which initiates and guides. The definition can be improved by eliminating the figurative language and by emphasizing the behavior, the physiological condition, and the external circumstances.

Instinct is another term which deserves close scrutiny. One may observe complex, patterned, adaptive behavior which is characteristic of all members of a species of the same age and sex, and which occurs abruptly without gradual development, extensive practice, or noticeable opportunity for imitation and communication through social contact. An example is nest building by birds. Behavior of this sort may be said to be instinctive, and there is little or no involvement of figurative meaning. When the definition of instinct involves initiation and control, or other expressions suggesting these, there is again the possible suggestion of agent and an involvement with figurative meaning.

Concrete and Abstract Words

Words can be classified as concrete or abstract with respect to their referents. The referents of concrete words, established by repeated and consistent usage, are actual objects—material or physical things which can be seen and touched. Concrete words include the names or labels of specific persons, animals, objects, materials, and places. Of special interest to the psychologist are three groups of concrete words: the names of persons, of interest because he must identify and distinguish them without error in his work; words that refer to specific products of human scholarship and workmanship, including paintings, books, poems, musical compositions, handicraft, articles of manufacture, and exact quotations of what people say, because these are behavioral products which he may wish to study; and words like timer, pencil, answer sheet, color wheel, stylus, finger maze, aesthesiometer, memory drum, and stop watch, because these are names of pieces of equipment employed in psychological work.

A concrete noun may designate a particular single object such as that student, the one sitting opposite me in the laboratory and waiting to be tested, or it may be used as a collective to designate a specific group of objects such as those students, the ones gathered around the entrance to the laboratory.

Because the referents of concrete words are easily identified, reports of the presence or absence of objects by different observers usually exhibit a substantial degree of agreement. Observers can agree on the presence or absence of food pellets in the feeding tray of an animal cage. In examining an answer sheet for a certain kind of test, they can agree as to the particular answers chosen by a student. With the aid of a good tape recorder, they can agree on what was said and by whom in an interview. They can agree as to which one of several objects a child selects as a prize. It is also true that repeated reports by only one observer concerning the presence or absence of objects may be quite consistent under certain circumstances. Thus it is that the use of concrete language does not involve serious difficulties in achieving agreement in observing.

Concrete language also presents relatively little difficulty in communication. Usage peculiar to the speaker or writer is not ordinarily a problem. Conventional usage agreeing with that of observers-in-general can, under normal circumstances in most situations, be taken for granted. Failures in communication which occur because people use the same word for different objects are relatively infrequent. The referents of concrete words such as projector, color wheel, and audiometer are seldom confused in psychological communications. Nor are other referents likely to be confused, such as *child* in "the child who was tested this morning by Dr. James"; *drawing* in "the crayon drawing done by Johnny Jones"; *hose* in "the thirty dozen hose produced by J. L. Brown"; and *solution* in "the salt solution on the shelf in the laboratory."

The antonym of concrete is abstract. An abstract word refers to an attribute of objects, an attribute of events, or an attribute of other attributes. Abstract words may be classified as activities, qualities, conditions, classes, and relations. Activities are designated by words such as walking, drinking, talking, selling, learning, crying, and judging; qualities, by words such as length, speed, whiteness, sourness, femininity, honesty, and beauty; conditions, by words such as deprivation, poverty, sleep, pregnancy, mental illness, pneumonia, and hypnosis; classes, by words such as animal, primate, man, infant, adolescent, female, and teacher; and relations, by words such as analogy, association, best, coincidence, comparable, equal, and subordinate. It should be obvious that these five categories and the list of words within each category are not exhaustive.

In any quantitative science a place of importance is held by abstract terms expressing mathematical constructs. The referents of mathematical terms employed in psychology are constructs resulting from deduction applied to numerical data. Mathematical constructs are designated by words such as constant, variable, sum, difference, variation, covariation, mean, ratio, proportion, rate, slope, correlation, approximation, equation, and asymptote.

Abstract words are general, not particular. It follows that summarizing requires abstract terms. The salient features of collections of psychological data require abstract terms for their expression.

The referents of abstract words are not visible and tangible as are those of concrete words. Assigning an abstract word to its referent is the last step in the abstracting process. Prior to this assignment, there must be identified an attribute common to the matters of concern. Confirmation of the correctness of abstract language usage depends, therefore, not on pointing to objects as can be done for concrete language, but on establishing the adequacy of the abstracting process. More will be said later about the criterion for evaluating this process.

The same word can be concrete in one context and abstract in another. In the sentence, "That woman applied for a job at the factory today," woman is a concrete word; but in the sentence, "Woman has a subordinate role in our society," it is abstract. Similarly, in the sentence, "There is a slide projector on the table in Room 203," projector is concrete, but in the sentence, "The slide projector is widely used in psychological laboratories," it is abstract. There are many words which are concrete in referring to particular pieces of apparatus and abstract in referring to classes of apparatus. Neither usage is a problem in psychology.

Important in psychology are abstract words denoting procedures, such as practice, testing, interviewing, counseling, judging, rating, and scoring. Although each of these words is very general and covers numerous specific procedures, none of them poses any special problem. The classes to which they refer are distinguished very satisfactorily.

Definite and Indefinite Abstract Words

Abstract words can be conceptualized as lying on a continuum running from definite to indefinite. A definite word refers to an attribute common to two or more objects or events. Words such as redness, length, triangularity, blinking, running, and talking, as well as expressions such as hitting a home run, catching a fish, eating a sandwich, making a speech, serving a summons, or buying a house, are definite.

An indefinite word refers to an attribute common to two or more previously abstracted attributes. Consciousness, dimension, shape, reflex, locomotion, and communication are examples of indefinite words.

The difficulties of reporting and communicating observations by means of abstract language vary with the indefiniteness of the terms. The more indefinite the terms, the greater the opportunity for uncertainty and disagreement. With the most indefinite terms, the difficulties are so great as to be insurmountable. Even recognition and understanding of the problem of indefiniteness coupled with a determined effort to solve it by examining, evaluating, and defining terms will not necessarily overcome the difficulties.

Abstraction and Reification

An abstraction is the joint result of a thought process and an attempt at expression in language. Although an abstracted attribute may have been derived from a set of real objects or events, it exists only in a way of thinking and verbalizing about them. It is a common fault to attempt the reification of an abstracted attribute. (The meaning of *reify* is *to make concrete*.) This fault occurs when the origin of the abstraction is forgotten and the attribute is credited with an existence in physical reality. There may even be a search for something visible or tangible as the referent. When the search fails, as it must, the reaction is usually to declare that the abstraction is erroneous. The reaction is not justified, for it is the attempt at reification that was erroneous. The attribute never had the existence in physical reality which was incorrectly imputed to it.

The process of abstraction is the forming and naming of a common property. Whether or not a given attempt at abstraction is successful depends on the amount of agreement exhibited by the participants. It would be possible, of course, to contrive a situation which produced temporary agreement among a few people, but such agreements would have trivial significance. The agreement of many persons on numerous occasions in different situations, however, would clearly justify an abstraction. Some abstractions are characterized by a very high degree of agreement so that the terms adopted for them are extremely useful in a practical way. There is hardly ever any question about abstractions such as length, weight, and time, but some others, such as liberal, conservative, and socialist, are agreed upon so little that the terms are continually the subject of disagreement.

Since abstracting is a human activity, the success of which is reflected in the amount of agreement accompanying it, the criterion for validating it is procedural, not existential. If a term is called into question and it is necessary to settle the issue, then a situation must be devised to permit examination of the set of objects or events, and the assessment of agreement in naming attributes. Since agreement is the only validator of abstract language usage, idiosyncratic usage is meaningless. Furthermore, deliberately using a term with intended meaning peculiar to oneself, when the term will be interpreted according to a general meaning by one's audience, is pure misrepresentation.

Research Language

In psychological research, language problems arise at two points: in stating aims and procedures, and in reporting results and conclusions.

AIMS AND PROCEDURES

In stating the purpose of a psychological investigation, there is the problem of choosing terms at an appropriate level of definiteness. The investigation may involve only a few procedures with a small group of subjects on a particular occasion. For example, a test involving definitions of words and a questionnaire requiring expressions of satisfaction with college life may be administered to students in a class which happens to be available. The investigator may state his purpose as one of determining the relation between test scores and ratings of satisfaction for those students; that is, he may choose very definite language. If he does, everyone will understand very well what his purpose is and will accept his procedures as suitable to that purpose. If he says, however, that his purpose is to determine the relation between intelligence and adjustment among college students in general, he will be severely criticized for the disparity between his terms and his procedures. Psychologists exert great care to keep the level of definiteness or indefiniteness of language appropriate to the actual procedures of their investigations. An indefinite abstract term is not used when a definite one represents the situation adequately.

There is, of course, the other side of the problem. It would be foolish to use a definite term when the scope of the investigation clearly justified an indefinite one. The goal of science, which is greater generality of knowledge, is not approached by adhering slavishly to definiteness of language.

In undertaking the study of psychology for the first time, however, most students have the problem of learning to speak about psychological topics in terms more definite than those they have been accustomed to using.

Results and Conclusions

The statement of results and conclusions of a psychological investigation poses much the same problem as the statement of aims and procedures. Results are formulated by summarizing and analyzing data. Conclusions are reached by reasoning about the results in relation to the conditions of the investigation. The psychologist may observe the behavior of his subjects and record it in symbols consisting of words and numbers. After he has accumulated numerous records, he may examine them and formulate summary statements concerning characteristics of his data. Finally, having reasoned about the limitations and possible implications of the entire investigation, he may state his conclusions. Results are seldom absolutely clear-cut and conclusions are usually tentative. For these reasons, psychologists are cautious in their choice of language to report their findings. High levels of indefiniteness are avoided. Definite terms or modest and appropriate levels of indefiniteness are preferred.

Language and Logic

To a very great extent the emphasis in the preceding discussion has been upon the problem of expressing observations in words and formulating propositions which express the agreement in those observations. All this has to do with setting forth empirical knowledge. The account of the role of language in psychology will not be complete, however, until its connection with logic is acknowledged, for language provides the psychologist with the means of recording, evaluating, and communicating his reasoning. The psychologist deals with language and logic in four related areas: formal logic, common sense, mathematics, and theory.

Formal logic is an account of the certainties and successes of reasoning, and the exposure of many of its common uncertainties and failures. Reasoning pervades many areas of life, and people in those areas would benefit by training in formal logic. It will not be discussed here even briefly, for that is the proper task of a philosopher and not at all the task of a psychologist.

Much of the reasoning done by psychologists in their work is expressed, not in formal logic, but in what is usually called common sense. Of course, common sense has its limitations, for it cannot serve as a substitute for observation and is not a source of empirical fact. When it is properly employed, however, it is of very great value not only in psychology but in all the sciences. Common sense, as the term is used here, refers to everyday reasoning of a sound and valid nature. It is the basis for intelligent decision and action on the part of a psychologist as he carries on his work. It is applied by reducing an issue to terms in which the correct resolution is obvious to any intelligent and competent person. Not all issues can be resolved in this fashion. Those which require evidence cannot be resolved by reasoning of any form.

Although applications of common sense can be given expression in the traditional statements of formal logic, they seldom are made explicit in this way. More of them should be, even though much more time would be required, for formal expression would reduce the amount of error in reasoning.

Another substantial part of the reasoning done by psychologists is mathematical. Mathematics is essentially deductive and is certainly the most elegant form of logical reasoning achieved by man. It is far superior to common sense in the way it combines highly abstract and complicated operations with absolute certainty as to the correct outcome. Mathematics is, of course, simply not applicable to many of the issues dealt with by common sense.

Much valuable psychological knowledge is not quantitative and little or no training in mathematics is needed for expressing or assimilating it, but much is quantitative and some training in mathematics is needed for dealing with it. The student who aspires to be a psychologist should not limit himself in his preparation for that role. Quantitative psychology is not the whole of psychology, but it is already a significant part and may continue to grow in importance.

Theory is another of the areas in which the psychologist deals with language and logic. Theorizing begins with formulating one or more assumptions and ends with deducing one or more hypotheses. In simple terms, the psychologist may say, "I have an idea about these subjects. I have reasoned from this idea to a conclusion. My observations will confirm or deny the empirical validity of the conclusion." *Reasoned to a conclusion* is the expression of immediate concern. It is a process of logical thinking to obtain a hypothesis. If the conclusion is logically correct, other competent persons should be able to verify its being so and should agree with the theorizer. Sometimes what is intended as a conclusion or hypothesis turns out, on close scrutiny, to be no more than a plausible statement which cannot really be verified.

Experiential and Behavioristic Language

In earlier sections, words were classified as concrete and abstract, and abstract words were described as varying from definite to indefinite. Words can also be classified as experiential and behavioristic.

Psychology draws many of its terms from everyday language. These terms are adopted for the relevance of their original meanings. Everyday language contains many words which are descriptive of people. Roget's *Thesaurus*[6], a classification of words according to the ideas they express, devotes almost two-thirds of its 400 pages to intellect, volition, and affection, three of its six principal classes of words. In addition, it has a large section on sensation and smaller sections on motion and vitality, all of which contain many terms applicable to people and their behavior. The significance of everyday language as a potential source of psychological language is also indicated by the survey of G. W. Allport and H. S. Odbert[1] who found 17,953 words descriptive of human traits. Furthermore, an informal inspection by the present author revealed that in a list of 2506 different words appearing in the glossaries of five introductory psychology texts, more than 600 words, approximately twenty-five per cent of the total, were in common use and not in their origin attributable to psychology or any other special field. Although everyday language provides many words for psychology, it is, of course, not the only source. Essentially new words are deliberately invented and introduced into the technical literature from time to time.

Many words which are descriptive of humans and which have been adopted from everyday language for use in psychology can be differentiated with respect to their relation to experience and behavior. Some words refer to experience; some, to behavior. The class of experience-related words includes red, sour, loud, pain, seeing, hearing, thinking, reasoning, fear, and thirst. Words related to experience will be called experiential words. The class of behavior-related words includes blinking, walking, climbing, talking, grimacing, shrugging, crying, announcing, acting, and clowning. Words related to behavior will be called behavioristic words.

Whether a word is related to experience or behavior may depend on the way it is used. For example, the verbs debate, question, resist, consent, and agree may refer to either covert or overt activities on the part of an individual. A student may debate inwardly in the course of thinking about an issue or outwardly in the course of arguing the issue in one of his classes.

The Redefinition of Everyday Terms

Some words taken from everyday language and adopted as part of a technical language are redefined. Even so, their common meaning may have relevance to their technical meaning. An example from physics is *pressure*. A common meaning of pressure is squeezing. The technical meaning in physics is pounds of force per square inch of surface. The common meaning is not satisfactory for the physicist's purposes, but it is not irrelevant. Consider a tank of compressed air under a pressure of 100 pounds per square inch. Thinking of the tank as squeezing the air it contains is inaccurate and primitive, but relevant. Although it would be simple enough to invent a new technical term for pounds of force per square inch of surface, the word pressure has some value in that its common meaning mediates the acquisition of the new meaning. An example from psychology is the word *blink*. In common use it means closing and opening the eye quickly. It may be given a more precise definition in psychology to take account of partial closures of the eyelid. For example, a blink may be defined as a movement of the eyelid through some minimal arbitrary distance.

Some behavioristic words require redefinition, but all experiential words require it. Furthermore, the change of meaning with redefinition is more drastic for experiential words than for behavioristic ones. Redefinition of an experiential term involves establishing a behavioral referent for a term which, according to its common meaning, has a referent in experience. An example of an experiential word which must be redefined is *seeing*. In everyday usage it refers to a variety of experiences, including that of color. Thus *seeing a blue paper* is accepted as descriptive of a common experience. In psychology the expression is redefined to have a meaning which does not deny the possibility of a certain experience on the part of the subject but does affirm that what the psychologist observes is the subject's behavior, not his experience. Strictly speaking, what is observed may be one or more of the following behaviors: orienting of the subject's head and eyes in the direction of the paper, his naming the color of the paper, his selecting a paper of the specified color, his matching papers of the same specified color, his verbalizing about differences among colored papers or his acting in a particular way to the paper presented as a signal. Insisting on redefinition of the expression amounts to saying that a psychologist cannot study a person's seeing of colored papers except as orienting, naming, selecting, matching, verbalizing, and acting on signal. The candor of this statement is a distinguishing quality of modern psychology. It is achieved by acknowledgment on the part of the psychologist as to the exact nature of his observations and knowledge.

Another example of a statement requiring redefinition is "The man's fear was extreme." In ordinary usage the word fear refers to the man's inner feeling. An inference regarding the existence of the man's inner fear may be correct, but the claim cannot be made that it was observed. What can be observed, among other things, is his verbalization. The man talked at length about being afraid. If fear itself cannot be observed, what then is the justification for use of the term? It is, first, that the original meaning of fear is relevant to what has been observed and, second, that the term has been redefined to give it stricter meaning consistent with the reality of the situation.

The psychologist cannot afford to be misunderstood in matters of this sort. He is fully aware of the fact that the individual's experience is private. He knows that his investigations will involve observations of behavior and that no other choice is open to him. His terms must be defined accordingly—that is, to give recognition to the real nature of psychological knowledge. Pretense on his part is futile, for if his language is interpreted as implying that he studies experience, the intelligent and skeptical layman will quickly challenge and reject psychology.

Some psychologists believe that it would be better to dispense with experiential terms and employ only behavioristic ones. The exercise of this preference is sometimes easy. There are situations in which behavior can readily be described without recourse to experiential words. If the language does justice to the observations, there is good reason to insist on behavioristic terms. The chances of misunderstanding, especially on the part of students and the public, will be reduced considerably if behavioristic words are used.

A strict avoidance of experiential terms, however, has not been achieved by those who recommend it. Consider the simple statement, "The child looked at the block." Does the statement have behavioral or experiential referents, or some combination of both? The correct answer may be debatable. Could the statement be rewritten in strictly behavioral terms— head, neck, eyelids, eyeballs, position, angle, distance, and the like—about which there could be no argument? Possibly, but the result may be a translation which is fantastically long and complicated. Furthermore, the translation, for all its detail, may be unrecognizable without the word *looked* itself. The complexities of behavior often defy description if no experiential terms are allowed. In the past, those who have wished to avoid such usage, but could not, have sometimes employed the expression *as if* as a last-ditch stand against experiential language. Thus a psychologist might say, "The child handled the two parts of the puzzle and turned his head in various positions *as if* he was trying to see a relation between the parts."

Other psychologists have revealed their uneasiness about experiential words by putting them in quotations in their writing. Thus an allusion may be made to "fear" responses on the part of a child. What the psychologist may observe is complex action in which a child, while crying, tries to avoid some object and tries to escape from the situation. (Even *tries to avoid* and *tries to escape* may not be free of experiential meaning. Purpose is a familiar and common feature of experience, but as a characteristic of behavior it is very difficult to verbalize.) The psychologist can say something behavioristic at length and in detail, but he may prefer to say simply that the child displayed fear responses, if he is not going to be misunderstood. He adds the quotation marks as a kind of reminder of his qualification of the experiential word.

Still other psychologists accept experiential terminology and, in fact, insist upon its use. It is impossible to generalize regarding the reasons for their views, but those views represent, at the very least, a strong, intuitively-based conviction regarding the importance of experience to psychology. Although they are sometimes accused of being unscientific, they are certainly as aware as anyone that psychological language is always reducible to statements about behavior and the circumstances under which it occurs. Certainly they can describe the specific action or verbalization given by their subjects. It may be that they continue to insist upon the importance of experience to psychology because they sense the language is necessary; that is, a complete and comprehensible account of psychology could not be given without the terminology of experience. There are, of course, no valid *a priori* reasons for concluding that the language of experience can contribute absolutely nothing to psychology.

In this discussion of the redefinition of experiential words, a central issue of psychology has been exposed. The issue involves experience and behavior, and their places in psychology. Our viewpoint is that experience and behavior are different. Experience is privately real but publicly unobservable; behavior is publicly real and observable. Consequently, the psychologist who wishes to participate with other psychologists in establishing a field of knowledge studies behavior, not experience, and a student who wishes to participate with a psychologist in exploring that field of knowledge also studies behavior, not experience. But to be clear about what psychologists and their students can know from collaborative observation is not to deny the reality of experience to the individual or the value of experiential language to psychology. In this respect psychology is different from the physical and biological sciences. Experience and its language have no place in those sciences.

There can be no doubt that psychology is to be a field of knowledge about behavior. Although a man may be interested in knowing about others in the way he knows about himself, he cannot. To say he cannot know others as he knows himself, however, does not mean he cannot know anything of relevance to the matters which interest him. It is possible to associate certain forms of behavior with certain forms of experience. After the connection has been established, the behavior can be described in the language of experience, and no other language will serve the interests of some men as well. Thus there is no proof that experience and its language are expendable. As long as men think about men in experiential terms and contrive their research in those terms, experience will have a place in psychology. One may believe in the futility of the endeavor in this respect but one cannot make a law out of a belief. The possibility remains that psychological knowledge will increase by reason of its connection with human experience.

The Redefinition of Experiential Words

In the process of redefinition, experiential terms are given behavioral referents. The behavioral referent for a given experiential term is not arbitrarily chosen. There are ways of determining the relevance of the one to the other. Five ways in which relevance is determined will be described next.

1. Experiential terms may be assigned to specific forms of behavior according to the judgment of a psychologist. Detailed rules for the assigning do not exist. There is no manual listing experiential terms and their appropriate behavioral referents. There is no formula which can be applied mechanically. The judgment cannot be made as a deduction.

The psychologist observes the behavior of another person. He judges the relative appropriateness of the various experiential and behavioristic terms with which he is familiar and makes his choice, tentatively. It is impossible to list all the variables which could conceivably be related to his choice of an experiential term. One could speculate at length about the psychologist's personal background and how it might be related to his choice of language. Having made a tentative choice, the psychologist checks with others in his field to assess the amount of agreement he can expect with regard to his use of the term. If he encounters a fair amount of agreement, he goes on to employ the selected language, but he fully expects his choice to be questioned, reviewed, and debated repeatedly. Eventually, the term of his choice may be widely accepted as having the behavioral referent he intended.

The steps in the judgmental process cannot be made explicit with any degree of certainty. Several ways exist as possibilities for its conduct. They may be employed singly or in combination.

(a) The psychologist may identify actions of the subject which in his own behavior would be associated with certain of his own experiences.

Example: He observes a flushed face, a loud voice, and an out-pouring of words. He recognizes that he sometimes acts that way when he is angry. He describes the person he is observing as "being angry."

(b) The psychologist has learned that a certain experience is typically reported when the behavior occurs which he is now observing.

Example: In a physician's waiting room, a psychologist observes a stout, elderly man enter and seat himself. The man's face is flushed and he is perspiring heavily. Soon he removes his suit coat, loosens his tie, and opens his shirt collar. He then takes out a large white handkerchief and mops his forehead. The psychologist describes the man as "being uncomfortably warm" because that is the experience usually reported when someone behaves in this fashion.

(c) A psychologist has learned to predict certain subsequent events from what he observes at a given moment. The subsequent events could be verbal reports or other actions, as in (a) and (b), which support his choice of an experiential term for the observed behavior.

Example: A psychologist observes several students at the rear of the classroom leaning forward, with frowns on their faces and with heads turned slightly to one side or the other. He recognizes that these actions often precede the raising of hands and the reporting of an inability to hear him, so he describes the students as "not hearing what is being said" and raises his voice.

(d) The psychologist has learned that taking account of the setting in which the behavior occurs often supports descriptions by the method of (a), (b), or (c) above. Where he observes is relevant to the experience of his subject.

Example: A psychologist observes a little boy about three years old, unaccompanied, in one of the aisles of a large supermarket on a busy day. The child looks around with a solemn expression on his face. He calls out several times for his mother and then begins to cry. The psychologist describes the child as "afraid." He may make his choice of this term by any of the previous methods, but the setting, the huge busy supermarket with its unaccompanied small boy, facilitates the decision by providing additional information.

2. An experiential term may be applied to a verbal report of an experience. The verbal report is, of course, behavior. What a person says about his experience is assumed to be relevant to that experience. The psychologist reports that a young woman is afraid. His reason for so reporting is that she has said that she is afraid. Putting it in somewhat different terms, what the psychologist means when he says, "The young woman is afraid," is "The young woman says she is afraid." He does not pretend to know what he cannot know, how the young woman actually feels, but he does accept what she says as establishing the relevance of an experiential term for describing her behavior. The skeptic may be quick to point out that the young woman may not be telling the truth. The psychologist makes no defense because he considers none is necessary. He never meant that he really knew how the young woman felt. A similar treatment can be given to the statement, "Mr. and Mrs. Smith are happily married." It can be translated into a more accurate statement, "Mr. and Mrs. Smith say they are happily married," or a still more accurate one, "Mr. and Mrs. Smith both answered 'Yes' to the question, 'Are you happily married?' " Although the degree of correspondence between a subject's experience and his verbal report of that experience cannot be determined, an accurate statement about the subject's behavior, making explicit reference to the subject's verbal report and its exact nature, can be formulated. Such statements would, however, be unwieldy and burdensome if they were employed on all occasions.

3. Use of an experiential term may be justified by administering a

test to a subject. The subject's behavior in taking the test qualifies as the referent for the experiential term. Testing provides referents for many terms in perception and thought, but it provides very few, if any, in feeling.

Earlier, certain attributes of perception were indicated as having specific physical correlates. These correlates can be manipulated to provide perceptual tests. There are many varieties of tests. Five types will be described briefly.

(a) Accuracy of detection. *Example:* A subject is asked to report the presence or absence of a light. In a series of trials, the light is sometimes presented and sometimes not. On each trial the subject says whether or not he perceives it. His report can be characterized as correct or incorrect. If he is correct on a high percentage of trials, he can be said to see the light.

(b) Consistency in labeling in relation to a physical scale. *Example:* A subject is asked to name the hue of each one of a series of presented lights. Wave lengths of the lights vary. Each different wave length is presented a number of times. A subject who is very consistent in naming the different wave lengths can be said to see the hues. One form of consistency is conformity to conventional practice in naming hues. It is conceivable that a subject could be consistent without agreeing with anyone else. It is a fact, however, that consistent people exhibit a high degree of agreement.

(c) Correspondence of ranking to a physical scale. *Example:* A subject is asked to rank a number of tones, according to their pitch, from low to high. A subject whose ordering of the tones corresponds very closely to their order on the frequency scale can be said to hear the pitch of tones.

(d) Consistency in labeling in relation to qualitative physical differences. *Example:* A subject is asked to name the taste of a number of solutions. If he is highly consistent, he is said to experience the various taste qualities. One form of consistency is conformity to general practice in applying the words salt, sweet, sour, and bitter to solutions of sodium chloride, sucrose, hydrochloric acid, and quinine.

(e) Matching a sample. *Example:* A subject is presented with a block of a peculiar shape. He is asked to select a block having the same shape from a pile of blocks having varied shapes. His repeated success justifies the statement that he can perceive the shape of blocks.

For practical purposes, knowing that someone passes a test may be as valuable as it would be knowing that he had a given experience, if that were possible. In other words, it may be just as valuable to know that a man can respond consistently and conventionally to signals consisting of lights of certain wave lengths as to know what one cannot know, what the man sees. In driver training, if a student makes correct responses to all colored traffic signals and signs, what he actually sees is of no concern to anyone. That he does make correct responses in all situations to which he will subsequently be exposed is important to determine. If the test is not exhaustive, he may pass it and he may subsequently stop and start correctly as long as red lights are larger than green ones or as long as red lights are above green lights, but if he encounters lights of the same size or lights reversed in position, he may violate a law and be the cause of an accident.

Attributes of feeling do not have physical correlates which allow for testing as do those of perception. Life itself involves many situations which are conceptualized as tests of courage, patience, resoluteness, endurance, perseverence, love, friendship, confidence, and the like, but relatively little has been done by way of contriving such tests in the laboratory and in the field. The everyday tests are characterized by the occurrence of some event which puts the experiencer on trial and sets the stage for his success or failure under that trial. Success or failure, of course, in these real-life tests may be a matter of life and death, literally. Men undergo these tests in life situations, but it is obviously very difficult, if not impossible, to contrive comparable situations for the sake of psychological research.

Thought does not have physical correlates as perception does. Nevertheless, tests can be devised which qualify behaviors as referents for certain thought processes. A psychologist may ask a subject to read a list of words; he may then remove the list from view and ask the subject to write as many of the words as he can. If he writes a number of the words correctly, he is said to have remembered. A psychologist may show a set of pictures to a subject, remove them, then show the original pictures mixed with new ones, and ask the subject to identify as many of the original pictures as he can. If he succeeds in identifying a relatively large number of the original pictures, he is said to have recognized them. A subject may be given an algebra problem and asked to solve it. If the problem has a known solution and the subject obtains it, he is said to have reasoned. A subject may examine a set of objects and name their common property. If he is correct, he is said to have abstracted the property. A child may learn to move the larger of two wooden cubes from a desk to obtain a prize concealed under the larger cube. Confronted with two wooden cylinders, he may move the larger to obtain the prize. His behavior is taken as the referent for his having the concept of *larger than*. Although tests have been devised for remembering, recognizing, reasoning, and abstracting, they have not been devised for reflecting, dreaming, imagining, and some other thought processes.

4. An experiential term may be applied to a subject to denote the state of the subject after some condition has been imposed on him. For example, a subject who has been deprived of food for twenty-four hours is said to be hungry. On occasion, the referent of the experiential term may be solely the condition imposed. At other times, the referent may be complex. It may

include the condition plus some specific behavior. A baby may be said to be hungry after a period of deprivation of four hours at the end of which he begins to cry. The referent for *hungry* includes the deprivation and the crying.

5. An experiential term may be applied to a subject who exhibits certain physiological responses. The experience of strong emotion has come to be associated with a number of physiological responses, including heart beat, pulse, respiration, and perspiration. Unfortunately, the correspondence between these responses and the typical verbal reports, facial expressions, and voice inflections associated with emotional experiences is far from perfect. Furthermore, the correspondence among the physiological responses themselves is not high. No single pattern of physiological and behavioral characteristics can clearly qualify as the referent for anger, fear, love, or any other emotion.

The preceding account of ways in which the relevance of behavior to experiential language might be established is not exhaustive but covers the more important ones. These ways are not necessarily employed singly. There are many situations in which a combination of them may account for the terminology employed.

Listed below are eight experiential terms with their behavioral and situational referents. Use of a term with more than one referent could imply any one or combination of the referents.

Experiential Term	Behavioral and Situational Referents
Aesthetic appreciation	Statement that something is beautiful
Anger	Verbal report, voice tremor, verbal castigation, physical assault, scowling, flushed face, hand tremor, increase in pulse rate
Effort	Strained facial expression, verbal report
Fatigue	Sleep deprivation, long period of work, verbal report, slouching, shuffling, unsteadiness
Fear	Verbal report, pale face, trembling, perspiring, avoidance of a high place, running away from a barking dog, cringing before a threatening person, cowering in battle
Hunger	Verbal report, food deprivation, stomach contractions, low blood sugar, restlessness, attempts to secure food
Insight	Sudden change in facial expression from strain to relaxation, report of sudden understanding, quick solution of a problem after a delay
Monotony	Verbal report during repetitive events

Summary

In psychology experiential terms denote behavior. The procedure for assigning these terms to behavior is not standardized and remains somewhat informal and unstructured. It is certainly not arbitrary and not devoid of criteria, however, for there is a set of practices which have evolved as psychology has developed. Although this set of practices is only vaguely defined, an attempt has been made to describe its principal features within the context of a description of psychological language.

Motive: A Special Problem of Redefinition

Motive is a term whose definition merits special consideration, because it is widely used but variously defined in terms of experiential, behavioral, and biological referents. It is defined in *Webster's Collegiate Dictionary*[7] as "that within the individual . . . which incites him to action; any idea, need, emotion, or organic state that prompts to an action," referents which, except for organic state, are experiential. In their dictionary of psychological terms, English and English[2] give three definitions: the consciously assigned basis of one's behavior; the consciously sought goal which determines one's behavior; and a state or event within the organism which initiates or regulates behavior relative to a goal. They say the term has lost most if not all its original experiential connotation.

There have been other technical definitions in which terms such as need, impulse, urge, aspiration, purpose, desire, and intention have appeared. Some of these terms are clearly experiential in everyday usage and, for technical work, require behavioral referents.

Goal appears in numerous definitions of motive. (*Incentive* is considered to be equivalent to supplementary goal.) In general terms *these* definitions refer to a biological state of the organism and related action in achieving an external goal, meaning which is clearly not experiential. Goal is a technical term corresponding roughly to everyday purpose, whose meaning is experiential.

Two important parts of this word puzzle have now been identified: biological state and external goal. Two other parts are necessary in the formulation of a satisfactory final definition: the external circumstances associated with the biological state and the individual's behavior. A psychologist may observe a biological state, such as the level of blood sugar, but he more often observes a related circumstance, the deprivation of food. In fact, on many occasions he observes the circumstance and only conjectures about a biological state. Therefore, it is reasonable that the definition of motive should incorporate a reference to the circumstance associated with the internal state. What about the individual's behavior and its place in the definition? There are two possibilities: action to achieve the goal and a verbal report of purpose. Putting these four parts together, we propose as the definition of motive: the concept of a combination of external circumstance, internal biological state, and a goal associated with behavior. The behavior may be either action which, if it achieves the goal, will terminate the circumstance and the state, or a verbal statement of purpose to achieve the goal. Thus the hunger motive is the combination of food deprivation, lowered blood sugar, and food goal associated with either some action to obtain that food or a statement of the individual's intention to obtain it.

It should be obvious that motive is an indefinite abstract term. The form motivation has similar meaning but is more indefinite. Motivation is equivalent to *the general nature of a person's varied motives.*

We have said nothing in this section about the statements that a motive directs, incites, initiates, guides, or regulates. Our opinion, as expressed earlier in this chapter, is that these are figurative expressions. If they imply anything of importance to psychological knowledge, it can be expressed literally. They may, for example, indirectly suggest knowledge of prediction and control based on external circumstances, internal states, goals, or behaviors; but, if so, it would be better to say just that.

One reason has already been given for the special consideration of motive: the term is widely used in psychology. Another reason is that the definition of a test raises a question regarding the subject's motivation. In *Webster's Collegiate Dictionary*[7] one of the definitions of a test is "subjection to conditions that show the real character of a person in a certain particular." Psychological definitions say nothing about the real character of a person, but they do reveal concern about a matter which bears some resemblance to it. For example, English and English[2] point to usage in which test means "test of maximum performance," in which the subject is challenged "to his best execution." It is difficult to express this concern in strictly behavioristic words; it is easy to express it in experiential words. There is concern about the subject's attending, concentrating, and trying. There is concern about the subject's accepting the task given him by the psychologist.

Especially in the testing of children is this concern encountered. Does the child treat the testing as an idle game, one that can be interrupted, modified, ignored, or abandoned? Does the child deliberately think up nonsensical answers? Does he understand that he is, in a mild sense, on trial? Does the examiner, on leaving the testing room, say, "He could have done much better but just didn't try"?

Instructions for standardized tests usually include some reminder such as "Do your best," "Work as efficiently as possible," "Don't waste time," and the like, for results of tests have little value when the subject doesn't care and simply guesses at the answers. There is also concern about motivation in situations where the individual may benefit, or may think he will benefit, by turning in a poor performance. The term "malingering" has been applied when subjects hold down test performances deliberately.

The point is that the complete definition of a test involves the psychologist in experiential language having to do with motivational variables such as purpose, effort, concentration, and the like. These terms must, of course, be redefined so that they have behavioral and circumstantial referents. English and English[2] have suggested as a definition of purpose: a series of acts in which the organism persists until it attains some specific environmental situation or biological state.

Language and Theory

Theory has already been mentioned briefly on two occasions. When the distinction was first made between rational and empirical knowledge, it was pointed out that theory had an important place in psychology and that logical reasoning was a necessary part of theorizing. In the brief discussion of language and logic, the place of logic in theory was again emphasized. Although logical reasoning is a part of theorizing, it is not the whole of it, for a psychological theory has empirical connections.

Psychological theory will be defined here as a kind of language. In the most general terms it is abstract language employed in giving an account of behavior. This definition is so broad, however, that any abstract description of behavior, from a single word to a lengthy book might qualify as a theory.

We shall add a restriction to this very general definition by saying that a minimal psychological theory is a sentence expressing a relation. The relation involves at least two parts, one of which must be behavior. The other parts may be nonbehavioral characteristics and circumstances. Many different kinds of relations are possible and the nature of some of them will be described in later chapters.

Language has been divided into two kinds: behavioristic and experiential. Theory can be divided into two corresponding kinds: one is expressed in behavioristic language; the other, in experiential language. It is too early in the history of psychology to assess the ultimate value of either kind of theory. Both may prove to be of great value. It is possible that one will eventually prove to be of more value than the other. There are no valid a priori grounds for rejecting either one.

Psychological theory has two possible empirical connections: old and new evidence. The original formulation of a theory may be an inference from what is already known; that is, a theory may be based on existing evidence. If deductions from the theory yield hypotheses which can be tested by observing behavior, the observing may produce new evidence. Thus a theory may link old and new evidence.

EXAMPLES OF THEORIES

A system is a conceptual framework for the organization of knowledge in a particular field. It usually embraces a number of interrelated theories.

There have been distinguishable and, at times, rival systems in psychology in the past. Three prominent ones were structuralism, functionalism, and gestalt psychology. To provide some fairly specific examples of theories and to indicate how they might be translated into ways of studying behavior, a statement representative of each of these systems will be presented, and observations which are relevant to the statement will be suggested.

A theoretical statement from structuralism is "The basic elements of consciousness are sensations, images, and feelings." For the statement to be of value, it must have an implication which can be tested by observation. If basic elements are defined as those which intelligent people would identify and report in analyzing their conscious experience, then the statement implies that people will agree in naming sensations, images, and feelings. Observations of behavior might be obtained under the following circumstances. One hundred students in an introductory psychology course are interviewed individually by a graduate student. He instructs each one, "Think carefully about the content of your conscious experience for the next five minutes. Try to detect the basic elements out of which your experience is constructed. At the end of the period, report your results to me." When the subject reports, everything he says in three minutes is written down by the graduate student. The records are then examined to see how much agreement there is among the subjects and how frequently the hypothesized classes of elements occur.

A theoretical statement representing functionalism is "All mental states are followed by bodily activity of some sort." Since consciousness and activity are continuous, at least during waking, there is the problem of identifying particular mental states and particular bodily activities. There is also the problem of identifying the activity which follows any given state. Mental state would, of course, have to be redefined. One possibility for a behavioral referent would be the subject's verbal report of a perception, a feeling, or a thought. Bodily activity could be defined as the secreting of specific glands or the occurrence of action potentials in particular muscles. A method of observation would have to be devised for the specific bodily activities. After a record had been obtained of verbal reports and bodily activities, it would be examined for concomitance. If every report of an emotion was followed by the action of a particular gland, that finding might be interpreted as supporting the original theoretical statement.

From gestalt psychology come the statements: "The causes of behavior are in the psychophysical field, which combines the perceptual field of consciousness and the physiological field of the brain. There is a close correspondence between the perceptual and physiological fields." Characteristics of the perceptual field would have to be redefined in terms of behavior, one possibility being verbal reports of experience. Characteristics of the physiological field would have to be defined as physicochemical variables. A limited number of characteristics in each field would be selected for investigation. Observations of these selected characteristics would be made on a group of subjects. The relation between the two sets of characteristics would be examined. If there was positive evidence of a relationship, it could be expressed in a number of ways, either verbally or mathematically. This evidence would be taken as support for the statement of correspondence.

PSYCHOANALYTIC THEORY

The theory of unconscious mental processes, formulated by Sigmund Freud around 1920 and modified in many ways by other psychoanalysts who came after him, has also been prominent in psychology. One version employs the concepts of id, ego, and superego. The individual's id is said to be his original source of psychic energy. It is directed toward immediate self-satisfaction of natural impulses and desires. In coping with external realities, the individual develops an ego, whose function is conscious control in the physical environment. In coping with the rules of society, he develops a superego whose function is believed to be much like that of conscience.

There are numerous versions of the theory of unconscious processes. The main problem with any one of them is establishing observable referents for the words in which hypotheses are expressed. The principle which must be followed is that the terms of the hypotheses must be defined to permit observation of behavior and its attendant circumstances.

An example of the kind of approach necessary is found in Freud's early discussion of slips of the tongue. A slip of the tongue is a behavioral event. Freud proposed that when a person committed a slip of the tongue, it was not just an accident. He assumed the existence of mental processes which made the slip a communication. If a speaker in eulogizing a military officer says "battle-scared veteran," when, as he quickly insists, he really intended saying "battle-scarred veteran," then one might assume there is a mental process, not necessarily conscious, which involves *scared* and an intention different from that claimed. The slip is a communication, a kind of expressive behavior. By similar assumptions many of the terms of psychoanalytic theory can be connected with observable behavior. Consider repression. In theory it is the internal action of expelling some idea from consciousness into the unconscious. It must, however, be given behavioral and circumstantial referents. If Mr. Jones is introduced to Mr. Smith under circumstances unpleasant and embarrassing for Mr. Jones, and if, on subsequent occasions, he fails to remember Mr. Smith's name, he is said to have repressed it. Consider sexual symbolism in dreams. If a young woman reports a dream in which she is chased by a terrifying man with a knife, there is nothing sexual immediately apparent, but if in continuing to talk about the dream she eventually admits to panic at the thought of sexual relations, then an assumption might be made that the dream was a symbol for the panic. Notice that the word employed is *assumption.*

SUBLIMINAL PERCEPTION

Theories about subliminal perception present problems similar to those of unconscious processes. Subliminal perception is defined as a subject's response to an external event without awareness of the event. The expression *without awareness* is itself experiential and must be redefined. One possibility is to give it the referent: a subject's verbal denial of experiencing the event. It now becomes clear that the referent for subliminal perception is a combination of inconsistent actions: a positive response to the external event and a simultaneous verbal denial of awareness of it. It is easier to pose the definition of subliminal perception than it is to demonstrate its occurrence. The evidence remains uncertain and controversial. In a typical situation, the various actions which follow the external event are consistent most of the time. It is doubtful that the few inconsistencies can be legitimately interpreted as supporting a concept of subliminal perception, for the presence of error could be expected to account for those few.

Ambiguity

A serious problem of psychological language is ambiguity. An ambiguity occurs when a term has two or more definitions and neither the user nor his audience identifies or distinguishes the intended definition. That more than one definition exists is not made explicit by the user and may not be known by either party.

An example of an ambiguity follows: An incandescent bulb is located in a light-proof room. There is no living organism in the room. An automatic switching device closes an electrical circuit containing the bulb. An energy-sensitive instrument indicates the bulb is functioning. Is light emitted by the bulb, when there is no one to see it?

A correct answer to the question cannot be given until an ambiguity is removed. The ambiguous word is *light.* If its definition is *radiant energy of certain wave lengths,* then the answer is "Yes." If its definition, however, is a *perceived quality of radiant energy,* then the answer is "No."

In everyday life and in psychology, ambiguities occur in the use of the words intelligence, personality, habit, and drive. They will be taken up in that order.

THE DEFINITION OF INTELLIGENCE

There have been numerous definitions of intelligence. The definitions agree that intelligence is a variable attribute of behavior; that is, people differ in intelligence. The definitions disagree in two ways: in being definite or indefinite; in being conceptual or operational. (Procedural may be substituted for operational.) Logically then, there are four possible kinds of definitions: definite-conceptual, indefinite-conceptual, definite-operational, and indefinite-operational. An example of each is given below:

1. A definite, conceptual definition: success in solving problems involving symbols.

2. An indefinite, conceptual definition: success at tasks characterized by difficulty, complexity, abstractness, and social value with performances characterized by speed, accuracy, efficiency, adaptiveness, and originality.

3. A definite, operational definition: scale of scores on the Army General Classification Test. (The Test consists of vocabulary, arithmetic, and block counting.)

4. An indefinite, operational definition: scale of scores on the Stanford-Binet Intelligence Test, which contains a large variety of items; or the scales of scores on the Tests of Primary Mental Abilities, a battery of eleven different tests.

A first encounter with an ambiguous word such as intelligence is usually followed by the question, "But what is it, really?" The answer is that intelligence is not really anything but a conceptualized attribute of behavior. That is the only reality. There is a definite trend in psychology toward greater use of operational or procedural definitions, but there is no trend with respect to definiteness. In some situations specific definitions are satisfactory; in others, general definitions are preferred.

THE DEFINITION OF PERSONALITY

Personality has been defined in many ways. Four of the more important definitions will be given here. The broadest of the four makes personality synonymous with individuality. In describing a personality, one tries to characterize the individual's behavior in every respect. Defined as individuality, the word is so indefinite as to be of only limited value. Perhaps its greatest appeal comes from its emphasis on the whole individual and his uniqueness.

The behavioral referents are more narrow in the other three definitions: the individual's motivational and emotional characteristics; characteristics of the individual's social behavior—his behavior in relation to others; and characteristics of the individual's behavior as perceived by others. Although they point out that the last definition can be found in psychological literature, English and English[2] consider it obsolescent.

Proposed here as an improved definition of personality is one that combines the second and third definitions given above. It is that personality combines the characteristics of the individual's motivational, emotional, and social behavior. In this definition, personality is obviously an indefinite abstract term, but not nearly so indefinite as individuality.

The Definition of Habit

Habit has been defined as a persisting state of the organism necessary but not sufficient for evoking an action; an acquired way of speaking or acting; an acquired sequence of actions which give the appearance of being automatic; and an action showing increased facility of performance or decreased power of resistance after many repetitions. These do not agree in every respect. It is suggested here that the definition could be improved by placing emphasis on the acquisition and repetition of behavior, as in the following statement: A habit is an acquired act which occurs repeatedly, possibly displaying a trend in some characteristic such as dexterity or facility.

The Definition of Drive

An examination of six different definitions of drive reveals several possibilities for ambiguous usage. Drive is said to be a synonym for motive or need; a physiological condition distinguished from a motive; an internal condition; the consequence of need by means of which need is translated into motive; a hypothetical state identified by behavior and circumstances; and an equivalent of motivation. These expressions do not exhibit a high degree of common meaning. Five of the six agree in imputing to drive the role of inciter, impetus, control, initiator, and guide of behavior. The possible figurative meaning in these terms and its objectionable features have already been mentioned. They may suggest an agent functioning in the organism and doing things to it. A recommendation for an improved definition was also given earlier. It was that a drive is a concept based on behavior, a biological state, and external circumstances, all three of these being interrelated in their occurrence.

New Definition for Old Words

Giving everyday words new definitions increases the possibilities for the occurrence of ambiguities. A psychologist may lecture intending certain meanings and his students may listen attributing different meanings to what he says. To ensure against ambiguities in studying psychology, one may have to go over new definitions many times, paying close attention to the difference between the old and the new. In this connection, words such as attitude, opinion, frustration, and compulsion require special vigilance on the student's part.

In *Webster's Collegiate Dictionary*[7], attitude has the definitions: "position assumed to serve a purpose; position or bearing as indicating action, feeling, or mood; the feeling or mood itself." The definitions have both behavioral and experiential features represented in "position" and "feeling," respectively. Most psychologists emphasize behavior in their definitions and qualify the behavior as expressing a favorable or unfavorable position. A new definition will be presented in Chapter 7.

The common definition of opinion is "belief stronger than impression, less strong than positive knowledge; a formal expression by an expert"[7]. Experiential meaning is indicated by "belief"; behavioral meaning is indicated by "formal expression." Technical definitions, which have varied considerably, have included overt expression on a controversial matter, belief or verbal expression on a matter involving some knowledge, and meaning synonymous with attitude. The following definition is recommended: An opinion is an overt expression involving some—but not complete—knowledge about the matter in question.

Confusion about frustration arises because two kinds of meanings are widely used. Frustration has been defined as the thwarting of behavior directed toward a goal, and as the state of the organism resulting when behavior is thwarted. Our solution to the problem is to have the term refer to the thwarting itself. The state of the organism after frustration, if it can be identified, can be described in definite physiological or behavioral terms.

The common definition of compulsion is "an impulse or feeling of being irresistibly driven toward the performance of some irrational action"[7]. This definition is clearly experiential. The technical definitions do not agree: some give behavioral referents; others, experiential referents. The definition proposed here is behavioral: A compulsion is a useless or undesirable act which, nevertheless, occurs repeatedly in the life of an individual.

MIND

In their first encounter with psychology, people are often surprised to learn that *mind* is no longer in good standing as a technical term. The reason is that it is highly indefinite and ambiguous, as revealed by the three common meanings: "consciousness; the subject of consciousness, that which feels, perceives, wills, thinks, etc.; the perceptive and thinking part of consciousness, exclusive of will and emotion"[7]. The first definition makes mind equivalent to consciousness; the second makes it equivalent to the person; and the third makes it equivalent to two categories of consciousness: perception and thought. If mind is taken as equivalent to consciousness, then it is experiential and highly indefinite. On redefinition, its referent would be a very large number of varied behaviors. All the behaviors which qualified as the referents for all the categories and properties of experience would together be the referent of mind. There is nothing to recommend adoption of the second definition as person, or adoption of the third definition as perception and thought.

Technical and Mediating Language

The acquisition of new knowledge in psychology culminates in the formulation of propositions in technical language. Technical language is, however, only a part of the total language of psychologists, for there is much informal but serious communication between one psychologist and another and between the psychologist and his students. Furthermore, this informal communication, involving everyday language, to a considerable extent, has a very important function: it helps psychologists formulate propositions in the technical language; and it helps students acquire and understand the technical language. Since this informal communication is different from technical language and since it is facilitative in its function, we shall call it mediating language. In studying psychology, one may benefit by recognizing the progression from mediating language to technical language, as it occurs repeatedly. The mediating language is almost always chosen to open the exposition on a given topic. It provides the psychologist with the means of introducing his work to the scientific community and the public, and the means of introducing the various topics of psychology to his students.

Chapter Summary

The acquisition of psychological knowledge depends very much on the success with which observations of behavior can be transformed into written records. Literalness of language is the goal in scientific psychology. Definiteness facilitates communication, while indefiniteness often obstructs it. Experiential words are important in concept and theory, but they must be redefined to have behavioral referents. Language is the means of expressing reasoning as well as observation. Psychological theory, which is abstract language giving an account of behavior, can be differentiated as behavioristic and experiential. Ambiguous words add to the difficulties of communication. Much of the language of psychologists is nontechnical and has a mediating function, facilitating the acquisition and understanding of the technical language.

References

1. Allport, G. W., and H. S. Odbert. "Trait-Names: A Psycholexical Study." *Psychological Monographs,* 47, No. 211 (1936).
2. English, H. B., and A. C. English. *A Comprehensive Dictionary of Psychological and Psychoanalytical Terms.* New York: Longmans, Green and Co., 1958.
3. Freud, S. *A General Introduction to Psychoanalysis.* New York: Garden City Publishing Co., Inc., 1943.
4. Jacobi, J. *The Psychology of Jung.* New Haven, Conn.: Yale University Press, 1943.
5. Menninger, K. A. *The Human Mind,* 3rd ed. New York: Alfred A. Knopf, 1945.
6. Roget, S. R. *Thesaurus of English Words and Phrases.* Cleveland: The World Publishing Company, 1941.
7. *Webster's Collegiate Dictionary,* 2nd ed. Springfield, Mass.: G. & C. Merriam Co., 1936.

PART 2

MEASUREMENT

5

Psychological

Measurement

QUANTITATIVE PSYCHOLOGY IS THAT PART OF PSYCHOLOGY IN which observations are expressed as measures. Since measures are used in reporting and communicating, they are a kind of language. The basic procedure in measurement is the assigning of numbers to attributes of behavior.

One cannot assume that any haphazard method of assigning numbers to behavior will aid the search for knowledge. It is a widely accepted belief that for measurement to have any value, there must, in some sense, be correspondence between the attributes of numbers and the attributes of behavior. The degree of correspondence is, however, never known in advance of the assigning. Thus the original assigning of numbers results only in provisional measures, and attempts at confirmation of the correspondence must always follow the assigning. In this chapter ways of achieving provisional measures will be described. Ways of confirming the correspondence for provisional measures will be described in Chapters 7 and 8.

Current measurement practices in psychology are many and varied. One way of classifying them involves four categories: physical measurement, counting, judgments, and psychophysical methods. This way of classifying measurement practices directs attention to the procedures themselves, which, to a very great extent, define the psychological concepts.

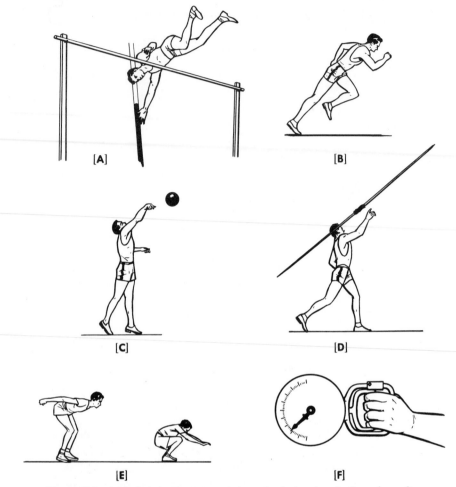

Figure 5-1. Athletic behaviors measured on physical scales. **A:** the pole vault measured in terms of height. **B:** the sprint measured in time. **C:** the shot-put measured in distance. **D:** the javelin throw measured in distance. **E:** the standing broad jump measured in distance. **F:** strength of hand grip measured as pounds of force on a dynamometer. [**A, B, C,** and **D** after G. T. Bresnahan, W. W. Tuttle, and F. X. Cretzmeyer, *Track and Field Athletics*, 6th ed., 1964, by permission of the authors and The C. V. Mosby Company, publishers. **E** after H. M. Barrow, and R. McGee, *North Carolina Fitness Test*. Raleigh: North Carolina State Department of Public Instruction, 1961.]

Physical Measurement

Length, weight, and time are the fundamental dimensions in physical measurement. Derived from these are measures in degrees, area, volume, pressure, and speed. Physical measures can be obtained for simple or complex actions, intimate concomitants of behavior, and behavioral products.

As every student knows, physical measures of behavior are used in athletics to evaluate agility, stamina, and strength. The length of a broad jump, the height of a pole vault, the distance of a shot put, the strength of a hand grip, and the time required to run a specified distance are expressed in familiar physical units of feet, pounds, minutes, or related units. Illustrations of certain athletic behaviors measured in this way are shown in Figure 5-1.

Physical measures are also employed by psychologists in investigations of a wide range of motor behavior. At one extreme are the movements of specific parts of the body such as the pupil of the eye, the eyeball, and the eyelid. When a light is presented to a subject's eye, the pupil can be observed to contract. When the light is removed, the pupil dilates.

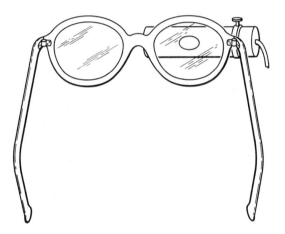

Figure 5-2. Apparatus for measuring eyelid movement. Mounted on the spectacle frame is a photo-electric cell. [Adapted from Franks and Withers.[9]]

The extent of the contraction or dilation can be measured in millimeters. It is known that, in reading, one's eyes move a short distance, stop for a short time, and then move again. This action is called saccadic movement. It is possible to measure the extent of the movement in degrees, and the duration of the movement or the fixation in thousandths of a second. The accurate measurement of movement may require special apparatus.

Apparatus for measuring eyelid movement was devised by Franks and Withers[9]. It involved an ordinary spectacle frame and a photo-electric cell, shown in Figure 5-2. The method was based on the principle that a photo-electric cell passes a current proportional to the intensity of the illumination which falls upon it. The cell employed was sensitive to room lighting reflected from the subject's eyelid, if a high constant level was maintained in the room. Uniform distribution of light was necessary so that slight movements of the subject's head would not produce changes in the intensity of illumination falling upon the cell.

The cell was mounted in a small can, in one side of which was drilled a hole to admit light. The can, which was mounted on a plain disk fitted in place of one of the lenses in the spectacle frame, was small enough that the subject's vision was relatively unobscured. When the eyelid moved, there was a change in the amount of light reflected on the cell. The variation in energy generated by the cell was then amplified and recorded automatically. Information about eyelid movements could then be obtained from the record.

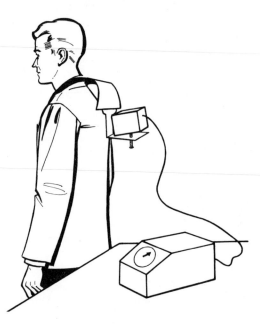

Figure 5-3. Apparatus for measuring body sway. The subject wears an aluminum yoke which supports a box containing a coil and pendulum. An adjustable screw under the box controls its position. On the table is a millivoltmeter. [Adapted from Furneaux.[10]]

Eye movements represent one extreme of the range of motor behavior. At the other extreme are movements of the whole body, such as body sway, which may be measured for the purpose of assessing steadiness. Apparatus for measuring body sway has been described by Furneaux[10]. The apparatus as worn by a subject is shown in Figure 5-3. It consisted of a small box held by means of an aluminum yoke on the subject's back. Within the box was a pendulum which swung as the subject swayed. Any movement of the pendulum produced a change in the magnitude of a current produced in the box. Thus a subject's sway could be recorded and measured by a meter connected to the current. The box was attached to the yoke by a bracket, the position of which could be adjusted horizontally by means of a screw, regardless of the subject's build or posture. By means of this screw an adjustment of the needle of the meter to a setting of zero was made at the outset. Any subsequent sway would then be registered by a deflection of the needle.

Characteristics of sensorimotor behavior are frequently investigated through measurements expressed in physical units. Psychologists have observed the distance of a subject's hit from the bull's-eye of a target, the

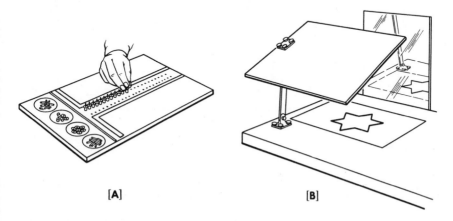

[A]   [B]

Figure 5-4. Performance of the sensorimotor tasks, assembly and mirror drawing may be measured on the physical dimension of time. **A:** The Purdue Pegboard being used in an assembly task. In the four wells are supplies of pins, collars, washers, and pins. The subject places a pin in a hole, and a washer, a collar, and a washer on the pin, alternating hands in doing so. The standard method of scoring is counting the number of parts assembled in one minute. It would be possible, however, to measure the performance on a physical dimension, the time required to assemble a certain number of units. [Adapted from Examiner Manual, *The Purdue Pegboard*, developed by the Purdue Research Foundation under the direction of Dr. Joseph Tiffin; Science Research Associates, Inc., publishers.] **B:** Mirror-drawing apparatus. The subject traces the star which he can view only indirectly by means of the mirror. The performance might be measured in terms of time required to complete the tracing.

force applied to a control wheel by his hand grip, the time required to trace a star pattern while viewing it indirectly in a mirror, the time required to trace the true path of a maze, and the time required to turn wooden disks in a manipulation test. Illustrations of sensorimotor tasks are given in Figure 5-4.

Tracking behavior, which is one kind of sensorimotor behavior, receives much attention in psychology and is often measured on physical dimensions. In every tracking task there is a target and a follower. The target is manipulated by the investigator. The follower is manipulated by

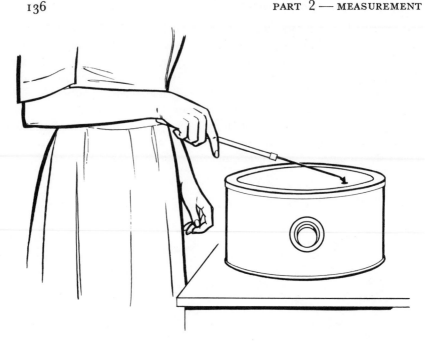

Figure 5-5. Tracking on a pursuit rotor may be measured as the amount of time the subject keeps the stylus in contact with the target on the rotating table.

the subject whose task it is to track the target—that is, to keep the follower on or near the target. Tracking, as it is performed in a student laboratory, often involves a revolving turntable, on which there is a target disk, and a stylus which the subject tries to keep in contact with the target (see Figure 5-5). His success can be measured in terms of the amount of time the contact is maintained.

Figure 5-6. The tracking box and pen with felt point. [Adapted from Slack.[20]]

More complex apparatus and procedures are sometimes employed in tracking, as in a task devised by Slack[20], which required the subject to keep a pen on a segment of line viewed through a slit. The position of the line could be varied continuously or discontinuously. The apparatus and the position of the subject's hand in performing the task are shown in Figure 5-6. An input line of any desired frequency, amplitude, and

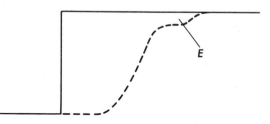

Figure 5-7. The solid line is a segment of an input line for the tracking box. The dashed line shows the path of the subject's tracing. The separation between the target line and the subject's tracing is the error (*E*), measurable as distance in physical units. [Adapted from Slack.[20]]

Figure 5-8. An arrangement of a tracking display and the target control. The target was a bright vertical line above; the follower was a similar line below. The measure of behavior was time on target. [Adapted from Hartman and Fitts.[13]]

complexity was drawn on a strip of paper which was inserted in the apparatus so that only a small segment of the line was visible to the subject through the slit. The paper moved behind the slit at a constant rate. The subject was instructed to keep his pen on the line. Lines of many types could be employed, one of which, called a step function, is shown in Figure 5-7. The solid line is the input; the dotted line is the track of a subject's response. The distance E is the magnitude of the error in the subject's initial response.

An electronic tracking apparatus which had as its principal components a target generator, a programming unit, a display tube, a tracking control, and a scoring and recording unit was employed by Hartman and Fitts[13] to measure tracking behavior. Subject and apparatus are shown in Figure 5-8. The subject worked in a booth with the display on a cathode ray tube located in front of him. The target and the follower were bright, narrow, vertical lines. The follower appeared below and slightly overlapped the target. Both lines moved across the middle of the display tube. The task of the subject was to keep them in vertical alignment by manipulating a lever. He placed the elbow of his right arm

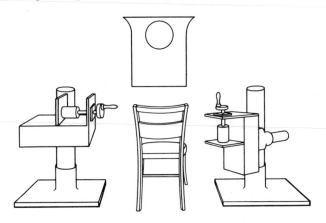

Figure 5-9. Tracking apparatus consisting of subject's chair, two cranks for controlling the follower circle, and the cathode-ray-tube display on which the target spot and the follower circle appeared. [Adapted from Gerall, Sampson, and Spragg.[11]]

above the pivot point of the lever and extended his arm forward, grasping a knob at the end of the lever.

Two types of displays were employed: pursuit and compensatory. When the pursuit display was used, the target moved and the subject tried to align the follower with it. When the compensatory display was used, the target line remained stationary in the center of the display and only the follower moved. The subject's task was to return the follower to the position of the target. The measure of performance was time on target.

Tracking in two dimensions was measured on a two-hand tracking apparatus designed by Gerall, Samson, and Spragg[11]. The apparatus consisted of the subject's control, the display, the programmer, and the recorder. The arrangement of the apparatus is shown in Figure 5-9.

By manipulating two cranks, the subject controlled the movement of the follower (a circle) over the display (a cathode ray tube). One crank fixed the horizontal position of the follower; the other fixed its vertical position. The programmer was designed to present the target (a spot) at various locations on the display. When the spot appeared, the subject rotated the cranks until the circle surrounded it. Soon after he accomplished the task, the circle and the spot would disappear from the display; after an interval, the target appeared at a new location.

The subject's time off the target in each direction was recorded on an electric clock. Another automatic device graphically recorded the direction and magnitude of his errors. From these records the total time required by the subject to reach the target could be obtained.

Handwriting is a familiar and important kind of everyday sensorimotor behavior. It has been of interest to psychologists but has always posed serious difficulties of measurement. One approach to its measurement was devised by Smith and Bloom[21]. Apparatus was constructed to measure the duration of contact and travel movements in a writing task. The principle of the apparatus was that the writer served as a switch.

The subject sat at a writing table. In his left hand he held a metal electrode which was connected in the circuit with a clock. He wrote with a metal pencil containing a special conductive lead. The writing paper, which was also conductive, was connected in the circuit. When the subject put his pencil on the paper, he closed the circuit which operated the clock; when he lifted the pencil from the paper after writing a letter or word, the clock automatically stopped and another clock automatically started. After he completed one line of writing across the paper, he touched a metal plate on the right with his pencil, automatically stopping both clocks. The subject could not detect the very weak current which passed through his body in operating the clocks.

The specific behavior studied was the writing of single numerals and letters of the alphabet. A subject wrote one letter or numeral repeatedly on each trial. He was instructed to begin at the left writing a given letter or numeral across the paper to the right, where the last character was to be written on the stopping plate. He was also instructed to write at his usual speed. Typically, 10 to 15 distinct characters were written in one line. The average times of contact and travel for each character for a given subject were computed by dividing the accumulated time per trial by the number of distinct letters written in that trial.

In addition to measuring sensorimotor behavior as it occurs originally, one can measure the accuracy of attempts at reproducing it. Bahrick, Fitts, and Schneider[3] have reported a method of measuring a subject's reproduction of simple movements of a control which offered resistance. The task was to make either triangular or circular movements in time to a metronome.

The control was a "joy stick." Springs were attached to the stick so that a given force in any direction would displace the stick the same distance from its center position. The fulcrum was located at floor level. The lower end of the stick projected below the floor into a large tank filled with water. Damping, the reducing of oscillation, was achieved by attaching hollow aluminum drums to the lower end of the stick. Inertia was controlled by attaching lead weights to the stick above and below the fulcrum.

Visual guides, one triangular and the other circular, indicated to the subject the required patterns of movement. The control stick was moved within the guides along the figure defined by them. An electric metronome was used to pace the movement during practice trials.

Two small lights were mounted side by side on top of the joy stick. One light was on continuously; the other flashed regularly. A camera with an attachment for exposing a single frame was mounted directly above the joy stick and recorded each movement of the control on a frame of the film as two lines traced by the lights, one continuous and the other intermittent.

Following a series of practice trials, the metronome and guide were removed, a curtain was dropped to hide the control from the subject's view, and the room was darkened. The subject was then instructed to duplicate the movement he had practiced, with respect to spatial pattern and timing. By projecting each photographic record on a screen and comparing the record with the guide, twenty-three different measures of spatial and temporal accuracy were obtained.

LATENCY

All the temporal measures described up to this point are measures of the duration of behavior. There is another important class of temporal measures called measures of latency. The latency of a given action is the interval between the occurrence of some event, which is a stimulus or a signal, and the beginning of the action. The action may be a simple movement, a vocalization, or a complex activity. Three behaviors often measured in this way are the eye blink, word association, and finger or hand withdrawal in releasing a telegraph key. The latency of the eye blink may be measured from the occurrence of an air puff directed at the edge of the cornea. The puff and the reflexive blink constitute an important sequence of events in conditioning procedures which will be described later. Word association refers to the verbal response a subject makes when a word is presented to him and he is under instruction to say the first word that comes to mind. The latency of the verbal response is measured from the presentation of the original word. Finger or hand withdrawal in releasing a telegraph key is behavior which occurs under instruction to release the key as quickly as possible after some specified signal, usually visual or auditory. Latency is measured from the signal to the withdrawal and is commonly referred to as reaction time. Apparatus may be designed so that presentation of the signal starts a clock and releasing the key stops it. An arrangement for measuring hand withdrawal reaction time in a student laboratory is shown in Figure 5-10.

[A]   [B]

Figure 5-10. A: An arrangement of apparatus for measuring handwithdrawal reaction time in a student laboratory. On the left is the subject, a signal light, and a telegraph key. On the right is the observer wearing earphones, a clock, and a telegraph key. When the observer closes her key, the clock starts and signal light is activated. The subject releases her key as quickly as possible and stops the clock. **B:** An electric clock widely used in psychological laboratories. [Adapted from The Standard Electric Time Company.]

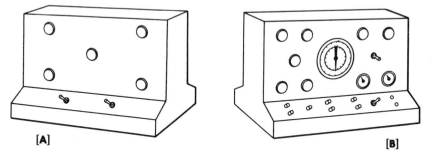

[A]   [B]

Figure 5-11. Two views of a reaction timer. **A:** The subject's view. **B:** The tester's view. [Adapted from Pierce and Pascal.[18]]

In research on reaction time, more complicated apparatus and procedures are sometimes required. Pierce and Pascal[18] devised the reaction-time apparatus shown in Figure 5-11. The subject's view of the apparatus is on the left. Five lights of different colors were arranged on the upright panel, and two switches were mounted on the sloping base. After a warning signal, a clock, the subject crooked the forefingers of both hands around the switches. After the main signal, the flash of one or more lights, he responded by pulling one or the other of the switches toward himself. The switches were mounted so that the subject could rest his hands on the table in the ready position and maintain that position for long periods of time with little movement.

The tester's view of the controls of the apparatus is on the right in Figure 5-11. On the upright panel were five lights corresponding to the five lights on the subject's panel, a clock, and two lights which indicated whether the subject responded with his right or left hand. The tester could select in advance the light which would be the main signal. He could also set the apparatus so that the clock would be stopped by the hand which was correct for a given trial, and so that an interval timer would control the presentation of the warning signal and the main signal. In measuring reaction time, it is a general practice to insure that the subject is not caught off guard by the main signal but, at the same time, cannot anticipate its occurrence successfully. Consequently, the length of the period between the warning signal and the main signal was varied randomly over a range of several seconds.

For simple reaction to a light signal, the subject crooked one forefinger around one of his switches. He was told to watch the center light and, when it came on, to respond as quickly as possible by pulling the switch toward himself. In one complex-reaction procedure, he had to respond with his right hand to a blue light and with his left hand to a red light. If the blue light was accompanied by the center white light, he had to respond with his left hand. If the red light was accompanied by the center white light, he had to respond with his right hand. In every kind of procedure, the time between signal and response was recorded on each trial.

FIRST OCCURRENCES OF BEHAVIOR

One of the most important temporal measures is the time between birth and the first occurrence of some specified behavior. This time, of course, corresponds to the age at which the specified behavior is first observed. An investigation by Aldrich and Norval[1] illustrates the procedures employed in determining first occurrences. They studied 215 normal infants from birth to the early part of their second year. Parents of the infants came from all strata of society in Rochester, Minnesota.

Information concerning the occurrence of the various behaviors was obtained by testing the infants at monthly intervals and by having their mothers watch for behaviors not easily tested in the clinic. The age of an infant at which a given behavior occurred for the first time was taken as a measure of that infant's behavior. The average age of the group of infants for the first occurrence of a given behavior was taken as a measure of the group's behavior.

The behaviors whose first occurrences were determined and the average group ages in months are listed below.

1. Smiling in response to an adult or to his voice, 0.9 months.
2. Vocalizing of sounds such as "ah," "eh," and "uh" spontaneously or on stimulation, 1.7.
3. Control of head when the infant is lifted by his hands from the supine to the sitting position, 2.9.
4. Grasping of toy dangled in the midline above the infant's chest, 4.0.
5. Rolling from back to abdomen, 5.1.
6. Sitting alone for several moments, 6.2.
7. Crawling in any manner across the room or pen toward some distant object, 7.3.
8. Prehension or bringing together the thumb and index finger to pick up a small object such as a bright-colored button, 8.1.
9. Pulling himself up to a standing position, 8.7.
10. Walking with support by holding to his playpen, a piece of furniture, or an adult, 9.5.
11. Standing alone, without any support, for several seconds, 10.7.
12. Walking alone for several steps, 12.0.

PHYSICAL MEASURES OF INTELLECT AND PERSONALITY

Intellective characteristics of behavior, such as remembering, reasoning, and abstracting, are measured by both verbal and nonverbal tests. The latter are also known as performance tests. Physical measures can be obtained for behavior on either kind of test.

Verbal remembering may be measured in terms of the time a child can be delayed, after exposure to a series of letters, and still repeat the letters in proper order. Verbal reasoning may be measured as the time required to solve a logical problem and state the correct answer in words. Verbal abstracting may be measured by determining the time a student takes to name the common characteristics of groups of objects.

Nonverbal or performance characteristics of intellective behavior can also be measured in terms of time. Nonverbal remembering may be measured as the time a child can be delayed, after the solution to a puzzle has been demonstrated, and still solve the puzzle; nonverbal reasoning, as the time required for a student to complete the task in the test of systematic procedures (see Figure 5-12). Performance may be timed on a spatial-relations test, which might involve assembling a jigsaw puzzle, forming a design out of colored blocks, or placing blocks of different shapes in their proper positions in a formboard (see Figure 5-13). Abstracting could be measured as the time required to sort blocks of different sizes into the shape categories: triangles, squares, and circles.

Abstracting was called for in a performance test developed by Heidbreder[14]. Card sorting was the task. Drawings were made on rectangular white cards which a subject classified by sorting into piles. The drawings were instances of three concepts of concrete objects: face, bird, and hat; three concepts of spatial forms: a circle and two special figures; and

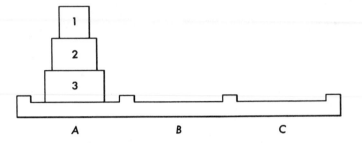

Figure 5-12. A schematic drawing of materials employed in a test of reasoning. The subject's task is to transfer the three blocks to position *B* moving one at a time without placing any block on top of a smaller one. Blocks may be stored in position *C*. The measure would be time required.

three concepts of numbers: three, four, and six. There were 144 drawings, consisting of sixteen different drawings for each of the nine concepts.

The cards were divided into three packs: concrete objects, spatial forms, and numerical quantities. One pack at a time thoroughly shuffled was presented face down to the subject. Instructions were that the pack should be sorted into three equal piles, each containing cards which were similar in some way. On signal, the subject turned the pack over and began sorting as rapidly as possible until all forty-eight cards had been

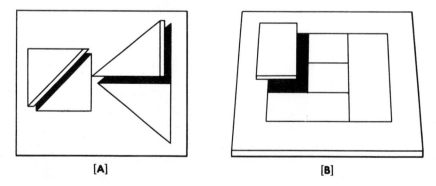

[A]   **[B]**

Figure 5-13. Formboards employed in spatial relations testing. **A:** Gwyn Triangle Test. **B:** One of the Healy-Fernald Construction Tests. [Adapted from C. H. Stoelting Company.]

sorted. He was allowed to discard drawings temporarily or to take cards from the discard pile whenever he desired. Only one correct classification was possible. When the subject completed the classification correctly, he was considered to have attained the concept represented by the drawings. The measure of an individual's performance was the time required to sort the cards.

According to the definition given in Chapter 4, personality has to do with motivational, emotional, and social characteristics of behavior. Some personality measurement is accomplished by expressing observations in physical dimensions. A child draws a man on a sheet of paper and the height of the figure is interpreted as revealing a feature of the child's view of adults. A child who indicates his choice of two prizes by moving a lever in one of two directions vacillates in making his choice, and degree of conflict is defined as the distance over which he moves the lever in vacillating. A college student writes a standard passage on a pressure-sensitive surface and the physical force exerted by his hand is adopted as a definition of tension. The force with which a child applies a mallet in mashing a plasticine doll is interpreted as an index of hostility. A word printed on a card is displayed to a client in a psychiatric clinic, and a record is made of the time between the presentation of the card and the vocalization of a word by the client, who is under instructions to say the first word that comes to his mind. When a very long latency occurs, an interpretation is made that the word relates to some disturbing situation or problem. The duration of an infant's sucking on a finger guard is one possible measure of oral activity. The per cent of time an infant is active between feedings could be taken as an indication of energy level.

Characteristics of intellect and personality are named with abstract words which are defined, in part, by procedures of observation and measurement. Any given procedure may appear to be so specific that it does not fit the abstract characteristic very well. A large part of the psychologist's job is to establish and justify a connection between the abstraction and the procedure of measurement. The nature of this part of the job is nowhere more apparent than it is in using physical measures to assess intellect and personality.

PHYSICAL MEASURES IN EVERYDAY LIFE

Physical measures of behavior are employed in everyday life, often as applications of developments in psychology. In education, business, industry, government, the military, and the health services, physical measures may be used to provide information for important decisions. In a nursery school there may be interest in determining children's food preferences, so the weights of specific foods consumed by children at meal-time are observed and recorded. In driver training programs, there is emphasis on the driver's braking reaction time. An oil company may wish to find out how far the driver of an automobile can go on a gallon of gasoline. A department store may want information on the time required by clerks to wrap packages. The time a housewife takes to choose between two products can help a manufacturer evaluate them. In an industry, the personnel department may evaluate a job applicant, in part at least, by recording the time he requires to pick up, transfer, and place metal pins in a test of finger dexterity; or the time he takes to put a nut on a bolt, place the assembly in a container, remove the assembly, and remove the nut in a test of mechanical skill. In an industrial training program, a painter's apprentice may be evaluated in terms of the area of a wall covered in a specified period of time; or a machinist's apprentice may be evaluated in terms of the inaccuracy in the diameter of a rod he produces. Investigation of fatigue on the job may involve registering the force exerted by a worker as he depresses keys during the performing of a task. Productivity may be evaluated by recording the per cent of time a worker keeps a silk loom in operation, the time required for a worker to polish spoons, the pounds of women's hose produced per hour by the operator of a knitting machine, or the pounds of cartridge shells visually inspected per minute by a factory worker. The traffic department of a municipal government may be interested in observing and recording the length of time truck drivers park in making deliveries. A hospital may institute procedures for determining the daily intake of water, measured in cubic centimeters, for patients with certain illnesses. These physical measures of behavior are only a few out of many which have very valuable applications in every area of life.

Counting

The second major category of measurement practices is counting. After the psychologist decides on the particular kind of action which interests him, he counts all the identifiable instances of that action by a subject on a given occasion. He reports, as a measure of the subject's behavior, the frequency or relative frequency of the action. The frequency is simply the number of occurrences; the relative frequency is a proportion or percentage of occasions on which the action occurred.

To be counted, an action must, of course, be identifiable. Some actions are so extensive that there is little room for disagreement in identifying them. Others such as eyelid movements, which vary from a slight quiver to full closure, are sometimes so slight that their occurrence is

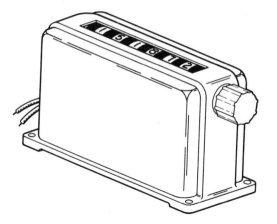

Figure 5-14. A reset magnetic counter which can be connected in series with any one of a variety of devices providing an electrical contact arrangement operated by the subject's response. [Courtesy of Veeder-Root Inc., Hartford, Connecticut.]

debatable. Self references in conversation vary from the obvious use of first-person pronouns to vague allusions to the speaker's relations with others. At times an arbitrary rule must be adopted for identification so that counting can be accomplished. When actions are observed and identified as they occur sequentially, it is sometimes necessary to employ a mechanical device of some sort to record and accumulate the occurrences. Commonly used are counters which may be activated by the psychologist or the subject according to the circumstances in which observing is done. An electromagnetic counter of a type used in psychology is shown in Figure 5-14.

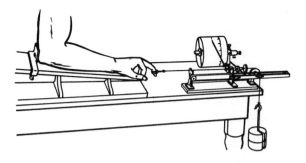

Figure 5-15. An ergograph. By moving his finger, the subject pulls the weight as far as he can at each beat of a metronome. Each pull is recorded on the revolving kymograph drum. The number of pulls in a specified period could be counted. [Adapted from Mosso's Ergograph in J. F. Dashiell, *Fundamentals of General Psychology*, 3rd ed. Boston: Houghton Mifflin Company, 1949.]

THE COUNTING OF MOVEMENTS

Psychological investigations of motor activity may involve the counting of events such as eye fixations per line of print, underlining of nouns on a page of print, errors made in tracing the true path of a maze, and finger flexions in operating an ergograph (see Figure 5-15). Dynamic balance, tapping, and finger dexterity were measured by counting in an investigation by Fleishman[8].

In the dynamic balance test, the subject stood on a seesaw with one foot on each side of the fulcrum so that the board could be balanced in horizontal position (see Figure 5-16). Next to the board was a panel of lights in two rows—one red, the other green. When a red light came on, the subject had to shift his weight on the board to match the red light with a green one, whose position was controlled by tilting the board. When the board was tilted correctly and matching was achieved, the red light shifted to another position. The subject had to achieve as many of these matchings as he could in the time allowed. His score was the number of matchings accomplished in that time.

In the tapping test, a subject was required to strike two adjacent metal plates with a stylus as rapidly as possible (see Figure 5-17). He struck the plates alternately, first one, then the other, making taps as fast as he could. The number of taps was recorded by electromagnetic counters, and his score was the number of taps in the time allowed.

In the finger dexterity test, the subject was required to pick up three small pins at a time from a tray of pins, using his preferred hand, and place them three at a time in a small hole. He had to fill a series of small holes in this manner as rapidly as he could (see Figure 5-18). The number of pins placed in the time allowed was his score.

COUNTING IN INTELLECTIVE MEASUREMENT

Counting has been employed very extensively in testing intellective characteristics of behavior such as information, achievement, remembering, reasoning, and abstracting. The instances of behavior which are identified and counted are usually answers or solutions which the subject gives in response to questions, problems, or other kinds of items presented to him by the tester. Knowledge of vocabulary is tested by requiring a subject to choose a correct definition, a synonym, or an antonym for a given word. When the subject is a young child, his vocabulary may be measured by observing and counting the number of different words he uses, or the number of different words he recognizes in print.

Achievement refers to knowledge or skill acquired in some specific period of time. The assumption is sometimes made that the individual did not possess the knowledge or skill prior to the period in question.

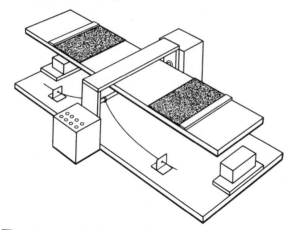

Figure 5-16. The teeter-totter for the dynamic balance test. [Adapted from Fleishman.[8]]

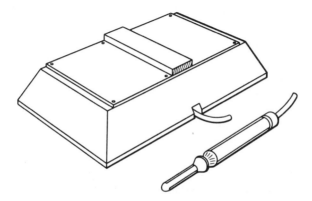

Figure 5-17. The two-plate tapping apparatus. [Adapted from Fleishman.[8]]

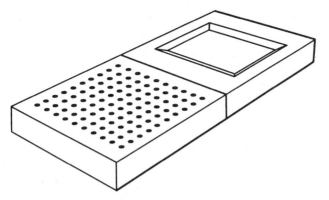

Figure 5-18. The board for the finger dexterity test. The bin at the right contained metal pins. The subject had to place them in the holes at the left. [Adapted from Fleishman.[8]]

It may, of course, be possible to test beforehand to confirm this assumed lack of knowledge or skill. For example, achievement in a history course may be tested simply by asking a student a number of questions concerning topics covered in the course. One possible score would be the number of correct answers. It might be assumed that he would not have answered correctly before he took the course, but if the questions were asked at the beginning of the course as well as at the end, there would be more certainty about his achievement in the course.

Remembering is measured in three ways: recall, recognition, and relearning. To test recall, one may ask a child to tell a story he has heard, a student to give the events of a movie he has seen, a shopper to name the items he saw in a window display, or a subject to reproduce a list of words some time after he has memorized them. A count of the parts of the story, the events of the movie, the items in the display, or words in the list, correctly stated, is a measure of success in remembering. A somewhat different approach is to determine how long a list of items a person can recall correctly immediately after the list is shown or read to him. The items may be numbers, letters, words, or other symbols, and his score is the number of items in the longest list correctly recalled. In testing recognition, a person is shown a set of words, faces, drawings, or other objects. After the objects are removed and a period of time elapses, the person is shown a larger set including new objects as well as old and is asked to indicate which ones he recognizes as having been shown to him earlier. The number of objects correctly recognized is his score.

In testing remembering by the relearning method, the subject's task could be memorizing a list of words. If it is, he is allowed to read through the list repeatedly, each reading constituting a trial. Between trials he tries to recite the list. His score is the number of trials required to memorize the list so that he can recite it without error. After a lapse of time, he is given the task of memorizing the list again. If he remembers at all, the number of required trials in relearning will be less than the number originally needed. The difference is taken as a measure of his success in remembering. Suppose he learns in ten trials and, after a lapse of time, relearns in five trials. The difference, which is five trials, may be thought of as a kind of saving in trials and, consequently, as a measure of remembering.

Reasoning is measured by having an individual solve logical problems and counting his correct solutions. Arithmetic, algebra, and other mathematical topics are familiar sources of problems for reasoning tests. Formal logic is a source of problems based on syllogisms.

One approach to measuring abstracting is to require a subject to identify concepts from examples or instances and then count his successes. Cahill and Hovland[5] have described a method of this kind. An instance of a concept was composed of one of three values on each of three dimensions. The three dimensions were form, shading, and number. The three values for form were triangle, circle, and cross; for shading, white, gray, and striped; for number, 1, 2, and 3.

The simplest concept involved only one value of one dimension. It could be represented by either positive instances or negative instances. If the concept was circularity, positive instances were one, two, or three white, gray, or striped circles; negative instances were one, two, or three white, gray, or striped crosses or squares. Two positive instances, properly chosen, provided sufficient information to identify the concept. The presentation of one white circle and two gray circles would indicate that circularity was the solution. Three negative instances, properly chosen, provided sufficient information to exclude all concepts except circularity. The presentation of one white square, two gray crosses, and three striped squares, as negative instances, would exclude the three values of number, the three values of shading, and two values of form, leaving only circularity. Only negative instances were actually employed in the testing done by the investigators.

A more complex concept involved a value from each of two dimensions. An example was whiteness and circularity. Positive instances were one, two, or three white circles; negative instances were one, two, or three gray or striped crosses or squares. Two positive instances were sufficient for identification, whereas ten negative instances were required. These could have been one white cross, one gray circle, one striped square, two white squares, two gray crosses, two striped circles, three white crosses, three gray circles, three gray squares, and three striped crosses. "White circle" does not, of course, occur among these negative instances. There is some redundancy. "Three gray," "gray circle," "three crosses," and "white cross" occur twice.

A subject was presented with negative instances and required to guess the correct concept. After each instance was presented, he recorded his guess in a booklet. His score was the number of correct answers after presentation of the minimum number of negative instances for each of several problems. Before the test, the subject received instructions which indicated, by verbal definitions and pictorial examples, the dimensions, their values, the ways in which dimensions and values were to be combined, and the nature of negative instances. He also received practice problems.

In addition to correct responses, trials required to reach some specified level of performance may be counted. The level is called a criterion. If a list of names is exposed to a subject on repeated occasions and he is instructed to try to reproduce the correct order of the names after each presentation, then his score may be taken as the number of presentations or trials required for him to achieve a perfect reproduction of the order of names. If a problem is presented to a student repeatedly in a standard fashion with a certain amount of time allowed for the student to attempt its solution, then the number of presentations or trials required for him to reach a correct solution can be taken as his score. If a child is allowed to work on a jigsaw puzzle on successive occasions for a fixed period of time, the number of occasions he requires to assemble the puzzle may be assigned to him as his score.

A method of counting trials required to reach a criterion level was employed by Heidbreder[15] to measure the attainment of concepts of concrete objects, spatial forms, and numbers. A subject was required to learn the names of drawings presented to him in series. The names were nonsense syllables, arbitrarily assigned to the drawings. A given syllable was used as the name of drawings which differed in some respects but which, as a group, possessed a common characteristic distinguishing them from other groups. For example, the syllable *relk* was used as the name for each of the different drawings of the human face, *fard* was applied to each of the different drawings of a circular object, and *ling* was applied to drawings containing two similar items: two vases, two bees, two designs, and so on. The instances of each concept varied widely. Each instance of *mulp* was a drawing of a tree—an oak, a willow, a palm, a pine, and so on. There were three concepts involving concrete objects; three, spatial forms; and three, numerical concepts. There were sixteen drawings for each of the nine concepts.

The subject sat before an apparatus which exposed the drawings one at a time for four seconds. During the first trial for each series of nine drawings, the investigator pronounced the name of each drawing as it appeared and the subject immediately repeated it. In each subsequent trial, the investigator waited after the appearance of the drawing and then prompted the subject if he did not himself name the drawing. If the subject named the drawing incorrectly, the investigator corrected him. Each series was repeated until the subject had correctly and, without being prompted, named all the drawings on two successive trials.

One of the measures devised by Heidbreder was called concept attained or *CA*. The number of the series in which a subject gave correct, unprompted responses to instances of a concept on their first appearance in the first trial and maintained this level throughout the remaining trials and series was taken as the point at which he attained that concept and as the measure of his performance. Thus a *CA* score could vary from two to sixteen.

COUNTING IN PERSONALITY MEASUREMENT

The definition of personality, given originally in Chapter 4, referred to the motivational, emotional, and social characteristics of an individual's behavior. Interests and attitudes are personality characteristics according to this definition. What is the behavioral referent for an interest? There are at least three possibilities: the individual's statement of interest, his actual participation in some activity, or his knowledge of the activity. A boy's interest in collecting stamps can be evaluated by what he says, the amount of collecting he does, or how much he knows about the hobby. What is the referent for an attitude? A person's statement of his approval or disapproval of some position, or his actual activity in working for or against it. Interests and attitudes, along with other motivational, emotional, and social characteristics are measured by counting responses in a variety of situations.

Vocational interest can be measured by counting the number of items checked as "liked" in a list of activities associated with different kinds of jobs. An individual's moral attitude can be measured by counting the number of actions of which he disapproves, in a list of items such as drinking, swearing, and gambling. Level of economic aspiration might be defined as the number of material needs and wants a man checks on a list. Diligence in academic work might be the number of answers on a questionnaire concerning study habits. Emotional characteristics may be measured by counting the following responses: bodily symptoms of fear in combat checked on a list by a flyer; affirmative answers on a questionnaire concerning neurotic symptoms; inspiration-expiration cycles per minute in breathing during a test; swallowing actions as a subject reads aloud; and contacts between a stylus and the perimeter of a small hole in a steadiness test.

Counting was employed to obtain scores in connection with a diary method of reporting fears and angers, devised by Anastasi, Cohen, and Spatz[2]. The method required their subjects, twenty-eight women enrolled in a course in psychology at Barnard College, to keep a diary of the occurrence of fears and angers. A subject was asked to record, at the end of each day, all instances of fear or anger experienced during that day, together with a brief statement describing the situation associated with the emotion. She was also to indicate for each instance of fear or anger whether the situation was recalled, present, or anticipated. To guarantee anonymity, reports were submitted in sealed envelopes with names on detachable flaps which were removed before the envelopes were opened.

The number of reports of each emotion was determined for each subject for the one-week period covered by the records. The average number of fears was 12.2; of angers, 15.7. Individual fear scores ranged from two to thirty-six; individual anger scores, from zero to forty-two. Reports of fear were most often concerned with anticipated situations, whereas reports of anger were most often concerned with present situations.

Personality characteristics include social aspects of behavior as well as motivational and emotional ones. In studying psychiatric patients, psychologists often concentrate on social behavior, as did Farina, Arenberg, and Guskin[7] in constructing a scale for measuring the appropriateness of behavior in simple, conventional social situations. The scale was developed for use with male patients. It was administered as a brief standardized interview which was intended to require behaviors indicating how the patient dealt with other people.

The interview was conducted in a room containing only a desk, two chairs, and a wastepaper basket. An aide brought the patient to the door and introduced him. If the patient entered and approached the examiner, he was given one point. The examiner said, "Hello, Mr. Blank." For any discernible response to the greeting, verbal or motor, the patient was given one point; if the response was verbal and appropriate, he was given another point. The examiner extended his hand. If the patient shook hands, he was given a point. The examiner said, "Won't you have a seat?" If the patient sat without further urging, he was given a point. The examiner said, "How are you today?" Any discernible response to the question was scored one point; a verbal and appropriate response received another point. The examiner pushed a pencil off the edge of the desk, as if by accident. If the patient picked up the pencil spontaneously, he was given a point. If he did not, the examiner said, "Will you please pick up that pencil for me?" If the patient complied, he was given a point. The examiner said, "Would you mind moving your chair closer?" A point was given if the patient did so. There were twenty-two other items in which the examiner made some request or comment. The patient's response was noted in each instance, and his score was the total number of points awarded for making appropriate social responses.

The Vineland Social Maturity Scale by Doll[6], developed for measuring social competence, contains more than one hundred items in age groupings from one year to over twenty-five. An examiner checks items in the Scale on the basis of information obtained by interview with a subject or from an informant who knows him. Items are classified as pertaining to self-help in general, self-help in dressing, self-help in eating, communication, self direction, socialization, locomotion, and occupation (see Figure 5-19).

An item in the first-year level under socialization is "reaches for familiar persons." A socialization item at ages one and two is "plays with other children"; at four and five, "plays competitive exercise games"; at five and six, "plays simple table games"; at seven and eight, "disavows literal Santa Claus"; from twenty to twenty-five, "contributes to social welfare"; and from twenty-five up, "promotes civic progress."

In the category of occupation, behavior at ages eight and nine includes "does routine household tasks"; at ten and eleven, "does small remunerative work"; from twelve to fifteen, "performs responsible routine

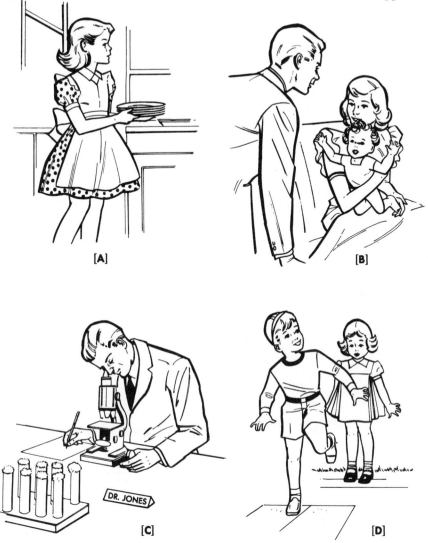

Figure 5-19. Drawings illustrating items from The Vineland Social Maturity Scale. **A:** Does routine household tasks. **B:** Reaches for familiar persons. **C:** Performs expert or professional work. **D:** Plays competitive exercise games. [Adapted from E. A. Doll, *Measurement of Social Competence*, 1953, published by Educational Test Bureau, division of the American Guidance Service, Inc.]

chores"; from eighteen to twenty, "has a job or continues schooling"; and from twenty-five up, "performs expert or professional work."

The number of items checked is converted to a social age score (SA). Another score, social quotient (SQ) is obtained by dividing SA by CA, the subject's chronological age, and multiplying the quotient by 100.

Another example of personality measurement based on the counting of items is an inventory constructed by Lorr, O'Connor, and Stafford[17] for describing the behavior of psychotic patients in a psychiatric hospital. (A psychotic individual is one with serious intellective and personality problems arising from unrealistic, highly emotional, or extremely asocial behavior.) The inventory consisted of eighty-five items divided into four groups or scales. The scales were given the labels: thinking disorganization, agitated depression, withdrawal, and paranoid belligerence. The first is intellective; the last three pertain to personality characteristics in emotional and social behavior.

Observations of behavior were made by nurses and aides on a representative group of patients. Inventories were completed under the supervision of either a psychologist or a psychiatrist after an observation period of one week. An observer checked statements in the inventory as true, not true, or doesn't apply, with reference to a particular patient. Scores were based on the number of items checked in each scale and the direction of the item. For example, in scoring withdrawal, "true" for "usually stays by himself" would be counted in the same way as "false" for "nearly always chatting with someone."

The definitions of thinking disorganization, agitated depression, withdrawal, and paranoid belligerence can be obtained from an examination of items in each scale.

Thinking disorganization was defined by ratings of behaviors such as talking to himself, seeing and hearing things that were not there, talking whether or not anyone was listening, giggling in a silly way, repeating words and phrases in a meaningless way, making faces and strange movements that did not make sense, not knowing where he was, and drifting off the subject when he talked.

Agitated depression was the general label for ratings on the patient's appearance of sadness, unhappiness, tiredness, fear, worry, and nervousness.

In the scale for *withdrawal* were ratings of the extent to which the patient stayed by himself, ignored the activities around him, took part in conversation, had to be pushed to follow routine, responded to entertainment, spoke too softly to be heard, mixed with other patients, had friends on the ward, and listened to radio or watched television.

The definition of *paranoid belligerence* was contained in ratings of the patient's telling other patients what to do, doing the opposite of what he was asked to do, resisting treatment from the doctors, acting as though the hospital was persecuting him, hitting someone for no apparent reason, shouting and yelling, bossing the other patients, quickly flying off the handle, yelling at an attendant when he was dissatisfied, swearing and using obscene language, and threatening to assault others.

COUNTING MEASURES IN EVERYDAY LIFE

Perhaps the most familiar use of counting to obtain scores occurs in sports. The golfer counts his strokes over the eighteen holes of a course. The baseball player counts the number of hits he gets in each game and his team counts the number of runs it scores. In basketball, the number of field goals is recorded for each player. In some sports, a score is simply the number of successes, but in some, one kind of success is given more points than another. In football, a touchdown is given more credit than a field goal. In basketball, a field goal earns more points then a free throw.

In psychology, similar variations in scoring can be found. On a given test, a correct answer to one problem may be worth five points while that of another is worth only two points. On a personality inventory, a "yes" given to one item may count one point, whereas the same answer, given to another item, may count three points. These variations are introduced to improve the test or inventory.

In business and industry there are many uses for counting measures. An automobile dealer holds a contest in which the number of cars sold per month by each salesman is determined. In training telegraphers or radio operatiors in Morse code, a record of their progress is kept in terms of letters per minute sent and received correctly. Production in a shoe factory is measured in terms of the number of heels trimmed each day by each worker. A stenographer is hired after being tested to find out how many words she can type per minute. A cosmetic manufacturer eliminates certain items from a new line of lipsticks after he has found out the number of times the members of a consulting panel have chosen each item in comparisons with every other one.

In developing aircraft control systems, there has been much concern about confusion in identifying knobs and handles. Accidents have been traced to the confusion of controls which were close together and not easily distinguished. Jenkins[16] investigated the extent of confusion among control knobs of varied shapes by counting errors made in identifying knobs by touch. Forty Army Air Force pilots were tested. The purpose of the investigation was to find a set of knobs which could be easily discriminated.

Twenty-two plastic objects, 1.25 inches in the largest dimension, were mounted on shafts and attached to a turntable. Standard control knobs used in cockpits and on radar and radio sets, as well as some new kinds, were selected for testing. Each blindfolded pilot sat before the turntable. After the instructions were read to him, a test knob was presented and he felt it for one second. The examiner then rotated the turntable

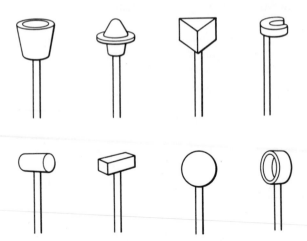

Figure 5-20. Eight knobs with shapes yielding the fewest errors in an investigation of their use in coding aircraft controls. [Adapted from Jenkins.[16]]

to a predetermined point and the pilot felt each knob, in order, until he reported what he thought was the test knob. The same test procedure was repeated for each of the knobs.

Two types of errors were recorded: incorrect identifications and hesitations. A hesitation was defined as handling a comparison knob for more than one second. An error score was obtained for the pilot on each knob. The total number of errors for a knob of a given shape could then be determined. Figure 5-20 shows eight knobs which yielded no errors.

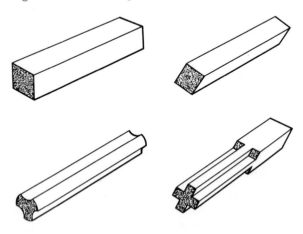

Figure 5-21. Four small handles of the sixteen employed in an investigation of their use on the switches of an electronic control panel. [Adapted from Green and Anderson.[12]]

A similar attempt was made to code the switches of an electronic control panel by using handles of different shapes. Green and Anderson[12] suggested that the operator of a control panel might work more efficiently if he could select the appropriate switch without looking at it. The purpose of their investigation was to select a set of differently shaped switch handles which could be identified easily. Twenty-seven enlisted men in the United States Army were subjects.

Sixteen small handles were made of black lucite (see Figure 5-21). Confusions were determined by two methods: learning and finding. In the learn method, the soldier had to associate a number from one to sixteen with each of the handles. The handles were mounted near the edge of a circular disk behind a shield, and the tester could, by rotating the disk, position any handle at an aperture through which the soldier could then reach to feel it. On each trial the subject was given approximately two seconds to feel the handle and report its number. After he responded, the tester announced the correct number. Identifications were said to be learned when the subject responded correctly on a complete set of trials for all sixteen handles.

In the find method, a set of handles was mounted in a row on each of the four sides of a long narrow box. On each trial, the tester presented a sample handle on the rotary disk. The blindfolded subject felt the handle and then tried to locate a matching handle in one of the four rows on the box.

The data from both methods were combined. The number of specific mismatchings or confusions was determined for each soldier on each pair of handles. Four handles which were seldom confused are shown in Figure 5-21.

Standardized Measures

A standardized test is one for which instructions, procedures, circumstances, and methods of scoring have been formally adopted, usually after investigations to determine the desirable combination. A substantial part of current psychological measurement is not standardized. Whether in research or application, many measurement systems are invented for and adapted to particular situations. A research psychologist may devise a method for the investigation of abstracting in a laboratory setting. An industrial psychologist may devise a method of testing dexterity for selecting employees in a particular factory. Most of the counting measures described so far have been of this sort: methods invented to serve special but limited purposes.

This is only a part of the picture, however, for a number of measurement systems have been standardized and accepted for general use in a wide range of situations. Although counting measures are not the only ones which have been standardized, they account for a large proportion of those which are better known and more widely used.

Standardized Tests of Intelligence

Intelligence tests can be classified in two categories: individual and group. An individual test requires, as part of the standard procedure, that the test be administered to a single subject. The administration should be done by a person who has been trained and supervised. A group test may be administered to a single subject or a group of subjects. A group test does not require as much training in administration as does an individual test.

The Stanford-Binet Intelligence Scale is an individual test with a relatively long history. In this country, there have been three "revisions," in the years 1916, 1937, and 1960. The first was published by Lewis M. Terman; the second, by the same author and Maud A. Merrill; the third, by Merrill after the death of Terman in 1956. The first was a revision of a test developed by Alfred Binet and Théodore Simon in France between the years 1905 and 1913. The work of Binet and Simon stemmed from a public commission in which they undertook to devise a test for detecting and measuring mental defect.

The Stanford-Binet Scale is intended to measure general intelligence from early childhood through adulthood. To achieve this end, a large number of heterogeneous test items were included in it. Test items were selected which provided standard situations in which *intelligent behavior* could be observed, as that term was understood and agreed upon by various experts. Items were arranged in age levels according to their difficulty, which was defined in terms of the percentage of subjects passing at each age. A very easy item for ten-year-olds would be one passed by ninety-five per cent of them. A very difficult item would be one passed by only five per cent. Items within a medium range of difficulty were selected for each age level. For example, a vocabulary item might be assigned to the ten-year level because sixty per cent of children tested at that level passed it.

To convey some impression of the kinds of test items in the Stanford-Binet Scale and at the same time avoid an undesirable public exposure of their specific content, there are listed below, with their age levels, the general names of selected items:

> Year II, Form board
> Year III, Stringing beads
> Year IV, Naming objects from memory
> Year VI, Maze tracing
> Year IX, Verbal absurdities

Year XII, Vocabulary
Adult, Differences between abstract words

The subject may be given a score called mental age (MA), which is based upon the items he passes. His basal mental age is the highest

Figure 5-22. Pictorial items adapted from the 1937 Revision of the Stanford-Binet Scale. **A:** Dog and rabbit. The child was asked, "What's funny about that picture?" **B:** Familiar objects. The child was asked, "Show me the one that we cook on." [By permission of The Houghton Mifflin Company.]

age level at which he passes all items before his first failure. Added to this basal age is credit for passing items at higher levels. The credit is expressed as months and, without going into the specific variations in procedure, is determined generally in the following way: If there are six items at a given age level, then each item is said to represent two months of mental age. Since an age level is one year, which is twelve months, the whole year's credit is divided among the six items. If a child's basal age is eight years and he earns ten months credit from the nine-year level and two months from the ten-year level, he is given a total of eight years and twelve months, or nine years of mental age.

The original idea in having a score called an intelligence quotient (IQ) was to provide a comparison of mental age and chronological age. The comparison was obtained by dividing mental age by chronological age. The quotient was computed to two decimal places and then multiplied by 100, to eliminate the decimal point. In the example of the preceding paragraph, the child's mental age turned out to be nine years. If his chronological age was nine years, then his IQ would be 9/9 or 1.00, which would be expressed as 100. If his chronological age was eight, then his IQ would be 9/8 or 1.12, approximately, and would be expressed as 112. Some pictorial test items from the 1937 Revision of the Stanford-Binet Scale are shown in Figure 5-22.

The Wechsler Adult Intelligence Scale, originally published in 1939 and revised in 1955, is another widely used individual test. (There is also a companion test called the Wechsler Intelligence Scale for Children.) The former was devised primarily for, and adapted specifically to, the measurement of adult intelligence. Items were selected which had long been accepted as relevant to the evaluation of intellective characteristics and which had a content suitable for adults.

The Adult Scale contains items grouped in eleven subtests: information, comprehension, arithmetic, similarities, digit span, vocabulary, digit-symbol substitution, picture completion, block design, picture arrangement to tell a story, and object assembly, a kind of jigsaw puzzle. The first six are considered verbal tests; the last five, performance tests.

The Adult Scale was constructed as a point scale, one in which a subject's final score is obtained from a summation of credits or points given for items passed. In deciding on the number of points for each subtest, an assumption was made that all subtests should be given the same share of the total score. Tables were established by means of which the original scores on each subtest could be converted to so-called scaled scores which were equivalent from one subtest to another. These scaled scores are used in determining an intelligence quotient, which expresses an individual's score in terms of its position in his chronological age group. There is no mental-age score on the Wechsler Scale as there is on the Stanford-Binet Scale. It is important to note that IQs on the two scales are not obtained in the same way. On the Wechsler Scale, verbal and performance IQs, as well as a full-scale IQ, can be determined. Items similar to some of those used in the Wechsler Scale for Children are shown in Figure 5-23. They have been modified extensively to prevent undersirable exposure of the real items.

There are several standardized group tests of intelligence in use at the present time, but the one to be described here has special significance, for it was based on Louis L. Thurstone's pioneering investigations of the nature of mental ability reported in 1938. His findings indicated that the

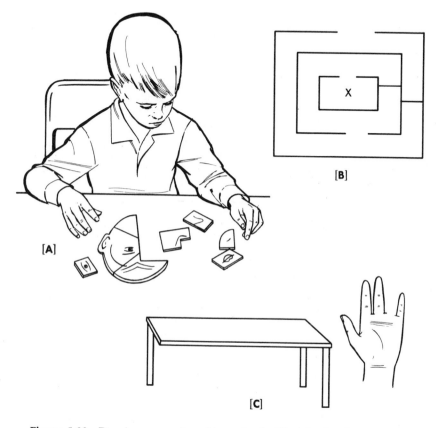

Figure 5-23. Drawings suggestive of items in the Wechsler Intelligence Scale for Children. **A:** A six-year-old tries an object-assembly test. **B:** A maze similar to one of those in the Scale. **C:** Picture-completion items from the Revised Beta Examination, suggestive of items in the WISC. [By permission of The Psychological Corporation.]

use of a single term (such as general intelligence) and a single score (such as an intelligence quotient) did not do justice to the variations in human test scores. They could be more adequately represented by a battery of tests and a set of scores. Out of his work came an original battery of eleven tests of *primary* mental abilities. The SRA Primary Mental Abilities for Ages 11-17, first published in 1947, was based on

[A]

[B]

[C]

[D]

[E]

[F]

[G]

[H]

[I]

Figure 5-24 (*opposite page*). Illustrations of items from a number of intellective tests for children or adults. **A:** A tracing test. (Adapted from The Macquarrie Test for Mechanical Ability.) **B:** A picture-order item. (Adapted from The Chicago Non-Verbal Examination by Brown, Stein, and Rohrer.) **C:** A spatial-relations item. If the two parts at upper left are put together, what figure results? (Adapted from The Revised Minnesota Paper Form Board Test by Likert and Quasha.) **D:** Three of twelve faces which in the original have names below them. The subject studies the faces and names. Later he must try to recognize them in a larger group. (Adapted from The Social Intelligence Test of the George Washington University Series.) **E:** An item requiring the counting of blocks. How many blocks touch each of the blocks marked with an "X"? (Adapted from The Macquarrie Test for Mechanical Ability.) **F:** An item suggestive of one of the simpler plates in the Design Judgment Test by Graves. The subject is instructed to indicate which design he prefers. **G:** A portion of an item from a test for children. The subject is told to mark the prettiest house. (Adapted from the Pintner-Cunningham Primary Mental Test.) **H:** A portion of an item used in testing rhyming. The child is to mark the picture which sounds most like "big". (Adapted from The Gates Reading Readiness Test.) **I:** An item for testing number readiness. The child locates the third horse from the gate. (Adapted from The Metropolitan Readiness Test.) [**A** and **E** by permission of California Test Bureau. **B, C,** and **F** by permission of The Psychological Corporation. **D** by permission of the Center for Psychological Service, Washington, D.C. **G** and **I** by permission of Harcourt, Brace and World, Inc., New York. **H** by permission of Bureau of Publications, Teachers College, Columbia University.]

---

research in this area by the author and his wife, Thelma Gwinn Thurstone. The SRA test was designed to measure five primary mental abilities: verbal, spatial, reasoning, number, and word-fluency. Verbal ability refers to the understanding of ideas expressed in words and is tested by items requiring the identification of synonyms. Spatial ability refers to the visualization of objects in two or three dimensions. It is tested by items requiring the rotation of figures in one's imagination. Reasoning pertains to the solving of logical problems. Number is the ability to handle quantitative problems quickly and accurately. Word-fluency is the ability to produce words easily. It is measured by having a subject write as many words as possible, beginning with a certain letter, in a specified time.

Figure 5-24 presents a selection of items from several standardized intellective tests for children and adults.

Standardized Measures of Personality

The personality measures to be described here are based on the counting of responses made by a subject to the items of an inventory. The inventory may be administered to an individual or a group. Some training is necessary for the proper administration of personality inventories, but a great deal of training is required for interpretation of the scores. A subject can easily misunderstand and exaggerate the significance of his scores if he is not carefully and skillfully handled.

The Minnesota Multiphasic Personality Inventory (MMPI) was designed to provide scores on a number of personality characteristics for persons sixteen years of age and older. The inventory contains 550 statements. The subject is asked to describe himself by sorting them into three categories: True, False, and Cannot Say. His responses are counted to yield scores on thirteen scales. The statements have to do with a variety of topics: general health, coordination, habits, family and marital relations, occupation, education, sexual attitudes, religious attitudes, political attitudes, social attitudes, moods, phobias, morale, and others.

Nine of the thirteen scales are clinical in nature: hypochondriasis or amount of concern about bodily functions; depression; the degree to which the subject is like patients who display symptoms of hysteria; the psychopathic deviate scale, which measures the subject's similarity to persons who lack emotional response, are unable to profit from experience, and disregard social mores; masculinity-feminity; paranoia as indicated by suspiciousness, oversensitivity, and delusions of persecution; psychasthenia or the similarity to persons troubled by phobias and compulsions; schizophrenia or the similarity to persons who reveal bizarre and unusual thoughts or behavior; and hypomania or marked overproductivity in thought and action.

Four of the MMPI scales provide the examiner with information about the adequacy of the subject's responding to the items. Unusual scores invalidate the subject's description of himself.

The nine clinical scales of the MMPI suggest important dimensions of personality. It would not be correct, however, to leave the impression that there is complete agreement on what the basic dimensions of personality are. For this reason, two other inventories will be described briefly and their dimensions listed.

The Guilford-Zimmerman Temperament Survey contains 300 items divided equally among ten traits: general activity, restraint, ascendance, sociability, emotional stability, objectivity, friendliness, thoughtfulness, personal relations, and masculinity. Items are stated affirmatively and the examinee indicates assent or dissent by answering "Yes," "?," or "No." The Survey may be used with high school seniors, college students, young adults, and older adults.

The Edwards Personal Preference Schedule contains 225 items. Each item consists of two statements. The subject chooses the statement which is more characteristic of what he likes. The Schedule has been used primarily with college students.

A subject is given scores on fifteen dimensions which are called manifest needs. (Manifest means "as revealed in what the individual says about himself." Needs refers to personal and social requirements of the individual.) The needs have been given the names: achievement, the need to be successful; deference, the need to acknowledge the authority of others; order, the need to be neat and have one's affairs organized; exhibition, the need to draw attention to one's good qualities; autonomy, the need to be independent; affiliation, the need to be friendly; intraception, the need to analyze one's own behavior and the behavior of others; succorance, the need to receive help, sympathy, and affection; dominance, the need to control others; abasement, the need to be submissive and to engage in self-punishment; nurturance, the need to give help, sympathy, and affection; change, the need to do new and different things; endurance, the need to complete a task; heterosexuality, the need to be involved with members of the opposite sex; and aggression, the need to be critical of others.

Each of the three personality inventories which have been described attempts to provide a fairly comprehensive coverage of personality characteristics. An inventory of preferences for personal activities, The Kuder Preference Record (Personal), is more limited in its scope. The preferences which the subject must express are representative of five scales: sociable, practical, theoretical, agreeable, and dominant. The inventory can be used with both high school students and adults. It contains 168 items. There are three activities listed in each item. A subject responds by choosing the activity he likes most and the one he likes least in each triad.

Judgments

Two classes of measures, physical and counting, have already been described. Judgments constitute the next class to be considered. As the consequence of a judgment, a number may be assigned directly to behavior. There is, of course, no guarantee in advance that the assigned number will be, in any sense, a good measure. It has only a provisional status and must be investigated before a decision can be made as to its adequacy or value.

Psychologists distinguish two broad categories of judgments in terms of the kind of instruction given to the judge. Judgments made without explicit instructions to compare one thing with another are called absolute judgments. There is, of course, no guarantee that the judge will not covertly make a comparison even when he is told not to do so. Judgments given under explicit instructions to make a comparison are called comparative judgments.

ABSOLUTE JUDGMENTS

A person may be instructed to judge a specific property of something and to express his judgment as a number. This number can be employed in two different ways: it can be taken as a measure of what is judged and assigned to it; or it can be taken as a measure of the judge and assigned to him. These two uses will be described separately and examples of each will be given.

Assigning the Number to What Has Been Judged

A person is asked to make a judgment on some physical dimension such as length, height, distance, weight, time, intensity, concentration, or frequency. In making the judgment he may or not use the special, standardized instruments commonly employed in physics, chemistry, and engineering. If what is judged is behavior, the number obtained is a provisional psychological measure. Thus an observer may judge the distance of a flyball in a baseball game. Knowing the size of the diamond and the distance of the fences, he may give a judgment which could be taken as a provisional measure of the batter's behavior. If he used a surveyor's tape and measured carefully from the batter's box to the point of impact of the ball in the outfield, he could give a better judgment of the batter's behavior. In fact, his judging would now be identical with the common practice for physical measurement of behavior described earlier. Judging on physical dimensions without benefit of standardized instruments is important only when those instruments are not available, since it is not as accurate as when instruments are employed.

A person may be asked to make a judgment or rating on an abstract psychological dimension. Typically, but not necessarily, the rater uses a graphic scale; that is, he places a mark at an appropriate point on a printed line to represent the degree to which the object possesses the specified property.

In psychology, ratings are used extensively in assessing personality characteristics. Only infrequently are they employed at the present time for measuring intellective characteristics, such as remembering, reasoning, and abstracting; for verbal and nonverbal tests, in which correct answers are counted, have largely supplanted ratings in this area. However, when an attempt is made to measure a motivational characteristic such as initiative, a characteristic such as emotional stability, or a social characteristic such as friendliness, rating methods are often employed. In fact, it may be very difficult to find any other method which can be applied to assessing such characteristics as the constructiveness of children's play, the aggressiveness of psychiatric patients, parents' solicitousness for their children's welfare, effectiveness in teaching, and success in supervising. Very indefinite abstract dimensions such as the merit of architectural designs, the artistic value of paintings, the literary value of books, and the originality of English compositions—dimensions which may be so general as to cover both intellective and personality characteristics—may, of course, be impossible to measure in any other way.

How ratings can be employed with very young infants for whom other kinds of measurement would have been inappropriate is illustrated in an investigation by Bell[4]. Subjects were thirty-two white male infants, four days old, whose mothers were wives of noncommissioned personnel in the United States Navy and Marine Corps. Sound and color motion pictures were made of the infants in the hospital nursery. Very brief film records were made, without any special intervention by the observer, over a three-hour period following one feeding and preceding the next. In addition, when the infant appeared to be asleep, as evidenced by closed eyes, infrequent bodily movements, and regularity of breathing, film records were made of behavior before and after deliberately introduced interventions. The interventions were repeated two or three times as conditions allowed.

Among the measures obtained were ratings of perceptual sensitivity, oral behavior, and crying. The measures of perceptual sensitivity for cutaneous, auditory, and visual stimuli were averages of ratings by two judges on a seven-point scale. The ratings of cutaneous sensitivity were based, in part, on reactions to removal of the blanket on approximately eleven occasions while the infant was sleeping. Auditory sensitivity was based on reactions to three high sharp clicks in rapid succession produced by a small metallic frog snapper, and reactions to a noise of 84 to 88 decibles produced by a blow on a metallic resonating chamber below the infant's crib. One kind of visual sensitivity rated was the amount of looking, based on openness of the eyes and movement of the infant's head and eyeballs while his eyes were open. In evaluating oral behavior, ratings were obtained for the frequency of empty sucking or mouth movements and extent of tongue, mouth, and jaw movements. Loudness was one of the characteristics of crying on which ratings were made.

Assigning the Number to the Judge

A person is asked to judge something on a physical dimension. He may do the judging with or without standardized instruments. The value is to be assigned to the judge and not to what he judges. The number he produces is a measure of his behavior. If he makes several judgments, the average is taken as a measure of his behavior. The purpose of obtaining judgments on physical dimensions and assigning the values to the judge is usually to determine how accurate he is. It may be to find out how accurate an individual is in estimating the length of a room, the area of a building lot, the volume of a tank, the height of a tree, the weight of a steer, the frequency of a tone, or the time required for some event to take place.

Judging is also done on abstract psychological dimensions. The judge may or may not use a graphic rating scale. He may give a single rating or a series. If he gives just one rating, that value is a measure of his behavior. If he gives a series, the average becomes his measure. The purpose in obtaining a rating and assigning it to the judge is to indicate his preferences, values, interests, attitudes, or opinions. In a sense, the judge rates himself when he rates the pleasantness of the weather, the sourness of pickles, the bitterness of tea, the honesty of politicians, the seriousness of juvenile delinquency, the quality of a concerto, the importance of a congressional action, or the extent of his approval of a civic project.

Ratings which are self-descriptions are very valuable in personality assessment. A person may describe himself by means of ratings on a variety of motivational, emotional, and social characteristics. He may rate his ambition for professional advancement, his fear of unemployment, his hostility toward his brothers and sisters, and many other features of his behavior about which his judgments must surely be important to consider.

COMPARATIVE JUDGMENTS

In psychology, comparative judgments are made in two ways: by ranking objects, or by comparing each with every other. If ranking is employed, the rank assigned to any one object may be taken as a measure of the judge's behavior in reacting to that object. In studying appreciation of literature, a psychologist instructs a student to rank, in order of literary merit, the titles of a number of novels, only one of which is a widely acclaimed, prize-winning book. The rank given to that book is a measure of the student. If he ranks it high, he is considered to be a good judge of literary merit; if he ranks it low, he is considered to be a poor judge.

When the method of judging is that of comparing each object with every other, the number of possible comparisons for n objects is $n(n\text{-}1)/2$. The number of comparisons for any one object is $(n\text{-}1)$. In making each comparison, the judge says which object is "greater" in some respect specified in advance. The number of times a judge says "greater" for any one object can be determined, and that number is assigned to the judge as a measure of his behavior.

The method of comparing each object with every other has been applied to the study of nationality perferences. If ten nationalities are chosen, $10(10\text{-}1)/2$ or 45 pairs can be formed. A student may be instructed to express a preference for one name in each pair. If the investigator is interested in characterizing a student with respect to his attitude toward the Japanese, he counts the number of perferences for Japanese given by that student in the nine pairs involving that particular nationality.

Psychophysical Measurement

Descriptions have been presented for three of the four categories of current practices in measurement: physical measures, counting measures, and judgements. The fourth consists of psychophysical measures, which are values obtained by procedures combining physical measures of perceptual stimuli and judgments of those stimuli. The principal uses of psychophysical methods occur in the measurement of various kinds of perceptual accuracy and sensitivity—visual, auditory, olfactory, and so on.

Perceptual accuracy may be measured by the method of adjustment, in which the subject is instructed to adjust one stimulus to equality with a standard on a given dimension. The method yields a measure of the subject's error in judging, the difference in physical units between the subject's adjustment and the standard. The subject is usually required to make a number of adjustments, half of them starting with a setting greater than the standard and half with a setting smaller. The two kinds of trials may be alternated. If the subject makes a number of adjustments, the measure assigned to him is the difference between the average and the standard. The difference is expressed in physical units such as inches, cycles per second, volts, or decibels.

To determine accuracy in judging loudness, the subject's task may be to adjust the intensity of one sound source so that it is equal in loudness to a standard on each of a number of trials. On half the trials, the subject begins with an intensity obviously louder than the standard; on the other half, with an intensity obviously softer. The difference in decibles between the standard intensity and the average of his adjustments is a measure of his error and an index of accuracy.

Perceptual sensitivity is measured in two ways, as the least detectable magnitude of a stimulus or the least detectable difference between stimuli. The former is called an absolute threshold; the latter, a differential threshold. Either kind of threshold can be obtained by a procedure known as the method of limits.

When an absolute threshold is obtained by the method of limits, the tester varies some property of a stimulus and asks the subject whether or not he can perceive it. The variable property of the stimulus is decreased in one series of trials and increased in another. The first is called a descending series; the second, an ascending series. A physical measure of the stimulus when it is just detected by the subject is obtained on each series. The average value for all series, descending and ascending, is the absolute threshold.

To determine an absolute threshold for pitch, the frequency of a tone might be varied, in an ascending series of trials, from seven to twenty-four cycles per second in steps of one cycle. In a descending series, it might be varied from twenty-four to seven cycles per second in steps of one cycle. Both series would be repeated a number of times. The subject would be told to report on each trial whether or not he heard a continuous tone. In each series, the highest frequency reported as not heard and the lowest frequency reported as heard would be recorded. A value midway between these two frequencies would be computed. The average of midpoints for all series of trials would be the subject's absolute threshold for pitch.

To determine a differential threshold by the method of limits, the tester varies a property of the stimulus and asks the subject whether or not he can detect a difference between the stimulus and a standard. Both ascending and descending series of trials are employed. A physical measure of the difference between the stimulus and the standard, when the difference is just detected by the subject, is obtained on each series of trials. The average of the differences from all series is the subject's differential threshold.

A differential threshold for grayness may be obtained by varying the composition of a rotating disk, in one series of trials, from 216 degrees of white and 144 degrees of black to 144 degrees of white and 216 degrees of black by steps of four degrees. In another series, white is increased and black is decreased. Both series are repeated a number of times. A rotating disk composed of 180 degrees of white and 180 degrees of black serves as the standard. The subject is asked to report on each trial whether the variable disk is lighter than, equal to, or darker than the standard. In each series, two transition points are determined. In a series descending with respect to white, one transition point is located midway between the successive settings on which the subject says "lighter" and "equal"; the other, between the successive settings on which he says "equal" and "darker." In a series ascending with respect to white, the transition points are between "darker" and "equal," and "equal" and "lighter." The difference in degrees between each transition point and the standard (180 degrees) is computed. The average of all the differences, disregarding signs, is the subject's differential threshold for gray expressed in degrees.

Psychologists have devised many different kinds of apparatus and many variations in procedure to test perceptual sensitivity. Even kinesthetic sensitivity has been measured. An example of a procedure for measuring kinesthetic thumb and forefinger discrimination has been described by Rodger and McEwen[19]. They constructed apparatus from a woodworker's vise, a few pieces of smooth hardwood, and a dial gauge (see Figure 5-25). A rider is omitted in the drawing. Bolted to opposite jaws of the vise were two strips of hardwood on which the subject placed his thumb and index finger. The strip under his index finger was moved by means of the handle on the vise and the amount of movement was registered in thousandths of an inch on the dial. It was found that subjects could easily discriminate a movement of 0.04 inches after only a little practice.

The authors do not report the exact procedures they employed in measuring kinesthetic discrimination, but the device would be suitable for the method of limits. In one possible procedure, the tester sets the opening of the vise and the subject places his thumb and forefinger on the strips of hardwood. On the first trial, the tester increases the size of the

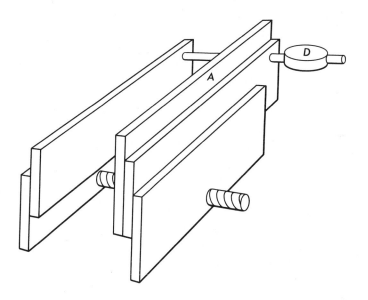

Figure 5-25. A device for measuring kinesthetic thumb and forefinger discrimination. *A* is a rider attached to one of the test strips to guide the hand. The rider on the other test strip is not shown. *D* is a gauge to register movement of the test strip. [Adapted from Rodger and McEwen.[19]]

opening by a small amount and the subject has to say whether the opening remained the same or became larger. On the second trial, the tester starts with the original setting but increases the size of the opening by a larger amount. On the third trial, he increases it by a still larger amount. These and additional trials like them make an ascending series. The transition point between "same" and "larger" is noted. A descending series is contrived of similar steps and trials with successive openings decreasing. A differential threshold is computed from the transition point for each kind of series separately or for both kinds combined.

Abstract Dimensions

By definition, a specific procedure of measurement yields a score on a definite dimension of behavior. The scale of scores on a test in which a child adds three two-digit numbers in each of twenty items is a definite dimension. Another, only a little different, is the scale for a test requiring the child to add two three-digit numbers. Another, more different, is a scale of scores for a test involving subtraction.

It is possible to conceptualize a dimension of behavior not as definite as the scale for a particular test. The scale of scores on an adding test is not as definite as the scale on a test of twenty problems, each with three two-digit numbers to be added. This less definite dimension could be represented by total scores on all the tests in a battery of varied adding tests. It is also possible to conceptualize a dimension of behavior, the scale of scores on an arithmetic test, which would be less definite or more indefinite than an adding test, and which would require adding, subtracting, multiplying, and dividing. Finally, a highly indefinite dimension of behavior would be the scale of scores on a mathematical test, which would include arithmetic, geometry, algebra, trigonometry, calculus, and possibly other topics.

Similar conceptualizations can be developed for tests involving words. Spelling could be measured by a test constructed of 20 five-letter words or by a battery of tests on several classes of words. A word test of a different kind might ask for definitions, synonyms, or antonyms. A very general verbal test could be constructed out of problems involving spelling, definitions, synonyms, antonyms, analogies, and others.

It is now possible to propose a test at a more indefinite level than either mathematical or verbal—a test of symbolic behavior. The test would contain problems expressed in a variety of symbols, including numbers and words. There are many other areas in which conceptualizations can be developed around groups of measures. The concepts and groups are not formed according to well-defined rules, but according to consensus developed over some period of time among experts in those areas.

The grouping or classifying of measures described above is based on an examination of the subject's task. It is not the only way in which abstract dimensions are formulated. Psychologists also arrive at abstract dimensions from an analysis of the actual numerical scores subjects make, and the relations among sets of scores on different tests and inventories. These mathematical and statistical procedures are complicated and, although something more will be said about them later, it will be done in very general and elementary terms. These abstract dimensions derived from an analysis of scores do not always correspond to those derived from an examination of tasks. This failure in correspondence complicates the psychologist's use of abstract language.

Summarizing Measures for a Group

Since interest often focuses on the behavior of subjects in a group, it is desirable to have ways of describing and communicating information contained in a number of measures. One approach is to summarize the information by computing an average and an index of variablility for the set of measures.

An average is obtained by summing all the measures and dividing by the number of them. This average is sometimes called the arithmetic mean or simply the mean. Sometimes the middle score or median, a score with equal numbers of scores above and below it, is used in place of the mean. If there is no single score which qualifies as the median, a hypothetical value is determined by simple interpolation. Sometimes the mode, the score which occurs most often in the group, is used in place of the mean. It is easily determined by inspection, if there is one score which occurs more often than all others. If there is more than one score occurring with the largest frequency, the mode is not employed.

When measures obtained on a group of subjects differ somewhat, they are said to exhibit variability. That they do or do not vary is, of course, easily determined by inspection, but it is also possible to compute an index of variability. A simple numerical index is the range of the measures, the number of units encompassed by the lowest and highest values. The range is obtained by subtracting the lowest value from the highest and adding one unit to the difference. A more sophisticated index of variability is a value called the variance. It is computed in the following steps: the mean is obtained; each measure is transformed to a deviation from the mean by subtracting the mean from that measure; each deviation is squared; the squares of the deviations are summed; and the sum of the squares is divided by the number of measures. Another commonly used index of variability is the standard deviation, which is obtained by computing the square root of the variance.

Comparing Measures

A measure obtained on one person provides little or no useful information unless that measure can be compared with a standard. The magnitude of a single score depends so much on the test, its particular content, instructions, and so on, that it cannot be interpreted. One common standard for comparison is the group average. An individual's score can be compared with the group average by subtracting the average from his score, yielding a difference or deviation of positive, negative, or zero value. A positive deviation indicates that his score is above the group mean; a negative deviation, that it is below the mean. Sometimes the individual's deviation score is divided by the standard deviation, yielding a value called a standard score with the same sign as the deviation from which it is computed. A standard score indicates, in units of the standard deviation, how far a person's performance is above or below the group mean. Thus an individual may be one standard deviation above the mean, 2.5 standard deviations below the mean, or some other number of standard deviations from the mean in one direction or the other.

Another standard with which an individual's score is sometimes compared is a hypothetical mean obtained by deduction. A hypothetical mean can only be deduced for certain kinds of tests, one of which is the multiple-choice achievement test. Consider a test of twenty items in which each item has four answers, three incorrect and one correct. The subject's task is to choose the correct answer. There are many ways in which the subject can choose answers to all twenty items. To be exact, there are 4^{20} ways, the number of possible combinations of twenty answers with one for each item. It is not so difficult to deduce what different scores go with these combinations and how many ways each different score can be obtained. Nor is it difficult to compute the mean of all possible scores. This hypothetical mean is often called a chance score. For a test of 20 four-choice items, the hypothetical mean is five.

The hypothetical mean has been called a chance score because of its relation to results obtained by means of gambling devices. There have been many demonstrations in which a complete set of answers for a test has been chosen many times by means of a die, a roulette wheel, or a lottery. Each set of answers was scored. The average of the many scores approximated the hypothetical mean derived strictly by deduction.

A subject's score could be compared to the hypothetical mean or chance score. Thus a subject who scored fifteen points in a twenty-item four-choice test would be ten points above the hypothetical mean of five. A subject who scored four would be one point below it.

Chapter Summary

Psychological measurement is the assigning of numbers to behavior. In this process, observations are made and transformed into numbers. It is not difficult to invent new procedures for assigning numbers, but there is no gurantee that the provisional measures which result will be worth anything. Confirmation of their value requires certain kinds of empirical investigation which will be described in later chapters.

Current measurement practices can be placed in four categories: physical, counting, judging, and psychophysical. Behavior can be measured on physical dimensions, and the values obtained can be given a psychological interpretation. Counting is a large category which includes some of the best and most widely used standardized intelligence tests and personality inventories. In some situations the identification of actions to be counted is a problem. Judging yields numbers which are sometimes assigned to what is judged and sometimes to the judge himself. Judgments are distinguished as absolute and comparative. Important methods of obtaining judgments include the use of graphic rating scales, the ranking method, and the method of pair comparisons. Psychophysical measures combine physical measures of stimuli and judgments of those stimuli in the determination of perceptual accuracy and sensitivity. Accuracy is determined by the method of adjustment; sensitivity, absolute or differential, is determined by the method of limits.

Abstract concepts can be formulated for the content of tests and inventories. The scale of a test or inventory may be quite definite if the content is homogeneous, but it may be quite indefinite if the content is heterogeneous.

Individual scores have little meaning unless they are compared to some standard. The group average is frequently taken as a standard for comparison. In some tests, a so-called chance score can be used as a standard.

References

1. Aldrich, C. A., and M. A. Norval. "A Developmental Graph for the First Year of Life." *The Journal of Pediatrics,* 29 (1946), 304-308.
2. Anastasi, A., N. Cohen, and D. Spatz. "A Study of Fear and Anger in College Students Through the Controlled Diary Methods." *The Journal of Genetic Psychology,* 73 (1948), 243-249.
3. Bahrick, H. P., P. M. Fitts, and R. Schneider. "Reproduction of Simple Movements as a Function of Factors Influencing Proprioceptive Feedback." *The Journal of Experimental Psychology,* 49 (1955), 445-454.
4. Bell, R. Q. "Relations Between Behavior Manifestations in the Human Neonate." *Child Development,* 31 (1960), 463-477.
5. Cahill, H. E., and C. I. Hovland. "The Role of Memory in the Acquisition of Concepts." *The Journal of Experimental Psychology,* 59 (1960), 137-144.
6. Doll, E. A. *The Measurement of Social Competence.* Minneapolis: Educational Test Bureau, Educational Publishers, Inc., 1953.
7. Farina, A., D. Arenberg, and S. Guskin. "A Scale for Measuring Minimal Social Behavior." *The Journal of Consulting Psychology,* 21 (1957), 265-268.
8. Fleishman, E. A. "Dimensional Analysis of Psychomotor Abilities." *The Journal of Experimental Psychology,* 48 (1954), 437-454.
9. Franks, C. M., and W. C. R. Withers. "Photoelectric Recording of Eyelid Movements." *The American Journal of Psychology,* 68 (1955), 467-471.
10. Furneaux, W. D. "An Apparatus for Measuring Bodily Sway." *The American Journal of Psychology,* 64 (1951), 271-273.
11. Gerall, A. A., P. B. Samson, and S. D. S. Spragg. "An Electronic Apparatus for Studying Tracking Performance." *The American Journal of Psychology,* 68 (1955), 297-305.
12. Green, B. F., and L. K. Anderson. "The Tactual Identification of Shapes for Coding Switch Handles." *The Journal of Applied Psychology,* 39 (1955), 219-226.

13. Hartman, B. O., and P. M. Fitts. "Relation of Stimulus and Response Amplitude to Tracking Performance." *The Journal of Experimental Psychology,* 49 (1955), 82-92.
14. Heidbreder, E. "The Attainment of Concepts: I. Terminology and Methodology." *The Journal of General Psychology,* 35 (1946), 173-189.
15. ———. "The Attainment of Concepts: VI. Exploratory Experiments on Conceptualization at Perceptual Levels." *The Journal of Psychology,* 26 (1948), 193-216.
16. Jenkins, W. O. "The Tactual Discrimination of Shapes for Coding Aircraft-Type Controls" in *Psychological Research on Equipment Design,* Report No. 19, ed. P. M. Fitts. Washington, D. C.: Government Printing Office, 1947, pp. 199-205.
17. Lorr, M., J. P. O'Connor, and J. W. Stafford. "The Psychotic Reaction Profile." *The Journal of Clinical Psychology,* 16 (1960), 242-245.
18. Pierce, J. F., and G. R. Pascal. "A Flexible Reaction- and Interval-Timer." *The American Journal of Psychology,* 64 (1951), 591-596.
19. Rodger, R. S., and P. McEwen. "A New Device for the Study of Kinesthetic After-Effects." *The American Journal of Psychology,* 72 (1959), 290-291.
20. Slack, C. W. "Learning in Simple One-Dimensional Tracking." *The American Journal of Psychology,* 66 (1953), 33-44.
21. Smith, K. U., and R. Bloom. "The Electronic Handwriting Analyzer and Motion Study of Writing." *The Journal of Applied Psychology,* 40 (1956), 302-306.

PART 3

PREDICTION

6

Functions

QUANTITATIVE PSYCHOLOGY BEGINS WITH MEASURES OF BEHAVIOR and ends with functions incorporating them. In mathematics, a function is a specification of the relation between two sets of paired numbers. In psychology, it is that and more. It is, in addition, a major form of expression for psychological knowledge. Some of the ways in which functions can be written symbolically will be reviewed in this chapter. In succeeding chapters there will be described applications of functions in which the numbers are measures of behavior or values representing characteristics of the situation in which the behavior occurs.

Exact Prediction

To predict means to compute according to a rule. Two sets of numbers may be so related that it is possible to predict exactly one set from the other. The nature of exact prediction and the rules employed in it will be revealed in the examples which follow.

CONSTANT POSITIVE CHANGES

Given below are two sets of paired numbers. The two sets, labeled

		PAIRS			
	Y	9	3	7	5
SETS					
	X	4	1	3	2

X and Y, correspond to the two rows of the table. Each set contains four numbers. There are four pairs, corresponding to the four columns of the table. The order of the columns is arbitrary. Certain features of the table of numbers will be varied but the pairing is to be considered fixed.

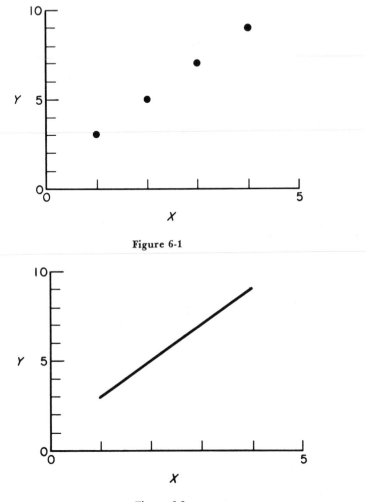

Figure 6-1

Figure 6-2

Consider the first pair, counting from the left. The numbers are 4 and 9. The latter can be computed by multiplying the former by 2 and adding 1 to the product. In each of the other three pairs, the Y value can be computed from the X value by the same rule: Multiply X by 2 and add 1. In symbols the rule is $Y = 2X + 1$. Computing Y from X according to a rule is predicting Y from X. Verify that the rule works for all pairs. Notice that the prediction is exact in each instance, that Y can be computed exactly from X by the rule given.

The numbers have been rearranged below, but the pairing has not been changed. After rearrangement the X values increase reading from

PAIRS

	Y	3	5	7	9
SETS					
	X	1	2	3	4

left to right. They will always be rearranged and ordered in this way. Values of Y will be rearranged to preserve the original pairing. The increase from one X value to the next, reading from left to right, is one unit. Thus the change in X is a constant.

Although the numbers have been rearranged only with reference to X, is there any discernible order in the new arrangement of Y values? Yes, they increase, reading from left to right. The amount of change from one Y value to the next is a constant of $+2$. Thus there are constant positive changes in Y.

The four pairs of numbers can be represented graphically, as shown in Figure 6-1. There is a point for each pair. The position of the point representing the pair, 4 and 9, is determined by locating 4 on the horizontal scale and drawing a vertical line through it, and by locating 9 on the vertical scale and drawing a horizontal line through it. The point is placed at the intersection of the two lines. The position of each of the other three points is determined by the same method. Determining the position of a point is called plotting the point. The four points of the graph lie in a straight line. If a straight line was drawn through the points, the graph would appear as shown in Figure 6.2.

Given below is another table containing two sets of paired numbers. There are five pairs. Consider the first: 5 and 17. The latter number can

Y	17	8	5	11	14
X	5	2	1	3	4

be computed by multiplying the former by 3 and adding 2. Each of the other Y values can also be computed from its corresponding X value by the same prediction rule: Multiply X by 3 and add 2. In symbols the rule is $Y = 3X + 2$. Verify that the rule applies to all pairs. The prediction is exact in each instance.

The numbers have been rearranged below, but the pairing has not been altered. The X values increase, reading from left to right. The amount

Y	5	8	11	14	17
X	1	2	3	4	5

of each change is a constant of $+1$. The Y values also increase, reading from left to right. The change is a constant of $+3$.

Four of the five pairs of numbers have been represented graphically in Figure 6-3. Identify the ones which have been plotted. A straight line can be drawn through the four points. The point not plotted would also

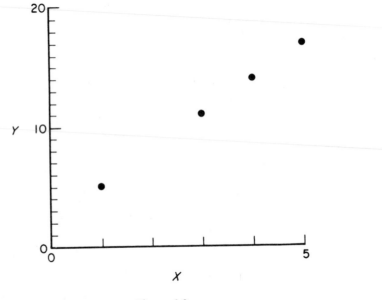

Figure 6-3

lie on this line. If X is assigned a value of 2.5, the Y value which must be paired with it is 9.5. A point representing this new pair would, if plotted, also lie on the line through the others. In fact, if any decimal or fracional value between 1 and 5 is assigned to X and the corresponding Y value is computed, the resulting pair of values will locate a point on the line.

Another table containing two sets of paired numbers is given below. There are five pairs. Consider the pair: 8 and 3. The latter can be com-

Y	3	0	2	1	4
X	8	2	6	4	10

puted by multiplying 8 by ½ and subtracting 1. The same computation holds for the other pairs: Divide X by 2 and subtract 1. In symbols the prediction rule is $Y = X/2 - 1$. Verify that the rule works.

The numbers have been rearranged in the next table but again the pairings have not been altered. Observe that X and Y both increase. The amount of change from one value of X to the next is a constant, $+2$; the

Y	0	1	2	3	4
X	2	4	6	8	10

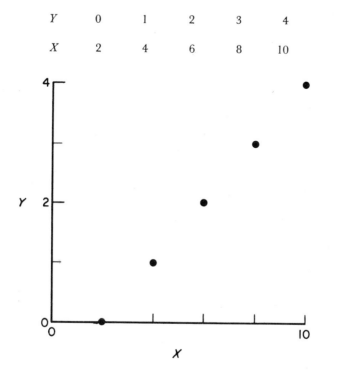

Figure 6-4

change from one value of Y to the next is a constant, $+1$. The five points, which are plotted in Figure 6-4, lie in a straight line. Any new value of X, between 2 and 10, and the corresponding predicted value of Y will be a pair whose point lies on the same straight line.

In all three of the examples given so far, changes in Y have been positive. It is also possible to have negative changes after the numbers have been rearranged.

CONSTANT NEGATIVE CHANGES

A relationship different from the previous ones will be found in the two sets of paired values given next. There are six pairs, all of which satisfy

Y	13	3	7	5	11	9
X	1	6	4	5	2	3

the prediction rule: Multiply X by 2 and subtract the product from 15. In symbols the rule is $Y = 15 - 2X$. Verify that the rule applies to all pairs exactly. The numbers have been rearranged below. Values of X

Y	13	11	9	7	5	3
X	1	2	3	4	5	6

increases from left to right. The amount of each change is a constant of $+1$. Values of Y decrease from left to right with each change equal to -2.

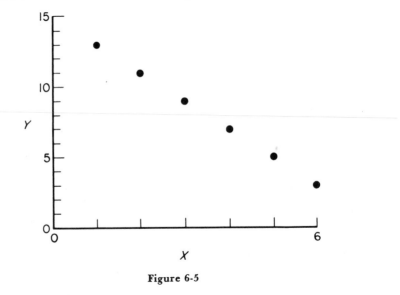

Figure 6-5

Thus changes in Y are constant and negative. The six points have been plotted in Figure 6-5. A straight line can be drawn through them.

Rate of Change

Any change in Y can be compared to the corresponding change in X by computing a ratio. Dividing the change in Y by the change in X gives the amount of change in Y per unit change in X. This quotient or ratio will be called the rate of change in Y with respect to X, or simply the rate of change.

Four examples have already been given. In the first, the change in X was a constant of $+1$; the change in Y, a constant of $+2$. Since both changes were constants, the ratio of any change in Y to the corresponding change in X is a constant of $\frac{2}{1}$ or 2.

In the second example, the change in X was a constant of $+1$; the change in Y, a constant of $+3$. Since both changes were constants, any ratio is a constant of $\frac{3}{1}$ or 3.

In the third example, both changes were constants: in X, $+2$; in Y, $+1$. The rate of change is a constant of $\frac{1}{2}$.

In the fourth example, both changes were again constants: in X, $+1$; in Y, -2. The rate of change is a constant of $-\frac{2}{1}$ or -2.

VARIABLE CHANGES

The relations illustrated by the previous examples involved constant positive or negative changes in Y. There are many possibilities for predictive relations in which changes in Y vary systematically.

Two sets of paired values are given below. There are six pairs. The

Y	7	2	1	11	4	16
X	4	2	1	5	3	6

rule for predicting Y from X will not be given in words but in symbols it is $Y = X^2/2 - X/2 + 1$. Verify that the rule applies to all pairs. The advantage of symbols over words should be apparent. Only a few simple symbols are required for expressing the prediction rule whereas many words would be required.

The numbers are rearranged below. Both X and Y increase. The

Y	1	2	4	7	11	16
X	1	2	3	4	5	6

change from one X value to the next is a constant of $+1$, but the change from one Y value to the next varies. The successive changes, obtained by subtracting a value of Y from the next on its right, are $+1$, $+2$, $+3$, $+4$, and $+5$. Notice that the changes in Y increase systematically. Since the changes in Y are not constant, rates of change vary, too. Dividing each change in Y by the corresponding change in X yields the rates: $\frac{1}{1}$, $\frac{2}{1}$, $\frac{3}{1}$, $\frac{4}{1}$, and $\frac{5}{1}$; or simply 1, 2, 3, 4, and 5.

The six points are plotted in Figure 6-6. A single straight line cannot be drawn through all of them simultaneously. A curved line, representing the locations of all points in this system, can, however, be drawn through them. The curve is drawn in Figure 6-7. Given any value of X between 1 and 6, and the corresponding predicted value of Y, the pair of values would determine the position of a point on this curved line.

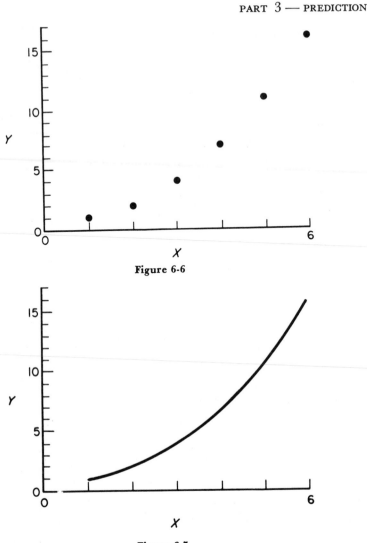

Figure 6-6

Figure 6-7

Another predictive relation in which changes in Y vary systematically is illustrated by the two sets of paired values which follow. There are six pairs. The rule for predicting Y from X will not be given in words. In symbols

Y	4	9	13	3	6	3
X	4	2	1	5	3	6

it is $Y = X^2/2 - 11X/2 + 18$. Verify that the rule applies to all six pairs. The numbers are rearranged in the next table. X increases; Y decreases

Y	13	9	6	4	3	3
X	1	2	3	4	5	6

in the first four changes but not in the fifth. The changes in X are a constant of $+1$. The changes in Y vary, being -4, -3, -2, -1, and 0. They are obtained by subtracting 13 from 9, 9 from 6, 6 from 4, 4 from 3, and 3 from 3. Since the changes in Y vary systematically, increasing from -4 to 0, and the changes in X are constant, the rates of change necessarily vary. The successive rates are $-\frac{4}{1}$, $-\frac{3}{1}$, $-\frac{2}{1}$, $-\frac{1}{1}$, and $\frac{0}{1}$; or -4, -3, -2, -1, and 0.

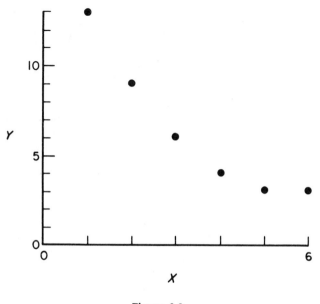

Figure 6-8

The six points are plotted in Figure 6-8. A straight line cannot be drawn through them. A curved line which would fit the points and indicate the position of all points in the system is drawn in Figure 6-9.

A different relation obtains for the two sets of paired values displayed and rearranged in the next two tables. The prediction rule is $Y = -X^2/2 + 11X/2 - 4$. Verify its appropriateness. Observe that, while X increases, Y increases and then decreases. Changes in X are constants of $+1$ whereas changes in Y vary. They are 4, 3, 2, 1, 0, and -1, decreasing from 4 to -1.

Y	11	1	10	5	8	10	11
X	5	1	4	2	3	7	6

Y	1	5	8	10	11	11	10
X	1	2	3	4	5	6	7

The rates of change also vary, being $\frac{4}{1}$, $\frac{3}{1}$, $\frac{2}{1}$, $\frac{1}{1}$, $\frac{0}{1}$, and $-\frac{1}{1}$; or 4, 3, 2, 1, 0, and -1.

The seven points are plotted in Figure 6-10. A straight line cannot

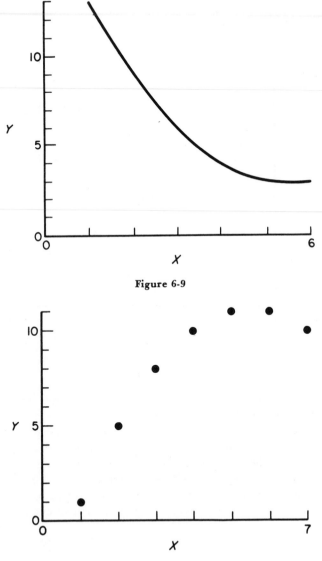

Figure 6-9

Figure 6-10

be drawn through all of them. A curved line which would fit every point
in the system is drawn in Figure 6-11.

For the two sets of paired values displayed and rearranged in the
next two tables, the prediction rule is $Y = X^2/2 - 7X/2 + 9$. Verify it.

As X increases, Y decreases, then increases. Changes in X are a con-

Y	3	4	3	4	6	6
X	3	5	4	2	1	6

Y	6	4	3	3	4	6
X	1	2	3	4	5	6

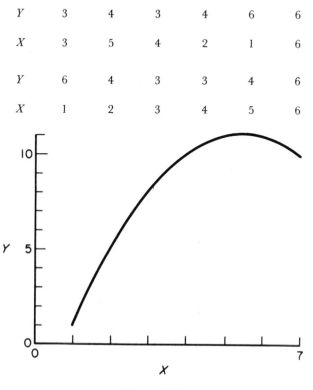

Figure 6-11

stant value of $+1$. Changes in Y, which are -2, -1, 0, $+1$, and $+2$,
increase systematically from -2 to $+2$. Since changes in X are constant
and corresponding changes in Y vary, rates of change vary. They are
$-\frac{2}{1}$, $-\frac{1}{1}$, $\frac{0}{1}$, $\frac{1}{1}$, and $\frac{2}{1}$; or -2, -1, 0, 1, and 2.

The six points are plotted in Figure 6-12. A straight line cannot be
drawn through them. A curve showing the position of all points in the
system is drawn in Figure 6-13.

In the next example, the arbitrary arrangement has been omitted
and only the ordered rearrangement is presented. The prediction rule is
$Y = 2^{-X}$. (The student may not recall that a negative exponent in the
numerator can be changed to positive by moving the factor to the denom-
inator.) When X is 2, Y is equal to 2^{-2} or $1/2^2$ or $\frac{1}{4}$. Verify the appropriate-

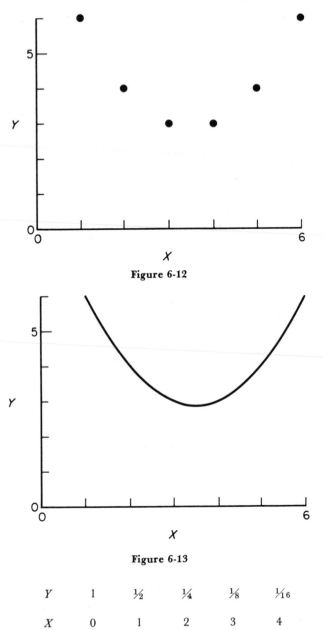

Figure 6-12

Figure 6-13

Y	1	½	¼	⅛	¹⁄₁₆
X	0	1	2	3	4

ness of the rule for the other pairs. Observe that Y decreases as X increases. In X, the change is constant; in Y, it varies. Successive changes in Y are $-\frac{1}{2}$, $-\frac{1}{4}$, $-\frac{1}{8}$, and $-\frac{1}{16}$. Since the changes increase, the rates of change also increase. The rates are $-\frac{1}{2}$, $-\frac{1}{4}$, $-\frac{1}{8}$, and $-\frac{1}{16}$. Notice that each

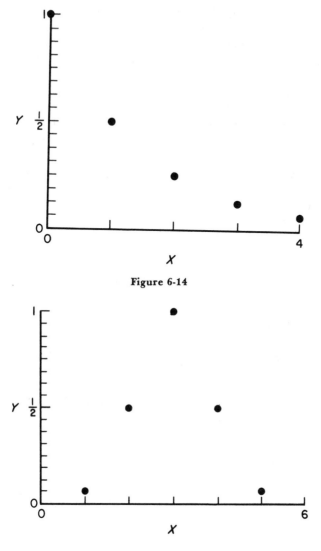

Figure 6-14

Figure 6-15

Y value is one half the preceding one. This implies that although Y decreases, it would never reach zero, no matter how far the series was extended. The points are plotted in Figure 6-14.

Another ordered rearrangement is given in the following table. The

Y	⅟₁₆	½	1	½	⅟₁₆
X	1	2	3	4	5

prediction rule is $Y = 2^{-(X-3)^2}$. When X is 4, Y is equal to $2^{-(4-3)^2}$ or 2^{-1} or $\frac{1}{2}$. Verify the appropriateness of the rule for the other pairs.

As X increases, Y increases, then decreases. The change in X is constant; the change in Y varies. Successive changes in Y are $\frac{7}{16}$, $\frac{8}{16}$, $-\frac{8}{16}$, and $-\frac{7}{16}$. The changes increase, decrease, and increase. The rates of change vary, being $\frac{7}{16}$, $\frac{8}{16}$, $-\frac{8}{16}$, and $-\frac{7}{16}$. The points are plotted in Figure 6-15.

In the first four examples, where the rate of change was constant, a straight line could be drawn through the points. A function of this type is said to be linear. In the next six examples, where the rate of change varied, an appropriate curved line could be drawn through the points. A function of this type is said to be nonlinear or curvilinear.

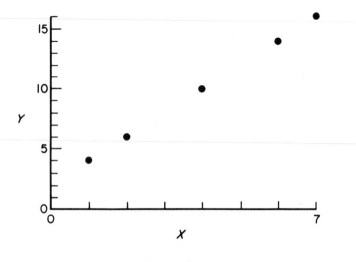

Figure 6-16

Unequal Changes in X

It is possible to have unequal changes in the succession of ordered X values and still have exact prediction. Consider the following sets of numbers. The prediction rule is $Y = 2X + 2$. The graph is given in Figure

Y	4	6	10	14	16
X	1	2	4	6	7

6-16. Notice that the points lie in a straight line. Successive changes in X are 1, 2, 2, and 1; corresponding changes in Y are 2, 4, 4, and 2. Rates of change are $\frac{2}{1}$, $\frac{4}{2}$, $\frac{4}{2}$, and $\frac{2}{1}$; or 2, 2, 2, and 2. It is evident that the rate is constant and the function is linear.

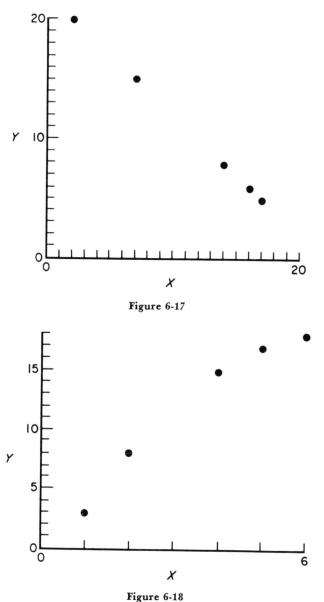

Figure 6-17

Figure 6-18

The two sets given next have unequal changes in X and negative changes in Y. The prediction rule is $Y = 22 - X$. The points are plotted in Figure 6-17. Successive changes in X are 5, 7, 2, and 1; corresponding changes in Y are -5, -7, -2, and -1. Rates of change are $-\frac{5}{5}$, $-\frac{7}{7}$, $-\frac{2}{2}$, and $-\frac{1}{1}$. Thus the rate is a constant of -1, and the function is linear.

Y	20	15	8	6	5
X	2	7	14	16	17

The next example has a gap in the successive of X values and represents a nonlinear relation. The prediction rule is $Y = -X^2/2 + 13X/2 - 3$. The plot is in Figure 6-18. A value of 3 for X does not appear in the table. If it did, the corresponding value of Y would be 12, and the point would lie on a curve passing through the five given points.

Y	3	8	15	17	18
X	1	2	4	5	6

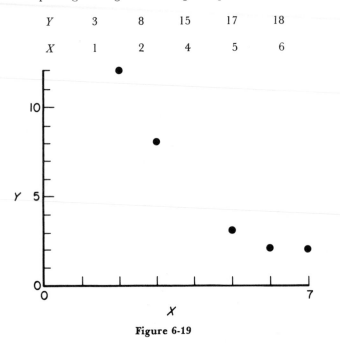

Figure 6-19

There is again a gap in X in the next example. The prediction rule is $Y = X^2/2 - 13X/2 + 23$. The plot is in Figure 6-19. A curve could be

Y	12	8	3	2	2
X	2	3	5	6	7

drawn through the points given and any other points for pairs of values satisfying the equality in the rule.

Approximate Prediction

In actual practice, psychological data seldom display the regularities possessed by the sets of paired values in the previous examples, where Y

values could be computed exactly from X values by applying an appropriate rule. Although irregularities in real data make exact prediction impossible, approximate prediction is often possible and worthwhile. When irregularities occur, a rule cannot be formulated for the exact computation of Y from X. Any single rule applied to all pairs will yield values of Y different from those given. The solution is to formulate a rule which gives the best approximation. Although . there are no absolute standards for deciding what is best, there are some conventional practices.

If there are irregularities in the numbers, the plotted points will be scattered so that a straight line or a simple curved line cannot be drawn through them. When a rule for approximate prediction has been formulated, it can be represented by a straight or curved line which is said to be a line of best fit for the plot of points. If the points lie in a cluster along and near the line, the configuration is said to display a trend, and the approximation is considered satisfactory. There is, of course, no guarantee that a configuration of points representing real data will display a trend; that is, there is no guarantee that the line of best fit will be a good or satisfactory fit. Real psychological data may display no trend and even approximate prediction of any value may not be possible.

A POSITIVE LINEAR TREND

The next table shows two sets of numbers which display a definite positive linear trend. Y increases as X increases. Changes in X are constant.

Y	5	7	11	15	16	20
X	1	2	3	4	5	6

Changes in Y are 2, 4, 4, 1, and 4—positive but not constant values. They vary unsystematically. The prediction rule, $Y = 3X + 2$, does not permit exact prediction. Y values computed by the rule are 5, 8, 11, 14, 17, and 20. It is conventional to compute errors in prediction by subtracting the predicted values from the actual values. Errors for the predicted values 8, 14, and 17 are -1, $+1$, and -1, respectively. Errors for the other values are zero. The six points are plotted in Figure 6-20.

A straight line cannot be drawn through all points but can be drawn near them. The line for the prediction rule, $Y = 3X + 2$, would pass through the first, third, and sixth points, and near the second, fourth, and fifth. Other straight lines could be drawn to fit the configuration in other ways. A curved line could, of course, be drawn through all of the points, but it would not be a simple curve and its rule would be quite complicated. Since a straight line can be drawn to fit fairly well, the relation would be considered to be approximately linear.

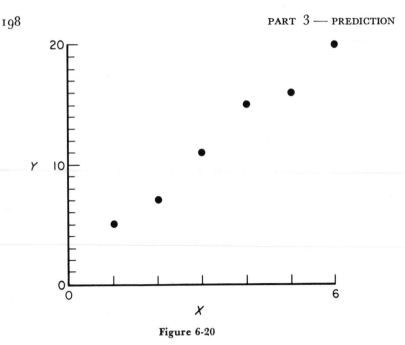

Figure 6-20

A NEGATIVE LINEAR TREND

In the next example, X increases and Y decreases. Changes in X are constant. Changes in Y are -3, -3, -1, -3, and -1—all negative but not constant values. The linear rule, $Y = 15 - 2X$, yields predicted values of 13, 11, 9, 7, 5, and 3. The first, third, and fifth predicted vaues

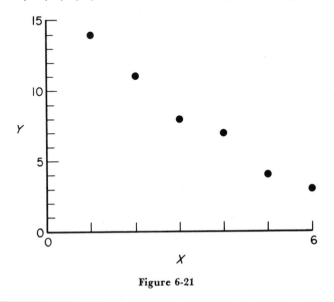

Figure 6-21

Y	14	11	8	7	4	3
X	1	2	3	4	5	6

have errors of $+1$, -1, and -1, respectively. The graph is in Figure 6-21. Although a complicated nonlinear rule could be devised to predict perfectly and to yield a curve which would fit the six points exactly, it would be much easier to use a linear rule as an approximation, and in actual practice that is what would very likely be done. Although a straight line cannot be drawn through all the points, it can be drawn very close to them. The line for the rule already mentioned would pass through the second, fourth, and sixth points, but would miss the others by small distances. Other straight lines could be drawn to give a very good fit.

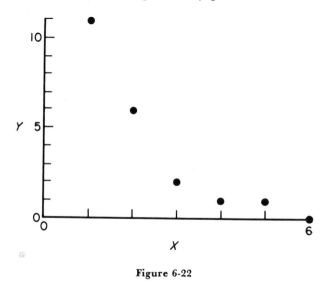

Figure 6-22

NONLINEAR TRENDS

In the next example, X increases and Y decreases. Changes in X are constant. Changes in Y, which are -5, -4, -1, 0, and -1, vary, increasing

Y	11	6	2	1	1	0
X	1	2	3	4	5	6

irregularly with one exception. The prediction rule, $Y = X^2/2 - 11X/2 + 15$, yields values of 10, 6, 3, 1, 0, and 0 for Y. Errors for the first, third, and fifth predicted values are $+1$, -1, and $+1$, respectively. Errors for the others are zero. Figure 6-22 is a graph of the six points.

The curved line for the rule already mentioned would pass through the second, fourth, and sixth points, but would miss the others. Other rules could be formulated for curved lines which would fit satisfactorily. A straight line representing a linear rule would yield a very poor fit to the configuration of points.

The two sets of numbers which follow also display a nonlinear trend. As X increases, Y increases, then stops. Changes in X are constant. Changes in Y are 3, 3, 2, 2, and 0. One could say that changes in Y decrease generally but not without exceptions. The prediction rule, $Y = -X^2/2 + 11X/2 - 4$, yields values of 1, 5, 8, 10, 11, and 11. The first, fifth, and

| Y | 1 | 4 | 7 | 9 | 11 | 11 |
| X | 1 | 2 | 3 | 4 | 5 | 6 |

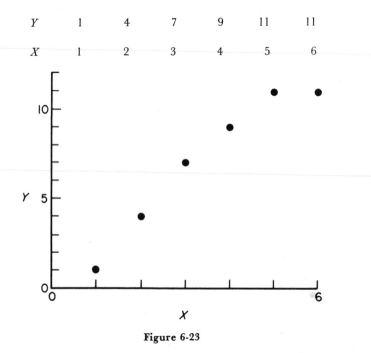

Figure 6-23

sixth are not in error. The error for each of the others is -1. Figure 6-23 is a graph of the six points. The curve for the rule used would pass through the first, fifth, and sixth, but would miss the others by small distances. Other nonlinear rules could be formulated which would give a good fit. Although a straight line would give a crude fit, a linear function would not likely be considered appropriate.

Statistical Curve-Fitting

In advanced work in psychology, formulating a rule for computing Y from X, approximately, and choosing the best-fitting line, straight or curved, are accomplished by statistical procedures; that is, the conventional standard employed for selecting a prediction rule is mathematical. The topic of curve-fitting can, of course, be treated only briefly and in a very elementary fashion in an introductory text. At least a general impression of the nature of the topic is necessary, however, if one is to achieve an understanding of the nature of much psychological knowledge.

When data are judged to display a linear trend, the statistical procedure involves, in part, computing a coefficient of correlation. The coefficient is a number indicating the degree of accuracy or the lack of error in predicting by a linear rule. The coefficient can take any value from -1.00 to $+1.00$. When changes in Y are positive, or generally so, it is positive. When changes in Y are negative, it is negative. When positive changes in Y are exactly constant, the coefficient is $+1.00$, the predictions are without error, and all the points lie in a straight line. When negative changes in Y are exactly constant, the coefficient is -1.00, the predictions are without error, and all the points lie in a straight line. The poorer the approximation in the prediction, the nearer the coefficient is to zero. When the coefficient is zero, using the prediction equation is equivalent to predicting the mean of the Y values no matter what value of X is under consideration.

COMPUTATION OF A CORRELATION COEFFICIENT

The numbers in the first table below do not permit exact prediction but they do display a definite positive trend; that is, as X increases, Y also increases without exception. Steps in one method of computing a correlation coefficient will be given.

Y	1	2	4	6	7
X	1	2	3	4	5
Y deviations	—3	—2	0	2	3
X deviations	—2	—1	0	1	2

The mean of each set of numbers is computed. The mean of Y is 2% or 4; the mean of X is 1% or 3. In each set the numbers are converted to deviations from the mean by subtracting the mean from each of them. The deviations, which are shown in the second table, are employed in the three computations:

1. The product of the two deviations in each pair and the sum of the five products.

$$(-2)(-3) + (-1)(-2) + (0)(0) + 1(2) + 2(3) = 16$$

2. The square of each Y deviation and the sum of the five squares.
$$(-3)^2 + (-2)^2 + 0^2 + 2^2 + 3^2 = 26$$
3. The square of each X deviation and the sum of the five squares.
$$(-2)^2 + (-1)^2 + 0^2 + 1^2 + 2^2 = 10$$

Finally, the sum of products, 16, is divided by the square root of the product of the two sums of squares, 26 and 10. The result is the correlation coefficient. The computation is
$$16/\sqrt{(26)(10)} = 16/\sqrt{260} = 0.99.$$
The correlation between the two sets of numbers in the example is very high but not 1.00.

The Prediction Rule

The general linear prediction rule can be expressed in literal symbols as
$$Y = bX + a.$$
In general the value of b is obtained by dividing the sum of products by the sum of squares for X. In the example, b is equal to $16/10$ or 1.6. The value of a is obtained by multiplying the mean of X by b and subtracting the product from the mean of Y. Therefore, a is equal to $4 - (1.6)(3)$ or -0.8. The prediction rule can then be written as
$$Y = 1.6X - 0.8.$$
The predicted Y values are 0.8, 2.4, 4.0, 5.6, and 7.2, all but one of which are in error.

When data are judged to display a nonlinear trend, formulating a rule for predicting Y from X, approximately, and choosing the best-fitting curved line are accomplished by complex statistical procedures which will not be described here.

Psychological Prediction

Prediction in psychology involves two sets of paired values. Frequently, but not always, both sets are measures of behavior. For example, X may be a set of scores on a vocabulary test and Y may be a set of scores on a test in general psychology. When both sets of measures are obtained on the same subjects, the necessary pairing is achieved by having two measures on each subject. Thus there are as many pairs of values as there are subjects. Predicting has been defined as computing a Y value from a given X value according to a rule. A score for any subject on the general psychology test could be predicted or computed from his score on the vocabulary test after the rule had been formulated. Because of the irregularities in real psychological data, the rule usually yields only approximate prediction.

The commonly used rules in psychological prediction are those for linear functions. Consequently, the accuracy of predictions is frequently expressed in terms of a correlation coefficient. There are occasions, of course, when it is obviously necessary to use a nonlinear rule, regardless of its complexity and the inconvenience of doing so. A large part of the work in psychology can, however, be handled satisfactorily by means of simple linear approximations and correlation coefficients.

OTHER COMPLICATIONS IN APPROXIMATE PREDICTION

Repeated Xs, Varied Ys

A common feature of real data is the repetition of a particular value of X with varied values of Y, as illustrated in the next table. There are two values of X equal to 2. One is paired with a value of Y equal to 5; the other,

Y	5	5	7	6	7	8	8	9	8	10	11
X	1	2	2	3	3	3	4	4	5	5	6

with 7. There are three values of X equal to 3. One is paired with 6; one, with 7; and one, with 8. There are two values of X equal to 4. One is paired with 8; one, with 9. There are two values of X equal to 5. One is paired with 8; the other, with 10.

It should be obvious that errors of prediction cannot be avoided when a given value of X is paired with two or more different values of Y. If one of the Y values is predicted exactly, the others will necessarily be missed. Of course, all of them could be missed.

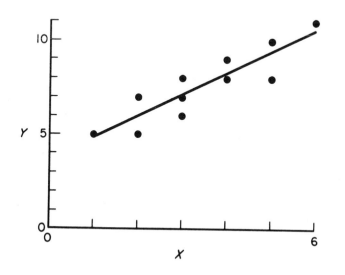

Figure 6-24

The eleven points are plotted in Figure 6-24. The correlation coefficient is 0.90; the prediction rule is $Y = 1.14X + 3.74$. The computation of these values will not be shown. The best fitting straight line, which represents the prediction rule, is also drawn in Figure 6-24.

Repeated Pairs

When there are two or more identical pairs of numbers, representing each pair by a point in the graph is not satisfactory because points will be superimposed on one another and will not be distinguishable. A better procedure is to plot a number, the frequency of identical pairs, instead of a point. Examine the table below for identical pairs. The plot is shown in

Y	3	3	3	4	5	5	6	6	7	7
X	1	2	2	2	3	3	4	4	4	5

Figure 6-25. The two identical pairs—2, 3 and 2, 3—are represented by a frequency of 2 in Figure 6-25. The two identical pairs—3, 5 and 3, 5— and two others—4, 6 and 4, 6—were plotted in the same way. The correlation coefficient is 0.95; the prediction rule is $Y = 1.21X + 1.27$. The computation will not be shown here. The line of best fit is also drawn in Figure 6-25.

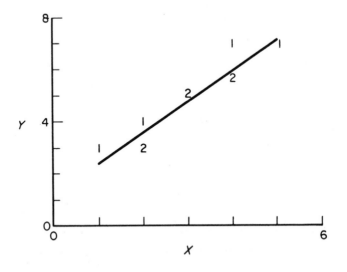

Figure 6-25

Chapter Summary

The relation between two sets of paired values, X and Y, can be given expression even when it is not possible to formulate a rule for predicting Y from X exactly. Despite the irregularities often found in real psychological data, prediction rules can be formulated by means of statistical procedures. In psychology, the most widely used prediction rules are those which allow for approximate linear prediction. Occasionally, however, there is need for an approximate prediction rule which takes account of nonlinearity.

In psychology paired measures are obtained as data in many different kinds of investigations. The most frequent application of correlation methods and prediction rules occurs when there is a pair of measures for each one of a number of subjects. The two numbers in each pair may both be measures of behavior, but that is not always the case. One set of numbers may be measures of a biological, biographical, or environmental characteristic of the individuals. In the chapters which follow, correlation coefficients will be employed frequently to express psychological information, but even where they are not explicitly stated, the concepts of prediction and correlation can be applied and, if they are, will be accompanied by a deeper understanding and appreciation of the information. Evidence of predictive relations among sets of observations is a very important kind of knowledge in many fields of study and in many applied areas. It is so in psychology. The function concept and its use in prediction constitute a powerful approach to the comprehension of natural phenomena, including those having to do with human behavior.

7

Distribution

and Reliability

A PROVISIONAL METHOD OF MEASUREMENT, IN PSYCHOLOGY, IS A new and untried procedure for assigning numbers to behavior. The method's ultimate value depends on the extent to which the measures it yields satisfy three criteria: distribution, reliability, and validity. Evaluating a method in terms of these criteria is facilitated very much by the use of functions.

In quantitative psychology, the variability in measures is knowledge or, at least, potential knowledge. Although the differences which appear in data are often irregular and difficult to interpret, data without differences would be of little value. The presence of variability offers the possibility of making useful distinctions.

Distribution, as a criterion for evaluating measurement, refers to the occurrence of some number of different values in a set of measures. One situation in which distribution is a matter of interest is the measuring of a group of subjects to find out about differences among them. There is no law which says that any set of measures will necessarily display variability, but its occurrence is a common event. It is rare that measurement of a group of people does not yield different values for the individuals in the group. Another situation in which distribution is of interest is the measuring of a single person repeatedly. Repetition of measurement may yield variable results.

The Frequency Distribution

Given a set of measures, a simple way of displaying or communicating the nature of its distribution is to arrange them in a tabular form called a frequency distribution. A frequency distribution is a function relating frequency and the magnitude of some scale. The distribution shows each different measurement value and the number of times it occurs. A frequency distribution for the scores of 100 subjects on a short algebra test is shown below.

Score	Frequency
20	0
19	1
18	6
17	11
16	15
15	26
14	14
13	14
12	9
11	4
10	0

A frequency distribution can be represented graphically by a histogram, a graph in the form of a step function. Figure 7-1 is a histogram for the algebra scores.

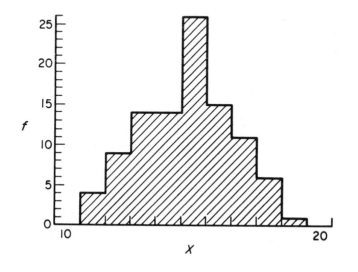

Figure 7-1. A histogram for the frequency distribution of 100 algebra scores.

A frequency distribution can be described in terms of its location, dispersion, and shape. Location refers to the position of the distribution on the scale of measures. One way of giving its location is to compute the mean. If the mean is high, the distribution is located high on the scale; if it is low, the distribution is low on the scale. Dispersion refers to the spread of the measures along the scale. One distribution may be broad; another may be narrow. One way of gauging dispersion is to determine the range, the number of intervals on the scale encompassed by the distribution. Another way is to compute either the variance or the standard deviation.

Shape has to do with two highly abstract characteristics: skewness and kurtosis. Skewness refers to lack of symmetry. In a symmetrical histogram, for every point to the right of its midpoint on the horizontal scale there is a corresponding point to the left. It is also true that the midpoint coincides with the mean. If there is not this point-by-point correspondence around the mean, the distribution is asymmetrical or skewed. Asymmetrical distributions are characterized as positively or negatively skewed. Positive skewness obtains when many scores are concentrated at the low end of the scale and few are spread out toward the high end. Negative skewness has the heavy concentration at the high end with relatively few scores spread out toward the low end. It is easy to detect symmetry or the lack of it by inspection of a histogram, but it is not always easy to distinguish between positive and negative skewness. There is a statistical index of skewness which takes either a positive or a negative value and which can be used to distinguish between positive and negative skewness.

The other characteristic of shape is kurtosis, the concentration of scores in the middle relative to the concentrations at both ends. One extreme possibility is no scores in the middle and half of them concentrated at each end. Another extreme possibility is a very large concentration in the middle with a very small number of values at each end. In actual practice one seldom encounters such extreme degrees of kurtosis. Typically, one finds distributions which are flat—their scores spread out unevenly over a large part of the scale; or one finds those which are peaked—their scores piled up near the middle. There is a statistical index for kurtosis. It is low for flat distributions and high for peaked ones. Judging kurtosis from an inspection of the histogram is often difficult.

There was a time when it was thought that the form of a frequency distribution was a feature of behavior having very great generality—a kind of absolute. The particular form which received most of the attention was that of a function called a normal probability function or a normal curve. Its equation is

$$p = \left(\frac{1}{\sqrt{2\pi}} \right) e^{-Z^2/2}$$

It is a symmetrical curve with a degree of kurtosis between flat and peaked. In other words, a normal distribution has many values in the middle and few at the extremes, with as many at one extreme as at the other (see Figure 7-2). If an attribute of behavior is said to be normally distributed, the implication is that a frequency distribution of measures of that attribute is well-fitted by a normal curve.

It is now known and widely accepted that normal distribution is not a natural law of behavior. The form of a distribution of measures is related to many features of the entire measurement procedure. It is quite possible that a given measure will be normally distributed for a certain

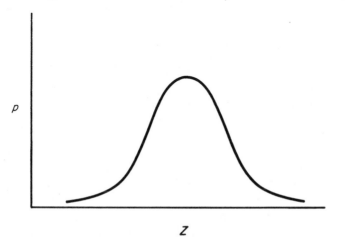

Figure 7-2. A normal probability function or a normal curve.

group of subjects, certain specific procedures, and certain specific circumstances. Change any one of these features, however, and the form of the distribution may change. If a test of language usage is administered with a time limit of one hour, to high school students in their first year, the distribution of scores will have a certain location and dispersion. It could also have the shape of a normal curve. If the same test is administered with a thirty-minute time limit, to applicants for admission to college in the spring of the year in which they wish to enter, the resulting distribution of scores may very well have a different location, dispersion, and shape. Used as a college admissions test, it may have a higher location, a more narrow dispersion, and a greater concentration of high scores, features which indicate a better performance, a more homogeneous group, and a predominance of high scores in the group. Thus normal distribution may be a specific fact but it is not a general law.

Recognition that distribution is relative turned out to have considerable importance. It was realized that the form of a distribution might be modifiable by judicious choice of testing circumstances, materials, instructions, and scoring systems. Thus, to some extent, the form of a distribution can be manipulated or determined to suit the psychologist's purposes.

Distributions of test and inventory scores are often manipulated for normative purposes. There is a procedure by means of which test scores in a distribution of some nondescript form can be transformed to scores which are normally distributed. The value in doing so is that the position of an individual in the distribution is immediately known from his transformed score. Each score in the normalized distribution is known to exceed a certain percentage of ,all scores and to be exceeded by a certain percentage. Thus a student may have a normalized score of sixty on a certain scale. Anyone familiar with that scale will know that the average is fifty and that the score of sixty, in addition to being above the average, exceeds the scores of approximately eighty-four per cent of persons who have taken the test and is exceeded by the scores of sixteen per cent. In this connection, the percentage exceeded (eighty-four) is said to be the individual's percentile rank. Normalized distributions are of great value in educational and vocational counseling, and in industrial selection and placement.

If measures are distributed over a number of intervals of a scale with a concentration at or near one of the limits, a skewed distribution is obtained. Characteristic of this kind of situation is one in which the measure for each person is number of accidents. The lower limit is obviously zero since the number can not be less than zero. A concentration on and near this value was found by Brown and Berdie[2], who reported frequency distributions for driving violations and accidents among college freshmen. Subjects were 993 residents of Minnesota registered as freshmen in the General College of the University of Minnesota. The average age of the group was about nineteen. The names of entering students were obtained and checked in the records of the Minnesota State Highway Department. From the drivers' folders, information was obtained regarding violations and accidents. Figure 7-3 is a histogram showning violations; Figure 7-4, accidents. Both histograms are quite asymmetrical, being positively skewed. Many students had no violations or accidents; few had a large number.

That circumstances in which observations are made may be related to the form of distribution obtained is shown by the results of a study by Allport[1], reported in 1932. Observations were made of the behavior of motorists at different street corners.

One set of observations was made in Syracuse, New York, on 208 motorists. They were observed at a corner where there was cross traffic but no traffic signal. At the corner were buildings obscuring the motorist's view from all directions. Other cars were crossing the corner or approach-

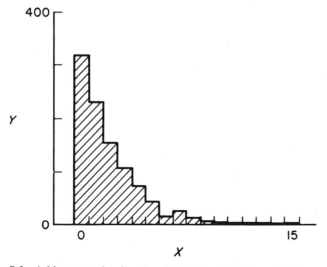

Figure 7-3. A histogram showing the distribution of driving violations among 993 college freshmen. X is the number of violations. Y is frequency. [After Brown and Berdie.[2]]

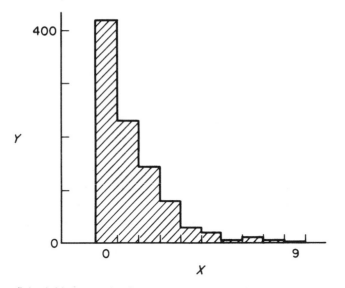

Figure 7-4. A histogram showing the distribution of driving accidents among 993 college freshmen. X is the number of accidents. Y is frequency. [After Brown and Berdie.[2]]

ing the corner from other directions at about the same time as the subject. As each subject crossed the corner, an observer classified his behavior in one of four categories: coming to a stop; crossing at very slow speed; crossing at a slightly slower speed; and crossing with no apparent reduction of speed. Figure 7-5 is a histogram for the distribution of the 208

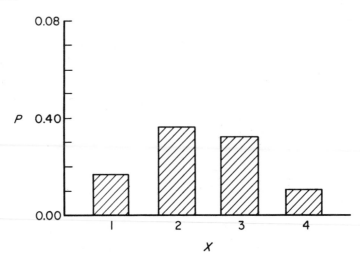

Figure 7-5. Relative frequency distribution of motorists according to their behavior at an intersection with cross traffic. X is a ranking of the categories employed in order of increasing disregard of the traffic. (1, stop; 2, very slow; 3, slight reduction of speed; 4, no reduction of speed.) P is relative frequency. [After Allport[1]]

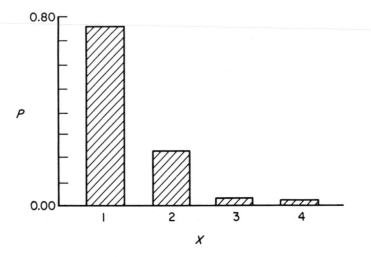

Figure 7-6. Relative frequency distribution of motorists according to their behavior at an intersection with boulevard stop signs. X is a ranking of the categories employed in order of increasing disregard of the signs. (1, stop; 2, very slow; 3, slight reduction of speed; 4, no reduction of speed.) P is relative frequency. [After Allport[1]]

observations. Another set of observations was made in Syracuse and Los Angeles on 2,114 motorists. They were observed at corners where there were both cross traffic and boulevard stop signs. Behavior was classified in the same four categories described above. Figure 7-6 shows the distribution of the 2,114 responses over the four categories. The two distributions are quite different. Allport suggested that the first was similar to a normal curve, being symmetrical with concentration in the middle. He called the second a reverse-*J* distribution.

That a characteristic of social behavior might be revealed by the form of a frequency distribution was shown by an investigation of conformity by Chin[3]. The arrival of undergraduate students for a morning class at Columbia University was observed. The hypothesis was that times of arrival would be distributed so as to reveal conformity, defined in terms of skewness and kurtosis.

The class of eighty-eight students met three times a week at nine in the morning in a large amphitheatre. Two observers sat in the back of the room. One gave the names of the students as they entered; the

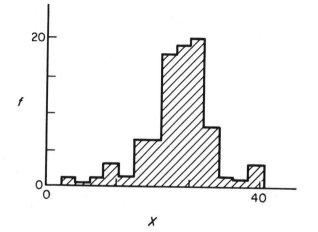

Figure 7-7. The distribution of times of arrival at class. *X* is time in minutes after 8:30 A.M.; *f* is frequency. [After Chin.[3]]

other recorded the names and also times, by drawing a line, every thirty seconds, under the last name listed. Observing began at 8:30 a.m. at each of fourteen meetings of the class.

Figure 7-7 is a frequency distribution of the average time of arrival for the eighty-eight students. Indexes of skewness and kurtosis were computed. They indicated that the distribution was negatively skewed and peaked. The interpretation of the investigator was that skewness indicated the presence of prohibitive pressures—the forbidding of late behavior—and that peakedness indicated prescriptive conformity to a social norm in the massing of behavior around the central point.

A frequency distribution can also be employed to represent the variation in measures obtained on a single subject. Certain kinds of measures such as reflex latencies, reaction times, and perceptual thresholds may be obtained repeatedly for the same subject. One reason for doing so is that when behavior of a subject is variable from one occasion to another, an average of a number of determinations may be considered a better representation of his behavior than any one value. An example of this usage of a frequency distribution is contained in an investigation of pain thresholds by Hardy, Wolff, and Goodell[6]. They employed a dolorimeter, a device for administering a pain stimulus, in obtaining judgments of pain. An exposure unit incorporated an electronically controlled shutter, a special lens, and a powerful projection lamp. A control unit incorporated a timer for starting the exposure and the means of adjusting intensity.

The skin surface which was to be stimulated was blackened with India ink. By that procedure a high degree of absorption of the radiation was insured regardless of the natural pigmentation of the skin. The blackening also prevented penetration of the radiation below the skin surface. By means of the lens, the light from the projection lamp was focused on the subject's blackened forehead. The shutter, which was interposed between the lamp and the lens, gave a brief, constant exposure time.

The nature of the judgment which the subject was required to make was carefully defined since the radiation had been found to evoke sensations of warmth and heat before pricking pain. The sensation of pricking pain was described as a distinct, sharp, very small stab of pain experienced at the end of the exposure to the light. The prick was preceded by warmth, heat, and burning which seemed to "swell" and then "draw together" into a prick at the end of the interval. The subject was told to focus attention on the barely perceptible prick. He was also told that the procedure was not a test of his ability to endure pain but a test of his ability to perceive and report the first trace of pain.

The initial exposures were for purposes of orientation. The first was a light radiating a low number of millicalories per second per square centimeter to which the subject was asked to report his sensations. He reported a mild sensation of warmth. The second exposure, at a high level, was focused on an adjacent spot. The subject reported a definite pricking pain. For the next exposure the intensity of the light was lowered to a level judged by the investigator to be below the pain threshold. If no pricking pain was reported, the intensity was increased for another stimulation. The procedure of increasing intensity by steps at intervals of 15 to 20 seconds was continued until the lowest setting at which the subject reported pricking pain was determined. The entire procedure was repeated until the investigator was sure that the subject understood it. A subject was considered trained when his estimates were consistent. Then a series of measurements was made without further instruction. Figure 7-8 represents a frequency distribution of thresholds for one trained subject. Notice the location, dispersion, and shape of the histogram. Thresholds varied, but the number at each extreme was not as large as the number near the middle.

Reliability

For a method of measurement to have value, distribution is a necessary but not sufficient condition. If a method is employed only once to obtain measures on a group of subjects, it is of relatively little interest to anyone. Its value begins to become apparent when it is applied a second time to the same subjects.

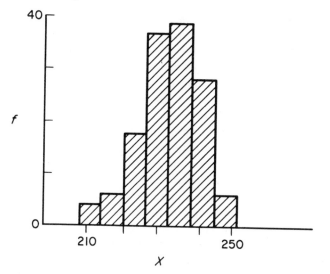

Figure 7-8. Frequency distribution of threshold measurements on one trained subject. X is millicalories per second per square centimeter; f is frequency. [After Hardy, Wolff, and Goodell.[6]]

If each individual in a group is measured twice on the same test and his obtained scores do not vary much, the measures are said to be reproducible; and if the scores vary from one individual to another on each occasion, the measures of the second occasion can be predicted from those of the first and the two sets will be positively correlated. Thus a positive correlation between two sets of scores on the same test is evidence of the reproducibility of individual scores and is said to indicate the reliability of the test for that group.

There is a difference between reproducibility and reliability which may not yet be apparent. A reliable test yields reproducible scores, but it does not follow that a test yielding reproducible scores will necessarily be reliable. If each subject gets approximately the same score on both occasions but scores on each occasion do not vary much between subjects, the scores are reproducible but the correlation is low. For a high correlation, differences among subjects must be relatively large. Thus the relative homogeneity or heterogeneity of the group is critical in determining the reliability of a test.

It follows that the reliability of a test is not a fixed attribute. It varies, depending on the group of subjects. A test may be unreliable for elementary school students, reliable for secondary school students, and unreliable for college students. If the test is too difficult for elementary school pupils, each child may be fairly consistent, but the scores of all children may be low and not different from one another. If the test is too easy for college students, each student may be consistent, but the scores of all students may be high and not different from one another. Secondary school students, however, may be consistent, and scores for different students may vary considerably. Thus reliability is the extent to which individuals in a group are consistently differentiated. For this reason, high reliability is interpreted as indicating large differences among subjects or large *individual differences*. High reliability is indicated by a correlation coefficient above 0.80; moderate reliability, by one between 0.60 and 0.80; and low reliability, by one below 0.60.

Psychology has been very successful in developing a great variety of measures which are reliable for specific groups and circumstances. Although there is no advance guarantee of success, it is now a fairly routine procedure for psychologists to devise a reliable method of measurement for a particular group and situation. The basic procedure in determining the reliability of a test is to administer it on two occasions to the same group of subjects. The index of reliability is the coefficient of correlation between the two sets of scores. There are situations, however, in which it does not make sense to administer the same test twice to the same subjects. If the first exposure to the test results in fairly permanent changes, such as knowing the answers to problems, then the second exposure cannot yield the same kind of assessment. This problem is solved by constructing two equivalent or parallel forms of a test. To determine reliability both forms are administered to a group. The correlation between the two forms is accepted as an index of reliability.

The Concepts of Ability and Attitude

The definition of a specific ability as the scale of scores on a particular test is correct as far as it goes, but it can be improved by adding a qualification. The definition does not convey all the meaning of ability as a *state of being able*, which suggests consistency or predictiveness of success. The definition can be improved by taking account of reliability. Predictiveness of success can be made explicit by saying that a specific ability is the scale of scores on a particular *reliable* test. The ability of an individual is his success on the test and the measure of his ability is his score. Success on a reliable ability test is inferred to be predictive of later success on that test.

The definition of attitude is also improved by denoting what is sometimes only connoted with respect to reliability. Definitions of attitude usually incorporate expressions such as "a tendency to respond," "a predisposition to react," "a readiness to react," "a determining tendency," "an enduring organization of processes," "a disposition to respond," and "a tendency to react consistently." Consistency or predictiveness is the common attribute in these expressions. It is made explicit, by reference to reliability, in the following improved definition: An attitude is an expression of some degree of favorableness or unfavorableness on a scale which has been demonstrated to yield reliable scores. Thus the subject's score is inferred to be predictive of a similar degree of favorableness or unfavorableness on another occasion.

Evidence of Reliability

Evidence of reliable and unreliable methods of measurement can be found in every category of measurement, under every theoretical topic, and in every area of psychological activity, whether in research or in everyday applications. As stated earlier, there is no advance guarantee that a given attempt to devise a reliable method will be successful but, in general, there has been considerable success. Since a comprehensive review of reliability would be appropriate in an advanced text in psychological measurement but inappropriate here, only a limited amount of evidence in the form of examples will be presented. It has been organized in two sections: findings from selected investigations of special-purpose measures; and results for some widely used standardized measures.

RELIABILITY OF SPECIAL-PURPOSE MEASURES

The evidence to be presented has to do with the reliability of body sway, olfactory thresholds, handwriting pressure, flying maneuvers, and interaction in a clinical interview.

Fisher, Birren, and Leggett[4] determined the reliability of measures of body sway, made by means of an instrument called an ataxiagraph. Figure 7-9 shows a subject, the ataxiagraph, and a kymograph, on which body sway was graphically recorded. Subjects were 133 enlisted personnel in the Navy.

The ataxiagraph recorded the anterior-posterior movements of a subject as he stood erect with his heels together and his feet spread in a *V* position. He wore a helmet from the top of which protruded a short rod. Fastened to the rod was a cord which ran over a pulley and trans-

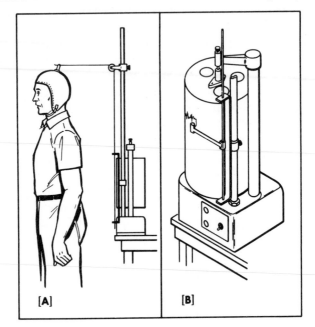

Figure 7-9. A: The ataxiagraph, a kymograph modified to record body sway in one plane. **B:** Detail of kymograph. [Adapted from Fisher, Birren, and Leggett.[4]]

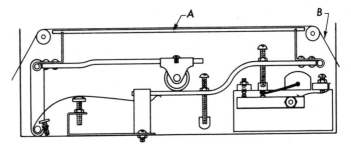

Figure 7-10. Apparatus for measuring pressure of handwriting. *A* is the pressure-sensitive writing surface; *B* is the paper on which writing was done. [Adapted from Wenger.[9]]

lated his movement into equivalent vertical movements of the pen on the kymograph. The test consisted of four two-minute trials, on which the subject's eyes were alternately open and closed. A brief rest period was allowed between trials. The graphic record was scored by measuring the line traced vertically by the sway of the subject's body. Reliability was determined for scores for both conditions, eyes open and eyes closed, by computing the correlation between two-minute trials for each condition. The reliability of scores with eyes open and with eyes closed was the same, 0.89. Another reliability coefficient was determined by retesting eighty-five subjects within a few days after the initial test. The correlation was 0.87. The reliability of these measures of body sway turned out to be quite satisfactory. It is interesting that the reliability held up so well over a few days. It is not unusual for it to drop substantially with a longer period of time between measures.

The reliability of measures of olfactory thresholds obtained by simple sniffing methods was investigated by Jones[7]. Subjects were twenty-four advanced undergraduate psychology majors and graduate students in psychology.

Three sets of odorous solutions were prepared in wide-mouth bottles. The solutions in each set were obtained by successive dilutions of a basic solution with mineral oil. The first set contained varied concentrations of n-butanol; the second set, safrol; the third set, n-butyric acid. The subject was given a preliminary sniff of each odor for identification purposes and a preliminary sniff of pure mineral oil as a reference point for no odor. The threshold was determined by the ascending method of limits. The subject's task was to recognize the odor.

The bottles were given numbers in order from the highest to the lowest concentration and the data used for computing reliability were the numbers of the bottles to which a response of positive recognition was given. The reliability coefficient for n-butanol was 0.82; for safrol, 0.77; and for n-butyric acid, 0.80. Considering the difficulty of measuring olfactory thresholds, these results are very good.

In an investigation of handwriting, the reliability of measures of pressure was reported by Wenger[9]. Measures were obtained by means of a pencil designed to register the amount of pressure exerted upon it during writing. Subjects were 427 cadets in the Air Corps.

An ordinary mechanical pencil was set in a cylinder of plastic. In the side of the cylinder was a lever with the fulcrum near the top and the end at the gripping point. In use, the end of the lever was under the index finger. Beneath the lever were four tiny switches constructed so that they would close consecutively as greater pressure was exerted on the lever. The pencil switches were connected to four clocks. As pressure on the lever increased, one clock after another was activated and then stopped. Recording of the duration of each of four levels of grip pressure was therefore possible.

Figure 7-10 shows a cross section of the apparatus containing the writing surface. A metal plate with adding-machine paper constituted the writing surface. The metal plate was suspended at each end over a movable bar so that equal pressures on any parts of the plate would depress the bar equal extents. The bar in turn moved a switching mechanism. As was true of the pencil, increasing pressure on the plate activated four electric clocks in succession. Duration of writing at each of four levels of point pressure was recorded.

A subject was instructed to write with the pencil in his usual style and at his usual speed at a location which kept his fingers off the paper. The subject's task was to write a phrase, "a donkey loaded with salt," a series of E's, a series of O's, and finally a sentence: "every army pilot goes through preflight primary basic and advanced training." He was then asked to repeat the entire performance.

Pressure scores were determined for the phrase, the letters, and the sentence on the initial test and the immediate retest. The grip-pressure reliability coefficient for writing the phrase was 0.88; the letters, 0.92; and the sentence, 0.94. The point-pressure coefficient for the phrase was 0.85; for the letters, 0.85; and for the sentence, 0.90. The magnitude of these coefficients indicates that handwriting grip pressure and point pressure can be measured well enought to distinguish among individuals.

Fleishman and Ornstein[5] described the testing of pilots in flying twenty-four different maneuvers and reported the reliability of the resulting scores. Subjects were sixty-three graduates of the Primary Pilot Training Program at Goodfellow Air Force Base, Texas.

Pilots were tested in a training plane. Daily records of student performances were made by each student's instructor on a form containing items obtained from an analysis of the performances required by the maneuvers. After each item was scored correct or incorrect, the number of incorrect items was taken as an error score for a trial. The subject's score for a given maneuver was the sum of errors on four trials. Only the first performance of a maneuver during any flight was included in the test, and no instruction on that maneuver was given until after the first performance. Thus the error scores for four trials on a given maneuver were from four different, successive flights. Scores were obtained for twenty-four maneuvers, all of which involved contact flying, which means flying with unrestricted vision.

The reliability of each maneuver test was determined by computing the correlation between the first and second flights, and the correlation between the third and fourth flights. These two coefficients were averaged, and the result was considered to be the reliability of a single-flight test. By means of statistical procedures, an estimate was then made of the reliability of a four-flight test.

Brief descriptions and estimates of reliability are presented here for six maneuvers:

1. Straight and level. The pilot was required to maintain a specified

altitude and heading. When deviations occurred, he made corrections in bank and pitch. Reliability, 0.47.

2. Ninety-degree climbing turn. The pilot established and maintained a specified bank, air speed, rate of turn, and power setting, until the appropriate recovery point. A carefully controlled combination of stick and rudder pressures was required throughout the maneuver. Reliability, 0.60.

3. Gliding turns. The pilot executed several preparatory procedural items and established certain flight conditions, including reduction of power, before initiating a bank and turn. This maneuver required the anticipation of control pressure changes and coordination of elevator, aileron, and rudder. Reliability, 0.58.

4. Take-off. The pilot was required to maintain a specific track and establish a proper climb attitude while accomplishing a number of procedural items. Rudder corrections and changes in elevator pressures were necessary. Reliability, 0.34.

5. Power-off stall. The maneuver was performed from a normal glide. The pilot established and maintained a specific pitch attitude until the stall occurred. The recovery from the stall required gross control movements. Reliability, 0.72.

6. Traffic pattern at home field. The pilot executed a number of procedural items while flying a predetermined pattern over the ground. Reliability, 0.75.

None of the coefficients of reliability for these flying performances was high; three were moderately high; and three were low. It should be recognized, however, that this kind of testing is very difficult and has very great practical significance. With results like these, there is no doubt that more work would be done in an attempt to improve the reliability of the measures.

The psychiatric interview is another situation which is difficult to measure but which is of very great practical importance. Saslow, Matarazzo, Phillips, and Matarazzo[8] investigated the reliability of measures obtained from a standard interviewing procedure. The variables measured were characteristics of the verbal and gestural interaction of subject and interviewer. Subjects were twenty outpatients, nine men and eleven women, at a psychiatric clinic. They varied in age from 16 to 61 years and displayed typical symptoms.

The interviewing procedure required the interviewer to act in a prescribed way during each of five defined periods. The first, third, and fifth periods were occasions for free give-and-take interviewing. In the second period, the interviewer was required not to respond to the subject. In the fourth period, he was required to interrupt the subject. The second and fourth periods were intended to be periods of stress for the subject.

The first, third, and fifth periods had fixed durations of 10, 5, and

5 minutes, respectively. The second and fourth had variable durations. The second was terminated after twelve failures to respond on the part of the interviewer or the lapse of 15 minutes, whichever occurred first. The fourth was terminated after twelve interruptions by the interviewer or the lapse of 15 minutes, whichever occurred first.

A device called an interaction chronograph was employed for recording behavior. By means of this device, an observer could record the occurrence and termination of different kinds of interaction of subject and interviewer. The device involved electrically controlled counters. The observer activated the appropriate counter whenever one of the two participants was talking, nodding, or gesturing.

Subjects were interviewed twice with a lapse of seven days between interviews. One of the investigators did the interviewing; one, the observing. Reliability was determined by computing the coefficient of correlation between scores for the two occasions. The coefficient for the frequency of the subject's actions was 0.89; for the average duration of his actions, 0.46; for the average duration of his silences, 0.65; and for the frequency with which he failed to synchronize with the interviewer either by failing to respond to him or by interrupting him, 0.53.

The investigators concluded that these interpersonal interaction measures exhibited considerable stability. According to the standard suggested earlier, only one reliability coefficient could be considered high; one, moderate; and the remaining two, low. They are, however, large enough to justify further research.

Reliability of Standardized Measures

Intelligence

The reliability of scores on the 1937 Revision of the Stanford-Binet Scale was determined by computing the correlation between two equivalent forms. Coefficients were obtained for twenty-one separate age groups from two to eighteen years. The coefficients varied from 0.85 to 0.95. The median value was 0.91. These are excellent results considering the homogeneity of the groups. The 1960 revision is comparable in reliability.

Reliability for the Wechsler Adult Scale was determined on three age groups: 18-19, 25-34, and 45-54. Each subtest was divided into two equivalent forms and the correlation between the two halves was computed. By means of a special statistical method, estimates were then obtained for the whole subtests. These estimated coefficients varied from 0.71 to 0.94 for the verbal subtests, and from 0.65 to 0.93 for the performance subtests. These, too, are excellent results considering that they apply to the individual subtests. The reliability of the whole combination of subtests would be quite high. The results for the Wechsler Scale cannot be compared to those for the Stanford-Binet, for different age groupings and different methods of analysis were employed.

The reliability of the SRA Primary Mental Abilities for Ages 11-17 was determined on high school students. Each of four subtests was divided into two equivalent forms and the correlation between the two was computed. By statistical procedures, an estimate was then obtained for each whole subtest. The estimated reliability for the verbal subtest was 0.92; for the spatial subtest, 0.96; for the reasoning subtest, 0.93; and for the number subtest, 0.89. For the fifth subtest, word fluency, reliability determined by a different method was 0.72. These are also excellent results.

The evidence for all three of these standardized tests of intelligence indicates reliable measurement, which means they can be used, with appropriate groups, to differentiate among individuals.

Personality

When normal subjects were tested twice within one week on the Minnesota Multiphasic Personality Inventory, the reliability coefficients for the nine clinical scales were found to vary from 0.56 for paranoia to 0.91 for masculinity-femininity. The median value was 0.80.

College students were tested on the Guilford-Zimmerman Temperament Survey. The various methods employed to determine reliability yielded values which varied from 0.75 for friendliness to 0.87 for sociability over the ten scales. The median value was 0.81.

Two administrations of the Edwards Personal Preference Schedule were given one week apart to college students. The correlation between the two administrations varied from 0.74 for achievement to 0.88 for abasement.

Reliability for the Kuder Preference Record (Personal) was determined on high school and college students. Coefficients varied from 0.79 for high school girls on the practical scale to 0.89 for high school boys on the sociable scale.

These results for standardized personality measures indicate the possibility of satisfactory differentiation among individuals. The reliability coefficients for personality inventories, however, are in general somewhat lower than those for intelligence tests.

Chapter Summary

Provisional measures of behavior must be evaluated by reference to three criteria: distribution, reliability, and validity. Distribution has to do with the way individuals fall on the scale of scores. This information is represented conveniently by a frequency distribution or its histogram. The location, dispersion, and shape of the frequency distribution are abstract characteristics which can be given psychological interpretations.

A reliable method of measurement is one which consistently differentiates subjects in a group. A method is not reliable or unreliable in any absolute sense. It may be reliable for one group and unreliable for another. Reliability is expressed in terms of a correlation coefficient computed for two sets of measures on the same subjects.

The reliability of psychological measurement in many situations is indicated by a vast amount of evidence. What this means is that psychologists can consistently distinguish among people in terms of their performances. This consistency is interpreted as revealing individual differences.

References

1. Allport, F. H. "Psychology in Relation to Social and Political Problems" in *Psychology at Work,* ed. P. S. Achilles. New York: Whittlesey House, 1932.

2. Brown, P. L., and R. S. Berdie. "Driver Behavior and Scores on the MMPI." *The Journal of Applied Psychology,* 44 (1960), 18-21.

3. Chin, R. "An Analysis of Conformity Behavior." *The Archives of Psychology,* 40, No. 289 (1943).

4. Fisher, M. B., J. E. Birren, and A. L. Leggett. "Standardization of Two Tests of Equilibrium: The Railwalking Test and the Ataxiagraph." *The Journal of Experimental Psychology,* 35 (1945), 321-329.

5. Fleishman, E. A., and G. N. Ornstein. "An Analysis of Pilot Flying Performance in Terms of Component Abilities." *The Journal of Appliea Psychology,* 44 (1960), 146-155.

6. Hardy, J. D., H. G. Wolff, and H. Goodell, *Pain Sensations and Reactions.* Baltimore: The William Wilkins Co., 1952.

7. Jones, F. N. "The Reliability of Olfactory Thresholds Obtained by Sniffing." *The American Journal of Psychology,* 68 (1955), 289-290.

8. Saslow, G., J. D. Matarazzo, J. S. Phillips, and R. G. Matarazzo. "Test-Retest Stability of Interaction Patterns During Interviews Conducted One Week Apart." *The Journal of Abnormal and Social Psychology,* 54 (1957), 295-302.

9. Wenger, M. A. "An Apparatus for the Measurement of Muscular Tension During Hand Writing." *The American Journal of Psychology,* 61 (1948), 259-267.

8

Validity

THE ULTIMATE VALUE OF A METHOD OF MEASUREMENT DEPENDS
on its properties with respect to validity, as well as distribution and reliability. Speaking generally, validity is defined in terms of correlation. The basic procedure in determining validity is to measure a group of subjects by two *different* methods and compute the correlation between the two sets of measures. Reliability was also defined in terms of correlation, but the procedure was to measure a group twice by the *same* method and compute the correlation between the two sets of measures.

Validity is related to distribution and reliability in that both set limits on it. The distribution of both sets of measures is a matter of concern. If all subjects get the same score in one set, the correlation between it and another must be zero. If the distribution of one set differs from the other in certain respects, there is a limit on the magnitude of the correlation. Reliability also sets a limit on validity. Logically, a coefficient of validity should not be higher than a coefficient of reliability, for one scale should not correlate with another higher than it correlates with itself.

Although validity is broadly defined in terms of correlation, psychologists commonly distinguish three kinds: predictive, congruent, and factorial. All three are closely related and based on correlation data. Each kind, however, emphasizes an aspect of psychological data different from the others.

Predictive Validity

When two different sets of measures on the same subjects are obtained for the purpose of predicting one set from the other, the set being predicted is called the criterion variable; the set from which predictions are made is called the predictor variable. When there is a linear relation between a criterion variable and a predictor variable, the predictor variable is said to be valid. A valid predictor may have either a positive or a negative correlation with the criterion. Although the degree of validity is expressed by the correlation between the predictor and the criterion, the prediction rule or equation, not the correlation, is the center of interest.

The degree of predictive validity is reflected in the magnitude of the correlation coefficient. The highest possible degree is represented by a coefficient of either $+1.00$ or -1.00, which is seldom, if ever, obtained in practice. The lowest degree is a coefficient of zero, but positive or negative values near zero (say between -0.10 and $+0.10$) are also interpreted as indicating no validity. The interpretation of values between $+0.10$ and $+1.00$, as well as the corresponding negative values, depends somewhat on the size of the group of subjects. More confidence is placed in a correlation of some given magnitude when it is obtained for a large group than for a small one. Generally speaking, validity coefficients above 0.60 are considered high; those between 0.40 and 0.60, moderate but substantial; those between 0.20 and 0.40, low. Values between 0.10 and 0.20 would be taken seriously only for very large groups of subjects. These various intervals ought not to be considered rigidly defined or fixed. Bear in mind, also, that negative correlations are just as good as positive ones.

A vast amount of evidence on predictive validity has been accumulated. Especially in education, industry, government, and the military, where the selection of personnel is a practical problem of tremendous proportions, there has been a great volume of work on the predictive validity of a wide variety of measures, including motor, sensorimotor, perceptual, and intellective abilities, as well as attitudes, interests, and other personality characteristics. Since the results can be classified in a large number of different ways, they provide many specialized topics for courses in psychological measurement.

The evidence from studies of predictive validity is put to different kinds of use; that is, the consequences of establishing a predictive relationship are not always the same. One can distinguish three purposes served by knowledge of predictive relations: selection, test construction, and description.

Selection refers to the evaluation of applicants for admission to college or employment in business, industry, government, and other situations.

After a relation has been found between criterion and predictor measures for one group of subjects, the prediction rule is often used in other situations with other subjects for whom only the predictor measures are available. The rule is applied to obtain predicted values of the criterion. In the selection of students and personnel, if applicants who have predicted criterion values above some arbitrary point are admitted or employed, those below are rejected.

In the process of constructing a test, the psychologist may validate it against a certain criterion in order to justify substituting the test for the criterion, on which adequate measures may be difficult or expensive to obtain routinely. What the psychologist wants is a simple and inexpensive test which will eventually take the place of the criterion. In the early development of measures of intelligence, tests were validated in terms of their correlation with ratings of intelligence given by teachers. Eventually, the tests themselves became accepted as better measures of intelligence than teachers' ratings, and today it would be thought strange indeed if one were to construct an intelligence test for the purpose of predicting a criterion such as teachers' ratings. In the development of a new interest inventory, however, criterion measures might be obtained by having a number of associates of each subject rate him on his interests. In the development of a method of measuring children's popularity, a new technique for deriving scores from drawings made by the children might be validated against their popularity as indicated by the number of times they were chosen by their peers to participate in some social activity.

The use of a predictive relation purely for descriptive purposes is a simple and straightforward matter, but there is a danger in jumping from this evidence to conclusions not justified by it. In their research, psychologists have established many predictive relations for which there are no immediate applications in selection or test-construction procedures. What then are the consequences of obtaining this evidence? One could say that the predictive relation is descriptive of the subjects who were studied and that having this information is important just for the sake of having it. This limited use of description is not satisfying to many people. One can point to other possibly legitimate uses, but in doing so there is the risk of being misunderstood and of appearing to recommend jumping to unjustified conclusions. Nevertheless, an attempt will be made to delimit these other uses very strictly.

A predictive relationship may suggest further research. Consider, as an example, the relation between education and delinquency among adolescents. If it was established that delinquency was predictable from amount of education, it would be reasonable to undertake research to show that educating adolescents to a higher level reduced the incidence of delinquency. (This anticipates a later discussion of experimentation, so none of its details will be presented at this point.) Notice that knowledge of the predictive relation is *not* knowledge that educating adolescents will reduce delinquency. Strictly speaking, knowledge of the predictive relation merely furnishes the idea for research to obtain the other knowledge. This process whereby the "idea for further research" is obtained may involve incorporating the fact of the predictive relation in a theory about delinquency and its causes. The degree of uncertainty which accompanies this process will become apparent in considering the prediction in the opposite direction—level of education predicted from classification as a delinquent or nondelinquent. This way of stating the prediction could just as reasonably furnish the idea for further research to determine whether or not reducing delinquent activities would result in adolescents attaining higher levels of education. The arbitrary nature of the choice of direction for the prediction (in other words, the arbitrary choice of a criterion) is revealed in this example. The uncertainty increases when one realizes that it is also quite reasonable to propose that neither of these actions—increasing education nor reducing delinquent activities—would have the desired effect, and that only some, as yet unspecified, action would be necessary to increase education attainment *and* reduce delinquent activities among adolescents.

A predictive relationship is sometimes made the basis for practical decision. Consider again the relation between education and delinquency. Given the information that delinquency is predictable from educational level, a practical administrative decision may be made to enforce school-attendance laws more strictly. Is this decision justified? Any answer is controversial here. The scientific-minded individual will say that the decision goes far beyond the evidence. The practical-minded individual will say that with no better evidence available and no opportunity to engage in research to obtain it, the decision based on the prediction alone is justified.

In the present discussion predictive relations which, strictly speaking, serve only descriptive purposes will be described in just those terms. Doing so will be taking the conservative position of the scientific-minded person. This is done in the belief that it is the position to which beginning students need to be exposed.

PREDICTIVENESS OF INTELLIGENCE TESTS

Scores on intelligence tests have been investigated as predictors of both educational and vocational success. The correlations between test scores and grades in school and college are frequently of moderate positive magnitude. For example, three subtests of the SRA Primary Mental Abilities for Ages 11-17 were found to be predictive of grade-point averages for ninth grade students in the Chicago area. Moderate positive correlations were obtained for the verbal, reasoning, and number subtests.

The relation between intelligence scores and vocational success depends very much on the criterion selected. Average scores for a number of occupations ranked according to level increase from the lower to the upper levels. There is, however, considerable overlap in scores for adjacent occupational levels. Low positive correlations have been obtained for test scores and job success as rated by supervisors or indicated by productivity. Job satisfaction has been found to be predictable from intelligence scores, but whether the correlation is positive or negative depends on the kinds of demands the job makes on workers. On jobs which require little ability, workers with high scores may become dissatisfied; on jobs which require some higher degree of ability, workers with low scores may find the demands too great and become dissatisfied.

APTITUDES

Predictive validity has a place in the definition of an aptitude as the scale of scores on an ability test which has been shown to be predictive of some criterion of success. Thus a test of scholastic aptitude is a test which has been found to be correlated with a criterion of success in scholastic activity, one possible criterion being grade-point average.

The Differential Aptitude Tests (or DAT) is a well-known battery constructed to measure abilities in grades eight through twelve for purposes of educational and vocational guidance. It provides multiple scores on intellective variables, not just a single score. This differential measurement yields much more detailed information about abilities than does a unitary scale.

The battery contains seven tests: verbal reasoning or the understanding of concepts expressed in words; numerical ability, the understanding of numerical relationships and handling of numerical concepts; abstract reasoning, nonverbal reasoning which requires the detection of principles in changing diagrams; space relations, identifying objects constructed from patterns and other objects after they are rotated; mechanical reasoning, answering simply worded questions about pictures of mechanical situations; clerical speed and accuracy, identifying on an answer sheet the number and letter combinations marked in the test; and language usage, distinguishing among correctly and incorrectly spelled words and inspecting sentences for errors in grammar, punctuation, and word usage (see Figure 8-1).

The predictive validity of the Differential Aptitude Tests has been demonstrated in many investigations. For example, certain ones were found to predict course grades in high schools with a correlation of 0.50 and

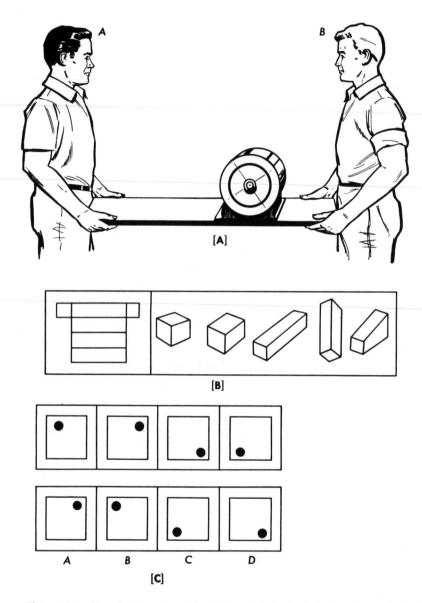

Figure 8-1. Sample items from the Differential Aptitude Tests. **A:** Mechanical Reasoning. Which man has the heavier load? **B:** Space Relations. Which figure can be made from the pattern at the left? **C:** Abstract Reasoning. Which of the figures in the lower row shows the next position of the moving dot? [By permission of The Psychological Corporation.]

higher. Verbal reasoning and the sentence part of language usage were predictive of grades in English; numerical ability was predictive of grades in mathematics; verbal reasoning and numerical ability were predictive of grades in science, social studies, and history.

The Scholastic Aptitude Test (or SAT) should be familiar already to many students. It is sponsored by the College Entrance Examination Board and administered by the Educational Testing Service. It was given for the first time in 1926. In the academic year 1961-62, 819,339 students planning to go to college took it.

The Scholastic Aptitude Test measures the level of development of verbal and mathematical skills important in performing the academic tasks required in college. Verbal skill includes knowledge of meaning and the relationships of words, reasoning with words, and comprehension of prose passages. Mathematical skill pertains to the solving of problems in mathematics through elementary algebra and geometry.

Many investigations have been made of the predictive validity of the Scholastic Aptitude Test. Typically, the correlation with college freshman grades has been around 0.60 for SAT verbal scores in liberal arts colleges and SAT mathematics scores in engineering colleges.

The Flanagan Aptitude Classification Test series (FACT) was constructed for the prediction of success in particular occupational tasks. The series consists of fourteen tests: inspection for imperfections; coding typical office information; memory for the codes learned; precision in making small circular finger movements; assembly, the visualization of the appearance of an object from its separate parts; scale reading; coordination of hand and arm movements; judgment and comprehension; arithmetic; reproduction of simple patterns; identification of important components in drawings and blueprints; reading of tables; understanding of mechanical principles; and knowledge of correct expression in English. These tests were designed for two uses: in vocational counseling as an aid to prediction of job success, and in programs of selection and placement for employees (see Figure 8-2). Combined scores were found to have moderate correlations with a criterion based on rate of salary increase in the occupations: sales work, electrical, structural, mechanical, and drafting.

PREDICTIVENESS OF PERSONALITY MEASURES

It is very difficult to summarize the evidence concerning the predictive validity of personality measures, for there is a vast amount of evidence, and it varies considerably. In general, the validity of personality measures is not as high or consistent as the validity of intellective measures. There are situations in which certain personality measures may have moderate validity; there are others in which the same measures may have low or even zero validity. A great deal of research is undertaken to determine the circumstances under which various measures are valid. The evidence concerning the predictive validity of personality measures is of two kinds: evidence for the standardized widely used inventories, and evidence for the special methods of measurement developed for research situations.

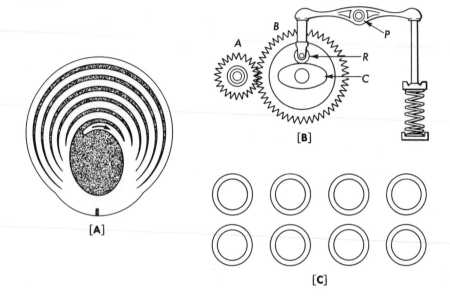

Figure 8-2. Sample items from the Flanagan Aptitude Classification Tests. **A:** Coordination. A test of speed and accuracy in following a circular path with a pencil, starting at the arrow and working out gradually to the last ring. **B:** Mechanics. For every two revolutions of gear *A*, how many times is the spring compressed? (*A*, small gear; *B*, large gear; *C*, cam; *P*, pivot; *R*, roller.) **C:** Precision. Draw a circle in the space between the inner and outer rings. [By permission of Science Research Associates, Inc., the publisher (1951), for John C. Flanagan, the author.]

Standardized Inventories

Each of the nine clinical scales of the Minnesota Multiphasic Personality Inventory has been found to predict with moderate success the corresponding final clinical diagnosis of new psychiatric admissions; that is, scores on a given scale were correlated with the classification of a patient as belonging to or not belonging to the corresponding diagnostic category. Thus the Inventory is moderately valid in distinguishing among various kinds of clinic cases.

In investigations of the relations between scores on the ten scales of the Guilford-Zimmerman Temperament Survey and the performances of supervisory and administrative personnel, eight of the correlations were between 0.20 and 0.50.

Three of the five scales of the Kuder Preference Record (Personal) were found to be correlated with the classification lawyers and men-in-general. The correlation between the classification and the practical scale was −0.18; the theoretical scale, 0.39; and the dominant scale, 0.48. Scores from the three separate scales could be combined to yield a score whose correlation with the classification was 0.67. Thus scores on the scales differentiated between lawyers and men-in-general. Lawyers were less practical but more theoretical and dominant than men-in-general.

Prediction from Personality Measures in Special Situations

Merenda and Clarke[9] have reported part of a long-range investigation by an insurance company for the purpose of evaluating procedures used in the selection of life insurance agents. Subjects were 522 male life insurance agents hired by one company in a four-year period. The predictor variables were a personality inventory and items of personal history obtained from a questionnaire.

The personality inventory was the Activity Vector Analysis (AVA). It consisted of a list of eighty-one words which could be used in self-description of personality. Instructions to the subject were, "Check those words you believe actually describe you." There were four scales: aggressiveness, sociability, emotional control, and social adaptability. In the aggressiveness scale were words such as nervy, argumentative, opinionated, stubborn, and dominant; in the sociability scale, words such as charming, admirable, smooth, attractive, and magnetic; in the emotional-control scale, words such as willing, pleasant, kind, and obliging; and in the social-adaptability scale, words such as harmonious, God-fearing, open minded, and tolerant. The inventory was administered to each agent at the time he applied for employment.

The personal history questionnaire contained twenty items: age, marital status, number of children, educational level, percentage of educational expenses earned, number of memberships in organizations, number of years of previous work experience, length of stay at present residence, amount of outstanding debts, amount of life insurance purchased for self, employment status of wife, type of recreation normally engaged in, previous sales experience, total number of friends, and six other items. Personal history data were recorded at the time the agent applied for employment.

The criterion was success or failure at the end of the third year after employment. Success was defined as meeting the training allowance program quotas or achieving 200,000 dollars production the first year and at least 300,000 dollars in either the second or third year; or advancing to a supervisory or a management position within the company; or leaving the company to become an agent, supervisor, or general agent for another company before the end of the third year, if the agent had achieved the production goals stated. Failure was defined as failing to meet the stated production goals, whether or not he remained as an agent with the company; or having his contract terminated by the company; or leaving the insurance industry within a three-year period.

The correlation between the criterion and aggressiveness was 0.14; sociability, 0.12; emotional control, −0.15; and social adaptability, −0.18. Thus successful agents were more aggressive, more sociable, less emotionally controlled, and less socially adaptable than unsuccessful agents. Four personal history items were correlated with the criterion. The coefficient for number of children was 0.13; educational level, 0.10; monthly living expenses, 0.18; and amount of insurance owned, 0.17. All these coefficients are very low, but because of the large number of salesmen in the group, they were judged to be of value. Employed in combination, the personality scales and the personal history items improved selection enough to justify their use.

As mentioned earlier, predictive relations may be taken simply as descriptions of behavior. This possibility is illustrated by the relation between academic success and self-ratings found in an investigation by Worell[15]. Academic success was defined as decile rank for the year's academic performance. (Decile rank is a standing in percentage from zero to 100 in units of ten percentage points.) Subjects were 138 freshman volunteers in a small liberal arts college.

Measures of level of aspiration were obtained by having each student rate himself on a decile scale in answer to the questions:

(a) How do you think your average grades compare with those of your classmates?

(b) If you plan to return next year, how well do you expect to do in comparison with other members of your class?

(c) If you really tried to do well and worked near the limits of your capacity, how would your average grades compare with those of your classmates?

(d) How well would you like to do in order to be reasonably well-satisfied according to your own standards?

The predictor variables were differences in self-ratings on three combinations of the questions:

Rating on (b) minus rating on (a), the extent to which rating of future grades exceeded rating of past grades. Correlation with the criterion was −0.56, indicating that poorer students exceeded better students in the improvement they expected.

Rating on (c) minus rating on (a), the extent to which estimated capability exceeded past performance. The correlation was −0.57. Capability exceeded performance more among poor students than among good ones.

Rating on (d) minus rating on (a), the extent to which aspiration exceeded past performance. The correlation was −0.65. Aspiration exceeded achievement more for poor students than for good ones.

A descriptive relation between marital happiness and self-acceptance was reported by Eastman[2]. Subjects were fifty couples who had been married for two years or more. Marital happiness was measured by means of a questionnaire. Self-acceptance was measured as the discrepancy between a subject's rating of himself as he was and his rating of the person he would, ideally, like to be.

Subjects were contacted in small groups brought together by colleagues ostensibly for social purposes. All couples in every group agreed to complete the questionnaires anonymously. Husbands and wives were separated before they completed the forms, and each couple put its completed questionnaires in the same envelope before returning them, thereby identifying for the investigator the husband-wife combinations. The correlation between marital happiness and self-acceptance for the husbands was 0.37; for the wives, 0.35. Although these correlation values are low, they indicate some degree of relation between marital happiness and self-acceptance.

A descriptive relation between absences from work and feelings about promotions was found by Patchen[11], who studied 1,500 nonsupervisory employees of an oil refinery located in a small Canadian city. Most of them worked in the maintenance of equipment or at watching and adjusting control dials in regulating the actual production of oil. The remainder worked on assembly-line jobs such as packaging and manufacturing oil drums, on jobs in the laboratory, at common labor and janitorial tasks, or on miscellaneous jobs such as driving trucks.

Because of the hazards associated with inefficiency and confusion in the refinery, absences were considered important. The management kept close check on absences among all employees. Men with five or more absences in a year without sufficient cause were interviewed.

To select a sample of subjects for the study, the total group of nonsupervisory workers was classified by occupation and by rate of pay. A random subsample was obtained from each category, proportional to the size of that subgroup in the total group. The number of men interviewed was 487. The number of times a man was absent from work in the preceding year, without regard for the length of each absence, was obtained from company records. To obtain expressions of attitude conconcerning promotions, the question was asked, "Do you feel that you deserve to have been promoted higher by now?" In answering, a worker had four possibilities: "Yes, I definitely feel that way." "Yes, I feel that way a little." "No, I don't feel that way at all." "I am not sure."

Absences were found to be related to expressions of attitude. Men who said they had been treated fairly with regard to promotion were absent less often than were those who said they deserved to have been promoted higher or those who had doubts on the matter.

Congruent Validity

Congruent validity is demonstrated when two tests or scales, each labeled provisionally with the same abstract term, are found to be correlated. For example, two different tests may be developed by different authors, each one proposed by its author as a test of verbal ability. If they are both administered to the same subjects and found to be correlated, the validity of each test as a measure of verbal ability is considered to be supported. There is obviously only a relative, not an absolute, evaluation involved in congruent validity. Another example would be two different inventories purported to measure neuroticism. The finding of a correlation between them would be evidence of congruent validity.

Earlier, a specific ability was defined as the scale of scores on a particular reliable test. Congruent validity has a place in the definition of a general ability. A general ability is defined here as the scale of combined scores on two or more reliable tests demonstrated to possess congruent validity. Thus a general ability is a dimension of behavior abstracted from two or more tests shown to be correlated.

Determinations of congruent validity have been made routinely in connection with many kinds of psychological measurement. One intelligence test has been correlated with another; one test of verbal ability, with another; one interest inventory, with another; one personality scale, with another; and so on. In general, there has been some success with both intellective and personality measures, but more in intellective than in personality areas. Motivational, emotional, and social characteristics of behavior appear to be more difficult to measure than remembering, reasoning, abstracting, and the like.

Following are some specific results for congruent validity in the measurement of intelligence. IQs for the original Stanford-Binet Scale and Form L of the 1937 Revision had a correlation of 0.88. High correlations were obtained for the two parts of the Wechsler Adult Intelligence Scale and the 1937 Stanford-Binet Scale: The coefficient for WAIS verbal scores was 0.86; for WAIS performance scores, 0.69. The correlation for WAIS full-scale scores and Stanford-Binet scores was 0.85. Two subtests of the Primary Mental Abilities for Ages 11-17 were found to be related to the Kuhlmann-Anderson Intelligence Test. The correlation between combined scores on the verbal and reasoning subtests and scores on the Kuhlmann-

Anderson Test was 0.63. The same combination of subtest scores on the PMA had a high correlation with the Otis Self-Administering Test of Mental Ability. All these results for measures of intelligence indicate a high degree of congruent validity.

In an investigation of the congruent validity of the Edwards Personal Preference Schedule, low positive correlations were obtained between the agreeableness scale of the · Guilford-Martin Personnel Inventory and the four scales: affiliation, deference, abasement, and nurturance. A moderate negative correlation was found for the aggression scale. These results can be interpreted as supporting the congruent validity of the five scales from the Edwards Schedule and the one scale from the Guilford-Martin Inventory.

The Congruent Validity of Judgments of Behavior

One problem of interest to many psychologists is the validity of judgments of behavior. There have been few investigations which have clearly demonstrated that there is a general ability to judge others. One very extensive study, which yielded evidence of a moderate degree of congruent validity, was reported by Cline and Richards[1]. Subjects or judges were fifty students of both sexes, volunteers from classes in psychology, education, sociology, and anthropology in a summer session at the University of Utah.

Interviews with adults were recorded in sound colored motion pictures. The interviews were filmed at three different locations in the metropolitan area of Salt Lake City: an anteroom to a suburban supermarket, a downtown theatre lobby, and a University research laboratory. Interviewees were recruited from customers at the supermarket, passers-by on the street, and students in University classes. A member of the University theatre staff conducted the interviews, which were structured but did permit the interviewer some freedom. Interviews dealt with the interviewee's personal values, personality strengths and weaknesses, reactions to the interview, hobbies and activities, self-concepts, and temper. During the filming, camera and sound equipment were in full view.

Finally selected for use were the films of ten interviewees: a 19-year-old engaged male geology major at the University of Utah; a 36-year-old married female of Greek parentage, with three children; a 40-year-old married male oculist of Italian parentage; a 22-year-old divorced female waitress with no children; a 32-year-old married grammar school teacher with three children; a 65-year-old widow who had two married children and worked as supervisor of a church cafeteria; a 22-year-old single male Mexican-American working in a meat-packing plant; a 17-year-old single female high school student of German parentage; a 41-year-old married male IBM worker with one child; and a 25-year-old divorced female who had two children and lived with her parents.

After the interview was film recorded, information about the interviewee was obtained in the course of several visits to his home. Information included biographical material and personal characteristics in addition to responses to the Minnesota Multiphasic Personality Inventory (MMPI), Strong Vocational Interest Blank, California Psychological Inventory, a word association test, the Otis Intelligence Test, a multiple-choice sentence completion test, an adjective checklist, a group of eighty items from the MMPI, and a fifty-item self-rating scale. Five close associates of each interviewee were questioned about his behavior and history. They were also asked to rate him on the fifty-item rating scale.

From the information obtained about an interviewee, five inventories were constructed for judges to complete after seeing each filmed interview. The inventories were given the names behavior postdiction, trait rating, opinion prediction, sentence completion, and adjective checklist.

1. On the behavior-postdiction inventory, the judge was required to identify past behavior of the person seen in the filmed interview. Items were written for each interviewee separately. Correct answers were determined from biographical material obtained from the interviewee and his five close associates.

2. On the trait-rating inventory, the judge rated the interviewee on a six-category scale for each of twenty-five traits used for all interviewees. After the mean rating on each trait given by the five associates of the interviewee was obtained, the judge's error score was computed from the differences between his ratings and the mean ratings of the associates. These error scores were transformed to accuracy scores.

3. The opinion-prediction inventory consisted of twenty MMPI items for each interviewee. The judge was required to check whether the interviewee answered "true" or "false" to each item in describing himself.

4. On the sentence-completion inventory, the judge had to indicate how the interviewee had answered multiple-choice sentence-completion items. Items varied from one interviewee to another.

5. On the adjective checklist, the judge had to indicate which one of two adjectives an interviewee had checked as being descriptive of himself.

The film of the first interview was shown and judges completed the inventories for the interviewee. This procedure was repeated until all ten films had been shown and the corresponding inventories had been completed.

The correlations among the five inventories are given in the table below. Most of the correlations are moderate. Thus the interpretation could be made that these five different ways of measuring judging ability

	2	3	4	5
1	.30	.50	.47	.24
2		.52	.48	.65
3			.47	.54
4				.58

were congruently valid. They agreed in placing some judges high and some low. The investigators concluded that the existence of a general dimension of judging ability had been demonstrated.

Factorial Validity

It is only a short conceptual step from congruent validity to factorial validity. Evidence regarding factorial validity is obtained from the presence and absence of correlation observed in the interrelations of a number of tests or scales. The pattern exhibited by the correlation coefficients is interpreted in terms of, and taken as justification for, the use of abstract dimensions or *factors*. Crudely speaking, a factor is a hypothetical dimension abstracted from and considered representative of a group of tests or scales correlated among themselves and uncorrelated with other groups.

A simple example of factorial validity can be constructed from four imaginary tests with labels A_1, A_2, B_1, and B_2. From an examination of the tests themselves, the investigator may hypothesize two unrelated dimensions or factors, A-ness and B-ness. He would expect to find that A_1 and A_2 were correlated, that B_1 and B_2 were correlated, but that no A test was correlated with a B test. If his data confirmed his hypothesis, the abstract dimensions or factors labeled A-ness and B-ness would be considered justified, and factorial validity would have been demonstrated.

Sometimes the results of investigations of factorial validity do not conform to expectation. For example, the investigator's data may show that tests A_1 and B_1 are correlated, that A_2 and B_2 are correlated, and that no 1-test is correlated with a 2-test. His results may be taken as suggesting two unrelated dimensions or factors, 1-ness and 2-ness. They do not support the concept of A-ness and B-ness. The theory and method employed in analyzing correlations among tests for the purpose of establishing abstract dimensions is called factor analysis. The computational procedures are quite complex.

The practical consequences of establishing factorial validity are found mainly in the selection of items for tests or scales and in the selection of tests or scales to make up batteries. From items which are representative of a given factor, the test constructor may select a number to constitute a test; from items representative of a different factor, he may choose a number for another test. The same kind of procedure can be employed in selecting tests for a battery.

FACTORIAL VALIDITY OF STANDARDIZED MEASURES

It is highly appropriate to begin this discussion of factorial validity with evidence concerning the Primary Mental Abilities, the authors of which were the Thurstones, for it was Louis L. Thurstone who did much of the pioneer work in factor analysis in this country. One of the early practical consequences of his work was the development of a factorially valid battery of tests of intellectual abilities. A battery of tests which are not highly correlated can provide much more detailed information about an individual's ability than can a test providing only a single score. This does not mean that the problem is merely one of finding uncorrelated tests. The tests must, of course, be reliable, and it should be possible to demonstrate the congruent validity of each one. These standards have been met very satisfactorily by the five PMA subtests: verbal, space, reasoning, number, and word fluency. Their intercorrelations, averaged over six investigations, varied from 0.13 to 0.50. These generally low intercorrelations are evidence of factorial validity, but they also indicate a low level of congruent validity supporting the idea of a very general intellectual ability.

Attempts to develop factorially valid personality measures have also been successful. The fifteen scales measuring manifest needs in the Edwards Personal Preference Schedule have low intercorrelations and are therefore relatively independent measures. This is also true of the ten scales in the Guilford-Zimmerman Temperament Survey and the five interest scales in the Kuder Preference Record (Personal).

FACTORIAL VALIDITY IN SPECIAL INVESTIGATIONS OF PERCEPTUAL, SENSORIMOTOR, AND INTELLECTIVE BEHAVIOR

As any specific area of psychological knowledge is developed, a multiplicity of distinguishable methods of measurement inevitably accrues from the inventiveness of workers in that area. The set of measures yielded by each of these methods typically varies in its degree of correlation with other sets. One of the goals of psychological science is to find out the smallest number of methods of measurement necessary for adequate coverage of a given area. This involves examining the intercorrelations for all methods in the area and determining the few factors which can satisfactorily represent the many scales. What happens next? There are several possibilities. Having determined what the factors are, one might then search for a biological correlate of each, or present them as very general descriptive concepts, or incorporate them in a theory from which new hypotheses and research might come. In varying degrees, these possible consequences of factor analysis can be seen in the investigations described next.

Dimensions of Olfactory Sensitivity

A classification of odors and odorous substances was attempted by Jones[6], who measured the absolute olfactory thresholds of eighty-four subjects for twenty substances, computed all possible correlations, and performed a factor analysis on them. Subjects were undergraduate or graduate majors in psychology and a few staff members. Both sexes were represented.

A blast of odorous air of measured volume and duration was injected into a subject's nostril. The air was drawn into a syringe from an evaporation bottle kept under constant temperature and delivered by a motor. During the threshold determinations, the subject sat in an air conditioned, glass-lined booth kept at a comfortable constant temperature. The air in the booth was constantly recirculated and filtered. The twenty odorous substances were organic compounds.

One ascending series of concentrations was employed in determining a recognition threshold for each substance. Since the subject's task was to report when he detected each odor, he had to be given a whiff of the odor before the threshold for each new substance was determined. The order of substances was random for each subject. For practice, a preliminary threshold determination was made for citral.

Correlation coefficients were calculated for all possible pairs of substances. All the correlations were positive and varied from 0.08 to 0.68. When the correlations were factor analyzed, four groups of variables were obtained. Substances grouped together under Factor 1 were pyridine, n-butyric acid, eugenol, and benzaldehyde; under Factor 2, the isomeric butanols (iso, sec, tert), n-octane, safrole, and methyl salicylate; under Factor 3, ethyl acetate, ethylene chloride, and n-propanol; and under Factor 4, n-caprylic acid and amyl acetate.

In general, substances under a given factor were positively correlated. For example, pyridine and n-butyric acid had a correlation of 0.56; iso-butanol and sec-butanol, 0.68; ethyl acetate and ethylene chloride, 0.54; n-caprylic acid and amyl acetate, 0.33. A study of the groups of substances revealed that the factors did not represent either chemical dimensions or homogeneous odor qualities. The general positive correlation among substances supported the idea of a general ability in olfactory discrimination.

Dimensions of Sensorimotor Behavior

Sensorimotor behavior can be measured on specific dimensions corresponding to a multitude of tasks. The goal of psychology, however, is to reduce complexity and achieve simplicity and economy in its account of behavior. Reducing the multiplicity of dimensions and tasks in the measurement of sensorimotor behavior to a smaller number, without loss of scope and predictiveness, would be a great advance indeed. Factor analysis lends itself to this kind of endeavor, and it was employed by Fleishman[4,5] in two very extensive investigations. In each of them, a battery of sensorimotor tests was administered to a large group of subjects and a factor analysis of the correlations among the tests was performed.

Fleishman distinguished between positioning movements, static reactions, and movement reactions. Positioning movements were defined as those in which the body members are moved to a specified position in space. In positioning movements, the primary feature is the terminal accuracy of the response. Static reactions involve holding a body member for a time in a fixed position in space. In static reactions, the primary feature is the maintenance of position. Movement reactions were defined as movements of a body member at a given rate, in a rhythm, in sequence, or along a path.

In the investigation of positioning movements and static reactions, subjects were 200 basic trainee airmen at Lackland Air Force Base. They were given twenty-four tests which included the following positioning movements:

1. *Track tracing.* The subject had to trace a path in the frontal plane from one end of an irregular slot to the other and then retrace it. He used a T-shaped stylus which was inserted in the slot and held at arm's length. Errors were recorded when his stylus touched any part of the slot. His score was the number of contacts in four trials. The apparatus is shown in Figure 8-3.

2. *Steadiness precision.* The subject had to move a long stylus forward through a long cylindrical tube. He held the stylus slightly below shoulder height, moved it slowly and steadily away from his body, and withdrew it. He was instructed to avoid hitting the sides. His score was the number of contacts in four trials.

3. *Position finding.* The subject, blindfolded, had to reach out and grasp one peg in a semicircular arrangement of pegs on a table before him. All the pegs were white except for three black ones. One black peg was directly in front of him; one was in each of the right and left quadrants. First, without the blindfold, the subject inspected the peg arrangement and practiced reaching for the black pegs. In the test, after putting on black goggles, he was told to reach for either the center, right, or

left black pegs. His score was the sum of his errors, which were the number of pegs deviation to the right or left of the correct peg on each attempt in a number of trials.

4. *Stick reaction.* The subject moved a control stick into one of a number of slots in a semicircular horizontal panel before him. The stick and the panel with its slots were hidden from him by a shield and a curtain. Above the apparatus was a panel of lights positioned to correspond with the slots. A light indicated the slot to which the subject must move the stick. After each trial the stick was returned by a spring to the center position. The subject's score was the sum of his errors, each of which was the number of slots deviation from the correct slot on each attempt in a series of trials.

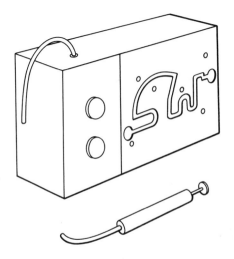

Figure 8-3. Apparatus for track tracing. The stylus is inserted in the track at one end and moved to the other end. [Adapted from Fleishman.[4]]

5. *Target location, front.* The subject had to reach out with a wax pencil and mark as close to the bull's eye of a set of wall targets as possible. He sat on a stool in front of a panel containing six targets in two rows of three each. He was allowed to practice reaching the center of each target without goggles and then had a series of test trials during which he wore black goggles. He made one thrust at each target and his score was the sum of his errors, each of which was measured from the center of the target.

6. *Forward stick positioning.* The subject's task was to reproduce the extent of movement, forward and backward, of a stick control. His score was the accumulated error from the target position in a number of trials.

Only a few of the twenty-four tests were static reactions. One of them was called steadiness tremor. In it the subject had to hold a stylus steadily in the opening of a cylindrical tube and try to avoid hitting the sides. His score was the number of contacts in a series of one-minute trials.

Correlations among all twenty-four tests were computed, but only

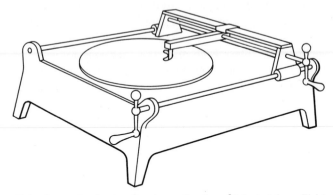

Figure 8-4. Apparatus for two-hand coordination. [Adapted from Fleishman.[5]]

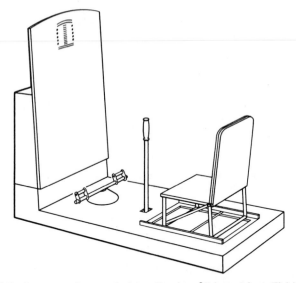

Figure 8-5. Apparatus for complex coordination. [Adapted from Fleishman.[5]]

those for thirteen tests were analyzed. Eleven tests were dropped because they did not correlate with any others. The analysis produced three factors: arm-hand steadiness, which included track tracing and steadiness precision; position estimation, which included stick reaction and forward stick positioning; and position reproduction, which included position finding and target location, front.

In the study of movement reactions, subjects were 204 basic trainee airmen at Lackland Air Force Base. They were tested on thirty-one tasks, five of which will be described here.

1. *Two-hand coordination.* The subject tried to keep a follower on a small target disk as the disk moved irregularly and at varying rates in a horizontal plane. Movement of the follower to the right and left was controlled by one handle; movement toward and away from the subject was controlled by another. Simultaneous rotation of both handles moved the follower in a direction representing the resultant of the combination of movements. The subject's score was the total time on target during four one-minute trials. The tracking apparatus is shown in Figure 8-4.

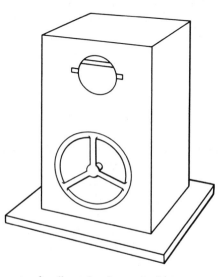

Figure 8-6. Apparatus for dimensional pursuit. [Adapted from Fleishman.[5]]

2. *Complex coordination.* Patterns of lights were presented to the subject on a panel. He had to match these lights by adjusting a stick-and-rudder control (see Figure 8-5). A correct response was accomplished only when both hands and feet had completed and maintained the appropriate adjustments. When the pattern was matched correctly, a new pattern of lights was presented. The subject's score was the number of matchings completed during two two-minute test periods.

3. *Single-dimension pursuit meter* (see Figure 8-6). The subject made compensatory adjustments of a control wheel to keep a horizontal line in its original position as it deviated from center in irregular fashion. His score was the time the horizontal line was held on center during four one-minute trials.

4. *Dial setting.* The subject had to set four dials to the number

indicated in four apertures, corresponding to the dials. When all four dials were set correctly, four new numbers appeared in the apertures. His score was the number of settings completed in three two-minute trials.

5. *Rudder control.* As the subject sat in a mock airplane cockpit, he tried to keep it lined up with a target light. His own weight threw the seat off balance unless he applied and maintained proper correction by means of foot pedals. His score was the total time the cockpit was held lined up with the light during three short trials.

The correlations among all thirty-one tests were analyzed. Among the factors obtained were the following: response orientation, which included the dial-setting task; fine control sensitivity, which included complex co-ordination; reaction time, which represented four different measures of reaction time not described above; speed of arm movement, which represented tasks requiring a gross arm movement; and multiple-limb coor-dination, which included the rudder-control task.

Dimensions of Connotation

The attempt to achieve simplicity and economy in descriptions of behavior has been extended to intellective characteristics, as well as to per-ceptual and sensorimotor behavior. Consider the connotation of words. One might reasonably ask, "What is the nature of connotation? Does it have one characteristic, a dozen, or many? If many, what are its principal characteristics?" Osgood and Suci[10] developed a method for measuring connotative meaning and employed factor analysis in an attempt to identify its general dimensions. They labeled the resulting set of scales *the semantic differential* because, in their opinion, it represented a differentiation of connotative meaning in terms of a limited number of scales with known interrelations. The basic idea was that subjects would rate a given term on different scales of connotative meaning. The scales which were highly correlated could be interpreted as being equivalent, and a few uncorrelated scales could be chosen to represent satisfactorily the much larger original number. The method of factor analysis was, of course, ap-propriate for this undertaking.

The original rating scales were constructed from information obtained about the most frequent ways in which people describe certain words. A list of forty nouns was read fairly rapidly to a group of approximately 200 undergraduate students, who were instructed to write immediately the first descriptive adjective which occurred to them after they heard each noun. After hearing "tree," a particular student may have written "green"; after "house," "big"; and after "priest," "good."

The associations were examined to determine the frequency of oc-currence of adjectives, without regard for the nouns with which they had

occurred. The fifty adjectives which occurred most frequently were identified. The adjectives *good* and *bad* were used more than twice as often
as any others. Almost half of the fifty were clearly evaluative. Among the
fifty were most of the common perceptual dimensions such as heavy, light,
sweet, sour, hot, and cold.

The investigators selected twenty terms to which the fifty adjectives
might be applied: lady, boulder, sin, father, lake, symphony, Russian,
feather, me, fire, baby, fraud, God, patriot, tornado, sword, mother, statue,
cop, and America. Descriptive scales for the fifty adjectives were listed,
with each of the twenty terms yielding 1,000 rating-scale items. Each
rating-scale had the form:

LADY

rough   :   :   :   :   :   :   *smooth*

A subject was instructed to check a position on each rating scale indicating the nature of his association to a given term. Subjects for this part
of the study were 100 students in introductory psychology.

All possible intercorrelations were computed for the fifty rating scales.
The analysis yielded three factors: evaluation, which represented good-bad,
beautiful-ugly, sweet-sour, clean-dirty, tasty-distasteful, valuable-worthless,
kind-cruel, pleasant-unpleasant, bitter-sweet, happy-sad, sacred-profane,
nice-awful, fragrant-foul, honest-dishonest, and fair-unfair; potency, which
represented strong-weak, heavy-light, deep-shallow, loud-soft, and thick-
thin; and activity, which represented fast-slow, active-passive, hot-cold,
sharp-dull, and angular-rounded. The authors concluded that the evidence
from judgments of connotative meaning pointed to the existence of three
general characteristics: evaluation, potency, and activity.

FACTORIAL VALIDITY IN SPECIAL INVESTIGATIONS OF PERSONALITY

In no area of psychology has there been any greater proliferation
of specific methods of measurement than in personality. The characteristics
of motivational, emotional, and social behavior are legion. There is a
strenuous effort in progress to achieve the information necessary to settle
upon the fundamental dimensions of personality. In this connection the
task of psychologists is far from complete, but much has been achieved.
The investigations described in the following sections reveal the typical
approaches to the solution of this problem and the kinds of results obtained.

Personal Problems of High-School Girls

The personal problems of adolescents were investigated by Schutz[13]
for the purpose of determining the major characteristics of those problems.
The method, which involved identifying groups of correlated items called

clusters, was a simple approximation to factor analysis. Subjects were 500 girls in grades 10 and 11 in two high schools in Pinellas County, Florida.

The girls reported their problems by checking items in a list. The 441 items of the checklist included problems mentioned in compositions and free answers of a large number of high school students whose responses were obtained in the original development of the list. The items were classified according to content in eleven areas: physical health, fitness, and safety; getting along with others; boy-girl relationships; home and family life; personal finance; interests and activities; school life; heredity; planning for the future; mental-emotional health and fitness; and morality and religion. The checklist was administered in classrooms by the students' teachers. Forms were returned with signatures.

The 156 items selected for further analysis had been rated as serious problems by a panel of twenty guidance specialists and had been checked by at least five per cent of the girls.

Three clusters or groups of correlated items were identified. The first cluster, which corresponded to the category of mental-emotional health and fitness, included the items:

> People don't understand me.
> I'm afraid of making mistakes.
> I worry about what others say.
> I feel I'm not wanted.

The second cluster embraced three categories. "Getting along with others" included the items:

> I'm nervous when I talk to people.
> I'm not good at talking with people.
> I don't like to meet people.

"School life" included the item:

> I'm nervous in front of the class.

"Physical health, fitness, and safety" included the item:

> I get tired easily.

The third cluster, which corresponded to the category of home and family life, included the items:

> My father is always criticizing me.
> I can't discuss things with my mother.
> I am thinking of leaving home.

The three clusters were designated general personal anxiety and insecurity, tension concerning relations with others, and difficulty in getting along with parents.

Attitudes Toward Child Rearing

An attempt was made by Schaefer and Bell[12] to determine the principal dimensions of attitudes toward child rearing and the family. The correlations among twenty-four attitude scales were subjected to a factor analysis. Subjects were 100 unmarried student nurses in their freshman and sophomore years.

An inventory called the Parental Attitude Research Instrument was developed to measure a variety of attitudes toward child rearing and the family. Each of the twenty-four attitude scales in the inventory consisted of eight items. The names of the scales, with a sample item from each one, are listed below. (It is a good exercise to try to see the connection between the name and the sample item.)

1. *Encouraging verbalization.* Children should be allowed to disagree with their parents if they feel their own ideas are better.

2. *Infantilization.* A well-trained child always keeps the same close bond with its mother.

3. *Seclusion of the mother.* Too many women forget that a mother's place is in the home.

4. *Breaking the will.* Children need some of the natural meanness taken out of them.

5. *Harsh punishment.* If small children refuse to obey, parents should whip them for it.

6. *Fostering dependency.* A mother should do her best to avoid any disappointment for her child.

7. *Martyrdom.* Children should realize how much parents have to give up for them.

8. *Marital conflict.* Sometimes it is necessary for a wife to tell off her husband in order to get her rights.

9. *Strictness.* Strict discipline develops a fine strong character.

10. *Irritability.* Children will get on any woman's nerves if she has to be with them all day.

11. *Excluding outside influences.* Children should never learn things outside the home which make them doubt their parent's ideas.

12. *Deification.* The child should be taught to revere his parents above all other grownups.

13. *Suppression of aggression.* There is no good excuse for a child hitting another child.

14. *Rejection of the homemaking role.* Having to be with children all the time gives a woman the feeling her wings have been clipped.

15. *Autonomy of the child.* Children should be given a chance to try out as many things on their own as possible.

16. *Avoidance of communication.* If you let children talk about their trouble, they end up complaining even more.

17. *Ignoring the baby.* Handling a baby too much makes him spoiled and demanding.

18. *Suppression of sexuality.* It is very important that young boys and girls not be allowed to see each other completely undressed.

19. *Intrusiveness.* An alert parent should try to learn all her child's thoughts.

20. *Ascendance of the mother.* A married woman knows that she will have to take the lead in family affairs.

21. *Comradeship and sharing.* If more parents would have fun with their children, the children would be more apt to take their advice.

22. *Demand for activity.* The sooner a child learns that a wasted minute is lost forever the better off he will be.

23. *Abdication of the parental role.* Some children are so naturally headstrong that a parent can't really do much about them.

24. *Acceleration.* A mother should make an effort to get her child toilet trained at the earliest possible time.

The inventory was administered in psychology classes. Subjects were instructed to indicate whether they strongly agreed, mildly agreed, mildly disagreed, or strongly disagreed with the statements in each item. Inventories were completed and returned anonymously. Responses to each item were given weights of 1, 2, 3, or 4. Scores for each scale were computed by summing the responses for the eight items in that scale.

The correlations among the twenty-four scales were computed and subjected to a factor analysis to determine the general dimensions which might be taken as representing the specific scales. The five dimensions are listed below with the names of related scales. (It is a good exercise, but certainly a difficult one, to try to verify the abstraction which yielded each dimension.)

1. *Suppression and interpersonal distance:* comradeship and sharing, autonomy of the child, suppression of sexuality, avoidance of communication, and encouraging verbalization.

2. *Hostile rejection of the homemaking role:* rejection of the homemaking role, abdication of the parental role, irritability, marital conflict, and ignoring the baby.

3. *Excessive demands for striving:* strictness, acceleration, and demand for activity.

4. *Over-possessiveness:* martyrdom, suppression of aggression, fostering dependency, intrusiveness, and infantilization.

5. *Harsh punitive control:* excluding outside influences, breaking the will, ascendance of the mother, deification, seclusion of the mother, and harsh punishment.

Neuroticism and Extraversion

Two personality characteristics which have been given much attention by psychologists are neuroticism and extraversion. The factorial validity of two short inventories for measuring these characteristics was demonstrated by Eysenck[3]. Subjects were 1,600 adults from all over England. The sample was made up to have correct proportions of urban and rural dwellers and correct proportions from different regions of the country. Equal representation was given to the two sexes, male and female; two age groups, under 35 and over 35; and two social classes, upper and lower.

Interviews were conducted by representatives of a British market-research organization. In the interview, questions were first asked concerning a number of commercial products. Subjects were encouraged to think that obtaining answers to these questions was the purpose of the interview. A few personal questions about age and occupation were then asked. Finally the items of the personality questionnaire were presented. The questions were asked by the interviewer and the answers were written down by him. An answer of "Yes" was scored $+1$; an answer of "No," -1.

Neuroticism can be defined as an abstraction appropriate to the questions: Do you sometimes feel happy, sometimes depressed, without any apparent reason? Do you have frequent ups and downs in mood, either with or without apparent cause? Are you inclined to be moody? Does your mind often wander while you are trying to concentrate? Are you frequently "lost in thought" even when supposed to be taking part in a conversation?

Similarly, extraversion can be defined as an abstraction appropriate to the questions: Do you prefer action to the planning for action? Are you happiest when you get involved in some project that calls for rapid action? Do you usually take the initiative in making new friends? Are you inclined to be quick and sure in your actions? Would you rate yourself as a lively individual? Would you be very unhappy if you were prevented from making numerous social contacts?

Correlations among the answers to the twelve items were obtained and analyzed. Two general dimensions were identified. They corresponded to the two inventories, neuroticism and extraversion, thus confirming their factorial validity.

Dimensions of Neuroticism

In the study by Eysenck[3], the factorial validity of measures of neuroticism and extraversion was demonstrated by showing that the items in one inventory were related to one factor; those in the other inventory, to another factor. Demonstrating the validity of a general dimension such as neuroticism does not preclude the possibility that neurotic behavior may itself have varied characteristics or dimensions whose factorial validity might be investigated. To determine the dimensions of neurotic behavior as represented by a large number of rating scales, Lorr and Rubinstein[8] obtained ratings of neurotic adults, computed correlations among the scales, and subjected the correlations to a factor analysis. Subjects were 215 neurotic, male veterans with psychiatric disabilities incurred during service in World War II and the Korean War. All were newly accepted for treatment at Veterans Administration mental hygiene clinics.

Rating scales were put in graphic form with four- or six-point scales. Each subject was rated once by his own therapist on each of the rating scales after his third or fourth treatment interview. Therapist raters were predominantly psychiatrists, clinical psychologists, and social workers, with a few advanced psychology trainees and psychiatric residents. In each clinic several training sessions were conducted for raters, at which times there was opportunity for discussing and comparing practice ratings. Fifty rating scales were selected for a factor analysis. All correlations among the scales were computed and then analyzed.

The investigators had hypothesized in advance what the factors would be and which rating scales would be related to each factor. Listed below are the hypothesized factors, with illustrative rating scales. (The name of each factor is an abstraction appropriate to the scales.)

1. *Lack of emotional restraint:* expression of hostility, frequency of mood changes, and impulsiveness.
2. *Distortion of reality in thinking and perception:* blaming others for difficulties, feeling the world is hostile, defensiveness, and suspicion.
3. *Obsessive-phobic reaction:* distortions of reality, insistent thoughts, and morbid fears.
4. *Anxious tension:* tension, frequent difficulty sleeping, frequent irritability, and depression.
5. *Sense of personal adequacy:* feelings of inadequacy, weak belief in self, and troubled by guilt.
6. *Dependent immaturity:* dependent on others, weak interests, and low motivation for achievement.
7. *Lack of conscientiousness:* carelessness with tasks, little concern for orderliness, and no concern for anyone.
8. *Gastro-intestinal reaction:* complaints of headaches, complaints of tiredness, and severe gastric symptoms.
9. *Cardiac-respiratory reaction:* severe respiratory and cardiovascular symptoms.
10. *Conflict between sex impulses and moral standards:* concern over homosexual tendencies, and guilt over masturbation.

Seven of the ten factors yielded by the analysis corresponded to those hypothesized in advance. The seven confirmed factors were emotional responsiveness, sense of personal adequacy, drive toward long-term goals, conscientiousness or careless indifference, gastro-intestinal reaction, cardiorespiratory reaction, and conflict between sexual impulses and moral and social standards.

Dimensions of Abnormal Behavior

Attempts at classifying abnormal behavior have a long history in which many different schemes have been suggested. These schemes were not always simple. Numerous categories and subcategories have been employed, and people have even been classified in two or more sets of categories simultaneously. Classifying is, of course, a qualitative approach to the problem.

There is a quantitative approach to the description of abnormal behavior, in which measures are employed in place of categories. The problem with the quantitative approach is that abnormal behavior has many characteristics, and it is impractical, if not impossible, to employ measures of all of these characteristics when a description of that behavior is to be given. One solution to the problem would be to determine a few measurable characteristics or dimensions which give a satisfactorily comprehensive and economical description. As indicated earlier, factor analysis is suited to this purpose. The following investigation illustrates the approach.

Data obtained on 250 psychiatric patients newly admitted to a Connecticut State Hospital over a six-month period were subjected to a factor analysis by Lorr[7]. The data had been obtained originally by Wittenborn and Holzberg[14]. Patients who were alcoholic, senile, or physically ill in certain ways were excluded.

In the original investigation, psychiatrists observed and rated each patient during a standard period when he was not under treatment. All possible correlations were computed among fifty-one rating scales. In his analysis, Lorr identified seven factors. One was paranoid-schizophrenia, an abstraction for the scales: unjustified sexual beliefs, thinking bizarre or obscure, feels conspired against, feels others control his behavior, grandiose notions, distorts facts to defend opinions, has hallucinatory experiences. The other factors are given below with the rating scales which define their abstract labels.

1. *Disorganization of thinking:* difficulty in carrying out plans, bizarre or obscure thinking, slowed or delayed overt activity, difficulty in making decisions, poor memory of life history, and words irrelevant to recognizable ideas.

2. *Excitement with hostile belligerence:* belligerent or combative, reluctant to conform or cooperate, difficulty in sleeping, impudent or impolite, expresses irritation, does not give in easily to others, little concern for others, and eats very little.

3. *Anxiety:* unrealistic self blame, feeling of impending doom, doubts he can be helped, suicidal thoughts or impulses, avoids people, difficulty in sleeping, slowed or delayed overt activity, and performance of tasks affected by anxiety.

4. *Conversion hysteria:* use made of physical disease symptoms, organic pathology with emotional basis, and little concern over physical handicaps.

5. *Excitement with expansiveness:* conspicuously optimistic, engrossed in plans, demands attention, speech stilted, and grandiose notions.

6. *Phobic-compulsive reaction:* obsessional thinking, behavior affected by phobias, acutely distressed by anxiety, and exhibits compulsive acts.

The analysis by Lorr does not, of course, give a final answer to the problem of describing abnormal behavior quantitatively, but it does illustrate very well the kind of approach widely used in psychology, and the results support the validity of the groups of rating scales employed.

Chapter Summary

Definitions and illustrations were given of three kinds of validity: predictive, congruent, and factorial. All three are based on relations expressed in terms of correlation coefficients. Predictive validity, which is indicated by the correlation between a predictor variable and a criterion variable, is important in selection procedures, test construction, and the description of behavior. Evidence of predictive validity is furnished routinely by the authors of standardized tests and inventories. An aptitude test is an ability test which has been shown to be predictive of a criterion of success.

Congruent validity is indicated by the correlation between two sets of measures which are assumed to represent the same dimension of behavior. It is especially valuable when no suitable criterion is available for validating a test. There is substantial evidence of congruent validity for the widely used intelligence tests.

Factorial validity is indicated by the pattern of relatively low and relatively high values among all possible intercorrelations for a number of tests or scales. A factor is a hypothetical dimension representing some number of correlated real variables. Factor analysis is the formal computational method by means of which the salient dimensions are determined from the intercorrelations. A factorially valid battery of tests provides much more detailed information than does a single test.

There are three important ideas connected with the three kinds of validity:

1. Information about prediction is a major form of psychological knowledge.

2. Consistency of performance is observed not only in repeated administrations of the same test, as in the determination of reliability, but also in administrations of similar tests, as in the determination of congruent validity. In many situations people are consistently different from one another.

3. One goal of psychology is to reduce the countless complexities of behavior to a comprehendible number of salient characteristics. The general method is one of abstracting attributes. This is a major purpose of factor analysis.

References

1. Cline, V. B., and J. M. Richards, Jr. "Accuracy of Interpersonal Perception—A General Trait?" *The Journal of Abnormal and Social Psychology,* 60 (1960), 1-7.
2. Eastman, D. "Self-Acceptance and Marital Happiness." *The Journal of Consulting Psychology,* 22 (1958), 95-99.
3. Eysenck, H. J. "A Short Questionnaire for the Measurement of Two Dimensions of Personality." *The Journal of Applied Psychology,* 42 (1958), 14-17.
4. Fleishman, E. A. "An Analysis of Positioning Movements and Static Reactions." *The Journal of Experimental Psychology,* 55 (1958), 13-24.

5. Fleishman, E. A. "Dimensional Analysis of Movement Reactions." *The Journal of Experimental Psychology,* 55 (1958), 438-453.
6. Jones, F. N. "An Analysis of Individual Differences in Olfactory Thresholds." *The American Journal of Psychology,* 70 (1957), 227-232.
7. Lorr, M. "The Wittenborn Psychiatric Syndromes: An Oblique Rotation." *The Journal of Consulting Psychology,* 21 (1957), 439-444.
8. Lorr, M., and E. A. Rubinstein. "Personality Patterns of Neurotic Adults in Psychotherapy." *The Journal of Consulting Psychology,* 20, (1956), 257-263.
9. Merenda, P. F., and W. V. Clarke. "The Predictive Efficiency of Temperament Characteristics and Personal History Variables in Determining Success of Life Insurance Agents." *The Journal of Applied Psychology,* 43 (1959), 360-366.
10. Osgood, C. E., and G. J. Suci. "Factor Analysis of Meaning." *The Journal of Experimental Psychology,* 50 (1955), 325-338.
11. Patchen, M. "Absence and Employee Feelings About Fair Treatment." *Personnel Psychology,* 13 (1960), 349-360.
12. Schaefer, E. S., and R. Q. Bell. "Patterns of Attitudes Toward Child Rearing and the Family." *The Journal of Abnormal and Social Psychology,* 54 (1957), 391-395.
13. Schutz, R. E. "Patterns of Personal Problems of Adolescent Girls." *The Journal of Educational Psychology,* 49 (1958), 1-5.
14. Wittenborn, J. R., and J. D. Holzberg. "The Generality of Psychiatric Syndromes." *The Journal of Consulting Psychology,* 15 (1951), 372-380.
15. Worell, L. "Level of Aspiration and Academic Success." *The Journal of Educational Psychology,* 50 (1959), 47-54.

9

Age and

Other Nonbehavioral

Predictors

THE PREDICTIVE RELATIONSHIPS EXAMINED SO FAR HAVE INVOLVED two sets of paired measures of behavior. One set served as the criterion; the other served as the predictor. The pairing was accomplished in the measuring of each subject twice, once on each of two different scales. Thus the number of pairs of measures was equal to the number of subjects in the group.

Behavior can be predicted from other kinds of information. Quantitative data which are not measures of behavior can be employed as a predictor. The criterion is still a set of measures of behavior. Pairing is achieved by measuring each subject twice, once on the behavioral criterion and once on the nonbehavioral predictor. Thus the number of pairs of measures is again equal to the number of subjects in the group.

Nonbehavioral predictors include age, body measurements, biographical data, biological variables, and characteristics of the physical and social environments. Since age as a predictor of human behavior has been investigated extensively by psychologists, we shall give brief illustrations of the others and then return to it.

256

Prediction involving body measurements was demonstrated by Schrock and McCloy[12], who obtained ratings of basketball ability and measures of height and weight on forty-three subjects. The correlation between ratings and height was 0.50; between ratings and weight, 0.65. Weight turned out to be a better predictor of basketball ability than did height.

Biographical data in the form of school grades are shown to be predictive of test performance in the Manual for The Differential Aptitude Tests[1]. Scores on the subtest, verbal reasoning, were obtained for 3,400 boys in grades eight to twelve in widely scattered parts of the country. The average score for each of the five grades was obtained, yielding the five pairs of values plotted in Figure 9-1. The correlation between grade and average score is 0.99, indicating nearly perfect prediction. If

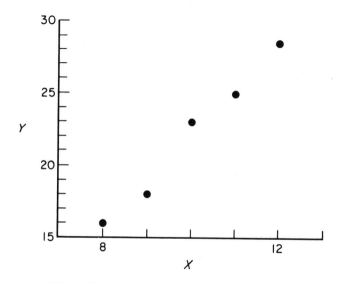

Figure 9-1. Relation between school grade and average score on the DAT subtest, verbal reasoning. X is grade. Y is average score.

individual scores had been plotted against grade instead of average scores, however, the correlation would have been lower. There would have been 3,400 points, one for each subject, and the points for each grade would have been dispersed or scattered in the vertical array. The results obtained illustrate a general principle. Average scores for groups can often be predicted with much greater accuracy than scores for individuals. In many practical situations, however, interest centers on prediction for individuals, not groups.

Personal history data were employed in an investigation by Soar[14] in which success in the management of service stations was predicted. Subjects were twenty-nine dealers who operated service stations in a metropolitan area of about 300,000 population in a southeastern state.

The criterion measures were ratings of the dealers by the five supervisors. Since territories had been systematically rotated, all supervisors knew the work of each dealer. Each dealer was also rated by one person at the next higher level of management. All raters were involved in selecting and training new dealers as part of their regular responsibilities.

Dealers were rated on fifteen aspects of service station management, categorized as business sense, promotion, emotional maturity, responsibility, and personality. Since the correlations between categories varied from 0.56 to 0.95, they were considered high enough to justify combining ratings on all aspects into one over-all criterion rating, the measure of success in service station management. Personal history data were collected from the dealers as they recalled their circumstances at the time they accepted dealerships. Among the fourteen personal history items related most highly to the criterion were the following: two or more subjects listed as liked in school; held office in high school organizations; held job in high school; wife not working; own home or paying on it; owe money; carry other insurance in addition to life insurance; have 500 dollars or more in savings; no more than 200 pounds in weight; between 25 and 39 years of age; and no more than one child.

Additional data were collected on twenty-three dealers from two somewhat smaller metropolitan areas in the same state for purposes of confirming or cross validating the findings. The correlation between the criterion, rated success, and personal history scores based on the fourteen items was +0.47, a substantial correlation for a situation in which criterion measurement is difficult and uncertain. This predictive relation could then have been employed in the selection of dealers in the future.

Biological predictors of behavior are studied intensively in courses in physiological psychology. Among the more important ones are structural, chemical, and electrical variables. Certain characteristics of behavior may be predicted from changes in the structure of the nervous system, internal organs, bones, and muscles as a consequency of disease or injury; from cellular chemical reactions involved in the transformation of energy and the chemical reactions whereby energy is obtained from food; and from the electrical activity of neurons, muscles, skin, and the brain. Numerous biological predictors represent conditions of the internal environment which, in the normal healthy organism, are maintained within fairly definite limits—a set of circumstances conceptualized as homeostasis. These conditions include body temperature, blood-sugar level, hydrogen-ion concentration in the blood, blood pressure, and others. Complex predictive relations have been found between the biological variables and sleep, sexual behavior, hunger, thirst, and emotion.

The behavior of subjects from different physical environments might be predicted from a characteristic of those environments. Humidity, temperature, altitude, barometric pressure, rainfall, distance from the ocean, distance from a metropolitan area, amount of some chemical in the drinking water, and amount of fall-out radiation are some possibilities. One could, if he wished, determine the relation between sociability scores of college students on a personality inventory and the average daily high temperatures in the communities from which they came.

Just as characteristics of the physical environment can be used as predictors, so can characteristics of the social environment. The number of siblings in a person's family, the number of people in his household, the population of his home community, an index of cultural activity in his home community, and the number of incidents of racial conflict reported in the newspaper of his home community might be of interest to a psychologist. He could, for example, determine the relation between students' scores on a scale of attitude toward racial integration and the frequency of racial conflicts in their home communities, as reported in the newspapers serving those communities.

There have been studies in which measures of behavior for certain people have been assigned, as a predictor variable, to subjects related to those people or connected with them in some way. In this situation, the measures do not pertain to the behavior of the subject and constitute, therefore, a nonbehavioral predictor. A group of students, whose behavior is to be predicted on some criterion, such as leadership in extracurricular activities, may have assigned to them their fathers' scores on an inventory designed to measure interest in political affairs. The fathers' interest in political affairs as expressed by their answers on an inventory is the predictor. A group of children, whose play behavior with respect to constructiveness is to be predicted, may have assigned to them scores representing their parents' agreement in answers on an inventory of practices in child rearing. The hypothesis might be that constructiveness can be predicted from agreement between a child's parents.

Age Classifications

A great amount of information is available on the relation between various characteristics of behavior and age. Since there are two clearly distinguishable procedures for investigating this relation, and one cannot assume that they will yield the same results, it is important to keep them separate and to exercise caution in interpreting the results.

One of the two procedures involves classifying subjects by age. Studies using age classifications are sometimes referred to as cross-sectional studies. Subjects in a given group are measured on an attribute of behavior and classified according to age. For each subject there is a measure of behavior and a measure of age. The predictive relation between behavior and age can then be determined. This predictive relation may be of value in telling how people of different ages in a similar group can be expected to differ in their behavior.

The other procedure involves measuring each subject repeatedly at successive ages. We shall refer to the predictor variable in this procedure as developmental age. Studies employing this procedure are sometimes called longitudinal studies. The predictive relation between behavior and developmental age expresses the course of development of that behavior over some period of time. The relation could be of value in anticipating future behavioral events.

The relation between behavior and classification age cannot be assumed to express the course of development. There is no law or logic which precludes the two procedures from giving the same result, but they may not, and therefore they should be distinguished. Since developmental studies are more difficult to conduct than classification studies, there is a greater danger of misinterpretation in one direction than the other—namely, treating classification results as developmental.

If it can be safely assumed that the different age groups are comparable in all important respects, classification age can be interpreted as developmental age with little or no risk of error. This assumption can be justified more often with children than with older people, and with a narrow range of ages than with a broad one. In a given small community, children of preschool age may be comparable from one age group to another, whereas young people between fifteen and twenty may not be, if many of them go off to college or to the city for jobs after graduation from high school. If the group studied covers an age range of fifty years, there is the possibility of very great differences in background characteristics, such as amount of education, from one age group to another. Therefore, the predictive relation involving classification age might reflect selective migration or changes in level of education and, if it does, would not fairly represent the anticipated course of future development for a given group of infants, children, adolescents, or adults.

The Prediction of Children's Behavior from Classification Age

Differences in motor, intellective, and personality characteristics of children's behavior have been predicted from classification age. Some typical findings in these three areas will be described next. The findings are illustrative of the kinds of age-related differences one can expect to find within similar groups of children.

Motor and Sensorimotor Characteristics

Motility, which is defined as general spontaneous or operant movement, is a kind of motor behavior which has been predicted from classification age. In one study, infants who varied in age from one to sixteen days were found to vary in motility. There was a trend in which
motility increased from lower age groups to higher ones.

In 1932, Irwin[5] reported measurements of motility for seventy-two
full-term infants born in the obstetrical ward of the State University of
Iowa General Hospital. A bassinet-like stabilimeter, connected by string
and pulleys with a polygraph, was employed. Motility was measured in
oscillations per minute of the polygraph pens. Measurements were made
during a three-hour period in the afternoon. A plot of average number

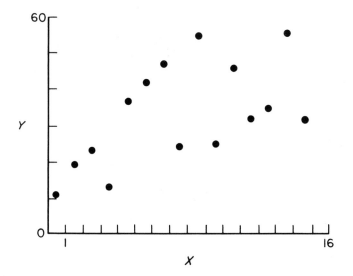

Figure 9-2. Motility of infants classified by age. *X* is age in days. *Y* is number of
oscillations per minute, averaged for a varying number of infants. [After Irwin.[5]]

of oscillations per minute for the infants classified by age in days is
presented in Figure 9-2. The number of infants represented by each point
varied from two to seven.

Prehension, the act of grasping, is a kind of sensorimotor behavior
which has been widely investigated. Typical grasps employed by infants
at varying ages were identified by Halverson[4] in 1931. Observations
were made by moving-picture camera in the observatory of the Yale Psycho-
Clinic. Subjects were twelve or more normally developing infants at each
of the ages 16, 20, 24, 28, 32, 36, 40, and 52 weeks.

The behavior studied was prehension of small red cubes. The infant

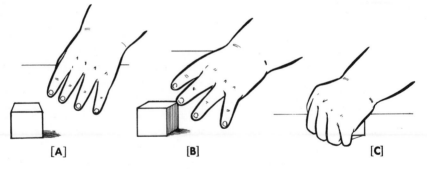

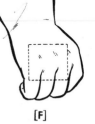
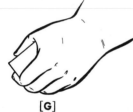

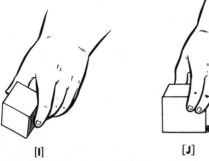

Figure 9-3. Typical grasps employed by infants at various ages in weeks. **A:** No contact, 16. **B:** Contact only, 20. **C:** Primitive squeeze, 20. **D:** Squeeze grasp, 24. **E:** Hand grasp, 28. **F:** Palm grasp, 28. **G:** Superior palm grasp, 32. **H:** Inferior forefinger grasp, 36. **I:** Forefinger grasp, 52. **J:** Superior forefinger grasp, 52. [Adapted from Halverson.[4]]

was seated on a platform in an experimental crib before a table top at elbow height. He faced the longer edge of the table top, which was divided into six equal lanes by lines extending from its far edge to a line parallel with the near edge.

Observations were made in three situations, each of twenty seconds duration. In the first, the examiner took a cube in the palm of her hand and carried it, below the table top, to the middle line. She then tapped the cube against the far edge. As the infant fixated the cube, the examiner advanced it along the middle line at a rate which brought it, in two seconds, to the standard position, a point not far from the near edge. The examiner then released the cube so that one of its surfaces fronted the infant. If, within nine seconds, he gave no indication of reaching for the cube, the examiner advanced the cube nearer him and again released it. This procedure was repeated with the second and third cubes, except that the second cube was presented while the infant held the first cube in his left hand, and the third cube was presented while he held a cube in each hand. Two cameras recorded the infant's behavior.

To analyze the film records, apparatus for stilling individual frames was constructed. Images were projected on ground glass, marked to facilitate the determination of position, direction, and distance. Movements of the hand, arm, and body were charted on special forms.

Infants of different ages were found to vary greatly in their manner of grasping objects. Figure 9-3 shows the different types of grasps employed by the various age groups. There were infants who did not succeed in reaching the cube and others who reached the cube but could not grasp it.

In 1935 Goodenough[3] found that children's reaction times to visual and auditory stimuli, measures of sensorimotor behavior, decreased from one age group to the next. The children, whose ages varied from 3.5 to 9.5 years, were enrolled in the nursery school and kindergarten of the University of Minnesota Institute of Child Welfare, or were brought in for testing the Institute's laboratory.

Reaction time was measured by means of an electric clock which made a buzzing noise. It was started and stopped by either a telegraph key or a push-button switch which the examiner held. With a child seated before a low table containing the apparatus, the examiner said: "I have a clock here that makes a loud noise and its hands go around just like your clock at home. You can stop the clock if you put your finger down hard on this button like this." After demonstrating, the examiner said, "Now let's see how quickly you can stop it. Put your finger on the button so you will be all ready and, as soon as I start it, you stop

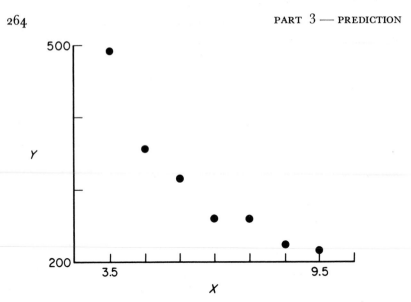

Figure 9-4. Reaction time of male children classified by age. *X* is age in years. *Y* is reaction time in thousandths of a second. The value plotted is the median of all trials for each age group. [After Goodenough.[3]]

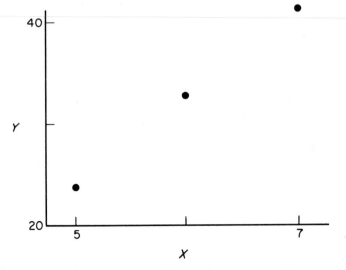

Figure 9-5. Motor performances of children selected by age. *X* is age in years. *Y* is average distance in feet for boys on the baseball throw. [After Jenkins.[7]]

it." After two practice trials with each hand, twenty test trials were given with hands alternating.

The median reaction time of all trials for a given age group was determined. Figure 9-4 is a plot of such values in thousandths of a second for both hands for males. Numbers of children in the successive age groups vary from 13 to 54. Reaction time decreases as the age of the various groups increases.

Some simple measures of athletic behavior were obtained by Jenkins[7] in 1930, on children from five to seven years of age in schools in Englewood and Montclair, New Jersey. In each of the three age groups were 100 children, equally divided according to sex. The differences between the age groups indicated improvement from the lowest to the highest age on every measure. As one would expect, boys were generally superior to girls in these performances.

The children performed in the following events: three trials on a 35-yard dash; tossing a bean bag for accuracy at distances of 10, 25, and 35 feet; three trials on a baseball throw for distance; throwing a baseball at a circular target from distances of 5, 10, 20, and 35 feet; three trials on the standing broad jump; and jumping and reaching. Most of the tests were given out-of-doors.

Figure 9-5 is a graph of distance and age for the baseball throw by boys. Distance of throws increases from the lowest to the highest age group.

Intellective Characteristics

Many intellective characteristics are measured in terms of verbal behavior. An example is the length of children's sentences. It was predicted from classification age in an investigation reported in 1926 by Smith[13]. The 124 children, who varied in age from two to five years, were contacted at the baby-examining and preschool laboratories of the Iowa Child Welfare Research Station, the University elementary school, a private day nursery, and a boarding home.

Each child was observed for an hour while he played with other children, and an attempt was made to record every word he spoke. A few children who were very quiet had to be observed for several days before a sufficient amount of vocalizing could be recorded. After the numbers of words and sentences were determined, the average length of sentences was calculated for each child.

Figure 9-6 is a plot of average number of words per sentence for children in six-month age groups from two to five years. The numbers of children in the successive age groups varied from 11 to 23. Sentence length obviously increased from the lower age groups to the higher but then appeared to level off.

Intellective characteristics of children, measured in terms of talkativeness and vocabulary size, were studied in 1938 by Jersild and Ritzman[8]. Both characteristics were found to increase with the age of the groups.

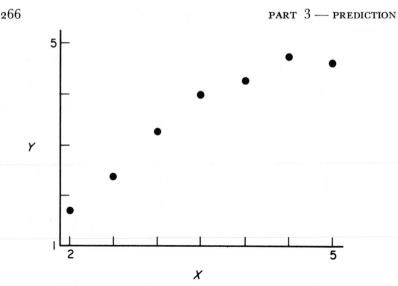

Figure 9-6. Sentence length of young children classified by age. X is age in years. Y is average number of words per sentence. [After Smith.[13]]

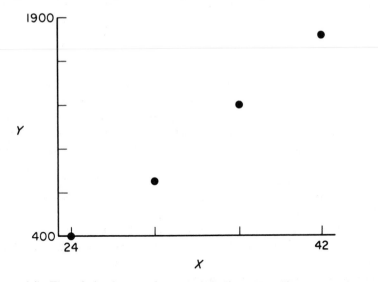

Figure 9-7. The relation between language behavior and age in a group of nursery school children. X is lowest age in months for each subgroup. Y is average number of words spoken. [After Jersild and Ritzman.[8]]

The seventy-nine children, two to five years of age, were enrolled in the nursery schools of the Child Development Institute.

Verbatim records of the language used by children during two or three mornings in the nursery school, representing approximately six or nine hours of observation, were obtained. During each one of the days devoted to a given child, he was followed by an observer. The period of observation began when the child entered school in the morning and ended when he had finished his lunch and was ready for his afternoon nap. All vocalizations made during this period were recorded as they sounded to the observer. The situation in which each vocalization occurred, the behavior of playmates or teachers, and other events occurring in the subject's immediate environment were also recorded.

Two scores were obtained for each child: a count of the total number of words spoken and a count of the total number of different words used. In determining the number of different words, no proper nouns were counted; no plural forms were counted if the singular had been

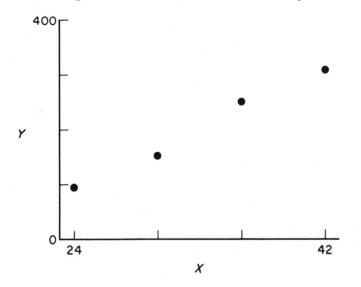

Figure 9-8. The relation between language behavior and age in a group of nursery school children. X is lowest age in months for each subgroup. Y is average number of different words used. [After Jersild and Ritzman.[8]]

used; childish forms of the same word, such as mother and mammy, were counted as different words; a combination of two or more words, such as kiddie car, was counted as one word; childish expressions such as choo choo for train were counted; incomprehensible vocalizations were not counted; slang expressions were counted; and a contraction such as can't or won't was counted as one word.

Figure 9-7 shows the average number of words spoken by children in four age groups, the lowest age in each group being indicated on the scale. Figure 9-8 shows the average number of different words used for the same age groups. There is a definite positive linear trend in each graph.

The prediction of the intellective characteristic, memorizing, from classification age was investigated in a study reported in 1933 by Stroud and Maul[15]. Memorizing of poetry and nonsense syllables was found to improve from age seven to eleven years. The 172 children who were tested made up the major part of the enrollment in grades two to six of the training school at Kansas State Teachers College.

A child's task was to memorize poetry and nonsense syllables. Three poems with four lines to a stanza and six lists of three-letter nonsense syllables were employed. The children, who were tested individually, spent fifteen minutes memorizing poetry and ten minutes memorizing syllables. A child was required to read the poetry aloud and to spell out the syllables with presentation and recall alternated. He memorized a unit, a pair of syllables or a stanza, memorized the next unit, then integrated the units, and so on. Scores were the number of lines of poetry and the number of syllables memorized in the time allowed.

Figure 9-9 is a plot of average number of lines of poetry against age; Figure 9-10, average number of syllables against age. Both show increases in amount memorized with increases in the age of the different groups.

Personality Characteristics

Negativism, a social characteristic of personality, was investigated in 1928 by Reynolds[11] and found to decrease between the second and fifth years. Negativism was measured by the number of failures to comply to requests made by an examiner. The 229 children were from the nursery school of the Institute of Child Welfare, the psychological clinic of the Institute, seven day nurseries, and the kindergarten of the Horace Mann School.

Painted blocks were spread out on a small table placed, with two chairs, where they could be seen from the door of the observation room. The examiner would approach a child and say, "Come on, John, let's go play some games." When they entered the room and approached the table, she would say, "See the pretty blocks, let's go over here and play with them." Then she would choose four blocks and, putting one of them on top of another, say to the child, "Let's play blocks this way, John. See, I'll put a block on top, like this, now you put one on." She would hold a block in her outstretched hand for about five seconds and then lay it down near the child. If, at the end of ten seconds, the child had made no move to comply, the request was repeated four times. For each request made of the child, the examiner recorded whether or not he complied.

In another situation, the examiner picked the child up, without ex-

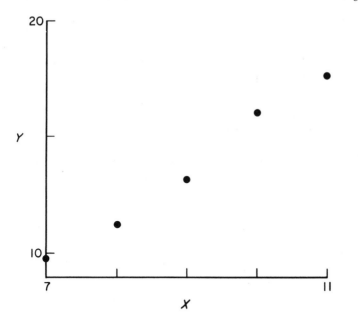

Figure 9-9. Amount of poetry learned among children classified by age. X is age in years. Y is average number of lines of poetry learned. [After Stroud and Maul.[15]]

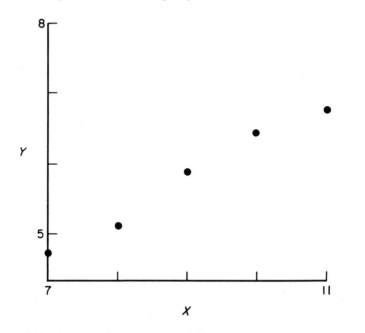

Figure 9-10. Amount of nonsense material learned among children classified by age. X is age in years. Y is average number of syllables learned. [After Stroud and Maul.[15]]

planation, and held him on her lap for one minute. As soon as she had him on her lap, she said, "Go ahead, play with the blocks some more," and extended her hands to the edge of the table to prevent him from falling or getting down. If the child protested, the examiner made no comment. If the child succeeded in moving the examiner's hands, he was allowed to get down.

Other situations involved requests for the child to imitate the examiner by waving his hand, shaking his head, and clapping his hands. Each request was repeated four times. The requests were given as follows: "John do this. John do this. Come on, John, do this. Oh John, come on; you can do this, can't you?" A record was made of every compliance or failure to comply.

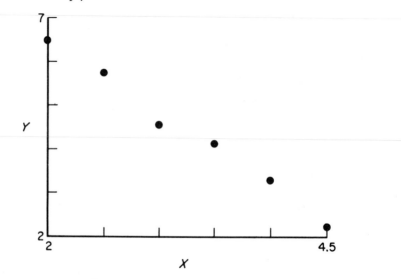

Figure 9-11. Negativism of young children classified by age. X is age in years. Y is average number of failures to comply to a series of requests. [After Reynolds.[11]]

The entire series consisted of thirteen situations involving thirteen opportunities to refuse. The child's score on negativism was based on his reactions to first requests in the different situations. Figure 9-11 is a plot of average number of failures for the children in six-month age groups from two to 4.5 years. As already noted, negativism scores decreased from the lower age groups to the higher ones.

In another investigation of the prediction of personality characteristics from age, the perception of social differences by children was measured by Jahoda[6]. Scores on the test were found to increase with age in four groups from six to nine years. The subjects were children from schools in Glasgow. Ten children, five boys and five girls, were selected randomly at each of four ages from six to nine years in each of four schools. In a fifth school, five boys were selected at each age.

The test material consisted of pairs of pictures. Each member of a pair was divided into two pieces so that the four pieces could be put together in two different ways. Both solutions were physically correct, but only one gave a socially probable picture. A child was told that he would see a series of cards, that the pieces could be put together in different ways, and that he was to choose the way that was more usual.

The first set, which dealt with football and cricket, was intended merely to introduce the child to the task and nearly all children quickly solved the problem correctly. When a child had gotten a correct solution, the investigator put the cards together incorrectly and asked, "Woud it be all right like this?" The correct answer was "No." The second set consisted of two versions of a husband and wife at a dining table; the third, two versions of a woman sitting in a chair in a living room; the fourth, two versions of two men meeting on the street and shaking hands; the fifth, two versions of a father, mother, son, and daughter, and their house.

A child was scored on the second, third, and fourth sets of pictures for both performance and verbal response to the question. The fifth set consisted of two large cards with pictures of houses and cards showing parents and children. The child was asked to put together two families and to put each family on the house in which it lived. Four scores were given on the fifth set, two for performance in assembling the families and assigning them to their correct houses, and two for verbal responses to the incorrect arrangements.

Children in each of the four age groups were placed in two classes: middle and working. Figure 9-12 is a plot of boys' mean performance against group age for the two classes. At all ages middle-class boys had higher scores than working-class boys. Scores increased with the age of the groups, but not in a perfectly regular manner. Middle-class boys were also superior to working-class boys at every age on verbal-response scores. Middle-class girls were superior to working-class girls at every age on both sets of scores.

An emotional characteristic of personality in children from one to eight years of age was studied in 1931 by Goodenough[2]. The frequency of occurrence of anger outbursts was determined for forty-five children whose mothers volunteered from study groups of clubs for college women in Minneapolis and St. Paul. The results showed a peak at the age of two years.

Mothers were asked to keep daily records of anger outbursts by their children at home. Records were to be kept for one month. The instructions were to record any manifestation of anger, rage, or marked irritation; the child's occupation at the time of the outburst; and the event which appeared to be the immediate source of the difficulty. The mothers were asked not to analyze or explain in recording and to base their classifications on overt behavior. Records included the categories: undirected energy, a discharge of physical energy without apparent direction or purpose; resistance, pouting or sulking and pulling or tugging on some object; and retaliation, attacking an offending person or object.

The mothers reported kicking, stamping, jumping up and down, striking, throwing self on floor, stiffening the body, refusing to budge, pulling away, struggling, running for help, turning away bodily, turning away the head, closing the mouth tightly, refusing to swallow food already in the mouth, pouting, frowning, pulling, pushing, throwing objects, running away, running at the offender in a threatening manner, reaching for objects, grabbing for objects, pinching, biting, crying, screaming, fussing, scolding, whining, snarling, mumbling, muttering to self, refusing verbally, threatening, calling names, arguing, and insisting. Figure 9-13 is a plot of frequency of outbursts per hour of observation against age of groups. As already noted, the frequency of outbursts shows a peak for the second-year group.

THE PREDICTION OF ADULT BEHAVIOR FROM CLASSIFICATION AGE

In studies of intellective behavior covering a wide age range, attention has been focused largely upon determining the age at which maximum performance is displayed and whether or not performance at later ages is as high. There is considerable evidence of lower performance at higher ages, but the results are not uniform for all tests as will be shown in the first investigation to be described. Furthermore, there is the possibility that people in the age range from fifty to sixty years have, on the average, much less education than those from fifteen to twenty-five. These results must therefore be interpreted cautiously with respect to the anticipated future performance of the highest performing age groups. The results can be interpreted unequivocally as indicating the distribution of scores over the age classifications.

In 1933, Jones and Conrad[9] reported on a survey conducted in nineteen villages of Massachusetts, New Hampshire, and Vermont to determine the relation between scores on an intelligence test and age. They found that scores increased rapidly over the early age groups, reaching a maximum around age twenty. People in progressively higher age groups obtained lower scores on most tests.

In villages with a hall where commercial silent films were shown once a week, arrangements were made for rental of the hall and projection service. In smaller villages, a portable projector was used in the

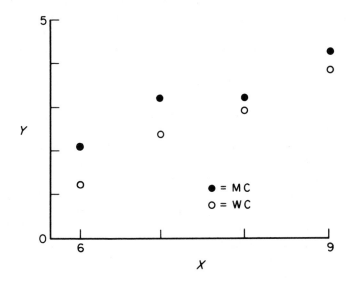

Figure 9-12. Social perception scores of children classified by age and class. X is age in years. Y is average score. The two sets of points represent two categories: middle class and working class. Data are for boys only. [After Jahoda.[6]]

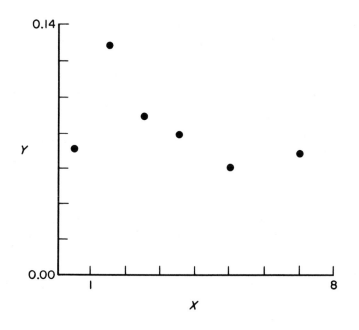

Figure 9-13. Frequency of outbursts of anger among children classified by age. X is age in years. Y is average frequency per hour of observation. [After Goodenough.[2]]

town or parish hall. Where electric lines were not available, current was obtained from a portable generator. Advertising consisted of announcements in church, at preceding moving-picture showings, and at meetings of the Grange and other local societies; newspaper notices; placards posted in the village and along country roads; and free tickets of invitation, circulated by local canvassers. The halls were usually filled by a group of 60 to 150 people.

In the earlier part of the survey, the Army Alpha Intelligence Test was administered at the end of the main feature of the show and before the final reels of short subjects. Monitors distributed pencils, lap boards, and test blanks. Two different forms were distributed to alternate persons to prevent copying. In the meantime, the examiner gave a brief talk designed to stimulate people's interest. In the later testing, a moving picture test was given prior to the Alpha Test to stimulate interest and cooperation and to provide experience in group measurement. The Alpha Test was then usually administered in the intermission of a second show, scheduled a week or so later.

In later testing, the title on the Alpha Test was concealed by pasting a printed slip across the top of each test blank. In place of the intelligence test title, a title was given which was designed to interest people in the test as a measure of practical judgment, information, speed of reading, and understanding.

When members of a family were absent or asked to be excused from participating, the family was visited and tested later at home, where a technique was used similar to that employed in the group measurements, except that no entertainment was given. In some communities an attempt was made to test every family containing two parents and two or more children. In others, a family census was drawn up from town records and a random sample was obtained of two-child families.

Total and subtest scores on the Army Alpha Intelligence Test were obtained. Figure 9-14 contains plots of total scores; scores for Subtest 4, Vocabulary or Opposites; scores for Subtest 7, Analogies; and scores for Subtest 8, General Information.

All four kinds of scores were averaged and plotted against age. The plot of total scores indicates successive increases from one age group to another up to a maximum for groups between the ages 18 and 21. Scores then decrease until the 55-year group is at a level with the 14-year group. The plots for the individual subtests vary. Subtest 4, Vocabulary or Opposites, and Subtest 8, General Information, do not show a postadolescent decline. Subtest 7, Analogies, shows a rapid decline.

The 1933 survey by Jones was confined to New England villages. A standardization project for the Wechsler Adult Intelligence Scale (WAIS), described by Wechsler[16] in 1958, covered the United States. The results showed a maximum performance around twenty-five years and successively lower performances at higher ages.

The project involved two groups: 1,700 subjects of both sexes, ages 16 to 64, and an additional 475 subjects of both sexes, ages 60 to 75 and over. In planning the composition of the groups, occupation and education, as well as sex and age, were considered. Thus an examiner who participated in obtaining standardization data could have been asked to

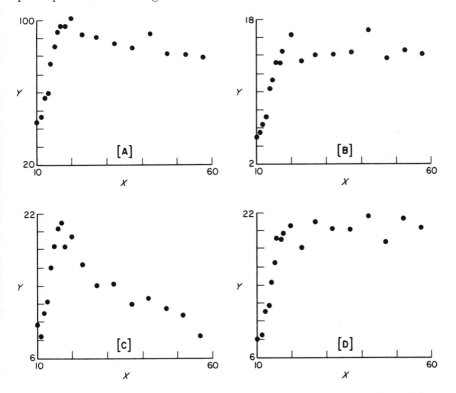

Figure 9-14. The relation between test performance and age in a rural population. *X* is age in years in all four graphs. **A:** *Y* is average *total* score on the Army Alpha Intelligence Test. **B:** *Y* is average score on the vocabulary subtest of the Alpha Intelligence Test. **C:** *Y* is average score on the analogies subtest. **D:** *Y* is average score on the general-information subtest. [After Jones and Conrad.[(9)]]

obtain a male, semi-skilled laborer, age 30 to 34, who had completed eight grades or less; or a housewife, age 25 to 29, who was a college graduate.

Subjects were obtained from all parts of the country in rough proportion to the population of the different sections. Nonwhite subjects made up ten per cent of the sample. This percentage corresponded approximately to the percentage of nonwhite persons in the United States

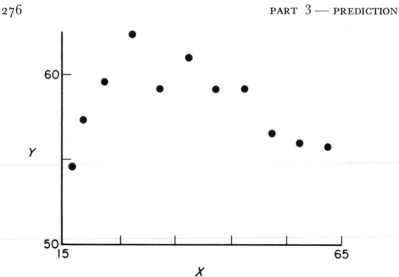

Figure 9-15. The relation between test scores and age in a cross-section of the population. X is age in years. Y is the average of sums of scaled scores on six verbal tests from the Wechsler Adult Intelligence Scale. [After Wechsler.[16]]

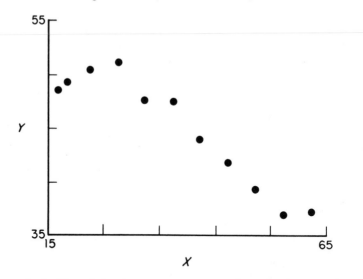

Figure 9-16. The relation between test scores and age in a cross-section of the population. X is age in years. Y is the average of sums of scaled scores on five performance tests from the Wechsler Adult Intelligence Scale. [After Wechsler.[16]]

at the time of the 1950 census. All subjects were volunteers. Figure 9-15 is a plot of scores on six verbal tests against group age. Figure 9-16 is a plot of scores on five performance tests against age. Both plots show an initial rise followed by a decline. It is evident that people in the higher age groups did not do as well as those around twenty-five. Can one assume that the people who did best will, in the future, decline? They may, of course, but the assumption is made with some risk of error. If their education differs from that of the higher age groups, they may not show the same decline.

Prediction of Sales Effectiveness

An investigation of sales effectiveness by Kirchner, McElwain, and Dunnette[10] illustrates the kind of interest an industry may have in age as a predictor. Subjects were 539 salesmen from two sales divisions of Minnesota Mining and Manufacturing Company. There ages averaged

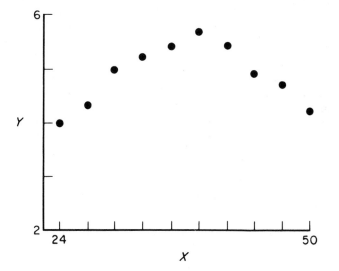

Figure 9-17. Sales effectiveness of men classified by age. X is age in years. Y is average rating of sales effectiveness. Total number of salesmen was 539. [After Kirchner, McElwain, and Dunnette.[10]]

34.07 years and varied from 23 to 65 years. Ratings of sales effectiveness were obtained from the salesmen's managers. The ranks assigned by each manager were converted to an index which varied from one to nine. Figure 9-17 is a graph of average sales-effectiveness scores for salesmen classified by age. Ratings of sales effectiveness are highest for age groups around age forty and lower for younger and older groups.

Chapter Summary

Behavior can be predicted from the nonbehavioral variables: age, body measurements, biographical data, biological characteristics, and attributes of the physical and social environments. Classification age should be distinguished from developmental age, for their predictive relations with behavior are not necessarily the same. Prediction from classification age embodies the idea that people who differ in age may display concomitant differences in behavior. Developmental age will be considered in the next chapter.

References

1. *Differential Aptitude Tests,* 2nd ed. New York: The Psychological Corporation.
2. Goodenough, F. L. *Anger in Young Children.* Child Welfare Monograph IX. Minneapolis: University of Minnesota Press, 1931.
3. ———. "The Development of the Reactive Process from Early Childhood to Maturity." *The Journal of Experimental Psychology,* 18 (1935), 431-450.
4. Halverson, H. M. "An Experimental Study of Prehension in Infants by Means of Systematic Cinema Records." *Genetic Psychology Monographs,* 10 (1931), 107-286.
5. Irwin, O. C. "The Amount of Motility of Seventy-Three Newborn Infants." *The Journal of Comparative Psychology,* 14 (1932), 415-428.
6. Jahoda, G. "Development of the Perception of Social Differences in Children from 6 to 10." *The British Journal of Psychology,* 50 (1959), 159-175.
7. Jenkins, L. M. "A Comparative Study of Motor Achievements of Children Five, Six, and Seven Years of Age." *Contributions to Education,* No. 414. New York: Teachers College, Columbia University, 1930.
8. Jersild, A. T., and R. Ritzman. "Aspects of Language Development: The Growth of Loquacity and Vocabulary." *Child Development,* 9 (1938), 243-259.
9. Jones, H. E., and H. S. Conrad. "The Growth and Decline of Intelligence: A Study of A Homogeneous Group Between the Ages of Ten and Sixty." *Genetic Psychology Monographs,* 13 (1933), 223-298.
10. Kirchner, W. K., C. S. McElwain, and M. D. Dunnette. "A Note on the Relationship Between Age and Sales Effectiveness." *The Journal of Applied Psychology,* 44 (1960), 92-93.
11. Reynolds, M. M. "Negativism of Pre-School Children." *Contributions to Education,* No. 288. New York: Teachers College, Columbia University, 1928.
12. Schrock, H. D., and C. H. McCloy. "A Study of the Best Combination of Age, Height, and Weight for Basketball Classification." *Journal of Physical Education* (October 1929).
13. Smith, M. E. "An Investigation of the Development of the Sentence and the Extent of Vocabulary in Young Children." *University of Iowa Studies in Child Welfare,* 3, No. 5 (1926).
14. Soar, R. S. "Personal History Data as A Predictor of Success in Service Station Management." *The Journal of Applied Psychology,* 40 (1956), 383-385.
15. Stroud, J. B., and R. Maul. "The Influence of Age Upon Learning and Retention of Poetry and Nonsense Syllables." *The Journal of Genetic Psychology,* 42 (1933), 242-250.
16. Wechsler, D. *The Measurement and Appraisal of Adult Intelligence.* Baltimore: Williams and Wilkins, 1958.

10

Predictors

of Changes

in Behavior

A GIVEN CHARACTERISTIC OF BEHAVIOR MAY VARY, AND THAT IT does so may be revealed by repeated measurement of the same subject. By definition, change is the predictable part of this variation. The unpredictable part is error. Narrowly conceived, change is the difference between two successive measures; more broadly conceived, it is a series of such differences. There are numerous predictors of change and they have been widely investigated. A substantial part of psychological knowledge consists of predictive relations which have been demonstrated between changes in behavior and a variety of predictor variables.

The single subject is the basic unit in the prediction of change. A pair of values, X and Y, is obtained for the subject on one occasion. (X is the predictor variable; Y is the measure of behavior.) Another pair is obtained on a second occasion. Additional pairs may be obtained on succeeding occasions. This repeated measurement results in two sets of paired values. For the one subject there are as many pairs of values as occasions. An attempt is made to establish a rule for predicting Y from X on the set of paired values for that subject.

Although the basic unit in the prediction of change is the single subject, data from a number of subjects can be combined by averaging measures for each occasion. Changes in averages can then be studied and an attempt can be made to formulate a prediction rule for the group of subjects.

Predictors of change fall in five classes: developmental age, time, conditioning trials, practice trials, and operant training trials. All five classes have a common feature—that occasions are ordered temporally. A child's birthdays from age four to eight are ordered occasions of developmental age. The hours between two infant feedings are ordered time intervals. Trials of any kind are necessarily ordered temporally by their occurrences.

Developmental Age

Developmental age is expressed as successive hours, days, weeks, months, or years in some part or the whole of the life span of an individual. To predict change, the successive ages are the occasions for measurement of some aspect of the individual's behavior. Developmental age is, of course, different from classification age. A difference in behavior from one developmental age to another is a change. A difference in behavior from one classification age to another is, strictly speaking, a difference between two groups which may not be comparable in other respects. The relation between some aspect of behavior and developmental age could be quite different from the relation between that same aspect of behavior and classification age. The most certain knowledge about the course of development comes from studies of developmental age.

LOCOMOTION

The development of locomotion in the first two years was described in 1933 by Shirley[31,32] after she made extensive observations of babies in a hospital and in their homes. The twenty-four babies were from families in professional, managerial, and business occupations.

Observations were made every day during the first week in the hospital and every two days during the second week. During the remaining fifty weeks of the first year, observations were made in the babies' homes at intervals of one week, and during the second year at intervals of two weeks. The weekly observations of the first year were supplemented by the mothers' daily records of food intake and habits of sleep and by their reports of behavior.

Complete records for the first year were obtained on the twenty-four babies; for the second year, on sixteen of them. The records included a

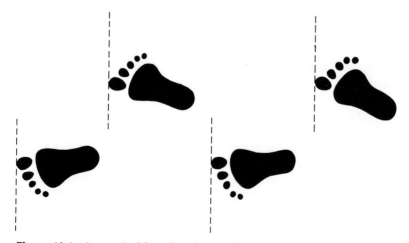

Figure 10-1. A record of footprints from which measurements of step length were obtained. [Adapted from Shirley.[31]]

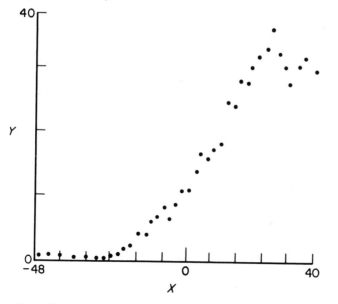

Figure 10-2. The development of walking. X is weeks before and after walking. Y is median distance in meters traversed in a one-minute interval of walking. [After Shirley.[31, 32]]

variety of data: anthropometric measures; reports of health, nutrition, and physical conditions; observations of motor coordination; observations of sensory development; notes on the development of speech; notes concerning interest in objects, choice of toys, and the like; and notes on incidental behavior which occurred during the examinations.

A graphic record of each baby's walking was obtained periodically by means of a strip of unglazed white wrapping paper laid out on the living room floor. After the soles of the baby's feet were lightly greased with olive oil he was encouraged to walk along the paper path. Until he walked alone, he had to be supported. At the end of the day, the oil prints were taken to the laboratory and treated with a black powder, which adhered to the oil and made the footprints clearly visible.

Stepping distance was measured as the distance between a line drawn perpendicular to the walking path at the tip of the first right toe print and a line similarly drawn at the tip of the next left toe print. Stepping widths and angles were also measured. Figure 10-1 shows a part of a foot-print record. Rate of walking, expressed as the median number of meters traveled in one minute, is plotted in Figure 10-2 against successive weeks for all babies combined.

First occurrences of twelve different behaviors were observed for twenty-two infants. Typically, the ages for each behavior varied considerably. For example, measures of creeping varied from 32 to 50 weeks. The median age was 44.5 weeks.

The next table shows the median age in weeks at which each of the behaviors was first observed. The corresponding age for each of four children is also given.

Behaviors	Median	Martin	David	Winifred	Walley
Chin up	3	3	5	10	5
Chest up	9	18	7	19	9
Sit on lap	18.3	19	18	19	15
Sit alone momentarily	25	24	27	25	20
Stand well with help	29.5	27	27	29	37
Sit alone 1 minute	31	25	27	27	34
Stand holding to furniture	42	35	37	37	47
Creep	44.5	32	35	45	45
Walk when led	45	29	34	41	54
Pull to stand	47	33	37	42	50
Stand alone	62	50	54	62	66
Walk alone	64	50	60	62	68

The list of median ages gives an impression of regularity in the order of occurrence of the twelve behaviors not supported by the lists for individuals. The extent of agreement between an individual list and the group list can be seen in a plot of the twelve pairs of values. Figure 10-3 is a plot of Martin's age measures against the median ages for the whole group. If the order of occurrence for Martin were the same as for the order of the medians, there would be no inversions; that is, no point to the right of another would be lower. If the age measures for Martin were the same as the median ages, then all points would lie on a straight

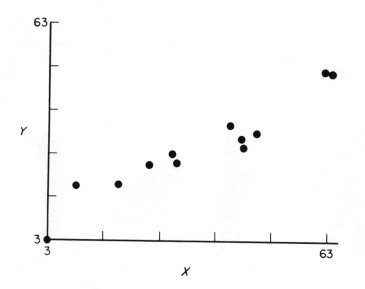

Figure 10-3. The relation between Martin's development and the group's development. X is median age of first occurrence of twelve motor behaviors. Y is Martin's age of first occurrence of the same behaviors. [After Shirley.[31, 32]]

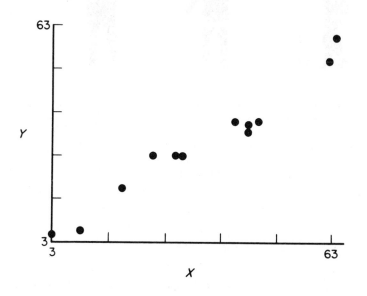

Figure 10-4. The relation between David's development and the group's development. X is median age of first occurrence of twelve motor behaviors. Y is David's age of first occurrence of the same behaviors. [After Shirley.[31, 32]]

Figure 10-5. The motor sequence prior to walking: 1 mo., chin up; 2 mo., chest up; 5 mo., sit on lap; 7 mo., sit alone; 8 mo., stand with help; 9 mo., stand holding furniture; 10 mo., creep; 11 mo., walk when led; 12 mo., pull to stand by furniture; 14 mo., stand alone; 15 mo., walk alone. [Adapted from Shirley.[32]]

line with a constant rate of change of +1. Figure 10-4 is a plot of David's age measures against the median ages. Figure 10-5 illustrates the typical developmental changes in locomotion with age.

CHANGES IN INTELLIGENCE SCORES

Changes in scores on intelligence tests have been reported by Bayley[3,4,5] and Jones[18] as part of the results of the Berkeley Growth Study. Testing began on sixty-one infants, one month of age, soon after the Study was undertaken in 1928. The Study continued on forty of them for most or all of their eighteen years, and on a substantial proportion of them for twenty-five years. Infants were selected who had parents considered to be permanent residents of Berkeley, California. They were above average in measures of socio-economic status such as parental occupation, income, and education.

Infant and preschool tests were developed especially for the Study. For the infant test, the California First-Year Mental Scale, the literature was searched for descriptions of infant behavior suitable for evaluating intellective development during the first year. Items were devised and tried out on the babies in testing at monthly intervals. Ratings and descriptions were made of each infant's responses during testing. Items

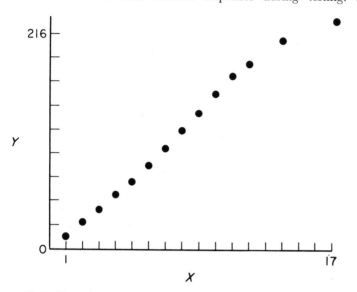

Figure 10-6. The relation between mental age and chronological age in a longitudinal study. X is chronological age in years. Y is mental age in months. Four different tests were employed at successive ages of one year, 2 to 5 years, 6 and 7 years, and 8 to 17 years. [After Bayley.[3]]

finally placed in the Scale were selected according to the following criteria: occurrence in all or most of the infants; increasing percentage of success on the items with increasing age; positive correlations among the items; and apparent relevance as intellective tasks. In a similar program, the California Preschool Scale was constructed.

The First-Year Scale was administered at one-month intervals through fifteen months; the Preschool Scale, at three-month intervals through three years and at six-month intervals through five years. The 1916 Revision of the Stanford-Binet Scale of Intelligence was given at six and seven years; the 1937 Revision, Form L, at 8, 9, 11, and 14 years; and Form M, at 10, 12, and 17 years. Form C of the Terman-McNemar Group Test was

given at thirteen years and Form D at fifteen years. The Wechsler-Bellevue
Intelligence Scale was given at 16 and 18 years.

Figure 10-6 is a plot of means of mental ages against chronological
age from one year to seventeen years. Mental age increases with chronological age. Figure 10-7 shows a plot of intelligence quotients for thirty-
three subjects on the Wechsler-Bellevue Intelligence Scale at the ages of
16, 18, and 21 years. Average IQ increases over the three ages.

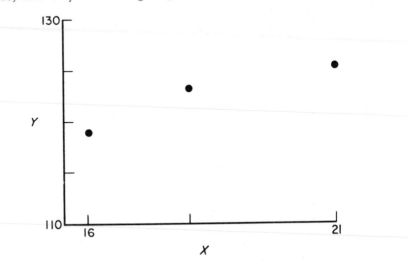

Figure 10-7. The relation between Wechsler-Bellevue intelligence quotients and
chronological age in a longitudinal study. X is chronological age in years. Y is average
full-scale intelligence quotient for thirty-three subjects. [After Bayley.[5]]

Changes Predicted from Time

Changes in motility during the time between infant feedings were
described in 1932 by Irwin[16]. He found that motility increased throughout
thirteen periods between two nursings.

The seventy-two infants, born in the obstetrical ward of the State
University of Iowa General Hospital, varied in age from eight to 373.5
hours. Motility was registered by means of a bassinet-like stabilimeter and
expressed in oscillations per minute as recorded on a polygraph. Measurements were made on the infants for each of thirteen fifteen-minute periods
between two consecutive feedings. Figure 10-8 is a plot of average number
of oscillations per minute against hour of the day after noon. Motility increases steadily throughout the thirteen periods.

Movement in response to a signal was recorded and measured over a
very brief period by Jones, O'Connell, and Hanson[17]. They employed
multiple-image photography for recording a signal and movement of a

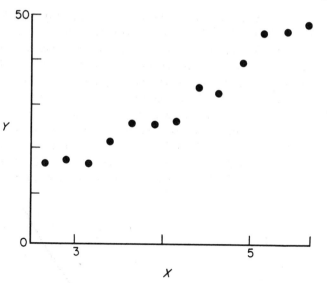

Figure 10-8. Motility of infants during thirteen successive fifteen-minute periods between consecutive feedings. X is hour of the day, after noon. Y is average number of oscillations per minute. [After Irwin.[16]]

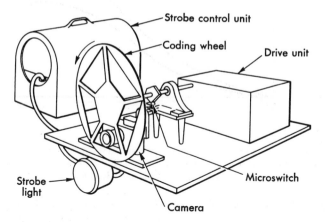

Figure 10-9. Apparatus for color coding stroboscopic multiple-image photographs. [Adapted from Jones, O'Connell, and Hanson.[17]]

subject's arm in response to the signal. By color coding successive photographic images, they obtained a record of latency, direction, and rate for each arm movement.

Recording was done on color film. Both the signal object and the subject's arm were marked with reflecting tape. The photograph was obtained by leaving the shutter of the camera open and having a stroboscope flash at rates of 5, 10, or 20 cycles per second. Color coding was achieved by means of a rotating aluminum wheel with five apertures, each of which was covered with a gelatin filter of a particular color (see Figure 10-9). The wheel rotated in front of the camera so that the appearance of a given aperture before the camera was synchronized with a flash of the strobo-scope. Thus the direction of movement and the time relations between positions were indicated by the colors recorded on a single photograph.

The subject wore a black jacket of nonreflecting cotton. A stick covered with silver tape and fastened to an arm served as a marker. The investigator supported the subject's arm in a horizontal position by means of a thin board covered with reflecting tape. The subject was instructed to let his arm drop when the board was dropped. There was

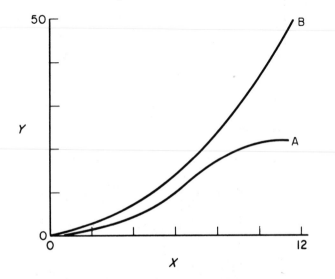

Figure 10-10. The relation between vertical displacement and time. X is time in twentieths of a second. Y is displacement in inches. The two curves represent the board and the subject's arm. [After Jones, O'Connell, and Hanson.[17]]

some rebound at the end of a drop, but color coding made it possible to interpret the rebound pattern of images. Figure 10-10 is a plot of inches of displacement against time for the drop of both board and arm for one subject. Successive changes in displacement for the falling signal board increased while successive changes for the arm increased and then decreased.

Conditioning Trials

Conditioning is a kind of training procedure. It requires two stimuli: one that elicits a reflex or unconditioned response (UR) and one that does not elicit the designated UR. The first is called an unconditioned stimulus (US); the second, a conditioned stimulus (CS). The purpose of conditioning is to train a subject to respond to the CS as he does to the US.

An essential feature of conditioning is the pairing of CS and US in presentations to a subject; that is, the two stimuli are presented close together in time with CS before US. A presentation of both is called an acquisition trial.

With many different kinds of stimuli in many varied circumstances, repeated acquisition trials accomplish the desired training; that is, after a number of acquisition trials, the presentation of CS alone is followed by the response which is now called a conditioned response (CR). Presentation of CS alone is called a test trial. CR is measured in terms of the relative frequency of its occurrence on repeated test trials, its magnitude on a given test trial, or its average magnitude for a number of trials.

If test trials are repeated without interruption over an extended period, it is a common observance that the concomitance of CS and CR is reduced—that is, the measure of CR diminishes with continued presentation of CS alone. This procedure is called extinction. Each presentation of CS alone in a series of such trials is called an extinction trial. When CR no longer occurs to any measurable degree on an extinction trial, it is said to be extinguished.

If test trials are resumed with CS after a lapse of time following extinction, CR may occur again. This reoccurrence of CR following extinction is called spontaneous recovery.

If conditioning is achieved for CS_1 and a given CR, presentation of CS_2, a different but similar stimulus, may be followed by CR. This phenomenon is called generalization. If trials are continued in which CS_1 is always followed by US but CS_2 is never followed by US, subsequent test trials with CS_1 may yield CR and test trials with CS_2 may not yield CR, a phenomenon called differentiation.

If conditioning is achieved for one CS and a given CR, it may be possible to employ that CS as US in a new conditioning procedure. Let the original CS be CS_1 and the new CS be CS_2. Acquisition trials are carried out until CS_1 is followed by CR. A new series of acquisition trials is then instituted in which CS_2 and CS_1 are paired, in that order, until CS_2 is followed by CR. Thus CS_1 functions as US in the second acquisition series. This procedure is called higher-order conditioning.

The reflexive eye blink which occurs on presentation of a sudden puff of air to the cornea of a subject's eye has been the unconditioned response in numerous investigations of conditioning in psychology. In 1936, Hilgard and Campbell[15] described the acquisition and extinction of conditioned eye blinks for fifty-one students of Stanford University.

Movement of the left eyelid, recorded photographically, was the UR.

The *US* was a controlled air-puff striking the margin of the right eye. The *CS* was a sudden increase in brightness of a circular field of frosted glass located in front of the subject. A small black cross was attached to the center of the frosted glass. The subject, who viewed the field with both

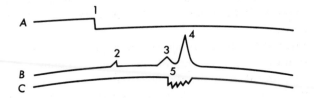

Figure 10-11. Specimen photographic record of *UR* and *CR* in eyelid conditioning. *A* shows light *CS* with onset at *1*. *B* shows paper eyelash movement record with reflex to *CS* at *2*, *CR* at *3*, and *UR* at *4*. *C* shows air-puff record with onset at *5*. Interval between light *CS* and air puff is 400 milliseconds. [Adapted from Hilgard and Campbell.[15]]

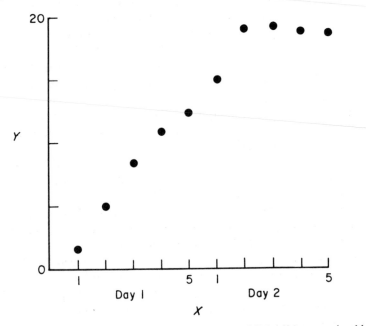

Figure 10-12. The acquisition of the conditioned eyeblink. *X* is successive blocks of ten trials on each of two days. *Y* is the mean amplitude of conditioned eyeblinks in millimeters. [After Hilgard and Campbell.[15]]

eyes, was instructed to look at the cross when a ready signal was given. On an acquisition trial, the light increased in brightness just before the air-puff occurred and remained at that level until after the response to the air puff.

A subject served for one period on each of two consecutive days. The acquisition series on each day consisted of fifty joint presentations of light and air-puff at intervals of 20 to 40 seconds. Each trial was preceded by the verbal signal "Ready." Each session began with five and ended with ten extinction trials, in which the light was presented without the air-puff. During the acquisition trials, five records of responses to the air-puff alone were obtained at equally spaced intervals. A specimen photographic record is shown in Figure 10-11. It was possible to determine from each record whether or not CR occurred, and its amplitude in millimeters and latency in milliseconds when it did.

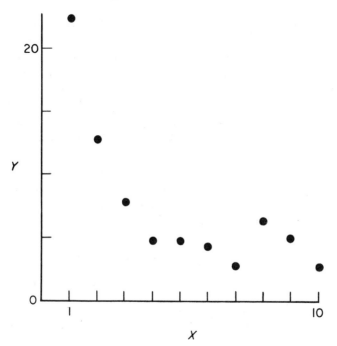

Figure 10-13. The extinction of the conditioned eyeblink. X is successive trials following acquisition. Y is the mean amplitude of conditioned eyeblinks in millimeters. [After Hilgard and Campbell. [15]]

Figure 10-12 shows the plot of means obtained by averaging values for each successive block of ten trials for all subjects. The amplitude of conditioned responses shows a gradual increase throughout the first day. Values of the second day are higher than those of the first day. Figure 10-13 shows the result of the ten extinction trials at the end of the second day. Amplitude decreases rapidly and then appears to level off.

Measures on successive trials, or blocks of trials, will show the course of acquisition and extinction of a conditioned response, and that is often the purpose of an investigation of conditioning. A psychological study may go beyond the conditioning procedures, however, in a variety of ways. One possibility is to obtain a conditioning score for each subject and attempt the prediction of other behavior. For example, the prediction of depth of hypnosis from eyelid conditioning scores was demonstrated by Das[8].

Conditioning and hypnotic sessions were conducted in succession with the same subjects. Conditioning scores and hypnosis scores were obtained and found to be moderately correlated. The sixty-three male students, 16 to 26 years of age, volunteered to participate and were paid for their services.

Before hypnosis, a student was told he would participate in a test of relaxation. During induction of hypnosis, he lay on a sofa with the room partially darkened. After being told to fixate a small bright light held a short distance above his forehead, he was given repeated suggestions to relax and suggestions that he felt heavy, drowsy, and sleepy. After fifteen minutes the depth of hypnosis attained by the subject was tested by giving him seven specific suggestions. An induction procedure of fifteen minutes duration was found suitable to induce a light to medium depth of hypnosis.

Das did not state explicitly the suggestions he employed but indicated they were similar to ones described by Friedlander and Sarbin in 1938[14]. They said their suggestions involved much repetition of language and gave the following statements as representative:

1. No matter how hard you try, you cannot open your eyes. . . Try to open your eyes.
2. You cannot raise your left arm. . . Try to raise your left arm.
3. Extend your right arm. Your arm is rigid. You cannot bend your right arm. . . Try to bend your arm.
4. Interlock your fingers. You cannot separate your fingers. . . Try to separate your fingers.
5. You cannot say your name. . . Try to say your name.
6. After you awake, you will hear someone calling your name. . . Do you hear anything? Did you hear your name being called?

The subject was awakened by the investigator's counting to fifteen in a firm voice. The hypnosis session lasted for about twenty-five minutes. The subject's hypnosis score was based on the number of suggestions he did not reject, but it also took account of his answers to oral questions given after hypnosis. These questions included, "Did you feel relaxed? Heavy? Sleepy? How did you feel when you were suggested that. . .?"

The response conditioned was the eye blink. Subjects were told that the conditioning was a test of relaxation, but they were to keep their eyes open. The conditioning session lasted for about thirty minutes.

The *US* was a puff of air delivered to the subject's right eye. The *CS* was a pure tone of 1,110 cycles. The tone preceded the puff and continued for its duration. Both terminated simultaneously.

Each subject was given thirty acquisition trials and eighteen interspersed test trials. After the acquisition procedure, there were ten extinction trials. The acquisition score was the total number of blinks during the test trials; the extinction score, the number of blinks during the extinction trials. Correlation coefficients were computed between the hypnosis scores and the scores for acquisition and extinction. The correlation between hypnosis scores and acquisition scores was 0.51; between hypnosis scores and extinction scores, 0.42. Thus greater depth of hypnosis was associated with higher scores on acquisition and extinction.

Early in the present century extensive investigations of conditioning were begun by Ivan Petrovich Pavlov, the Russian physiologist whose achievements in conditioning dogs are now quite famous. One of the unconditioned responses he employed was salivation, the secreting action of the salivary gland, after stimulation by meat powder placed in the dog's mouth. One conditioned stimulus was a tone produced by a tuning fork.

In the survey of recent research on conditioning in Soviet psychophysiology, Razran[29] has described semantic conditioning in which the original unconditioned response was salivation by a human subject. Semantic conditioning is generalization from a word *CS* to another word *CS* with similar meaning but different letters or sounds. In an investigation by Volkova, Yuri, the thirteen-year-old subject, was conditioned to give a salivary response to the Russian word for ten. Differentiation procedures were carried out for the word for eight. The subject was then given arithmetic problems in simple addition, subtraction, multiplication, and division, to some of which the answer was ten and to others, eight. Solving the problems with answers of ten was accompanied by a number of drops of saliva which varied from seven to twenty-five in thirty seconds with a median of seventeen. None of the problems with answers of eight yielded more than three drops.

Practice Trials

A practice trial in psychological research is a planned behavioral event occurring with instruction of the subject by the investigator to carry out a specified action. Changes in behavior which occur with repeated practice trials are classified as learning, adaptation, fatigue, and adjustment.

Learning is a change in behavior in acquiring knowledge or skill. Acquiring knowledge takes the form of remembering, recognizing, abstracting, or reasoning. Acquiring skill has to do with judging or discriminating in perceptual tasks and performing on motor or sensorimotor tasks. Characteristics of behavior which are measured in assessing learning include amount, quality, accuracy, speed, and efficiency.

Adaptation has several meanings, but it is used here in two ways: for either perceptual or motor change. Perceptual adaptation refers to a change in threshold. A change from a lower to a higher threshold is a decrease in sensitivity; a change from higher to lower is an increase. Motor adaptation refers to a change in a reflex—a reduction of its magnitude in some respect.

Fatigue, as it refers to changes in behavior, involves reduction in amount, quality, accuracy, speed, or efficiency in the performance of a task. As it relates to feelings, it designates verbal reports of an individual's experience. It might also be defined in terms of the production of waste products in the body. The first definition is the one of interest at the moment.

Adjustment, as an activity, refers to changes in behavior which can be conceptualized as accommodation to physical or social circumstances. As a state, it designates the kind or degree of accommodation displayed by the individual. The term is sometimes used very generally or indefinitely to include a complex of changes, but it can be used to refer to a specific or definite change.

Sensorimotor Learning

Learning occurs with practice in a great variety of sensorimotor tasks. Even repeated measures of a simple reaction time have been found to show improvement in terms of shorter times, as in a study by Evans[12] who measured the foot-withdrawal reaction times of three female college students. Each student participated in more than twenty irregularly scheduled sessions. A session consisted of thirty trials.

The subject sat in a chair with her foot on a telegrapher's key fastened to a board on the floor in front of her. When the investigator pressed a foot-pedal switch, a timer and a ready-signal light were activated. The timer controlled the interval between the ready signal and the main signal, the buzzing of an electric clock as it started and ran. The interval varied from two to four seconds. The subject responded to the buzzing of the clock by withdrawing her foot from the key.

Reaction time was measured and recorded on each trial. Figure 10-14 is a plot of the means of the first five sessions against the ordinal number of those sessions for one subject. Each point is based on thirty measures. Reaction time diminishes over the five sessions. The subject's performance indicated learning.

Sensorimotor learning was demonstrated by Franklin and Brozek[13] who studied performance during practice on a complex reaction and pattern tracing. Subjects were thirty-six young men whose ages averaged 25.7 years and varied from 20 to 33. Gross body reaction time was measured as the subject walked on a treadmill which moved at a slow constant rate. The treadmill was set on an angle and three signal lights were mounted five feet ahead of the subject at approximately the height of his head. A green light was at the left, a white one in the center, and a red one at the right. On each side of the subject was a paddle-key mounted a short distance from the floor of the treadmill. He had to assume an upright position to see the signal and then bend to tap the appropriate paddle-key.

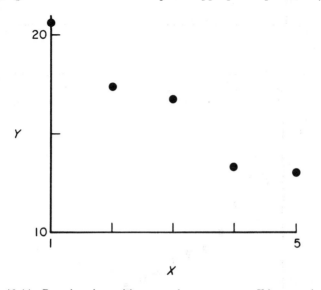

Figure 10-14. Reaction time with repeated measurement. X is successive sessions. Y is the average of thirty reaction times per session in $^1/_{120}$ of a second. Data are for one subject. [After Evans.[12]]

The subject's task was to turn off the signal light by tapping a key. The green light was turned off by tapping the left key, the red by tapping the right one, and the white by tapping both simultaneously. The time between the presentation of a signal and the subject's depressing of the proper paddle-key was automatically registered.

The pattern-tracing test required the subject to trace a grooved pattern using a stylus. When the metal tip of the stylus contacted the side of the pattern, the event was electrically recorded on a counter and the length of the contact was registered on a clock. Before the test, the subject was practiced at pacing himself in tracing the path twice in approximately forty-five seconds.

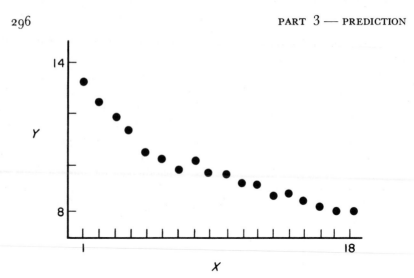

Figure 10-15. Gross body reaction time on eighteen successive trials. X is trial number. Y is average time score in seconds. Each score was the sum of twenty-five reaction times. [After Franklin and Brozek.[13]]

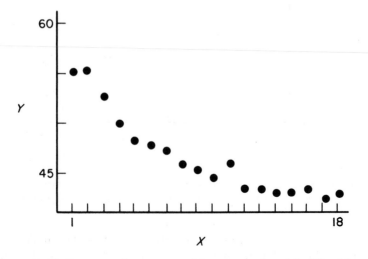

Figure 10-16. Pattern tracing scores on eighteen successive trials. X is trial number. Y is average time in seconds of error contacts. [After Franklin and Brozek.[13]]

Reaction times were summed and averaged for each set of twenty-five trials. Figure 10-15 is a plot of average reaction time against successive sets of trials. Figure 10-16 is a plot of total time of error contact against successive trials. The plots are for one group of six subjects. The reductions in reaction time and error time represent learning with practice. A smooth continuous curve fitted to the points would, in each case, be called a learning curve.

Sensorimotor Learning-to-Learn

In many situations practice trials are repeated on essentially the same task, and learning, if it occurs, is referred to that task. It is possible, however, to vary the task markedly, but within limits, and to obtain improvement over repeated trials. This change in behavior cannot properly be described as learning a particular task, because the task changes from trial to trial. If the subject improves in his performance of each task as trials continue, the change is called learning-to-learn.

Duncan[11] has reported an investigation in which learning to learn sensorimotor tasks was demonstrated. Subjects were forty male and female undergraduate students who were paid for their services. They learned the tasks by the method of paired associates, in which they had to make an appropriate movement to each of a number of visual forms. A task involved the learning of thirteen pairings, each of which consisted of a particular visual form and a particular movement of a lever. The lever could be moved into any one of thirteen slots arranged in a semicircle in a steel plate with its concave side toward the subject. There were ten different tasks corresponding to ten sets of visual forms. Each of the thirteen visual forms within a set was a variation on a theme, produced by drawing surplus lines on a single basic figure such as a circle or a letter.

The slots were numbered from one to thirteen, from left to right. Above each one was a red light. Movement of the lever into any slot switched on the light above the correct slot for that trial. Immediately above the numbers and lights was the aperture of a memory drum on which the visual forms appeared. Each task was practiced for twenty trials. The order of the tasks was varied from subject to subject so that the different tasks occurred equally often in each ordinal position.

The number of correct responses was recorded for each trial and the average was computed for each ordinal position of tasks. Figure 10-17 shows increases in skill as ordinal position increases, even though the task changed. These successive increases, which decrease in magnitude, constitute the changes in behavior called learning-to-learn.

Perceptual Learning

Evidence of learning has been found in all the categories of perceptual behavior: visual, auditory, gustatory, olfactory, cutaneous, kinesthetic, and static. Typical of methods and results in this general area are those of two investigations: one in vision, the other in static sensitivity.

Cohen[7] found that reported reversals of a two-dimensional cube increased with successive periods of viewing over an initial period and then remained at the level reached. Subjects were twenty-six clerical and pro-

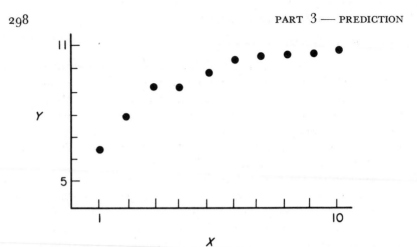

Figure 10-17. Measurement of learning to learn. X is ordinal position of task. Y is mean number of correct responses per trial. [After Duncan.[11]]

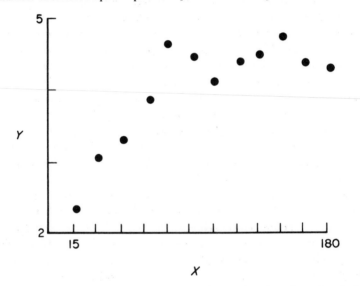

Figure 10-18. Rate of reported cube reversals as a function of continued viewing. X is time in seconds. Y is average number of reversals per fifteen-second period. [After Cohen.[7]]

fessional employees of various research laboratories at New York University. A subject sat with his chin in a rest and one of his fingers on a typewriter key. He was instructed to fixate a homogeneous white field before him. After one minute, the investigator shifted the cube into view. The subject had been instructed to strike the typewriter key each time a change in the apparent perspective of the cube occurred. Every fifteen seconds the investigator struck a key different from that of the subject, thereby pro-

ducing a typewritten record from which the number of reported fluctuations per fifteen-second period could easily be determined. The subject
viewed the cube for twelve consecutive periods, a total of three minutes.
Figure 10-18 is a plot of average number of reversals against successive
time periods. The rate of reported changes increased during the first
minute of viewing and was maintained at this level for the remaining two
minutes. Thus learning was limited to the initial minute.

Evidence of learning in static sensitivity was found by Solley[33], who
obtained repeated judgments of the alignment of the longitudinal axis of
a subject's body with gravitational vertical. Subjects were thirty-four male
undergraduates at Tulane University.

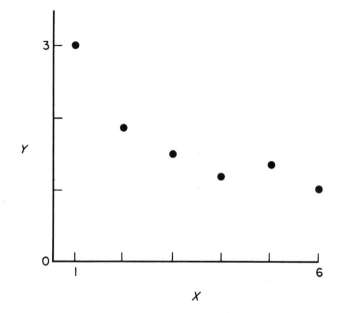

Figure 10-19. The reduction of error in successive trials of judging postural vertical. X is successive blocks of trials. Y is average error in degrees. Data are for the left-
tilt group only. [After Solley.[33]]

A large chair, specially built for the purpose, could be tilted in a
lateral plane—that is, from side to side. While a subject sat in the chair,
its tilt could be controlled either by the investigator or the subject. The
latter controlled it by means of a key mounted on the right arm of the
chair. Moving the key to the left tilted the chair to the left; moving it to
the right tilted the chair to the right; placing it upright stopped the
movement.

The subject was told that the purpose of the investigation was to
determine how well he could tell when his body was upright with respect

to the outside world. After receiving instructions, he was blindfolded and given thirty trials in blocks of ten. A single trial consisted of the following events: The investigator placed the chair in vertical position and said "Upright." Five seconds later he tilted it thirty degrees to the right or to the left. In doing so, he moved the chair five to fifteen degrees in one direction before moving it in the opposite direction to its final position. When the investigator said "Return yourself," the subject used his key to move the chair. After the subject made his judgment, he said "Now." The investigator then put the chair through a series of random movements, returned it to vertical, and said "Upright."

On each trial the investigator recorded the subject's error—the number of degrees he was off vertical. Figure 10-19 shows average degrees of error for sixteen subjects tested on left tilt, plotted against successive blocks of five trials. Learning in terms of improved accuracy in perceiving postural vertical occurred with practice.

INTELLECTIVE LEARNING

Intellective learning refers to improvement in remembering, recognizing, reasoning, or abstracting with repeated trials of practice on appropriate tasks. There is a great body of positive evidence concerning these changes for many specific tasks in laboratory studies, and this body of evidence overlaps to a considerable extent our everyday knowledge about practice. A common task for a subject in the laboratory is the memorizing of a list of so-called nonsense syllables. A nonsense syllable is a combination of letters which is not a conventional word.

Deese and Kresse[10] had ten subjects memorize a list of nonsense syllables by the method of anticipation and then analyzed their errors with respect to the kinds made and their locations in the list. Syllables were spelled with three letters: a consonant, a vowel, and a consonant, in that order. In the method of anticipation, the subject's task was to spell each syllable before it was presented. The list, which contained twelve syllables, was put on a film strip and presented by means of a projector. At the beginning of a trial, the investigator gave the subject a signal, after which a syllable was exposed for two seconds and followed by a blank exposure of two seconds. The next syllable was then exposed, and so on. The interval between trials was six seconds. Trials were continued until a subject correctly anticipated all twelve syllables. Two orders were devised for presenting the syllables. To obtain the second order, the two halves of the first order were exchanged and reversed. Syllables previously at the middle were placed at the ends by this reordering; and syllables previously at the ends were placed at the middle. Each order was used with a separate group of subjects.

Responses were recorded and classified in three categories: failures to respond, intrusion errors which resembled other syllables in the list, and extraneous errors which did not resemble items in the list. Figure 10-20 shows the plot of total errors against the serial position of syllables in both orders. It has the classical form with many more errors in the middle than at the extremes. Intrusion errors occurred with relatively low frequencies. The plots show that rote serial learning is accompanied by more errors in the middle than at either end of the list.

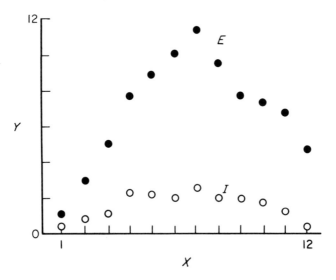

Figure 10-20. Errors in rote serial learning. X is serial position of syllables. Y is average number of errors. The two sets of points represent total errors and the special subclass of intrusion errors. [After Deese and Kresse.[10]]

Intellective Learning-to-Learn

Learning-to-learn has already been defined and described in connection with sensorimotor behavior. Learning to recall nonsense syllables, a form of intellective behavior, was demonstrated by Meyer and Miles[21], who had subjects practice a list of nonsense syllables for five trials and then go to another list for five trials, and so on for twenty lists, with the order of lists varied from subject to subject. They found that recall improved from one list to another in the order of presentation.

The subjects who learned to recall nonsense syllables were sixty-four students in two sections of an elementary course in psychology. Twenty typewritten lists of syllables were constructed, each list containing twelve syllables. Booklets were made up of the lists and blank cards. Twenty booklets, one for each list, were prepared for each subject. They were presented to subjects in twenty different random orders.

Each subject studied the list on the first page of a booklet. After thirty seconds, the instruction "Recall" was given and the subject was allowed thirty seconds to reproduce the syllables on the first blank card in the booklet. At the end of the reproduction period, which marked the end of a trial, the instruction "Turn" was given. The subject folded over the recall card and studied the same list which appeared again on the third page of the booklet. Five trials were given on each booklet. The subject was told that he did not have to reproduce the syllables in order; that his score would be the number of syllables which were correct with respect to all letters.

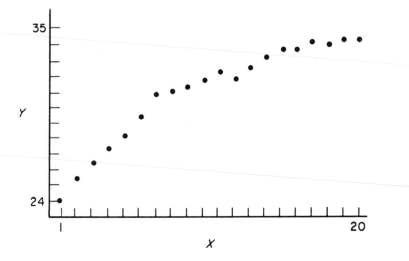

Figure 10-21. Learning to learn. X is ordinal position of lists of nonsense syllables. Y is mean number of syllables reproduced in five learning trials. [After Meyer and Miles.[21]]

Figure 10-21 shows average number of syllables reproduced for all five trials plotted against the ordinal position of lists. The plot is negatively accelerated: successive increases decrease in size. The changes represent learning-to-learn, since the content of the lists varied from one position to the next.

APPARATUS FOR CONDUCTING PRACTICE

The scheduling of practice trials uniformly with respect to time and other circumstances often requires special apparatus. Noble and Farese[25] constructed a device providing automatic control of the presentation of materials for learning with many possible variations in patterns of responding. A view of the apparatus is shown in Figure 10-22. The subject sat on the left. In front of him was a panel with keys and lights. In responding, he depressed one or more of the keys. At the subject's eye level was a projection screen, and behind the screen was an automatic slide projector. To the right was a recorder. The investigator sat on the far right before a control unit consisting of clocks, timers, and switches. In normal operation, the subject and the investigator faced each other with a screen interposed.

The subject's reponse panel was set at an angle, and around the panel's perimeter were arranged nineteen push-button keys which operated switches under the panel. The keys were equally spaced around a semicircle on radiuses of the same length measured from a base position

Figure 10-22. The selective mathometer, a device for studying human behavior in multiple-choice situations. The subject is on the left; the tester is on the right. P is a slide projector; S is an opaque projection screen; R is a continuous-feed recorder. Keys which the subject manipulates are arranged on the perimeter of the half-circle panel in front of him. The tester sits in front of the control panel. [Adapted from Noble and Farese.[25]]

for the subject's hand. Any number of the keys could be covered when they were not in use. A variety of handles and levers could be substituted for the push buttons. At the top and in the center of the subject's response panel was a green light which was automatically illuminated following a correct response. Delay and duration of the green light could be varied separately. The green light could be turned on after each correct response, or after the last response of a correct sequence.

On the investigator's control panel, in positions corresponding to the subject's response keys, were nineteen switches. By means of one or more of these switches, the investigator chose the correct response and a counter to register the number of correct responses made. After the choice was made, a correct response by the subject actuated a timer controlling the green light. The investigator could also set counters to register errors.

It was possible to schedule the green light only for those correct responses which occurred while the projected material remained on the screen, or for all correct responses given before and after the material was removed from the screen. Under conditions of pacing by the subject himself, successive problems were presented as rapidly as he solved preceding ones. The period between presentations of material could be controlled by the investigator by means of the timer.

The automatic slide projector, which had a magazine with storage for forty-eight slides, was equipped for remote control and continuous operation. Timers provided variable durations of exposure and periods between exposures. The period between trials was established by inserting one or more blank slides between the end of one trial and the beginning of the next in the magazine.

The recording instrument was an ink-writing, electromagnetic recorder with twenty pens. By means of the first nineteen pens, automatic recording of the time of occurrence, sequence, and duration of response was achieved. By means of the twentieth pen, which was activated by turning on the projector, the onset and duration of presentations were recorded.

To demonstrate how practice could be conducted on the apparatus, four distinctive visual forms and a signal or cue symbol were prepared on slides. Each slide was duplicated eight times, making forty slides in all. In addition, eight blanks were inserted, one between each set of five slides. The magazine of the projector was then full.

The timer controlling the green light was set so that the light came on for 0.75 seconds immediately after a correct response, but only when the response occurred during the exposure of a slide. Other timers were set for a slide exposure of two seconds and a period between slides of 1.44 seconds. Task performance was paced by the investigator.

The subject's task was to learn a sequence of four keys by viewing a sequence of the four visual forms. One of the twenty-four orders in which four events can occur was arbitrarily designated correct. The investigator uncovered the four keys: 4, 8, 12, and 16. The correct sequence for a given subject was 8-16-12-4. If the subject selected key "8" when the first form appeared, the correct response was counted and recorded along with its time, and the green light came on, indicating that the subject was correct. If the subject selected "12," the incorrect response was counted as an error and recorded, but the green light did not come on. The correct key for the second form was "16"; for the third, "12"; and for the fourth, "4." This sequence of events was continued trial by trial until a criterion of success was achieved, a number of trials was given, or a time period elapsed.

ADAPTATION

Dark adaptation, the change in absolute threshold for visual brightness after general illumination has been removed, is a well-established perceptual event. It should be familiar in everyday life, for it is related to the experience one has in leaving a brightly lighted room and entering a dark room. Initially one can not distinguish objects, but after a period of time, can do so fairly well. Dark adaptation is not always studied by successive determinations of thresholds for stimuli of diminishing intensity but that is the method used by Mote, Briggs, and Michels[23].

A bright patch of white light, subtending a large visual angle, was employed for exposure prior to dark adaptation. The light for threshold measurements during adaptation passed through a violet filter and formed a violet test patch subtending a small visual angle. Both patches of light were positioned off the subject's fovea on the retina of his right eye.

A subject was exposed to white light for two minutes prior to dark adaptation. Approximately eight seconds after the white light was extinguished, the first threshold for the violet light was determined. Additional threshold determinations were made every half minute for the first five minutes and then every minute for the next thirty-five minutes. The duration of the violet light was 0.2 seconds. This entire procedure, which lasted approximately forty minutes, was repeated.

To obtain a given threshold, a violet light with an intensity slightly higher than the previous threshold was first presented. The intensity was then reduced below threshold and increased by steps until the subject reported the light as visible for two successive presentations of the same intensity. This had to be done very quickly to be completed in the time available between thresholds.

Each subject participated in twelve sessions, irregularly scheduled over a period of eleven months. Figure 10-23 shows the average threshold for one inexperienced subject plotted against time in dark. Measures averaged were from the first series in each of the twelve sessions.

The investigators characterized the results as conforming to the classical picture of the course of dark adaptation following a moderate degree of light adaptation. Each plot showed a rapid descent which continued for three or four minutes. The threshold values dropped only slightly for the next two or three minutes, indicating that the end of the period of adaptation of the cones in the retina was approaching. A second rapid descent began at approximately six minutes, representing the beginning of adaptation of the rods in the retina. Within a minute or two, the subject reported a change from violet to colorless light.

In dark adaptation there is an increase in sensitivity. In other kinds of perception, adaptation often involves a decrease in sensitivity—that is, an increase in threshold. Taste, odor, pressure, and temperature thresholds often show large decreases in sensitivity with repeated stimulation. In fact, adaptation of this sort complicates research in these areas very much. Evidence of visual adaptation with increases in thresholds was found by Bakan[1] who investigated the differential threshold for brightness during a prolonged vigil. During the vigil, the subject was required to report the occurrence of a flash presented irregularly and differing in brightness from a standard flash. Subjects were ten males and ten females, whose ages varied from 16 to 35 years. They were paid to participate.

The subject viewed a test area which subtended a small visual angle. It was located within a larger, uniformly illuminated surround. The test area had a base brightness less than its surround, with a duration of 0.33 seconds. Its flash was a standard brightness greater than the surround,

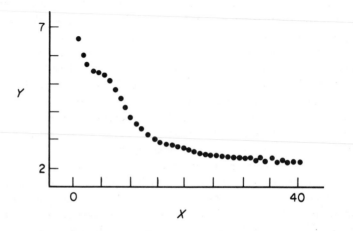

Figure 10-23. The course of dark adaptation. X is time in dark in minutes. Y is threshold in luminance units. Data are for one inexperienced subject. [After Mote, Briggs, and Michels.[23]]

with a duration of 0.66 seconds. Irregularly, the test area flashed to a level brighter than standard. The subject's task was to push a button when he detected a flash brighter than standard.

The ascending method of limits was employed. For the first step, a flash with the smallest increment of brightness over the standard was presented. If the subject did not detect it, the next level was presented later, and so on, until he indicated detection by pressing a button. There were two test sessions, each of which lasted for 1.5 hours. Six trials were scheduled irregularly in each fifteen-minute period.

The subject's difference threshold was the average brightness increment detected by him in each fifteen-minute period. Figure 10-24 is a plot of difference thresholds against successive periods. The two sets of points represent the two sessions on different days. Although the trend of the points is irregular, the investigator concluded that the difference threshold increased throughout the vigil and that the threshold for the second day was lower than that for the first day.

Adaptation of a reflex is a decrease in its magnitude in some respect with repeated stimulation. The galvanic skin response or *GSR*, which is a sudden change in the electrical resistance of the skin, has been found to show adaptation with repetition of any one of a variety of stimuli. If two electrodes are placed some distance apart on a subject and a weak current is passed between them, skin resistance and changes in it can be measured in ohms. (Skin resistance can be transformed to conductance by computing

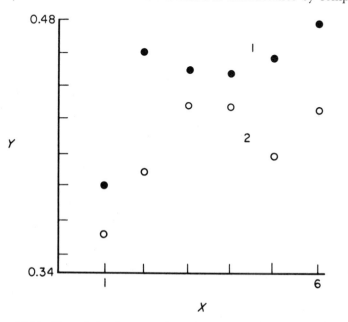

Figure 10-24. The relation between visual difference threshold and time spent in a vigil. *X* is successive fifteen-minute periods. *Y* is average difference threshold in luminance units. The two sets of points represent successive days of testing. [After Bakan. [1]]

the reciprocal of resistance.) It is not certain what all the events associated with *GSR* are, but the evidence seems to indicate that it is an intimate concomitant of the reflex activity of the skin's sweat glands. The *GSR* may be antecedent to the actual secreting of the glands but is closely associated with it. Psychologists have been interested in the *GSR* because of its association with emotional behavior. It cannot be taken as a certain indicator of emotion, however, because it occurs at times with other kinds of behavior and in situations not suggestive of emotion.

In 1934, Davis[9] measured the *GSR* when the stimulus was a loud tone repeated daily. Subjects were three women and five men who served for five consecutive daily sittings at the same hour each day. The tips of a subject's first two fingers were immersed in a sodium chloride electrolyte. To insure that the same skin area was in contact with the electrolyte at each sitting, adhesive tape was placed on the fingers at the top of the nail.

Readings, from which the subject's resistance could be computed, were taken at varied intervals from a voltmeter and an ammeter. Small changes in resistance which completed recovery within a recording interval were disregarded, and only those which exhibited no recovery during the interval were recorded. For a definite period after the initial reading, nothing was done to the subject by the investigator. Readings were taken at intervals of one minute during the first five minutes and at half minutes thereafter.

The subject sat in an arm chair in a booth. The investigator controlled the presentation of a tone of 1,000 cycles per seconds through earphones. The sound produced was unpleasantly loud and rough. The subject was told that he would have a seven-minute period of rest, the end of which would be indicated by the signal "Ready," and that fifteen seconds after the signal, the noise would begin and continue for two minutes. Additional readings were made of minima, the lowest resistances observed, after the ready signal and after the onset of the noise.

After readings were converted into ohms of resistance, the average for eight subjects was computed for each reading time for each day. These averages are presented for the first day in Figure 10-25, and for the fifth day in Figure 10-26. There was a drop in resistance immediately after the onset of the noise. Over the five days, the size of the drop became smaller. This change represented adaptation.

Mundy-Castle and McKiever[24] tested subjects for adaptation of the GSR with repeated presentation of a loud noise. They found evidence of differences among subjects in adaptation: some showed decreases in response; others did not. The subject lay on a couch in a partially lighted and soundproofed room. Electrodes were attached to the palmar sides of the thumb and third finger of his left hand, the skin of which was cleaned with alcohol and impregnated with electrode jelly. The subject was instructed to close his eyes and keep them closed during the entire session. He was informed that there would be a loud noise and that the testing might continue for as long as thirty minutes.

The noise, which was harsh and loud, was presented for one second at regular intervals. Its occurrence was controlled mechanically by a device which connected the subject's earphones to the noise every thirty seconds. Presentations were terminated when complete adaptation occurred, the criterion being three successive noises which failed to elicit a GSR. If adaptation did not occur within thirty-five presentations, the testing was

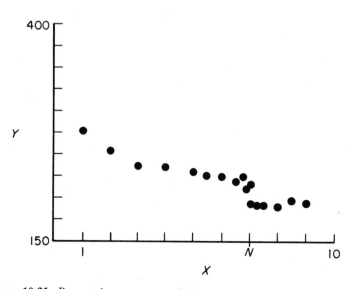

Figure 10-25. Repeated measurement of skin resistance on the first of five days. *X* is time in minutes. *Y* is average resistance in hundreds of ohms. Ready signal at 6.75 minutes; noise (*N*) at 7.0 minutes. [After Davis.[9]]

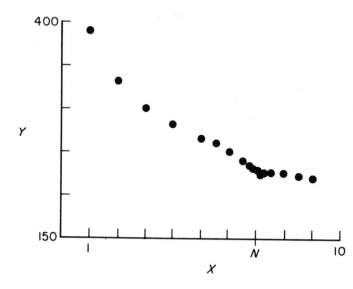

Figure 10-26. Repeated measurement of skin resistance on the fifth day. *X* is time in minutes. *Y* is average resistance in hundreds of ohms. Ready signal at 6.75 minutes; noise (*N*) at 7.0 minutes. [After Davis.[9]]

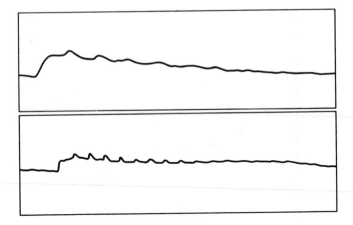

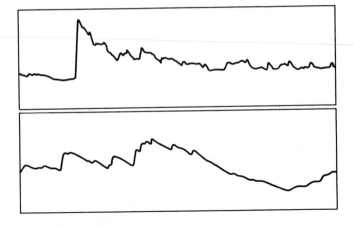

Figure 10-27. *GSR* records for four subjects. The two records at the top show adaptation after seven and sixteen stimuli, respectively. The two at the bottom show no adaptation; that is, continuing endogenous responses in addition to responses to stimuli. [Adapted from Mundy-Castle and McKiever.[24]]

discontinued. Level of skin resistance was recorded continuously. Figure 10-27 contains the records of four subjects. Two reveal no adaptation; two reveal adaptation after seven and sixteen presentations of noise, respectively.

FATIGUE

Although fatigue is sometimes evaluated in terms of verbal reports of feelings or amount of certain waste products of the body, the matter of interest at the moment is its definition in terms of changes in behavior with repeated practice trials. In this connection, fatigue refers to a variety of changes: increase in error, reduction in rate of work, decrease in steadiness, slump in posture, increase in rate of blinking, frequency of yawning, and decrease in dexterity. Berger and Mahneke[6] described the development of fatigue, measured in terms of decrement in performance, during the exercise of two visual discriminations: acuity and flicker fusion.

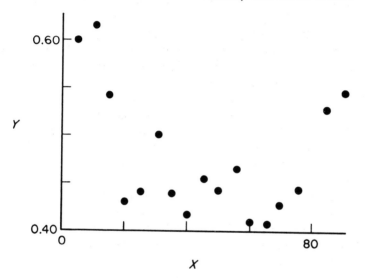

Figure 10-28. The measurement of fatigue defined as decrement in performance during the exercise of a visual discrimination. X is time in minutes. Y is visual acuity measured as the reciprocal of visual angle in minutes of arc using a broken ring. Data are for one subject. He was given five minutes rest before the last twenty determinations on which the last two points are based. [After Berger and Mahneke.[6]]

In the test of visual acuity, the subject sat before a white background, his head held in position by a chin rest, and viewed a broken ring monocularly through an artificial pupil. The distance between the subject and the broken ring was varied by moving the ring at a constant rate of five centimeters per second. Repeatedly throughout a period of nearly an hour, the subject, by pressing a button, gave reports of the apparent presence and absence of the break in the ring. There followed a five-minute period of rest in the dark, after which he gave twenty additional judgments.

Figure 10-28 shows the plot of acuity thresholds for one subject. Each point is the average of ten determinations. Visual acuity decreased for this subject, as it did for two others. Acuity increased after the five-minute rest but did not reach the initial level. The decrease in acuity was interpreted as fatigue.

The second discrimination task involved critical flicker frequency. Flicker was produced by means of a rotating disk which interrupted a beam of light illuminating a circular diffusing glass surface. Thresholds were determined by the method of limits with both ascending and descending series of trials in which frequency was varied by regular steps. Each of two subjects gave repeated judgments during a fifty-minute period. After a ten-minute rest in the dark, he was required to give twenty additional series of judgments.

Figure 10-29 shows a plot of means for one subject. Each point is the average of ten determinations. This subject showed a decline in critical flicker frequency with repeated determinations, as did the other one. The decline was interpreted as fatigue.

Fatigue was defined as the decrement in the number of correct answers given during continuous addition in an investigation, in 1928, by Poffenberger[26,27]. In addition to measures of correct additions, reports were obtained from subjects about their concomitant feelings. Contrary to what one might expect, there was no evidence of a relation between work output and reported feelings.

Subjects were eleven graduate students in psychology. The task consisted of adding, to a two-place number, first 16, then 17, then 18, then 19, then 16, and so on. At the end of each successive thirty-second period, a new two-place number was given. When the sum reached 100 or more, the subject was instructed to drop the third figure. His score was the number of correct additions per period. The work was continued for approximately 5.5 hours or until the subject refused to continue. At the end of each half hour of work, he was asked to report how he felt.

The subject reported his feelings on a scale of seven steps: 1, extremely good; 2, very good (as after a good night's rest); 3, good; 4, medium; 5, tired; 6, very tired (as at the end of a hard day's work); and 7, extremely tired. Each subject's time at work was arbitrarily divided into fourteen successive and equal parts. The average number of correct responses per thirty-second period for each part was then computed. Figure 10-30 is a plot of the averages against the fourteen successive parts. Output remains high for the first six parts and then begins to decline. This change was conceptualized as fatigue. There was no evidence of a relation between changes in output of work and reported feelings. This lack of relation is indicative of some of the difficulties encountered in formulating a definition of fatigue.

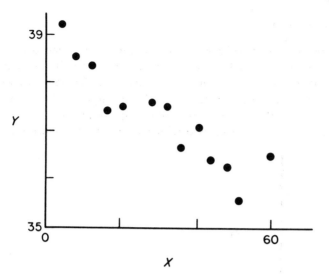

Figure 10-29. The measurement of fatigue defined as decrement in performance during the exercise of a visual discrimination. X is time in minutes. Y is critical flicker frequency in flashes per second. Data are for one subject. He was given a ten-minute rest in the dark after fifty minutes. [After Berger and Mahneke.[6]]

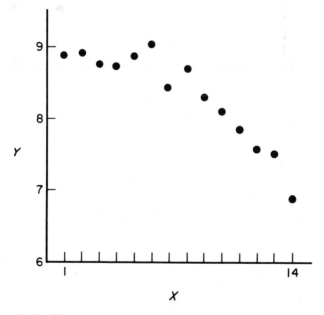

Figure 10-30. Output in continuous addition. X is successive parts of work. Y is average number of correct answers per thirty-second period in each of the fourteen parts. [After Poffenberger.[26, 27]]

ADJUSTMENT

Adjustment is sometimes broadly conceived, as when one speaks of a persons's adjustment to life, and sometimes less broadly, as in a student's adjustment to college, but it may also refer to a change in a specific form of behavior in a particular situation. An example is the change in self-ratings of fear with repeated parachute jumps from a high tower. Walk[34] found that fear ratings decreased with repeated performance of the jumps.

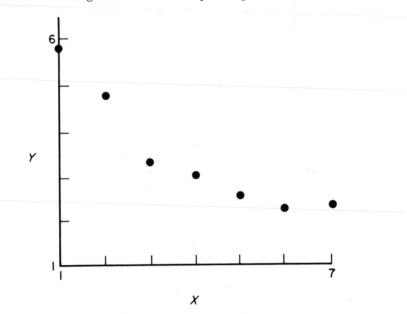

Figure 10-31. Self-ratings of fear in a training situation. X is successive jumps from a tower. Y is median fear rating just before jumping. [After Walk.[34]]

Subjects were 107 airborne trainees who were required to jump from a tower thirty-four feet high as a part of learning the proper form of exit from an airplane in flight. A trainee fell eight feet before his fall was snubbed by straps fastened on the rear of his parachute harness and connected to a pulley arrangement on a steel cable. After falling, he rode the cable some distance to a mound where he was unhooked. Trainees were graded on their performance in jumping. Those who could not learn the proper form failed the airborne training course. The training procedure was generally considered to be frightening. Many trainees displayed overt signs of fear such as pallor and trembling.

A trainee had to rate the degree of fear he felt just before jumping from the tower. The rating scale, a sketch of a figure somewhat like a thermometer, was divided into ten equal parts. The trainee had to place a mark on the figure to indicate the degree of his fear. The highest rating was at the top of the thermometer; the lowest, at the bottom. The distance from the base to the subject's mark was taken as a measure of fear. During the orientation period, the investigators displayed a permissive attitude toward the admission of fear and told trainees that it was expected they would be afraid on some of the jumps.

One squad of 15 to 20 trainees was studied per week for seven weeks. Each trainee made from 10 to 25 jumps. He had to make three satisfactory jumps before he was graduated from the first week of training. Complete records were available on 107 men. The data included self-ratings of fear on the first seven jumps. Figure 10-31 is a plot of the median rating of fear against successive jumps. Ratings declined with successive jumps and leveled off during the fifth, sixth, and seventh jumps. The trainees reported hand trembling, nervousness, heart beating hard, shortness of breath, hand sweating, upset stomach, and cold sweats during early jumps.

Operant Training Schedules

In conditioning procedure, an acquisition trial consists of the presentation of CS and US, and a test trial consists of presentation of CS only. In practice procedure, a trial is a planned event in which the subject performs a task according to instructions from the investigator. In scheduling practice, trials may be suspended for a period of time. Conditioning trials and practice trials have been demonstrated to be predictive of changes in behavior under widely varied circumstances and with many different kinds of behavior.

There is another procedure, called operant training, which is closely associated with conditioning and practice but distinguishable from them in certain respects. Schedules of operant training have been demonstrated to be predictive of changes in behavior in a variety of situations. There is some overlapping of terminology between operant training and conditioning. Operant training is also called operant conditioning; the behavior acquired during operant training is referred to as a conditioned response; and this change in behavior is considered to be a form of learning. Conditioning, as we have described it, is often called classical conditioning to distinguish it from operant conditioning. Some of this overlapping usage of terms results from attempts to achieve maximum generality on a theoretical level. However, terms will be employed here to maintain the distinctions which exist among the procedures of conditioning, practice, and operant training.

An operant training schedule is a rule which the investigator adopts and follows in acting upon a subject for purposes of training him to behave in some specified way. The rule makes the occurrence of the investigator's action contingent upon the occurrence of the subject's action. Thus an operant training schedule does not have the planned regularity of conditioning trials or practice trials.

The action of the investigator in operant training will be called a conditional event; the action of the subject will be called an operant response. The rule for the occurrence of the conditional event must, of course, designate the operant response. The rule may state that the conditional event is to occur only after a specific operant response or that it is to occur after successively better approximations to a specific response. The rule also indicates the occasions on which the conditional event is to occur. The conditional event may be scheduled to occur after each operant response, after every third operant response, after odd or even numbered operant responses, after nine randomly selected operant responses out of ten, or any other temporal pattern of interest to the investigator. The period during which the conditional event occurs repeatedly will be designated the period of acquisition. The period after suspension of the conditional event will be called the period of extinction. Although this usage overlaps that of conditioning procedure, it appears to be the most convenient of any presently available.

An operant training schedule might be employed by a teacher for purposes of increasing participation by students in classroom discussions. The operant response might be the student's asking a question; the conditional event might be the teacher's using the student's name in replying to the question. If the adopted schedule called for the conditional event on every occurrence of the operant response, then the teacher would use the student's name in replying to every question asked by a student during the discussion period. Implicit is the assumption that participation would increase as the teacher continued to use students' names.

A rule for the classroom situation might be devised to restrict conditional events to those operant responses which were better approximations to some desired response. Suppose the teacher wished to improve discussion by training students to make prefatory statements before they asked their questions. One possible rule would be that the conditional event would occur only when the student's operant response was more elaborate in appropriate ways than his preceding response; that is, the teacher would use the student's name in replying to his question only when the student's statement of his question was better than his preceding one. Execution of a training schedule of this sort in the classroom would be very difficult for the teacher. In research situations, electronic programming equipment is frequently used to evaluate the subject's operant response and to control the occurrence of the conditional event.

The term *reinforcement* is widely used in a general way to refer to the unconditioned stimulus in conditioning procedure or to the conditional event in operant training schedules. The term is also used in theoretical discussions to refer to hypothetical consequences of the conditioning or training. The value of the term is considerably reduced by the number of different meanings given to it. We shall adopt the practice of making explicit reference to the unconditioned stimulus or the conditional event and avoid the possible ambiguity of reinforcement.

The acquisition and extinction of vocalizations by infants was demonstrated by Rheingold, Gewirtz, and Ross[30]. In their operant training procedure, the conditional event was a complex of social acts resembling those an attentive adult would make when an infant vocalizes. Subjects were twenty-one infants, residents of an institution in Washington, D.C. Their median age was three months.

In two days of preliminary observation, a female investigator leaned over the crib with her face a short distance above the infant's face. She looked at the infant with an expressionless face and moved her head as necessary to remain in his line of vision. A collaborator, out of the infant's sight, tallied his vocalizations.

In two days of main observation, the investigator again leaned over the crib with an expressionless face but, when the infant vocalized, she executed the complex of social acts: giving a broad smile, making three "tsk" sounds, and applying a light touch to the infant's abdomen with thumb and fingers. The three acts, performed simultaneously, required no more than a second of time. At the beginning of training, the conditional event occurred after each vocalization. Later, the investigator responded to every second or every third vocalization.

In two final days of observation, the investigator leaned over the crib with an expressionless face and made no response to the infant's vocalizations.

Most of the infants were observed in nine three-minute periods in the morning and early afternoon. Every discrete voice sound produced by an infant was counted as a vocalization, but straining sounds, coughs, whistles, squeaks, and snorts of noisy breathing were not counted. Protests, fussing, and crying were categorized separately. For each half minute during which a vocalization occurred; the infant was given one point. A mean score was obtained for each infant for each day. Figure 10-32 is a plot of mean number of vocalizations on consecutive days. Means for the third and fourth days were greater than those for the other four days. Those results were interpreted as evidence of successful training in vocalizing on the third and fourth days and extinction of the operant response on the fifth and sixth days.

A procedure for operant training of nursery school children has been described by Lambert, Lambert, and Watson[19]. The children were

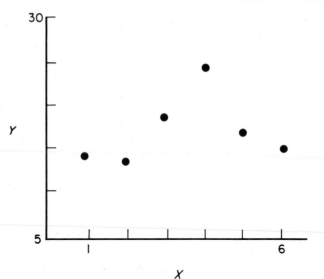

Figure 10-32. Conditioning of infant vocalizations. *X* is successive days. *Y* is mean number of vocalizations for twenty-one subjects. Preliminary observations were made on the first two days. Acquisition took place on the third and fourth days. Extinction took place on the fifth and sixth days. [After Rheingold, Gewirtz, and Ross.[30]]

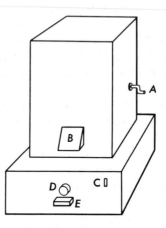

Figure 10-33. A token-reward vender, showing the turning handle (*A*), the token chute cover (*B*), the token inset slot (*C*), the candy chute opening (*D*), and the candy trough (*E*). [Adapted from Lambert, Lambert, and Watson.[19]]

trained to operate a vending machine, from which they received tokens, as well as candy, as rewards. Figure 10-33 shows the Solomon token-reward machine. A child turned the handle on the right a number of turns, received a poker chip from the chute at upper center, inserted the chip in the slot at lower right, and, after a number of repetitions of this sequence, received a small piece of candy from the trough at bottom center.

During training, according to one schedule, the child turned the handle a number of times determined by the investigator. After the last turn, the token vendor emitted a clear click and ejected a token into the chute. The child obtained the token and inserted it in the slot. The candy vendor emitted a clear but distinctly different sound and ejected a small piece of candy into the trough.

A variety of training schedules could be imposed on children. A child might be put through the procedure once a day or several times a day for any number of days. He could be required to turn the handle some number of times after inserting the first token to obtain a second token, which could then be inserted to obtain candy.

After training, a variety of procedures could be employed for suspending the conditional events. A child might turn the handle with no further result; or turn the handle with the click emitted periodically and no further result; or turn the handle with the click emitted and the token ejected, and insert the token with noise emitted by the candy vendor. In none of these procedures would he obtain candy.

A child was scored finally in terms of the number of turns, occurring after suspension of the conditional events, until a period of time of some specified length passed with no turning. Thus a score represented resistance to extinction.

A successful program for dealing with tantrum behavior—a program based on ideas about operant acquisition and extinction—was reported by Williams[35]. The program of treatment was undertaken with one male child who exhibited extreme tantrum behavior at the age of twenty-one months. During the first eighteen months of his life he had been seriously ill. Although his health had improved considerably, he continued to demand and receive special care and attention. He engaged in tantrums, apparently to control the actions of his parents, especially at bed time.

The parents and an aunt rotated in putting the child to bed at night and in the afternoon when he was supposed to nap. When the adult left the bedroom after putting the child in his bed, the child would scream and fuss until the adult returned. For this reason, the adult did not leave the bedroom until after the child went to sleep. If the adult began to read while he was in the bedroom, the child would cry until the reading was terminated. The parents stated that they believed the child enjoyed his control over them and tried to stay awake as long as he could. At the time, an adult was spending from one half to two hours at each bedtime waiting in the bedroom until the child went to sleep.

On the assumption that the adult's behavior was a conditional event in a training schedule in which the child's tantrum was the operant response, the parents decided to suspend the conditional event in an attempt to extinguish the operant response. After the parents had received medical reassurance regarding the child's physical condition, they decided to institute a program of leaving the bedroom and ignoring the tantrums. In carrying out this program, a parent or the aunt put the child to bed in a leisurely and relaxed fashion. After the usual bedtime pleasantries, the adult left the bedroom and closed the door. The child put on a tantrum complete with screaming and crying, but the adult did not reenter the room. A measure of the duration of screaming and crying was obtained beginning with the closing of the door.

By the tenth occasion, the child no longer protested when the adult left the room. He smiled and, in the opinion of the parents, made happy sounds until he went to sleep. About a week later, however, he put on another tantrum, at which time the aunt returned to the bedroom and stayed there until the child went to sleep. The program was then instituted a second time. Figure 10-34 shows the results for the second series of occasions on which the program was tried. Duration of crying reached zero by the ninth occasion. The data for the first series were quite similar. No tantrums at bedtime were observed during the next two years. No undesirable sideeffects or aftereffects of this program were detected. At the age of four years, the child appeared to be a friendly, expressive, outgoing person.

Change as a Predictor of Change

If Y is a set of successive measures for an individual, successive differences in Y are changes. If X is a set of values paired with the Y values, X is a potential predictor of those changes. We have already shown that age, time, and trials are potential predictors. There is another possibility. If X is a set of successive measures, as it can be, then successive differences in X are themselves changes and constitute a potential predictor of changes in Y. Thus changes in a subject's behavior in one respect may be predictive of changes in his behavior in another respect. To implement this plan of prediction, data are obtained by measuring a subject's behavior on X and Y on each one of a number of occasions. The pairing of values is achieved by obtaining two measures on each occasion. Consequently, the number of pairs is the number of occasions.

Following is a fictitious example of a situation in which change might be predicted from change. Beginning on his eighth birthday, a boy is measured on each of five successive birthdays with respect to two characteristics: the length of his maximum stride and the distance he achieves in a standing broad jump. There result five pairs of values for the five occasions of measurement. The pairs could be plotted as five points in a graph and an attempt could be made to establish a rule for predicting distance from length. Changes in distance jumped might turn out to be predictable from changes in length of stride.

Biological change represents another important class of predictors of behavioral change. Structural, chemical, and electrical changes in the skin,

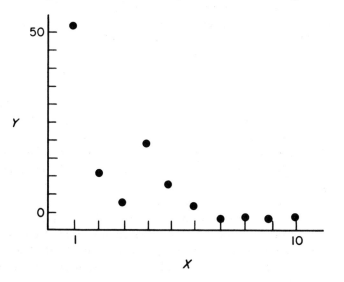

Figure 10-34. Tantrum behavior on successive occasions when it was ignored. X is successive times of putting child to bed. Y is duration of crying in minutes. Data represent second program of treatment. Similar results were obtained for first program. [After Williams.[35]]

bones, muscles, nerves, and organs of the body can be measured on successive occasions. If measures of some characteristic of behavior are obtained on the same occasions, the biological changes may be predictive of the behavioral changes. Thus increases in blood-sugar level are often predictive of increases in the frequency of urination.

Changes in Behavior with a Special Order of Circumstances

Situations sometimes arise in which the psychologist has an opportunity to measure the behavior of a subject repeatedly with each measure obtained under a circumstance different from those under which the other measures are obtained. In situations of this kind, there is a special order of circumstances, and changes in the behavior may be predictable from that order. The special order of circumstances may be simply the natural order of events in the life of a subject or an order of events contrived and staged by the investigator.

A simple hypothetical case can be constructed from two circumstances, A and B, occurring in that order. A measure of a subject's behavior under circumstance A is obtained. After a change of circumstance takes place or is arranged, a measure of the subject's behavior under circumstance B is obtained. The change in behavior, if there is one, can be related to the change of circumstances. It is entirely possible that a valuable predictive rule would result.

A serious problem of interpreting the relation between the change and the circumstances arises, however, for there are usually several questions of interest which one may ask but cannot answer from the data. The questions concern comparisons which cannot be made, since only part of the necessary data is available.

In the simple case involving circumstances A and B, in that order, one could ask what the relation between behavior and circumstances would be if A followed B. That is, one might wish to compare the order of circumstances AB with the order BA. If the investigation has not included both orders, the comparison cannot be made. One could also ask how the behavior of one or more subjects under circumstance A compared with the behavior of similar subjects under circumstance B. If A and B have not been arranged for separate and different subjects, the comparison cannot be made.

The issues in interpreting data from investigations involving special orders of circumstances are usually resolved in discussions of psychological experimentation; that is, the questions about comparisons of the various kinds mentioned above give rise to special kinds of investigations called experiments. The term experiment will be defined and the topic of psychological experimentation will be introduced in the next chapter. In succeeding chapters the findings in a number of areas of psychological experimentation will be presented.

Some examples of prediction from a special order of circumstances will be given. This kind of prediction is important because so much information about it is so readily available. Strict limits should be observed in interpreting the information, however, and it should be clearly distinguished from experimental knowledge.

Following is a simple example involving a situation with which students are familiar. The teacher of a course in the psychology of adjustment believes that his students benefit from the course in ways which can be measured by a personality inventory. He decides to administer the inventory at the beginning and again at the end of a semester. Scores on a neuroticism scale from the inventory are obtained for both administrations. Do the scores show improvement? They may. If they do, to what should the improvement be attributed? They cannot be attributed to the course, for no similar group of students who did not take the course is available for comparison. It may be that students in other classes or that young people outside of school improve in this way. What does the evidence show? It shows that improvement in neuroticism scores can be predicted from time.

Mosel and Kantrowitz[22] found that before-and-after exposure to monosodium glutamate was the special order of circumstances predictive of taste thresholds. They determined absolute thresholds for the four primary tastes before and after subjects had tasted a strong solution of monosodium glutamate, a chemical food additive, for which claims have been made that it enhances the palatableness of a wide variety of foods. The substance is available to consumers under several trade names. The results were that thresholds for sour and bitter were lower after exposure than before, but thresholds for salt and sweet did not change. Thus sensitivity for sour and bitter increased from the first to the second occasion.

Subjects were four graduate students in psychology. Absolute thresholds for salt, sweet, sour, and bitter solutions were measured by a modification of the method of limits, before and after a subject tasted a solution of monosodium glutamate. A series of solutions was presented to the subject in ascending order of concentration. The four solutes were sodium chloride, sucrose, tartaric acid, and quinine hydrochloride. The first solution was tap water without any solute. The subject was instructed to judge each solution and to report whether it had the taste of water or the taste of the solute under study. Thus the task was one of recognizing a particular taste. The subject was not told the solutions increased in concentration, and solutions of tap water were presented irregularly in the series, without the subject's knowledge, to prevent him from discovering the ascending order. When he reported the taste on two consecutive presentations, the presentations were stopped.

On each trial of a series the subject held a small measured volume of a solution in his mouth for five seconds. Trials were separated by an interval of forty-five seconds. Ten ascending series were given each subject, with successive series separated by an interval of two minutes. Between series, the subject rinsed his mouth three times with tap water and dried his tongue with filter paper. Solutions and rinses were expectorated, not swallowed. After his threshold for one solute had been determined, the subject tasted a strong solution of monosodium glutamate by working a small volume of it about his mouth for seven seconds. He then rinsed his mouth and dried his tongue. Five minutes later, the threshold for the solute was measured again. Only one solute was investigated each day for any subject. All sessions were held at least one hour after eating.

As noted earlier, sensitivity for sour and bitter increased. Would it have changed without the monosodium glutamate? One cannot say, since the necessary observations were not made.

Decreases in the constructiveness of children's play were found to occur when restrictions were imposed following a period of free play. Barker, Dembo, and Lewin[2] recorded the behavior of children in a nonfrustrating situation and a subsequent frustrating situation. Each child was observed on two occasions: first, when he was placed in a standardized play room and allowed to play without restriction, and second, when he was placed in the same room with the same toys as on the first occasion but with a number of more attractive toys in view and not accessible. Subjects were children from three age groups of the preschool laboratories of the Iowa Child Welfare Research Station. There were ten children from two to three years of age, twelve from three to four years, and eight from four to five years.

In the first situation, free play, an effort was made to establish conditions which would maximize constructive play. Each child was asked, "Do you want to come and play with me?" Children who appeared reluctant were excused from participating.

The play room had two doors, a window, and a removable partition consisting of two wooden frames covered with wire mesh netting. In the free-play situation, the frames, which could be moved up and down like windows, were in position as a partition. An opaque canvas covering was fastened on the back of each frame. One door was the entrance to the room. In the other was a one-way observation screen, behind which an observer sat. The investigator sat in a child's chair at a small table near the window.

On the floor of the room were three large squares of paper. On the first square were various play materials: a child's chair on which a small teddy bear and a doll were seated, a small truck and trailer, a cup, a saucer, a teapot without a lid, an ironing board with an iron, and a telephone receiver which squeaked when shaken. On the second square were a box of crayons and two pieces of writing paper. On the third were a small wooden motor boat, a sail boat, a celluloid duck, a frog, and a fishing pole with line on the end of which was a magnet.

After entering the room with a child, the investigator approached the first square and, picking up each toy, said, "Look, here are some things to play with. Here is a teddy bear and a doll. Here is an iron to iron with," and so on. Then he said, "You can play with everything. You can do whatever you like with the toys, and I'll sit down here and do my lesson." The investigator then sat on the chair at the table.

The child was allowed to play for a period of thirty minutes, at the end of which the investigator made the first suggestion about leaving: "I am about through. Will you be ready to go pretty soon?" If the child said "No" or did not answer, the investigator waited for about a minute and then said, "Shall we go to the school now?" If this second suggestion was not accepted, the investigator made a third after a minute or two. If the child still did not want to leave, the investigator started to leave the room saying, "I have to go now." This statement never failed in its purpose.

During the next period, before the frustration was introduced, the partition was lifted so that the room was twice the size it had been. The three squares were in place, but all the toys except those on the second square had been removed and placed in the new part of the room among more attractive new toys: a big doll house which a child could enter and which contained a bed, a doll, a chair, a teddy bear, the ironing board with the iron on it, and the telephone; a cupboard and a stove with cooking utensils; a laundry line on which the doll's clothes hung; a rubber bunny placed near the entrance to the house; a large toy truck and the small truck and trailer used earlier; a child's table on which were cups, saucers, dishes, spoons, forks, knives, a small teapot, and a large teapot; a toy lake which was filled with real water and had sand beaches, an island with a light house, a wharf, a ferryboat, small boats, fishes, ducks, and frogs. Every child showed great interest in the new toys and started at once to play with them. Each one was allowed to explore and play freely and if, after several minutes, he had played with only a few toys, the investigator demonstrated the others. Then the investigator returned to his chair and waited from five to fifteen minutes until the child became thoroughly involved in play.

The frustration period then began. The investigator collected all the old play materials which had been used in the first situation and distributed them on the empty squares. He then said, "Now let's play at the other end," and pointed to the old part of the room. The child went or was led to the old part of the room and the investigator lowered the partition and fastened it with a large padlock. The new part of the room containing the new toys was inaccessible but visible through the wire netting from which the cover had been removed. The child was allowed to play for thirty minutes, at the end of which the investigator suggested leaving. Usually the child was willing to leave at the first suggestion. After the investigator had made certain that he wanted to leave, the partition was lifted. Usually the child was pleasantly surprised and hurried into the new part of the room to play with the new toys. If he did not do so spontaneously, the investigator suggested that he do so. The lifting of the partition at the end of the frustration period was done to obviate any undesirable after-effects of the frustration period. The child was allowed to play until he was ready to leave.

Observations were made by the observer and the investigator. The data consisted of two synchronized running accounts of the events of each session. For purposes of analysis, the record of behavior was divided into parts. A part judged to be guided by a single purpose on the part of the child was considered a unit of action. Units of action varied in length from five seconds to several minutes.

Behaviors in the free-play and restricted play periods were compared in terms of average time in seconds spent in a particular kind of activity. The results showed an increase, from the first period to the second, in barrier behavior: attempts to lift or climb over the partition; requests or threats to get the investigator to raise the barrier; and actions such as looking at or talking about the inaccessible toys. At the same time there was a decrease in constructive behavior defined as playing with the toys, and an increase in escape behavior: attempts to open or kick the door; requests or threats to get the investigator to open the door; and actions such as looking at or talking about the regions outside the door.

The evidence regarding the predictiveness of the sequence of situations is unequivocal. Constructiveness of play decreased. Would it have decreased if the first free-play situation had been extended? Perhaps so, perhaps not. There is no data on which to base an answer to this question.

Changes in the interpersonal behavior of children were observed by Raush, Dittmann, and Taylor[28] while the children were under psychological treatment. Observations were made of spontaneous behavior in the daily activities of a small group of disturbed boys over a period of a year and a half while the boys were in a residential treatment program. The changes, which were consistent with the aims of the treatment program, were a decrease in hostile-dominant behavior and an increase in friendly-submissive behavior.

The six boys were patients on a hospital ward which they entered when they were eight to ten years old. Prior to hospitalization, the behavior of the boys was characterized by aggressiveness so extreme they were not tolerated by community, schools, foster parents, or parents. Four of the boys had been referred to courts because of destructive behavior. Three of the four had been sent to a reformatory shortly before their admission. Two boys, who had not been before the courts, had been excluded from several schools because of their antisocial actions. All the boys had had numerous contacts with social agencies. Out-patient clinical treatment and special school programs had not been effective. None, however, was identified as a delinquent belonging to a gang. Each appeared to be highly disturbed personally. All were physically healthy and of normal intelligence. Their socioeconomic backgrounds varied from lower-lower through lower-middle class.

During the study, the boys lived on the hospital ward. Their program was planned in detail. They had four hours per week of psychotherapy and continued their schooling in the hospital with specially trained teachers. Their interpersonal behavior was observed at two points in time: after they had had numerous opportunities to become acquainted and to become familiar with the general pattern of living on the ward, and eighteen months later.

At each point, a boy was observed twice in each of six settings: breakfast, snack periods just before the boys went to bed at night, other meals, structured games, unstructured group activities such as conversation, and an arts-and-crafts period. A number of observers participated, but each boy in a setting was observed by only one person. The observer reported the interactions between the boy and other children or adults, as well as what went on among the other children within the situation. He did not take notes but observed as much activity as he thought he could remember. After leaving the setting, he dictated, on tape or disk, a descriptive report of his observation. Periods of observation varied from several minutes to half an hour.

Actions were classified on two dimensions: friendliness-hostility and dominance-submissiveness. They were also rated on intensity. Four categories resulted from combining two terms, one from each dimension. Hostile-dominant interactions included actively refusing to comply with adult requests, making boastful demands on adults, threatening or challenging adults, attempting to argue down an adult, poking unfriendly fun at an adult, ordering adults around in a boastful or unfriendly manner, and attacking an adult authority with the attempt to negate or degrade his authority. Hostile-submissive interactions included whining and complaining in relation to adults, accusing adults of punitive behavior or attitudes, demanding something of an adult in such a way as to imply that the adult was an ungiving monster, sulky withdrawal from interaction, and tearful refusals. Friendly-submissive interactions included affiliative behaviors, cooperative actions, and the seeking of help. Friendly-dominant interactions included sympathizing with or reassuring adults, offering help to adults, and teaching or advising adults. Friendly-dominant responses constituted only a small proportion of behavior toward adults. Over the eighteen months hostile-dominant behavior decreased and friendly-submissive behavior increased.

According to the observations made, the order of events in the hospital was predictive of changes in the boys' behavior. However, what would have happened if the treatment program had been different in one or more respects? One cannot say, for there is no comparison group.

An attempt was made by Levitt and Grosz[20] to find measures of anxiety which would vary appropriately over three successive conditions: hypnosis, hypnosis with suggested anxiety, and the waking state. The measures employed were twenty-five different scores on the Rorschach Test, a set of ink blots to which a person responds by reporting what he sees in each blot. (The Test was introduced by Hermann Rorschach in 1921.)

Subjects were twelve medical and nursing students, six males and six females, who volunteered and were paid for participation in the research. They were selected from a larger number of volunteers on two criteria: demonstration of amnesia for performance in hypnosis and general psychological adjustment. All subjects scored within normal limits on a scale measuring anxiety and a scale measuring ego strength or stability of general adjustment. They were also screened in psychiatric and medical examinations.

Three Rorschach records were obtained from each subject on a single day. The three conditions were instituted in the same order for every subject: hypnosis, first; hypnosis with suggested anxiety, second; the waking state, third. Suggestion of amnesia for the blots was given after the first and again after the second condition. In suggesting anxiety, a psychiatrist used the word anxiety and synonyms such as fear, apprehension, and panic to avoid differences in private meanings of anxiety. Subjects were told by the psychiatrist that they did not know what was making them anxious. After the suggestion of anxiety, all subjects expressed feelings of anxiety verbally, and all displayed some physical manifestations commonly associated with anxiety, including trembling, agitation, and pallor.

Twenty-five different scores were obtained on the responses to the blots. Only four scores showed changes which distinguished the second condition from the first and third. For each of the four the score under suggested anxiety differed from the scores under hypnosis and the waking state in the same direction. One of the four, average reaction time, was longer under anxiety than in the other two states. The investigators concluded that these four scores could be interpreted as measures of anxiety since they all varied in the expected way with the order of the three circumstances.

Interpretation of the relation between the sequence of conditions and the change in scores must be limited to the prediction itself. Although there are six possible orders of the three conditions, only one order was employed. It is possible that the change in scores would be the same for all six orders, or that it would vary from one order to another. One cannot say.

The difficulty in measuring an emotional characteristic of personality such as anxiety by means of a so-called projective test such as the ink-blot test is certainly illustrated by this investigation. Only four of twenty-five measures actually showed promise. Nevertheless, work will continue with the Rorschach and other similar tests because of the interest in them and the possibility that they can contribute in an important way to psychological measurement, especially in the area of personality.

In his review of Russian psychophysiological research on conditioning, Razran[29] described briefly an investigation by Lisina on vasomotor activity, the constriction and dilation of blood vessels, as it related to the so-called orientation of subjects. Certain kinds of changes in vasomotor activity were found to occur when opportunity was provided for subjects to observe their records.

Five adults were subjected to prolonged and moderately painful electrical shock. Records were made of concomitant changes in the volume of the blood vessels of their arms. Constriction occurred frequently; dilation, infrequently.

The procedure was instituted of terminating shock when dilation occurred. Thus termination of shock became a conditional event in an operant training situation. There was the possibility that the frequency of dilation would increase and the frequency of constriction decrease. No changes were observed, however, in the records of subjects through eighty terminations of shock. Operant training was not successful in this first phase.

The investigator then arranged for the subjects to observe their records as the procedure continued. A change to less frequent constrictions and more frequent dilations occurred rapidly. After subjects were allowed to observe their records and to observe the termination of shock when dilation occurred, dilation increased in frequency. Operant training was successful in the second phase.

The special order of circumstances here is not-observing-records followed by observing-records. What would the results have been for observing before not-observing? For not-observing over the entire period? For observing over the entire period? It is not possible to answer these questions from the available evidence.

Chapter Summary

Changes in behavior are revealed by successive measurement of an individual. There is a great deal of evidence that they can be predicted from developmental age, time, and trials in conditioning, practice, and operant training. Changes with practice are classified as learning, adaptation, fatigue, and adjustment. Changes can also be predicted from other changes, psychological and biological.

Prediction from a special order of circumstances is an important kind of psychological knowledge, but it should not be confused with experimental knowledge. One must be careful not to go beyond the data and make unwarranted inferences about matters for which there is no evidence.

References

1. Bakan, P. "Discrimination Decrement as a Function of Time in a Prolonged Vigil." *The Journal of Experimental Psychology,* 50 (1955), 387-390.

2. Barker, R. G., T. Dembo, and K. Lewin. "Frustration and Regression: An Experiment with Young Children." *University of Iowa Studies in Child Welfare*, 18, No. 386 (1941).

3. Bayley, N. "Consistency and Variability in the Growth of Intelligence from Birth to Eighteen Years." *The Journal of Genetic Psychology*, 75 (1949), 165-196.

4. ———. "On the Growth of Intelligence." *The American Psychologist*, 10 (1955), 805-818.

5. ———. "Data on the Growth of Intelligence Between 16 and 21 Years as Measured by the Wechsler-Bellevue Scale." *The Journal of Genetic Psychology*, 90 (1957), 3-15.

6. Berger, C., and A. Mahneke. "Fatigue in Two Simple Visual Tasks." *The American Journal of Psychology*, 67 (1954), 509-512.

7. Cohen, L. "Rate of Apparent Change of a Necker Cube as a Function of Prior Stimulation." *The American Journal of Psychology*, 72 (1959), 327-344.

8. Das, J. P. "Conditioning and Hypnosis." *The Journal of Experimental Psychology*, 56 (1958), 110-113.

9. Davis, R. C. "Modification of the Galvanic Reflex by Daily Repetition of a Stimulus." *The Journal of Experimental Psychology*, 17 (1934), 504-535.

10. Deese, J., and F. H. Kresse. "An Experimental Analysis of the Errors in Rote Serial Learning." *The Journal of Experimental Psychology*, 44 (1952), 199-202.

11. Duncan, C. P. "Description of Learning to Learn in Human Subjects." *The American Journal of Psychology*, 73 (1960), 108-114.

12. Evans, Diana "The Relationship Between Level of Activation and Reaction Time." Unpublished Honors Paper. Greensboro, N.C.: The Woman's College of the University of North Carolina, 1960-61.

13. Franklin, J. C., and J. Brozek. "The Relation Between Distribution of Practice and Learning Efficiency in Psychomotor Performance." *The Journal of Experimental Psychology*, 37 (1947), 16-24.

14. Friedlander, J. W., and T. R. Sarbin. "The Depth of Hypnosis." *The Journal of Abnormal and Social Psychology*, 33 (1938), 453-475.

15. Hilgard, E. R., and A. A. Campbell. "The Course of Acquisition and Retention of Conditioned Eyelid Responses in Man." *The Journal of Experimental Psychology*, 19 (1936), 227-247.

16. Irwin, O. C. "The Distribution of the Amount of Motility in Young Infants Between Two Nursing Periods." *The Journal of Comparative Psychology*, 14 (1932), 429-445.

17. Jones, F. P., D. N. O'Connell, and J. A. Hanson. "Color-Coded Multiple-Image Photography for Studying Related Rates of Movement." *The Journal of Psychology*, 45 (1958), 247-251.

18. Jones, H. E., and N. Bayley. "The Berkeley Growth Study." *Child Development*, 12 (1941), 167-173.

19. Lambert, W. W., E. C. Lambert, and P. D. Watson. "Acquisition and Extinction of an Instrumental Response Sequence in the Token-Reward Situation." *The Journal of Experimental Psychology*, 45 (1953), 321-326.

20. Levitt, E. E., and H. J. Grosz. "A Comparison of Quantifiable Rorschach Anxiety Indicators in Hypnotically Induced Anxiety and Normal States." *The Journal of Consulting Psychology*, 24 (1960), 31-34.

21. Meyer, D. R., and R. C. Miles. "Intralist-Interlist Relations in Verbal Learning." *The Journal of Experimental Psychology,* 45 (1953), 109-115.
22. Mosel, J. N., and G. Kantrowitz. "The Effect of Monosodium Glutamate on Acuity to the Primary Tastes." *The American Journal of Psychology,* 65 (1952), 573-579.
23. Mote, F. A., G. E. Briggs, and K. M. Michels. "The Reliability of Measurement of Human Dark Adaptation." *The Journal of Experimental Psychology,* 48 (1954), 69-74.
24. Mundy-Castle, A. C., and B. L. McKiever. "The Psychophysiological Significance of the Galvanic Skin Response." *The Journal of Experimental Psychology,* 46 (1953), 15-24.
25. Noble, C. E., and F. J. Farese. "An Apparatus for Research in Human Selective Learning." *The Journal of Psychology,* 39 (1955), 475-484.
26. Poffenberger, A. T. "The Effects of Continuous Mental Work." *The American Journal of Psychology,* 39 (1927), 283-296.
27. ————. "The Effects of Continuous Work Upon Output and Feelings." *The Journal of Applied Psychology,* 12 (1928), 459-467.
28. Raush, H. L., A. T. Dittmann, and T. J. Taylor. "The Interpersonal Behavior of Children in Residential Treatment." *The Journal of Abnormal and Social Psychology,* 58 (1959), 9-26.
29. Razran, G. "The Observable Unconscious and the Inferable Conscious in Current Soviet Psychophysiology: Interoceptive Conditioning, Semantic Conditioning, and the Orienting Reflex." *Psychological Review,* 68 (1961), 81-147.
30. Rheingold, H. L., J. L. Gewirtz, and H. W. Ross. "Social Conditioning of Vocalizations in the Infant." *The Journal of Comparative and Physiological Psychology,* 52 (1959), 68-73.
31. Shirley, M. M. *The First Two Years, A Study of Twenty-Five Babies,* Vol. I: *Postural and Locomotor Development.* Child Welfare Monograph VI. Minneapolis: University of Minnesota Press, 1931.
32. ————. *The First Two Years, A Study of Twenty-Five Babies,* Vol. II: *Intellectual Development.* Child Welfare Monograph VII. Minneapolis: University of Minnesota Press, 1933.
33. Solley, C. M. "Reduction of Error With Practice in Perception of the Postural Vertical." *The Journal of Experimental Psychology,* 52 (1956), 329-333.
34. Walk, R. D. "Self Ratings of Fear in a Fear-Invoking Situation." *The Journal of Abnormal and Social Psychology,* 52 (1956), 171-178.
35. Williams, C. D. "Case Report: The Elimination of Tantrum Behavior by Extinction Procedures." *The Journal of Abnormal and Social Psychology,* 59 (1959), 269.

PART 4

EXPERIMENTAL
CONTROL

11

The Nature
of Experimentation

PSYCHOLOGICAL KNOWLEDGE TAKES THREE FORMS: MEASUREMENT, prediction, and control. (Classification is an equivalent of measurement.) The acquisition of knowledge in the form of measurement requires that characteristics of behavior be observed, recorded, and summarized. When behavior is classified, a typical result is a description of the categories and the numbers of behavioral events in them, a kind of presentation usually facilitated considerably by tables. When behavior is measured, the results may be presented in a frequency distribution or in terms of summary statistical values such as the mean and standard deviation, computed from the data. Included in this first form of knowledge are collections of normative data: measures obtained on some specified group of people under standardized conditions. Normative data are valuable in providing a standard with which an individual's behavior can be compared. Practical decisions in selection and placement programs are often based on the result of comparing an individual's performance with a set of norms. Prediction is implied in the making of these decisions. Success is predicted for a person if he stands high or compares favorably; failure is predicted if he is low or compares unfavorably. The prediction, however, is not made explicit in the form of a rule or an equation. We shall have nothing

335

more to say about this first form of knowledge. Our purpose in describing it briefly at this point is merely to ensure that it will be distinguished from knowledge of control.

Predictive knowledge is based on procedures for establishing relations. One kind of result is a prediction rule or equation for two sets of paired values. A practical consequence of establishing predictive relations is their application in new situations. An example in academic life is the selection and admission of new students to college. After a predictive relation is established between test scores on an admissions test and freshman grade-point averages for one group of students, the prediction rule is applied to a new group of applicants for whom only scores on the admissions test are available. Predicted grade-point averages are obtained, and applicants with predicted averages above some arbitrary value are accepted, while those with predicted averages below it are rejected. Predictive knowledge and knowledge of control are different and the distinction between them should be maintained.

Knowledge of control is based on procedures involving more than measurement and more than prediction. Data are gathered which yield facts concerning the control man can exercise over the behavior of others. At first glance, the expression *control of the behavior of others* may appear to have a sinister connotation, but a little thought will reveal that it represents the purpose of a variety of highly valued activities in most modern societies. Educating, training, advising, counseling, motivating, propagandizing, advertising, and selling are familiar ways in which people try to control the behavior of others.

The word control requires definition, for it is used in at least three related but distinguishable ways: holding a condition constant; manipulating a condition; and holding all conditions constant except those which are intentionally manipulated. Holding a condition constant is done to prevent an extraneous and unwanted influence from affecting the outcome of an investigation. If a horticulturist wishes to compare two kinds of plant food, applied to two like groups of plants, he sees to it that both groups of plants get the same amount of water. Thus amount of water is held constant or controlled. If a psychologist compares two methods of practice on a sensorimotor task by having one of two like groups practice by each method, then he controls amount of practice, holding it constant for the two groups. Manipulating a condition is done to find out the effect it has. When manipulating is incorporated in an investigation, determining its effect is usually the central purpose of the investigator. In the horticulturist's investigation of plant food, applying two kinds of food to two like groups of plants is the manipulation. In the psychologist's study of the sensorimotor task, imposing two methods of practice on two like groups of subjects is the manipulation. The third definition of control is the broadest since it actually encompasses the other two. It makes control equivalent to experimentation and knowledge of control equivalent to experimental knowledge. Psychological experimentation is arranging the conditions, subjects, procedures of measurement, and occasions of measurement so that a comparison can be made of the behavior of subjects observed under circumstances alike in all respects except those varied intentionally by the experimenter.

Knowledge about the control of behavior is obtained only by trial. In other words, one finds out about control by attempting it. There is no substitute for executing the actions which constitute a given instance of attempted control and observing the effects of those actions. It is a gross error to interpret data from an investigation which did not incorporate control as if the data came from one which did; that is, it is incorrect to call an investigation an experiment when it is not one.

The distinction between experimental investigations and nonexperimental investigations can be well illustrated by reference to some nonpsychological problems of concern to everyone. Suppose one wanted to determine whether or not adding a particular fluoride to drinking water would reduce the incidence of tooth decay. What should one do? Given a common supply of water, he should add the fluoride to the drinking water of one group of subjects and withhold it from the drinking water of a like group. After a period of time, the incidence of tooth decay should be determined for both groups. The two groups could then be compared to find out the effect of adding the fluoride and the possibility of controlling tooth decay by that operation.

It would not be surprising to have someone suggest what he thinks is an easier way to get the answer. The suggestion would be to survey a number of communities whose water supplies varied in the amount of the fluoride present by natural processes. The survey would involve determining the incidence of tooth decay in each community and relating these values to amounts of fluoride in the supplies. A predictive relation might be found. If so, is one justified in concluding that adding the fluoride to drinking water will have the desired effect? The answer is "No." There is the possibility that some other chemical, deposited by natural processes in amounts correlated with amounts of fluoride, is the effective substance and that the fluoride is not. The survey might be valuable, of course, in suggesting the need for an experiment, but the survey is no substitute for the experiment.

The controversy over the connection between lung cancer and smoking centers upon this same issue. There is evidence of a predictive relation between incidence of lung cancer and the practice of smoking. Much of this evidence is based on surveys. There is no experimental evidence of a connection as far as human smoking goes. Experiments with human subjects would, of course, be very difficult to perform. One possibility for an experiment would require two like groups of children who had not yet started to smoke. At some age, one group would start smoking; the other would not. In other respects the two groups would be treated alike. After a number of years, they would be compared with respect to the incidence of lung cancer in each.

Insistence on a distinction between experimental and nonexperimental research should not be interpreted as a denial of the value of nonexperimental research in making decisions when no experimental evidence is available. Everyone must make decisions without adequate evidence.

The research on the Salk vaccine for poliomyelitis was a remarkable achievement in medical experimentation on human subjects. Two like groups of children were constituted by random assignment. Children in one group received the vaccine; children in the other group received a placebo, an inert substance which looked like the vaccine and was known to have no effect. The administering physician or nurse could not distinguish between the vaccine and the placebo. When the evidence was in, there was little room for doubt or controversy: the vaccine was effective in preventing poliomyelitis.

In a psychological experiment, certain circumstances are contrived by the experimenter and arranged for subjects according to a plan which the experimenter carefully formulates in advance. These contrived circumstances are called conditions or treatments. A psychologist is said to impose them and the respect in which they differ is called the independent variable. In imposing conditions or treatments, the experimenter is said to manipulate the independent variable. After the imposition, the experimenter measures some characteristic of his subjects' behavior. The characteristic measured is called the dependent variable. The measures from the different conditions are then compared to determine the differential effects of the conditions on behavior.

Experiments with Groups of Subjects

One way of arranging conditions and subjects is to have as many comparable groups of subjects as there are conditions and to impose one condition only on each group. It is convenient to represent an experiment schematically. A simple plan involving two conditions and two groups of subjects can be represented by the following rectangular table of two cells. Each cell represents a group of subjects. The letters above the cells represent the conditions imposed on the groups. The letters A and B suggest two qualitatively different conditions, which, in an experiment on taste thresholds for sour, might be two solutions: one of tartaric acid,

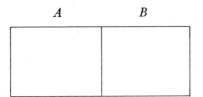

the other of acetic acid. One could imagine a set of measures of behavior in each cell, with one measure for each subject. The two conditions would be compared by computing the mean for each group and the difference between the two means.

When conditions can be designated quantitatively, the schematic representation is slightly different. An experiment involving three conditions, distinguishable quantitatively, may be represented by the following rectangular table of three cells. Each cell is a group of subjects. When

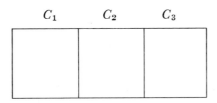

conditions are quantitatively different, they are called levels. In an experiment on learning to reason, three levels might be three different amounts of practice in solving logical problems. The three conditions would be imposed and subjects would be measured on the dependent variable. After the three means were computed, they would be compared to determine the outcome of the experiment. When conditions are levels, the results can be plotted graphically. With three conditions there are three pairs of values, each pair consisting of a mean and a level. A fictitious plot is given in Figure 11-1. The independent variable is labeled C for conditions; the dependent variable is labeled Y.

When the plot of points is linear or nearly so, a correlation coefficient can be computed to express the relation between Y, the dependent variable, and C, the independent variable. In actual practice, however, the most common way of reporting results involves computing the differences among the means. There are statistical procedures for making decisions about the reproducibility of such differences. The general idea is that having adopted a theory about the nature of errors in his experiment, the researcher can decide that a difference is large enough not to be attributed to error, or so small it should be.

Experimental designs can be elaborated by combining two sets of conditions. Suppose one set is designated as A_1 and A_2, and another as

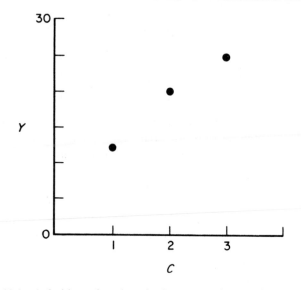

Figure 11-1. A fictitious plot of results for an experiment with three quantitative conditions or levels of treatment. Y is the scale of means for the dependent variable.

B_1 and B_2. Following is a hypothetical example of conditions which might be employed in an experiment in clinical psychology. A_1 and A_2 might be two different dosages of a tranquilizer drug, administered by a physician or a psychiatrist collaborating in the experiment. B_1 and B_2 might be two different amounts of psychotherapy: one or two sessions per week with a clinical psychologist. The two levels from both sets can be combined. The logically possible combinations of two levels, with one from each set, are four in number: A_1B_1, A_1B_2, A_2B_1, and A_2B_2. A convenient schema is the following table of two rows, two columns, and four cells. Each cell represents a group of subjects. The evaluation of the results would require computing and comparing the means for the four cells. There are three possibilities. Comparing the two means in the left column with those in the right one would reveal the apparent effect of

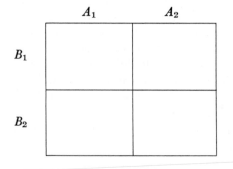

drug dosage. Comparing the two in the top row with those in the bottom one would reveal the apparent effect of amount of psychotherapy. Comparing the two in the one diagonal with those in the other would reveal the interaction between drug dosage and amount of psychotherapy. Interaction is specifically defined as the difference between the therapy effect at the lower dosage and the therapy effect at the upper dosage. In other words, the comparison of diagonal groups shows how the effect of therapy depends on drug dosage. A design having two or more sets of conditions is called a factorial design. Each set of conditions is a factor. The expression "factorial design" should not be confused with "factor analysis," to which reference was made in the chapter on validity. Nor should "factor in experimental design" be confused with "factor in factorial validity."

Experiments with Repeated Treatment of Subjects

When it is *not* known that the effects of conditions are temporary, an experiment is performed with a separate group of subjects for each condition. With separate groups, the effects are kept separate. When it *is* known that the effects are temporary, one group of subjects may be employed, in which case the conditions of the experiment are imposed in succession on each subject. The behavior of each subject is measured after each condition is imposed. Thus there is repeated treatment and repeated measurement of each subject. The schema for an experiment involving two conditions and three subjects is given below. The rectangular

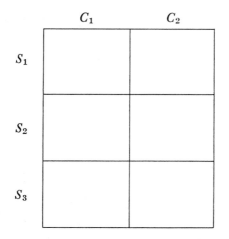

table has three rows, two columns, and six cells. Each row represents a subject. Each column represents a condition. One can imagine a measure in each cell for a particular subject after a particular condition has been imposed on him. The evaluation would require comparing the means of the two columns. In an experiment on visual acuity the two conditions might be two levels of illumination. Repeated treatment of subjects with different levels of illumination is permissible, because it is known that the effect of any level within the ordinary range is only temporary.

An important precaution which must be taken in imposing two or more different treatments on a subject is varying the order of the treatments. If the same order is used for all subjects, then learning, adaptation, or fatigue may be measured along with the effects of the treatments. In an experiment with two conditions, C_1 and C_2, there are two possible orders: C_1C_2 and C_2C_1. Both orders would be employed equally often, with the order for any subject determined randomly by the toss of a coin or some other mechanical method. Thus in the experiment on visual acuity, half the subjects would have the lower level of illumination imposed before the higher level; half would have the higher before the lower. In an experiment with three conditions, *A, B,* and *C,* there are six possible orders in which the conditions can be imposed: *ABC, ACB, BAC, BCA, CAB,* and *CBA.* If there were six subjects, one order would be used for each subject. This procedure would insure that changes predictable from the successive occasions would be distributed equally over all three conditions.

Experiments with Repeated Treatment of a Single Subject

Repeated treatment, as the expression has been used up to this point, has meant imposing a full set of conditions on each subject. It has not meant repeating a condition on a subject, a procedure which is often objectionable. If the three conditions in an experiment on visual thresholds in identifying geometric figures were a triangle, a square, and a circle, all three conditions could be imposed on a subject once, but any further repetition might be accompanied by learning, a change in behavior which the experimenter might wish to exclude. When it is known that the effects of all conditions are temporary and that the effect of a given condition does not vary with repeated imposition of that condition, then it is possible to perform an experiment with only a single subject. The several conditions are imposed in succession on one subject and the entire procedure is repeated for that subject. The behavior of the subject is measured after each condition is imposed. The schema for a hypothetical experiment involving three conditions and one subject is given below. The table of three rows, three columns, and nine cells represents one subject. Each column is a condition. Each row is a set of conditions numbered according to the order of imposition. The order of imposition of the

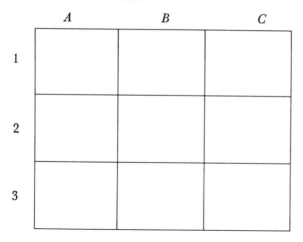

conditions within each set would be varied. One possible arrangement for the three sets would be *CAB, BCA,* and *ABC.* It has the advantage that each condition appears once and only once in each position. There would be one measure per cell. In evaluating the experiment, the means of columns would be compared. Examples of experiments requiring only one subject will be given in the next section.

PSYCHOPHYSICAL EXPERIMENTS

Psychophysics is an area of psychological experimentation in which the design with repeated treatment of a single subject has been widely employed. In a psychophysical experiment the conditions are stimuli which vary along some dimension. In an experiment on vision, three different wave lengths of light could be a set of stimulus conditions. The subject's task could be to make judgments concerning an object illuminated successively by the lights of different wave lengths. It is known that the effect of light of a specific wave length is only temporary. Furthermore, it is known that with moderate exposure the effects of repeated illumination by a given wave length are relatively constant. Therefore it is justifiable to perform an experiment of this type on one subject.

One standard procedure for a psychophysical experiment is called the method of constant stimuli. A number of stimuli are chosen to be the conditions of the experiment. The stimuli are presented to the subject in a random order. The subject is instructed to report, on each presentation, whether or not he can perceive the stimulus by saying either "Present" or "Absent." The entire series of stimuli is repeated a number of times. A count is made of the subject's judgments of "present" with respect to each stimulus. The frequency count may be converted to a percentage.

A fictitious account of an experiment with frequency of a tone as the stimulus dimension follows. Four tones with frequencies of 12, 18, 24, and

30 cycles per second are the stimulus conditions. They are presented in ten different random orders to a subject. The subject's task, on each presentation, is to report "Yes" if he perceives the stimulus as a smooth continuous tone and "No" if he does not. Since there are ten presentations of each of four tones, the experimenter records forty judgments. The results consist of the numbers of yesses: two for the 12-cycle tone; four for the 18-cycle tone; nine for the 24-cycle tone; and ten for the 30-cycle tone. These numbers may be expressed as the percentages: 24, 40, 90, and 100. The absolute threshold obtained by this method is defined as the stimulus value detected on fifty per cent of presentations. The value is determined by simple linear interpolation. It lies between 18 and 24 cycles as fifty lies between 40 and 90, and is, therefore, 19.2 cycles.

The method can be extended to the judgment of differences, but it is then called the method of constant stimulus differences. Stimuli called comparison stimuli are chosen to be the conditions of the experiment. One stimulus is chosen as a standard. The comparison stimuli are presented in random order. Before each one, the standard stimulus is presented. The subject's task is to report whether the comparison stimulus is "greater" or "less" than the standard. The entire series is repeated a number of times. A count is made of the subject's reports of "greater" for each comparison stimulus. The frequency count may be converted to a percentage.

A fictitious experiment follows. Seven comparison weights of 185, 190, 195, 200, 205, 210, and 215 grams are presented to a subject in random order. The subject lifts a standard weight of 200 grams before each comparison weight. He reports whether the comparison weight is heavier or lighter than the standard. One hundred series of judgments are obtained, and a count of judgments of "heavier" for each comparison weight yields the numbers: 1, 20, 40, 55, 60, 76, and 92. The seven percentages are the same. Two differential thresholds can be determined by this method: the upper threshold is the difference between the standard weight and the comparison weight judged heavier on seventy-five per cent of presentations; the lower threshold is the difference between the standard and the comparison judged heavier on twenty-five per cent of presentations. Interpolation yields 209.7 grams as the value judged "heavier" on seventy-five per cent of presentations. Thus the differential threshold is 9.7 grams. The value judged "heavier" on twenty-five per cent of presentations is 191.25 grams, and the lower differential threshold is 8.75 grams.

Cause

Few terms are more widely used in lay and scientific circles and, at the same time, less satisfactorily defined than *cause*. The term has been the subject of discussion and debate for centuries. It would not be difficult to formulate a definition in highly indefinite abstract terms, controversial though it might be, but, if we were to do so, the serious problem would remain of connecting the concept with the realities of psychological investigations.

There are, of course, no absolute standards for deciding on any definition. There is no proof that one is correct and others incorrect. The only standard is usage, and when usage is uniform, there is no problem. When usage varies, different definitions may have equal merit. When usage is chaotic, however, there is no standard, and the term in question should be defined arbitrarily to some good purpose, or abandoned.

Over the years cause has been defined in a variety of ways: The cause of one event is a prior event. One event is the cause of another when the former precedes the latter on a large percentage of occasions. A cause is designated in stating a theory from which one can deduce the occurrence of an event as a logical consequence of prior or attendant circumstances. When the occurrence or nonoccurrence of an event is concomitant with the occurrence or nonoccurrence of another event, either event can be said to be the cause of the other. The cause of an event is the act of an agent who instigates or regulates the event. Cause is the experimental manipulation of conditions by a human agent to produce some effect.

Our position here is that we can do without the word. Everything that needs to be said about methods and results in psychology can be said very satisfactorily and uncontroversially without it. If we had to choose one of the definitions listed above, we would choose the last one, experimental manipulation. The basis for this choice is our opinion that, in common usage, *cause* has the connotation of *agent*.

If literalness is accepted as a proper standard for psychology, then impersonal objects and events should not be conceptualized as agents. Thinking of the experimenter's manipulation as a cause fits the common idea of cause as the act of an agent but does not violate the literalness standard. The experimenter is, properly speaking, an agent.

Heredity and Environment

There is an old controversy over the "relative effects of heredity and environment" which can be put in proper perspective by examining the nature of the evidence with which participants were actually concerned. Since a full appreciation of the nature of the evidence regarding heredity requires an understanding of the nature of experimentation, we have chosen to discuss the issue here. This does not mean that the evidence on the "effect of heredity" was experimental. To the contrary, there was little or no experimental evidence, especially on humans. There was no evidence from direct and precise manipulation of the structure, function, location, and interaction of genes, which with cytoplasm are passed bodily in the chromosomes from parents to offspring. There was some evidence from radiation treatments deliberately imposed on lower animals, but little or none on humans. There was a great deal of evidence from studies of selective breeding of animals but none, of course, for humans. There was evidence of family resemblances, but these could be interpreted as related to either similarity of environments or hereditary factors with equal justification. There was positive experimental evidence of the tremendous effects of instruction, practice, and other conditions, but there was also a kind of negative evidence with respect to the limits of those effects. Whenever experimental manipulation appeared to have a limited effect, especially in reducing differences among individuals, an inference was made concerning the effect of heredity. There was also evidence from studies of twins, fraternal and identical; but the volume was not large; the studies were not always good; and the results were not unequivocally interpretable for some of the reasons already given above.

For many participants in the controversy, the problem appeared to be at best theoretical and at worst philosophical. The real problem, of course, was obtaining evidence concerning the possibilities of prediction and control in a wide range of circumstances having to do with human genetics. Theoretical principle and philosophical argument had to give way to empirical and experimental research. The evidence as it bears upon human behavior, distinguished from organic structure and disorder, is still scant. The evidence concerning organic matters is, of course, very largely in the field of medical genetics.

Maturation

Maturation is a concept often discussed in connection with developmental age but sometimes, too, in connection with heredity. Consideration of the concept has been delayed until measurement, prediction, and control were distinguished. Maturation is an indefinite abstract term which has been given varied referents: completion of developmental processes in the body; the hereditary aspect of development; developmental changes in behavior as a result of growth and not training; and developmental changes in behavior related to age. Although development, the idea of orderly or predictable early change with age, is common to all the definitions, the possibility of ambiguity in the use of the term should be evident. What it is that one observes in studying maturation is not clear. Is it a change in behavior or a change in the body anatomically, neurologically, and physiologically? If it is a change in behavior, what is the class of behavior which maturation designates, and how is that behavior measured? Is it behavioral change predictable from age? From measures of the body, its structures, and its functions? Or from genetic variables? Is it behavioral change predictable from age with or without specific kinds of conditioning, practice, or training? Is it an inferred process? If so, from what?

The value of a term such as maturation is difficult to assess. The methods and results of psychological research on development can be communicated in terms more definite and less ambiguous than maturation. The word may have value for theory but, if it does, its use in that connection has not progressed very far. Until the term is defined, at least in general terms, with respect to operations of measurement, prediction, or control, it is of questionable value.

The Systematization of Experimental Evidence

Experimental findings can be systematically organized in several different ways. They can be classified by kind of subject to which they apply, area of application in which they have been put to practical use, characteristic of behavior observed, and type of condition or treatment imposed. Consequently, it is not surprising that reports of the same experiments appear in different settings in psychological literature. Organizing evidence by kind of subject yields categories such as infant, child, adolescent, and adult; by area of application, categories such as clinical, educational, and industrial; and by characteristic of behavior, categories such as perceptual, motor, and sensorimotor; or normal and abnormal; or intellective and personality; or learning, adaptation, fatigue, and adjustment.

It is our purpose here to emphasize the *control* of behavior. These are the relevant questions: In what ways can man control the behavior of others? In what ways can he control his own behavior? What knowledge is there that pertains directly to this control? What are the facts obtained by actually attempting it? The remaining chapters constitute an answer. Organizing the experimental evidence by type of condition—an approach which serves the purpose of emphasizing control—provides the chapter topics.

There is a type of condition which has great potential significance for the control of human behavior, but is not represented in the following chapters except, in a very limited way, by the material on drugs. It is the class of biological interventions involving—in addition to the administration of all kinds of drugs—dietary, surgical, radiation, and various other chemical and physical treatments. Psychologists employ many of these biological interventions in experiments on the lower animals, but most of the experimentation on humans is done by medical researchers.

Chapter Summary

A psychological experiment is a planned event in which conditions are imposed on subjects and the effects on their behavior are observed. Thus experimental knowledge has to do with ways of controlling behavior.

An experiment may be conducted by imposing each one of two or more conditions on a separate group of subjects, on the same group of subjects, or on a single subject. When conditions vary quantitatively, they are called levels, and the results of the experiment can be expressed by stating the relation between the measures of behavior and the levels of treatment. Two or more sets of conditions can be employed in the same experiment, yielding what is called a factorial design.

Cause is a controversial term. A suggested definition is "the experimental manipulation of conditions by a human agent to produce some effect." The old argument about the relative importance of heredity and environment has been supplanted by research on various aspects of genetic prediction and control. Maturation is an abstract term for an inferred developmental process, but the operations by which it is defined have not been made explicit. Succeeding chapters will emphasize the control of behavior by focusing on various types of experimental conditions.

12

Perceptual

Stimulus

Conditions

AN INTRODUCTION TO THE EXPERIMENTAL PSYCHOLOGY OF PER-
ception is presented in this chapter, organized in terms of the stimulus conditions: visual, auditory, gustatory, olfactory, cutaneous, kinesthetic, and
static. Since these stimulus conditions are readily manipulatable as independent variables in both laboratory and field experiments, a great amount
of research has been done with them, and a substantial portion of present
psychological knowledge concerns their effects. This knowledge is among
the most certain and uncontroversial in psychology.

There are many opportunities in everyday life to become familiar with
connections between perceptual stimuli and judgments. It is a common
experience to adjust a three-way lamp and make a judgment about its
brightness; to adjust the volume control on a radio and judge its loudness; to add sugar to a drink and judge its sweetness; or to adjust the
control on a heating pad and judge its warmth. Thus it is easy to learn
the practical manipulations of physical variables by means of which one
can control perceptual behavior—either one's own or that of others—in

the form of judgments of brightness, loudness, sweetness, warmth, and other perceptual dimensions. In addition to these personal experiences of controlling perceptual behavior, there are many opportunities to witness others doing the manipulation. A stage hand dims the lights in a theater; a violinist produces a melodic variation in pitch; an orchestra plays a crescendo in a symphony; a technician changes the color of a spot of light thrown on a principal in a ballet; an operator projects figures which appear to move on a theater screen. On all these occasions the manipulation of stimuli may be observed to produce perceptual behavior in the form of verbal responses or other kinds of overt activity in the audience.

Familiarity with this practical control comes from everyday experience, but an understanding of it comes only through study of the experimental knowledge. Specific laws relating stimuli and judgments have been established as the consequences of a vast amount of psychological experimentation. An attempt will be made in this chapter to represent some of the principal experimental relationships which are fundamental to an understanding of this control.

Visual Stimulus Conditions

Experimentation with visual stimulus conditions requires that the investigator change either the light itself or the objects from which it is reflected, and that he observe the effects of the change on the judgments of subjects. Light may be varied with respect to wave length, intensity, and duration; objects may be varied with respect to orientation, size, distance, number, and other characteristics.

Wave Length

Wave length can be varied by the experimenter in three ways: changing filters, changing colored papers, and changing the position of a prism. Presented below are the findings of some typical investigations in which these methods have been employed to determine the relation between wave length and the response variables: sensitivity, brightness, and discrimination.

It has been shown that the normal human eye is not equally sensitive to all the hues of light. By measuring absolute thresholds for various wave lengths, Wald[36] established that the lowest threshold occurred at approximately 562 millimicrons, a yellow-green hue. The threshold value was the least intensity which could be detected. Since the reciprocal of a threshold was called the sensitivity, the wave length for the lowest threshold was the point of maximum sensitivity.

To obtain the thresholds, Wald isolated ten spectral lines or narrow bands of wave lengths from a light source by means of color filters. The intensity of each line or band could be regulated very accurately. Measurements were obtained with monocular viewing of a small circular test field. The test field was exposed by means of a shutter for durations of 0.04 seconds. Since the small test field was fixated centrally, the image fell entirely within the fovea of the retina and stimulated only cones, the color-sensitive receptors. Subjects were twenty-two persons whose average age was twenty years. Each subject was dark-adapted before measurements of thresholds were obtained. Figure 12-1 is a plot of relative sensitivity against wave length. On both sides of the maximum, sensitivity declined rapidly.

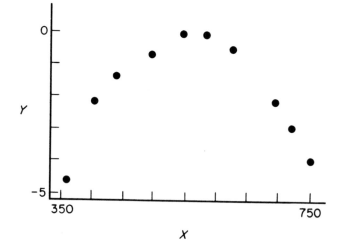

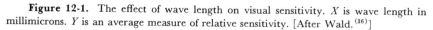

Figure 12-1. The effect of wave length on visual sensitivity. X is wave length in millimicrons. Y is an average measure of relative sensitivity. [After Wald.[36]]

When the intensity of the visible spectrum is reduced to a very low point, and the individual viewing the spectrum has been in the dark for a period of time, the spectrum appears without hue but varies in brightness. This corresponds to a common experience in viewing objects in a dimly lighted room. Objects are seen in shades of gray even though they would possess vivid hues in a brightly lighted room. In 1922, Hecht and Williams[15] reported on this relation between wave length and brightness of the spectrum at low intensities. They found that the center portion of the spectrum, around green, was much brighter than either the red or the violet end. Subjects were forty-three men and five women, graduate students and members of the teaching staff in chemistry and physics at the University of Liverpool. Their average age was twenty-five years.

Light from the incandescent portion of a lamp mounted in a light-tight box was focused on the slit of a spectrometer, a device which employs a prism to separate light into its component hues. The monochromatic light which emerged from the spectrometer passed through a pair of special prisms, employed for varying the intensity of the light, and impinged on a ground glass at the end of a viewing box. A subject viewed the other side of the ground glass from the opposite end of the viewing box.

A constant standard light was provided by a layer of radium paint on a pattern cut out of cardboard. The intensity of the standard was well below the threshold for any hue but bright enough to be seen easily by a dark-adapted subject. The relative energy necessary to produce this degree of brightness at various wave lengths was determined. The cardboard pattern, shown in Figure 12-2, covered the ground glass inside the viewing box. The radium paint gave a constant and continuous light.

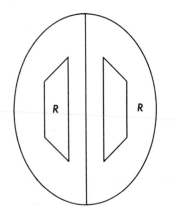

Figure 12-2. The cardboard pattern employed in an investigation of the relation between wave length and brightness at low intensities. R identifies the areas covered by radium paint. Other areas were cut out, revealing the ground glass which was illuminated from the back. [Adapted from Hecht and Williams.[15]]

The subject sat in front of the viewing box in a darkened room. He was allowed half an hour for dark adaptation during which time the pattern formed by the radium paint became visible and then increased in brightness and clearness. In the test, the subject looked into the viewing box and observed the radium pattern for a few seconds, after which the spectrometer was adjusted to admit a weak light of a given wave length. The subject was instructed to notice whether the shadows of the pattern were as strong as they were before. Then a stronger light was admitted and he again examined the pattern. This procedure was continued until he reported the shadows had completely disappeared and the pattern had become uniform in brightness. The intensity of the light relative to its source was determined and recorded. Similar measurements were obtained with lights of different wave lengths one after the other.

The data for each subject were plotted and the minimum point in the plot was found. An arbitrary value was assigned to the minimum and the results at the other wave lengths were then expressed in terms of it. The results for each wave length for the forty-eight subjects were then averaged. Figure 12-3 is a plot of relative energy against wave length. Each point is the average for forty-eight subjects. The wave length at which the minimum energy was necessary to produce the given brightness was near 510 millimicrons, a green hue. The energy values for wave lengths on each side of the point rise quickly.

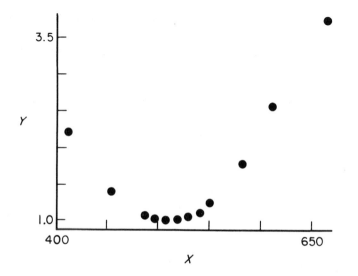

Figure 12-3. The effect of wave length on brightness matching. X is wave length in millimicrons. Y is average relative energy required to match the standard. [After Hecht and Williams.[15]]

It is a matter of common observation that children, in distinguishing colors, have more difficulty with some than with others. Discriminating between blue and green was found to be more difficult than discriminating between black and white in tests given by Clifford and Calvin[6]. Subjects were 120 elementary school children in six grades from kindergarten to the fifth. Within each grade level children were assigned randomly to two groups: one tested on a black-white discrimination; the other tested on a blue-green discrimination.

The test materials were arranged on a table and concealed by a screen. Two different cards were placed behind the screen in front of identical red cups, under one of which a plastic toy was hidden. A child sat at the table facing the screen while the experimenter manipulated the screen and arranged the materials from a position behind the table. The child was told, "We are going to play a little game. Behind this screen are two cups and under one of them there is a toy. If you can guess which cup the toy is under, you can keep it." After the experimenter arranged the material, gave a signal, and raised the screen, the child chose one of the cups. If his choice was correct, he was immediately given the toy. If his choice was incorrect, both cups were raised to show him where the toy was, the screen was lowered, and the materials were arranged for the next trial. The positions of the toy and the cards were varied.

Black and white cards were used for one group; blue and green, for the other. For half the children in the first group, black was correct; for the other half, white was correct. For half of the second group, blue was correct; for the other half, green. A child was considered to have learned the discrimination when he achieved ten successive correct trials. The procedure was terminated if he did not learn in thirty trials.

The median number of trials required to learn the black-white discrimination was twenty-one; to learn the blue-green discrimination, forty. The results supported the conclusion that the blue-green discrimination was more difficult than the black-white discrimination for the children studied.

INTENSITY OF LIGHT

The intensity of a light source is measurable in terms of candlepower, the number of units being the number of "candles." (A candle is a standard electric bulb.) The illumination of a surface some distance from a light source is measurable in terms of foot-candles, the number of units being the candlepower of the source divided by the square of the distance in feet. For light reflected from the surface to the eye, the property measured is called luminance. It is expressed in terms of apparent foot-candles, the number of units being the illumination in foot-candles multiplied by a percentage representing the reflecting quality of the surface. (Distance can also be expressed on the metric scale as meters or centimeters.) Intensity, illumination, and luminance can be measured directly by instruments sensitive to the energy level of light, but are often measured by visual comparison with a standard. Measurement by visual comparison is called photometry, and a device employed in making the comparison is called a photometer.

In an experiment, intensity, illumination, or luminance can be varied in several ways: changing the voltage to the light source, varying the distance of the light source, inserting neutral or gray filters in the path of the light, rotating certain special kinds of prisms, varying the mixture of black and white on a color wheel, or presenting cards which differ in grayness. The variations produced by any of these methods may constitute a set of conditions imposed on subjects in the experiment. After the conditions are imposed, measurements of the subjects' behavior are obtained and differences in behavior under the varied conditions are evaluated.

Control of the brightness of lights is a familiar feature of many everyday situations. Evidence that the control of brightness is achieved by manipulation of intensity was reported in 1929, by Kellogg[19] as the result of a psychophysical experiment. Judgments of brightness were obtained by the method of constant stimuli. A subject gave his judgments by pressing telegraph keys.

The reflecting surfaces judged were presented by means of a photometer. Light from a bulb of known candlepower was reflected by mirrors upon two diffusion surfaces in the photometer. When the bulb was centered between the diffusion surfaces, the illumination on the two surfaces was the same. Sliding the bulb nearer to or farther away from one surface produced, concomitantly, inverse variation in the illumination on the opposite surface.

The subject viewed with his left eye through an artificial pupil. In looking through the telescope of the photometer, he viewed a circular field, which was bisected vertically. Each half of the field contained a smaller semicircle framed by a border of uniform width. The illumination from one diffusion surface appeared in the inner semicircle of one side of the field and in the bordering edge of the other semicircle. Thus illumination from each surface was present in each half of the circular field. The bulb flashed, under the control of a timer. The duration of each light interval was one second; the duration of each dark interval was two seconds.

The subject gave judgments of the relative brightness of the two semicircles by pressing his left key to indicate that the left semicircle was darker and his right key to indicate that the right one was darker. The keys operated electromagnetic markers. In three of seven pairings, the right surface was darker than the left; in three, the left surface was darker than the right; and in one, the two surfaces were equal. Figure 12-4 is a plot of percentage of judgments of the right semicircle as darker for one subject. The number of judgments for each of the seven settings was 144.

That objects are more clearly distinguishable under higher levels of illumination than they are under lower levels is known from everyday experience but specification of the relation between acuity and illumination requires experimentation of the kind performed by Leibowitz[22], in which acuity was found to improve with increases in luminance. Acuity was defined as precision in aligning two straight edges. Since this task resembled

the use of a vernier, a device employed in physics to make fine adjustments, the experimenter called the dimension "vernier acuity." Subjects
were university undergraduates possessing normal vision.

The test objects were two adjacent rectangles, the edges of which
were off-set at the start of a trial. A subject's task was to adjust the rectangles so that their edges coincided. The lower one was stationary; the
upper one was movable and could be adjusted by turning a knob at the
end of a flexible cable. A plate of ground glass, illuminated from the
rear by a large bulb, was located in back of the test objects. The subject
viewed the test objects with his natural pupil through a lens which gave
an apparent distance of one meter.

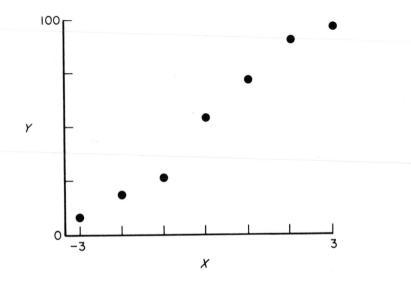

Figure 12-4. The effect of intensity on judgments of brightness by the method of
constant stimuli. X is level of intensity for the left semicircle relative to the right. In the
seven pairs from -3 to $+3$, the left semicircle gets brighter while the right one gets
darker. Y is per cent of judgments "right screen darker." Data are for one subject. [After
Kellogg.[19]]

After the subject adapted to the dark for ten minutes and then
adapted to the lowest test-field luminance at which he could perform the
task, the experimenter displaced the upper rectangle and the subject tried
to realign it. These two actions constituted a trial. Twenty trials were
conducted at each level of luminance. The direction and magnitude of
the displacement was varied randomly with the restriction that the numbers of displacements right and left should be equal. Levels of luminance
were presented in an ascending order.

Measurements were obtained with two black rectangles presented in a vertical position in a light field, the same black rectangles in a horizontal position, and with vertical light bars on a dark field. Figure 12-5 is a plot of a measure of variability, the standard deviation, against seven luminance levels for one subject's judgments of the light bars. As luminance increased, variability decreased, rapidly at first and then more slowly as it approached an apparent limiting value. The trend of the plot for black bars and for bars in either horizontal or vertical positions was quite similar. The decrease in variability was an increase in precision.

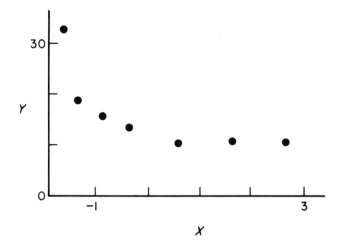

Figure 12-5. The effect of luminance on vernier adjustment for one subject. X is a measure of luminance. Y is the standard deviation of settings in seconds of arc. [After Leibowitz.[22]]

Critical flicker frequency (CFF) is the lowest frequency at which a flashing light is judged to be continuous. It is a measure of ability to discriminate between flashes. CFF depends on a number of conditions, including the brightness of the light and the area of the test patch, as shown in an experiment by Kugelmass and Landis[21]. It was found to increase with both luminance and area.

A subject viewed the test patch through a binocular microscope while his head was held in position by means of a hood. When he looked through the oculars or eyepieces, he saw a large circular uniform field of light surrounded by darkness. In the center of the light field was a smaller darker circular patch defined on opal glass. The area of the patch could be varied by means of a template with thirty-six different holes. The subject was instructed to fixate the center of the dark patch and was allowed to do so for approximately five minutes. He was then instructed to press a key, an action which eliminated the dark patch for one second with controlled intermittent light. Frequency was decreased in steps of one half cycle per second until the subject changed his report from "steady" to "flicker." Luminance was varied over five different levels.

Figure 12-6 shows the relationship between *CFF* and area at three different levels of luminance. The plots are based on averages for two subjects.

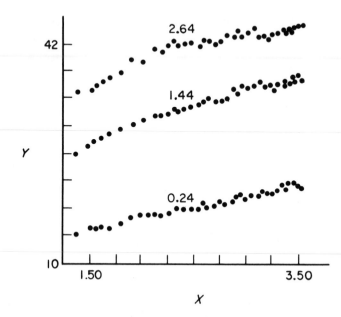

Figure 12-6. The effect of area and luminance on critical flicker frequency. *X* is log area in square millimeters on the retina. *Y* is the *CFF* in number of flashes per second. The three sets of points represent three conditions of luminance. [After Kugelmass and Landis.[21]]

DURATION

Either the presence or the absence of light stimulation can be varied with respect to its duration to provide a set of experimental conditions. Assuming the presence of illumination, how does its duration affect visual perception? The question is not difficult, for surely one answer is that the individual can see more in a longer period of viewing than he can in a shorter one. This answer is supported by the experimental evidence obtained by Hunter and Sigler[16] who investigated the effects of duration on judgments of the number of black dots in a luminous test field. Intensity was also varied. The results showed that the number of perceived dots increased as both duration and intensity increased. Two subjects served in the experiment which lasted for two years.

A subject sat in a dark cubicle at some distance from the test field, which he viewed with both eyes through the hood of a stereoscope adapted as a head rest. The test field was a circular opal glass plate which at the distance used subtended only a small visual angle. A white circle painted around the test field was illuminated from the sides by dim light shielded from the subject's direct view.

The subject was instructed to report, after each exposure, the number of dots he saw. He was told not to guess and that he could report, "I do not know." If a great many dots appeared, he was to report only the number that he had seen. When the experimenter gave a ready signal, the subject fixated the center of the test field. Approximately two seconds after the ready signal, a pattern of dots was presented.

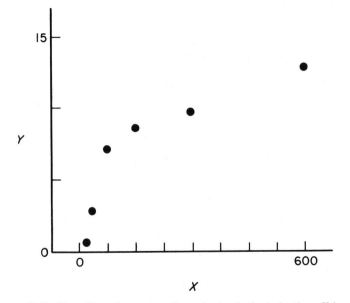

Figure 12-7. The effect of exposure time on visual discrimination. X is exposure time in milliseconds. Y is number of dots for which fifty per cent of judgments were correct. Data are for one subject at one level of intensity. [After Hunter and Sigler.[16]]

The dots were printed in black India ink on a sheet of translucent tracing paper which was then placed between two pieces of clear glass to form a test plate. Five different irregular patterns were made for each number of dots from one to sixteen. The single dot was placed in the center. Where two or more dots were employed, the distance between dots was kept constant. For exposure a test plate was placed behind the opal glass and illuminated. The light source was a powerful projection bulb. Intensity was controlled by means of filters. Exposure times were obtained by automatic mechanical devices.

A measure of amount perceived was defined as the number of dots for which fifty per cent of judgments were correct. Figure 12-7 is a plot of the measures of amount against six exposure times for one subject at one of six intensity levels.

If a person goes from a brightly lighted room into a relatively dark room, he cannot see very much, if anything, at first, but with the passage of a few minutes he may be able to distinguish objects and features of the dark room fairly well. There is experimental evidence that sensitivity increases in the absence of light. As mentioned earlier, this increase in sensitivity is called "dark adaptation."

The course of dark adaptation for foveal vision was determined in 1922 by Hecht[14]. The conditions of the experiment were varied amounts of time in the dark. Determinations were made of the minimum intensity at which a subject reported a test object as just visible.

The test object was a small cross, obtained by cutting an opening in cardboard. Its red color was produced by a Wratten red filter. It was assumed that only the cone receptors were stimulated for two reasons: The cross was small enough for its projection to fall well within the fovea, the rod-free area of the retina; and the subject had to report the object visible as a *red* cross.

A translucent screen illuminated from behind was located below the viewing box. The subject could look at the screen and then raise his head to the opening in the viewing box. Although only one eye was used at a time, and it was selected by the experimenter's moving a slide near the viewing end of the box, the subject acted as if he were looking with both eyes. The red cross was illuminated by means of a small lamp on a movable carriage in a long box. Illumination was varied by moving the lamp along the length of the box. After the intensity of the light emitted by the red cross was measured for a given position of the lamp, the intensity for any other position could be calculated.

The testing procedure in broad outline involved three steps: light adaptation during which the subject viewed the illuminated translucent screen; dark adaptation during which neither the screen nor the cross was illuminated; and determination of the position of the red cross at which it was reported as just visible. A description of the procedure in detail would be much more complicated, for light adaptation was not scheduled before every dark adaptation, the subject's eyes were alternately stimulated, and some of the longer dark adaptation periods were merely continuations of others.

Measures were obtained on each eye of fifteen subjects for eight periods of dark adaptation: five seconds, thirty seconds, and 2, 3, 6, 10, 15, and 20 minutes. Figure 12-8 is a plot of the results of one experiment on one subject. Each point represents a single determination with one eye.

The ordinates indicate the illumination emitted by the red cross when it was reported just visible. Dark adaptation proceeded at a very rapid rate during the first few seconds. Most of it took place during the first thirty seconds. The process was nearly complete after ten minutes.

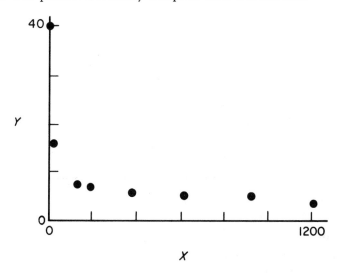

Figure 12-8. The effect of time in the dark on the threshold for identifying a red cross. X is time in seconds. Y is intensity of illumination. Data are for one eye of one subject. [After Hecht.[14]]

ORIENTATION CONDITIONS

Orientation refers to the view a subject has of a scene or some object in it. How often the statement is made, "I wish I had a better view." It suggests the possibility for experimentation to determine what circumstances contribute to improved visual perception of a scene or an object. Orientation can be varied by manipulating either the individual or what he views. In either case, the resulting positions may be the experimental conditions under which his judgments are obtained as measures on the dependent variable.

Dusek, Teichner, and Kobrick[8] performed an experiment to compare the effects of sloping surrounds around a target, distance from the target, and eye-level height of a judge, on the precision of judgments of the target's distance. Subjects were four enlisted men who possessed good stereoptic acuity.

Figure 12-9 shows the apparatus, which was painted black except for two small white square targets. The targets were mounted on hidden parallel tracks on a large table. The slope of the table could be varied by placing blocks under the back legs. The separation between the targets could be varied so that the visual angle subtended by the separation was maintained constant. The experimenter controlled the near-and-far position of the left target by means of a tape-chain device at the center of the table.

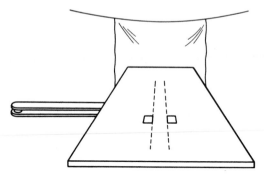

Figure 12-9. Apparatus for relative depth discrimination. The position of the small target on the left could be varied along the dashed line by means of a tape-chain device on the arm at the left. [Adapted from Dusek, Teichner, and Kobrick.[8]]

There were three sets of conditions in the experiment: three slopes of the table, two distances of the target, and two eye levels of the judge. The three slopes were zero, 1.7, and 2.9 degrees; the two distances were 50 and 100 feet; the two eye levels were achieved by having the subject stand on the floor and on a box. The number of possible combinations of conditions, formed by taking one from each of the three sets, was $3 \times 2 \times 2$ or 12. Each subject served under all conditions.

At the signal, "Ready," the experimenter moved the variable target toward the standard at a very slow rate. The subject said "Stop," when he judged the targets to be about equally distant. Ten judgments were obtained under one of the twelve conditions, after which the subject was given a rest. Then a new condition was imposed.

A measure of variability, the standard deviation, was computed as a measure of precision for all judgments under each condition. Figure 12-10 is a plot of standard deviations against slope for the distance of 100 feet and the lower eye level. The experimenters concluded that variability of judgments decreased as slope increased. They also found that variability decreased as height of eye level increased, but that variability increased with viewing distance. A decrease in variability was interpreted as an increase in precision.

Changes in the orientation of projected figures were found to affect the success with which younger children identified the figures in an experiment by Ghent[13]. Subjects were sixty-nine children, between the ages of three and seven years, in a day-care center. The numbers of boys and girls in each age group were approximately equal but the total number of children varied from one age group to another.

A realistic figure was projected tachistoscopically on a screen. A child was asked to identify the picture by naming it or by pointing it out in an array of pictures projected on the screen continuously throughout the procedure. There were twelve figures in the array: a toy wagon, a cup and saucer, a rectangular table with four legs, a sailboat, a face, a squirrel, a house, a clown, a flower in a flower pot, a horse, a tree, and a large carpet tack. There were four test figures projected one at a time: the wagon, boat, clown, and horse. The orientation of the test figures was varied over four positions: right side up, upside down, rotated ninety degrees to the left, and rotated ninety degrees to the right.

Before testing began, the child was asked to name each of the pictures in the array. He was then told that he would be shown some of the pictures on the screen, that they would go by very quickly, that they would sometimes be right side up and sometimes upside down and sometimes turned to the side, and that he was to see if he could tell which picture it was. Before each picture was exposed, he was told to look at a black circle on the screen. The circle, which was surrounded by pictures in the array,

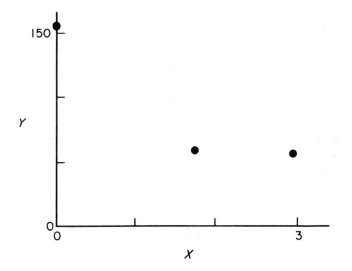

Figure 12-10. The effect of sloping surround on judgments of target distance. X is slope of table in degrees. Y is the standard deviation of settings in millimeters. [After Dusek, Teichner, and Kobrick.[8]]

marked where the figure would be projected. The child either named the picture he had seen or approached the screen and pointed to the picture in the array. Exposure times were chosen to suit each child on the basis of results from preliminary testing. The results showed that orientation was effective with the two groups at the lower ages but not with the three groups at the upper ages. Performance was better on right-side up figures than on the others at the lower ages only.

There is a familiar illusion of movement in viewing a stationary point of light. It may occur in looking at a star or a planet and trying to decide whether or not the point of light is an airplane or a satellite moving across the sky. In the psychological laboratory, the illusion is called autokinetic movement. Evidence that head position may affect the illusion was found by Bridges and Bitterman[4] in an experiment on sixteen undergraduate women. The subjects had no prior knowledge of the phenomenon under investigation.

By means of a lever, a subject could vary the position of a point of light in the frontal-parallel plane. She was told that the point of light would be moved from its original position by a special mechanism and that she was to return it to its original position. The apparatus is shown in Figure 12-11. It consisted of a lever pivoted in both horizontal and vertical directions with a point source of red light on one end. To produce a movement of the light through any given distance, the subject had to move her end of the lever five times as far. A small electrical motor, attached to the lever just below the light, provided noise and vibration intended to give the subject the impression that the movement for which she was to compensate was real. Threads attached to the lever ran to two pens on a kymograph. Simultaneous recording of the horizontal and vertical components of the subject's movements were made. Sample records are shown in Figure 12-12.

The subject sat with her head in a headrest, the position of which could be adjusted. She was given seven trials with a pause between successive ones. On certain trials, her head was tilted, twisted, or tilted and twisted, by adjustment of the headrest into one of eight positions. On the other trials her head was placed in a normal position. The experimenters hypothesized that autokinetic movement would be opposite to head positions involving tilt or twist.

Measures were obtained from records like the two in Figure 12-12. Each record contained two tracings: the upper one indicated the vertical component of the movement of the light; the lower indicated the horizontal component. Each record in Figure 12-12 is for two trials: the first, a trial on which there was no tilt and no twist; the second, a trial on which the head was tilted or twisted. The upper record shows little movement with no tilt or twist but marked movement down and to the left when the head was tilted down and twisted to the left. Thus the upper record supports the hypothesis that movement would be opposite to head position. The lower record does not. A method of scoring each subject's record was devised. The average score for all subjects confirmed the hypothesis.

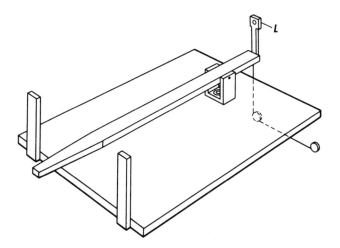

Figure 12-11. Device for measuring autokinetic movement. *L* is a point source of light. [Adapted from Bridges and Bitterman.[4]]

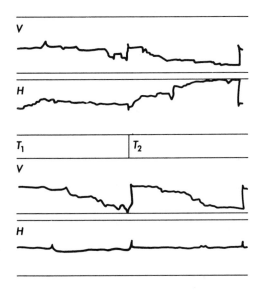

Figure 12-12. Two records of compensatory movements of the light in the experiment on the autokinetic phenomenon. T_1 and T_2 are consecutive two-minute trials. *V* is a record of the vertical component and *H* is a record of the horizontal component. On the first trial in the upper record, the head was in a normal position; on the second trial, it was tilted down and twisted to the left. On the first trial in the lower record, the head was in a normal position; on the second trial, it was twisted to the left. [Adapted from Bridges and Bitterman.[4]]

There is an illusion which is well-known to psychologists but not commonly identified in everyday situations. It is that the length of a vertical line in an inverted T is typically overestimated when it is compared to the horizontal line. Finger and Spelt[10] investigated this illusion for an L, as well as an inverted T, and varied the orientation of each. Overestimation of the vertical occurred with all figures but appeared to be affected by both orientation and the junction of the lines. Subjects were seventy-two college students, fifty women and twenty-two men.

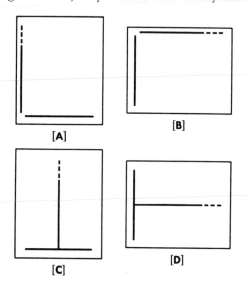

Figure 12-13. Apparatus for investigating the horizontal-vertical illusion. **A** and **B** differ only in orientation. The same is true of **C** and **D**. Solid lines within each rectangle represent black sections of tapes. Dotted lines represent white sections. [Adapted from Finger and Spelt.[10]]

A subject equated a horizontal line and a vertical line in an L and a T, with each letter in two positions, as shown in Figure 12-13. Each letter consisted of a standard line of fixed length and, perpendicular to it, a line whose length could be varied. In Figure 12-13, A and B differ only in their orientations; the same is true of C and D. The solid lines within each of the four figures represent black tapes; the dashed lines indicate white tapes. The subject determined the length of a line by adjusting the proportions of black and white tape exposed.

The background for the figures was a white sheet of wood, four by five feet. The standard line was a steel tape painted black and fastened to the board. The variable comparison line was another steel tape painted black for part of its length and white for the remainder. The end of the black section of the variable tape passed through a slot near the fixed tape; the end of the white section passed through a second slot four feet distant. By pulling on cloth tapes, the subject varied the amount of black tape visible. At a distance of twenty feet, where the subject sat, the black tapes appeared as black lines on a white surface. Ten determinations were made by the method of adjustment on each of the figures.

The median of the ten judgments for each subject and each figure was determined. If the variable vertical was shorter than the fixed horizontal, overestimation of the vertical was indicated; if the variable horizontal was longer than the fixed vertical, overestimation of the vertical was again indicated. For the *L*, the average shortening of the variable vertical line below equality was 0.39 inches. For the rotated *L*, the average lengthening of the horizontal was 3.22 inches. Subjects shortened the vertical in the inverted *T*, on the average, 2.72 inches. They lengthened the horizontal in the rotated *T*, on the average, 1.2 inches. All of these differences were overestimations of the length of the vertical. A change in orientation decreased the illusion for the *T* but increased it for the *L*.

Constancy Conditions

As an automobile moves away from a viewer, its retinal image becomes smaller, but the viewer does not report that the automobile shrinks in size. As a person looks at the wheel of his car from an angle, the shape of its retinal image is an ellipse, not a circle, but he does not report that the wheel has changed its shape. The fact that judgments of size or shape do not always closely follow changes in the size of the visual angle or the actual shape of the projection on the retina, but instead often remain somewhat constant, provides a background for some interesting experiments in which the possibility of this disparity is exploited. Objects of varied heights may be placed at varied distances from a viewer so that the visual angles corresponding to the different heights are equal. The viewer is then asked to judge the heights of the objects. Will he judge them all to be of the same height or will he accurately judge their real and varied sizes? A subject is shown a set of rectangular forms, displayed on a sloping surface, and asked to find a square. Does he choose a rectangle with height greater than that of a square to achieve a square retinal projection or does he allow for the slope? If the slope is varied, how are his judgments affected? If a subject, standing some distance from a table on which there lies a drawing of a circle, is asked to match the figure by choosing from a set of varied ellipses, does he choose one corresponding to the projected shape or does he choose a circle? If his distance from the table is varied, how are his judgments affected? All these questions concern the relation of judgments to visual angle or retinal projection. Attempts to find answers were made in the experiments which will be described next.

Zeigler and Leibowitz[38] varied the distances and lengths of wooden dowels displayed vertically so that a constant visual angle was maintained by their heights. Subjects, who were asked to judge the heights of the objects, were eight boys whose ages varied from seven to nine years and five men whose ages varied from 15 to 24 years, all residents of a summer camp.

Five wooden dowels, whose lengths varied so that at each one of five different distances one of the dowels subtended a visual angle of less than one degree, constituted the standard objects. The comparison object was also a dowel, arranged so that the visible portion of its length could be continuously varied by raising it or lowering it through a hole in the center of a board. The five distances of 10, 30, 60, 80, and 100 feet were paired with the five dowel lengths of 2, 6, 12, 16, and 20 inches. The five combinations of distance and length constituted the five conditions of the experiment. The subject's task was to adjust the exposed length of the variable comparison dowel until it appeared equal to a chosen standard. He made four judgments at each distance: two with ascending adjustments and two with descending adjustments.

Figure 12-14 contains a plot of matched size in inches against distance in feet for each of the age groups. Perfect matching of actual size would have yielded a linear plot with a slope of 0.2, since size was related to distance by the formula: size in inches equals 0.2 times distance in feet. The experimenters concluded that the data for adults were close to matching of actual size. Perfect matching of projected size would have yielded a plot with a slope of zero or a horizontal line of points since visual angle was constant for all distances. The experimenters concluded that the data for children were close to matching of projected size. In a sense, the children were not as realistic as the adults.

The slope of a surface on which rectangular forms were presented was found by Stavrianos[32] to affect judgments of the shape of the forms. There were five subjects whose task was to select a square from a number of rectangular forms having the same base but altitudes which varied around that of the square. The rectangles, which were made of light gray paper, were presented simultaneously on a rectangular black background in one of five different arrangements throughout the experiment. The experimental conditions were degrees of inclination of the background from a frontal parallel position: 0, 15, 30, 45, and 55 degrees. The angle was varied randomly from trial to trial.

Figure 12-15 is a plot of error in judging height against the angle of the background. An error was computed by subtracting the height of the chosen rectangle from the height of a square. Thus choice of a rectangle taller than a square would have yielded a negative error. Accuracy decreased as a function of angle of inclination over all five conditions. In

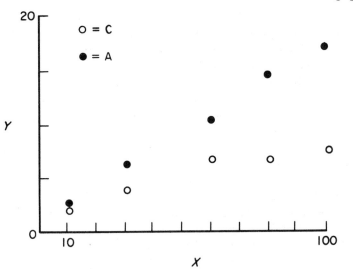

Figure 12-14. The effect of distance on judgments of size. X is distance in feet. (Objects varied in size so that the object at each distance subtended a visual angle of 0.96 degrees.) Y is average matched size of comparison object in inches. Two sets of points are for adults and children. [After Zeigler and Leibowitz.[38]]

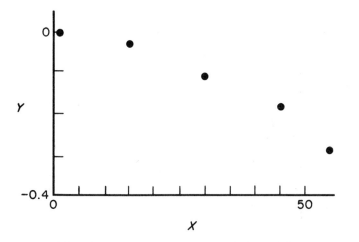

Figure 12-15. The effect of tilt on judgments of shape. X is angle of presentation in degrees. Y is average error of judged shape in millimeters. [After Stavrianos.[32]]

other words, subjects chose rectangles of increasing altitude as the tilt of the background increased. If they had chosen the square regardless of angle of inclination, they would have demonstrated perfect shape constancy.

In 1931, Thouless[34] studied the effect of angle of inclination on judgments of the shape of a circle. He found that judgments varied with inclination but fell between the projected and actual size of the circle.

A white cardboard circle was placed on a dark table and was observed by a subject with his eyes at a fixed level above the surface of the table but at three different distances from the point of the circle nearest him. Thus the angle of inclination of the circle varied with distance. The subject matched the apparent shape of the circle with one of a series of cardboard ellipses. The ratio of the short axis to the long axis varied by constant steps from one ellipse to another in the series. The ellipses were presented to the subject in both ascending and descending series. He was instructed to judge whether the presented ellipse was fatter or thinner than the circle, or equal to it.

A number of matchings was obtained from each of four subjects. Figure 12-16 is a plot of the average matched ratio for one subject. At all three distances the average was intermediate to the ratio of 1.00 for the physical object and the ratio for its projected ellipse. The experimenter gave this outcome the name *phenomenal regression to the real object*. The expression was intended to represent the fact that judgments did not correspond to the shape of the image on the retina but were closer to the real object than was the image.

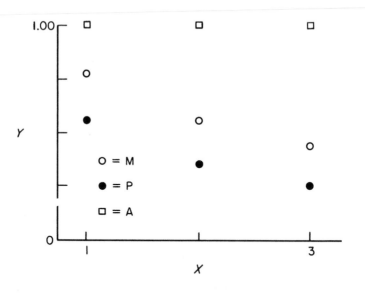

Figure 12-16. The effect of angle of inclination on the reported shape of a circle. *X* is distance of the subject from circle, in centimeters. *Y* is the average ratio of the short axis to the long axis for the matched ellipses. Data are for one subject. There are three sets of points; actual ratios for the circle (A); matched ratios (M); ratios for retinal projections of the circle (P). [After Thouless.[34]]

VISUAL LOAD

When someone says, "It was like a three-ring circus," he is implicitly recognizing another important perceptual problem. He means that there was too much to see. The problem, one of *visual load,* can be attacked experimentally. By varying the number or complexity of stimuli, the experimenter can vary the subject's load, one aspect of the difficulty of a task. At the same time, the accuracy of the subject's judgments can be determined.

Span of attention was measured by Saltzman and Garner[27] under varied conditions of load consisting of different numbers of concentric circles. Measures were expressed in terms of a subject's accuracy in estimating the number of concentric rings presented to him in a brief exposure. The results showed that accuracy decreased as load increased.

Two projectors and a vertical ground-glass projection screen were employed. One projector presented the concentric rings; the other provided illumination of the screen before and after exposure of the rings. The subject sat on one side of the screen, twelve feet from it; the projectors were located on the other side. The concentric rings were drawn on slides with the distance between rings equal to the radius of the innermost ring, and with the diameter of the outside ring constant at three feet, regardless of the total number of rings on the slide. The projected circles appeared as black lines on a white ground. The number of circles varied from two to ten.

By means of a camera shutter the experimenter exposed a slide for a half second, once every six seconds, with a warning signal one second before the exposure. The slides were presented in a random order. The subject was told to write down the number of circles that appeared on the screen for each presentation and, if he was not certain, to guess. Ninety presentations, ten exposures of each slide, were made in each of five sessions.

Figure 12-17 is a plot of percentage of correct responses against number of circles. The percentage decreases as the number of circles increases. Each point is based on ten judgments by five male college students. Data are for the fourth session.

In 1924, Oberly[24] obtained judgments as to the number of black dots under varied conditions of numerousness. The visual load was number of dots; the judgment made was number of dots. He found that accuracy decreased as load increased. Subjects were six members of the staff of the Department of Psychology, University of Pennsylvania.

Black dots were pasted in haphazard arrangements on five sets of small white cards. Cards in each set contained from two to fifteen dots. They were exposed in a dark room by means of a tachistoscope, with a brief constant exposure time. The order of the cards in each set was haphazard and differed from set to set. After the five sets were exposed, they were turned ninety degrees so that the right edge of each card became the bottom for the next exposure. This method of rotating the cards was continued.

The subject was instructed to report verbally the number of dots and the certainty of his judgment. The scale of certainty had five steps: a hundred-to-one bet, five-to-one bet, one-to-one bet, one-to-five bet, and guess. Only those reports which were correct and which had ratings of certainty of hundred-to-one, five-to-one, or one-to-one were counted. For each number of dots, 250 judgments were obtained from each subject. Figure 12-18 shows the results for one subject, the observed relative frequencies for a number of dots from two to twelve inclusive.

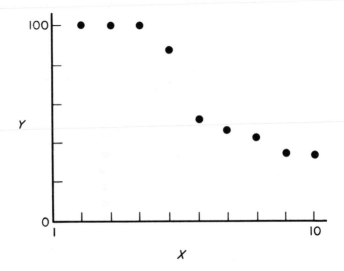

Figure 12-17. The effect of number of concentric circles on accuracy in estimating the number during a brief exposure. X is number of circles. Y is per cent of correct judgments. Data are for diameter of three feet for the outermost circle and a viewing distance of twelve feet. [After Saltzman and Garner.[27]]

In an experiment by Ellis and Ahr[9] visual load was the density of errors in reading materials. Its effect on proofreading was determined. The results indicated that the percentage of errors increased and then decreased with increasing density. Subjects were 216 students from classes at the University of New Mexico.

The proofreading material was chosen to be relatively homogeneous in content, and interesting but not emotionally stimulating. It was typed, double spaced, in a booklet of fifteen pages. Three kinds of typographical errors were introduced: omissions, transpositions, and substitutions. An example of an error of omission, one letter deleted from *your*, was *yor;*

an example of transposition, an exchange in the position of two adjacent letters in *time,* was *tmie;* an example of substitution, one letter wrong in *work,* was *wark.* The three kinds of errors were employed in equal numbers. The position of the error, the specific word to be changed, and the specific letter in each word to be changed were determined randomly.

In the initial phase of the experiment, the six conditions were six levels of error density: 6, 9, 15, 30, 60, and 120 errors per five pages in the first ten. Subjects were divided randomly into six groups of thirty-six. Each level was imposed on one group.

In the final phase of the experiment, there were three conditions, three levels of error density for the last five pages. The levels, which

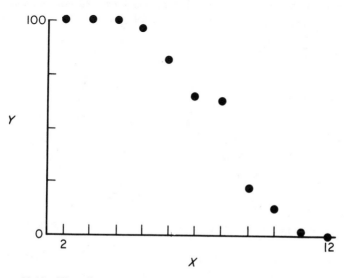

Figure 12-18. The effect of numerosity on judgments of numerosity. X is number of dots. Y is percentage of correct judgments given with some confidence. Results are for one subject. [After Oberly.[24]]

were 6, 30, and 120 errors, were imposed on three random subgroups in each of the original groups. Subjects were allowed fifty minutes for the entire task.

Figure 12-19 is a plot of percentage of detected errors as a function of error density for the first phase of the experiment. Percentage of detected errors increased and then decreased. This result deserves comment. Are errors harder to detect when there are few or many? Obviously any given number of errors would be detected more easily when there were many than when there were few. Consequently the number of errors detected would be expected to increase with the number occurring. For this reason, the experimenters expressed the results in terms of percentages.

Still there was improvement; at least, up to a point. Beyond this point the percentage began to decrease, although the number itself continued to increase. The levels imposed for the last five pages did not affect error detection.

The rate at which signals are presented is another way in which perceptual load can be varied, as in an experiment by Jenkins[17]. The situation was a vigil, in which a subject was required to carry on a continuous search for a visual signal which occurred intermittently and independently of his performance. As in the preceding experiment on proofreading, success was expressed as a percentage. It was found that detection improved as signal rate increased: the percentage of signals detected increased with increases in the four rates employed. Subjects were 125 enlisted men of the Air Force assigned to the laboratory for testing purposes.

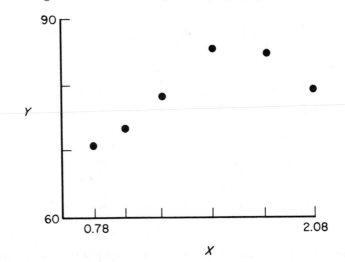

Figure 12-19. The effect of error density on detection of errors. X is log frequency of errors per block of five pages. (The six frequencies were 6, 9, 15, 30, 60, and 120.) Y is per cent of errors detected. [After Ellis and Ahr.[9]]

The display consisted of a voltmeter with a blank white circular face and a pointer resting at the left. The pointer was deflected from its resting position to the middle of the dial at the regular rate of one deflection per second. Occasionally it was deflected a greater amount. A subject's task was to discriminate between regular movements and the occasional movement of greater amplitude. The subject was given a concurrent task of responding to a second signal, a light located where he could easily see it when he viewed the main display. This concurrent task was employed so that gross failures to carry out the main task would be apparent. Pointer signals and light signals were interspersed randomly. Signals and responses were recorded on a graph automatically.

Subjects performed during two ninety-minute sessions, one in the morning and one in the early afternoon of the same day. Signals were presented at randomly varied intervals but at four average rates: 7.5, 30, 60, and 480 signals per hour. Subjects were assigned randomly to the four signal rates which were the conditions of the experiment.

Figure 12-20 is a plot of percentage of signals detected in the morning watch. Performance improved as signal rate increased but the rate of improvement decreased. Performance was poorer in the afternoon watch.

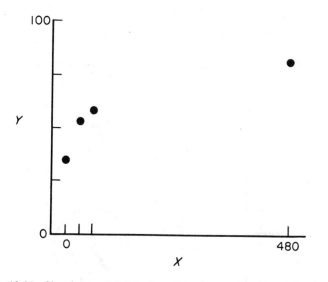

Figure 12-20. Signal rate and detection. X is average number of signals per hour. Y is mean percentage of signals detected. [After Jenkins.[17]]

PRACTICAL EXPERIMENTS

There are many everyday situations in which people must give judgments to visual stimuli in the form of signals or displays of information. These situations pose problems, for the designers of instruments and equipment, which can only be solved satisfactorily by experimentation. The problems have to do with developing a design which suits the man who must use it. Scale numbering and dial shape have been investigated for this purpose and some of the findings will be described next.

Barber and Garner[1] performed an experiment with twelve subjects to determine the influence of scale numbering on accuracy and speed of interpolation in making scale readings. The experiment involved three different scales and two sets of instructions. The three scales varied only in the numbers assigned to the marks. One scale had numbers of 0, 5, 10, 15, and 20; a second had 0, 10, 20, 30, and 40; a third had 0,

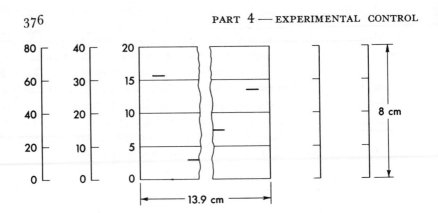

Figure 12-21. Methods of numbering the scales on three rectangular displays. Dashes are targets. [Adapted from Barber and Garner.[1]]

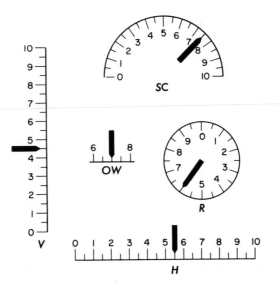

Figure 12-22. Dial shapes: vertical (*V*), open window (*OW*), semicircular (*SC*), round (*R*), horizontal (*H*). [Adapted from Sleight.[31]]

20, 40, 60, and 80. Figure 12-21 shows the way scales were numbered. In one set of instructions, a subject was told to estimate the positions of small dashes on the scales, or *targets*, as accurately as he possibly could regardless of the time. In a second set of instructions, he was told not to take time to refine his judgments but to read the positions as rapidly as possible. There were six conditions in the experiment: the six logical combinations of the three scales and the two sets of instructions.

The subject gave eighty readings in each of the six conditions of the experiment. Six subjects worked first under instructions to be accurate and second under instructions to be fast; the other six had the instructions in reverse order. The three different scales were presented in all possible orders.

The apparatus consisted of a special projection table, a set of three photographic plates each with a different scale printed on it, and a set of eight photographic plates bearing the targets. Ten targets were placed on

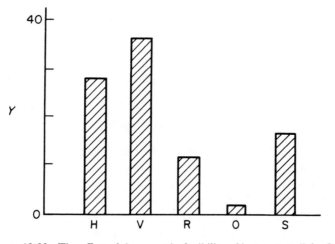

Figure 12-23. The effect of shape on the legibility of instrument dials. On the horizontal axis are the labels for the five types: horizontal, vertical, round, open window, and semicircular. Y is average per cent of incorrect readings. [After Sleight.[31]]

a photographic plate, distributed over all parts of the area. A display consisted of a scale plate on top of the target plate. This display was placed on the translucent area of the projection table.

A trial consisted of estimating the position of the ten targets on one of the target plates. A subject was given either the "speed" or "accuracy" instructions and told to estimate the target position by visual interpolation. When the display was illuminated the subject called out his estimates to a recorder. After he read all eight targets for one scale, a new scale was introduced. When all three scales had been used, the instructions were changed and the whole procedure repeated.

Performance was evaluated in terms of both time and errors. As one would expect, less time was taken under speed instructions than under accuracy instructions, and fewer errors were made under accuracy instructions than under speed instructions. The "five" scale—the scale with increments of five—was clearly inferior to the other two. The "twenty" scale was superior to the "ten" scale in time but not in accuracy.

The effect of the shape of dials on accuracy of readings made from the dials was investigated by Sleight[31]. Simple numerical information was presented to sixty male university students possessing normal visual acuity.

A mirror tachistoscope was employed to give a very brief constant exposure time. The test materials consisted of the five dials shown in Figure 12-22. They were drawn to have certain constant features: dimensions, form, and position of numerals; size of graduations and distance between them; and dimensions of pointers. Pointers could be adjusted by the experimenter.

The experimenter showed a dial to a subject and pointed out the location of the zero and nine. He then told the subject that as the lights flashed on briefly he would have a view of the dial and should report the setting. Figure 12-23 shows per cent of incorrect readings on each of the five types of dials. The open-window dial was clearly the best.

Auditory Stimulus Conditions

Stimuli for auditory perception can be manipulated by an experimenter in many ways. A tone is frequently employed as a stimulus. It may be conveniently produced and controlled by means of the electronic device called an audio-oscillator. The characteristics of a tone which are often varied are its frequency, intensity, duration, and rate of occurrence. The judgments of subjects, evaluated in terms of accuracy, often have to do with the corresponding characteristics: pitch, loudness, duration, and rate. Of course, auditory stimuli can be studied experimentally as signals and conveyers of information. Combinations and sequential patterns of tones, as well as clicks and noises, offer many possibilities for the conditions of an experiment. Speech, which is a very complex auditory stimulus, can also be varied with respect to a variety of characteristics.

FREQUENCY OF A TONE

Variations in the number of cycles per second produced by a sound source can be the experimental conditions imposed on subjects, and judgments of pitch, the principal psychological correlate of frequency, can be the behavior observed under those conditions, but judgments of loudness, the principal correlate of intensity, are also of interest. Some typical results are described below.

Can you tell when a vocalist sings "off key" or when a piano is out of tune? Have you ever tried to tune a violin, a clarinet, a trumpet, or any other instrument? Have you ever known a person who possessed absolute pitch? If you can answer "Yes" to any of these questions, then you already have some appreciation of the task of judging pitch, and are probably aware of the differences among people in their ability to carry out that task. The next experiment involved subjects who would be said to possess absolute pitch—meaning that they possessed the ability to make very accurate judgments of pitch.

Van Krevelen[35] has reported on the accuracy of judgments of pitch made by students in the Eastman School of Music. Forty were selected for having given a very good performance on an entrance test requiring identification of piano tones. These subjects were tested again as a group, at which time they were required to identify all eighty-eight tones on the piano. Tones were presented singly and subjects wrote their answers. Twenty-three, who either identified all eighty-eight notes correctly or made only occasional half-step errors in the extreme upper and lower octaves, were selected for a third test given individually with forty-eight pure tones produced by means of an audio-oscillator and transmitted through headphones. Each subject gave his judgments aloud. Ten women and seven men identified all tones correctly. These seventeen subjects were employed in two experiments.

In the first experiment, a subject wore earphones and test tones were produced by an oscillator at an intensity of a fixed level above his threshold. The duration of each tone was one second and a period of ten to fifteen seconds separated tones in the series. The frequency of tones varied by steps of two cycles from 404, which was about a quarter tone below G-sharp, to 478, which was a quarter tone above A-sharp. Two exceptions were the correct frequencies for G-sharp and A. Each of thirty-nine different frequencies occurred ten times. The entire series consisted of 390 tones presented in a random order. The subject judged 100 tones per session. He was instructed to report in terms of the closest musical tone. Thus he might report one tone as a C, another as a flat A-sharp, another as a sharp G, and so on.

In the second experiment, the apparatus was the same. A subject's task, however, was to produce the tones G-sharp, A, and A-sharp by turning the dial of the oscillator. He produced each tone 100 times, fifty times starting the adjustment from settings below the designated tone and fifty times from above. The order of requested tones was random. The subject gave fifty judgments per session and the experimenter recorded them in hundredths of a semitone deviation from the requested tone.

In the first experiment, 510 tones—thirty for each of the seventeen subjects—were actually G-sharp, A, or A-sharp. Figure 12-24 shows the mean of judgments for these three tones. Figure 12-25 shows the means of judgments for the three requested frequencies, 415.30, 440.0, and 466.16, in the second experiment. The results indicated a high degree of accuracy by both methods of judging the tones.

As already mentioned, people vary in the accuracy with which they can judge pitch. They also vary in their sensitivity to differences in pitch. Some people can detect very small differences; others can detect only

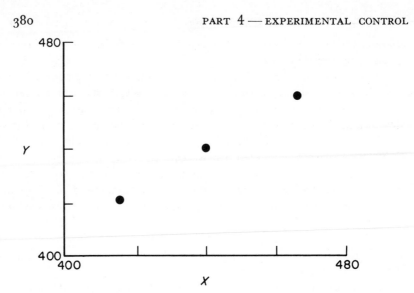

Figure 12-24. The effect of frequency on judgments of pitch by expert subjects. X is frequency of standard tone. Y is average frequency for the obtained judgments. Data are for judgments in terms of the closest musical tone. [After Van Krevelen.[35]]

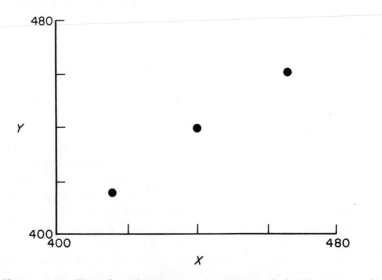

Figure 12-25. The effect of frequency on judgments of pitch by expert subjects. X is frequency of standard tone. Y is average frequency for the obtained judgments. Data are for judgments given by adjustment of the oscillator dial. [After Van Krevelen.[35]]

relatively large differences. This differential sensitivity varies in another way. The detectable difference in frequency of a low tone is not the same as the detectable difference for a high tone. In other words, the detectable difference depends on the base frequency. This was shown, in 1931, by

Shower and Biddulph[30], who determined the effect of frequency and intensity on the differential threshold for pitch. Their subjects were five men between the ages of 20 and 30 years. A trial consisted of three parts: presentation of a tone of constant frequency for a short interval; a change of frequency to a new level for another short interval; and finally a return to the original level. Changes were varied in steps of two cycles. The tone was presented through a single earphone. Both ears were tested.

The differential threshold, the minimum perceptible change, was obtained by finding the setting of the apparatus at which the subject just detected a variation in pitch. The threshold was determined for different base frequencies at each of a number of intensities which varied from five decibels above threshold to a maximum level the subject could tolerate. Figure 12-26 is a plot of the differential threshold in frequency against the base frequency. The threshold increases with frequency. In other words, as frequency of a tone increased, the smallest detectable variation in the tone increased. Figure 12-27 shows the ratio of the differential threshold to the base frequency plotted against the base frequency. The ratio decreases with frequency. It was once thought that this ratio was a constant, but these data show that it can only be so considered over a limited part of the range.

Although pitch is the principal psychological correlate of frequency, loudness also varies with it, as shown, in 1933, by Fletcher and Munson[12]. Audio-oscillators were used to generate pure tones, delivered through headphones to each of eleven subjects. A subject was required only to listen and operate a simple switch. Threshold measurements were obtained by slowly reducing the intensity of a test tone below threshold and then raising the level until it again became audible. The subject signaled, by operating his switch, when he could no longer hear the tone and again when it was just audible. The average voltage level of these two occasions, expressed on a decibel scale, was taken as the threshold. Figure 12-28 shows thresholds for eleven different frequencies for the eleven subjects, plotted against frequency. The plot shows that the range of greatest sensitivity is from 500 cycles per second to 8,000. In other words, less energy is required to produce a detectable tone within this range than outside it.

INTENSITY OF A TONE

Is there anyone today who has not adjusted the volume control of a radio or television set? It is taken for granted by most people that turning the knob will be effective, but what exactly does it do? It increases or decreases the amount of energy employed in producing the sound. This is often referred to as a change in intensity.

That variations in the intensity of a tone produce variations in judg-

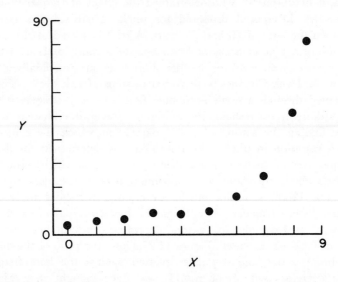

Figure 12-26. The effect of frequency on differential pitch sensitivity. X is a transformed frequency scale. Y is the minimum perceptible change in frequency. Intensity level was five decibels above the threshold. [After Shower and Biddulph.[30]]

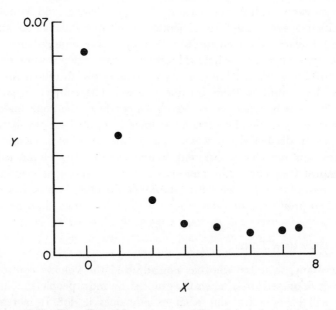

Figure 12-27. The effect of frequency on differential pitch sensitivity. X is a transformed frequency scale. Y is the ratio of the minimum perceptible change in frequency to the base frequency. Intensity level was five decibels above threshold. [After Shower and Biddulph.[30]]

ments of loudness was demonstrated in 1929 by Kellogg[19]. He had subjects compare tones of the same frequency, 1,000 cycles per second, but
of different intensities. The method of constant stimulus differences was
employed. Each of seven tones which varied in intensity was compared
with a standard tone of fixed intensity. Tones were presented in pairs with
the standard first and the comparison tone second. The subject's task was
to judge whether the second tone was stronger or weaker than the first.
The duration of each tone was one-half second; the interval between tones
in each pair was also one-half second; the interval between pairs was 2.5
seconds. Figure 12-29 is a plot of percentage of judgments "stronger" for
one subject. The total number of judgments for each tone was 144. Loudness increased with intensity.

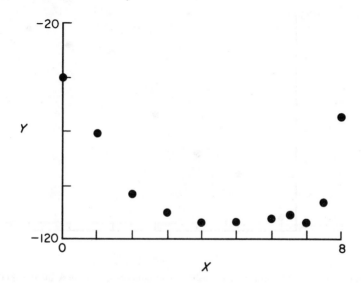

Figure 12-28. The effect of frequency on loudness thresholds. X is frequency transformed to a logarithmic scale. Y is the average threshold voltage level in decibels. [After
Fletcher and Munson.[12]]

Just as the smallest detectable difference in pitch depends on the
base frequency, so the smallest detectable difference in loudness depends
on the intensity of the base tone from which the difference varies, as reported in 1928 by Riesz[26]. In his experiment, intensity was varied and the
effect on a subject's differential threshold for loudness was determined.
Riesz made use of the fact that two pure tones which differ by only a
few cycles per second will produce that many beats per second when one is
audible and the other is adjusted from an intensity below threshold to be
nearly equal in intensity.

Tones were produced by two audio-oscillators and delivered to a receiver held against a subject's ear by an elastic strap. The absolute threshold intensity was determined for a tone of a given frequency. The first oscillator was set at that frequency; the second, at a frequency lower by three cycles per second. The first oscillator was then set at an intensity far below threshold; the second, at an audible intensity. Finally, the intensity of the first was increased until the subject indicated that he heard beats. After about twenty trials of this sort, the tester located the setting for which the subject reported he was just able to detect the fluctuations in loudness. Measurements were made on each subject at frequencies of 35, 70, 200, 1,000, 4,000, 7,000, and 10,000 cycles per second, and at intensities from tones near the threshold of hearing to tones near the threshold of feeling.

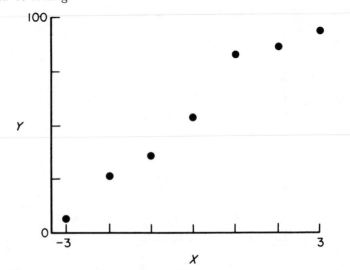

Figure 12-29. The effect of intensity on judgments of loudness by the method of constant stimuli. *X* is level of intensity with reference to the standard. *Y* is per cent of judgments "stronger." Data are for one subject. [After Kellogg.[(19)]]

Figure 12-30 shows a plot of differential sensitivity as a function of intensity for a tone of 10,000 cycles per second. Differential sensitivity is the ratio of the just-detectable difference in intensity to the base intensity. Each point is the average for twelve male subjects. It was once thought that this ratio was a constant, but it is so only approximately through a part of the range of intensity.

Auditory judgments of loudness are often given by reports of the presence or absence of a tone, and by reports of loudness and softness in comparing tones. A different method has been devised by Stevens[(33)]. The method requires judging the attribute on a numerical scale. A subject is presented with a standard stimulus and given an arbitrary number to characterize the magnitude of some attribute of the stimulus. He is then asked to judge and report verbally the magnitude of other stimuli on this same scale. The effect of intensity on estimations of loudness made by eighteen subjects using this method was clearly demonstrated in the following experiment.

The frequency of the tones employed was constant at 1,000 cycles per second. Intensity was controlled by the experimenter. The subject operated a pair of switches. One switch presented a standard tone; the other, a comparison tone. Tones were delivered to the subject's earphones. He was instructed to listen to the standard for one or two seconds, then

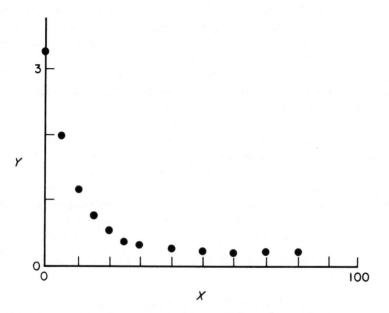

Figure 12-30. The effect of intensity on the differential threshold for intensity of a tone of 10,000 cycles per second. X is intensity expressed on a decibel scale. Y is differential sensitivity expressed as the ratio of the average detected difference to the base intensity. [After Riesz.[26]]

listen to the comparison for one or two seconds, and finally make a judgment of the numerical value to be assigned to the loudness of the comparison tone, assuming that the loudness of the standard was an arbitrary value of ten. The intensity of the standard tone was ninety decibels. There were nine different intensities for the comparison tones, covering a range of seventy decibels. The nine comparison tones were presented to each subject twice in an irregular order in a single session. Figure 12-31 is a plot of median judgments against intensity in decibels. Both scales are logarithmic transformations. There is obviously a very high correlation between judgments and intensity. Thus the experiment clearly indicates the effect of intensity on loudness.

THE EFFECT OF DISCREPANCY RATE ON DETECTION

The performance of men in long periods of listening, during which they are expected to remain alert for signals, and the conditions which affect their performance, are of considerable practical interest, especially in the military. Kappauf and Powe[18] performed an experiment to show the effect of one set of conditions, discrepancy rates, on the detection of discrepancies. Subjects were 235 basic trainees at Lackland Air Force Base.

A subject was required to perform an audio-visual checking task. He listened to a series of digits presented by tape recording for two hours without interruption and checked the digits against a nearly identical series in a mimeographed test booklet. He was instructed to mark a discrepancy whenever he detected one. The recording contained a practice series and the two-hour test series. Digits were spoken at the rate of one per second by a voice which was monotonous and without inflection.

The four conditions of the experiment were the four relative frequencies with which discrepancies occurred in the test series: 2, 5, 10, and 20 per fifteen-minute section. One condition was imposed on a group of subjects. Figure 12-32 shows plots of the proportion of discrepancies *not* detected, as a function of time for two of the four discrepancy rates. After the first period, the proportion not detected was higher for the higher rate. Thus performance was worse when there were more discrepancies to detect.

Stimulus Conditions for Taste

Experimentation is much more difficult with taste stimuli than with either visual or auditory stimuli. While the concentration of a substance in a solution to be tasted can be rigorously controlled, the administration of the stimulus to the tongue cannot be. Furthermore, adaptation, which is very likely to occur with repeated stimulation, cannot be eliminated with certainty, even with a great deal of mouth washing.

There are basic relations to be determined experimentally for taste just as there are for vision and audition. The principle attributes are quality—salt, sweet, sour, and bitter—and strength. One relation involves accuracy of judgments for different kinds of chemical substances and their varied concentrations in solution. Another involves sensitivity—both absolute and differential—for those substances and concentrations. Experimental determination of these relations provides detailed answers for the

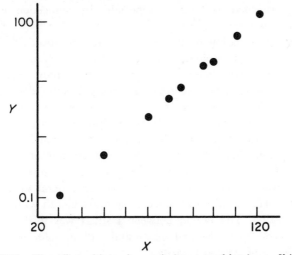

Figure 12-31. The effect of intensity on judgments of loudness. X is intensity in decibels. Y is estimation of loudness on an arbitrary scale. Standard was ninety decibels and called ten. [After Stevens.[33]]

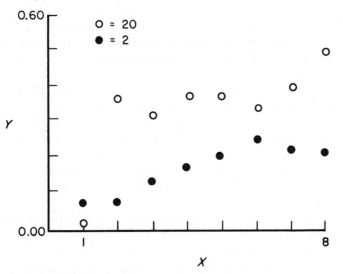

Figure 12-32. The effect of discrepancy rate on errors of detection. X is successive fifteen-minute periods. Y is proportion of discrepancies not detected. The two sets of points represent two of four conditions: two and twenty discrepancies per fifteen-minute section. [After Kappauf and Powe.[18]]

questions: How accurately can people identify taste qualities? How accurately can they judge strength? What is the weakest solution they can identify? What is the smallest difference in strength they can detect? In addition to these basic relations, there are many possibilities for experimentation with food and drink, especially in connection with people's preferences.

A basic investigation of the effect of concentration on the detection of differences in taste strength was conducted by Schutz and Pilgrim [28] Concentrations of salty, sweet, sour, and bitter solutions were varied and the effects on measures of differential thresholds were determined.

Subjects were five men and five women, volunteers from the employees of the Quartermaster Food and Container Institute for the Armed Forces. Their ages averaged thirty-three years and varied from 20 to 58. Subjects took the solutions from shot glasses. A small amount of a given solution was delivered by means of a calibrated, automatic pipette into a glass. The subject was instructed to swirl the solution around his mouth and to expectorate it. He was also instructed to rinse his mouth with distilled water after each tasting. The period between tastings was thirty seconds. Solutions were made up of distilled water and sodium chloride, sucrose, citric acid, or caffeine of standard purity.

As a first step, absolute thresholds were obtained by the method of constant stimuli. The threshold concentration for sodium chloride was 0.089 per cent; for citric acid, 0.004; for sucrose, 0.35; and for caffeine, 0.022. These threshold concentrations were established as the first and lowest of five different reference concentrations or levels for each substance. For each of the five reference levels, four different concentrations were prepared.

At the beginning of a session, a subject was told which substance would be tested in that session. Four practice solutions, consisting of the four concentrations at a given reference level, were presented one at a time in ascending order from the weakest to the strongest. Four identical test sets were then presented with the concentrations in random order. The subject's task was to assign each concentration a number from *1* to *4* to indicate his estimate of its intensity. The session was repeated the following day.

A judgment of *3* or *4* was interpreted as a judgment that the solution was stronger than the reference level. Thus the number of times out of eight that a solution was judged stronger than the reference level solution could be determined. Judgments of all subjects were combined, and the proportion of judgments of "stronger" was determined for each concentration at each reference level for each substance. An index of the differential threshold in units of concentration was computed by special methods for each substance at each reference level. For each substance the differential thresholds increased from the first to the fifth level. Thus increases in concentration had the effect of increasing the threshold size of the smallest detectable difference. This result is similar to those obtained for brightness, pitch, and loudness. In all four cases, the smallest detectable difference increases as the base dimension increases.

Olfactory Stimulus Conditions

The concentration of an odorous substance in air delivered into the nasal passages may be varied by an experimenter to determine the effect on judgments of intensity. The procedure is not without its problems. Varied methods of presentation have been devised in attempts to achieve the best possible control over the stimulus. Precautions must be taken to reduce adaptation, which may occur to a very great degree with repeated stimulation.

There are everyday situations which provide opportunity for convincing observations that intensity of an odor varies with the concentration of the odorous substance in the air. It may be the pleasant experience of sprayings from an atomizer containing a favorite perfume or the unpleasant experience of sprayings from a pressurized can containing insecticide. This relation between concentration and judgments of intensity has been demonstrated experimentally many times. An interesting example is an experiment by Reese and Stevens[25], in which concentration of stimuli derived from natural coffee was varied and the effect determined on judgments of the intensity of the odor. They found that intensity increased with concentration. Varied concentrations of the odorous gas were introduced into nonpermeable, collapsible containers called *sniffing bags*. Each container was fitted with a glass nose-piece connected to the bag by a short piece of tubing, which could be opened or closed by manipulation of a clamp. The subject could open the clamp and inhale the contents of the bag.

Five different concentrations of coffee odor were obtained by mixing odor-saturated air and ordinary air in various proportions. An appropriate amount of air saturated with coffee odor was first put in the bag and then the bag was filled with pure air. The odorous part of the mixture was obtained by passing air at a slow uniform rate through a half pound of ground coffee contained in a gas washing bottle, and filtering it through glass wool to remove the coffee dust. The amount of odorous air placed in a given bag was measured by timing its flow into the bag.

The subject's task was to judge the intensity of the odor in each bag. He was told the intensity of the first bag was to be represented as ten and that he was to assign numbers to the other intensities in proportion to their apparent strength. Each of the five concentrations was judged twice by each subject.

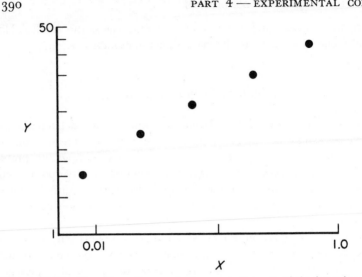

Figure 12-33. The effect of concentration on judgments of the intensity of coffee odor. X is concentration, measured by timing the flow of odorous air into a bag. Y is judgment of intensity on an arbitrary scale. Both scales are logarithmic transformations. [After Reese and Stevens.[25]]

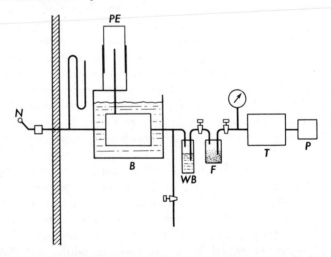

Figure 12-34. Apparatus for the presentation of olfactory stimuli. N is the nosepiece; PE, the pressure equalizer; B, the constant temperature bath; WB, the washing bottle; F, an activated carbon filter; I, a tank of air; and P, a pump. The shaded vertical bar at left is a wall separating two rooms. [Adapted from Wenzel.[37]]

The standard called "ten" was the middle concentration. It was presented first, followed by the five bags including the standard. This procedure was then repeated. The order of presentation of the five bags was different for each subject. Figure 12-33 shows the effect of concentration on judgments of intensity for twelve subjects. The judgments and concentrations were both transformed to logarithms before plotting. The trend of the points definitely indicates a linear function.

One of the problems in presenting an olfactory stimulus is the control of pressure, for there is the possibility that odor intensity varies with pressure as well as with concentration. Wenzel[37] investigated the effect of pressure on judgments of the intensity of phenyl ethyl alcohol. Subjects were three women and one man. The women were graduate students in psychology who had had some training as subjects in psychophysical experiments. The man had had experience as an employee of an aromatics company.

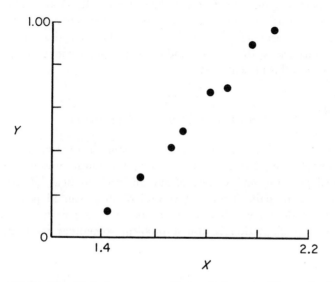

Figure 12-35. The effect of pressure on olfactory judgments. X is a scale of pressure. Y is proportion of judgments "strong." [After Wenzel.[37]]

Figure 12-34 is a diagram of the apparatus. Air moved through the system from right to left. The small square at the extreme right is an air pump. The next, larger square is a tank into which air was pumped under pressure and from which air flowed into a second tank, just left of center, when stopcocks were opened. In going from the first tank to the second, the air passed through an activated carbon filter to remove impurities, and a gas washing bottle filled with the stimulus liquid. Inside the second tank, which rested in a bath of constant temperature, was an evaporating dish also containing the stimulus liquid. Above the bath is a pressure control unit. The amount of pressure within the second tank varied according to the weight which the experimenter placed upon the upper cylinder of the control unit. When the system was opened to deliver a stimulus, the upper cylinder fell and the pressure was kept constant throughout the period of stimulation. The unit to the left of the bath is a manometer on which pressure could be read in millimeters of mercury.

At the far left, separated by a wall, is the nose piece and a valve for controlling presentations of the odorant. A warning light went on two seconds before the valve was opened. Stimulus duration was one half second and the interval between stimuli was 29.50 seconds. On any one day of testing only two different pressures were used. A session consisted of twenty presentations of those two pressures. The subject responded to each member of the pair with a judgment of odor as "strong" or "weak."

The data for each subject consisted of forty judgments for each pressure, obtained on two different days. Figure 12-35 is a plot of percentage of "strong" responses against pressure for the male subject. The percentage increases as pressure increases. The fact that intensity was found to increase with pressure indicates the importance of controlling pressure in stimulus presentation.

Cutaneous Stimulus Conditions

The control of judgments of cutaneous stimuli involves the manipulation of temperature conditions for cold and warmth, pressure conditions for judged pressure, and variety of stimuli, such as heat, electricity, and sharp objects, for pain. The strict control of these stimuli poses problems of equipment design which have been solved in a variety of ways. The elimination of adaptation is also a problem sometimes requiring special arrangements for its solution.

TEMPERATURE

It is common knowledge that the perceived warmth of water varies with its physical temperature and that expressed judgments of warmth follow the same relation. Experimental evidence has confirmed these facts. In 1926, Culler[7] reported an experiment on the judgment of warmth with himself as the subject. Warmth was found to increase with temperature.

Seven jars containing water were arranged on a table. Temperature of the water in each jar was controlled by a heating unit, an agitator, and a thermostat. The cooling device was a reservoir, filled with ice and water, from which cold water was siphoned into each jar through rubber tubes. On a given day, when a temperature of 24.00 degrees centigrade was to be investigated, the seven jars had temperatures of 23.85, 23.90, 23.95, 24.00, 24.05, 24.10, and 24.15 degrees. The jar at 24.00 degrees was the standard and also the preliminary adaptation jar in one series of experiments.

An assistant arranged the schedule so that the experimenter-subject was kept ignorant of the temperatures in use. On each trial the standard was compared with one of the other six jars. At the beginning of a trial, the subject placed the four fingers of each hand in the adaptation jar and kept them there for several minutes. After the assistant read the jar to be compared, the subject moved his hands in time with a metronome beating seconds. At the first stroke, he lifted his hands from the adaptation jar, held them two seconds in the air, immersed them in the standard or the comparison jar, held them again two seconds in the air, immersed

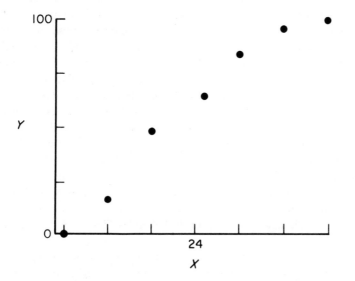

Figure 12-36. The effect of stimulus temperature on judgments of warmth. X is temperature of water bath in degrees centigrade. Y is per cent of judgments of "warmer." The temperature of the standard was twenty-four degrees. There was one subject. [After Culler.[7]]

them finally in the remaining jar for two seconds, then withdrew them at the ninth stroke and returned them at once to the adaptation jar. As he removed his hands from the second jar, he gave his judgment, either "the second jar is cooler" or "the second jar is warmer." Figure 12-36 shows the plot of percentage of "warmer" judgments against temperature. The trend of increasing warmth with increasing temperature is quite clear.

A normal individual can detect differences in cold and warmth. He can also adapt to various degrees of cold and warmth. Does the temperature to which he adapts affect his ability to detect differences in temperature? For example, when he has become accustomed to warmth is he more or less sensitive to a drop in temperature than when he has become accustomed to cold?

This was the subject of investigation by Kenshalo, Nafe, and Dawson[20]. In a psychophysical experiment, they determined the threshold of warm and cool as a function of the temperature to which the skin was adopted. Their single practiced subject was a white male, thirty-five years old.

The stimulating device delivered its thermal energy, obtained from circulating water of controlled temperature, by conduction. It consisted of a chamber formed from a small block of lucite. A silver plate, inserted in the bottom of the chamber, contacted the skin. The block of lucite was on an arm, counterbalanced so that the weight with which it rested on the skin could be adjusted. Two jets of water entered the chamber. Just above the chamber was a scoop which, upon rotation, interrupted one jet or the other before the stream of water reached the chamber. By switching from one stream to the other, a change in thermal energy delivered to the skin could be effected. The subject wore opaque goggles and sat in a chair. The skin area stimulated was the dorsal surface of the forearm approximately three inches below the bend of the elbow.

Thresholds were determined by the method of limits for a number of different adapting temperatures. To measure the warm threshold with an adapting temperature of 36 degrees centigrade, tanks were set to deliver water at the chamber at that temperature and at five higher temperatures in steps of one tenth of a degree. The subject was given at least twenty minutes for adaptation to thirty-six degrees and, after a ready signal, the experimenter changed to water of 36.1 degrees. This new temperature was maintained for a time and then a change was made back to the adapting temperature. Water of 36.2 degrees was presented one minute after the first had been presented and the procedure was continued to complete an ascending series. The descending series was similar. The subject was instructed to push a button when he detected a temperature change in the plate. Ten ascending and descending series were conducted for both warm and cool thresholds at each of six adapting temperatures. The threshold for a series was defined as the point midway between the temperatures, in both directions, beyond which the subject gave consistent reports.

Figure 12-37 is a plot of means of twenty differential threshold measures against adapting temperature. The threshold for "cool" decreased from approximately −0.15 degrees centigrade at lower adapting temperatures to approximately −0.65 degrees at higher temperatures. In other words, becoming accustomed to higher temperatures was accompanied by a decrease in sensitivity to a drop in temperature. The threshold for "warm" increased from approximately 0.28 degrees to 0.43 degrees for lower adapting temperatures, and then decreased to its smallest value at the highest adapting temperature. Therefore, becoming accustomed to the highest temperatures was accompanied by an increase in sensitivity to a rise in temperature.

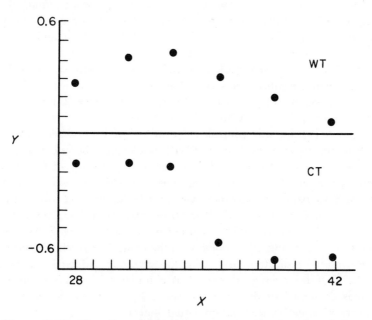

Figure 12-37. The effect of adapting temperature on detection of change. X is adapting temperature in degrees centigrade. Y is the difference threshold in degrees centigrade. The upper plot shows warm thresholds. The lower plot shows cool thresholds. Data are for one subject. [After Kenshalo, Nafe, and Dawson.[20]]

HEAT AS A PAIN STIMULUS

Do people become more sensitive to pain as the stimulation which produces it lasts longer? For example, do they become more sensitive to a dentist's drill as the periods of drilling increase in length? The answer, suggested by an experiment in which heat was employed to produce pain, is "Yes." Birren, Casperson, and Botwinick[2] employed radiant heat apparatus in an investigation of the effect of exposure time on pain thresholds. The ten subjects were laboratory personnel who were experienced with the pain apparatus. Pain thresholds were found to decrease with increasing duration of stimulation.

Radiation from a large incandescent lamp was focused upon a small area of a subject's forehead which had been blackened with India ink to maximize absorption of the radiation. The amount of heat was varied by changing the voltage to the lamp. Exposure time was controlled by a shutter. The subject was told he was to distinguish between the sensation of heat and drawing, pin-pricking pain. The whole experience was described to him as "a feeling of heat building up to a level where the skin seemed to feel as though it were drawing apart, with a final, sharp, stinging sensation." After several widely varied settings were used to provide opportunity for the subject to distinguish between heat and pain, an ascending series of stimuli was devised within the range defined by "heat" and "pain." Typically six stimuli with constant increments in millicalories separating them constituted a series. The pain threshold was defined as the lowest setting reported as painful. Each series was continued until at least two reports were obtained.

Skin temperature was controlled by means of water bags. After the subject's forehead was cooled or warmed a few degrees beyond the desired level, successive measurements of skin temperature were made until it reached that level. Within several seconds, his forehead was exposed to the lamp. Two pain measurements were made for each of two subjects, alternately, in a single session of 30 to 60 minutes. Initial skin temperature was maintained at ninety degrees Fahrenheit, a normal level. Four stimulis durations of 3, 5, 8, and 10 seconds were the conditions of the experiment.

The results indicated that stimulus duration affected thresholds. Figure 12-38 shows average threshold as a function of stimulus duration. Thresholds decreased as duration increased. In other words, subjects became more sensitive as stimulation lasted longer.

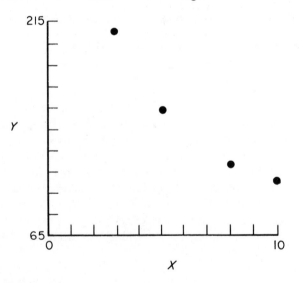

Figure 12-38. The effect of duration of stimulation on pain sensitivity. X is number of seconds. Y is average threshold in millicalories per square centimeter. [After Birren, Casperson, and Botwinick.[2]]

Pressure Stimuli

A person may become accustomed to light pressure on the surface of his body so that he reports he does not experience the pressure. This happens frequently with clothing, which exerts light pressure at many points on the skin. The person is said to adapt to the pressure. Suppose he wears a belt. Does the width of the belt affect his becoming adapted to its pressure? Does the tightness of the belt have such an effect? Common experience suggests that narrowness and tightness may both make adaptation more difficult. The evidence from the following experiment supports this idea.

Nafe and Wagoner[23] determined the effects of weight and area on pressure adaptation for two subjects, one familiar with the experiment and one naive as to its purpose. Figure 12-39 shows the device which lowered

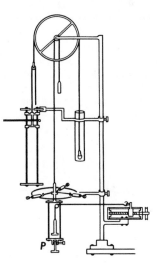

Figure 12-39. A device for controlling the weight and area of pressure stimulation. *P* is the applicator. [Adapted from Nafe and Wagoner.[23]]

a weight, at a constant speed, upon the skin and recorded on a graph the sinking of the weight into the tissue. The stimulating objects were six circular aluminum disks with areas of 6.25, 12.5, 25, 50, 100, and 200 square millimeters. The surface of each disk was covered with blotting paper. The weight was lowered or lifted slowly by means of a screw gear driven by an electric motor. The varied weights were 8.75, 17.5, 35, and 70 grams.

The subject sat in a chair with his knee beneath the stimulating disk. The skin area stimulated was about three inches above the knee cap. He was instructed to report, after the weight was delivered upon the skin,

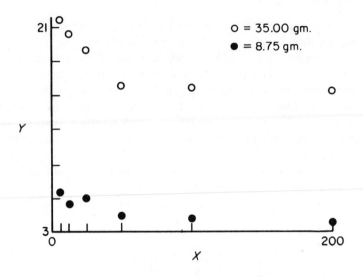

Figure 12-40. The effect of stimulus weight and area on pressure adaptation time. X is stimulus area in square millimeters. Y is average adaptation time in seconds for thirty measures on each of two subjects. The two sets of points represent two different stimulus weights. [After Nafe and Wagoner.[23]]

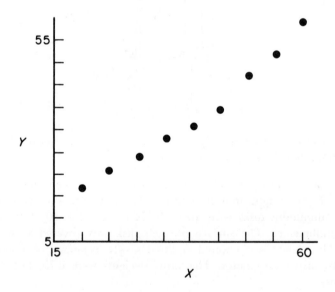

Figure 12-41. The effect of pressure on critical frequency of percussion. X is pressure in pounds per square inch. Y is average number of air bursts per second, at which subjects reported a constant sensation. [After Shewchuk and Zubek.[29]]

when adaptation was complete, that is, when he could no longer feel the pressure, by pressing a telegraph key which activated the signal marker on a kymograph. The twenty-four combinations of weights and areas were presented in a random order. The time interval between stimulations was never less than four times that of the adaptation time, to insure recovery of sensitivity.

Thirty measures were obtained for each subject for each of the twenty-four combinations of weight and area. Figure 12-40 shows the plot of adaptation times against area of the stimulus for two weights, 8.75 and 35.00 grams. The plots indicate that adaptation times diminish as areas of the stimuli increase and as the weights of the stimuli decrease.

Percussion discrimination was measured, in an investigation by Shewchuk and Zubek[29], by a technique analogous to that employed in the measurement of visual *CFF*. An interrupted stream of air at a constant pressure was produced and applied to the subject's skin. Its frequency could be systematically increased until a sensation of constant pressure was reported. The frequency at which this sensation was reported was called the critical frequency of percussion (*CFP*). The technique was employed in an experiment on the effect of air pressure on the tactual sensitivity of the finger tips. *CFP* was found to increase with air pressure.

A subject wore earplugs and earmuffs. His left index finger was placed in a stand so that its tip was very close to a nozzle which delivered air through a tiny aperture. After a thin film of petroleum jelly was applied to the finger tip, the subject was given one trial at each of nine air pressures which varied from 20 to 60 pounds per square inch by steps of five pounds. On each trial the frequency of the air bursts was increased until he reported a constant sensation. Trials were separated by brief rest periods. The entire procedure was repeated until the subject had received five trials at each of the nine pressures on one day. Five more trials were given on the following day. Thus each subject had ten trials at each of the nine pressures. Figure 12-41 is a plot of average *CFP* for ten university students, five men and five women. The fusion frequency increases with air pressure.

Conditions of Kinesthetic Stimulation

The receptors for kinesthetic stimuli, being located in the muscles, tendons, and joints of the body, are not stimulated in psychological experiments by methods as direct as those employed in visual, auditory, gustatory, olfactory, and cutaneous experiments. They can be stimulated, however, by movement of parts of a subject's body under instruction from the experimenter or actual manipulation by him. Planned variations in these movements may constitute the conditions of an experiment, under which the subject gives judgments. One difficulty encountered in an experiment of this kind is that kinesthetic stimulation may be accompanied by a considerable amount of pressure on the surface of the body—a kind of stimulation which cannot be controlled or reduced as effectively as can other kinds such as visual, auditory, gustatory, and olfactory. In everyday situations, the lifting of packages, chairs, tools and other objects provides a substantial amount of kinesthetic stimulation. It is commonly observed that in lifting things such as apples, bananas, cabbages, and melons for the purpose of comparing their weights, the judgments are easier when the differences are large than when they are small. This observation is supported by laboratory experiments. The lifting of small weights is one common laboratory task involving a large component of kinesthetic stimulation. In 1933, Bressler[3] described a psychophysical experiment to determine the effect of weight on comparative judgments of weights. Subjects were five adults, four males and one female. They were naive with respect to the purposes of the experiment.

A set of eleven weights was used, varying from 80 to 120 grams in steps of four grams. The weights were made from hard rubber bars, fashioned into cylinders. A hollow was drilled in each cylinder and then filled with shot and solder to a specified weight. The weights were arranged on a revolving table by means of which the experimenter could quickly and precisely place any weight in position under a subject's hand. The subject sat with his arm supported in a rest and his hand protruding through an opening in a screen. He raised a weight with a movement of the hand only; he kept his wrist on the edge of the rest.

The weight of 100 grams was designated as the standard. Each of the weights in the set was paired with the standard for comparison. The subject was instructed to lift the standard weight at the first signal, replace it immediately, lift the comparison weight at the next signal, replace it, and give his judgment while ignoring the third signal. At the fourth signal, he was to begin the process again for the next pair of weights. The subject's judgment was "heavier," "equal," or "lighter." The signal was a light which flashed regularly at an interval of a few seconds.

For one subject, the numbers of "heavier" judgments for the five central weights, each of which was presented 500 times, are presented as percentages plotted against weight in Figure 12-42. The percentage of "heavier" judgments increases with the weight of the comparison objects. What this means is that the percentage of incorrect judgments for weights lighter than the standard increased as did the percentage of correct judgments for weights heavier than the standard. In other words, weights were judged correctly more often when they were distant from the standard than when they were near it.

The importance of kinesthetic stimulation in a familiar and simple everyday situation was shown in an experiment by Brown[5] to determine the effect of wrapping materials on judgments of the freshness of bread. It had been found previously that consumers judge freshness largely by feeling the wrapped loaves, but it was not known that the technique actually worked or what effect different wrappers might have on judgments. Subjects in the first experiment were sixteen male and sixteen female university students.

Sixteen loaves of bread, all baked together during the night before the experiment and wrapped in the same material, were rewrapped in four different materials: cellophane, saran, regular wax, and a special wax paper with a subwrapper. A subject sat beside a table with his right arm

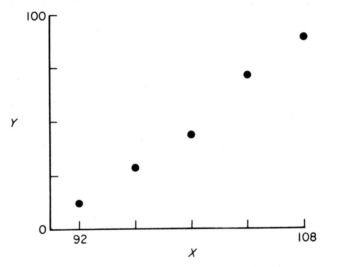

Figure 12-42. The effect of stimulus weight on comparative judgments of weight. X is stimulus weight in grams. Y is per cent of judgments of "heavier." The weight of the standard was 100 gm. The data are for one subject. [After Bressler.[3]]

around a screen. He was told that he was participating in an experiment to determine whether or not people can judge how fresh bread is by feeling it, that one loaf and then another would be presented under his hand, that he should feel one and then the other, and say which of the two seemed fresher. He was not allowed to judge the two loaves as equal in freshness. The four different wrappers were paired in all possible combinations which numbered six. The six pairs were presented in random order.

The percentage of judgments of "fresher" was computed by dividing the number of such judgments by the total number of times the wrapper appeared in the pairs. The result for cellophane was 68 per cent; for saran, 56; for regular wax paper, 42; and for the special wax paper with subwrapper, 34.

A second experiment was performed in the foyer of a large market with housewives as subjects. Fifty housewives who came to the market to shop volunteered.

Three conventional wrappers were selected: cellophane, cellophane with a band of wax paper, and wax paper. Eighteen round-topped loaves of sliced white bread were used. Six loaves were baked on the afternoon before the experiment; six were one day older; and six were two days older. All loaves were stored in their original wrappers until a few hours before the experiment when they were rewrapped in the three materials. An attempt was made to adjust all wrappers to the same degree of tightness on all loaves. A subject sat beside a table with her right forearm behind a screen on the table. Instructions were the same as in the first experiment. The three possible pairs of wrappers were presented in random order to each housewife.

The percentage of judgments of "fresher" was computed by the method of the first experiment. The result for cellophane was 62.2 per cent; for cellophane with a wax-band insert, 44.1; and for wax paper, 36.3. Judgments of "fresher" were more frequent for the freshest bread than for either of the other categories. Thus it was demonstrated in both experiments that different wrappers did affect judgments of freshness, and in the second experiment that housewives could discriminate between the freshest bread and the others by feeling it.

Conditions of Static Stimulation

The receptors for static sensitivity are not stimulated as directly in psychological experimentation as are the receptors for vision, audition, gustation, olfaction, and cutaneous sensitivity but, just as the kinesthetic receptors can be stimulated by instructed or manipulated movement, so can the static receptors be stimulated. The rotation of the body and the tilt of the body or the head can be varied, and the effect on judgments of rotation and tilt can be observed. It is true of static stimulation, as of kinesthetic stimulation, that pressure on the surface of the body constitutes a substantial component of stimulation and cannot be eliminated.

Stimulation from body tilt occurs in many everyday situations—for example, with the passenger in a jet plane climbing steeply from a take-off, the crew of a racing sloop which heels sharply as she beats to windward under a stiff breeze, and the driver of a car going around a steeply banked curve in the highway. It is critical to successful performance in the gyrations of a diver doing a jackknife, a gymnast on the parallel bars, a skier making a sharp turn in a slalom, and a figure skater performing a difficult routine. In many of these situations, being able to make accurate judgments of tilt is very important. Consequently it is not surprising that experiments, such as one by Fleishman[11], have been performed to demonstrate the effect of tilt on judgment of body position. In his experiment there were two sets of conditions: three degrees and three speeds of tilt. Subjects were ninety basic trainee airmen.

A tilting-chair arrangement, shown in Figure 12-43, could be displaced to one side or the other by either the experimenter or a subject. Speed of displacement was controlled by the experimenter and could be varied from three to seven degrees per second. The subject was strapped into the chair by means of a shoulder harness and belt arrangement. He was blindfolded with black opaque goggles, and his feet were positioned

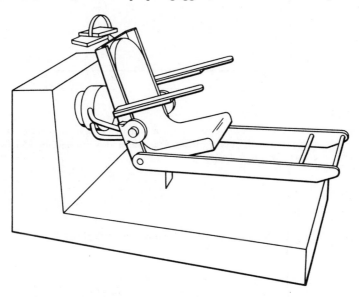

Figure 12-43. The tilting chair employed in the experiment on judging vertical body position. [Adapted from Fleishman.[11]]

on a foot rest. A head rest was available to immobilize the subject's head, but the rest was not used in this experiment. The experimenter gave the subject the following instructions: "This is an experiment to see how well you can adjust yourself to an upright position after you are placed in a tilted position. I will first tilt you to some inclined position, and when I instruct you to do so, you are to return the chair as nearly as you can to the position in which you are now. You can move the chair by pressing these buttons in the arm rest. Push the right button to move to the right, and the left button to move to the left. When you are satisfied that you are in an upright position, say 'Level.'"

Three displacement speeds constituted one set of conditions; three

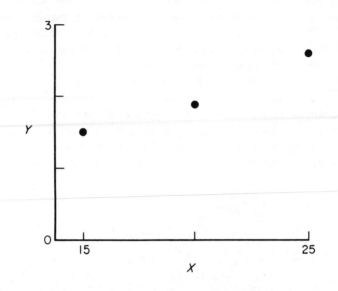

Figure 12-44. The effect of degree of tilt on judgments of body position. X is number of degrees displacement from vertical. Y is mean degrees deviation of judgment from vertical. [After Fleishman.[11]]

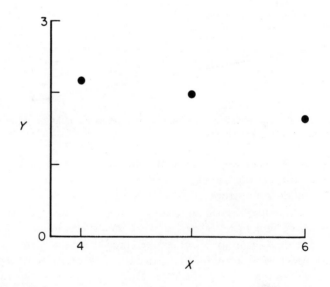

Figure 12-45. The effect of speed of tilt on judgments of body position. X is number of degrees per second. Y is mean degrees deviation of judgment from vertical. [After Fleishman.[11]]

amounts of tilt constituted the other set. The nine possible combinations of one speed and one tilt were the conditions of the experiment. Ten subjects were randomly assigned to each of the nine conditions. Each subject received twelve trials in a single sitting. The direction of tilt, to the right or to the left, varied from trial to trial in a randomly determined sequence.

Accuracy of judgment was measured in terms of degrees of deviation from the true upright position. Each group mean was based on twelve adjustments made by each of ten subjects. Figure 12-44 shows the plot of means for the three different amounts of tilt; Figure 12-45 shows the plot of means for the three different speeds of displacement. Error increased as amount of tilt increased and decreased as speed of displacement increased. This means that they were more accurate for small amounts of tilt than for large amounts, and that they were more accurate when the tilt was rapid than when it was slow.

Chapter Summary

In many everyday situations people manipulate perceptual stimuli and thereby control behavior. Sometimes it is their own behavior; sometimes, the behavior of others. Frequently, but not always, the behavior takes the form of judgments. The experimental knowledge of perception provides an explanation of this control in terms of the specific variables and relations involved. Only a superficial understanding of how perceptual behavior is controlled is possible without this knowledge.

Visual judgments can be controlled by manipulating the wave length, intensity, or duration of light, and the orientation or load of objects viewed; auditory judgments, by manipulating the frequency or intensity of tones, and the rate of sound signals; gustatory and olfactory judgments, by manipulating the concentration of the stimulating substance; cutaneous judgments, by manipulating heat and pressure; and kinesthetic and static judgments, by manipulating body movement and tilt. There are, of course, other possibilities for perceptual stimulus conditions, but a large proportion of research in this area has been concerned with the effects of conditions like those described in this chapter.

References

1. Barber, J. L., and W. R. Garner. "The Effect of Scale Numbering on Scale Reading Accuracy and Speed." *The Journal of Experimental Psychology,* 41 (1951), 298-309.
2. Birren, J. E., R. C. Casperson, and J. Botwinick. "Pain Measurement by the Radiant Heat Method: Individual Differences in Pain Sensitivity, the Effects of Skin Temperature, and Stimulus Duration." *The Journal of Experimental Psychology,* 41 (1951), 419-424.
3. Bressler, J. "Judgments in Absolute Units as a Psychophysical Method." *The Archives of Psychology,* 23, No. 152 (1933).

4. Bridges, C. C., and M. E. Bitterman. "The Measurement of Autokinetic Movement." *The American Journal of Psychology,* 67 (1954), 525-529.

5. Brown, R. L. "Wrapper Influence on the Perception of Freshness in Bread." *The Journal of Applied Psychology,* 42 (1958), 257-260.

6. Clifford, L. T., and A. D. Calvin. "Effect of Age on the Discriminative Learning of Color and Brightness by Children." *The American Journal of Psychology,* 71 (1958), 766-767.

7. Culler, E. A. K. "Thermal Discrimination and Weber's Law." *The Archives of Psychology,* 13, No. 81 (1926).

8. Dusek, E. R., W. H. Teichner, and J. L. Kobrick. "The Effects of the Angular Relationships Between the Observer and the Base-Surround on Relative Depth Discrimination." *The American Journal of Psychology,* 68 (1955), 438-443.

9. Ellis, H. C., and A. E. Ahr. "The Role of Error Density and Set in a Vigilance Task." *The Journal of Applied Psychology,* 44 (1960), 205-209.

10. Finger, F. W., and D. K. Spelt. "The Illustration of the Horizontal-Vertical Illusion." *The Journal of Experimental Psychology,* 37 (1947), 243-250.

11. Fleishman, E. A. "Perception of Body Position in the Absence of Visual Cues." *The Journal of Experimental Psychology,* 46 (1953), 261-270.

12. Fletcher, H., and W. A. Munson. "Loudness, Its Definition, Measurement and Calculation." *The Journal of the Acoustical Society of America,* 5 (1933), 82-108.

13. Ghent, Lila. "Recognition by Children of Realistic Figures Presented in Various Orientations." *The Canadian Journal of Psychology,* 14 (1960), 249-256.

14. Hecht, S. "The Nature of Foveal Dark Adaptation." *The Journal of General Psychology,* 4 (1922), 113-139.

15. Hecht, S., and R. E. Williams. "The Visibility of Monochromatic Radiation and the Absorption Spectrum of Visual Purple." *The Journal of General Physiology,* 5 (1922), 1-33.

16. Hunter, W. S., and M. Sigler. "The Span of Visual Discrimination as a Function of Time and Intensity of Stimulation." *The Journal of Experimental Psychology,* 26 (1940), 160-179.

17. Jenkins, H. M. "The Effect of Signal Rate on Performance in Visual Monitoring." *The American Journal of Psychology,* 71 (1958), 647-661.

18. Kappauf, W. E., and W. E. Powe. "Performance Decrement at an Audio-Visual Checking Task." *The Journal of Experimental Psychology,* 57 (1959), 49-56.

19. Kellogg, W. N. "An Experimental Comparison of Psychophysical Methods." *The Archives of Psychology,* 17, No. 106 (1929).

20. Kenshalo, D. R., J. P. Nafe, and W. W. Dawson. "A New Method for the Investigation of Thermal Sensitivity." *The Journal of Psychology,* 49 (1960), 29-41.

21. Kugelmass, S., and C. Landis. "The Relation of Area and Luminance to the Threshold for Critical Flicker Fusion." *The American Journal of Psychology,* 68 (1955), 1-19.

22. Leibowitz, H. "Some Factors Influencing the Variability of Vernier Adjustments." *The American Journal of Psychology,* 68 (1955), 266-273.

23. Nafe, J. P., and K. S. Wagoner. "The Nature of Pressure Adaptation." *The Journal of General Psychology,* 25 (1941), 295-321.

24. Oberly, H. S. "The Range for Visual Attention, Cognition and Apprehension." *The American Journal of Psychology,* 35 (1924), 332-352.
25. Reese, T. S., and S. S. Stevens. "Subjective Intensity of Coffee-Odor." *The American Journal of Psychology,* 73 (1960), 424-428.
26. Riesz, R. R. "Differential Intensity Sensitivity of the Ear for Pure Tones." *The Physical Review,* 31 (1928), 867-875.
27. Saltzman, I. J., and W. R. Garner. "Reaction Time as a Measure of Span of Attention." *The Journal of Psychology,* 25 (1948), 227-241.
28. Schutz, H. G., and F. J. Pilgrim. "Differential Sensitivity in Gustation." *The Journal of Experimental Psychology,* 54 (1957), 41-48.
29. Shewchuk, L. A., and J. P. Zubek. "A Technique of Intermittent Stimulation for Measurement of Tactual Sensitivity: Apparatus and Preliminary Results." *The Canadian Journal of Psychology,* 14 (1960), 29-37, published by the University of Toronto Press.
30. Shower, E. G., and R. Biddulph. "Differential Pitch Sensitivity of the Ear." *The Journal of the Acoustical Society of America,* 3 (1931), 275-287.
31. Sleight, R. B. "The Effect of Instrument Dial Shape on Legibility." *The Journal of Applied Psychology,* 32 (1948), 170-188.
32. Stavrianos, B. K. "The Relation of Shape Perception to Explicit Judgments of Inclination." *The Archives of Psychology,* 41, No. 296 (1945).
33. Stevens, S. S. "The Direct Estimation of Sensory Magnitudes—Loudness." *The American Journal of Psychology,* 69 (1956), 1-25.
34. Thouless, R. H. "Phenomenal Regression to the Real Object." *The British Journal of Psychology,* 21 (1931), 339-359.
35. Van Krevelen, A. "The Ability to Make Absolute Judgments of Pitch." *The Journal of Experimental Psychology,* 42 (1951), 207-215.
36. Wald, G. "Human Vision and the Spectrum." *Science,* 101 (1945), 653-658.
37. Wenzel, B. M. "Differential Sensitivity in Olfaction." *The Journal of Experimental Psychology,* 39 (1949), 129-143.
38. Zeigler, H. P., and H. Leibowitz. "Apparent Visual Size as a Function of Distance for Children and Adults." *The American Journal of Psychology,* 70 (1957), 106-109.

13

Nutrients
and Drugs

RECOGNITION HAS ALREADY BEEN GIVEN TO THE IMPORTANCE OF the large class of experimental conditions called biological interventions. It possesses an appeal which is universal, for who would not be interested in the discovery of medical treatments—dietary, pharmacological, radiological, or surgical—which would offer the successful control of behavior? The possibilities appear to be unlimited. There are now available vitamins and minerals for more energetic living, drugs for pain and anxiety, and surgery for defects of vision and hearing. The future may bring marvelous new treatments—ways of improving intellect and personality, preventing juvenile delinquency and mental illness, and insuring happiness and satisfaction in living.

As has already been noted, these biological interventions as they pertain to human behavior are very largely the province of medical research and practice. Even so, psychologists do participate in this experimentation, in collaboration with medical researchers. For the most part, participation has occurred in research on drugs, especially the new tranquilizers. One reason for collaboration in this area is that most modern psychiatric hospitals and clinics have both medical and psychological staffs. Since tranquilizers are used very extensively in these settings to quiet excited patients or socially activate withdrawn patients, and to make both groups amenable to psychotherapy, it is only natural that the two staffs would on occasion work together. Another reason for collaboration is that many different kinds of psychological testing are required to evaluate the effects of a drug on behavior. It is not sufficient to administer a drug and observe some general sort of improvement. It is possible that a given drug would reduce excited vocalizing, a beneficial effect, but impair problem solving, an undesirable effect. Consequently, an adequate evaluation of a drug would require a large amount of experimentation with measurement of numerous characteristics of behavior. Since psychologists specialize in the measurement of behavior, they can contribute a great deal to experimentation in this area.

There are possibilities for psychological experimentation with variations in the supply or deprivation of food and water. Periods of deprivation measured in hours, days, or other units are imposed on subjects and the effects on their behavior are observed. Food deprivation may apply to food in general or to specific items like salt, meat, or candy. Water deprivation may apply to water only or to all liquids.

Psychologists may experiment on humans with moderate variations in the supply or deprivation of food or water. When the variations are extreme and judged to involve some risk for the health of the human subject, experimentation in our society must, of course, be conducted with safeguards for the protection of the individual. One safeguard is supervision by a physician or a medical specialist. A safeguard for the public is the use of special groups of subjects who are asked and permitted to volunteer for participation in the research. In the past these groups have included men serving prison sentences, conscientious objectors, and other special groups.

Deprivation Conditions

There has been much discussion of many aspects of infant feeding schedules, including the length of periods between feedings. A delay in feeding after a regular schedule has been followed may be considered a mild form of deprivation. Even small variations of the kind which may occur in normal everyday situations have been shown to affect behavior.

The activity of newborn infants was found to increase with delay in feeding in an experiment by Marquis[5]. General bodily activity of one group of infants on a four-hour feeding schedule was measured and compared with general bodily activity of another group on a three-hour schedule for eight days and a four-hour schedule for the ninth day. Subjects were newborn infants on the pediatrics ward of the New Haven Hospital.

Infants were observed from the second day through the ninth day of their hospitalization. Eighteen were placed on a four-hour feeding schedule; sixteen, on a three-hour schedule. Two regulation nursery bassinets, equipped to measure general activity, were set up in a quiet, dimly lighted room in the Hospital. The foot end of each bassinet was supported by a bar which acted as a fulcrum; the head end was suspended by a coil spring. Movements of the bed were transmitted by means of string and pulleys to the pen of a polygraph. The apparatus was not sensitive enough to register a slight movement, such as breathing or muscle twitching, but did register a shift in position of the head or arm. Crying, hiccoughs, regurgitation, or any other unusual form of activity was recorded by an observer.

Two infants on the same feeding schedule were observed at the same time. They were placed in the bassinets, with light covering, after feeding at six AM and remained there until feeding at six PM. They were removed only for feedings, at which time diapers were changed. After six PM, the infants were returned to the regular nursery for the night.

Special precautions were taken to insure an adequate food intake. Infants were weighed before and after each feeding. Each infant was allowed to nurse as long as he would suck or until the milk supply was exhausted. If his increase in weight after feeding indicated that he had not taken an amount prescribed by the pediatrician as optimum for his age and weight, a supplementary formula was offered to him by bottle. After the infant ceased sucking, he was patted for air expulsion, an attempt was made to awaken him, and breast or bottle was offered to him again. If no sucking occurred, the infant was considered satiated. Bottle-fed infants were fed by their own mothers. Each was offered more of the formula than the amount prescribed and was allowed to suck until satiated.

Infants on the three-hour schedule were fed at 6, 9, 12, 3, and 6 o'clock; those on the four-hour schedule, at 6, 10, 2, and 6. Behavior was recorded during the last three periods for the three-hour group; during the last two for the four-hour group. Night feedings were carried out on the same schedule. On the ninth day, when the three-hour group was changed to a four-hour schedule, feeding times were 6, 9, 1, and 5.

Activity was measured as the per cent of half minutes the infant was active per unit of time. A half minute was counted if any activity occurred within it. The counts were converted to percentages because the periods between feedings were only approximately equal. Figure 13-1 is a plot of percentage of half minutes against successive ten-minute periods after feeding during the eight-day period. The curves are quite similar. Figure 13-2 is a similar plot for two four-hour periods on the ninth day. During the fourth hour, the three-hour group showed more activity and a more rapid increase in activity than did the four-hour group. This means that newborn infants are sensitive to mild deprivation.

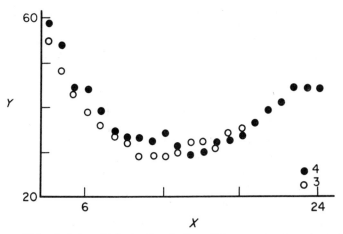

Figure 13-1. Activity of infants after feeding. X is successive ten-minute intervals after feeding. Y is per cent of half minutes during which activity was recorded. The two sets of points represent two schedules, three and four hours between feedings. [After Marquis.[5]]

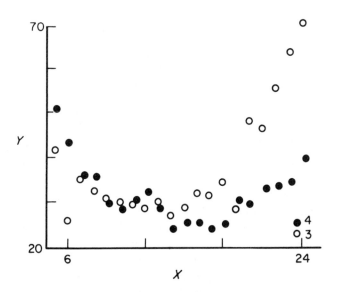

Figure 13-2. The effect of a change in feeding schedule on activity. X is successive ten-minute intervals after feeding. Y is per cent of half minutes during which activity was recorded. The two sets of points distinguish two groups of infants according to their original schedules, three and four hours between feedings. [After Marquis.[5]]

The effects of stimuli on perceptual behavior, as presented in the preceding chapter, are certainly not as surprising and perhaps not as interesting as the effect of deprivation on that behavior. The anecdotes about men, who were perishing from thirst, seeing mirages of lakes and rivers in the desert, may faithfully represent the effects of extreme deprivation. The effect of mild deprivation is represented by an experiment in which visual recognition thresholds for words were shown to be affected by deprivation of food and water. Wispé and Drambarean[8] experimented on sixty men and women in an introductory psychology course at Ohio State University. Students volunteered after having been told they would have to go twenty-four hours without food or water.

Two lists of twenty-four words were constructed. Twelve words in each list were called *need* words and twelve were called *neutral*. The need words included six related to food and six related to water; the neutral words were selected as words in common use and not related to hunger and thirst. In a preliminary study, words were rated by 250 college students in terms of commonness of usage. The words were then divided on the basis of these ratings into common and uncommon words. Among those which referred to food, the common words were feed, dine, meat, eat, cake, and steak; the uncommon ones were munch, waffle, chocolate, nibble, ham, and devour. Among those which referred to water, the common words were milk, drink, coke, sip, water, and drain; the uncommon were lemonade, imbibe, guzzle, soda, gulp, and cider. Common food and water words were assigned to one list; uncommon to the other list.

Words were presented to a subject by means of an episcotister and a slide projector. The openings in the disk of the episcotister permitted exposure times to be varied. Words were printed on amber-colored cellophane and mounted in slides, which were projected on a beaded glass screen containing two fixation points. The subject sat some distance from the screen with the projector behind him and to his right.

Three conditions of deprivation for both food and water were employed in the experiment: 1, 10, and 24 hours. Subjects were randomly assigned in equal numbers to the three conditions. Half in each group were tested on the list containing common words; half, on the list containing uncommon words. Subjects were told the experiment was concerned with deprivation and visual acuity. They were asked not to eat or drink prior to testing, to restrict their activities to study and attendance at classes, and to limit smoking. The one-hour deprivation group ate a normal lunch but ate it later than usual. The ten-hour group ate breakfast at 7:30 a.m., but no lunch. The twenty-four hour group ate dinner on the evening preceding the testing, but not breakfast or lunch. Testing began at 5:30 p.m. Each subject was called, on the night before he was to be tested, to remind him of his obligation.

The subject's task was to report each word as it was projected. He was told that he should report "blank" if he could not distinguish a word and that he should guess even if he was unsure. An ascending method of limits was employed: the exposure time was set at a level at which the subject reported seeing "only a flash of light" and then increased at intervals until he correctly reported the word. Two presentations were made at each exposure time and the subject was considered to have correctly identified the word when he gave two successive correct responses.

Figure 13-3 shows recognition time in seconds for the two classes of need words and the three conditions of deprivation. Words in both classes were recognized more rapidly as deprivation time increased. Thus visual sensitivity was affected by food and water deprivation.

The effect of food deprivation on perception was also demonstrated by Gilchrist and Nesberg[2]. The dependent variable was judgments of food pictures. Subjects were twenty-six students in elementary psychology

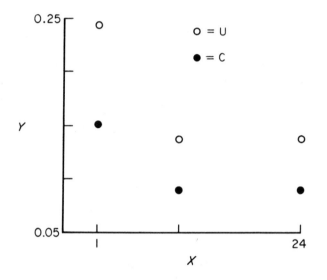

Figure 13-3. The effect of food and water deprivation on visual recognition thresholds for related words. X is hours of food deprivation. Y is average recognition time in seconds. The two sets of points represent two classes of words, common and uncommon. [After Wispé and Drambarean.[8]]

courses at the University of Wisconsin. All volunteered to go twenty hours without food and without liquids, except water.

A subject sat in front of a projection screen in a darkened room. The projector was placed on a stand behind and above his chair. A rheostat, for controlling the voltage of the projector, was placed so that the experimenter and the subject could both operate it but the subject could not see it. Four color slides of meals were reproduced from pictures in magazines. The main food items in the pictures were steaks, fried chicken, hamburgers, and spaghetti. The subject was told he was participating in an experiment on matching pictures. A picture would be projected on the screen and he was to look at it for fifteen seconds, after which the picture would be terminated. A few seconds later it would be turned on again but it would not look the same. His task was to make it look the same as before by turning the knob on the rheostat. The slides were presented in random order twice at each of two quite different standard settings of the rheostat. Matchings were made once from a voltage lower than each standard and once from a higher voltage.

Subjects were assigned randomly to two groups. Those in the first group were tested immediately after their noon meal, skipped their evening meal and were tested after the time they would have eaten it, skipped their breakfast and were tested after the time they would have eaten it the next morning. Thus at the three sessions they had been deprived of food for 0, 6, and 20 hours, respectively. Subjects in the second group were tested at the same times but they ate both dinner and breakfast.

Figure 13-4 is a plot of voltage settings for the hungry and satiated groups as a function of time from the start of the experiment. An exact average match was a setting of seventy-five volts. As the experiment progressed, the difference between the two groups became larger with hungry subjects using higher voltage settings than satiated subjects in matching the food pictures. Thus hungry subjects produced brighter pictures to achieve matching.

Drug Conditions

A major problem in psychological experimentation with drugs is the choice of a dependent variable—that is, the decision as to what specific characteristic of behavior will be observed and measured. This is a problem because there is a need to know all of a drug's effects, something a single investigation cannot possibly provide. Although the experiments reported here have to do specifically with palmar sweating, a visual threshold, the judgment of time, conditioning of the galvanic skin response, and relearning of paired adjectives, they are intended to convey some idea of the possible effects of drugs on a wide range of behaviors: reflexes and other motor behavior; perceptual behavior; conditioning; and learning. No experiments are reported here having to do with effects on personality characteristics, but there is, of course, considerable interest among psychologists in this area.

Palmar sweating was reduced by administration of a tranquilizer in an experiment by Laties[4]. The drug was meprobamate. Subjects were six male and ten female paid volunteers who varied in age from 21 to 38 years.

A subject held a bag of anhydrous silica gel for a fifteen-minute period on each of two nonsuccessive days. Prior to each period, he took 1,600 milligrams of either meprobamate or a placebo, an inert substance which looked like the drug, in four equal doses. Testing was scheduled in the middle of the afternoon. Either the drug or the placebo was taken the previous night, before retiring, and nine hours, five hours, and one hour before the measurement of palmar sweating. Ten subjects took the placebo first and the drug second; six took the drug first and the placebo second. The bag of silica gel was placed in a weighing bottle and weighed before and after it was held. The change in weight was taken as a measure of palmar sweat. As already noted, the drug was found to reduce sweating. If palmar sweating is assumed to be a correlate of excitement, then it is

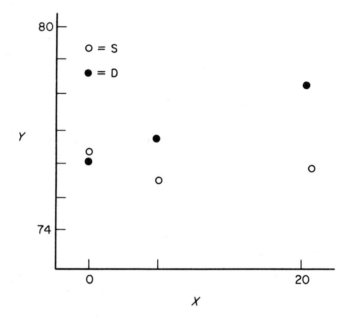

Figure 13-4. The effect of food deprivation on judgments of food pictures. X is number of hours elapsed from start of experiment. Y is average voltage for judgments. The two sets of points represent the two conditions, deprivation and satiation. [After Gilchrist and Nesberg.[2]]

reasonable to conclude that the drug had the effect of reducing excitement. This is not a matter of proof, for sweating might have diminished without a reduction of excitement.

Mitchell and Zax[6] investigated the effect of chlorpromazine, a tranquilizer, on conditioning of the galvanic skin response (GSR) in psychiatric patients. Their hypothesis was that subjects receiving the drug would be more difficult to condition than subjects not receiving it. They gave as justification for the hypothesis the evidence that chlorpromazine quieted disturbed patients, and other evidence that subjects who were less anxious were harder to condition. They reasoned that if the drug reduced anxiety, it should also make conditioning more difficult.

The subjects, who were sixty-nine psychiatric patients at St. Elizabeths Hospital in Washington, D.C., were divided into two groups, equated approximately for age, sex, length of hospitalization, and degree of anxiety as judged by the patient's psychiatrist. All subjects were conditioned initially under the same conditions. After approximately thirty days during which chlorpromazine was given to the patients in one group, another conditioning session was held. The experimenter was not told which patients were receiving the drug: the psychiatrist in charge of each case regulated the dosage level and method of administration. Typically, after ten days of gradually increasing dosages, a subject received orally 200 to 600 milligrams of the drug daily.

The conditioned stimulus (CS) in the initial conditioning session was the word *carry*. It appeared nine times randomly in a list which contained twenty-one other commonly used five-letter words. Words were presented on a memory drum with a constant exposure interval of 5.5 seconds and an interval between exposures of one second. The list was repeated as often as necessary for acquisition to a criterion of two sets of three consecutive GSRs to the CS alone. The unconditioned stimulus (US) was the sound of a bicycle horn at a moderately high frequency and intensity, delivered to the subject's ear through a pair of earphones. The CS and US both occurred on the first trial. On succeeding trials, the US occurred with every fourth CS. When both occurred, an automatic timer presented the US, the sound, after the CS, the word, and terminated it before the exposure of the word ended. The unconditioned response (UR) was the GSR. A response was defined as an observable rise accompanying the CS greater than that accompanying the word immediately preceding the CS. The response was measured by a galvanometer, finger electrodes, and a recorder which traced the GSR graphically and continuously throughout the conditioning session. The number of occurrences of US required before the criterion was achieved was the measure of conditioning. A different CS and list were used in the second conditioning session.

A difference between the number of occurrences of US to condition initially and the number required thirty days later was computed for each subject. The scores of subjects receiving chlorpromazine were then compared to the scores of those not receiving it. Those receiving the drug required an average of 6.78 more occurrences of US to the condition to criterion in the second session than in the first; those not receiving the drug required an average of only 0.52 fewer trials to condition in the second session than in the first. The experimenters concluded that the drug did have the hypothesized effect of making conditioning more difficult.

The effects of stimulant and depressant drugs on a visual threshold were determined in an experiment by Aiba[1]. The stimulant was dextro-amphetamine; the depressant was amylobarbital. The dependent variable was the threshold measure, the intensity of a red light necessary for it to become just visible when it was interrupted by a white surface of fixed luminance. Subjects were three men and two women in a postgraduate course in clinical psychology. Their ages averaged twenty-four years and varied from 21 to 33. All performed better than average in a test of visual acuity.

If, under certain conditions, a colored light is viewed through a sector cut out of a rotating white disk, the light's hue is not seen and in its place a negative after-image, the complementary hue, is seen. The effect occurs when the illumination and speed of rotation are properly adjusted. If the intensity of the colored light is increased, its hue will become apparent at some level. These are the general circumstances under which thresholds were measured. After fifteen minutes of dark adaptation, a subject was told to look at the center of a test patch, indicated by a fixation spot, and to increase the intensity of a red light by turning the knob of a rheostat until he could see the first suggestion of a reddish hue. As soon as he completed the adjustment, dark adaptation was resumed until the next trial. Four trials were conducted in each of six sessions. During intervals between sessions, dark adaptation was continued.

A drug was administered between the second and third sessions on a given day. Dextroamphetamine, amylobarbital, and a placebo were given in capsules of identical appearance. Each subject was given the three drugs in random order over three days, separated by at least a week.

Since a preliminary analysis indicated that thresholds varied widely from day to day, threshold measures were expressed as relative values based on the readings within a given day: the average for the four trials of the first session on a given day was chosen as a reference value for that particular day and this reference value was subtracted from the average for the four trials of each subsequent session on that day. Figure 13-5 shows the average difference measure for each drug plotted against the session number. Compared to the thresholds under the placebo, those under dextroamphetamine were lower in the fourth, fifth, and sixth sessions, while those under amylobarbital were higher on the sixth session. Thus the stimulant made subjects more sensitive to the red light and the depressant made them less sensitive.

There are occasions when time seems to pass very slowly and others when it seems to pass very quickly. If a person was asked to express a judgment when it passed slowly, he would overestimate it; when it passed quickly, he would underestimate it. Is it possible that drugs could affect him in this way? The effects of a stimulant and a sedative on judgments of time were demonstrated by Goldstone, Boardman, and Lhamon[3] in an experiment on ninety medical students and interns.

An audio-oscillator activated by an electronic timer transmitted to a subject, through headphones, a tone of 725 cycles per second for durations varying from one tenth second to two seconds by small steps. The intensity of the tones was moderate and constant. Subjects were divided into three equal groups which were treated differently in the experiment. The first group received quinalbarbital, a sedative drug; the second group received dextroamphetamine, a stimulant; and the third group received a placebo. All drugs were administered orally. Measurements were made prior to administration of the substance, thirty minutes after administration, and sixty minutes after administration.

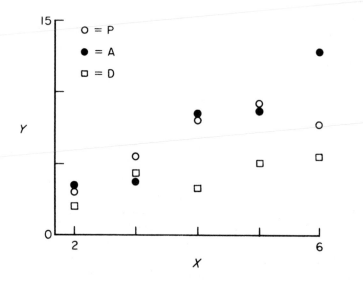

Figure 13-5. The effect of stimulant and depressant drugs on a visual threshold. X is ordinal number of session. Y is the average difference in threshold for each session, expressed in luminance units. The three conditions were amylobarbital (A), placebo (P), and dextroamphetamine (D). [After Aiba.[1]]

Each subject was presented with the tone in a series of varied durations by the method of limits. He was required to respond to each duration with "More" or "Less," indicating a judgment that the duration of the tone was more or less than one second. Twenty alternating ascending and descending series of durations were presented. Each series started at one second and changed by small regular steps. If the subject reported "More" to the first duration of one second, the series descended and terminated when he reported "Less" three consecutive times. If he reported "Less" to the first duration of one second, the series ascended and terminated when he reported "More" three consecutive times. It was possible to determine the length of interval which was judged "more" as often as it was judged "less." This duration was taken as a subject's judgment of the clock second.

All three groups, on the average, overestimated the value of the clock second before the treatments were imposed. Differences between measures obtained before and after treatment were computed. The placebo group and the quinalbarbital group had approximately the same differences for both times after treatment. The dextroamphetamine group was lower than the other groups at both times. Thus the stimulant made time appear to pass more rapidly than did the placebo or the sedative.

Promethazine, a sedative drug, was employed in an experiment by Payne[7] to determine its effect on relearning. Relearning turned out to be more difficult as a consequence of treatment with the drug. Subjects were 128 volunteer basic airmen.

Ten pairs of two-syllable adjectives were typed on the tape of an exposure device. One random order was produced for trials of original learning. Additional random orders were produced for trials of relearning. Three sets of conditions were employed in the experiment: degree of original learning; the order of the adjective pairs during relearning; and drug dosage. There were two conditions for degree of original learning: zero per cent overlearning and fifty per cent overlearning; two conditions for the order of the ten pairs during relearning: the original order fixed from trial to trial and a random order which varied from trial to trial; and two conditions of drug dosage: placebo and promethazine. The number of possible combinations of three conditions, one from each of the three sets, is $2 \times 2 \times 2$ or 8.

Subjects were assigned randomly to the eight combinations of conditions. All were practiced on the original list by the method of anticipation. The cue word in each pair was exposed alone. The subject was instructed to respond by pronouncing the word pair with it. Then both words of the pair were exposed. The next cue word appeared alone, followed by both words, and so on. Exposure of the ten pairs constituted a trial. The criterion of success in learning was two successive correct repetitions of the list. Practice was terminated at this point for subjects who were to have zero per cent overlearning but was continued without interruption for the remaining subjects until they had met the criterion of fifty per cent overlearning, defined as a number of additional trials equal to one half the number required to achieve two successive correct repetitions.

After original learning, subjects were given pink capsules containing either the placebo or the drug. Seventy-five minutes after taking the capsules, they undertook relearning. For half of the subjects, the paired associates were presented in the original order on each relearning trial. For the remaining half, a different order was employed on each relearning trial. Relearning was terminated when the subject had two successive errorless trials. Requirements of health safety were satisfied by appropriate medical supervision.

The dependent variable was the number of trials required to relearn the list to the criterion. Subjects given the drug required more trials in relearning than did those given the placebo; those who overlearned required fewer trials than did the others; and those who overlearned with the original order required fewer trials than did those for whom the order varied. The result of special interest here is that the sedative drug increased the difficulty of relearning.

Chapter Summary

Although biological interventions as conditions of experimentation on human subjects are primarily the business of medical researchers, psychologists do have an important part in this work, especially in the areas of nutrients and drugs. In general they have found that deprivation of food and water affects perceptual behavior; and specifically that perceptual sensitivity for need-related objects increases with deprivation. In experimentation on drugs, in collaboration with medical researchers, effects have been observed on sweating, GSR conditioning, visual perception, judgments of time, and relearning. Public interest in and demand for drugs, especially the tranquilizers, is very high, a circumstance which puts pressure on everyone concerned with public health, for the process of thoroughly evaluating the effects of drugs on behavior is lengthy and tedious. Psychologists with their specialized knowledge of measurement of behavior are making a valuable contribution to this work.

References

1. Aiba, S. "The Effects of Stimulant and Depressant Drugs on the Bidwell Phenomenon." *The British Journal of Psychology,* 51 (1960), 311-318.
2. Gilchrist, J. C., and L. S. Nesberg. "Need and Perceptual Change in Need-Related Objects." *The Journal of Experimental Psychology,* 44 (1952), 369-376.
3. Goldstone, S., W. K. Boardman, and W. T. Lhamon. "Effect of Quinalbarbitone, Dextroamphetamine, and Placebo on Apparent Time." *The British Journal of Psychology,* 49 (1958), 324-328.
4. Laties, V. G. "Effects of Meprobamate on Fear and Palmar Sweating." *The Journal of Abnormal and Social Psychology,* 59 (1959), 156-161.
5. Marquis, D. P. "Learning in the Neonate: The Modification of Behavior Under Three Feeding Schedules." *The Journal of Experimental Psychology,* 29 (1941), 263-282.
6. Mitchell, L. E., and M. Zax. "The Effects of Chlorpromazine on GSR Conditioning." *The Journal of Abnormal and Social Psychology,* 59 (1959), 246-249.
7. Payne, R. B. "An Extension of Hullian Theory to Response Decrements Resulting from Drugs." *The Journal of Experimental Psychology,* 55 (1958), 342-346.
8. Wispé, L. G., and N. C. Drambarean. "Physiological Need, Word Frequency, and Visual Duration Thresholds." *The Journal of Experimental Psychology,* 46 (1953), 25-31.

14

Motivating
Conditions

A CONDITION IMPOSED BY AN EXPERIMENTER FOR THE PURPOSE OF influencing directly the effort or persistence, and indirectly the speed, efficiency, quality, or productivity of a subject's performance is a motivating condition. This definition gives emphasis to the place of the condition in the over-all plan of an experiment. Describing a condition as motivating gives at least partial expression to the experimenter's purpose and hypothesis. One could, of course, distinguish between demonstrated and provisional motivating conditions: the former being those whose effectiveness was already established by research; the latter, those hypothesized to be effective but not yet tested. This distinction is not commonly observed in psychology.

Motive, as typically used, is an indefinite abstract term with a compound referent: an internal biological state, a set of external circumstances related to that state, and either a verbal report of experience or some other behavior associated with the internal state and external circumstances. *Motivating condition,* as defined above, is more definite than *motive* in that it refers to the actual procedures of an experiment and the experimenter's purpose in employing them.

Motivating conditions are positive or negative to some degree. There

421

are conditions of facilitation or frustration, incentive or deterrent, reward or punishment, approval or criticism, praise or reproof, and winning or losing, not all of which have been investigated to equal extents. If one considers amount of research actually done in the past, three major categories emerge: incentives, rewards, and frustrations. Incentives are positively valued objects such as money, candy, prizes, and tokens, offered to subjects for some specified behavior before it occurs, or positively valued treatments such as approval and praise, which subjects find they can earn by certain actions. Rewards are different from incentives in that they are presented after behavior occurs. It is sometimes difficult to distinguish between an incentive and a reward, for a reward given after one action may be an incentive for a subsequent one. Frustrations are negatively valued objects like barriers and obstacles, or events like interference, sensory deprivation, and discontinuance of rewards.

Motivating conditions, when they are effective, constitute a means of control over behavior of the greatest interest and importance to parents, teachers, coaches, leaders, supervisors, and others. The ways in which behavior might be improved are numerous and varied: faster learning, stronger competition, greater persistence in long and arduous undertakings, reducing error or the unnecessary expenditure of energy, achieving higher levels of excellence, getting more work done, surmounting obstacles, overcoming handicaps, concentrating more deeply, attending better to instructions and communications, and the like. Since conditions which—according to the values of a society—*improve* behavior are prized more highly than those which impair it, there is far more opportunity to study improvement than impairment. Nevertheless, knowledge of the effect of imposing frustrations is valuable in suggesting the possible benefit of preventing or removing them, and the wisdom of experimenting to confirm the benefit.

Incentives, rewards, and frustrations have been found to be effective in many experiments, and the conclusion would certainly be justified that, in many practical situations, incentives and rewards are worth trying and frustrations worth removing as ways of improving behavior. One cannot say, however, that incentives and rewards always produce improvement, and that frustrations always produce impairment. There is evidence that incentives and rewards are sometimes not effective and that frustrations occasionally produce improvement, not impairment. Considering these mixed results, it is not surprising that there are numerous and varied theories of motivation.

The Effects of Incentives and Rewards on Perceptual Behavior

We have seen that perceptual behavior is influenced in many ways by the manipulation of stimuli, that visual sensitivity to need related words can be increased by food and water deprivation, and that visual thresholds can be changed by stimulant and depressant drugs. That perceptual behavior can be controlled by incentives and rewards has also been demonstrated experimentally. A reward was shown to affect children's judgments of the size of a token in an experiment by Lambert, Solomon, and Watson[5]. Children engaged in a task using a poker chip to obtain a candy reward. After a time, the experimenters discontinued the reward, and then after another period of time reinstated it. The effects of these procedures on judgments of the size of the poker chip were determined. Subjects were nursery school children. In the first study, there were thirty-two children from the Harvard Nursery School; in the second, twenty-two children from a Salvation Army Nursery School. Their ages varied from three to five years.

Children in both studies were divided into two groups. In each study the task of a child in one group was to turn a crank on a vending machine eighteen times to obtain a white poker chip. When he put the chip into a slot, the apparatus automatically delivered a piece of candy. In the same study the task of a child in the other group was to turn the crank eighteen times, after which he was given a piece of candy. In the first study, both groups worked once a day for ten days; in the second, both worked five times a day for ten days. On the eleventh day, the reward was discontinued. The children worked but no candy was given. They were allowed to continue until they satisfied an arbitrary criterion, three minutes during which they did not turn the handle of the machine. On the twelfth day, the reward was reinstated.

Each child made judgments of the size of the poker chip on four occasions: prior to the experiment, after the ten days of reward, after removal of the reward, and after the reward had been reinstated. The apparatus for obtaining size judgments consisted of a rectangular box with a square ground-glass screen in the center of the front panel. By means of a control knob located at the lower right-hand corner, the diameter of a circular patch of light presented at the center of the ground-glass screen could be controlled. As a child stood in front of the apparatus, the light patch was about eye level and fifteen inches distant from him. The poker chip was pasted on a gray cardboard square, held by the experimenter so that the chip was near the patch. Each child made two adjustments starting from a larger patch, and two starting from a smaller patch.

Data for both nursery schools were combined. Figure 14-1 is a plot of judged size against the four successive occasions on which judgments were obtained. Judged size is expressed as a percentage of the actual diameter of the poker chip. The two sets of points represent the two conditions, chip present and chip absent. On the second occasion, children who had used the chip to get the candy overestimated its size by a larger amount than did the others. The difference between the two groups on each of the other three occasions was so small that it was attributed to error. The effect on the second occasion can be interpreted as indicating that judgments of an object can be influenced by associating it with a reward. Thus parents might be able to control children's judgments through the appropriate use of rewards.

Reward and punishment were shown to have an effect on judgments of length and weight in an experiment by Proshansky and Murphy[11]. College students judged lines and weights under two different conditions: one involving both reward and punishment, the other involving neither. Judgments differed under the two conditions.

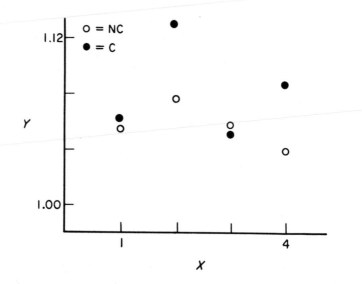

Figure 14-1. The effect of reward on size estimation. X is successive occasions of measurement: before the experiment, after ten days with reward, after removal of reward on the eleventh day, and after reinstatement of the reward on the twelfth day. Y is estimate as a proportion of the token diameter. The two sets of points represent two conditions, chip and no chip. [After Lambert, Solomon, and Watson.[5]]

Nine lines, including three long ones and six short ones, were drawn in black ink on pieces of white cardboard. Lengths varied in each group. Nine weights, including three heavy and six light ones, were made by filling small cans with buckshot. Weights varied in each group. In two sessions per week for five weeks, all subjects were asked to give estimates of the lengths of the lines and the magnitudes of the weights, in a partially darkened room. They were then divided into two groups. In two sessions per week for seven weeks, subjects in the reward-and-punishment group were asked to look at the lines and lift the weights without making any other overt response. As each long line or each heavy weight was presented, a subject was rewarded by giving him fifteen cents. As each of *three* short lines or *three* light weights was presented, he was punished by requiring him to pay fifteen cents. When the other short lines and light weights were presented, he was sometimes rewarded, sometimes punished, according to a planned haphazard schedule. Subjects in the other group were neither rewarded nor punished but were simply shown the lines and the weights. Finally, all subjects were asked to estimate the short lines and light weights which, in the one group, had been both rewarded and punished on a haphazard schedule. Subjects who were rewarded and punished increased the magnitudes of their judgments; the others did not. This means that when reward was connected with long lines and heavy weights, and punishment was connected with short lines and light weights, subjects increased their judgments of short lines and light weights. A conclusion is justified that judgments can in certain circumstances be controlled by the proper use of reward and punishment.

The Effects of Incentives and Rewards on Learning

The effects of incentives on learning in children were investigated by Terrell and Kennedy[14]. The motivating conditions of their experiment were praise, reproof, candy, and token reward, and the dependent variables were acquisition and transposition of a simple discrimination. In acquisition, the child's task was to learn to push a button corresponding to the larger of two three-dimensional geometric objects. In the transposition test, the task was the same, but the objects were changed. Subjects were 160 children, half of them four and five years old and half of them eight and nine years old, from preschools and elementary schools of Tallahassee, Florida.

A pair of cubes, a pair of cones, and a pair of cylinders were the training sets. The two members of each pair had different base areas. The set used for testing transposition consisted of the larger cube of the training set and another cube with a still larger base area. The order of presenting the sets and the spatial position of the members of a set during acquisition were randomly determined for each subject. Figure 14-2 shows the apparatus. A subject faced the narrow end of the base, near which were located two push buttons. Near the middle were two holes or receptacles into which plugs on the objects could be inserted. At the edge of the base distant from the subject was a panel containing a signal light. Pushing the button in line with the larger object was a correct response and turned on the light.

At each age level, children were randomly assigned in equal numbers to the five conditions. Each child in the praise group was told, "That's fine—you are doing well," after each correct response; in the reproof group,

"No, not that—you are wrong," after each incorrect response. Each child in the candy group was given a small piece of candy, which he immediately ate after each correct response, while each one in the token group was permitted to transfer a dried bean from one jar to another after each correct response and was told that as soon as all of the beans were transferred he could have a small bag of candy. Actually, each child in the token group received his candy immediately upon learning the training task, whether or not all the beans were transferred. Each child in a comparison group received no reward. After a child achieved nine out of ten correct responses on the training set, he was given a transposition test of four trials on the test set.

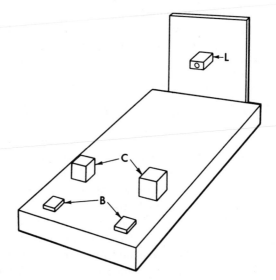

Figure 14-2. Apparatus for discrimination training. L is the signal light; C identifies the two cubes; B identifies the push buttons. [Adapted from Terrell and Kennedy. [14]]

The number of trials required in training and number of correct responses on the transposition test were determined for each child. In training, the candy group learned the task with fewer trials than did any of the other groups. On transposition, the candy group had higher scores than the other groups. Thus in this situation, direct reward with candy turned out to be the most effective motivating condition. This result does not justify a conclusion that candy is always more effective than praise and reproof, or that material rewards are always more effective than personal ones. It does justify the conclusion that, in some circumstances, a material reward may be the most effective.

Bahrick[2] measured the effects of varied incentive conditions on incidental learning, defined as the learning of materials not mentioned in instructions given a subject. His hypothesis was that incidental learning would be better in a group given a weak incentive for the main learning than in a group given a strong incentive. Subjects were seventy-four students in elementary psychology classes.

Fourteen geometric forms were exposed on a memory drum serially at a constant rate. Forms and colors were combined to yield red triangle, gray moon, blue cross, green circle, red moon, black rectangle, blue square, yellow circle, green diamond, brown rectangle, yellow triangle, black square, gray diamond, and brown cross. A complete presentation of all fourteen forms was a trial. Students were divided into two groups. All were told the task was anticipating each *form* before it was exposed, beginning with the second trial. Colors were not mentioned. Instructions intended to provide incentives of different strength for the two groups were then given. The high-incentive group was told, "We want to see how well you can do this task when you are trying your very best. We have been authorized to pay you a bonus ranging from ten cents to one dollar and a half, the exact amount depending upon how many times the list has to be presented before you can anticipate every one of the forms correctly." The low-incentive group was told, "We are interested in finding out whether this task can be learned when you are not trying very hard. Try to pay just enough attention to keep up with the task as you would in listening to a lecture which does not interest you." Training was continued in both groups until the subject could anticipate correctly all fourteen forms on one trial. Immediately after he reached this criterion, he was shown a chart containing seven rows and seven columns of colored forms, representing all possible combinations of form and color. He was asked to point out the color of each of the fourteen forms he had seen on the memory drum.

The high-incentive group required fewer trials than the low-incentive group to reach the criterion of correctly anticipating all forms on one trial. This meant that the high-incentive group had not been exposed as much to color as had the low-incentive group. When an adjustment was made to allow for this difference, however, the low-incentive group still had higher color recognition scores than did the high-incentive group. Thus the hypothesis that incidental learning under a weak incentive would be higher than under a strong incentive was supported. This result justifies the caution that while strong incentives may improve one aspect of learning, they may fail with other aspects. Therefore a teacher should consider the full range of desired outcomes before choosing incentives and formulating instructions as to what should be learned.

Arbitrary Rewards

The connection between a subject's actions and the presenting of a reward is typically defined in terms of the subject's actual success: the reward is given only when the subject achieves a certain kind or level of performance. There has been some experimentation, however, in which arbitrary conditions of reward obtain: the reward is given without regard for the subject's actual behavior. Rewarding on randomly determined occasions is an arbitrary condition; so is rewarding on a systematic schedule, such as every other occasion or every third one. This arbitrary scheduling has been found to be effective in certain circumstances.

Arbitrary rewards resemble many of the benefits which occur in everyday situations. Family life is a good example. Children may receive food, clothing, shelter, toys, attention, and care on a fairly consistent schedule over a long period of time without the precise timing of the presentations to coincide with actions desired by their parents. Even if parents wished to make all such rewards contingent upon specific behaviors, it would be impossible to do so. The program would make tremendous demands on parents' time and energies. Teaching is another situation in which arbitrary rewarding occurs. Some teachers perform many kindnesses for children with problems, regardless of their troublesome behavior. In other words, for a time at least, certain kinds of rewards, such as expressions of friendly interest and concern, are given unconditionally. In dealing with large numbers of students, teachers must necessarily be somewhat undiscriminating in handing out rewards. They cannot possibly manage the highly complex, irregular programming which would be required to make the act of rewarding concomitant with specific behaviors of particular individuals.

The frequency of rewards given arbitrarily as children played games was found to affect their later success in problem solving. Steigman and Stevenson[13] varied the frequency of rewards on three preliminary games and measured the effect on the learning of a discrimination afterwards. The larger number of rewards produced better scores on the learning task. Subjects were thirty-two children attending nursery schools in Austin, Texas. Their ages averaged 4.7 years and varied from 4.1 to five years.

There were three preliminary games: a card game which required a child to select twelve cards from a prearranged deck of black and red cards; a picture game which required him to match twelve cards of different colors with twelve pictures; and a nursery school game which required him to divide a set of twelve pictures of children into two groups corresponding to the nursery schools to which the children "belonged." The main task was the solving of a size discrimination problem, the apparatus for which included three black squares of different size, a gray tray containing three holes, and an opaque screen. The screen prevented a child from observing the experimenter arrange the squares to cover the holes in the tray.

A child was told that he would play some games and that if he played well he could win some prizes. He was also told that he would receive a marble when he made a correct response and that he had to fill a marble board in order to win the prizes, which consisted of balloons, small plastic figures, and other small toys. Two conditions were imposed on the children during the games. Half of them received marbles on two of twelve trials on each game; half received marbles on ten of twelve trials. In the card game, in which a marble was given for drawing a red card, the cards were arranged so that children in one group drew two red cards and those in the other group drew ten. In the picture game and the nursery school game, the experimenter arbitrarily gave marbles for two responses to children in the one group and for ten responses to those in the other group.

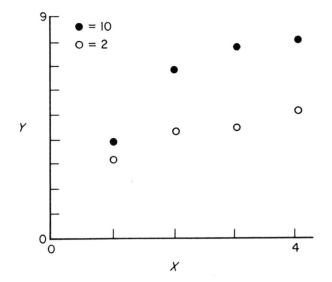

Figure 14-3. The effect of arbitrary rewarding on later problem solving. X is successive blocks of ten trials. Y is mean number of correct responses in problem solving. The two sets of points represent two conditions, rewarding on two and ten of twelve trials on each of three preliminary games. [After Steigman and Stevenson. [13]]

The child was told that the fourth game was his last chance to get enough marbles to fill his board. A marble had been hidden under one of the blocks on the tray and he was to try to find it by choosing a block. For a given child the block under which the marble was hidden was constant, but from one child to another it varied randomly. The criterion for learning was five successive correct responses. Training was stopped after forty trials if the child had not achieved the criterion.

Figure 14-3 is a plot of the number of correct responses made by children in each group against successive blocks of ten trials. After the first ten trials, the two groups differed consistently. Children rewarded on ten trials in the preliminary games had higher scores on the discrimination problem than did children rewarded on only two trials. Thus rewards may have an effect on learning after they have been given arbitrarily in another situation.

The frequency of arbitrary pay-offs in a card game was varied in the conditions of an experiment by Lewis and Duncan[6], and the effect on the number of hands played after pay-offs were terminated was observed. Subjects were 180 student volunteers from introductory psychology classes at Northwestern University.

A subject was instructed to play a kind of poker game with an ordinary deck of cards. He dealt four cards, face up, and then guessed whether or not the hand was a winner. If it was a winner, he was given a nickel; if it was a loser, he was given nothing. He was told to play through the deck, shuffle it, and begin again; to play as long as he wanted; and, when he was finished, to keep the money he had won. He was also told that his guesses had nothing to do with the pay-offs and that pay-offs were determined solely on the cards dealt. Actually, pay-offs were scheduled according to the experimental condition to which he was assigned. His total number of plays and his guesses were recorded.

There were two sets of conditions in the experiment: two percentages of hands—50 and 100—on which the pay-offs occurred; and three lengths of the series of hands—4, 8, and 16—during which pay-offs occurred. The number of possible combinations of two conditions with one from each set was 2×3 or 6. Subjects were assigned to one of these six conditions as they came to the laboratory.

Each student was given a score, the number of hands played after pay-offs were terminated. Percentage of pay-offs did not have an effect on these scores but length of series during which pay-offs occurred did, as shown in Figure 14-4. The longer the series, the smaller the number of hands played after pay-offs ended. In other words, the more accustomed subjects were to the occurrence of rewards, the sooner they quit when rewards were discontinued.

The percentage of guesses of winning was also determined for each subject. Percentage of pay-offs affected guesses: the average was higher for the 100-per-cent condition than for the 50-per-cent condition. Figure 14-5 is a plot of percentage guesses of winning against fourths of trials during pay-offs and sixths of trials after pay-offs were terminated. Points for the 100-per-cent group are higher than those for the fifty-per-cent group. It is not surprising that the largest differences occurred during the third and fourth quarters while pay-offs were given and during the first sixth after they were stopped. Subjects, who were winning more often, made guesses of winning more often. It is interesting to note that

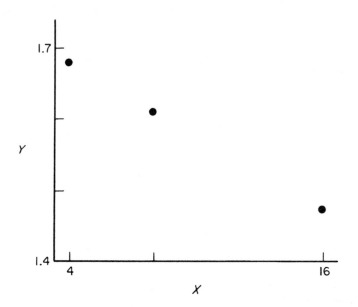

Figure 14-4. The effect of number of trials on hands played in a gambling situation. X is number of trials during which pay-offs were given. Y is mean log of number of trials to quitting after pay-offs were terminated. [After Lewis and Duncan.[6]]

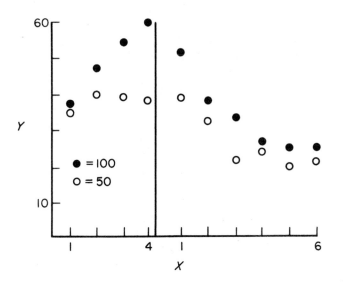

Figure 14-5. The effect of frequency of pay-offs on guessing outcomes in a gambling situation. X is fourths of trials with pay-offs and sixths of trials without pay-offs. Y is percentage of guesses of winning. The two sets of points represent two conditions of frequency of pay-off: 50 and 100 per cent. [After Lewis and Duncan.[6]]

the direction of this difference continued to the end; that is, the influence of different percentages of winning continued throughout the procedure after pay-offs were discontinued. Length of series did not affect guesses.

In an investigation of playing a slot machine after rewards were discontinued, Lewis and Duncan[7] found that playing decreased with increases in percentage of arbitrarily rewarded trials and increased with amount of reward. In other words, subjects who became accustomed to smaller and more frequent rewards quit playing sooner after rewards were terminated than did others. Subjects were 200 students in introductory psychology courses at Northwestern University.

An electrical slot machine, in which a disk the size of a quarter could be inserted, had two lights located near the top and center of its front. The left light was green; the right one, red. Sixteen push buttons were arranged in four columns in the middle of the front. A tray for receiving pay-offs was located at the bottom and near the center. A drawer on one side at the bottom contained a reserve supply of disks. On the right side was a lever.

When a subject put a disk in the slot, the green light came on and a motor inside the box began to run. His task was to push at least one button in each of the four columns. After he had done so, the green light went off, the red light came on, and the sound from the machine changed. The lever, which had been locked, could now be pulled; and when the subject pulled it, a disk dropped into the pay-off tray, if a pay-off was scheduled for that play. The machine was then ready for the next play. The number of plays was registered and accumulated on a counter inside the machine. The machine could be set to pay off on any of the plays. Pay-offs did not depend on the subject's responses.

There were two sets of conditions: five different percentages of plays on which pay-offs occurred; and four different amounts of money for pay-offs. The number of possible combinations of two conditions with one from each set was 4×5 or 20. Ten subjects were assigned to each of the twenty combinations of conditions. Each subject had a series of plays with and without pay-offs. Pay-offs were scheduled during the first nine plays and discontinued thereafter. The five percentages of plays on which pay-offs occurred were 0, 11, 33, 67, and 100, corresponding to pay-offs on none, one, three, six, or nine plays. The amounts of money in pay-offs were one cent, 10, 25, or 50 cents for each disk won.

The subject was told that he could win money if he could outguess the machine by choosing the correct combination of buttons. He was also told how much money he would receive for each disk and that he could play as long as he liked. After he decided to quit, he was paid off with coins. Figure 14-6 shows the effect of percentage of rewarded trials on the number of plays to quitting. Except for the initial small increase, play-

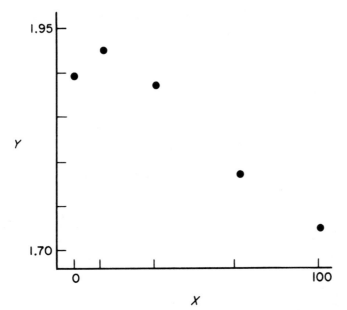

Figure 14-6. The effect of frequency of pay-offs on number of plays to quitting. X is per cent of initial plays with pay-offs. Y is mean log of the number of plays to quitting after pay-offs were terminated. [After Lewis and Duncan.[7]]

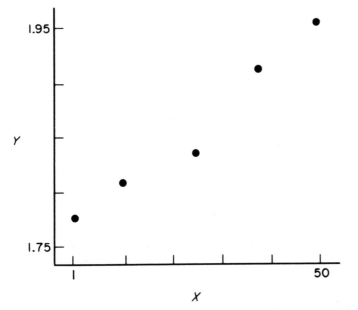

Figure 14-7. The effect of amount of pay-off on number of plays to quitting. X is pay-off in cents. Y is mean log of the number of plays to quitting after pay-offs were terminated. [After Lewis and Duncan.[7]]

ing decreased. Figure 14-7 shows the effect of amount of reward: playing increased with increases in reward.

The results of the three experiments on conditions of arbitrary reward indicate there are situations in which these conditions are effective. All three happen to be concerned with behavior after termination of rewards but it is, of course, possible that behavior is affected at other times. In trying to understand these results, it is important to keep in mind two points: first, subjects could not know the rewards were arbitrary; second, they could not tell when the arbitrary rewards were terminated. If we were to theorize regarding their expectations under the various conditions of the three experiments, their behavior would very likely appear to be consistent with these expectations. For example, we might theorize that children who were rewarded only twice in each of the preliminary games did not expect to get the required number of marbles, whereas those who were rewarded ten times did expect to be successful. Their performances on the size discrimination were consistent with these expectations.

Conditions Not Made Explicit for Subjects

In some experiments the motivating conditions are made explicit at the outset. When they are not made explicit, they are sometimes recognized by subjects as motivating conditions, as an experiment progresses, and sometimes not. When they are not recognized, results are often unpredictable and unexpected. For example, in an experiment on interviewing the occurrence of a nod from the interviewer may be intended as a sign of approval for the subject's behavior. If the experimenter does not say that the nod will occur and is to be interpreted as approval, it may go unnoticed by the subject or, if it is noticed, may be interpreted as disapproval.

There are probably many situations in everyday life where actions by certain people are intended to motivate others who have no idea what the actions signify. What an employer says by way of approval may be so crudely or vaguely expressed as to be interpreted by an employee as grudging acceptance or even veiled criticism. What a parent says by way of approval may be so casually, briefly, and infrequently expressed as to be unnoticed by a child. The failures of many attempts to motivate others may be explained as a failure to communicate approval or disapproval, and praise or reproof.

One way in which approval can affect verbal behavior, and at the same time be unrecognized by a subject, was demonstrated by Cohen, Kalish, Thurston, and Cohen[3] in an experiment in which the subject's choice of first-person pronouns in constructing sentences was approved by comment of the experimenter. Subjects were forty male patients at the

Veterans Administration Hospital in Iowa City. All were general-medical
patients under fifty-five years of age.

Eighty commonly used verbs, written in the past tense, were typed
individually on white cards. Below each verb were typed the six pronouns:
I, we, he, they, she, and you. The order of the pronouns was randomized
for each card. A subject was shown a card and instructed to make up a
sentence beginning with any one of the pronouns and incorporating the
verb. This procedure was repeated until the subject had completed the
eighty cards. The experimenter recorded the sentences verbatim.

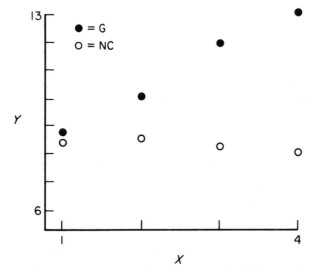

Figure 14-8. The effect of approval on verbal behavior. X is successive trials. Y is
average number of first-person pronouns used. The two sets of points represent two conditions, comment "good" and no comment. [After Cohen, Kalish, Thurston, and
Cohen.[3]]

The subjects were randomly divided into two groups of equal size,
on each of which one of two conditions was imposed. Under one condition, the experimenter said "Good" in a flat, unemotional tone at the end
of any sentence which the subject introduced with *I* or *we*. This treatment
began on the twenty-first card. Under the other condition, the experimenter made no comment on any of the eighty cards. Figure 14-8 shows
the average number of first-person pronouns for four successive blocks
of twenty cards. The number increases in the group given approval while
it does not in the nonapproved group. When questioned at the end, subjects gave no reports of awareness of the relation between their responses
and those of the experimenter. Thus approval was effective, even though
subjects were not aware—or *said* they were not aware—of the kind of
sentence approved.

The effect of an interviewer's behavior on the behavior of an interviewee was investigated by Rogers[12] in testing the hypothesis that an interviewer could produce changes in a subject's verbalization of self-references by consistently responding to the subject in a simple way. The experiment involved interviews with individual subjects in which the interviewee's self-reference verbalizations were followed by the interviewer's simultaneous "Mm-hm" and nod of the head. This behavior on the part of the interviewer is of special interest to psychologists because it is deliberately employed fairly extensively, although not so mechanically, in counseling and psychotherapy of a so-called nondirective type. Subjects were thirty-six male students drawn from an introductory psychology course at Stanford University.

A subject was told that he was participating in a study of how people think and feel about themselves. He was asked to describe his personality characteristics and traits spontaneously without questions or comments from the interviewer. Six interviews for each subject were recorded on tape. Each interview lasted ten minutes.

Subjects were randomly assigned to three conditions: positive, negative, and neutral. Those in the first condition received the interviewer's treatment when they made positive self-references; in the second condition, when they made negative self-references; in the third group, not at all. The interviewer was silent during the first of the six interviews for all subjects.

The tape recordings were studied to identify self-references, and the percentages of positive and negative self-references were determined for the first interview and for the other five interviews combined. The change in percentage, given by the difference between the two, was employed in evaluating the experiment. With respect to positive self-references, the positive group did not change but the other two groups showed a decrease, a result contrary to expectation. With respect to negative self-references, the positive group decreased, the negative group increased, and the neutral group showed no change, results supporting the original hypothesis.

In a structured interview following the experiment, subjects were questioned about the interviewer's behavior. From recordings of these interviews, it was found that not a single subject reported the head nodding. Twenty-three subjects noticed the interviewer's "Mm-hm," but only two reported correctly the connection between the type of verbalization and the interviewer's vocalization. It should be evident that there is much to be learned about the control of behavior through the manipulation of conditions of which people are only vaguely aware or completely unaware.

Odds and Stakes as Incentives

Gambling has incentive features which make it a situation of considerable interest to psychologists. At least two features of betting are usually of concern to the player: the odds or his chances of winning, and the amount at stake. In the long run, he can win a given sum by different combinations of odds and stakes: high odds against winning and high amount to be won; medium odds, and medium amount; or low odds, and low amount. The sum which can be won by any combination, in the long run, can be computed and is called the expected value of a bet. The same principles apply to losing.

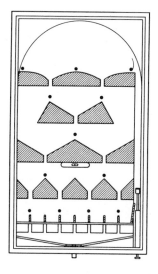

Figure 14-9. Top view of the pin-ball machine. [Adapted from Edwards.[4]]

If a player's goal is to win as much money as possible or lose as little as possible, his best strategy, in making a choice between two bets, is choosing the one with the larger expected value. If all bets have equal expected values, however, then a consequence of this strategy should be that his choices will be equally distributed over the bets. Odds and stakes were manipulated in an experiment by Edwards[4]. He had subjects, twelve undergraduates at Harvard University, express preferences for bets of the same expected value but different odds and stakes.

Figure 14-9 shows the pin-ball machine on which the gambling was done. At the bottom of the machine were eight cells into any one of which the ball could roll. The machine was adjusted to insure an equal distribution of balls into the eight cells.

Three sets of eight bets were formulated: those in the first set all had the same positive expected value; in the second set, a negative expected value; in the third set, an expected value of zero. The first set, in which the expected value was 52.5 cents won, had, as extremes, the two bets:

1. If you roll a four, you win $4.20. If you roll anything else, you win nothing.

2. Regardless of what you roll, you win 53 cents.

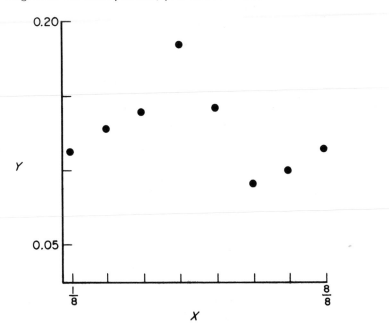

Figure 14-10. The effect of probability and pay-off on preferences for bets. X is probability of winning. (Amount won decreases as probability increases.) Y is number of preferences divided by total number of comparisons. The expected value of each bet was a gain of 52.5 cents. [After Edwards.[4]]

The second set, in which the expected value was 52.5 cents lost, were like those in the first set except *lose* was substituted for *win*. The third set, in which the expected value was zero, included the two extreme bets:

1. If you roll a four, you win $4.20. If you roll anything else, you lose 60 cents.

2. Regardless of what you roll, you neither win nor lose.

Within each set, each bet was paired with every other one. The result was twenty-eight pairs of bets at each of the three levels of expected value. Each pair of bets was typed on a card, yielding a deck of eighty-four cards.

A subject was given twenty-one dollars in chips at the beginning of each of four sessions and was required to return twenty at the end of a session. After he indicated his choice of one of the two bets on a card, he operated the pin-ball machine. If he won, he was given the amount in chips; if he lost, he paid the amount in chips. At the end of the session, his chips were counted and the amount by which they exceeded twenty dollars was his gain; the amount by which they were exceeded by twenty dollars was his loss. (Extra sessions not pertinent to the research were conducted later on to insure that no subject lost money on his participation in the project. He was permitted to recover the amount of his losses and enough more to earn himself one dollar per hour.)

A measure of relative preference was computed by dividing the number of times each bet was preferred by the total number of comparisons made on bets in that set. Figure 14-10 is a plot of relative preference against probability of winning for bets having a positive expected value. The important feature of the plot is its irregularity. The distribution of preferences over the different probability values was not uniform as they should have been if players based their choices solely on long-run winnings. The distribution of preferences in the other two sets was also not uniform. Thus apparently equal motivating conditions turned out to have different effects. This means that subjects chose bets on odds or stakes or some combination of both but not on the basis of long-run winnings.

Frustration

Life imposes many frustrations—some inconsequential, some serious. In psychological experiments, only relatively mild frustrations can be employed. The difficulty of a task may be varied. Subjects may be deprived of a reward they are accustomed to receiving for some particular action; or temporarily deprived of a sense by means of blindfolds, ear plugs, nose clamps, and the like; or deprived of sleep over some moderate period of time. There are also many possibilities for interfering with the completion of a task, placing barriers or obstacles in the way, or putting handicaps on the performer. From experiments with these mild frustrations comes knowledge which may be useful in dealing with serious frustrations on which it is not possible to experiment.

A way of varying the difficulty of anagrams in experimental conditions was devised by Mayzner and Tresselt[8] and the effect of difficulty on time required for solution was determined. Subjects were students from introductory psychology classes at New York University.

The letters in each of 20 five-letter words were numbered in order, 1-2-3-4-5. Ten orders for the letters of an anagram were selected for investigation. Five orders were designated *easy*, because of the similarity of anagram letter order and word letter order: 1-2-3-5-4, 2-3-4-5-1, 5-1-2-3-4, 3-4-5-1-2, and 4-5-1-2-3. Five orders were designated difficult, because of the lack of similarity: 1-4-2-5-3, 2-5-3-1-4, 5-2-4-1-3, 3-1-4-2-5, and 4-2-5-1-3. It was hypothesized that easy anagram orders would require less time for solution than difficult anagram orders, and that anagrams constructed from words used with greater frequency would require less time for solution than those based on words used less often.

Anagrams were constructed from five words from each of four levels of usage frequency: chair, sugar, train, party, and labor from the highest level; beach, model, clerk, halt, and giant from the next highest; patio, cobra, roach, baton, and jaunt from the next to the lowest; and tango, groin, peony, ghoul, and triad from the lowest. The twenty anagrams were typed on cards. Subjects were assigned randomly to the two conditions of the experiment: easy anagram order and difficult anagram order. Solutions were given orally by a subject and times were obtained by stop watch.

It was found that time required for solution of the anagrams was less for the easy condition than for the difficult condition with all four sets of words. The results support the idea that frustration can be manipulated in terms of the order of letters in an anagram. The results for word frequency confirmed the original hypothesis.

When rewards have been given regularly for certain actions over some period of time, terminating the reward is a kind of deprivation and may be considered a frustrating condition. In experimenting with frustrations the choice of subjects has considerable importance for the severity of the effect. Discontinuing a simple reward such as candy is more severe for children than it is for adults, and more severe for mentally deficient children than for normal children. In 1939, Mitrano[9] reported an experiment in which mentally deficient male children from the State Colony at Woodbine, New Jersey were taught to operate two vending machines in succession to obtain candy. For one group, the reward was terminated on one machine and then the other; for the other group, the rewards were terminated in reverse order. The effect on trials to quitting was determined.

Two groups of sixteen subjects were equated by selecting pairs of children roughly equivalent with respect to mental age, chronological age, weight, and body build. The experimenter accompanied a subject from his cottage to the laboratory and, on the way, would praise the subject by words or gestures. When the subject appeared fearful, apprehensive, or reluctant, he was excused from participating. A session with a subject was scheduled two hours after his last meal.

Two vending machines were employed: one yielded a poker chip when a marble was inserted; the other yielded chocolate candy when a poker chip was inserted. The first was called the *marble-chip* machine; the second, the *chip-candy* machine. Instructions on obtaining candy from the machines was given by means of gestures. The experimenter first pointed to marbles on a chair and to the slot in the marble-chip machine. After the subject succeeded in inserting a marble and obtaining a chip, the experimenter pointed to the chip and to the slot of the chip-candy machine. Typically, after obtaining the candy, the subject ate it with very little encouragement from the experimenter. As soon as the subject performed the task satisfactorily, the experimenter went behind a partition and observed him through a one-way vision screen as he continued to operate the machines. He was allowed to operate the machines ten times, after which he was taken to another room.

If the subject was from one group, the chip-candy machine was removed and the marble-chip machine was loaded with marbles instead of chips, so that inserting a marble produced another marble instead of a chip. The subject was then allowed to operate the machine again. After he failed to insert a marble for a period of five minutes, he was taken out of the room and the marble-chip machine was replaced by the chip-candy machine loaded with chips instead of candy so that when the subject inserted a chip he received another chip instead of candy. After he failed to insert a chip for a period of five minutes, the testing was terminated. If the subject was from the other group, the procedure was the same except the order of removing machines was reversed when reward was terminated.

The results showed that fewer trials to quitting were taken on the marble-chip machine when it was first in the termination procedure than when it was second. Thus the order of terminating rewards affected trials to quitting on the marble-chip machine. The order did not affect trials to quitting on the chip-candy machine. It was as if failure of the marble-chip machine was more discouraging when it came first than when it came second. Perhaps its initial failure was more easily comprehended as failure by these mentally deficient children, especially if they were disturbed by the continued frustration.

Deprivation of sensory stimulation while a subject performs a task is a kind of frustration—a handicap which can be imposed experimentally. The effect of auditory deprivation on the perception of obstacles was investigated by Ammons, Worchel, and Dallenbach[1]. They compared the performance of blindfolded subjects wearing ear plugs with the performance of blindfolded subjects not wearing ear plugs in perceiving a barrier erected in their path. Perception was, in general, poorer with auditory deprivation than without. From this result the inference was made that the blind perceive objects through sound reflected from them. Subjects were twenty students, seven women and thirteen men, majoring in psychology at Tulane University. They were naive as to the purpose of the experiment.

The experiment was conducted outdoors on a concrete walk which extended from a door of the psychological laboratory across the campus quadrangle of Tulane University. Both sides of the walk were bordered by grass. Traffic noises, the noises from nearby construction, and noises of students changing classes were clearly audible in the testing area. A blindfolded subject was placed at a starting position and instructed to walk toward an obstacle at a distance unknown to him. The obstacle, a large board, was placed at one of five different distances from the starting position: 6, 12, 18, 24, or 30 feet.

The subject was instructed to stop and raise his right arm when he first perceived the obstacle. If he did so without colliding with it, he was given a signal to approach as close as possible without touching it. He was instructed to stop at this point and raise his left arm. The return to a new starting point was made in a circuitous route over the grass. Thirty trials were completed by a subject during a session of one hour. Daily sessions were scheduled, except on Sunday when the noises were greatly reduced. The subject continued until he had completed eight sessions of thirty trials each or had clearly demonstrated that he had learned to perceive obstacles. The criterion of learning the task was twenty-five successes in thirty trials. Success was scored when the subject reported his first perception and near perception without touching the obstacle. If he did not achieve the criterion in eight sessions, testing was discontinued.

Subjects were divided by chance into two groups of ten each. Those in one group were blindflolded while those in the other group, in addition to being blindfolded, had their ears stopped. (Later, these conditions were reversed for the two groups and the entire experiment was repeated.) Even with their ears stopped, subjects reported hearing intermittently the noises from the area and the noise of their shoes on the walk. They could also understand the experimenter when he spoke very loud.

A general effort was made to encourage subjects to try. They were not prevented from crashing into the obstacle. Their greatest successes were highly praised; their poorer performances and failures were not praised. They were kept informed of the number of trials remaining and were given frequent rests during a session.

All ten subjects who were blindfolded learned to perceive the obstacles. Only six subjects who were blindfolded and had their ears stopped learned. When the experiment was repeated with conditions reversed for the two groups, all subjects except one, in the blindfolded and ear-plugged group, succeeded. The average number of sessions required for the blindfolded group, however, was less than the average number for the blindfolded and ear-plugged group. Subjects who were successful reported that their judgments were based upon "a change in the sound" of their footsteps, and upon the "sudden appearance of a black curtain or shade" before them. Those with ear plugs were observed to increase the loudness of the noise of their footsteps. All the results suggested that audition is important in the perception of objects, especially by the blind.

Preventing a person from satisfying a need is a frustration. This includes preventing him from obtaining food when he is hungry or water when he is thirsty; engaging in sexual activity or urinating when he has the urge to do so; and resting or sleeping when he is tired.

Murray[10] determined the effect of sleep deprivation on the occurrence of sleep themes in stories told to selected cards of the Thematic Apperception Test (TAT). Subjects were soldiers who had volunteered to participate in the research.

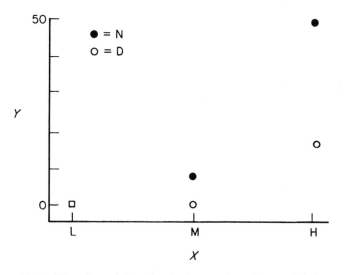

Figure 14-11. The effect of sleep deprivation on sleep themes. X is low, medium, or high level of sleep suggestion of selected TAT cards. Y is percentage of subjects expressing sleep themes. The two sets of points represent the conditions of deprivation and normal sleep. The square represents both conditions. [After Murray.[10]]

Ten subjects were divided into two subgroups, matched on intelligence test scores. There were two conditions in the experiment. Subjects in one subgroup were kept awake, by gentle means, for ninety-eight hours and then observed for four more days while they lived on a hospital ward. Subjects in the other subgroup slept on a nearby ward. Both subgroups were together during the day. Five groups were treated in this way during successive periods.

Ten psychologists selected three TAT pictures as representing high, medium, and low levels of sleep suggestion: several hobos lying around; a boy sitting and looking at a violin; and a man climbing a rope. The three cards were ranked by ten secretaries, assistants, and soldiers with complete agreement. A subject's story, given in response to a card, was scored for sleep themes by a clinical psychologist. Determination was made of the presence or absence of a general sleep theme and four subordinate themes: conditions which produce reports of sleepiness, including going without sleep, eating a full meal, or sitting in a stuffy room; subjective feelings of sleep, including descriptions of sleepiness, drowsiness or grogginess; responses for satisfying the need for sleep, including looking for an opportunity to sleep, making attempts to get to sleep, or lying down to sleep; and sleeping behavior.

Figure 14-11 shows the percentage of subjects in each condition expressing sleep themes plotted against the rank of the three cards. The two sets of points are for the two conditions: deprivation and no deprivation. The difference on the high card was large enough not to be attributed to error, with the deprived subjects giving fewer sleep themes than those allowed to sleep. The experimenter interpreted the results as indicating that subjects were avoiding thoughts and verbal responses which might arouse overpowering sleepiness. He concluded that the results represented the use of mild repression as a way of coping with a conflict between the need for sleep and social pressure to stay awake.

Chapter Summary

Conditions which are intended to control behavior by influencing effort or persistence are said to be motivating. Facilitation, incentives, rewards, approval, praise, and winning are positive conditions; frustration, deterrents, punishment, criticism, and losing are negative. There are many occasions in the family, in schools and colleges, in business, industry, and the military, when knowledge of how to motivate people is extremely valuable.

In general, positive motivating conditions have been found to improve behavior frequently enough to justify recommending their trial in practical situations. Negative conditions have been found to impair behavior, but not universally: some may actually improve behavior under certain circumstances.

Incentives and rewards may affect perception and learning. The arbitrary scheduling of rewards may affect behavior after they have been discontinued. When motivating conditions are not made explicit, they may not be noticed or may be misinterpreted by subjects, and the effects may be unpredictable.

Most of the frustrations investigated in psychology are mild ones like increasing the difficulty of a task, depriving a person of sensory stimulation temporarily, discontinuing an accustomed reward, preventing action to satisfy a need, or interfering with an activity. From them comes knowledge which may be useful in dealing with more serious frustrations.

References

1. Ammons, C. H., P. Worchel, and K. M. Dallenbach. "'Facial Vision': The Perception of Obstacles Out-of-Doors by Blindfolded and Blindfolded, Deafened Subjects." *The American Journal of Psychology*, 66 (1953), 519-553.

2. Bahrick, H. P. "Incidental Learning Under Two Incentive Conditions." *The Journal of Experimental Psychology,* 47 (1954), 170-172.

3. Cohen, B. D., H. I. Kalish, J. R. Thurston, and E. Cohen. "Experimental Manipulation of Verbal Behavior." *The Journal of Experimental Psychology,* 47 (1954), 106-110.

4. Edwards, W. "Probability Preferences in Gambling." *The American Journal of Psychology,* 66 (1953), 349-364.

5. Lambert, W. W., R. L. Solomon, and P. D. Watson. "Reinforcement and Extinction as Factors in Size Estimation." *The Journal of Experimental Psychology,* 39 (1949), 637-641.

6. Lewis, D. J., and C. P. Duncan. "The Effect of Partial Reinforcement and Length of Acquisition Series Upon Resistance to Extinction of a Motor and a Verbal Response." *The American Journal of Psychology,* 69 (1956), 644-646.

7. ———— and ————. "Expectation and Resistance to Extinction of a Lever-Pulling Response as Functions of Percentage of Reinforcement and Amount of Reward." *The Journal of Experimental Psychology,* 54 (1957), 115-120.

8. Mayzner, M. S., and M. E. Tresselt. "Anagram Solution Times: A Function of Letter Order and Word Frequency." *The Journal of Experimental Psychology,* 56 (1958), 376-379.

9. Mitrano, A. J. "Principles of Conditioning in Human Goal Behavior." *Psychological Monographs,* 51, No. 230 (1939).

10. Murray, E. J. "Conflict and Repression During Sleep Deprivation." *The Journal of Abnormal and Social Psychology,* 59 (1959), 95-101.

11. Proshansky, H., and G. Murphy. "The Effects of Reward and Punishment on Perception." *The Journal of Psychology,* 13 (1942), 295-305.

12. Rogers, J. M. "Operant Conditioning in a Quasi-Therapy Setting." *The Journal of Abnormal and Social Psychology,* 60 (1960), 247-252.

13. Steigman, M. J., and H. W. Stevenson. "The Effect of Pre-Training Reinforcement Schedules on Children's Learning." *Child Development,* 31 (1960), 53-58.

14. Terrell, G., Jr., and W. A. Kennedy. "Discrimination Learning and Transposition in Children as a Function of the Nature of the Reward." *The Journal of Experimental Psychology,* 53 (1957), 257-260.

15

Experimental Conditioning, Practice, and Operant Training

CONDITIONING, PRACTICE, AND OPERANT TRAINING ARE SOME OF the most effective ways of controlling behavior presently known. Their effectiveness has been demonstrated in a vast number of experiments in which treatments have consisted of variations in conditioning trials, practice trials, or operant schedules. This experimental knowledge of prediction *and* control should be distinguished from nonexperimental knowledge of prediction only. As indicated in an earlier chapter, changes in behavior can be investigated in relation to the successive trials of conditioning, practice, and operant schedules. The result may be the discovery of predictive relations, some of which are of considerable practical value. However, the correct interpretation of these predictive relations requires careful thought, for it would be a mistake to interpret them as evidence concerning a comparison of treatments not actually contained in the investigation.

How can the results of a nonexperimental investigation of conditioning be misinterpreted? If a series of acquisition trials is carried out with twenty pairings of *CS* and *US*, and if five test trials yield responses to *CS* which are considered to be *CR*s, it would be an unjustified interpretation that the pairing was a critical feature of the procedure and that the *CR*s would not have occurred on five test trials after twenty presentations of *CS* alone. It should be obvious that there is no evidence to support the interpretation.

If comparable subjects had been given twenty presentations of *CS* alone and then five test trials, the necessary evidence would be available, for the one group could be compared with the other. The entire procedure would constitute an experiment involving two conditions: twenty pairings of *CS* and *US*, and twenty presentations of *CS* alone.

There is another way in which the interpretation that the pairing was a critical feature of the procedure could be wrong. Suppose comparable subjects had been given twenty trials with *US* alone and then five test trials with *CS* alone. There have been instances in which this has been done and what appeared to be *CR*s occurred with *CS*s on the test trials, although no pairing was involved. This kind of result has been called *pseudoconditioning*.

A complete experimental demonstration of the effect of conditioning requires three comparable groups of subjects and three conditions: a set number of trials with *CS* alone; the same number with *US* alone; and the same number with pairing of *CS* and *US*. Each condition is followed by a given number of test trials with *CS*. If *CR*s occur in greater number or with greater magnitude under the pairing condition than under the others, the effect of conditioning is considered demonstrated experimentally and the interpretation that the pairing was a critical feature is justified.

Observed changes in behavior with successive practice trials can also be misinterpreted. If infants are given toilet training for an extended early period, near the end of which they begin to display some success in terms of bladder control and use of the toilet when they are placed on it, it is incorrect to attribute the success to the effects of the practice and to conclude that without it success would not have been achieved. It is entirely possible that a comparable group of infants without toilet training of any kind would have exhibited the same degree of success during the same period. If observations had been made on two comparable groups—one given training, the other not—the investigation would have been an experiment, and evidence on which to base the interpretation would have been obtained.

A final example of misinterpretation involves operant training. A teacher adopts a program to encourage participation in discussion with a new class of students. After each meeting of the class, the teacher approaches and speaks informally to each student who has made a comment or asked a question during that meeting. The student's response in class is the operant behavior; the teacher's action afterwards is the conditional event. The teacher observes a steady increase in participation and attributes it to his deliberate contacts with selected students. It is possible, however, that a similar new class would have shown the same improvement over the same period of time without any contact after meetings. If two similar classes treated differently had actually been observed, there would have been experimental evidence on which to base the conclusion that the training program had been effective.

Experimental Conditioning

Conditioning has been shown to be effective in a wide variety of experiments. These positive results are only achieved, however, when the procedures are carried out with proper care. Students, in their own laboratory work, sometimes fail to achieve success in conditioning experiments because of inadequacies in the procedure. The subject must be instructed so that his attitude neither helps nor hinders the attempt. The events must occur on schedule as predetermined before the procedure begins. Interruptions of all kinds must be avoided. Even with the best execution, of course, some variation in results can be expected. Nevertheless, the proposition that conditioning is an effective means of control of behavior is now so generally accepted that psychologists have turned their attention to many variations in the basic procedure.

Although any one of a variety of reflexes might be employed as the unconditioned response in conditioning, work with human subjects has largely involved two responses: the eye-blink reflex, given to an air puff; and the galvanic skin response, which is closely associated with the secreting reflex of the sweat glands and given to mild shock, a loud noise, or other stimuli.

Eyelid Conditioning

As already noted, acquisition trials in conditioning procedure involve both *CS* and *US,* whereas test trials involve only *CS*. Although the procedure may consist of an uninterrupted series of acquisition trials followed by a series of test trials, it is sometimes varied by interspersing test trials among acquisition trials. The effect of doing so in conditioning the eye blink was investigated in 1939 by Humphreys[11]. Subjects were students from elementary psychology classes at Stanford University. Nine men and thirteen women were assigned to each of three conditions: (1) acquisition with *US* occurring on 100 per cent of trials; (2) acquisition with *US* on fifty per cent of trials; and (3) as many trials with *CS* and *US* paired as in the second condition, but with rest intervals in place of trials with *CS* alone.

A subject's eyelid was connected, by means of a thread, to a light wooden lever on which a small mirror was mounted. Light, reflected from the mirror to a film, magnified any movement of the eyelid. The amplitude of magnified eyelid movement was measured to the nearest millimeter. The *CS* was an increase in illumination of a panel of glass; the *US* was a puff of air to one cornea.

Subjects in the 100-per-cent condition were given ninety-six pairings of light and air puff; those in the fifty-per-cent condition, forty-eight pairings of light and puff, and forty-eight presentations of light alone, randomly interspersed; those in the third condition, forty-eight pairings of light and puff, and forty-eight rest intervals, scheduled as in the fifty-per-cent condition. All subjects had twenty-four extinction trials.

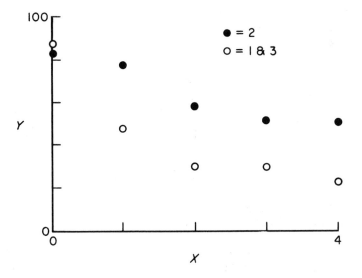

Figure 15-1. The effect of number of pairings of light and air puff in conditioning the eye blink. *X* is successive blocks of six trials during extinction. *Y* is per cent *CR*s. The upper set of points represents the condition of forty-eight pairings of light and puff and forty-eight presentations of light alone. The lower set of points approximates an average for the other two conditions. [After Humphreys.[11]]

The differences among the three conditions during acquisition were so small that they were attributed to error, but not so during extinction. Figure 15-1 is a plot of percentage of *CR*s during extinction as a function of successive blocks of trials: the upper set of points represents the condition with *US* on fifty per cent of trials; the lower set of points represents both of the other conditions. Subjects under the fifty-per-cent condition showed greater resistance to extinction. Thus interspersing test trials among acquisition trials affected extinction but not acquisition.

It has long been known that the magnitude of the temporal interval between the onset of *CS* and that of *US* is an important variable affecting the success of conditioning. In an experiment to demonstrate the effect on conditioning the eye blink, Kimble[13] imposed six different *CS-US* intervals on six groups of subjects formed from sixty-nine undergraduate women in psychology classes at the State University of Iowa. The *CS* was a reddish light; the *US*, an air-puff.

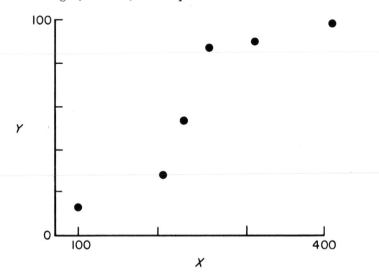

Figure 15-2. The effect of *CS-US* interval on conditioning of the eye blink. *X* is size of *CS-US* interval in milliseconds. *Y* is mean per cent of anticipatory *CR*s for the last block of ten trials in acquisition. [After Kimble.[13]]

The experiment involved six conditions, six different *CS-US* intervals: 100, 200, 225, 250, 300, and 400 milliseconds. One condition was imposed on each of the six groups. Eyelid movement was recorded by photographing the movement of a paper eyelash attached to a subject's eyelid. The air-puff was delivered by the fall of a column of mercury in a manometer, a device for measuring pressure. The tube which delivered the puff to the subject's eye was divided so that one part activated a plastic reed whose shadow was recorded on the photograph. The light was presented for 1,500 milliseconds on each trial; the puff was presented at the appropriate interval after the onset of the light.

Each subject was given fifty-four acquisition trials, with six test trials interspersed, and twenty extinction trials. The *CR* was defined as an anticipatory response, a blink occurring before the air puff. Figure 15-2 shows the mean percentage of anticipatory CRs for the last ten trials before extinction was undertaken, plotted against the length of the CS-US interval in milliseconds. The experimenter concluded that the level of conditioning was an increasing, negatively accelerated function of the length of the CS-US interval. In other words, CRs increased but at a decreasing rate. Figure 15-3 shows the mean percentage of CRs in twenty extinction trials plotted against length of interval. Resistance to extinction increased with length of interval.

The effect of the magnitude of the interval between trials was investigated by Spence and Norris[29] in conditioning the eyelid response to a light. Their subjects were sixty volunteers from an introductory psychology course at the State University of Iowa.

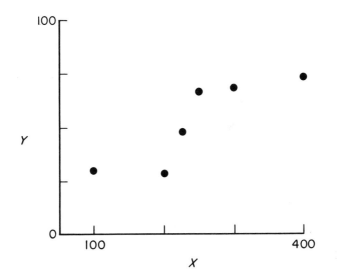

Figure 15-3. The effect of CS-US interval on conditioning of the eye blink. X is size of CS-US interval in milliseconds. Y is mean per cent of CRs during extinction. [After Kimble.[13]]

Eyelid movements were indicated by changes in potential, the electrical condition of the skin, registered by two electrodes placed at the outer edge of the right eye, one below the eyebrow and one just below the eye itself. (Muscle contractions and relaxations are accompanied by changes in electrical potential.) A subject sat in front of a black wall containing a small circular milk-glass window. The CS was an increase in brightness of the window. The US was a puff of air, produced by the fall of a column of mercury in a tube. The puff was delivered to the right cornea. A CR was a change in potential of specified magnitude and latency occurring before the US.

The experimental conditions were four average intervals between trials: 9, 15, 30, and 90 seconds. The intervals between trials varied randomly from six to twelve seconds for the nine-second condition, from ten to twenty for the fifteen-second condition, from twenty to forty for the thirty-second condition, and from 60 to 120 for the ninety-second condition. Subjects were divided into four groups. One condition was imposed on each group. *CS* and *US* were paired on 100 trials in acquisition. Figure 15-4 is a plot of percentage of *CR*s against successive blocks of ten trials. The two sets of points represent the conditions of nine and ninety seconds. The nine-second group was consistently below the other three groups. The conclusion is justified that acquisition depends on the magnitude of the interval between trials.

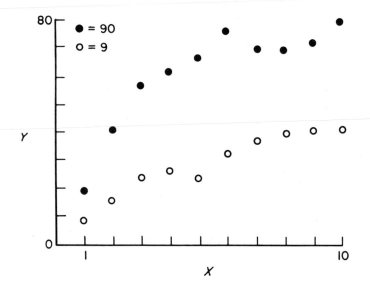

Figure 15-4. The effect of interval between trials on eyelid conditioning. *X* is successive blocks of ten trials. *Y* is per cent of *CR*s. The two sets of points represent the two conditions, nine and ninety seconds. [After Spence and Norris.[29]]

GSR CONDITIONING

The effect of the *CS-US* time interval on conditioning of the *GSR* was investigated by Moeller[22]. Subjects were seventy-five male students from an introductory psychology course.

GSR was recorded as a change in resistance of a subject's palms. The *CS,* white noise, was presented by means of headphones; the *US,* mild electric shock, was presented to the tips of the index and middle fingers of the subject's left hand. To reduce startle responses when the stimuli were presented, subjects were given a concurrent task: vocalizing a free-association to each of fifty nouns exposed on a memory drum. Nouns were presented at the rate of one every thirty seconds. Acquisition and test trials were interpolated between presentations of the words.

Subjects were assigned randomly to four conditions: 250, 450, 1000, and 2500 milliseconds between *CS* and *US*. They received twenty-three acquisition trials, with seven test trials interspersed, and five extinction trials.

Measures of *CR*s were obtained during the seven test trials and five extinction trials. (The first extinction trial was treated as an eighth test trial.) CR was defined as a decrement in resistance of a certain magnitude and latency but was transformed to a change in conductance. Figure 15-5 is a plot of amplitude of *CR* for the last four test trials against magnitude of the interval between *CS* and *US*. Differences among conditions were large enough not to be attributed to error. The optimal *CS-US* interval was 450 milliseconds.

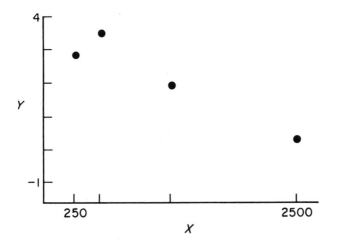

Figure 15-5. The effect of *CS-US* interval on conditioning of *GSR*. *X* is the interval in milliseconds. *Y* is mean amplitude of *CR* in units of conductance. [After Moeller.[22]]

VASCULAR CONDITIONING

Conditioning of changes in the size of blood vessels, demonstrated by Luria and Vinogradova[17] is of special interest because of the verbal stimuli employed. Subjects were ten normal children, eleven to fifteen years of age.

A subject was given a series of words spoken orally by the experimenter as evenly and constantly as possible. Neutral words, defined as words which were not judged likely to evoke any special emotional reaction in the subject, were employed. By means of a glass tube fixed tightly to the skin of a finger on the subject's left hand and connected pneumatically to the recording device, changes in the size of the blood vessels of the finger were registered and recorded on film. Changes in the size of the blood vessels in the temporal region of the head were also recorded by a similar device. When words were first spoken, it was found that they were accompanied by contraction of the blood vessels of the finger and dilatation of the blood vessels of the head surface. After fifteen to twenty different words had been pronounced, however, these reactions diminished and did not occur when additional words were given.

In the next stage, one word was designated as a signal: *koshka* (cat). The subject was told to press a button with his right hand every time he heard the signal word. The button pressing was registered on the photograph along with the vascular reaction of the finger of the other hand. Every time the signal word was given, it was followed not only by the motor reaction of the right hand but also by a vascular reaction, maintained for up to forty repetitions. The presentation of other words evoked neither a motor nor a vascular reaction. The experimenter then presented words belonging to the same semantic system as *koshka* to see if they would be followed by the vascular reaction. The subject gave no motor reaction of his right hand to these words.

Giving the subject a word like *steklo* (glass), *karandash* (pencil), or *oblako* (cloud), having nothing in common in sense or sound with the signal word *koshka,* was not accompanied by a vascular reaction. Giving a word like *kotyonok* (kitten), *mysh* (mouse), *zhivotnoye* (animal), or *sobaka* (dog), connected in meaning to the signal word, was followed by a distinct contraction of the blood vessels of the finger. It was also found that words closely and obviously connected with the signal word evoked larger vascular reactions than words of a general nature connected less closely and obviously with the signal word. Words like *okoshko* (window), or *kroshka* (crumb), which did not have a semantic link with the signal word but did have a phonetic resemblance to it, were not accompanied by the vascular reaction. The results indicate that meaning can be discriminated by the organism by body processes not usually under voluntary and conscious control.

EARLY CONDITIONING OF MOVEMENT

A very unusual experiment in conditioning the human fetus *in utero* was performed by Spelt[28]. It demonstrated that conditioning may occur very early in life situations, even prior to birth. The *CS* was a vibration applied to the abdomen of the pregnant mother; the *US* was a loud noise. Subjects were pregnant women attending the obstetrical clinic of an urban hospital. They were past the seventh month of gestation.

The source of noise was a large wooden box near the subject's bed. A metal framework mounted on the box carried a wooden clapper. When the clapper was raised and released, it struck the box sharply making a loud noise. Conditioned stimulation was achieved by means of a vibrator constructed from an ordinary doorbell. The vibrator, which was held by a movable support attached to the side of the subject's bed, could be positioned so that the striker would vibrate perpendicularly to the surface of any part of the subject's abdomen. Movements of the fetus were re-

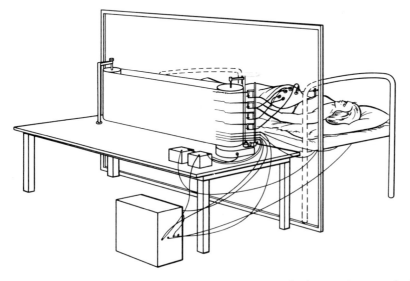

Figure 15-6. The arrangement of subject and apparatus in the experiment on fetal conditioning. The pregnant mother is in the bed behind the screen. Recording tambours are in place on her abdomen. On the table is a long-paper kymograph. The drawing does not show the clapper on the far side of the large box on the floor. [Adapted from Spelt. [28]]

corded by means of three pairs of receiving tambours taped to the subject's abdomen. (A receiving tambour is a device which transforms movement into pressure changes in air and transmits them through tubing to a recording device.) The subject gave a signal when she felt fetal movement by operating a push button which she held in her hand. The occurrence of stimuli and responses were recorded by ink writers which marked on an electrically driven long-paper kymograph. Figure 15-6 shows the arrangement of the subject and the apparatus.

When a subject went to the conditioning room, the operation of the apparatus was explained superficially but the purpose of the investigation was not explained. After the position of the fetus was determined, the recording tambours were put in position. The location of the vibrator was varied from one occasion to another. Typically, a subject had two sessions daily, each lasting from thirty to seventy-five minutes, depending on her reports concerning her comfort.

There were five subjects in the conditioning group. In preliminary testing three of them received a number of successive noises followed by a number of successive vibrations without noise to determine whether movement responses would occur without pairing of *CS* and *US*. The other two received a number of successive vibrations with no noises at all. The vibrator never elicited a response after three successive failures. Conditioning procedure involved presenting the vibrator for five seconds, with the loud noise immediately following. Successive trials were separated by intervals of increasing length.

There were two comparison groups which were treated somewhat differently: one group of six was tested with the vibrator alone during the last two months of pregnancy; another group of three *nonpregnant* subjects served for two conditioning periods.

The results varied considerably from subject to subject, but the investigator concluded that it was possible to establish a *CR* in the human fetus *in utero* during the last two months of gestation. His data indicated that fifteen to twenty paired stimulations were required so that three or four successive *CR*s would be given to the *CS* alone. Additional paired stimulations resulted in as many as eleven successive *CR*s. Experimental extinction, spontaneous recovery, and retention without the *US* over a three-week interval were demonstrated. Agreement was observed between records of fetal movements and reports of fetal movements by the mothers.

CONCLUSIONS

Conditioning has been demonstrated to be an effective means of controlling behavior in a variety of research situations. Since it is not feasible to perform conditioning experiments in everyday situations, the justification of applications must depend on inference. It seems reasonable to infer that conditioning does take place in everyday situations when there is a series of occasions on which pairings of the proper stimuli occur. It also seems reasonable to infer that parents, teachers, and others may deliberately achieve conditioning by appropriate scheduling of the proper stimuli for children. Conditioning has been discussed widely in connection with the development of personality. For example, emotional behavior is often thought to be the consequence of conditioning. There is also the possibility that conditioning may be effective in reducing or eliminating emotional reactions.

Practice Conditions

As everyone knows, practice is a powerful means to many desired ends in skill and knowledge. It would not be difficult at all to plan a great array of psychological experiments demonstrating what is, in fact, already known in everyday life: practice is highly effective in changing behavior of many kinds in many situations. True, it is not always effective, but that should not detract from our appreciation of it as an important way of controlling behavior. Since practice is known to be so widely beneficial, psychologists have turned their attention to some of its less obvious features, the conditions on which its effectiveness depends.

EARLY PRACTICE

Practice is known to be effective over a broad age range, but its benefits at very early ages have not been demonstrated in some areas. Toilet training was investigated and its ineffectiveness demonstrated by McGraw[19] in an experiment with identical twin boys: "One" and "Two". The experiment took place when they were between 41 and 800 days old. Seven hours a day for four days a week were devoted to toilet training. During that time, "One" was placed on a chamber every hour and his positive or negative response to the chamber was recorded. A record was also kept of occasions when he was found wet. "Two" was not placed on the chamber until the age of two years. The mother cooperated by withholding training when "Two" was at home.

A measure of achievement for "One" was calculated by dividing the number of his positive responses to the chamber by the total number of urinations during the seven hours of each day. Multiplication by 100 gave percentage of success. Figure 15-7 is a plot of this percentage against age in days. "One" 's performance was erratic until approximately 700 days. After that age his score was higher than ninety per cent. At the age of two years, "Two" was introduced to the training schedule, which was continued with both children for four months. During this period both children had scores higher than ninety per cent. The early training gave "One" no discernible advantage over "Two". It would be a mistake, of course, to conclude that toilet training in general is not effective, since only one kind of training method was tried. There is the possibility that other kinds will be demonstrated to be effective.

In 1932, Hilgard[8] reported an experiment in training preschool children on the simple skills of buttoning, climbing, and cutting. Subjects, who were children in the Merrill-Palmer Nursery School, were divided into two groups of fifteen, matched on chronological age, mental age, sex, and skill in buttoning, cutting with scissors, and climbing. There were two conditions: training for twelve weeks, and no training. One condition was imposed on each group.

The training group was tested at three weeks and at two-week intervals thereafter. Both groups were tested at the end of twelve weeks, after which the no-training group received intensive practice for four days. While the no-training group was receiving its four days of practice, the training group received no practice. Both groups were tested finally. (Sickness prevented five children in each group from completing the experiment.)

The climbing test required a child to mount a three-step ladder, to step on a table, and then climb down again. The table contained a number of toys. The child's score was the average time required for going up

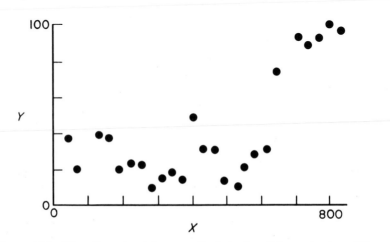

Figure 15-7. The effect of training on toilet behavior. X is age in days. Y is per cent success. Data are for one twin boy who received training. Data for the twin boy who did not receive training until the age of two years are not plotted. If they were, the four points would not be appreciably different from the last four plotted. [After McGraw.[19]]

and down. In the buttoning test, his performance was scored according to the degree of his success or the length of time he took to button cloth strips of varied difficulty. The easiest task involved a folded piece of cloth with four buttons and corresponding holes; a fifth button at the top was already buttoned, so that the four holes were in place over their buttons. In the cutting test, the material was graph paper. On one sheet two vertical red lines were drawn to a standard height and parallel to each other. On another, a line rising to a standard height was drawn at an angle to the base of the sheet. The experimenter gave the child a sheet and told him to cut as carefully as possible along one of the red lines. A scale of scores for successive levels of performance was devised. Deviations

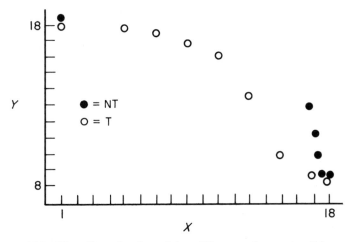

Figure 15-8. The effect of early training. X is successive weeks. Y is mean score in seconds for climbing. The two sets of points represent two conditions, training and no training. [After Hilgard.[8]]

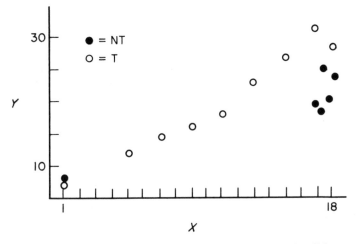

Figure 15-9. The effect of early training. X is successive weeks. Y is mean score for buttoning. The two sets of points represent two conditions, training and no training. [After Hilgard.[8]]

from the red line were obtained by counting the number of squares between the red line and the cut. A system was employed to allow for the distance attained by the child in cutting.

Figure 15-8 is a plot of climbing scores against successive weeks; Figure 15-9, buttoning scores; and Figure 15-10, cutting scores. The two sets of points in each figure represent the training and the no-training groups. The training group exceeded the performance of the no-training group on all tests. One week of practice by the no-training group, however, brought their scores up rapidly. Thus training could be interpreted as more effective in the later period than in the earlier one.

The possibilities of training very young children in discriminating toys are indicated by the report of an experiment by the Russian, Kal'tsova, summarized by Razran[24]. Ten children, twenty months of age, were shown a doll 1500 times in the course of several months. With five of the children the showing was accompanied by the experimenter saying "Here is a doll," "Take the doll," and "Give me the doll." The children reacted appropriately to these comments. With the five remaining children, thirty different comments, such as "Look for the doll," "Rock the doll," "Feed the doll," "Seat the doll," and the like were used. Again the children reacted to the comments.

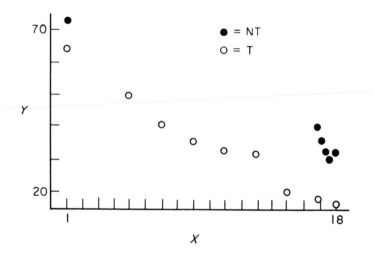

Figure 15-10. The effect of early training. X is successive weeks. Y is average error score for cutting. The two sets of points represent two conditions, training and no training. [After Hilgard.[8]]

After the training, the demonstration doll was placed before each child along with a variety of other dolls and a number of other toys. The child was told, "Pick a doll." Children in the first group selected the demonstration doll along with a number of other toys. Those in the second group selected the demonstration doll and other dolls but not other toys, and reacted much faster than those in the first group. The varied comments to and reactions of the second group apparently produced much more effective discrimination of the doll from other toys.

The evidence from the preceding three experiments on the effects of early practice is typical of many findings. Early practice is sometimes effective, sometimes not; and sometimes more effective at a later age than an earlier age. Parents should take heed and temper their enthusiasm for very early training. It could be a waste of time and effort.

METHODS OF PRACTICE

There are methods of practice which are valuable in controlling one's own behavior, as well as the behavior of others. Students may find the information from experiments on recitation, whole and part learning, overlearning, distributed practice, and knowledge of results more directly applicable to their own activities than any other category of psychological knowledge. This information about methods of practice is, of course, important to anyone responsible for training others.

Recitation

In 1917 Gates[6] reported an experiment in which he compared the effectiveness of different amounts of recitation on memorizing. The materials were nonsense syllables and brief biographies. The subjects were school children in grades three, four, five, six, and eight.

Nonsense syllables were arranged in columns on cards; biographies were typed on sheets of paper. The length of the syllable lists and the number of biographies varied for the different grades. Students in the fifth, sixth, and eighth grades memorized biographies similar to the following: "James Church, born in Michigan, February 15, 1869. Studied in Munich, and later studied forestry and agriculture. Director of Mount Rose Weather Observatory in 1906. Studied evaporation of snow, water content, and frost." Students in the third and fourth grade had simple biographies of boys.

A class of children was divided into a number of groups equal to the number of conditions in the experiment. Each group, consisting of seven or eight children, was tested once a day under one condition over the number of days required for the group to serve under all conditions. The order of conditions varied from one group to another so that each condition occurred once on the first day, once on the second day, and so on. Groups were scheduled so that each condition occurred once at each different hour of the day.

The conditions of the experiment were percentages of time spent in recitation: for nonsense material, five conditions varied from zero to eighty per cent; for biographies, six conditions varied from zero to ninety per cent.

After children were seated at a large table, a copy of the material was placed face down before each one. They were instructed to read the list of nonsense syllables repeatedly until they were given the signal to recite. On signal they were to try to say to themselves as many of the syllables as they could without looking at the card. If they could not remember a syllable, they were to look at the card for a prompt and then continue trying to recite. When time was called, they were to be tested. Instructions for memorizing the biographies were similar. At the end of each memorizing period, the children placed their papers face down and wrote their answers. After three or four hours, the retention tests were repeated.

Recall of nonsense syllables was scored by giving three points for a syllable correct in position and spelling, two points for one correct in position with one letter incorrect, two points for one correct in spelling but not correct in position, and one point for two letters correct but incorrect in position.

The biographies were scored by dividing the original text into units. One point was given for the correct reproduction of each unit given under the appropriate name. When a unit was correctly reproduced but attributed to the wrong name, half a point was given. Sometimes a fraction of a point was given for units partly correct, according to the judgment of the scorer.

Figure 15-11 is a plot of average scores and per cent of time spent in recitation for grades four and eight on nonsense syllables. For both grades, as per cent of time increased, average score increased. Figure 15-12 is a plot for the same grades on the biographies. Averages increased with per cent time up to about sixty per cent but then decreased slightly. The results clearly indicated the value of substantial proportions of time in reciting.

Whole and Part Methods of Practice

In mastering a large task, one may have a choice of approaches: practicing the task as a whole; or, after dividing it into parts, practicing each part separately before combining them. The evidence as to the relative effectiveness of the two approaches is mixed: for some tasks, the whole method is better; for some, the part method. The whole method was found to be superior to other methods in an experiment by McGuigan[20] in which subjects were trained to form a block design. Subjects were seventy-two undergraduate women at Hollins College.

Nine female undergraduate majors in psychology were trained as testers. Subjects were randomly assigned to four groups and two subjects in each group were randomly assigned to each tester. The subject's task was to reproduce a standard design from the Kohs Block Design Test. (The Test involves a set of sixteen cubes, the faces of which are either

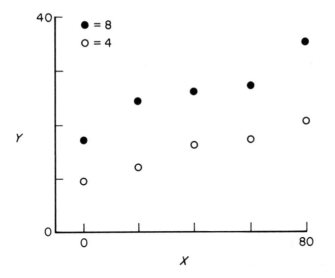

Figure 15-11. The effect of recitation on memorizing nonsense syllables. X is per cent time spent in recitation. Y is average score in recall. The two sets of points represent two different grades, four and eight. [After Gates.[6]]

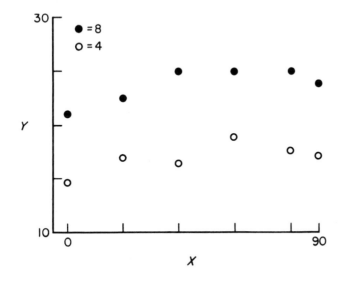

Figure 15-12. The effect of recitation on memorizing sense material. X is per cent time spent in recitation. Y is average score in recall. The two sets of points represent two different grades, four and eight. [After Gates.[6]]

solid colors or two-color designs made up of two triangles formed by a diagonal.) The design was shown to a subject according to each of the four conditions of the experiment: the part method, the very incomplete whole method, the incomplete whole method, and the whole method. Training by each method involved twelve trials on each part of the whole.

The block design was divided into four quadrants, which were covered with pieces of black paper as required for each condition. Subjects dealt with by the part method were given four blocks and only the first quadrant of the design was shown. They reproduced the first quadrant with the blocks, after which each of the other quadrants was shown and reproduced by the subjects. Subjects dealt with by the very incomplete whole method were given eight blocks and half of the design defined by a vertical division. They were instructed to reproduce that half, after which the other half was shown and reproduced. Subjects dealt with by the incomplete whole method had the design divided into two unequal parts. The first, second, and third quadrants were shown and subjects reproduced them. Then the fourth quadrant only was shown and reproduced. In the whole method, the entire design was shown and reproduced.

Following training by the four methods, subjects were presented with all sixteen blocks and the entire design was exposed. Instructions were to reproduce the design as rapidly as possible. Time required to complete the design was recorded. The results indicated that differences among the methods were large enough not to be attributed to error. The order of means from low to high was whole, incomplete whole, very incomplete whole, and part. Thus the least amount of time was required for the whole method, indicating its superiority.

Overlearning

In attempting to master a task one may practice until he achieves some arbitrary standard, such as one errorless performance, and then stop. Is there an advantage in continuing to practice? Going beyond the common standards of mastery is called overlearning. Its advantages have been demonstrated in many situations. Postman[23] investigated its effects on retention with serial lists of words of high and low frequency of usage. Retention was measured in terms of amount recalled and speed of relearning to complete mastery.

There were two types of lists: one containing frequently used words; the other containing infrequently used words. At each frequency level there were two lists, each of which consisted of twelve two-syllable nouns. Two different serial orders for each list were presented on a memory drum at a rate of one word every two seconds with an interval of six seconds between trials. Memorizing was by the method of anticipation.

There were three degrees of overlearning: zero, 50, and 100 per cent. For zero overlearning, practice was terminated at a criterion of one perfect trial; for fifty-per-cent overlearning, practice was continued beyond the criterion for half as many trials as had been required to reach it; for one-hundred-per-cent overlearning, the number of trials to criterion was doubled. The lists were relearned to criterion seven days after the end of original learning.

Figure 15-13 shows the number of items recalled on the first trial of relearning plotted against per cent of overlearning. For both lists the difference between the condition of 100-per-cent overlearning and the other two conditions was large enough not to be attributed to error. Figure 15-14 shows the number of trials required to relearn to criterion plotted against per cent of overlearning. The numbers of trials in relearning decreased steadily with degree of overlearning for both lists. Thus overlearning was shown to be effective in both instances.

Distributed Practice

Practice trials can be distributed temporally in many ways. They can be conducted continuously with no time lapse between successive trials; they can be separated by regular intervals measured in seconds, minutes, hours, or days; and they can be separated by intervals of varying length. Continuous trials with no time lapse are said to be *massed;* trials separated by time intervals are said to be *distributed.* The effects of distributed practice have been widely investigated. Although distributed practice has not been found to be superior to massed practice in every situation, it has been found to be so in a wide variety of circumstances and with many different kinds of tasks. In setting up a practice schedule for mastering a task, it is a good general principle to distribute practice over time.

DISTRIBUTED PRACTICE ON SENSORIMOTOR TASKS. Distributed practice was shown to be superior to massed practice in an experiment on star tracing reported in 1930 by Lorge[16]. Three groups of subjects, students in psychology classes at Teachers College, Columbia University, traced a star pattern under varied conditions of distributed practice.

The star-shaped path was cut in a sheet of brass, mounted on a heavy glass plate. Notches in the sides of the path prevented a subject from sliding his stylus along the edges. The brass star, the stylus, and a counter were wired so that contacts between the star and the stylus were registered on the counter. The subject's view of the star was obstructed by a screen placed so he could only see the image of the star in a mirror. The brass plate was marked with a black arrow indicating the direction of tracing, and by two black lines indicating the starting point.

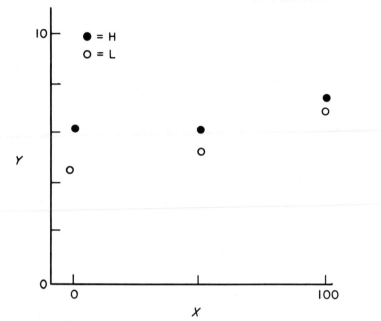

Figure 15-13. The effect of overlearning on recall of a list of words. X is per cent overlearning. Y is mean number of words recalled. The two sets of points represent lists of words of high and low frequency. [After Postman.[23]]

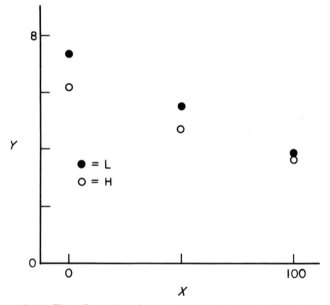

Figure 15-14. The effect of overlearning on relearning of a list of words. X is per cent overlearning. Y is mean number of trials to relearn. The two sets of points represent lists of words of high and low frequency. [After Postman.[23]]

The subject was instructed to trace the star with the stylus in such a way as to avoid touching the brass outline. His performance was paced by keeping the time in seconds and the number of contacts approximately equal. When the number of seconds was greater than the number of contacts, he was told to go faster; when the number of contacts was greater than the number of seconds, he was told to go slower. His score was the sum of the number of contacts and the number of seconds.

Subjects were divided into three groups equated for average score on the first trial. After the first trial, three conditions of practice were imposed: no interval between successive trials; an interval of one minute between trials; and an interval of twenty-four hours between trials. Each

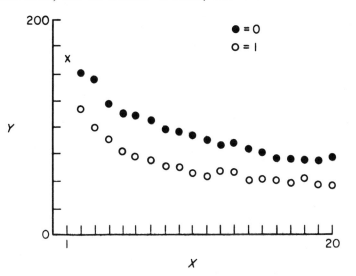

Figure 15-15. The effect of distributed practice on star tracing. X is ordinal number of trials. Y is the average score where an individual score was the sum of errors and seconds. Conditions were no rest and one minute rest between trials. The cross represents the average score for both groups on the first trial. [After Lorge.[16]]

group was given twenty trials. Figure 15-15 is a graph of average score per trial for the groups with no interval and one minute. A decrease in score represents improvement in the sense of a smaller sum for time required and number of contacts. The second group with one minute of time interpolated between trials was uniformly superior to the first group. The third group with one day interpolated between trials was uniformly superior to the second group but only by small amounts.

Distributed practice has been found to be effective in improving performance on a pursuit rotor, as shown by Bourne and Archer[3]. Subjects were 100 women students in introductory psychology courses at the University of Wisconsin.

The pursuit rotor operated at 54 rpm. The target was a silver disk, 0.75 inches in diameter, set in the turntable flush with the surface and five inches from the center. A subject tracked the target with a stylus hinged to prevent her from exerting pressure on the disk. Time on target per trial was recorded automatically. Each subject received twenty-one trials of thirty seconds each. The experiment involved five conditions of varied rest between trials: 0, 15, 30, 45, and 60 seconds. Subjects were assigned randomly to five groups and one condition was imposed on each group. After the twenty-first trial, the subject was given a five-minute

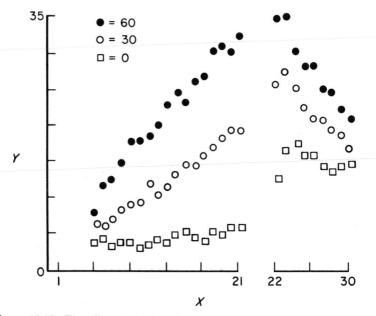

Figure 15-16. The effect of distributed practice on performance on a pursuit rotor. *X* is ordinal number of trials. *Y* is average per cent of time on target. The three sets of points represent three conditions: 0, 30, and 60 seconds of rest. There was a five-minute rest between trials 21 and 22. On the last nine trials, there was no rest between trials. Points are omitted for the first four trials. [After Bourne and Archer.[3]]

rest during which she read or talked with the experimenter. Following the rest, she was given nine trials of thirty seconds each with no interval between trials.

Figure 15-16 shows the percentage of total time on target as a function of the first twenty-one successive trials. The three sets of points represent rest conditions of 0, 30, and 60 seconds. Distribution of practice improved performance on the rotor. Figure 15-16 also shows the performance of the three groups on the last nine trials given with no rest. The groups differed on the first of the nine trials. Differences on the ninth trial were so small they were attributed to error. The improvement in performance on the first trial after the five-minute rest was considered an example of reminiscence.

DISTRIBUTED PRACTICE AND ROTE MEMORIZING. Psychologists have investigated very extensively the effects of distributed practice on the memorizing of nonsense syllables. The results have often shown some superiority for distributed over massed methods. In 1938, Hovland[9] described an experiment in which thirty-two Yale college students, who were paid for their services, memorized lists of nonsense syllables by massed and by distributed practice, with two rates of syllable presentation.

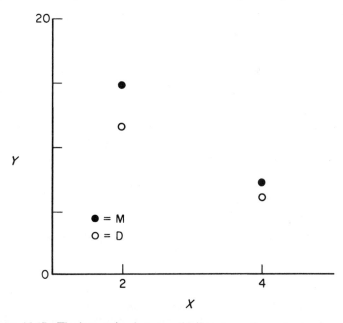

Figure 15-17. The interaction between distributed practice and rate of presentation in memorizing nonsense syllables. X is rate of presentation. Y is mean number of trials required. Condition M involved a rest of six seconds between trials; Condition D, a rest of two minutes and six seconds. [After Hovland.[9]]

In massed practice, only six seconds elapsed between successive presentations of a list; in distributed practice, two minutes and six seconds elapsed. During the period between presentations under distributed practice, subjects were required to name colors so that they could not rehearse. There were two rates of presentation: one syllable every two seconds, and one every four seconds. Four programs of memorizing representing the logically possible combinations of two methods and two rates were employed. A subject, of course, had to have the four programs in some order so they were represented equally often in each ordinal position.

The average numbers of trials required to reach the criterion of one perfect recitation by the four programs are plotted in Figure 15-17 against rate. The conclusion was that distributed practice was superior to massed practice for the two-second rate of presentation. With the four-second rate of presentation, however, the difference was so small that it was attributed to error.

In 1939, Cain and Willey[5] performed an experiment to determine the effects of distributed and massed practice on the recall of nonsense syllables with varied time interval between practice and recall. Subjects were graduate and undergraduate students at Stanford University.

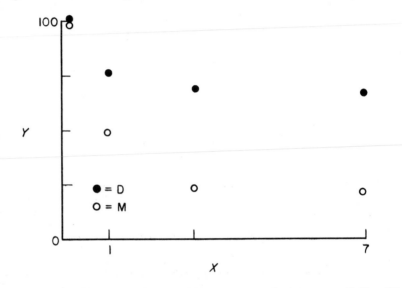

Figure 15-18. The effect of distributed practice on recall of nonsense syllables. X is time in days between learning and relearning. Y is average per cent of syllables recalled on first relearning trial. The two sets of points represent distributed and massed practice. [After Cain and Willey.[5]]

A subject's task was to memorize twelve three-letter nonsense syllables by the anticipation method. He was required to anticipate each syllable by spelling it aloud within the exposure period of the preceding syllable. He continued trials until he achieved one successful anticipation of the entire test. Syllables were exposed on a memory drum for two seconds with an interval of six seconds between trials.

There were two sets of conditions in the experiment: two kinds of practice, massed and distributed, and three different time intervals between learning and relearning. Under distributed practice, subjects worked until they achieved criteria of 6, 9, and 12 syllables on successive days; under massed practice, they worked until they achieved a criterion of twelve syllables in one day. The three time intervals between learning and relearning were one, three, and seven days. There were six possible combinations of conditions and one combination was assigned to each group of ten subjects. Figure 15-18 is a plot of recall scores on first trial of relearning against time interval. Distributed practice was superior to massed practice for all time intervals.

Knowledge of Results

An experimenter may deliberately vary the kinds or amounts of information subjects receive concerning the success of their performances during practice. In other words, he may vary their *knowledge of results*. There has been a substantial amount of experimentation with these conditions and they have been found to be effective in many situations and with respect to many different dependent variables. If one is interested in improving the efficiency of training procedures, it is a good principle to provide the trainee with knowledge of results.

The level of knowledge of a tracking performance was found to affect that performance in an experiment by Smode[27]. The higher level of knowledge produced higher scores for time on target. Subjects were 160 volunteer male undergraduate students from an introductory course in psychology at Ohio State University.

An electronic compensatory tracking apparatus was employed. The tracking display was a voltmeter with a zero at the center of the dial. Deflections of a needle from the zero position on the display were controlled mechanically and electrically. A subject's task was to keep the needle on zero by manipulating a knob. A panel of lights provided information about his achievement. There were three columns of red lights arranged on a black background. Each column of lights was numbered from zero to nine. The lights in the right column represented *units;* those in the middle, *tens;* those in the left column, *hundreds.* The subject's score in half seconds on target could be reported on this panel. Additional information about achievement was provided by clicks delivered through earphones. Clicks occurred at the rate of two per second when the subject was on target. Eleven training trials were given with one minute of rest between trials. Each trial lasted for ninety seconds.

There were two levels of knowledge of results during training trials: a high level consisting of the occurrence of clicks when the subject was on target and the display of his score on the panel of red lights; and a low level consisting of noise in the earphones, but no use of the panel. Subjects in this lower-level condition were told, at the end of each trial, their score for that trial to the nearest second. Subjects were divided randomly into equal groups and one condition was imposed on each group. Figure

15-19 is a plot of time on target against successive training trials. The two sets of points represent high and low levels of knowledge of performance. The high level produced a better performance than did the low level.

Knowledge of results can be given immediately or after a delay. Greenspoon and Foreman[7] found that delaying knowledge of results reduced success in drawing a line of specified length. Subjects were forty undergraduate students at Pomona College.

A subject sat at a small table on which a sheet of glass was fastened. On the glass and fastened to the top of the table was a large L-shaped strip of metal with points marked on it 2.75, 3.00, and 3.25 inches from

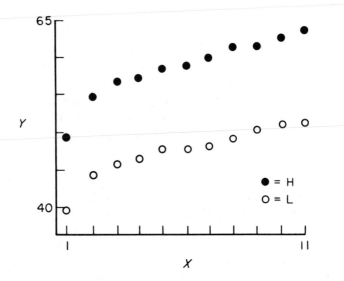

Figure 15-19. The effect of knowledge of performance on tracking. X is successive training trials. Y is average per cent of time on target. The two sets of points represent conditions of high and low levels of knowledge of performance. [After Smode.[27]]

the inner corner of the L. Heavy paper was passed between the glass and the metal strip. The blindfolded subject was instructed to draw a three-inch straight line along the marked branch of the L. When he completed the line, he was to leave his hand where he stopped and the experimenter would return his hand to the starting corner for another trial.

The experimenter placed the subject's hand so that his pencil was at the starting point, the inner corner of the L. The subject drew his line along the edge of the metal strip, after which the experimenter informed him that his line was "long," "short," or "right." A long line was one greater than 3.25 inches; a short line, one less than 2.75 inches; and a right response, one between those two dimensions. Each subject drew fifty lines with an interval of thirty seconds between trials.

The experiment had four conditions of delay: 0, 10, 20, and 30 seconds. Each condition was imposed on one of four groups. After the subject drew his line, the experimenter waited an appropriate interval and then gave the information. When a total of thirty seconds had elapsed, he picked up the subject's hand, advanced the paper, and replaced the hand at the starting point. Subjects in a fifth group were given no information. In this condition, the subject's hand was returned to the starting point thirty seconds after he completed a line.

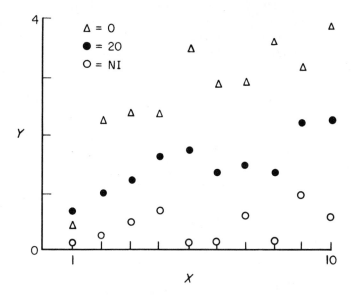

Figure 15-20. The effect of delay in knowledge of results on line drawing. X is successive blocks of five trials. Y is mean number of correct drawings. The three sets of points represent conditions of no information, information with no delay, and information with delay of twenty seconds. [After Greenspoon and Foreman.[7]]

There were differences among the five groups. Figure 15-20 is a plot of the mean number of right or correct responses for successive blocks of five trials. The three sets of points represent the condition of no information and the conditions of information with delays of zero and twenty seconds. The best performance occurred under the condition of no delay; the worst performance occurred under the condition of no information.

If a person, in choosing answers for multiple-choice test items, finds out whether or not his choice is correct, he is receiving knowledge of results. In this situation a correct choice provides positive information whereas an incorrect choice provides what might be called negative information. The larger the number of incorrect answers for an item, the greater the potential amount of negative information, assuming that the subject continues choosing until he gets a correct answer.

Kaess and Zeaman[12] imposed conditions of negative information on students enrolled in an introductory psychology course and observed their performances on a rudimentary teaching machine of the punch-board type. A subject received a test booklet containing 150 multiple-choice items and an IBM answer sheet stapled to a cardboard template with holes positioned beneath correct choices. A punch-board provided two types of knowledge of results: positive information—"This is the correct answer," when a subject's punch perforated the paper; negative information, "This is not the correct answer," when the punch did not break the paper. The subject was instructed to punch each item until there was a perforation signaling the correct answer.

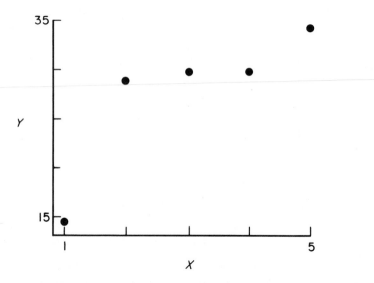

Figure 15-21. The effect of negative information on performance on a teaching machine. X is number of choices per test item. Y is average number of errors. [After Kaess and Zeaman.[12]]

Items for the test were based on definitions of psychological terms. One set of thirty items was used five times in what were called trials. On the first trial the thirty items were presented in a random order; on the second trial they were presented in a different order; on the third, in a still different order; and so on. The order of choices for each item was randomly determined.

Amount of negative information was varied in five conditions by having different numbers of incorrect answers on the first trial only. The first condition had one-choice items; the second condition, two-choice items; the third, three-choice items; and so on. On trials two to five, there were only five-choice items, which were the same for all conditions. The experimental condition under which any subject served was determined by the test booklet he received when the booklets were randomly distributed to a group. The number of subjects for each of the five conditions varied from sixty-two to seventy-five. Figure 15-21 shows the average number of errors on trials two to five for all five conditions. The first condition had the smallest number of errors; the fifth, the largest number. The differences among the second, third, and fourth conditions were small. These results pose an interesting problem of interpretation. A student can learn correct answers without going through the process of distinguishing them from incorrect answers, but does he know more when he can distinguish them? If the discriminations are important ones, then the answer is yes; if they are trivial, however, the answer is no.

Length and Difficulty of Task

The effects of practice depend on the characteristics of the task itself, especially its length and difficulty. Krueger[14] has described an experiment on the memorizing of nonsense syllables in lists which varied in length and difficulty. Subjects were 320 undergraduate students.

The task was to memorize a list of nonsense syllables, spelled by the experimenter at a rate of one every two seconds. After the experimenter completed the list, the subject was given a recognition test in which he was presented with a printed list containing the original syllables and an equal number of new syllables. During the recognition test, the experimenter again spelled aloud each syllable at the same rate and the subject had to mark each syllable as "original" or "new" during the two-second interval. The entire procedure was repeated until the subject had taken twelve recognition tests. His score on a test was the number of original items marked correctly.

The experiment had eight conditions, the possible combinations of one level from each of two sets. One set of conditions was four lengths of list: 5, 15, 50, and 100 items. The other set was two levels of difficulty: low, represented by syllables previously judged to have much meaning; and high, represented by syllables judged to have little meaning. One of the eight conditions was imposed on each of eight groups of subjects.

Figure 15-22 is a plot of averages, converted to per cent of the total, on successive tests for four of the eight lists: 15 easy items, 100 easy items, five difficult items, and 100 difficult items. The experimenter concluded that the nature of the trend with practice depended upon the length and difficulty of the list.

The effect of difficulty on practice on a sensorimotor task was also shown by Krueger[15]. The task was tossing rubber jar rings over a nail in a wall. Difficulty was defined as distance of the subject from the wall. Subjects were eighty undergraduate college students.

The four conditions were four distances of the subject from the wall: 2, 3, 6, and 9 feet. The subject was not allowed to lean forward to hang the rings on the wall. One of the four conditions was imposed on each of four groups of subjects. One trial consisted of ten tosses. The subject's score was the number of rings which remained hooked. Ten trials were completed in each practice session and two practice sessions were con-

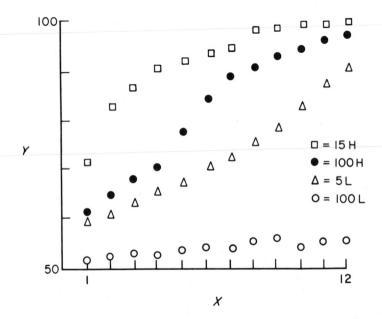

Figure 15-22. The effects of length and difficulty on memorizing lists of nonsense syllables. X is successive tests. Y is average per cent of syllables recognized correctly. The four sets of points represent four combinations of a number of syllables and a level of difficulty, either high or low meaning value. [After Krueger.[14]]

ducted in one day. Except in the two-foot condition, subjects worked on successive days until each one completed 100 trials. Subjects in the two-foot condition had only twelve trials because all of them had made perfect scores on successive trials by the time they completed the twelfth trial.

Figure 15-23 is a plot of average number of successes against every fifth trial. The four sets of points represent the four conditions. Level of performance and rate of change varied from one condition to another. Level decreased with increases in difficulty.

INTERPOLATED EVENTS

Practice on a task may be followed by a period of some other kind of activity before performance on the task is finally measured. What effect does the period of activity have? An answer requires experimentation with at least two conditions differing with respect to the activity interpolated between practice and final measurement.

The sequence of events under a single condition is often described as follows: original trials, intervening or interpolated events, and final

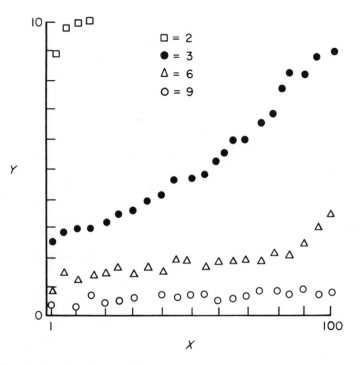

Figure 15-23. The effect of difficulty on perceptual-motor learning. X is the first and every fifth trial. Y is average number of successes. The four sets of points represent four conditions, throwing distances of 2, 3, 6, and 9 feet. [After Krueger.[15]]

measurement. In some experiments, the intervening events are unplanned; in some, they are planned. When they are unplanned, subjects may rest, read magazines, talk, or go on about their usual business. Frequently they are instructed not to practice during the period. It is convenient to designate these periods in terms of the lapse of time, although it should be clear that activity of some kind continues with the passage of time.

When intervening events are planned, they may involve activity quite different from the practice, like naming colors. The experimenter's intent in scheduling color naming is to prevent further practice during that period but not to impair the subject's later performance. The planned events may, however, be practice trials on some new task. For example, the original trials may be readings of a list of nonsense syllables and the intervening events may be trials with a new list. The period of interpolated activity may then be designated in terms of time, trials, or completion of a task.

Interpolated Rest

The effects of varied amounts of rest after varied amounts of practice was determined by Ammons[2] for performance on a pursuit rotor. One of the results was reminiscence—that is, performance at a higher level after rest than before it. His subjects were 510 undergraduate women.

Each of two pursuit rotors had a flat brass target on a disk which rotated clockwise at 60 rpm. A subject tracked the target with a hinged stylus which allowed no more pressure than its own weight on the disk. Duration of contact between stylus and target was recorded on clocks by periods of twenty seconds. Two subjects practiced at the same time. Brief encouraging remarks were made to each subject at intervals of several minutes but at different times for different subjects. Scores obtained in brief initial practice were employed in equating thirty-five groups of subjects. There were two sets of conditions: five initial practice periods of 1/3, 1, 3, 8, and 17 minutes; and seven rest periods of 1/3, 2, 5, 10, 20, 60, and 360 minutes. The number of possible combinations was 5×7 or 35. One combination was assigned to each group with rest always following practice. After rest, all subjects worked continuously for eight minutes. Subjects read magazines during the shorter rest periods but carried on their usual activities during the rest of 60 and 360 minutes.

Figure 15-24 shows percentage of time on target during the first minute after rest, plotted against amount of practice. As one would expect, performance improves with practice. Figure 15-25 shows percentage of time on target during the first minute after rest, plotted against amount of rest. Final performance improves and then falls off with increasing rest. Figure 15-26 is a plot of amount of reminiscence as a function of practice. The amount of reminiscence increased up to eight minutes, then decreased reaching a level at seventeen minutes below that at three minutes. Reminiscence was defined as the gain on the first minute after rest over the level which would have obtained if no rest period had been introduced. The level which would have obtained was extrapolated from a linear equation fitting the practice data.

Rock and Engelstein[25]) performed experiments in which recognition and reproduction of visual forms were measured after varied time intervals following exposure of the forms. There was no change in recognition, but reproduction deteriorated with time. Subjects were students at The New School for Social Research and undergraduates in psychology at The City College of New York.

A subject was shown a closed, rectilinear, asymmetrical form, made up of seven lines. He was then dismissed without being told that the study would be continued. After a time interval, he was recalled and asked either to reproduce the figure or to identify it among other figures. There were two separate experiments, each of which had four conditions —time intervals of fifteen seconds, one day, one week, and three weeks

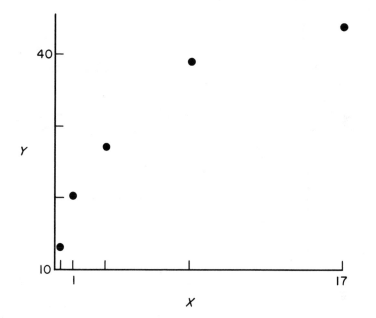

Figure 15-24. The effect of practice on performance on a pursuit rotor. X is minutes of initial practice. Y is average per cent of time on target on first minute after rest. [After Ammons.[2]]

between exposure to the figure and the final test. There were approximately twenty students in each condition in each experiment. Each subject's reproduction was rated by several judges working independently. His final score was the mean of the ratings of all judges. The ten figures used in the recognition test were chosen by four judges from a large group of actual reproductions obtained in another study. These figures were rated on similarity to the original and the ratings were used in scoring the subject's choices. It was found that reproduction deteriorated over time. The results for recognition showed no decline in accuracy over the periods of time employed.

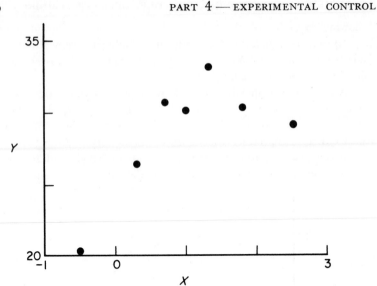

Figure 15-25. The effect of rest on performance on a pursuit rotor. X is log minutes of rest after practice. Y is average per cent of time on target on first minute after rest. [After Ammons.[2]]

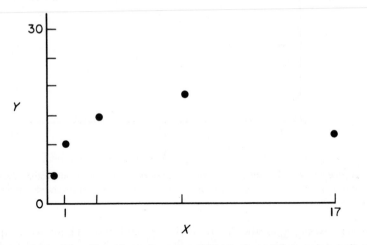

Figure 15-26. The effect of practice on reminiscence in training on a pursuit rotor. X is minutes of initial practice. Y is average amount of reminiscence after rest. [After Ammons.[2]]

Interpolated Color Naming

The effect of interpolated naming of colors on retention of words was investigated by Melton and Stone[21]. Retention declined as the periods of interpolated color naming increased in length. Subjects were twenty-four college students.

The subject's task was to memorize a list of sixteen two-syllable adjectives until he correctly anticipated twelve or more words. Words were presented on a memory drum. Each subject served under all four conditions: six seconds, two minutes, five minutes, and twenty minutes between memorizing and relearning. During the three longest intervals he had to name colors. Finally he relearned the list until he achieved two successive errorless trials. He learned and relearned a different list under a different condition on each of four days. The order of conditions was varied from subject to subject so that each of the twenty-four possible orders for the four conditions was the work schedule for one subject. All subjects practiced the same list on a given day. In naming colors, the subject read from a card containing fifty color samples, starting and stopping on signal from the experimenter.

Figure 15-27 is a plot of correct anticipations on the first relearning trial against interval in minutes. As already noted, retention decreased with increases in size of the interval. Figure 15-28 is a plot of the number of failures to recall adjectives in the various serial positions on the first relearning trial. The two sets of points represent the two intervals, six seconds and twenty minutes. Consistent with the other results, errors are more numerous at twenty minutes than at six seconds. The bow shape of each plot is characteristic of the frequency of errors in serial learning. Syllables near the beginning and the end of the list are memorized with fewer errors than those in the middle.

Interpolated Practice

The effect of interpolated practice on performance of a sensorimotor task has been reported by McAllister[18]. The task, which required coordination of two hands, was performed by eighty-four male student volunteers.

A small target was made to repeat an irregular circular pattern in the horizontal plane at the rate of one revolution per minute. A subject's task was to keep a small button on top of the target by manipulating two handles by a standard procedure and its reverse. In the standard task, the subject had to turn one handle to move the button to the right or to the left, and the other handle to move it toward himself or away. In the reverse task, he had to turn the handles in the opposite directions to produce movements the same as those of the standard task. A trial was defined as half a revolution of the target, the period of thirty seconds during which the target was near the subject. Original and final practice were done with the standard procedure but interpolated practice was done with the reverse.

The experiment had two sets of conditions: four levels of original practice on the standard task and two levels of interpolated practice on

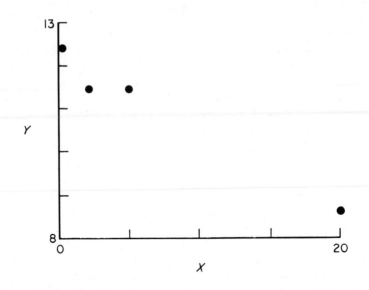

Figure 15-27. The effect of color naming on retention of two-syllable adjectives. X is size of interval in minutes. Y is mean number of correct anticipations on first re-learning trial. [After Melton and Stone.[21]]

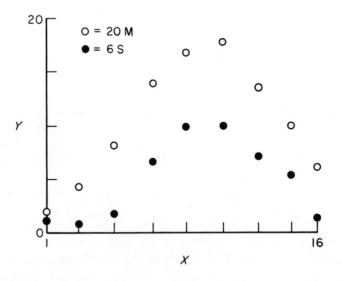

Figure 15-28. The effect of rest interval on retention of two-syllable adjectives. X is serial position. (Extreme scale marks represent the first and sixteenth positions, each intermediate mark represents two positions combined.) Y is number of errors on first recall trial. The two sets of points represent two conditions, six seconds and twenty minutes of rest. [After Melton and Stone.[21]]

the reverse task. Levels of original practice were amounts of time on target achieved in a single trial: 12, 20, and 28 seconds, and 28 seconds plus 30 more trials. Levels of interpolated practice were no practice and practice to the attainment of fifteen seconds time on target on a single trial. The number of possible combinations of conditions was 4 × 2 or 8. One combination of conditions was imposed on each of eight groups of subjects. All eight groups were given forty trials of final practice.

An error was defined as a movement of a handle which increased the distance between the target and the button. Figure 15-29 is a plot of differences in number of errors against the four levels of original practice.

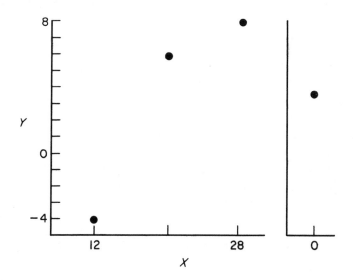

Figure 15-29. The interaction effect of original and interpolated learning on a psychomotor task. *X* is time on target, in seconds, required during original learning. *Y* is a measure of the differential effect of two levels of interpolated learning in number of errors. *O* is the condition of overlearning, 28 seconds on target plus 30 trials. [After McAllister. [18]]

For each group the number of errors on the last trial of original practice was subtracted from the number for the first trial of final practice. Then, for the two groups at each level of original practice, the difference between the two differences was computed. The four differences obtained are the ordinate values in Figure 15-29. Thus the differential effects of interpolated practice are plotted against the level of original practice. The variation in the ordinates is called *interaction*. The trend of the points indicates that the effect of interpolated practice increases with original practice up to a point and then decreases. The experimenter concluded that when practice on one sensorimotor task is followed by practice on a related task, relearning of the original task may be either facilitated or retarded depending on the levels attained during original practice and interpolated practice.

Twining[33] investigated the effect of interpolated practice on recall and relearning of nonsense syllables. Recall was poorer and relearning more difficult as interpolated practice increased. The subjects were seventy-five junior college students.

Five groups of subjects learned a list of nonsense syllables. During the next thirty minutes each group practiced on a number of other lists, the number varying from one group to another. The groups were then tested for their recall of the original list, after which they were required to relearn it. The effects of the interpolated practice could then be determined.

The syllables were exposed one at a time on a memory drum. A subject learned one of six lists by the anticipation method to a criterion of one perfect trial. For interpolated activity, he was given from one to five of the other lists, with ten presentations of each, according to the condition in which he had been placed. Work on the interpolated lists was scheduled in the middle of the thirty-minute period between the completion of the original learning and the beginning of recall and relearning. When he was not working on the interpolated lists, the subject engaged in the playing of a simple game of chance with the experimenter.

Figure 15-30 is a plot of the number of syllables recalled on the first trial for each group against the number of interpolated lists. The number of syllables recalled decreases as the number of interpolated lists increases. Figure 15-31 is a plot of the number of trials in relearning against the number of interpolated lists. The number of trials required for relearning increases as the number of interpolated lists increases. To sum up, interpolated memorizing had an adverse effect on recall and relearning.

The effect of interpolated memorizing of one sentence on recall of another sentence memorized earlier was determined by Slamecka[26] in an experiment on thirty-six students in general psychology at the University of Vermont. Interpolated memorizing had an adverse effect on recall. Memorizing was done by the method of anticipation. The materials were twenty-word sentences, all taken from the same book. Each word in a sentence was exposed on a memory drum. Each sentence constituted a trial.

The sentences were grouped into pairs, in each of which one was used for original memorizing and the other for interpolated memorizing. There were two sets of conditions: three amounts or levels of original memorizing and three of interpolated memorizing. Levels of memorizing were specified in terms of numbers of trials: 2, 4, and 8 for the original; 0, 4, and 8 for the interpolated. Each subject served in three of the nine possible combinations of conditions selected so that he had each level of each set

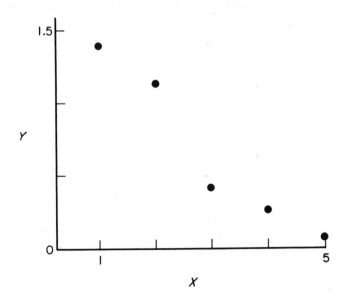

Figure 15-30. The effect of interpolated memorizing on the recall of nonsense syllables. X is the number of interpolated lists. Y is the mean number of syllables recalled. [After Twining.[33]]

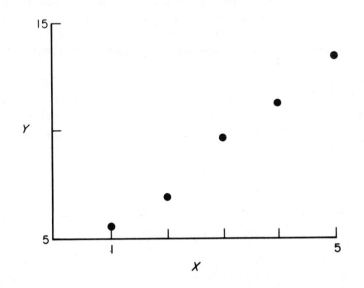

Figure 15-31. The effect of interpolated memorizing on the relearning of nonsense syllables. X is the number of interpolated lists. Y is the mean number of trials in relearning. [After Twining.[33]]

once only. Thus each subject had to memorize three pairs of sentences. The order of the three combinations of conditions and the three pairs of sentences was varied from subject to subject.

Relearning began approximately ten minutes after the completion of the original memorizing. To fill this period under conditions of zero and four trials of interpolated memorizing, subjects were engaged in guessing colors as they were presented in series. Four relearning trials on the original sentence were given finally. (Subjects were also required to relearn the interpolated sentence so they would not become indifferent with respect to interpolated learning in later sessions.)

The measure of recall was the number of correct anticipations on the first relearning trial. Figure 15-32 shows the number of correct anticipations on the first relearning trial for the three conditions of original memorizing. As one would expect, recall improved with increases in the original number of trials. Figure 15-33 shows the number of correct anticipations on the first relearning trial for the three conditions of interpolated memorizing. Recall decreased with interpolated practice.

Summary

In all six experiments on events interpolated between original practice and final testing, the effects with only minor exceptions were adverse. This was true whether the interpolated activity was planned or unplanned. Both kinds of planned activity—color naming and practice on a different task—impaired final performance, but the latter had the greater effect. In extending these results to practical situations, it is clear that a student would be wise to minimize the amount of potentially interfering activity between study and testing. Of course, it is not always possible to do so. Considering these results and the way in which college classes are scheduled, one wonders how much courses interfere with one another and whether there is some optimal schedule yielding minimal adverse effects.

TRANSFER AND TRANSPOSITION

Transfer is demonstrated by an experiment in which each condition requires that subjects practice one task and then another. The conditions vary in either the kind or amount of practice on the first task. Performances on the second task are measured after this practice and the different conditions are compared to determine their relative effects on the performances of the second task. The results of the comparisons are said to be transfer effects. Improvement on the second task is positive transfer; deterioration is negative transfer.

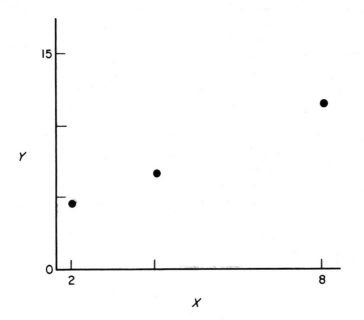

Figure 15-32. The effect of original learning on recall of prose. X is number of trials. Y is average number of correct anticipations. [After Slamecka.[26]]

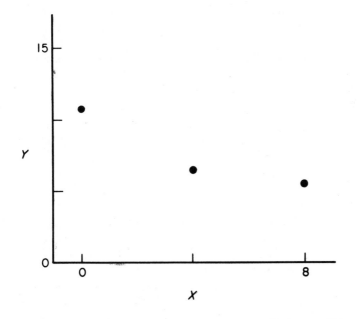

Figure 15-33. The effect of interpolated learning on recall of prose. X is number of trials. Y is average number of correct anticipations. [After Slamecka.[26]]

Transposition is demonstrated by an experiment in which each condition requires that subjects practice one task and then be tested on another related task. For example, a child may be trained to choose the larger of two blocks and then be tested with two balls of different size. In an experiment, two or more conditions which differ with respect to either the training or the testing can be arranged. The experimenter compares test performances to determine the effects of the different conditions. The results of the comparisons are called transposition effects.

If a subject is conditioned to respond to one stimulus and then tested on another stimulus which differs on some dimension, the conditioned response may occur to the different stimulus. If it does, *generalization* is said to have occurred. If one examines the procedures defining transfer, transposition, and generalization, some similarities will be noted. The different terms are useful, however, in distinguishing the procedures. The procedure for a condition in a transfer experiment could be characterized as *practice-practice;* in a transposition experiment, as *practice-test;* and in a conditioning experiment as *conditioning-test.*

Transfer Effects

Conditions of paired-associate learning, which yielded positive and negative transfer effects, were reported in 1933, by Bruce[4]. His experiment involved conditions of initial and subsequent learning of nonsense syllables by the method of paired associates. A syllable and its associate made up a pair in initial practice. A corresponding pair in subsequent practice could contain the old syllable with a new associate, a new syllable with the old associate, or a new syllable and a new associate. Subjects were twenty-seven college students.

An initial list of five pairs of syllables was presented to a subject, 0, 2, 6, or 12 times. A subsequent list of five pairs was then presented repeatedly until he reached a criterion of one perfect trial. Each exposure lasted for two seconds. The subject was presented a syllable, the syllable and its associate, and so on. Subjects were divided into three groups, each of which served under one of three conditions of subsequent practice: old syllable, new associate; new syllable, old associate; and new syllable, new associate. In the first condition, old syllable and new associate, an example of a pair in initial learning was *REQ* and *KIV;* a corresponding pair in subsequent learning was *REQ* and *ZAM.* In the second condition, new syllable and old associate, an example was the initial pair, *LAN* and *QIP,* and the subsequent pair, *FIS* and *QIP.* In the third condition, new syllable and new associate, an example was the initial pair, *XAL* and *POM,* and the subsequent pair, *CAM* and *LUP.* Each subject served under all four conditions of initial practice.

The averages of nine individual scores have been plotted in Figure 15-34 against the four amounts of practice. Individual scores were number of trials required to reach the criterion in subsequent learning. If performance under twelve practice trials is compared with performance under zero trials, slight negative transfer (larger number of trials) is revealed for the first condition, learning a new associate for an old syllable; positive transfer (fewer trials) is revealed for the second condition, learning an old associate for a new syllable; and slight positive transfer (fewer trials) is revealed for the third condition, learning a new associate to a new syllable.

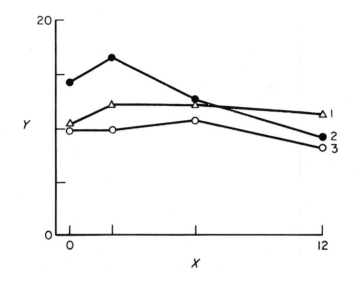

Figure 15-34. The relation between transfer effects and amount of practice. X is number of trials in initial learning. Y is average number of trials required in subsequent learning. Conditions of subsequent learning were: (1) new associate, old syllable; (2) old associate, new syllable; and (3) new associate, new syllable. [After Bruce.[4]]

Stevenson and Moushegian[32] gave three groups of subjects different amounts of training in making a size discrimination and then changed the problem without the subject's knowledge to a position discrimination. The effects of the initial training were determined by comparing performances on the position discrimination. The intermediate amount of initial training produced the best final performance. Subjects were eighty-one students who volunteered from introductory classes in psychology.

Three small square black blocks, a black tray containing three wells, a rubber eraser, and a screen were employed in the training and testing. On each of the blocks was a white square which varied in area from one block to another. The blocks were employed to cover the wells in any one of which the eraser could be concealed. The screen was used to block a subject's view of the arranging of the eraser and the blocks. The subject sat at a table across from the experimenter. After the experimenter showed the subject how the blocks could be used to cover the wells, he told the subject he was going to hide the eraser and the subject was to find it.

Each subject was required to solve two kinds of problems: In one, the location of the eraser was identified by a white square of a certain size; in the other, its location was identified by the position of a well. The experiment involved three conditions of 4, 16, and 40 successive

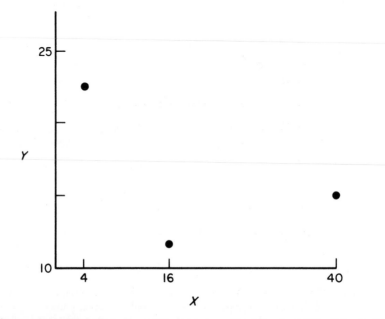

Figure 15-35. The effect of practice prior to a discrimination shift. X is number of correct trials required on a problem in size discrimination. Y is average number of trials required to learn a subsequent problem in position discrimination. [After Stevenson and Moushegian.[32]]

correct responses required during training on the first problem. After training, trials were undertaken on the second problem without comment from the experimenter. Testing continued on the second problem until the subject achieved four successive correct responses. The mean number of trials required to solve the second problem was determined. Figure 15-35 shows the effects of varied number of initial trials on solving the second problem. The experimenters concluded that small amounts of initial training may result in greater difficulty in solving later problems than larger amounts of training.

Transposition Effects

Transposition of size discrimination was investigated by Alberts and Ehrenfreund[1], who trained children in a visual discrimination and tested them for transposition on discriminations varied distances or numbers of steps from the original one. Distance was found to affect transposition for younger children but not older ones. Subjects were forty children from the nursery school of the Home Economics Department of the State College of Washington: a younger group of twenty-two whose ages varied from three years to three years and eleven months; and an older group of eighteen whose ages varied from four years and seven months to five years and five months.

A large black vertical panel with two square openings near its center and seven black boxes were employed. Each of the boxes could be inserted into either of the openings in the panel and curtains could be drawn to conceal both the boxes and the openings. In the front of each box, there was a square white door which varied in area, from box to box over the values: 128, 64, 32, 16, 8, 4, and 2 square inches. If a door was correct in the training trials, the floor of the box was lined with white paper; if it was incorrect, the floor was lined with black paper.

Each child was asked to take part in a game of finding gumdrops. He sat in a small chair about three feet from the center of the panel. The experimenter drew the curtains apart, pointed to the doors with areas of 128 and 64 square inches, and demonstrated how they could be opened. The experimenter said he would hide a gumdrop behind one of the doors and the subject should try to find it by opening one of them. The correct door was the smaller one. When the child was successful, he was given a gumdrop; when he was unsuccessful, the experimenter drew the curtains and told him he would have another opportunity to find the candy. A child was given fifteen trials per school day. Training on the two largest doors continued until he achieved nine correct choices in ten consecutive trials.

On the day after he reached the criterion, the child was given a transposition test of ten trials in which all choices were rewarded. Transposition was tested with door areas of 64 and 32 on four younger children only and, with 32 and 16, 8 and 4, and 4 and 2 on six children from each age group. Children were assigned to the pairs of doors randomly. Figure 15-36 is a plot of percentage of transpositions against the test pairs of areas arranged in order of their distance from the training pair. (The combination 64 and 32 was one step removed; 32 and 16, two steps; and so on.) The square point indicates the criterion score reached by all subjects on the training trials. The difference between the combined value for conditions 64-32 and 32-16, the first and second steps, and the combined value for 8-4 and 4-2, the fourth and fifth steps, for the younger children was large enough not to be attributed to error. The direction of the difference indicated that success in transposition diminished with increasing distance.

Distance of a transposition task from a training task was varied by Stevenson and Bitterman[31] in an experiment with children on the transposition of the concept of middleness in size relations. The results showed that children did better on a transposition task near the original task than they did on a far task.

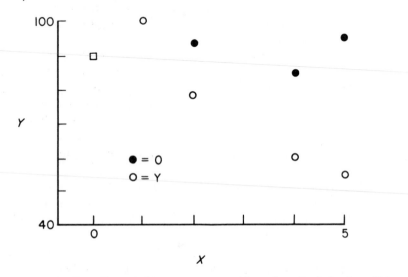

Figure 15-36. The effect of distance on transposition of a discrimination. X is distance in steps removed from the training pair. Y is average per cent of transpositions on ten test trials. The two sets of points represent two groups of subjects, older and younger children. The point plotted above zero is the training criterion. [After Alberts and Ehrenfreund.[1]]

Subjects, twenty-four preschool children between the ages of four and six years, were trained to choose the intermediate object in a set of three objects which varied in size. Tests for transposition were made with new sets of objects a number of steps removed from the training set in size. The materials and apparatus included a small brightly colored egg cut from paper, a set of eight blocks which varied in size, a black tray on which three blocks could be arranged in a row, and a black screen which could be interposed between a subject and the tray. The eight blocks were numbered in order of size from one to eight; the area of the smallest block was four square inches; the area of each successive block increased by a factor of 1.4.

Three blocks were arranged in random order in a row on the tray with the egg hidden under the block of intermediate size. The subject was told the egg was hidden under one of the blocks and he was to try to find it. His first choice terminated the trial. If his choice was incorrect, the blocks were rearranged for another trial. Training continued until the subject had made five consecutive correct choices.

The transposition test consisted of six trials with a set of blocks near to or far from the training set in area. One training set involved blocks one, two, and three. If the test involved two, three, and four, it was called a near test; if it involved six, seven, and eight, it was called a far test. The intermediate block in the transposition set was always correct.

Children were divided randomly into two groups. One condition was imposed on each group. For one group, the condition involved a near test; for the other, the condition involved a far test. The near-test group had a higher number of correct choices than did the far-test group, indicating that distance was effective and that the near test was easier than the far test.

CONDITIONS OF INCIDENTAL LEARNING

An experiment may show that practice on a task improves performance in some respect. If two comparable groups of subjects are employed with one given no practice and the other given ten trials, the practice group may be found to be superior. Suppose the two groups are now tested for skill or knowledge not specified in a statement of the original task and the instructions for performing it. The results may show that the practice group is superior again. This effect is called *incidental learning*. Psychologists have done a substantial amount of experimentation with the conditions on which incidental learning depends.

Stevenson[30] found that the effect of spatial arrangements of test objects on children's incidental learning of the location of those objects in a simple maze depended on age. The subjects were children residing in a housing project of Stanford University and a neighboring residential area. The task was to secure a reward contained in a locked box. A child had to find a key in another box which also contained several objects irrelevant to his task. After several trials at securing the reward, the child was asked to find one of the irrelevant objects.

A large maze in the shape of a V had its starting point at the apex of the V. Goals were located at the ends of the twenty-foot branches of the V. Two small boxes were placed on a small platform at each goal. One box on each platform was painted blue and the other yellow. Each blue box was locked with a large padlock; each yellow box was not locked. Each blue box contained the reward: a bird, flower, or animal sticker. Each yellow box contained the key to the blue box and the irrelevant objects. One of the irrelevant objects in each yellow box was designated the test object. In the yellow box on the left side, the test object was a small purple match box; on the right side, it was a small white flannel purse. The other irrelevant objects were the same in both yellow boxes.

Subjects were divided randomly into three groups of forty-five. In each group there were fifteen subjects at age 3, and ten at each of the ages 4, 5, and 6 years. Each child was tested under one of three conditions which were variations in the spatial relationships of the keys and the irrelevant objects. In one condition, the key lay on the test object and could be gotten without handling the irrelevant objects; in another, the key was under the irrelevant objects and a child had to move the objects to get the key; and in another, the key was in the test object and the child had to pick out the test object and open it to get the key. Each child was given six trials, three with each set of goal boxes, after which he was tested for incidental learning by being shown either a purse or a match box identical with the one in the yellow box, and asked to find another object like the test object. The purse was the test object for half the children; the match box, for the other half.

The proportion of successful children at each age in each condition was determined. The proportion of successful six-year-olds was uniformly high over the three conditions, indicating that the different locations did not affect their performance. The proportion of successful three-year-olds was highest for the condition in which the key lay on the test object, suggesting that the other locations were more difficult for them. The proportions for the intermediate age groups were highest for the third condition, a result which may indicate that the match box and the purse had some special interest for them.

Experimental Operant Training

Operant training is the administration of a schedule of events conditional upon the responses of a subject. The experimenter acts upon the subject in a certain way when the subject acts in a certain way. The subject's behavior is called an operant response; the experimenter's action is called a conditional event. The simplest schedule is the occurrence of the conditional event immediately after every operant response, but many variations of schedule are possible, a fact which implies that the effects of variations in schedule may be studied experimentally.

In an experiment by Hubbard[10], undergraduate men and women from psychology and journalism classes at Indiana University were trained to press keys corresponding to numbers as they were exposed. On initial trials, correct choices were indicated by a tone and light. Thus the operant response was a correct choice and the tone and light were the conditional event. On final trials, different conditions were imposed and the effects observed on correct choices.

A vertical panel mounted on a table separated a subject from the experimenter. To the left of a small aperture located near the top of the panel was a green light; and to the right, a red light. Three keys were mounted in a recess in the table top so that their tops were flush with the surface. The subject could reach any key with his index finger without moving his arm. Figure 15-37 shows the subject's side of the apparatus. Behind the aperture was a shutter, by means of which a number, *1*, *2*, or *3*, was exposed. Each of the three keys corresponded to one of the numbers, but was not so marked. The numbers assigned to the keys from

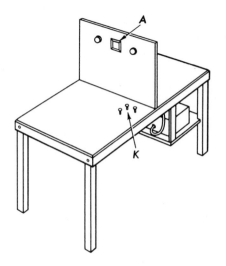

Figure 15-37. Apparatus employed in operant training. *A* is an aperture in which numbers were exposed. *K* is a set of three keys which the subject operated. [Adapted from Hubbard.[10]]

left to right were *3*, *1*, and *2*. The apparatus operated automatically: the green light came on for one second, then the shutter opened, exposing a number for eight seconds; one second after the shutter closed, the green light came on again. The three numbers were exposed repeatedly in random order.

The subject's task was discovering the key which corresponded to each number. The procedure from one green light to the next constituted a trial. Depressing the key corresponding to the number was a correct choice. The subject was told that the green light signaled that the shutter was going to open and that the red light signaled a correct choice had been made. An audio-oscillator emitted a tone of 850 cycles per second when the red light flashed but it was not mentioned as signaling a correct choice. Trials were continued until the subject made nine consecutive correct responses, after which he was given additional training until he had made twenty-one more correct choices. The red light was then suspended without warning while forty more trials were conducted.

Subjects were randomly assigned to two groups: one was given the last forty trials with both light and tone absent, the other was given the last forty trials with the tone only. The number of correct choices was recorded for the last forty trials. The mean number of correct choices with light and tone absent was 15.00; with tone only, 33.19. The difference was large enough not to be attributed to error. The experimenter called the last forty trials extinction trials and interpreted the results as indicating that extinction was slower with the tone present. Thus the tone became a conditional event, although at the beginning nothing was said about its indicating a correct choice. The implications are that events may acquire significance as conditional events in training when they are not explicitly designated as such. Furthermore, it is entirely possible that the person managing the training is not aware that this has happened. Operant responses may continue long after the original conditional events have ceased. One could imagine both desirable and undesirable consequences in everyday life.

Chapter Summary

Knowledge of how to control behavior implies knowledge of how to predict it, but knowledge of prediction does not imply knowledge of control.

Conditioning has been shown to be effective in controlling behavior such as the eye blink and the galvanic skin response. It has been inferred to be effective on emotional behavior, with and without intentional management by a human agent. The effectiveness of practice and operant training is so generally accepted that psychologists focus their attention on variables of which the effects of both are a function. Some kinds of practice are not effective at an early age but become so later.

Practice effects depend upon methods—recitation, dealing with a whole task or its parts, overlearning, distribution, and knowledge of results. It is a good principle, whether in practicing oneself or training others, to devote a substantial amount of time to recitation, to extend practice beyond achievement of a minimal standard, to intersperse practice with rest, and to arrange for continuing knowledge of results. With respect to whole and part methods, it is difficult to generalize but advisable to try different approaches and choose what appears to be the best in any given situation.

The length and difficulty of a task are conditions on which practice effects depend. If a task is very long or very difficult, small amounts of practice may be ineffective. If it is very short or very easy, varied amounts may all produce mastery at levels which are not distinguishable.

Events interpolated between practice and testing generally have an adverse effect on performance. This is especially so when the interpolated event is practice on another task, but is even true when it is rest or an apparently innocuous activity like naming colors.

Transfer is the effect of practice at one task, on practice at another. It may be positive or negative. Transposition is the effect of practice at one task on performance of another.

References

1. Alberts, E., and D. Ehrenfreund. "Transposition in Children as a Function of Age." *The Journal of Experimental Psychology*, 41 (1951), 30-38.
2. Ammons, R. B. "Acquisition of Motor Skill. II. Rotary Pursuit Performance with Continuous Practice Before and After a Single Rest." *The Journal of Experimental Psychology*, 37 (1947), 393-411.
3. Bourne, L. E., Jr., and E. J. Archer. "Time Continuously on Target as a Function of Distribution of Practice." *The Journal of Experimental Psychology*, 51 (1956), 25-33.
4. Bruce, R. W. "Conditions of Transfer of Training." *The Journal of Experimental Psychology*, 16 (1933), 343-361.
5. Cain, L. F., and R. De V. Willey. "The Effect of Spaced Learning on the Curve of Retention." *The Journal of Experimental Psychology*, 25 (1939), 209-214.
6. Gates, A. I. "Recitation as a Factor in Memorizing." *The Archives of Psychology*, 6, No. 40 (1917).
7. Greenspoon, J., and S. Foreman. "Effect of Delay of Knowledge of Results on Learning a Motor Task." *The Journal of Experimental Psychology*, 51 (1956), 226-228.
8. Hilgard, J. R. "Learning and Maturation in Preschool Children." *The Journal of Genetic Psychology*, 41 (1932), 36-56.
9. Hovland, C. I. "Experimental Studies in Rote Learning Theory. III. Distribution of Practice with Varying Speeds of Syllable Presentation." *The Journal of Experimental Psychology*, 23 (1938), 172-190.
10. Hubbard, W. R. "Secondary Reinforcement of a Simple Discrimination in Human Beings." *The Journal of Experimental Psychology*, 41 (1951), 233-241.
11. Humphreys, L. G. "The Effect of Random Alternation of Reinforcement on the Acquisition and Extinction of Conditioned Eyelid Reactions." *The Journal of Experimental Psychology*, 25 (1939), 141-158.
12. Kaess, W., and D. Zeaman. "Positive and Negative Knowledge of Results on a Pressey-Type Punch Board." *The Journal of Experimental Psychology*, 60 (1960) 12-17.
13. Kimble, G. A. "Conditioning as a Function of the Time Between Conditioned and Unconditioned Stimuli." *The Journal of Experimental Psychology*, 37 (1947), 1-15.
14. Krueger, W. C. F. "Rate of Progress as Related to Difficulty of Assignment." *The Journal of Educational Psychology*, 37 (1946), 247-249.
15. ———. "Influence of Difficulty of Perceptual-Motor Task Upon Acceleration of Curves of Learning." *The Journal of Educational Psychology*, 38 (1947), 51-53.

16. Lorge, I. "Influence of Regularly Interpolated Time Intervals Upon Subsequent Learning." *Contributions to Education,* No. 438. New York: Teachers College, Columbia University, 1930.

17. Luria, A. R., and O. S. Vinogradova. "An Objective Investigation of the Dynamics of Semantic Systems." *The British Journal of Psychology,* 50 (1959), 89-105.

18. McAllister, D. E. "Retroactive Facilitation and Interference as a Function of Level of Learning." *The American Journal of Psychology,* 65 (1952), 218-232.

19. McGraw, M. B. "Neural Maturation as Exemplified in Achievement of Bladder Control." *The Journal of Pediatrics,* 16 (1940), 580-590.

20. McGuigan, F. J. "Variation of Whole-Part Methods of Learning." *The Journal of Educational Psychology,* 51 (1960), 213-216.

21. Melton, A. W., and G. R. Stone. "The Retention of Serial Lists of Adjectives Over Short Time Intervals with Varying Rates of Presentation." *The Journal of Experimental Psychology,* 30 (1942), 295-310.

22. Moeller, G. "The CS-US Interval in GSR Conditioning." *The Journal of Experimental Psychology,* 48 (1954), 162-166.

23. Postman, L. "Retention as a Function of Degree of Overlearning." *Science,* 135 (1962), 666-667.

24. Razran, Gregory. "The Observable Unconscious and the Inferable Conscious in Current Soviet Psychophysiology: Interoceptive Conditioning, Semantic Conditioning, and the Orienting Reflex." *Psychological Review,* 68 (1961), 81-147.

25. Rock, I., and P. Engelstein. "A Study of Memory for Visual Form." *The American Journal of Psychology,* 72 (1959), 221-229.

26. Slamecka, N. J. "Retroactive Inhibition of Connected Discourse as a Function of Practice Level." *The Journal of Experimental Psychology,* 59 (1960), 104-108.

27. Smode, A. F. "Learning and Performance in a Tracking Task Under Two Levels of Achievement Information Feedback." *The Journal of Experimental Psychology,* 56 (1958), 297-304.

28. Spelt, D. K. "The Conditioning of the Human Fetus *in Utero.*" *The Journal of Experimental Psychology,* 38 (1948), 338-346.

29. Spence, K. W., and E. B. Norris. "Eyelid Conditioning as a Function of the Inter-Trial Interval." *The Journal of Experimental Psychology,* 40 (1950), 716-720.

30. Stevenson, H. W. "Latent Learning in Children." *The Journal of Experimental Psychology,* 47 (1954), 17-21.

31. Stevenson, H. W., and M. E. Bitterman. "The Distance-Effect in the Transposition of Intermediate Size by Children." *The American Journal of Psychology,* 68 (1955), 274-279.

32. Stevenson, H. W., and G. Moushegian. "The Effect of Instruction and Degree of Training on Shifts of Discriminative Responses." *The American Journal of Psychology,* 69 (1956), 281-284.

33. Twining, P. E. "The Relative Importance of Intervening Activity and Lapse of Time in the Production of Forgetting." *The Journal of Experimental Psychology,* 26 (1940), 483-501.

16

Instructions

and Communications

MUCH OF THE PSYCHOLOGIST'S WORK WITH HUMAN SUBJECTS involves instructions of some kind. Although certain conventional and standard ways of composing and presenting instructions have developed in the various areas of psychology, innumerable variations are possible and many are actually employed. Since different instructions may affect behavior differently, psychologists often experiment with them to determine how they do so.

Instructions are only one type of communication in which psychologists are interested. Others are messages, signs, exposition, suggestion, advertising, propaganda, and teaching. All are powerful means of controlling behavior, or at least they are assumed to be so. The demand for experimental evidence of their effectiveness continues to grow. There are, of course, many characteristics of communications which can be varied experimentally: the length and structure of messages; the size, shape, and color of traffic signs; the approach and organization of explanatory or descriptive writing; direct and indirect suggestion in both speech and writing including commands, hints, requests, threats, and the like; the layout or content of newspaper and magazine advertising; the form of propaganda directed to the public or some foreign country; and

499

ways of teaching such as the order of topics covered, the use of lectures or discussions, the scheduling of classes, and so on. It must be admitted that experimentation is not easy in the everyday settings in which these communications are important. Some of them can be simulated in the psychology laboratory, and when they are, the evidence provided is extremely valuable. It may be possible, of course, to collect data which are not experimental, and in the absence of anything better, decisions may have to be based on them. There is no satisfactory substitute for experimentation, however, and it is wise to try, at every opportunity, to get the best data. The most certain knowledge about the control of behavior through communications comes from their actual use as conditions in experiments.

Instructions

Instructions have been found to influence behavior in many ways intended by the experimenter. This does not mean that they always work, but they have been shown to influence judgments, conditioning, problem solving, learning, and choices. Parents, teachers, and employers would find it generally worthwhile and profitable to give special attention to the formulation of instructions in their dealings with children, students, and employees.

The Effects of Instructions on Judgments of Size

Judgments of the size of objects were shown to be influenced by instructions in an experiment by Gilinsky[3] on male high school students. One set of instructions required subjects to match the actual size of the object; the other required them to match the projected retinal size.

The experiment was conducted outdoors in daylight on a level stretch of grassy terrain. A subject's task was to match the size of a standard object placed at various distances directly ahead of him. He did so by altering the size of a variable object 100 feet distant and somewhat to the right of his line of regard. The objects were white isosceles triangles. They were seen against a background of grass, trees, and buildings at the far end of the field. The four standard triangles varied in size of base from 42 to 78 inches with the altitude of each equal to its base. They were placed upright at six different distances varying from 100 to 4,000 feet. The variable triangle was identical in color and shape to the standard triangles but its size could be varied by raising or lowering it into a pit in the ground. The subject adjusted it by remote control and the result in terms of its altitude was registered at the experimenter's station.

Each subject served under two sets of instructions: to make the variable triangle exactly the same size as the standard; and to make the image of the variable triangle, as it might appear in a photograph, exactly the same size as the image of the standard, as *it* might appear in a photograph. For every combination of a standard triangle and a distance, 32 to 36 subjects were tested. Figure 16-1 is a plot of size of matches against distance for the next-to-largest standard. The two sets of points represent the two sets of instructions. Under the instruction to match actual size the average judgment increases with distance and is

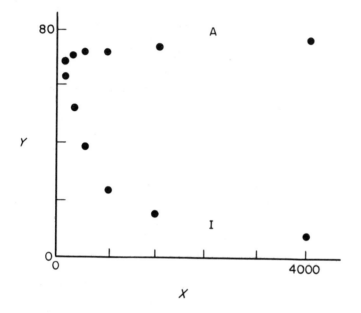

Figure 16-1. The effect of instructions on judgments of size. *X* is distance of standard object from subject in feet. *Y* is average size of matched object in inches. The two sets of points represent the two conditions, instructions to match actual size and instructions to match picture-image size. Data are for the 66-inch standard. [After Gilinsky.[3]]

greater than actual size. Under the instruction to match projected retinal size, the average judgment decreases with distance and is less than actual size. It is evident that instructions must be carefully worded if one is to obtain accurate judgments of either real size or image size.

THE EFFECT OF INSTRUCTIONS ON CONDITIONING

Does what a subject knows about the conditioning procedure make any difference in his responses? Indeed it may, as shown in an experiment on instructions, reported in 1938, by Hilgard, Campbell, and Sears[6].

Subjects in one group were told in advance which of two stimuli was to be the *CS* and which was not; subjects in another group were not given this information. The two groups were compared with respect to the course of a conditioned discrimination.

On the first day, a subject's eyelid response was conditioned to an increase of illumination on the left of two adjacent windows. The *US* was an air-puff delivered to the cornea of the left eye. Sixty pairings of light and air-puff were presented in sets of twelve.

On the second day, the subject was assigned to one of two conditions. Under one condition, he received no new instructions. On half the trials the illumination change occurred on the right window, which had not been illuminated on the first day, and was never followed by the air-puff. The light on the left window was followed by the air-puff as usual. The illumination of the right window was introduced without warning to subjects in this condition. Under the other condition, the subject was informed that the right window occasionally would be illuminated but that it would not be followed by the puff of air and that illumination of the left window would continue to be followed by the puff of air as on the first day. The procedure continued on the third day. Records of ten subjects, whose performances during the first day of conditioning were most nearly comparable, were identified and analyzed.

*CR*s were determined from the photographic records of eyelid movement. The frequency of *CR*s was expressed as a percentage of records on which these responses were found. Figure 16-2 shows the relative frequency of *CR*s within each block of twelve trials on the three days of acquisition. The two graphs represent the two conditions: prior knowledge and no prior knowledge. The difference between the performances of the two groups within the first block of the second day was substantial. The prior knowledge given to one group by instruction facilitated the discrimination. Within a few trials, however, the performances of the groups became nearly equal. In other words, knowledge about the procedure did affect responses but only for a brief period, after which subjects without knowledge caught up on the discrimination. These results are encouraging when one considers what may happen in everyday life. If one is without knowledge of the specific events which will be followed by some circumstance demanding a response, discrimination among them may be slowed but achieved nevertheless before too long a time. The results also indicate the value of instructing people to help them achieve a discrimination of this sort more quickly.

Can a person resist conditioning? Certainly most people would hope so, for the view that the individual is completely helpless when he encounters the stimulus events necessary for conditioning is not an encouraging one. Many kinds of evidence would bear upon the question. One kind would be the effect of instructions to resist conditioning. Specifically the instruction could be not to blink when the *CS* occurred. Evidence is provided by the results of an experiment on instructions by Norris and Grant[14]. Subjects were forty-eight men and women, volunteers from elementary courses in psychology.

The *CS* was an increase in illumination on a circular milk-glass window; the *US* was a puff of air. Movements of a subject's eyelid were recorded by photographing the shadow cast by a lever system connected to the eyelid by a thread and a small piece of adhesive tape. Two sessions were held on successive days. On the first day, there were forty acquisition trials with both *CS* and *US*. On the second day, there were thirty acquisition trials, followed by twenty extinction trials with *CS* alone.

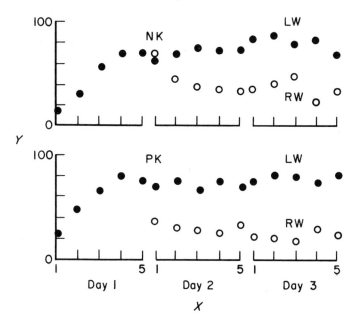

Figure 16-2. The effect of instructions on conditioning of the eye blink. *X* is successive blocks of twelve trials on three successive days. *Y* is per cent of *CR*s. The two plots represent prior knowledge and no knowledge that the left window and not the right window would be accompanied by the *US*. [After Hilgard, Campbell, and Sears.[6]]

Subjects were assigned to six conditions representing all possible combinations of two conditions of instruction and three of shock. The two kinds of instructions were called *inhibitory* and *passive*. Inhibitory instructions were, "Be sure you do not wink before you feel a puff." Passive instructions were, "Do not attempt to control voluntarily your natural reactions to these stimuli. Simply behave naturally and let your reactions take care of themselves." The three conditions in the other set were ways of employing a mild electric shock. In the first condition, shock was given, preceded by an explanation as to the occasions on which it would occur. In the second condition, shock was given with no explanation. In the third condition, no shock and no explanation were given. Subjects received the shock during each conditioned eyelid closure. The shock was delivered to a subject's right wrist.

The percentage and magnitude of CRs were determined for successive blocks of five trials in both acquisition and extinction. Inhibitory instructions reduced the percentage and magnitude of CRs on the last five acquisition trials of the first day, the acquisition trials of the second day, and the extinction trials. Differences among the three ways of employing shock were so small they were attributed to error. The positive results indicate that subjects can resist responding to a conditioned stimulus. One implication is that an individual is not completely at the mercy of conditioning events in life situations. One cannot tell from this experiment, however, just how much tension and fatigue might accompany the resistance to the conditioning.

The Effect of Instructions on Problem Solving

Success in problem solving may depend very much on the kind of instructions given, a fact of which anyone who gives instructions should be aware. This was demonstrated in 1928 by Waters[19]. The subjects were 210 students, most of them in introductory psychology courses at the University of Chicago and the University of Arizona.

A pile of beads was placed before a subject and the experimenter. They drew, alternately, one or two beads at a time. The subject was required to draw first and his task was to manage his draws so that he took the last bead. As soon as he succeeded on three trials in succession, the number in the pile was changed. There were no multiples of three: the first problem had seven beads; the second, eight; the third, ten; the fourth, eleven; the fifth, thirteen; and so on. Trials continued until the subject formulated the general principle upon which he could operate to draw successfully from any number of beads. When he stated the principle, he was considered to have solved the problem. The principle was that, on every draw, he should reduce the number of beads to a multiple of three, or stated in more general terms, he should reduce the number of beads to a multiple of the sum of the two possible draws. When the subject made an incorrect draw, the experimenter took advantage of the error and managed his draws to win. As long as the subject drew correctly, however, the experimenter drew by a systematic method so that all subjects would be treated alike in this respect.

Six different sets of instructions were the conditions of the experiment. (a) Correction. The subject was told that he would be informed whenever he made an incorrect draw and would be required to correct it. (b) Demonstration. He was informed that the experimenter would demonstrate the correct manner of drawing by drawing first and drawing so as to win. Two demonstrations were given at the beginning of each set. (c) Reporting. He was instructed to say aloud the number of beads remaining after each draw. (d) Specific suggestion. He was told, "Always draw so as to leave a multiple of three." (e) Brief general suggestion. He was told, "Always draw so as to leave a multiple of the sum of the highest and lowest possible draws." (f) Lengthy general suggestion. He was told, "The solution of the problem depends upon your leaving, at every draw, a number of beads such as will be exactly divisible by the sum of the highest and lowest possible draws." Subjects were divided into seven groups of thirty. One group was given no special instruction. Each of the remaining groups was given one of the six types of special instruction.

The percentage of successful subjects for the condition of reporting was 90; specific suggestion, 73; correction, 66; no instruction, 50; lengthy general suggestion, 43; brief general suggestion, 40; and demonstration, 33. It is interesting that the simple instruction to report the number of beads remaining after each draw was most effective. Demonstration was least effective but the limited number of occasions may have been its fault. It may be surprising that the general suggestions which actually gave the solution were relatively ineffective. Their generality or abstractness may have been their fault. The implication is that one should not expect the most general instruction necessarily to be the best. It is possible that some simple approach will provide information enough to be very satisfactory.

The advantage of instruction in a systematic approach to problem solving was shown by Katona[7]. He reported an investigation of the effect of instructions on solving a problem involving arranging a deck of cards so they could be dealt in a predetermined order. The subjects were graduate students of psychology in the New School for Social Research.

The experimenter demonstrated the dealing of eight cards alternately one to the table and one to the bottom of the deck with the cards prearranged so that they were placed on the table in the order: red, black, red, black, and so on. One group of subjects memorized the specific arrangement of cards necessary for achieving the desired outcome; another was instructed in using a logical system to discover the necessary arrangement of cards. Subjects were divided by lot into three groups: a memorizing group, a system group, and a group which received no training. The memorizing group learned the specific arrangement of the red and black cards already mentioned and then another problem—the specific arrangement of eight spades necessary for the placing of the cards on the table in order from ace to king. The learning period lasted four minutes. The system group listened for four minutes to an explanation of a systematic method of arranging four red and four black cards but was not shown the problem involving eight spades.

Six problems, the two original ones and four variations, were then given to the three groups. They were allowed four minutes of work on each problem. The results were that more subjects in the memorizing group were successful on the two original problems than in the system group; none of the subjects who received no training solved either of the original problems; and more subjects in the system group were successful on the four variations than in the memorizing group or the no-training group. The results indicate that memorizing should not be discredited completely, for those who memorized the original problems did better on those problems than the others. In undertaking new problems, however, the systematic approach was superior. There are probably many situations in which the quickest and most efficient way to master a particular solution is by memorizing it. If one desires more general mastery, however, it may be well worth the time and effort required to deal with a class of problems logically.

Abstracting is a kind of problem solving which has been found to be influenced by instructions. Underwood and Richardson[18] performed an experiment on abstracting or the learning of concepts with 144 students in elementary psychology. A subject was presented with the names of four common objects. His task was to discover the concept represented; that is, the single characteristic common to all four objects. If the names brick, cherry, tomato, and lips were presented, the common characteristic was their color, red. The words used were concrete nouns. The six concepts employed were descriptive of sense impressions: round, small, white, smelly, soft, and big. A list consisted of twenty-four nouns, four for each concept.

A list was presented on a memory drum twenty times. A subject was instructed to respond to each word with the name of the concept, even on the first trial. After each response, the experimenter said "right" or "wrong." The experiment involved three levels of information contained in instructions and three levels of word usage: high, medium, and low. Thus the number of combinations of conditions was nine. Each subject served under only one level of information but under all three levels of usage. Subjects were divided into three groups which received different instructions. Within each group there were three subgroups each of which received one of three lists. The twenty-four words in each list represented the six concepts equally often and the three levels of usage equally often.

The three sets of instructions differed in the amount of information they gave subjects concerning the concept. In the general instructions, they were told that there were twenty-four nouns in the list, that there were six groups of four, and that nouns in each group could be described by the same word. The unstructured instructions to one subgroup said nothing about the concepts to be learned but only that they were to respond with the first word that came to mind on the first trial, and that they should vary their responses on succeeding trials until they began to make correct responses. The partially structured instructions to another subgroup involved questioning by the experimenter until the subject displayed an understanding of the class of responses needed to form the concepts. The subject was asked to give simple ways of describing common

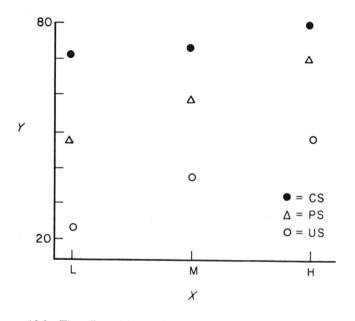

Figure 16-3. The effect of instructions on the learning of concepts. X is level of usage, low, medium, or high, in controlled association. Y is average number of correct responses. The three sets of points represent three conditions: completely structured, partially structured, and unstructured instructions. [After Underwood and Richardson. [18]]

objects and the questioning continued until he gave descriptions of sense impressions. The completely structured instructions to the third group made explicit the six correct responses. The subject was permitted to study a list of these terms until he could repeat them and to refer to the list during learning if he wanted to do so.

Figure 16-3 is a plot of number of correct responses against level of usage. The three sets of points represent the three kinds of instructions. The best performance was given by subjects who received completely structured instructions, not a surprising result. The poorest performance was given by those who received the unstructured instructions. One might react to these results as being obvious, but that would not do them justice. First, the unexpected occurs frequently enough to make one cautious until the evidence is in. Second, it is important to actually demonstrate the manipulation. Contriving different kinds of instructions is not as easy as it may seem at first thought.

THE EFFECTS OF INSTRUCTIONS ON INCIDENTAL LEARNING

Incidental learning is revealed when subjects are measured for mastery of some task not made explicit to them in the original instructions. Intentional learning is measured when the task *is* made explicit. One would expect that incidental instructions would not be as effective as intentional instructions. This result was obtained in an experiment by Saltzman and Atkinson[17], but the expected advantage of intentional over incidental appeared for larger numbers of trials and not for smaller numbers. There was, in other words, an interaction between instructions and number of trials. Subjects were 160 undergraduate students at Indiana University.

A subject's task was circling numbers on a sheet of paper as the numbers were exposed in the slot of a memory drum. The paper contained fourteen two-digit numbers. Four different random orders of the numbers were employed.

The experiment involved two sets of conditions: two kinds of instructions and four different amounts of repetition of the list of numbers. The number of combinations of conditions was eight. Subjects were divided randomly into eight groups of twenty and one combination of conditions was imposed on each group. Subjects given instructions for incidental learning were told that the experimenter was interested in finding out the best way to code numbers, and that, as soon as a number appeared in the slot of the memory drum, he was to circle that number on a mimeographed sheet. Each sheet contained the numbers 11 to 99 arranged in sequence. Subjects given instructions for intentional learning were told that the experimenter wanted to see how fast they could learn numbers, and that when a number appeared in the slot, they were to circle that number on the sheet. Subjects were given 2, 6, 8, or 16 trials according to the condition under which they served.

Finally each subject was given a sheet containing the original fourteen numbers plus forty-two new two-digit numbers randomly arranged in four columns. He was allowed two minutes to circle the numbers which he recognized as having appeared on the memory drum. His score was derived by subtracting from the number of correctly circled numbers the number which he might be expected to get correct by guessing. It was assumed that one of every four numbers circled was gotten correct by guessing.

Figure 16-4 is a plot of derived scores against number of trials allowed. The two sets of points represent the two kinds of instructions. With sixteen trials, intentional learners were higher than incidental learners but with other numbers of trials, differences were attributed to error. There were differences among the four intentional groups large enough not to be attributed to error, but differences among the four incidental groups were too small.

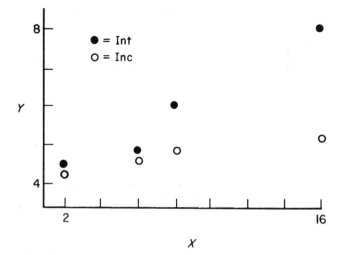

Figure 16-4. The effect of practice and instructions on recognition. X is number of trials. Y is the mean of scores corrected for guessing. The two sets of points represent the two kinds of instructions, incidental and intentional. [After Saltzman and Atkinson.[17]]

In a very similar experiment, intentional and incidental learning in the recognition of numbers were measured under different rates of presentation by Neimark and Saltzman[13]. Their subjects were 180 undergraduate students whose task was to learn a list of fourteen two-digit numbers, presented four times on a memory drum in different random orders.

There were two sets of conditions. One consisted of the conditions: intentional learning with orientation, defined as instructions to circle the numbers and to learn the list; intentional learning, defined as instructions to learn the list; and incidental learning, defined as instructions to circle the numbers. The other set of conditions consisted of three presentation rates: one item every two, three, or six seconds. The number of possible combinations of conditions was nine. Subjects were divided randomly into nine groups, on each of which one of the combinations of conditions was imposed.

After the fourth presentation, the subject was given a recognition test. The mean score was computed for each of the nine groups. Figure 16-5 is a plot of the nine means against rate of presentation. The three sets of points represent the three sets of instructions. The experimenters concluded that the three sets of instructions had different effects, that the three presentation rates also had different effects, but that the effects of instructions depended on the rate of presentation. The trend of points for the first condition, intentional learning with orientation, shows marked improvement in recognition scores with an increase in time per presentation; the trend for the second condition, intentional learning, shows a

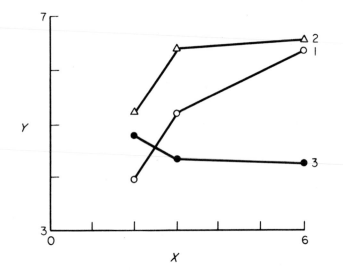

Figure 16-5. The effect of presentation rate on intentional and incidental learning. *X* is rate of presentation in number of seconds per item. *Y* is average corrected recognition score. Condition 1 was intentional learning with orientation; Condition 2 was intentional learning without orientation; and Condition 3 was incidental learning. [After Neimark and Saltzman.[13]]

sudden improvement and then a leveling off; the trend for the third condition, incidental learning, shows no improvement. Thus changes with presentation time vary with instructions. One could say that the two sets of conditions have an interaction effect on the results.

THE EFFECT OF INSTRUCTIONS ON CHOICES

One of numerous ways in which instructions to make choices may be varied has to do with whether the choices are to be real or hypothetical. The consequences of real choices are often so much more serious than those of hypothetical choices that it is not surprising when they differ. An experiment by Barker[2] showed that children's real choices of liquids differed from their hypothetical choices. He had children make choices of liquids, which varied in desirability, under two conditions: in one the choices were real, in the sense that the children acted upon them; in the other they were hypothetical in the sense that the children merely indicated their choices. Subjects were nineteen boys whose ages varied from nine to eleven years. They were paid a small amount of money for participating.

A boy was presented with two liquids at a time. His task was to indicate which one he wished to drink. There were seven different liquids: orange juice, pineapple juice, tomato juice, water, lemon juice, vinegar, and a saturated solution of salt water. Each of the seven was paired, for presentation, with every other one, yielding $(7 \times 6)/2$ or 21 pairs. As a preliminary, seven small glasses, each containing six cubic centimeters of a liquid, were placed before each boy. He was instructed to drink each of the liquids, to name it, and to say how he liked it.

In the main part of the session, the names of the liquids were exposed in pairs on cards side by side. Within easy reaching distance there was a lever, mounted so that it came to rest in a vertical position on a line midway between the two cards. The lever was easily moved to the right or to the left. When it was moved as far as it would go to either side, a buzzer sounded. A boy indicated his choice by moving the lever to the side corresponding to the card with the name of his choice. He was allowed to reverse his movement at any point before the buzzer sounded. A record was made on tape of the time of exposure of the two cards and the movements of the lever.

Each pair of cards was presented twice under real and twice under hypothetical conditions of choice. Positions of the two cards in each pair were reversed on the second occasion. Thus a subject made forty-two choices under real and an equal number under hypothetical conditions. Real choices were obtained first from nine boys; hypothetical choices followed after a rest. The order was reversed for ten other boys.

The order of preference for the seven liquids was determined for each boy from the choices he made. By reference to the ranks, the liquids in each pair could then be characterized in terms of the discrepancy—1, 2, 3, 4, 5, or 6 steps—between them. The time required for final movement of the lever was obtained in seconds. Figure 16-6 is a plot of time required for final choice against degrees of discrepancy in desirability. The two sets of points represent real and hypothetical choices. Less time was taken for hypothetical choices than for real ones but the difference became smaller as the discrepancies increased. The results confirm everyday experience that choices are harder to make when the alternatives are similar than they are when the alternatives are different, and that choices which have real consequences are made more carefully and deliberately than those which have no consequences.

How do people make choices when there is uncertainty as to which alternative is accompanied by success? This is the kind of problem one encounters when the same action sometimes succeeds and sometimes fails. The answer is that their approach will vary depending on circumstances, such as instructions, which define their task. Choices made by college students were observed by Goodnow[4] under two kinds of instructions: one describing the task as problem solving; the other describing it as gambling. The experimenter hypothesized that, in problem solving, choices

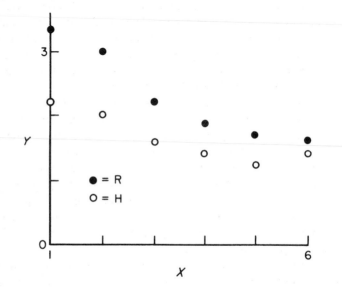

Figure 16-6. The effect of real and hypothetical conditions on children's choices of liquids. X is number of steps separation on preference scale. Y is average time in seconds required for choice. Two sets of points represent real and hypothetical choices. [After Barker.[2]]

would be divided according to the proportions of success associated with two events, and that, in gambling, choices would be concentrated on the event associated with the higher proportion. The hypothesis followed from the assumption that a subject in a problem-solving situation tries to discover a principle which will give him the correct choice on *every* trial and that a subject in a gambling situation only tries to discover the best bet. Subjects were sixty-eight Harvard undergraduates, paid for their participation.

A subject was asked to solve a problem actually not solvable. On each trial he was shown three cards containing geometrical designs. The first card contained a basic design. The other two contained variations. The subject's task was to connect the basic design with one of the variations and to find the principle by which the connection should be made. To form the variable designs, the basic design was altered by either adding or subtracting a line. The subject was, therefore, choosing on every trial between the two types of variation, adding or subtracting a line. There were ten different basic cards with four variations of each. The subject's success or failure was actually dependent on the agreement between his choices and a randomly predetermined schedule of answers devised by the experimenter.

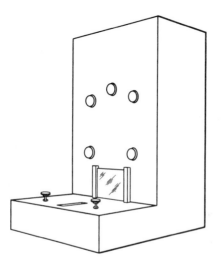

Figure 16-7. A slot machine employed in a gambling situation. The upper outer lights flashed as the machine came into operation on each trial. The upper central light flashed as the subject inserted a chip. One of the lower lights flashed as he pressed one of the two keys. The pay-off box was behind the cover on the panel. [Adapted from Goodnow.[4]]

The gambling task involved playing a slot machine with chips worth one cent each. The subject was given 200 chips. He inserted one of these chips into the machine and made his bet by pressing one of two keys. If the bet was successful, a chip dropped into the pay-off box with a clatter of noise. Winning followed a randomly predetermined schedule. Figure 16-7 shows the slot machine.

Three different schedules of success were employed for both tasks. The relative frequencies with which a correct or winning choice occurred were .50, .70, and .90, for the subtractive alternative in problem solving and the left key in gambling. Subjects were divided into six groups. One of the two tasks with one of the three schedules was assigned to each group. Each subject was given 120 trials, divided into twelve blocks of ten trials each. The mean proportion of choices of subtracting or left key were determined for each group. Figure 16-8 shows results for the last twenty trials. Proportion of choices is plotted against relative frequency of the correct or winning event. The two sets of points are for the two conditions, problem solving and gambling. The hypothesis was supported for the schedule with a relative frequency of .70, but the differences for the other schedules were so small they were attributed to error. When success accompanied the two possible choices equally often, the problem solver and the gambler both divided their choices equally. When

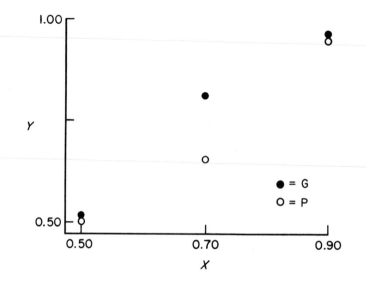

Figure 16-8. Choices in problem solving and gambling. X is relative frequency of correct or winning choice. Y is mean proportion of choices of subtracting and left key. [After Goodnow.[4]]

success accompanied one choice almost all the time, both concentrated their choices on the successful alternative. When success accompanied one choice most of the time, the two differed: the gambler concentrated; the problem solver divided his choices.

Messages

In communicating a message, does it help to give the recipient advance knowledge of the length of the message? The results of an experiment by Pollack, Johnson, and Knaff[15] indicate that it may, under some circumstances. They had subjects listen to messages and recall them under two conditions: prior knowledge of message length, and lack of knowledge. Subjects were students at the University of Maryland.

A subject listened to a tape on which instructions and sixteen spoken messages were recorded. The messages consisting of randomly selected digits were presented at four different rates: 0.5, 1, 2, and 4 digits per second. The subject was told that a group of numbers would be read and that he was to write, in order, as many of the last numbers in a group as he could. He was also told that a tone would signal the end of each group, that different rates would be employed and that messages would be between four and forty digits in length.

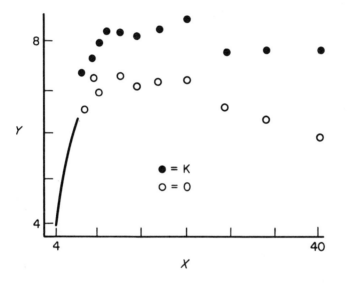

Figure 16-9. The effect of knowledge of message length on running digit span. X is length of message in digits. Y is average running digit span. The two sets of points represent two conditions, knowledge and no knowledge. For messages of four to seven digits, both sets of points fell on the solid curved line. [After Pollack, Johnson, and Knaff.[15]]

Five subjects were tested eight times under all possible combinations of conditions. There were four rates of presentation, fifteen lengths of messages, and two conditions of knowledge about message length. Thus the number of combinations of conditions was 120. Each subject was tested for five hours a day, with frequent rest pauses, for two days a week over thirteen weeks. His score was the number of digits correctly identified and positioned from the end of the message.

Figure 16-9 is a plot of average score as a function of length of message. The upper set of points represents the condition of prior knowledge of message length; the lower set represents lack of knowledge. Each point is based on 160 responses of five subjects. All points of lengths of four to seven digits fall on or very close to the segment of a curve drawn in the figure. It is evident that on the longer messages prior knowledge of length yielded higher scores than did no knowledge. The conclusion that communication of messages is facilitated by giving the receiver advance knowledge of their length seems justified. Rate of presentation had certain complex effects.

Varied messages were employed by Lykken[11] in a very successful method of detecting, from a number of persons, the individual who had committed certain acts. The method employed simple messages delivered by the experimenter to the subjects and *GSR* records obtained as the suspects listened to the messages. The committed acts were answers previously given by each subject to a questionnaire. The messages were simply an assortment of answers to each question. Each assortment contained the suspect's own answers. Subjects included medical students, psychologists, psychiatrists, and secretaries.

Preliminary to the detection, each subject completed a questionnaire containing twenty-five items, such as "What is your father's first name?," "What was the name of the street that you lived on when you were a child?," "What was the name of your high school?" The subject's answers to the questionnaire constituted the set of items said to be characteristic of him. The answers of five subjects were combined in an interrogation form. The first question on the form was "What was your mother's first name?" Six names were listed as answers: the first was a woman's name chosen randomly; five were the names of the mothers of the five students in random order. All of the questions had answers following this pattern. While he was being interrogated, the suspect, one of the five subjects, sat in a testing room wearing a blindfold and a pair of earphones. The investigator in an adjoining room read the questions and the various answers to the suspect over a microphone. The *GSR* electrodes were fixed over the fingerprint area of the first and third fingers of one hand.

An attempt was made to identify each subject by an analysis of his *GSR* record obtained as questions were read to him and answers mentioned. To identify a subject meant to determine which of the five sets of questionnaire answers was his. (The first randomly chosen answer was not scored.) For subjects interrogated after the first five, the form was modified by substituting the twenty-five answers of a new subject for those of one of the original group.

A suspect's record was scored by ranking his *GSR*s for the five answers under each of the twenty-five questions in order of amplitude. After this was done, each of the five sets of twenty-five ranks was inspected. On the assumption that a suspect would respond consistently to his own answers and inconsistently to the answers of others, the most consistent set of twenty-five *GSR*s was assigned to the suspect. The *GSR* records of all twenty subjects were correctly matched with their own sets of questionnaire answers. The success of this method is impressive but, of course, the results of one experiment cannot be taken as conclusive. It is too much to expect that the method would prove to be infallible for all kinds of people and circumstances. It would, however, be of interest to learn the results of further extensive experimentation. The sophistication of the method of scoring, based on the assumption that the individual suspect will be consistent only in responding to messages about his own acts, appears to have considerable value.

Suggestion

Suggestion is communication in one of two forms: it does not specify the action carried out by the subject; or, if it does specify the action the subject does not acknowledge that it does. The first is commonly encountered in everyday situations. Vague or ambiguous hints, cautions, and threats are all too often a part of parent-child, teacher-student, politician-voter, and other relations. Favorable associations between pain pills and the medical profession, cosmetics and movie stars, hair dressings and famous athletes are a familiar and substantial part of advertising. The second form of suggestion, in which the subject does not acknowledge that the communication specifies his action, even when it actually does, is represented by directions or commands given to the subject while he is in a state of hypnosis.

CAUTIONS AND PROBLEM SOLVING

It was demonstrated by Luchins[10] that cautions can be effective in improving problem solving. He gave subjects problems which could be solved by simple arithmetic reasoning. Problems solvable by only one method were followed by problems solvable by either the same method or a simpler one. The experimenter observed the choice of methods under two different conditions: caution and no caution. Subjects were senior students of Brooklyn College.

A subject's task was to determine, on paper, how to obtain a specified volume of water, given two or three empty jars of known volumes for measure. In the first problem, given as a sample, the specified volume was twenty quarts and the two jars had volumes of twenty-nine quarts and three quarts. The solution given to the subject was to remove three jars-full of three quarts each from the full jar containing twenty-nine, leaving the specified twenty. In the second problem, also given as a sample, the specified volume was 100 quarts and three jars had volumes of

21, 127, and 3 quarts, respectively. The solution given was to remove from the 127-quart jar a volume given by one filling of the 21-quart jar and two fillings of the three-quart jar, leaving 100 quarts of water. Another solution was also given. It involved filling the three-quart jar nine times from the 127-quart jar.

Other problems were then presented in succession. The first method of solving the second problem was applicable to problems three through six. Since the volumes in each problem were written on the blackboard in a standard order, the solution could be stated as "Fill the middle jar, and from it fill the jar to the left once and the jar to the right twice, leaving the specified amount of water in the center jar." The solution could also be stated as B minus A minus $2C$, if the jars were designated in the order written as A, B, and C, respectively. The same method could be applied to the seventh and eighth problems, but there were simpler solutions. The simpler solution for the seventh problem was $A - C$; the simpler solution for the eighth was $A + C$. The ninth problem could only be solved by the method, $A - C$. The tenth and eleventh problems were similar to the seventh and eighth in having two solutions.

In each of three classes, approximately half the students were asked to leave the room temporarily. These constituted the *uncautioned* group. Those remaining in the room constituted the *cautioned* group. While the uncautioned group was out of the room, the cautioned group was told that they were to write *Don't be blind* on their papers when they finished the sixth problem. Subjects in the uncautioned group were then recalled and the entire series of eleven problems was presented.

The cautioned group in each of the three classes gave fewer B-A-$2C$ solutions and more of the simpler solutions than did the uncautioned group on the seventh and eighth problems. Thus the vague caution, "Don't be blind," alerted students to the simpler solutions. On the tenth and eleventh problems, both groups showed a decrease in percentage of B-A-$2C$ solutions but the cautioned subjects in all three classes still gave fewer than did the uncautioned subjects. Having had their attention drawn to the simple solution, which was the only possibility for the ninth problem, subjects in both groups made more use of it.

AMBIGUITY AND VERBAL RESPONSES

That suggestion may be conveyed through ambiguous language was demonstrated experimentally by Postman and Crutchfield[16]. Skeleton words which suggested foods were constructed and subjects had to fill in the missing letters. The effects of word ambiguity and practice on the frequency of food-related verbal responses were determined. Subjects were 724 students in undergraduate psychology courses at the University of California.

Each skeleton word was formed by deleting two letters in various positions. A subject's task was to construct a meaningful English word by supplying letters for the blanks. Each skeleton word had at least two solutions, one of which was a food word and the other a nonfood word. Words chosen to be skeleton words varied in ambiguity, defined in terms of the relative frequency of food responses given in a preliminary investigation. When the relative frequency was very high or very low, the word was considered unambiguous; when it was near 0.50, the word was considered ambiguous.

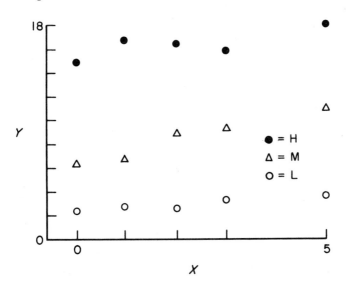

Figure 16-10. The effect of ambiguity and suggestion on food-related responses. X is the number of unambiguous, skeleton food words given in initial practice. Y is the average number of food responses. The three sets of points represent three lists of words of low, medium, and high relative frequencies in yielding food responses. [After Postman and Crutchfield.[16]]

Three lists of twenty-one words were finally selected to represent low, medium, and high relative frequencies of food responses respectively. One skeleton word in the low list was *gra _ _*. The food solution was gravy; the nonfood solution, grade. A word in the medium list was *pick _ _*. The food solution was pickle; the nonfood solution, picket. One from the high list was *bu _ _ er*. The food solution was butter; the nonfood solution, buffer.

There were two sets of conditions: the three lists which varied in relative frequency of food responses, and five amounts of practice in completing other high-frequency skeleton words. The five amounts of practice were 0, 1, 2, 3, or 5 completions. The high-frequency practice words in appropriate number were listed and followed by the twenty-one skeleton words in a list. Subjects were allowed eight minutes to complete the task.

The average number of food responses was determined for each group. Differences among the three lists and the five degrees of practice were large enough not to be attributed to error. Figure 16-10 is a plot of food responses against degree of practice for the three lists.

Hypnotic Suggestion

An unusual kind of suggestion was demonstrated by Leuba and Dunlap[9]. A subject asked to imagine a bell ringing reported a sensation of pain. The request was made after the subject had been put through a brief conditioning procedure in which the ringing of a bell was paired with a pin prick. The conditioning was carried out during hypnosis. Subjects were four college students who responded to a request for persons interested in being hypnotized, and displayed signs of deep hypnosis in preliminary sessions.

In a conditioning session under hypnosis, a subject was presented with the sound of a bell and a pin prick to the hand. After amnesia for the conditioning session had been suggested, he was awakened from hypnosis. In the waking state, he was asked to imagine a number of situations and to report any experiences which might occur in connection with the imagining. One of the situations he was asked to imagine was the sound of a bell. All four subjects reported sensations of pain in connection with instructions to imagine the sound of a bell. These reports were obtained even though a subject said he could not remember the conditioning session and was puzzled by suddenly experiencing the sensation when imagining some situation.

A typical result is shown by the record for one female student. When she gave evidence of being deeply hypnotized, the experimenter directed her attention to sounds and to sensations in her right hand. He sounded a door bell and simultaneously pricked her right hand with a sharp instrument several times. He then asked her what had occurred. She replied, "I heard a door bell and a pin pricked my hand." The presentation of the pair of stimuli was repeated three times. After suggesting that she would be amnesic for the hypnotic period, the experimenter awakened her. When he questioned her later, she reported that she could remember nothing except going to sleep. He then asked her to imagine experiencing certain events as he named them aloud and to report any ideas or experiences which might accompany the imaginings. First she was told to imagine as vividly as possible that she was smelling gasoline. Her response was, "Well, I like that smell." When she was told to imagine seeing a green light, her response was, "You mean a traffic light? Emerald green?

Well, I think of how a dark room with a green light looks very eerie."
When she was told to imagine hearing a door bell, she exhibited a puzzled
expression and said, "When I imagine a door bell ringing, I get a pain; a
sharp pain that goes through me." The experimenter said, "Where?"
She answered, "In my right hand." She then rubbed the area previously
pricked. "It's a sharp movement, like a needle; it comes and goes." When
she was told to imagine hearing a train whistle, she said, "I think of it
when I am in bed, not asleep, but just about to go to sleep; and how it
sounds far off but really isn't."

Varied life histories were suggested to college students during hypnosis and the effects on their judgments of the sizes of coins were determined by Ashley, Harper, and Runyon[1]. Subjects were volunteers from
the student body of Knox College. Nine subjects from an initial group of
volunteers qualified for participation by showing signs of experiencing
false visual perceptions in the hypnotic state.

A subject was hypnotized, told that he could remember nothing of
his former life except his name, and told that his life history would be
related to him. Then an account was given of a life history in which he
was either poor or rich. The wording of the life histories varied for different subjects but always followed the same general pattern. Nothing
was said in either kind of story about the size or value of coins. Each
poor subject, however, was told that he remembered seeing coins.

After the story, the subject adjusted a spot of light, by pulling on a
continuous cord, until the spot appeared to be the size of a specified coin.
Each subject gave two judgments of the remembered size of a penny,
nickel, dime, and quarter in all three states: rich, poor, and normal. He
made one adjustment after the experimenter had set the diameter of
the spot smaller than the coin; and the other, after the diameter was
set larger than the coin. Some subjects made their first judgment when
the spot was smaller; others, when it was larger. Some made their initial
adjustment in the rich state; others, in the poor state. The order of coins
was unsystematic. All subjects made their final set of judgments in the
normal state.

The size of the light spots judged by subjects as equal to the coins
differed in the rich and poor states. Figure 16-11 shows the effect of
coin value and hypnotic suggestion on the diameter of the spot of light
adjusted to equal each of the coins in size. For each coin, the matched
diameter was greater in the poor state than in the normal state and less
in the rich state than in the normal state. Considering how effective the
suggested life histories were, it would not be surprising to find that judgments of coin size are related to real life histories in many ways.

Posthypnotic suggestions are instructions given during hypnosis to act
in a certain way afterwards. Gordon, Martin, and Lundy[5] devised sugges-

tions to define repression, suppression, and verbalization of conflict with parents. (Repression and suppression are theoretical terms from psychoanalysis. Repression refers to the exclusion of events from consciousness by an unconscious process, whereas suppression refers to conscious exclusion of events or conscious inhibition of impulses to action.) The effects of the posthypnotic suggestions on the verbal behavior of twelve female undergraduates at the University of Wisconsin were observed, and the results were found to support the definitions. The criterion for selecting subjects was the achievement of complete amnesia for the hypnotic situation by the end of three preliminary sessions.

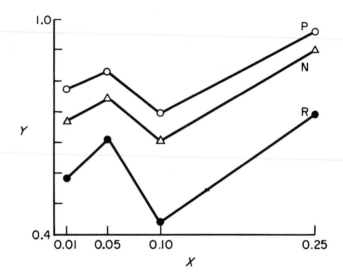

Figure 16-11. The effect of suggested life histories on judgments of coin size. X is value of coin. Y is median diameter, in inches, of spot judged equal to coin. The three sets of points represent the three conditions: poor, normal, and rich. Points for actual sizes were very close to normal points. [After Ashley, Harper, and Runyon.[1]]

After the third session, an appointment was made with each subject for an interview with a clinical psychologist. The interview was conducted in a nondirective manner for fifteen minutes; that is, the subject was told that she could talk about anything and the psychologist merely listened attentively.

The experiment involved two conditions, two orders in which the posthypnotic suggestions were given. Subjects were divided randomly into two groups and one condition was imposed on each group. Subjects in one group, *RVS*, received instructions to repress, verbalize, and suppress the conflicts, in that order; those in the other group, *RSV*, were instructed to repress, suppress, and verbalize, in that order. The instructions were to be followed in a later interview. Repression was defined by instructions not to think about conflict with parents; suppression, by instructions to think about it but not to talk about it; and verbalization, by instructions to talk about it.

In the main session, the subject was hypnotized and given one or the other of the two orders of instructions, to take effect in the subsequent interview. Conflict was defined for the subject as referring to arguments with parents, extreme parental strictness, unfair treatment by parents, or lack of understanding by parents. The subject was told that the signal marking the transition from one set of instructions to another during the interview would be the clicking of a key by the interviewer. Upon being awakened, the subject was interviewed again. The interviewer told her that she might start by telling something about herself. From that point on, the interview was nondirective. At the close of the interview the subject was informed of the hypnotic instructions she had been given and the purpose of the study.

Each interview was recorded on tape. Each half-minute interval of the recording was scored for the presence or absence of references to parental conflict. The results for both groups showed many more references to conflicts during verbalization than during either repression or suppression. There was little or no difference between repression and suppression. The fact that subjects talked about conflict with their parents more under the one kind of suggestion than under the others supports an inference that clients in counseling or psychotherapy might be similarly influenced to express themselves about matters which they were repressing or suppressing. Since it is widely assumed that free expression is beneficial in relieving emotional stress and providing opportunity for a person to understand and deal with his personal problems, the results emphasize the potential importance of suggestion.

Audio-Visual Aids to Communication in Education

Audio-visual aids have long been accepted as useful in teaching many different kinds of courses. Among the numerous possibilities for aids to teaching are charts, slides, film strips, movies, tape recordings, phonograph records, public address systems, radio, open- and closed-circuit television, so-called teaching machines, and a variety of mechanical devices. It is reasonable to inquire about experimentation in this area—and to encourage it—for one cannot safely assume that all such devices and the procedures involving them necessarily improve teaching and learning. Although the available evidence does not invariably recommend them in all situations, in general, their use is favorably viewed.

The teaching of arithmetic to a group of children by means of a machine has been described by Keislar[8]. Data were obtained for a comparable group given no instruction, but no data were obtained for a comparable group in regular arithmetic classes. Subjects were twenty-eight children from the fifth and low-sixth grades. They could do multiplication and division but were not familiar with the concept of area.

In the teaching machine, multiple-choice items, photographed on a film strip, were projected on a viewing plate. A subject indicated his choice of an answer by pressing one of five buttons. If his choice was correct, a green light came on. He could then bring the next item into view by pressing a special button. If his choice was incorrect, a red light came on. He had to choose the correct answer for one item before he could go to the next. The occurrence of correct and incorrect answers was recorded graphically.

The program consisted of 120 items. In ten of them the subject was instructed to operate the machine and informed of his task. In 110 items he was given arithmetic instruction. The initial items presented concepts of squares, rectangles, length, and width. The next items required the subject to determine the number of square units in rectangles. Then the concept of area, which followed logically, was presented along with practical applications like paint coverage, rug size, and tile laying. The next items were practice problems of adding and subtracting areas and finding the length or width of rectangles. The last items were problems of cost.

Children were divided into two groups, individually matched on intelligence, sex, reading ability, and pretest arithmetic scores. There were two conditions in the experiment: one group took a pretest, worked on the teaching machine, and took a final test; the other group took the pretest and the final test but received no special instruction. Those who worked on the machine did so for two or three periods on successive days. Total time on the machine varied from 1.5 to two hours. All children were given the final test on the day following the end of machine instruction.

The pretest and the final test were of the essay type. The pretest contained twelve problems involving multiplication and division, and eight problems dealing with areas of rectangles. The final test contained the same eight area problems of the pretest and eight new area problems which were more difficult. The results were that children who had worked on the machine had a higher average score on the final test than did those in the comparison group. These results indicate that children can teach themselves by means of a machine and certainly support the conclusion that opportunity to use it could be an important educational advantage. What the experiment did not show, of course, is whether time on the teaching machine was more profitable than time in class. It is possible that the teaching machine would prove to be inferior, equal, or superior to conventional instruction.

The effect of mental-health films on opinions and beliefs regarding mental illness was demonstrated by McGinnies, Lana, and Smith[12] in an experiment on seventy-six adults in parent-teacher and child-study groups in Prince Georges County, Maryland. An inventory of forty-seven items asking for opinions and beliefs about mental illness was given to groups of adults before and after they viewed a series of three films. Discussions were held in half the groups after the showing of each film but before the second administration of the inventory.

Six groups of subjects were formed. Four were shown the films; two were not. The films selected for use dealt with personality disturbances and institutional treatment of psychotic disorders. Films were viewed, one per session, at intervals of two weeks. In two of the four groups which viewed the films, each showing was followed by a thirty-minute discussion of the film or related topics. A professional psychologist was discussion leader for the groups. He adopted a non-directive approach to encourage expression of opinion. In the two other groups which viewed the films, no discussion was allowed. These groups were told they would discuss all three films at the final session. (This discussion was held after subjects had completed the inventory for the second time.) The two remaining groups completed the inventory twice with an interval of four weeks between administrations.

Responses to the items of the inventory were made on a five-point rating scale which varied from "strongly agree" to "strongly disagree." Among the items were the following: (a) It is better not to discuss a mental illness as one would a physical illness. (b) Few of the people who seek psychiatric help need the treatment. (c) An employer should avoid hiring someone who has been in a mental hospital. (d) Nervous breakdowns are due to overwork.

Each subject's ratings were scored for their correspondence to ratings by a panel of twelve staff members and graduate trainees at the University of Maryland Counseling Center. If his ratings were in the same direction as those expressed by the panel, he obtained a high score; if they were in the opposite direction, he obtained a low score. The opinions and beliefs of the panel were judged to represent the general points made in the films.

The four groups which viewed the films had higher scores than did the two groups which did not. The potential value of films in educating the public on topics like mental illness was clearly demonstrated. There were only differences attributed to error between the groups that had discussed the films and those that had not.

Chapter Summary

That people follow instructions in some situations and fail to do so in others is a common observation supported by psychological fact. There is much interest in this behavior, for it represents successes and failures in an important kind of control. It is not a simple matter to write instructions on how to take care of a power lawnmower; to bake a cake; to get to a specific destination in a strange city; to complete an income-tax form; to carry out a diplomatic assignment in a foreign country; or to take an intelligence test. Experiments, with variations in instructions as the conditions, can often provide information needed by the practical user of instructions to achieve his ends.

Instructions are only one kind of communication. Others—messages, signs, exposition, suggestion, advertising, propaganda, and teaching—provide almost limitless possibilities for experimentation. A great deal of information has already been accumulated. It is in the public interest to encourage experimentation on communication and application of the results, for there are great benefits to be realized when knowledge can be substituted for assumptions, beliefs, and guesses.

References

1. Ashley, W. R., R. S. Harper, and D. L. Runyon. "The Perceived Size of Coins in Normal and Hypnotically Induced Economic States." *The American Journal of Psychology,* 64 (1951), 564-572.
2. Barker, R. G. "An Experimental Study of the Resolution of Conflict by Children: Time Elapsing and Amount of Vicarious Trial-and-Error Behavior Occurring" in *Studies in Personality,* 1st ed., Q. McNemar and M. A. Merrill, eds. New York: McGraw-Hill Book Co., Inc., 1942.
3. Gilinsky, A. S. "The Effect of Attitude Upon the Perception of Size." *The American Journal of Psychology,* 68 (1955), 173-192.
4. Goodnow, J. J. "Determinants of Choice-Distribution in Two-Choice Situations." *The American Journal of Psychology,* 68 (1955), 106-116.
5. Gordon, J. E., B. Martin, and R. M. Lundy. "GSRs During Repression, Suppression, and Verbalization in Psychotherapeutic Interviews." *The Journal of Consulting Psychology,* 23 (1959), 243-251.
6. Hilgard, E. R., R. K. Campbell, and W. N. Sears. "Conditioned Discrimination: The Effect of Knowledge of Stimulus-Relationships." *The American Journal of Psychology,* 51 (1938), 498-506.
7. Katona, G. *Organizing and Memorizing.* New York: Columbia University Press, 1940.
8. Keislar, E. R. "The Development of Understanding in Arithmetic by a Teaching Machine." *The Journal of Educational Psychology,* 50 (1959), 247-253.
9. Leuba, C., and R. Dunlap. "Conditioning Imagery." *The Journal of Experimental Psychology,* 41 (1951), 352-355.
10. Luchins, A. S. "Mechanization in Problem Solving: The Effect of Einstellung." *Psychological Monographs,* 54, No. 248 (1942).
11. Lykken, D. T. "The Validity of the Guilty-Knowledge Technique: The Effects of Faking." *The Journal of Applied Psychology,* 44 (1960), 258-262.
12. McGinnies, E., R. Lana, and C. Smith. "The Effects of Sound Films on Opinions About Mental Illness in Community Discussion Groups." *The Journal of Applied Psychology,* 42 (1958), 40-46.

13. Neimark, E., and I. J. Saltzman. "Intentional and Incidental Learning with Different Rates of Stimulus Presentation." *The American Journal of Psychology,* 66 (1953), 618-621.
14. Norris, E. B., and D. A. Grant. "Eyelid Conditioning as Affected by Verbally Induced Inhibitory Set and Counter Reinforcement." *The American Journal of Psychology,* 61 (1948), 37-49.
15. Pollack, I., L. B. Johnson, and P. R. Knaff. "Running Memory Span." *The Journal of Experimental Psychology,* 57 (1959), 137-146.
16. Postman, L., and R. S. Crutchfield. "The Interaction of Need, Set, and Stimulus-Structure in a Cognitive Task." *The American Journal of Psychology,* 65 (1952), 196-217.
17. Saltzman, I. J., and R. L. Atkinson. "Comparisons of Incidental and Intentional Learning After Different Numbers of Stimulus Presentations." *The American Journal of Psychology,* 67 (1954), 521-524.
18. Underwood, B. J., and J. Richardson. "Verbal Concept Learning as a Function of Instructions and Dominance Level." *The Journal of Experimental Psychology,* 51 (1956), 229-238.
19. Waters, R. H. "The Influence of Tuition Upon Ideational Learning." *The Journal of General Psychology,* 1 (1928), 534-549.

17

The Physical

and Social

Environments

Does the individual's environment influence his behavior? There is widespread agreement among perceptive and thoughtful people that it does, in many different ways. Can advantage be taken of this relationship? Can people change environments and thereby control behavior —their own or that of others? The answer to both questions is, of course, yes. There is a substantial amount of experimental evidence supporting the answer. The relevant knowledge comes from actual attempts to manipulate characteristics of the environment in ways that permit the effects on behavior to be determined.

One can distinguish two kinds of environments: physical and social. The physical environment is the world of material things and processes. The social environment is the world of people and their behavior. Each has many characteristics which may be used as conditions in experimentation. Although much of value has already been realized from the results of such experimentation, the potential value is so great as to be difficult to describe or estimate.

528

The Physical Environment

Among the characteristics of the physical environment which can be manipulated are the following: distance, force, time, frequency, rate, or speed in the prescription of an individual's task; illumination, temperature, humidity, barometric pressure, air composition or pollution, and amount of living or working space; the spatial and temporal characteristics of events like music, noises, alarms, and explosions; the kind, color, texture, and quality of wall and floor surfaces; the specifications and arrangements of doors, windows, stairs, elevators, and escalators, as well as household furniture, kitchen appliances, office equipment, store fixtures, and industrial machinery; and the design of objects such as toothbrushes, combs, shavers, hearing aids, masks, gloves, tools, clothing, and shoes. Experiments which illustrate the manipulation of task specifications, illumination, music, the diameter of stair handrails, and the design of prosthetic devices will be described.

TASK SPECIFICATIONS

Physical Load

Physical load refers to the demand upon a person performing some task, when that demand is put upon him by the arrangements of materials or equipment he must use. The number of sources of visual signals to which a man has to respond is one kind of load. It was varied by Conrad[3] and the effects on responses in controlling dials were determined. Twelve navy enlisted men were subjects.

The apparatus, shown in Figure 17-1, consisted of a vertical bank of dials two feet wide. Each dial had a revolving pointer and marks at positions of 90 and 270 degrees. On a panel in front of and below the bank of dials were switches arranged to correspond spatially with the dials. The switches could be used to control the pointers. If the appropriate switch was depressed and held down as a pointer approached a mark, the pointer would cross the mark without stopping and would continue revolving. Each pointer revolved at a constant speed but speed varied from dial to dial. The subject was instructed to prevent the pointers from stopping and to start the pointers as soon as possible if any stopped.

A large clock with a single hand provided a continuous record of the subject's performance. When he prevented a pointer from stopping, the hand moved forward one scale division; when a pointer stopped, the clock hand moved back one division. During the time that a pointer was stopped, the hand moved back at a rate proportional to the running speed of that pointer. The subject's visual load was varied by using different numbers of dials: 4, 6, 8, 10, or 12. The five conditions were imposed on each subject in random order. The test for each load lasted ten minutes. Performance was recorded by a multipen ink writer.

Figure 17-2 is a plot of the number of stops per minute against the number of dials in the load. As one might expect, the number of stops increased as load increased. If one had to make a decision in some practical industrial or military situation as to the optimal load, he would have to have additional information such as the cost of the operator's time and the cost of his failures. If operator time was expensive and failures inexpensive, then a heavy load might be indicated. However, if operator time was cheap and failures costly, then a light load might be recommended.

Figure 17-1. Arrangement of dials, clock, and console of control switches. [Adapted from Conrad.[3]]

In another experiment, an auditory load consisting of recorded messages was varied by Conrad[4] with respect to the time interval between the messages. Subjects, who were twenty-four naval enlisted men, were required to repeat the messages. The number of intrusion errors in their responses was observed.

Each subject was tested under three different conditions: three time intervals of 15, 25, or 40 seconds between successive messages. Tape recordings were made of messages of eight digits, spoken at a rate of two digits per second in a fairly even monotone. Each subject served under all time intervals. He was told that he would hear an eight-digit number and that he should say aloud what he thought it was. His responses were recorded by the experimenter.

In each message, the frequency of occurrence of intrusions from a previous message was determined. An error was considered an intrusion

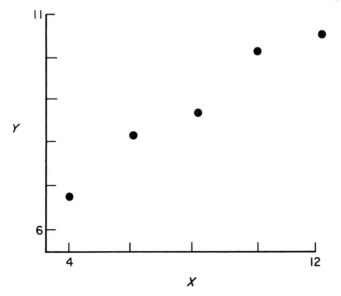

Figure 17-2. The effect of perceptual load on responses to signals. X is number of dials. Y is average number of pointer stops per minute. [After Conrad.[3]]

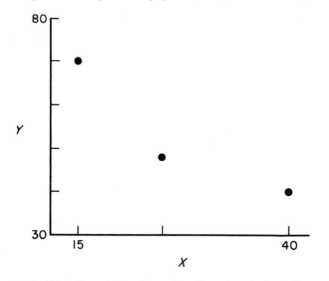

Figure 17-3. The effect of time interval on intrusions in immediate recall. X is time in seconds. Y is the number of intrusion errors. [After Conrad.[4]]

when it was a digit in the same serial position in the previous message, whether right or wrong in the previous message. Figure 17-3 is a plot of intrusion errors against time intervals in seconds. The number of errors decreases as the time interval increases. The implication is that messages can be received with greater accuracy if they do not follow one another too closely. In many situations it would be important to find some way of pacing messages to a receiver or distributing them over several receivers in order to achieve a high level of accuracy.

The effect of kinesthetic load on a simple motor performance, the turning of a crank, was investigated by Bilodeau[2]. Force required to turn the crank at a given rate was the independent variable; rate of turning was the dependent variable. The results were that rate of turning was slower for larger forces. Subjects were eighty trainees at Lackland Air Force Base.

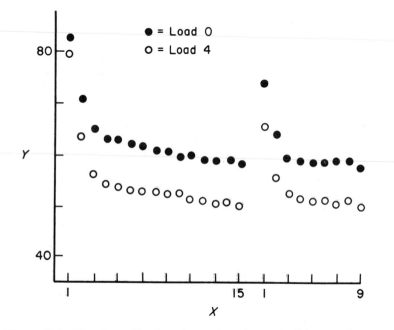

Figure 17-4. The effect of load on the turning of a crank. X is successive twenty-second scoring periods. Y is average number of revolutions. The two sets of points represent two conditions of load, zero and four. Subjects were given a rest of forty seconds between the first fifteen and the last nine scoring periods. [After Bilodeau.[2]]

The apparatus consisted of a manual crank with a system for controlling the force required to turn the handle at a given rate. The crank was mounted in the horizontal plane at the edge of a table. Each revolution was registered on a counter. The force required to turn the crank could be varied over settings from zero to four, representing increasing loads. The subject stood in front of the crank and rotated it, under instructions to do so as fast as he could, for a period of five minutes. He was then given a rest of forty seconds. After resting, he turned the crank for a period of three minutes.

The two conditions in the experiment were load settings of zero and four. One group of subjects performed with the minimum load; the other, with the maximum load. The number of revolutions of the crank per period of twenty seconds was recorded. Figure 17-4 is a plot of the number of revolutions against successive periods for initial and final sessions. The upper set of points is for the minimum load; the lower set is for the maximum. There is an initial decline for each set of points. Performance with the heavier load was poorer than with the lighter load. The result is certainly not surprising, but still important enough to demonstrate. This is the kind of information which is necessary in designing jobs for operators of industrial machinery. It could not be assumed that load made no difference, even though it might not within a limited range.

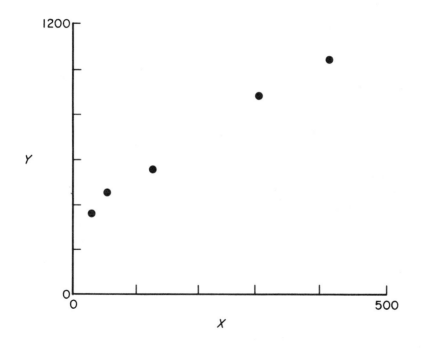

Figure 17-5. The effect of weight on prehension force. X is weight in grams. Y is prehension force in grams. [After Lyman and Groth.[16]]

A basic task in the assembly-line methods of modern industry is that of transporting an object from one place to another. How this task was affected by load defined in terms of object weight and distance was determined by Lyman and Groth[16] in an experiment on six male sophomore engineering students. The dependent variable was prehension or grasping force. The direction of the transporting movement and the kind of protective hand covering worn were also varied.

A semicircular piece of plywood, four feet in diameter, contained sixty-four large holes. One hole was located at the center; nine were spaced on each of seven radiuses at 0, 30, 60, 90, 120, 150, and 180 degrees. The seven directions were indicated by letters from A to G on the board. A subject's task was transporting a cylindrical object into which varied weights could be placed. Prehension force was measured by means of a special pressure-sensitive device incorporated in the cylinder. Force was recorded continuously on an oscillograph.

The experiment had four sets of conditions: five weights from 18 to 426 grams; the seven directions already noted; three distances measured from the center hole on the board to three holes on each radius; and three kinds of hand covering—no covering, latex gloves, and leather gloves. Each subject served under all conditions. The order of imposing the conditions was varied. The subject was instructed to grasp the cylinder as it rested in the center hole, pick it up, place it in the hole designated by the experimenter, release it, then pick it up again, and replace it in the center hole. Three sets of conditions—weight, distance, and hand covering—affected prehension force. Weight and distance increased it. Figure 17-5 is a plot of prehension force against weight. Prehension force was least for no hand covering and greatest for leather gloves.

The Effect of Target Shift on Tracking

Many tracking tasks in the laboratory involve a target which moves through a path the subject can anticipate, and his success is somewhat related to the regularity of the target movement. The task may be to follow the target, or to compensate for its movements from a specific position. In life situations, however, targets are sometimes highly irregular in their movements: the pheasant does not oblige the hunter with a predictable pattern of flight; the deviation of a boat from the intended compass course may vary with wind and tide in a highly irregular manner; the indicator on an automobile speedometer varies with the slope of the highway. Thus target movement is an important variable for experimentation. A typical investigation is one by Taylor and Birmingham[21], in which an irregularly moving target was presented in a compensatory tracking task. The subjects were ten adults, six men and four women.

Figure 17-6 is a schematic diagram of the tracking apparatus. It consisted of two parts: a presentation unit in one room and a recording unit in another. The presentation unit included a cathode-ray tube, a lens, and a "joy stick." The target appeared as a green dot against a vertical hair line on the tube. The subject viewed the target and the hairline through the lens, which gave a view as if he were at a very great distance from the target. When the target jumped away from the hairline to the

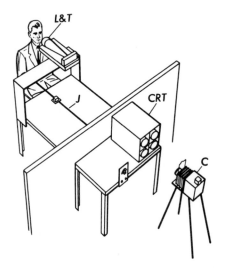

Figure 17-6. Electronic tracking apparatus. L and T show the location of the lens and target. J is the joy-stick control. CRT identifies a set of cathode ray tubes on which appeared a graphical display of position, rate, and acceleration of movement. C is the camera which photographed the display. [Adapted from Taylor and Birmingham.[21]]

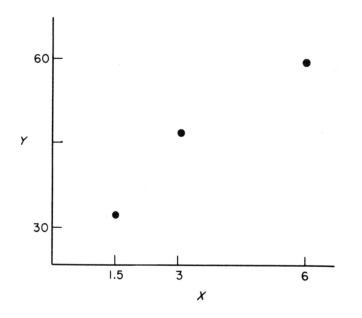

Figure 17-7. The effect of target shift on tracking behavior. X is shift in degrees of visual angle. Y is average rate of subject's movement in inches per second. [After Taylor and Birmingham.[21]]

right or to the left, the subject's task was to shift it back to the reference line by moving the joy stick in the appropriate direction. A warning bell sounded before each shift. The experimenter could select the direction and size of the target's shift. There were three sizes of shift for each direction: 1.5, 5, and 6 degrees of visual angle.

The subject's responses were transformed electronically into graphical representations of position, rate, and acceleration on cathode-ray tubes. A photograph of the tubes was taken each time he made a response. Measures were made from these photographs.

A subject was given thirty shifts to the right and thirty to the left with ten shifts of each of the three magnitudes in each direction. The order of the shifts was random. Figure 17-7 is a plot of rate of movement against size of target shift. The rate at which the subject moved the joy stick increased as the size of the target shift increased. This result represents only one part of a very detailed analysis of the subject's tracking behavior. Information gained from experiments of this kind is extremely valuable in designing control systems to be handled by human operators.

The Effect of Reference Lines on Control Efficiency

A fundamental task in the operation of many industrial and military control systems is the coordination of an operator's manipulation with signals from a display. When the display is large and complicated, its design, which is of critical importance to the operator's success, offers many possibilities for experimentation. If the display consisted of columns of lights, one feature which could be investigated would be reference lines as employed by Garvey and Mitnick[6]. They determined the effect of reference lines on rate of responding to lights by pressing corresponding buttons. Subjects were eight naval enlisted men.

There were two displays, one small and one large. The small one had two columns of ten lights; the large one, ten columns. There were two control panels with push buttons arranged to correspond to the two displays. Rows were marked with letters; columns, with numbers. In one condition there were reference lines on the displays and on the control panels; in the other, no reference lines. One light came on at a time. The subject's task was to press the button corresponding to the light. A light came on only after the button had been pressed for the preceding light.

Subjects were divided into two groups of four. All were given one trial of 100 successive lights per day on each of two different spatial arrangements of the large and small display-control systems for a period of thirty-six days. On the first twenty-six days, subjects in one group performed with one horizontal and one vertical reference line on the large display and its control panel, and one horizontal reference line on the small display and its control. Each reference line was located in the middle and ran from one edge to the other. Subjects in the other group performed without reference lines. On trials twenty-seven through thirty-six, subjects in both groups performed without reference lines. The subject was told to respond as fast as he could without making errors. Efficiency was measured in terms of the number of responses per second.

On both arrangements of the large display-control system, subjects with reference lines responded faster than those without reference lines. On the small system, the lines were not effective. After the lines were removed from the large system, subjects who had had the lines responded

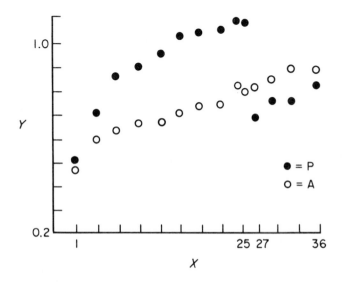

Figure 17-8. The effect of reference lines on display-control rate. X is ordinal number of trial. Y is mean responses per second. The two sets of points represent two conditions, lines present and absent on the first twenty-six trials for the large system. Lines were removed on the twenty-seventh trial. [After Garvey and Mitnick.[6]]

slower than those who had not had them. Figure 17-8 is a plot of responses per second against selected trials for the two conditions on one arrangement of the large display-control system. The advantage of the reference lines is clear. It is also interesting to note how much performance fell off when the lines were removed. It did not just fall off to equality with the other group: it fell below.

ILLUMINATION

It is a well-known fact that illumination is a condition which powerfully influences performance on many tasks. Study at home, in the library, and in the classroom proceeds with less strain and fatigue when lighting is good than when it is poor. Work at the office, in the store, and in the factory is more efficient with better lighting. An example of the effectiveness of illumination is provided by an experiment in which speed of reading six-point italic print was measured. The experiment was performed by Tinker[22] on 228 sophomores at the University of Minnesota.

There were two forms of a reading test, each containing 450 items of thirty words. A subject's task was to cross out the one word in each item that spoiled its meaning. The time allowed for each form was ten minutes. The four conditions in the experiment were levels of illumination: 1, 10, 25, and 50 foot-candles. One condition was imposed on each of four groups of subjects during the reading of the second form of the test.

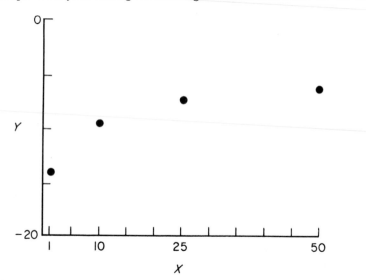

Figure 17-9. The effect of illumination on speed of reading. X is level of illumination in foot candles. Y is average difference between scores on the two forms of the reading test. [After Tinker.[22]]

The first form of the test, printed in ten-point Roman type on eggshell paper stock, was given to each subject under illumination of twenty-five foot-candles. Then the illumination was changed to the level under which he was to perform in the experiment. After five minutes, he was given the second form, printed in six-point, italic type on the same kind of paper. He was instructed that both speed and accuracy would count.

Reading speed was measured in terms of the number of items completed in the time allowed. Figure 17-9 shows the relation between the change for each group and level of illumination. The change was obtained by subtracting the mean number of items completed on the first form from the mean number for the second form. As illumination increased up to twenty-five foot-candles, speed of reading increased. The change from 25 to 50 foot-candles was so small it was attributed to error. The fact that reading speed does not increase in the last interval does not mean there is no advantage in higher levels of illumination. Effects would have to be measured in terms of fatigue and strain over longer periods of time for a variety of tasks to reach a general conclusion about the desirable levels of illumination. The experiment does illustrate, however, how this information could be obtained.

The visual illusion, overestimation of the length of a vertical line, was found to depend on illumination in an experiment by Künnapas[13]. He varied room illumination and measured the effect on judgments of the length of a vertical line in an L-shaped figure. His reasoning as to the expected effect of illumination started with the proposition that the visual field has the form of a horizontal ellipse. Two lines of equal length, one vertical and the other horizontal, in this elliptical field would not be seen as equidistant from its boundary: the vertical line would be nearer the boundary than the horizontal one. He hypothesized that, if the generally observed overestimation of the vertical line was related to the elliptical form of the visual field, it should be reduced in darkness where the field has no distinct boundary. His subjects were twenty university students in psychology, ten men and ten women. All had normal visual acuity, either corrected or uncorrected.

An L-shaped figure was projected in the central area of a circular white surface (see Figure 17-10). The figure consisted of two luminous lines, which were projected from behind the surface. One line was horizontal; the other was vertical. The length of the horizontal line, which was the standard, was fifty millimeters; the length of the vertical line was variable. A subject sat in front of the white surface, with his chin on a support, and viewed the figure binocularly. His task was to adjust the length of the variable vertical line by turning a knob, and equate it to the horizontal standard. The figure was exposed only while the subject made an adjustment.

Two conditions of room illumination were employed: light and dark. Under the light condition, the room was illuminated by a 150-watt lamp suspended from the ceiling behind the subject. Under the dark condition, the lamp was extinguished while he made his adjustment. Each subject served under both light and dark conditions, presented in various orders. He made thirty-two adjustments, half ascending and half descending, under each condition.

In the dark condition, the average length of the vertical line turned out to be 47.61 millimeters, which was overestimation of 4.8 per cent. In the light condition, the average was 46.46, overestimation of 7.1 per cent. Each percentage was computed by dividing the average value of the overestimation by the length of the standard. The hypothesis was supported by these results.

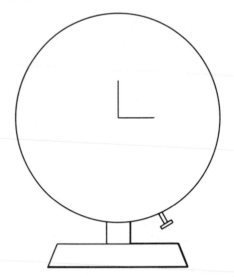

Figure 17-10. A device for investigating the horizontal-vertical illusion. The horizontal line was the standard. The length of the vertical line could be varied by turning the knob at lower right. [Adapted from Künnapas.[13]]

MUSIC

Most of us believe that music has an effect on people. It is not unusual to observe their reactions, usually vocal, expressing pleasure or annoyance on the occurrence of various types of music on radio or television. But are other kinds of behavior affected? An experiment by Ellis and Brighouse[5] showed that music could produce a change in respiration rate, a change usually associated with excitement or emotion.

In the experiment, thirty-six college students listened to three different recordings of musical selections. There were equal numbers of men and women selected from volunteers in undergraduate psychology courses.

The three conditions of the experiment were three recorded orchestral selections: Hall's *Blue Interval*, Debussy's *Prelude to the Afternoon of a Faun*, and Liszt's *Hungarian Rhapsody No. 2*. The experimenters described Hall's composition as "a subdued jazz selection in the blues idiom"; Debussy's as "a soothing classical selection"; and Liszt's as "a vivid and dynamic classical selection." The music was reproduced on a high-fidelity system.

Each subject served in all three conditions, the order of which was varied systematically. Conditions were imposed in thirty-minute sessions which were separated by at least twenty-four hours. Respiration rate was determined before, during, and after the presentation of a selection in each session. Respiratory activity was measured by a pneumograph, placed in the region of the subject's diaphragm, and recorded on a polygraph. The subject lay on a mattress with the testing room dimly illuminated.

Each session began with the reading of an article to the subject. After stable values of respiration rate were established, the music was reproduced. After the music, there was a rest period of five minutes. Then a second article was read. The subject was told that his task was to listen to the article and the music. Instructions were intended to convey the idea that the experiment was concerned mainly with the articles and only incidentally with the music. However, he was told that no questions would be asked about the articles. During music, values of respiration rate for *Hungarian Rhapsody* were higher than those for the other two selections; that is, subjects breathed faster, on the average, when they listened to the *Rhapsody* than they did during the other selections. If increased rate of breathing is accepted as a behavioral definition of increased excitement, then it could be said that the *Rhapsody* produced more excitement than did the other selections.

Applied Experiments

The Effects of Handrail Diameter on Preferences and Judgments

Some experiments are mainly intended to provide answers to basic or theoretical questions of interest to the psychologists working in a certain area. Others have obvious relevance to a large class of practical problems. Still others are directed mainly toward the solution of particular practical problems. We choose to call this last group applied experiments.

Handrail diameter was investigated in an applied experiment by Hall and Bennett[9]. The diameter of a handrail on a flight of stairs in an office building was varied and the effect on preferences and expressions of feelings of safety on the part of users was determined. Subjects were fifty-one female clerical employees, who varied in age from 20 to 60.

The four conditions in the experiment were four different handrail diameters. A subject's evaluations of the rails were obtained four times, twice after ascending and twice after descending. The existing handrail was removed and replaced by a handrail with four sections of different diameters: 1.5, 1.75, 2.00, and 2.25 inches. The four sections, which were equal in length, were placed in order of decreasing diameters going down. Subjects were asked to use the handrail while traveling the stairs.

When they reached the end of the test flight, they were asked questions about the handrail. Answers were scored for both preference and judgment of safety for each rail.

Figure 17-11 is a plot of scores against the diameter of the rail for both preference and feeling of safety. According to judgments of these women users, a rail with a diameter of approximately two inches was best. Notice that this experiment does not tell us what the safest handrail is. To find out, an experiment would have to be continued for a long period of time during which a record of accidents was kept. The experiment does show how many practical problems can be attacked in a systematic and objective way.

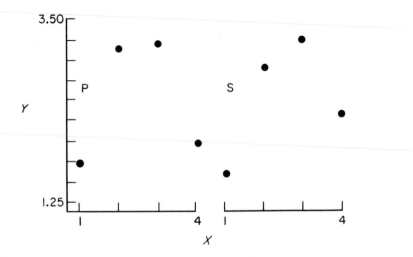

Figure 17-11. The effect of handrail diameter on judgments of users. X is rank of handrails for diameters: 0.50, 1.75, 2.00, and 2.25 inches. Y is average intensity score. The two plots represent questions concerning preference and safety. [After Hall and Bennett.[9]]

The Effects of Prosthesis Controls

Another applied experiment involved two kinds of prosthesis control. It was conducted by Groth and Lyman[8] with the terminal devices used by arm amputees. The various devices are operated for prehension or grasping by pulling a cable. The source of control and power is either a strap across the back or a pin inserted in a muscle. *Opening* devices, those for which a pull on a cable opens the device from a closed resting position, close on objects by spring force when the amputee releases the cable tension. *Closing* devices, those for which a pull on the cable closes the device from an open resting position, are kept open by spring force. The purpose of the experiment was to compare the performance of opening devices with the performance of closing devices as a step toward establishing criteria for future designs and prescriptions of terminal devices. Subjects were ten unilateral below-elbow amputees, five unilateral above-elbow amputees, and two bilateral amputees.

The motions of grasp, transport, and release of an object were required by the three simple manipulation tests: the Minnesota Rate of Manipulation Placing Test, a table-setting test, and a cup-handling test. Time for each test was taken with a stop watch. The cup test was omitted for some amputees because it was too difficult. Amputee preferences for the devices were obtained by means of a questionnaire listing twenty-five simple, manipulative motions from daily life.

The difference between opening and closing devices in average performance time was so small it was attributed to error. On the questionnaires, however, 76.6 per cent of the choices were for the opening device and 28.4 per cent were for the closing device. The results are interesting: no difference in actual performance but a large difference in preferences. It could be that the use of the favored opening device was accompanied by less effort and greater confidence while the use of the closing device was accompanied by more effort and less confidence.

The Social Environment

The social environment is made up of the behavior of individuals and groups. It is possible to experiment with ways of collaborating, cooperating, conforming, competing, imitating, and leading, as well as circumstances of social deprivation, isolation, stress, conflict, counseling, and psychotherapy. Experimental social and clinical psychologists investigate the effects of these conditions on behavior.

The person who would like to improve his social relationships will find much that is worth studying in the results of experimentation in this area. It is not that specific investigations will give him answers to his specific problems. It would be sheer misrepresentation to give the impression that this is so. It is rather that the results of specific investigations may suggest reasonable possibilities for action of a tentative sort in the management of his relations with others. One must act or refuse to do so in one situation after another, in one way or another, where other people are involved. To act on the basis of what appears to be the best available evidence is certainly a reasonable course to pursue. The whole point is that one should take advantage of any and all opportunities to control his behavior in relation to others and, within the ethical limits which society imposes and he accepts, to control the behavior of others in relation to himself.

INDIVIDUAL AND GROUP BEHAVIOR

Do people behave differently as individuals than as members of groups? There is evidence that they do, at least in some circumstances. Perceptual behavior was shown to differ in an experiment reported in 1935 by Sherif[18]. He investigated the autokinetic phenomenon, the apparent movement of a stationary point of light in a dark room, with subjects tested as individuals and then as groups, and with subjects tested as groups and then as individuals. Subjects were male undergraduate and graduate students at Columbia University, Teachers College, and New York University.

A small stationary point source of light was located on a table at one end of a darkened testing room. A subject sat at the opposite end of the room. The light was exposed periodically by means of a manually operated photographic shutter. The subject was instructed to press a key as soon as he detected movement of the light. The experimenter closed the shutter either two seconds after the subject pressed the key, or if he did not press it, thirty seconds after the exposure. In testing a group of subjects, keys were mounted on a table and subjects sat behind the table close to each other.

There were eight groups of two subjects. Those in four groups were observed individually in the first session and then as groups for three sessions; those in the other four groups were observed as groups for three sessions and then as individuals in the last session. Each individual subject gave 100 judgments in each session. Each subject in a group was told to respond as soon as he detected movement and not to wait for the other person.

When subjects began as individuals and ended in groups, judgments within each pair converged or became congruent. When subjects began in groups and ended as individuals, judgments within each pair displayed congruence throughout; that is, in all four groups the two subjects were much alike in all four sessions. The effect of group membership is clear: people become more alike in their judgments if they enter the group different from one another; and they continue to follow the judgment of the group after they leave it. It is important to keep in mind, however, that these results were obtained for a highly unstructured or ambiguous situation. In a different kind of situation where issues are clearly stated and individuals have standards for resolving those issues, the same convergence and continuing congruence might not be observed.

Are problems solved more efficiently by individuals working alone or in groups? To get some evidence bearing upon this question, Taylor and Faust[20] performed an experiment involving the game of Twenty Questions. Subjects solved a series of problems working individually and in groups. The efficiency of individual methods was compared with that of group methods. Subjects were 105 students in an elementary course in psychology.

Subjects were assigned randomly to three conditions of problem solving: fifteen worked individually; thirty worked in pairs; and sixty worked in groups of four. They were given four problems per day for four consecutive days. On the fifth day, all subjects worked individually on four problems.

The problems were typical of the game of Twenty Questions. The sixty answers were equally divided among animal, vegetable, and mineral objects. Examples were "newspaper," "Bob Hope," "scissors," "camel," "dime," and "rubber band." The order of presenting problems was varied but the three conditions did not differ in that respect.

Subjects were told that the number of questions was the important score. Those in groups were told that they could talk freely to one another in reviewing answers to previous questions or suggesting questions to ask. They were told not to compete among themselves but to cooperate to get the answers, and that their efficiency as a group would be compared with that of other groups. Because of the large number of failures which occurred in pretesting when the number of questions allowed was twenty, the number employed in the experiment was increased to thirty.

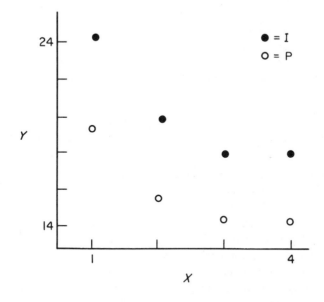

Figure 17-12. A comparison of problem solving by individuals and groups. X is successive days. Y is average number of questions per problem. The two sets of points represent two conditions, individual and pair activity. Points for groups of four are not plotted. They were not appreciably different from those for pairs. [After Taylor and Faust.[20]]

The score for an individual or a group for one day was the median number of questions required to solve the four problems on that day. Figure 17-12 is a plot of scores against the first four days. There are two sets of points, one for individuals, the other representing groups of two. Scores for individuals were higher than scores for pairs—a poorer performance for individuals than for pairs.

The difference between scores for groups of two and groups of four was so small it was attributed to error. The differences among the three conditions on the fifth day when all worked individually were also attributed to error. The advantage of the small groups in problem solving is apparent. Before deciding on the use of groups in some practical situation, however, one would have to consider the cost in manpower. Two people may do better than one, but the cost is twice as much. Notice also that the group experience in more rapid problem solving did not prove to be an advantage when those individuals separated and worked independently.

RELATIONS BETWEEN GROUPS

The effect of competition between groups of school children in performing addition was investigated in 1927 by Hurlock[11]. Subjects were 155 children from grades four and six of the Cameron Public School of Harrisburg, Pennsylvania.

On each of five successive days children were given one of five forms of a test containing thirty problems in adding six three-place numbers. On the first day all children were tested together with no explanation of the purpose of the testing. The results were used to divide the children in each grade into two groups, equated with respect to score, age, and sex composition. On succeeding days, one group was tested in a separate room. No comment was made to these children except that they were to perform the addition as quickly and accurately as possible. The other group was divided into two equated subgroups. These subgroups were told that they would compete with one another, that they were equal in ability, and that they had equal chances of winning. During the competition, the experimenter read aloud the names of the members of the winning subgroup, asking each child to stand as his name was called, and wrote the score for each subgroup on the blackboard. The experimenter explained just how much one subgroup had outperformed the other and urged the subgroup that was behind to work harder in the test that was to follow.

The average score made by the group of children in competition exceeded that of the separate group on every day except the first day of testing. Thus competition between the two groups was shown to be valuable in improving the performance of both. This is the influence, of course, which is generally assumed to be operating on a broad scale in many competitive sports but only infrequently is it introduced in education, business, and industrial situations with anything like the success it appears to have in athletics. Competition among individuals is naturally intense in many areas of everyday life, but planned competition among groups to achieve desirable goals for individuals has not yet been fully exploited.

Interaction between two groups is not always productive of benefits for either one of the groups or its members, a fact which certainly holds for conflict, as demonstrated in a remarkable investigation by Sherif and Sherif[19]. Their experiment, conducted in an isolated summer camp in northern Connecticut, was a deliberate attempt to produce friction between groups of boys. The first step was the establishment of in-groups, which displayed no friction between themselves at the outset; the second step was the creation of conditions which were followed by friction between these in-groups. Subjects were twenty-four boys, about twelve years of age, from settled, American Protestant families of the lower-middle-class income group in the New Haven area. None of the boys was considered to be a problem.

The experiment was conducted in three stages. During the first stage, the boys were allowed to develop informal groups according to their personal inclinations and interests. During this period, all activities were conducted on a camp-wide basis so that the boys could mix and choose friends freely in games and chores. During the second stage, two in-groups as much alike as possible in size and composition were formed. Separate activities were planned and conducted for all the members of each group. The activities were chosen to provide opportunities for participation on the part of all members of a group. Rewards were given to a group, not to individuals. During the third stage, the two in-groups were put in a series of competitive and frustrating situations so arranged that the actions of one group adversely affected the other. Most of the observations were made by two graduate students who were counselors to the two in-groups. Each observer had the assistance of a junior counselor. The principal investigator acted as a camp caretaker.

At the end of the first stage, which lasted for three days, the boys were interviewed on the pretext of getting suggestions for activities and improvements. During these interviews, friendship choices were noted casually. This information was used in assigning the boys to the two groups for the second stage, the period of in-group formation. Friendship groups were deliberately split in forming the two in-groups. A tabulation of choices showed that the boys in each group had expressed a much larger percentage of choices for boys in the other group than they had for boys in their own group.

At the end of the second stage, which lasted five days, friendship choices were again obtained informally. Sociograms, graphic representations of the friendship choices of the boys in each group, revealed their positions in terms of popularity. Figures 17-13 and 17-14 are sociograms for the groups at the end of the second stage. A tabulation of friendship choices showed that boys in each group had expressed a much higher per cent of choices for boys in their own group than for boys in the other group. This was just the opposite of the situation at the end of the first stage.

During the third stage, which lasted for five days, the groups engaged in activities which were competitive and mildly frustrating to one another. A series of competitive games was planned. The games were accompanied by considerable group friction and, for the losing group, considerable disappointment. Boys in the winning group were elated at their victory; boys in the losing group pretended they had no interest in the prizes. The leader of the losers became vindictive when the group showed signs of disintegration and disorganization.

Following the competitive games, situations were arranged in which it appeared that one group interfered with the other. At a party it was arranged that one group would have the opportunity to take refreshments in good condition, leaving only damaged refreshments for the other group. Friction at the party was followed by other conflicts and a series of raids and fights which had to be stopped by the counselors. A decision was then made to terminate the third stage and to break down the in-groups. The formal experiment ended at this point. The remaining days in camp were spent in activities designed to eliminate friction. Despite efforts on the part of the staff to reduce hostility, seating arrangements at meals and friendship preferences continued to follow in-group lines to a considerable degree.

The important implication of this experiment and its results is that relations within groups and between groups can be manipulated. The investigation is obviously limited. It was done with boys in a summer camp in connection with just a few events and relationships. Its methods and results do not apply specifically to all the life situations of interest and importance to psychologists and laymen, but it does strongly suggest the possibility of our learning a great deal more about methods of structuring and modifying group relations. There is no more important area of psychological research.

THE EFFECTS OF PEOPLE ON PEOPLE

People can be employed as conditions in psychological experimentation, and their effects on other people can be observed. This research is difficult in two respects: first, it is necessary to get the cooperation of

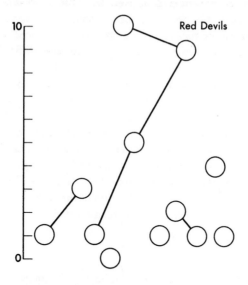

Figure 17-13. In-group formation at the end of the second stage. The number of boys choosing any given boy can be read on the scale at the left. Lines show reciprocated choices. [Adapted from Sherif and Sherif.[19]]

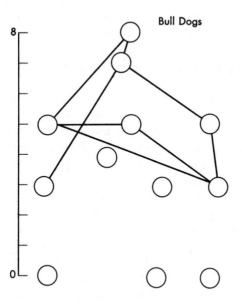

Figure 17-14. In-group formation at the end of the second stage. The number of boys choosing any given boy can be read on the scale at the left. Lines show reciprocated choices. [Adapted from Sherif and Sherif.[19]]

persons who will be treatments as well as those who will be subjects in circumstances acceptable to everyone; second, the behavior of persons who are the treatments has to be standardized, a procedure which almost always leaves something to be desired. Despite the difficulties of this research, it should be encouraged, for only through it can we get the best evidence on the management of interpersonal relationships: how parents should deal with their children; teachers, with their students; supervisors, with their workers; and therapists, with their clients. The situation in psychotherapy—whether in psychoanalysis, psychiatry, or clinical psychology—can appropriately be described as having to do with the effect of the therapist on the client. Furthermore psychotherapy possesses many features which are suitable for experimentation. The interest of clinical psychologists in experimentation with psychotherapy continues to grow despite the difficulties which must be surmounted.

Imitation

That children can be trained to imitate and not to imitate was demonstrated by Miller and Dollard[17]. Children were rewarded for imitating and for not imitating the behavior of a leader in three experiments.

Subjects in the first experiment were forty-two children in the first grade. Figure 17-15 is a diagram of the test situation. Two boxes, each of which had a hinged lid, were placed on chairs ten feet apart. A starting position was indicated by a chalk mark on the floor, ten feet from each box. Two children were used as leaders and were trained to go to the box to which the experimenter had pointed, and to stand so as to shield the box from a subject while he opened it. The leader was rewarded with candy for carrying out instructions and was punished by gentle verbal admonition for not doing so. Other children were randomly assigned to two conditions. Under the imitative condition, two gumdrops were placed in the same box. In the nonimitative condition, one gumdrop was placed in each box. The experimenter indicated to the leader, by pointing, the box to which he was to go. A subject was then brought into the room. The experimenter told the two children they were to find the candy. The leader was given the first turn; the subject was given the second turn. In the imitative condition, a subject's correct choice was the box to which the leader went. In the nonimitative condition, his correct choice was the opposite. If a subject went to the wrong box, he was not allowed to correct his error immediately; he was sent out of the room and then given another turn with the candy hidden in the same way and the leader going to the same box. These procedures were continued until the subject went to the correct box and obtained his reward. Thus a trial consisted of one or more turns with a correct response on the last turn. On trials after the first, the experimenter merely lined up the leader and the subject at the starting point, gave the leader his turn, and then gave the subject his turn. Each subject was given trials until his first choice was correct on two successive trials. After he had reached this criterion, he was given two additional trials.

On the first trial following achievement of the criterion, all twenty subjects in the imitative condition went to the same box as the leader; one of those in the nonimitative condition went to the same box as the leader. The different conditions of reward had produced different actions in the two groups: one group had learned to imitate; the other not to imitate.

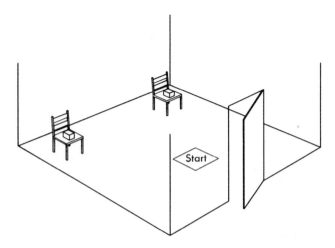

Figure 17-15. The situation employed to teach children to imitate. [Adapted from Miller and Dollard. [17]]

In a second experiment with the same children, the situation consisted of four boxes placed on chairs, arranged on the corners of an imaginary ten-foot square. A starting position was marked in the center of the square. While a subject was out of the room, the experimenter showed the leader which box to go to. The leader was sent to each of the four boxes ten times. Under the imitative condition, two gumdrops were put in the leader's box; under the nonimitative condition, one gumdrop was put into each box.

Seventy-five per cent of children who had been trained to imitate in the first experiment chose the same box as the leader, whereas none of those who had been trained not to imitate did so. The experimenters interpreted the results as generalization of the learning from the first experiment to the situation in the second experiment.

Subjects in the third experiment were twelve boys from the fourth

grade of a city school. The leaders were a boy from the third grade of
the same school and a male graduate student from Yale University. Figure 17-16 is a drawing of the apparatus to which a subject could make
one of two responses: grasping and depressing a handle; or grasping and
rotating the handle clockwise through an angle of ninety degrees. The
machine was designed so that the two responses were incompatible.

Gumdrops were the reward. An assistant dropped one of them
through a small tube in the front of the apparatus into a dish when a
child gave a correct response. In the first stage, children were trained in

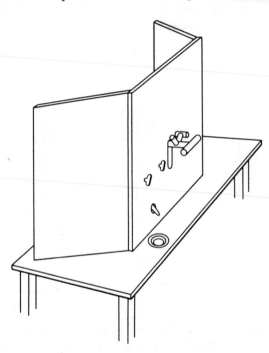

Figure 17-16. Apparatus for testing the prestige of a leader as a model. The handle
could be rotated clockwise through a 90-degree angle or depressed six inches in the slot.
Candy was dropped through the funnel into a dish on the edge of the table. [Adapted
from Miller and Dollard.[17]]

operating the apparatus. Half were rewarded for imitating the large leader;
half, for imitating the small leader. In the second stage those who had
been rewarded for imitating the large leader were rewarded for not imitating the small leader, and those who had been rewarded for imitating the
small leader were rewarded for not imitating the large. These stages were
repeated.

Finally, each subject was presented with the large leader and the
small leader in a random order. Shifts of responses by the leader were

made randomly. Subjects were consistently rewarded for imitating one leader and for not imitating the other and were given trials until they achieved a criterion of six successive errorless first turns, three with a child leader and three with an adult leader. They were then given four test trials.

The average number of errors on the four test trials was quite small. The results indicated that a child can be trained in the discrimination of imitating one person and not imitating another. The inference is justified that imitation can be manipulated. There must, of course, be limitations to the inference not brought out in this one series of experiments, but the possibility that imitation of behavior can be controlled should be of interest to everyone who has responsibility for the care and education of children.

Leadership

How do leaders affect the behavior of their followers? To get an answer to this question for boys' clubs, Lewin, Lippitt, and White[15], in 1939, experimented with three different types of leadership: authoritarian, democratic, and laissez-faire. The effects were observed on the aggressive behavior of twenty ten-year-old boys who volunteered from two school classes.

Four clubs of five boys were organized. Every six weeks for eighteen weeks each club was given a different leader with a different technique of leadership. Thus each club had a total of three leaders. An attempt was made to equate the clubs initially on interpersonal relationships, personality characteristics, and intellectual, physical, and socioeconomic variables.

A list of activities, which included mask making, mural painting, soap carving, and model airplane construction, was presented for discussion to the democratic clubs which met first. The members voted on their activity. The authoritarian leaders then initiated the same activity in their clubs without choice by the members. The laissez-faire groups were made acquainted with the opportunities and possibilities for activity but they were not influenced in their choice. There were five democratic, five autocratic, and two laissez-faire periods of leadership distributed among the three periods for each of the four clubs. During each fifty-minute club meeting, an observer recorded interactions between members including verbal comments and physical actions designated as aggressive.

The average number of aggressive actions per meeting was highest for the laissez-faire group, intermediate for the democratic group, and lowest for the autocratic group. One cannot say with any certainty whether a high or low number of aggressive actions is best. If the aggressive actions are free expressions of previously pent-up feelings, then a high number might be considered best. If, however, they are simply a product of the group activity and its leadership, a low number might be considered most desirable. As it turned out, the smallest average occurred with autocratic leadership, but the five autocratic periods displayed great variation, a fact which might be interpreted as indicating some uncontrolled influence in those periods.

An experiment of this kind is very difficult to perform. Prescribing roles is no simple matter, and having the leaders act in the prescribed fashion cannot be guaranteed. Furthermore, observation and measurement of social behavior presents many problems. The results of this particular experiment cannot be taken as conclusive, but the general idea of structuring groups and manipulating their leadership is a valuable contribution. One hopes that psychologists will continue to apply their ingenuity to the problem.

Social Deprivation

People can be imposed on people in special ways for purposes of determining the effects on behavior, but that is not the only way they can be manipulated. Another possibility is to deprive subjects of the usual social contact and observe the effects on their behavior. Knowledge of the effects of social deprivation has relevance to familiar life situations: children losing their parents by death, divorce, or war; mental patients being separated from normal social contacts; and delinquents and criminals being isolated from many of the community's positive social influences. An experimental approach to social deprivation in a play situation involving children was taken by Gewirtz and Baer[7]. They compared conditions of social deprivation, nondeprivation, and satiation with respect to their effects on a simple response by children in a game. Subjects were 102 children selected from the classes of the first and second grades of a university laboratory school.

Children were randomly assigned to three groups in which the sexes were equally represented. One condition was imposed on each group before they played a game. Under deprivation, a child was left alone in a testing room for twenty minutes before the experimenter returned with a toy for the final game in which the child's correct responses were approved. Under nondeprivation, the child played the game as soon as he arrived at the room. Under satiation, he was encouraged to draw pictures or cut out designs for twenty minutes while the experimenter tried to maintain friendly conversation with him and tried to induce him to talk about himself, if he did not do so naturally. The experimenter tried to administer praise and admiration thirty times during the twenty-minute period at an approximate rate of three times every two minutes, after which the final game was played.

The game which all children played after receiving the appropriate treatment was placing marbles into either of the two holes of a toy shown in Figure 17-17. The experimenter observed the child's play for four minutes during which no praise or admiration was given. There followed a ten-minute test period during which the experimenter administered approval by saying "good," "hm-hmm," and "fine." Approval, which was given for marbles dropped into the correct hole, was scheduled frequently in the early stages and infrequently in later stages. The correct hole was defined as the one used less during the last minute of the four-minute initial period.

The number of marbles dropped in the correct hole during each minute of play was recorded. The relative frequency of correct responses was determined by dividing the number of correct responses by the total number. The score employed as the dependent variable was the

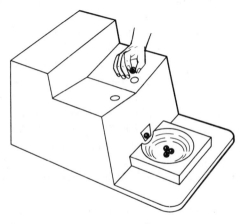

Figure 17-17. Apparatus for a simple game. [Adapted from Gewirtz and Baer.[7]]

difference between the relative frequency in the last minute of the four-minute initial period and the median relative frequency for the ten one-minute test periods. This difference represented a gain in relative frequency of correct responses associated with the approval given by the experimenter. Gains on the approval test were greatest after deprivation, intermediate after nondeprivation, and least after satiation. The interpretation seems justified that an adult's approval is more effective after a period of no approval than after a period of much approval. Thus it may be wise in our dealings with children to vary approval over time and concentrate it on those occasions which require it in some special way.

In a similar experiment on social deprivation, Hartup and Himeno[10] exposed preschool children to isolation from and interaction with an adult before a period of doll play. Aggressive behavior during doll play was measured. Subjects were twenty-four boys and the same number of girls attending the preschool laboratories of the Iowa Child Welfare Research Station.

Children were randomly assigned to two groups. The two conditions of the experiment were imposed on one group in one order and on the other group in the reverse order. Children in each of these groups were assigned randomly to four experimenters, two males and two females. The two successive conditions for each group were separated by a period which varied from five to eight days.

In the isolation condition, the experimenter left the child alone in the testing room for ten minutes. Two books, a puzzle, and a rubber-band game were available. The experimenter then reentered the room with a collection of materials for doll play: a plasticine male figure, a plasticine female figure, a plasticine child figure of indeterminate sex, doll furniture, a child's hammer, four one-inch wire nails, a wooden mallet, a wooden smasher, a wooden roller, a tongue depressor, a knife and fork of standard size, and a doll's nursing bottle. In the interaction condition, the experimenter suggested playing with the toys and interacted verbally with the child for ten minutes. Each experimenter was instructed to show interest in what the child did, to smile or laugh when appropriate, to give help and praise, and to answer his questions.

At the beginning of doll play, the experimenter handed the dolls to the child in the order: male, female, and child. After the child had identified each doll, the experimenter said, "You can play with them in any way you like." The session lasted for ten minutes. A record of the child's aggressive behavior during doll play was kept by an observer in a booth equipped with a one-way screen. Aggressive behavior was defined as actions which involved injury, destruction, and physical or verbal chastisement. The observer recorded a variety of aggressive actions: hammering, smashing, cutting, gouging, twisting, and tearing apart of the plasticine figures; scolding and threatening; and having a doll become sick or dead.

The frequency of aggressive behaviors during the ten-minute period was determined for each child. To make counting possible, units of aggressive behavior were distinguished by changes in the object of aggression, the agent of aggression, materials used to express aggression, and the type of aggression. The frequency of aggressive behavior in doll play was found to be greater after isolation than after interaction. It may be that this experiment and its result explains the everyday situation in which parents who have been away from their children for some period, perhaps unavoidably, return and are disappointed and distressed to find not a child happy to have them back but one who is upset and aggressive.

The Effect of an Observer on Children's Aggression

Does the mother's presence inhibit the expression of aggression by a child? Many psychologists would predict that it does, but the results of an experiment by Levin and Turgeon[14] did not confirm this idea.

Subjects were twenty children, ten of each sex, of ages three to five years. Each child was observed in a preliminary session of doll play when only the experimenter was present. In the main session, each child in one group was observed when his mother and the experimenter were present; each child in the other group was observed when a strange female adult and the experimenter were present. Each session of doll play lasted twenty minutes. Usually one day intervened between the preliminary and main sessions. The standard family of dolls included mother, father, boy, girl, and baby. The doll house had six uncovered rooms with movable furniture and fixed walls.

The child's remarks during doll play were divided into units. Each unit consisting of a subject and a predicate was recorded verbatim. Examples of units were "The boy runs," and "The daddy spanks the girl." Two scores were obtained: the total number of units per session; and the percentage of aggression per session, computed by dividing the number of aggressive units by the total number. Aggression was defined as statements of any action that irritated, hurt, injured, punished, frustrated, or destroyed a doll or equipment, such as "The boy jumps on the bureau," "The father breaks his leg," "The boy has his head sliced off," and "A storm breaks up the house." Scolding, threats, and occasions on which discomfort was attributed to a doll by statements that it was sick, sad, or lost were also counted.

The results indicated that aggressiveness increased from the first session to the second when the mother was watching the child and decreased when a stranger was present. How is this result to be interpreted? On the basis of the evidence at hand one cannot say whether the children were less inhibited in the mother's presence or whether her presence antagonized them.

Stress

Life provides many situations in which a person or a group produces stress for another person or group. Psychologists would like very much to study stress experimentally but there are obvious limits to what they can do or would want to do in imposing stress on human subjects. An unusual experiment by Barthol and Ku[1] demonstrated that stress could produce one kind of regressive behavior. They had subjects learn, in succession, two ways of tying a knot. Restrictive testing conditions were then imposed, after which observation was made of their choices of a way of tying the knot. Subjects were eighteen undergraduates, four men and fourteen women, at the Pennsylvania State University.

The knot employed was a bowline, for which there are two quite dissimilar methods of tying. The eighteen subjects were randomly divided into two groups. Both groups were taught both methods of tying the bowline, but the order of the methods was varied. Later, in a situation intended to be stressful, each subject was asked simply to tie a knot. His choice of methods, the one learned first or the one learned second, was observed.

The stress situation involved taking a difficult test late at night under restrictive conditions. Subjects were told that the test was designed for high school students and that the average college student could answer most of the questions without difficulty. Actually the test was much more difficult than described. College students usually required between forty minutes and one hour to complete the test. The subjects, however, were required to spend twelve minutes on each of sixteen parts, more than three hours total time, and were not allowed to proceed to the next section until the time had elapsed. They were not allowed to smoke, talk, leave the room, or direct any overt activity toward anything but the test proper. At the end of the testing session, they were called out of the room individually in random order, handed a cord, and told, "Tie a knot." After the experiment was finished, a complete explanation was given to the subjects, who departed quite amicably.

Sixteen out of eighteen tied the bowline by the method they had learned first. The remaining two tied it by the method learned second. Although the instruction was simply, "Tie a knot," no subject tied any other knot except the bowline. The experimenters called tying a bowline by the first method learned *specific regression*. The idea of specific regression is that a person under stress reverts to behavior which resulted in his earlier success under similar conditions.

Interpersonal Therapy

Although conventional psychotherapy varies from one clinical practitioner to another, depending on his theoretical orientation, it always involves the verbal interaction of the client and the therapist. Some therapists take a nondirective approach, which means they attempt to create a permissive atmosphere free of reproach and condemnation. They try to maintain an attitude of unconditional positive regard for their clients and encourage them to express themselves freely while they—the therapists—minimize their own control of the direction the interview takes. Other therapists are much more active, pursuing what they see as one clue to the client's difficulties and then another, with a good deal of analysis and interpretation.

In recent years interest has been growing in another kind of psychotherapy conducted by one or more therapists with a group of clients. Group therapy, as it is known, has two advantages: it is not as costly in terms of therapist time as individual therapy; and, what may be more important, it offers possibilities for using the interaction among clients as a therapeutic agent.

The amount of experimentation which has been done with psychotherapy is limited, but interest in its expansion continues to grow. It is difficult research, for the variables in the clinical interview and the therapist-client relation are not easily managed. There is much less experimental evidence concerning the specific benefits of psychotherapy in its various forms than clinical psychologists would like to have. But there is enough to stimulate new programs of research and to justify their continued use of psychotherapy in an effort to help their clients help themselves. There is also a firm and widespread conviction, based on personal observations made in clinical interviews, that some success is achieved in these endeavors; that some clients do achieve confidence, effectiveness, and satisfaction in their relations with other people and in their work.

Even though the amount of experimental work done with psychotherapy is limited, the methods and results can still not be covered here. To achieve some representation of experimentation in this area, an ambitious experiment by King, Armitage, and Tilton[12] will be reported. They studied the effects of four different therapies on hospitalized psychiatric patients who were characterized as being extremely withdrawn, lacking in energy, and uncommunicative. Subjects were obtained from a large locked ward which housed approximately 300 long-term male psychotic patients. All subjects had, at some previous time, undergone at least three of five treatment procedures: electro-shock therapy, insulin coma therapy, drug therapy, psychotherapy, and group therapy.

A complex vending machine shown in Figure 17-18 was built into a panel erected across an alcove in a large room. Three levers projected from the middle of the panel in a row about waist height. Below the first and third levers were slots with trays for dispensing candy and cigarettes. A small screen for projecting slides was located above the middle lever. To obtain candy, pictures, or cigarettes, a patient had to depress the appropriate lever until there was a click followed by the ringing of a chime. Beyond the levers on each side was an aluminum plate containing a cut-out cross into which a lever could be inserted. If a patient moved the lever of either cross from the position of rest to the end of a predesignated correct arm, a green light at the end of the arm came on.

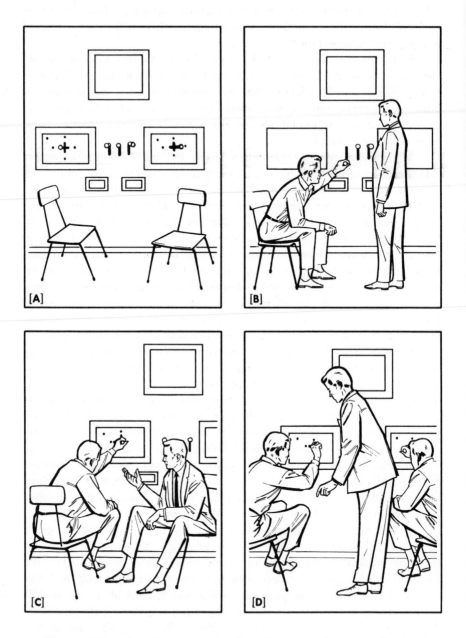

Figure 17-18. The apparatus employed in the operant interpersonal method of psychotherapy and illustrations of therapeutic phases. **A:** the apparatus showing levers, trays for dispensing candy and cigarettes, and a projection screen. **B:** simple operant behavior. **C:** problem solving. **D:** cooperative problem solving. The therapist stands by in each of the three situations. [Adapted from King, Armitage, and Tilton.[12]]

Problems could be introduced requiring from one to four movements in various patterns of right, left, up, or down. An amber light located at an upper corner of each plate flashed when a problem was solved. Located behind the panel and not visible to the patient was an assistant who projected scenic slides on the small screen, released chocolate candy and cigarettes, operated the system which set problems, and recorded the readings of the counters attached to the levers.

Four different treatments were imposed on four groups of patients. Those who underwent the special interpersonal therapy were seen three times a week for fifteen weeks. Sessions varied in length from 20 to 30 minutes. Although the therapy had to be adapted somewhat to the individual patient, the procedure could be divided into three phases. At the beginning of the first phase, a patient was lead into the therapy room and seated. The therapist directed his attention to the three levers and described their operation. He then demonstrated by manipulating each of the levers, taking time to give the candy and cigarettes to the patient and to call his attention to the picture on the screen. He then urged the patient to depress one of the levers. It was usually necessary to repeat the demonstration and sometimes, as a last resort, the therapist placed the patient's hand on the lever and then applied force enough to depress it. On one occasion the therapist actually unwrapped the candy and placed it in the patient's mouth. Although there were great differences among patients, all began to respond eventually. When a patient did begin to respond, he was frustrated by termination of the rewards. When he stopped pressing the levers after nonrewarded trials, special instructions and demonstrations were given by the therapist until the patient responded again. The first phase lasted approximately four weeks.

In the second phase, a lever was inserted in one of the crosses. The therapist showed that only one of the four possible movements of the lever turned on a green light at the end of the cross arm and subsequently the amber light at the upper corner of the plate. After making the correct response on the cross, the therapist depressed one of the levers and showed the patient the resulting reward. After the patient solved a variety of simple problems, he was introduced to more complex problems. After approximately three weeks, verbalization was included in the procedure. For example, the patient, when he had solved a problem several times, was stopped after making the first movement and asked, "Now where do you go next?" If he did not answer, the therapist would ask him to point to the next movement. The therapist also started to encourage more verbal interaction at the beginning and the close of sessions with topics not directly related to the problem solving.

At the beginning of the third phase, cooperative problem solving was undertaken. The therapist told the patient that they would have to work as a team to obtain rewards. In a simple problem, the therapist made the first movement on one cross and the patient made the second movement on the other cross. As the patient made progress in cooperating, they went on to more complex problems. When all patients had experience working with the therapist, two worked as a team. Then two additional patients were brought in to observe the cooperating pair and to give either motor or verbal advice. Eventually as many as six patients attended a session. Every patient had the opportunity to cooperate with every other one within a short period of time.

Three comparison groups were treated differently. One group had individual verbal therapy in three sessions of 20 to 30 minutes per week. The therapist adapted the verbal communication to the individual patient. Topics were explored ranging from routine daily events to the patient's feelings and concerns. With mute subjects monologs punctuated by pauses were carried on by the therapist. In the later stages, the verbal therapy was adapted to groups. Another group had recreational therapy. Varied activities were engaged in for three to five hours in a week in the company of a larger group not in the experiment. Activities included medicine-ball exercises, shuffleboard, playing in a rhythm band, singing, participating in social games, and dancing with volunteer workers. In this recreational therapy, subjects were given more attention than they would have received ordinarily. Subjects in another group were not given any special treatment but were allowed to participate in regular ward activities such as occupational therapy. Six patients from the interpersonal therapy group and six from the verbal therapy group were assigned to each of two therapists. Patients in the recreational therapy group were assigned to an experienced activity therapist.

Four different measures of behavior were employed as dependent variables:

1. An inventory for assessing low levels of adjustment. The inventory consisted of twenty-two items which were rated in an interview on four- or five-point scales. The first ten items were ratings on simple interpersonal behaviors like the response to a handshake, response to an offer of a chair, and response to an offer of a cigarette. The remaining twelve items were ratings of posture, sensorimotor action, peculiar gestures, and the like. The sum of the ratings on all the items yielded a score.

2. A special rating scale for assessing ward adjustment—that is, accommodation to ward personnel and routine.

3. A five-point scale for rating amount of verbalization.

4. A clinical improvement rating scale.

Before treatment, patients were measured on the interview inventory and the verbalization scale. After treatment, attendants and nurses rated the subjects on the ward adjustment scale; a psychologist not previously connected with the research administered the interview inventory and the verbalization scale; and an attendant observer rated patients on the ward adjustment scale and completed the clinical improvement scale.

The interpersonal therapy group was superior to the other three groups on all four dependent variables. Improvement scores on the interview inventory indicated the most improvement for the interpersonal therapy group, with the comparison groups following in the order: recreational therapy, no therapy, and verbal therapy. Scores on the ward adjustment scale showed interpersonal therapy highest followed by recreational therapy, verbal therapy, and no therapy. When the four groups were ranked in terms of the number of patients showing some improvement on the clinical improvement scale, they were in the same order as they were on the interview inventory. Changes in ratings on the verbalization scale showed the interpersonal therapy group to be superior to the others.

Chapter Summary

It is a widely accepted idea that people are, to a considerable extent, products of their environment. Experimental psychology gives this idea practical significance by providing evidence concerning the manipulation of environmental features and the effect on behavior. The experimental approach is not concerned with probable causes in a historical sense. It has to do with how man can make behavior what he wishes it to be at present and in the future.

Two kinds of environments can be distinguished. The physical environment is made up of material things and physical events. The social environment consists of the behavior of individuals and groups. Both are important. The physical environment can, however, be manipulated with greater ease and precision than the social environment. Relations between and within groups, including competition and conflict, are social conditions which have been demonstrated to affect behavior. People themselves have been employed as conditions in investigations of leadership, social deprivation, stress, and therapy. The methods and results of imposing these conditions constitute experimental social and clinical psychology.

References

1. Barthol, R. P., and N. D. Ku. "Regression Under Stress to First Learned Behavior." *The Journal of Abnormal and Social Psychology,* 59 (1959), 134-136.
2. Bilodeau, E. A. "Decrements and Recovery from Decrements in a Simple Work Task with Variation in Force Requirements at Different Stages of Practice." *The Journal of Experimental Psychology,* 44 (1952), 96-100.
3. Conrad, R. "Some Effects on Performance of Changes in Perceptual Load," *The Journal of Experimental Psychology,* 49 (1955), 313-322.

4. ———. "Serial Order Intrusions in Immediate Memory." *The British Journal of Psychology,* 51 (1960), 45-48.
5. Ellis, D. S., and G. Brighouse. "Effects of Music on Respiration- and Heart-Rate." *The American Journal of Psychology,* 65 (1952), 39-47.
6. Garvey, W. D., and L. L. Mitnick. "Effect of Additional Spatial References on Display-Control Efficiency." *The Journal of Experimental Psychology,* 50 (1955), 276-282.
7. Gewirtz, J. L., and D. M. Baer. "Deprivation and Satiation of Social Reinforcers as Drive Conditions." *The Journal of Abnormal and Social Psychology,* 57 (1958), 165-172.
8. Groth, H., and J. Lyman. "Relation of the Mode of Prosthesis Control to Psychomotor Performance of Arm Amputees." *The Journal of Applied Psychology,* 41 (1957), 73-78.
9. Hall, N. B., Jr., and E. M. Bennett. "Empirical Assessment of Handrail Diameters." *The Journal of Applied Psychology,* 40 (1956), 381-382.
10. Hartup, W. W., and Y. Himeno. "Social Isolation Versus Interaction with Adults in Relation to Aggression in Preschool Children." *The Journal of Abnormal and Social Psychology,* 59 (1959), 17-22.
11. Hurlock, E. B. "The Use of Group Rivalry as an Incentive," *The Journal of Abnormal and Social Psychology,* 22 (1927), 278-290.
12. King, G. F., S. G. Armitage, and J. R. Tilton. "A Therapeutic Approach to Schizophrenics of Extreme Pathology: An Operant-Interpersonal Method." *The Journal of Abnormal and Social Psychology,* 61 (1960), 276-286.
13. Künnapas, T. M. "The Vertical-Horizontal Illusion and the Visual Field." *The Journal of Experimental Psychology,* 53 (1957), 405-407.
14. Levin, H., and V. F. Turgeon. "The Influence of the Mother's Presence on Children's Doll Play Aggression." *The Journal of Abnormal and Social Psychology,* 55 (1957), 304-308.
15. Lewin, K., R. Lippitt, and R. K. White. "Patterns of Aggressive Behavior in Experimentally Created 'Social Climates'." *The Journal of Social Psychology,* 10 (1939), 271-299.
16. Lyman, J., and H. Groth. "Prehension Force as a Measure of Psychomotor Skill for Bare and Gloved Hands." *The Journal of Applied Psychology,* 42 (1958), 18-21.
17. Miller, N., and J. Dollard, *Social Learning and Imitation.* New Haven, Conn.: Yale University Press, 1941.
18. Sherif, M. "A Study of Some Social Factors in Perception," *The Archives of Psychology,* 27, No. 187 (1935).
19. Sherif, M., and C. W. Sherif, *Groups in Harmony and Tension.* New York: Harper & Brothers, 1953.
20. Taylor, D. W., and W. L. Faust. "Twenty-Questions: Efficiency in Problem Solving as a Function of Size of Group." *The Journal of Experimental Psychology,* 44 (1952), 360-368.
21. Taylor, F. V., and H. P. Birmingham. "Studies of Tracking Behavior. II. The Acceleration Pattern of Quick Manual Corrective Responses." *The Journal of Experimental Psychology,* 38 (1948), 783-795.
22. Tinker, M. A. "The Effect of Intensity of Illumination Upon Speed of Reading 6-Point Italic Print." *The American Journal of Psychology,* 65 (1952), 600-602.

Index